Legal Research and Writing:
A Practical Approach for Paralegals

First Edition

Robert P. O'Neill Jr., J.D.

PEARSON

Boston   Columbus   Indianapolis   New York   San Francisco   Hoboken
Amsterdam   Cape Town   Dubai   London   Madrid   Milan   Munich   Paris   Montréal   Toronto
Delhi   Mexico City   São Paulo   Sydney   Hong Kong   Seoul   Singapore   Taipei   Tokyo

Editorial Director: Andrew Gilfillan
Senior Acquisitions Editor: Gary Bauer
Editorial Assistant: Lynda Cramer
Director of Marketing: David Gesell
Marketing Manager: Thomas Hayward
Product Marketing Manager: Kaylee Carlson
Marketing Assistant: Les Roberts
Program Manager: Tara Horton
Project Manager Team Lead: Bryan Pirrmann
Project Manager: Yagnesh Jani
Operations Specialist: Deidra Smith
Creative Director: Andrea Nix
Art Director: Diane Six

Manager, Product Strategy: Sara Eilert
Product Strategy Manager: Anne Rynearson
Team Lead, Media Development & Production:
Rachel Collett
Media Project Manager: Maura Barclay
Cover Designer: Melissa Welch, Studio Montage
Cover Image: photogl/Shutterstock
Full-Service Project Management: Shylaja Gattupalli
Composition: SPI Global
Text Printer/Bindery: Edwards Brothers Malloy
Cover Printer: Phoenix Color
Text Font: 11/13 Goudy Oldstyle Std

Library of Congress Cataloging-in-Publication Data

Names: O'Neill, Robert P., author.
Title: Legal research and writing: a practical approach for paralegals /
   Robert P. O'Neill Jr.
Description: Columbus, Ohio : Pearson Education, 2015.
Identifiers: LCCN 2015040931 | ISBN 9780133808643 | ISBN 0133808645
Subjects: LCSH: Legal research—United States. | Legal composition.
Classification: LCC KF240 .O54 2015 | DDC 340.072/073—dc23 LC record available
at http://lccn.loc.gov/

2015040931

10 9 8 7 6 5 4 3 2 1

ISBN 10: 0-13-380864-5
ISBN 13: 978-0-13-380864-3

To my sister Stephanie, who, near completion of this book, was involved in a tragic and life-changing motor vehicle accident. With the power of faith and love from hundreds of people, her survival and ongoing recovery is nothing short of miraculous.

As her older brother, I wanted nothing more than to take her place and to eliminate all her hurt and pain. However, as I watch what she endures on a daily basis, I know that she indeed is the stronger sibling. I will forever be changed from witnessing the physical and mental strength, determination, endurance, hope, faith, trust, and love that she exhibits each day.

So I thank her for inspiring me, motivating me (and telling me) to finish this book.

SUMMARY OF CONTENTS

COMPREHENSIVE CASE STUDY – PART IV: DRAFTING LEGAL CORRESPONDENCE

CONTENTS

PREFACE

"We learn to do something by doing it; there is no other way."

John Holt, American Author and Educator

There are many legal research and writing textbooks on the market. However, as an instructor, I could not find a book that covered the material in a comprehensive yet easy-to-understand format. I wrote this textbook hoping to achieve that balance. Many books on this subject only present the general topics of legal research without any instruction on how to "search" for the law. It is not enough for the student to only learn the sources of law and where they are located. The true education comes from actually engaging in the process of research on a daily basis. This book provides the opportunity for the student to apply what they learn and to see results. Legal research is a complex subject, so it was crucial that my book not only be comprehensive, but engage the student in a way that builds a high level of knowledge, proficiency, and interest throughout the course. I trust that students and instructors will like the result.

■ MARKET RESEARCH

In developing this text, I not only implemented my own concepts and ideas through student feedback, but I also listened to the requests of instructors from numerous institutions who expressed *their* ideas of what material should be included in a legal research and writing textbook. The majority of responses included the top five requests:

- The book must be presented in a **basic** and **understandable** format for an **introductory** level course;
- The student must be able to learn and understand **core concepts** and **foundational** material prior to performing any actual legal research;
- The material must be **comprehensive**, yet **clear** and **well organized** with many graphs, charts, and visual aids;
- The material should be presented in a **step-by-step format** for both print and online sources, rather than presented in general terms found in most texts;
- The book must include many **practical** and **skill-based assignments** similar to what a paralegal would encounter in the legal profession.

This textbook addresses each of those concerns. Unfortunately, many instructors must utilize legal research and writing texts that are written for law students and not for paralegal students. Instructors know that the roles of lawyer and paralegal are different and unique. Therefore, this text is tailored for paralegal students and the skills *they* need to be successful in the profession. In addition, every instructor who anonymously reviewed the manuscript for this book provided positive feedback concerning its content and presentation, making comments such as, the author has an *"excellent and approachable style of writing that students will find easy to navigate,"* [and] *"this text seems to raise the bar academically,"* [and] *"I would choose this text over any other legal research book on the market."*

■ ORGANIZATION OF THE TEXT

The first two chapters provide the basic foundational concepts of legal research, including the US legal system and court structure and the various sources of law. In addition, the five components of legal research are introduced to the student in order to establish a foundation in the legal research process. In chapters three through nine, students will learn about the actual primary and secondary sources of research and how to locate each in print and online. In chapter ten, students will learn how to gather, organize, and analyze their research findings. In chapters eleven through fifteen, the student will see that once all the research has been located, read, and analyzed it is important to communicate those findings in writing to their supervising attorney in the form of a research memorandum. Emphasis is also placed on the basic and legal writing skills required for a paralegal, the importance of correctly drafting legal correspondence, as well as the importance of editing, proofreading and cite-checking skills.

Nothing unnecessary or beyond the skill of an entry-level paralegal has been included in the text. Students will learn how to conduct legal research that will stay with them beyond the classroom and throughout their legal employment. At the end of each chapter, students will utilize their knowledge and research skills within the "Critical Thinking and Application" section. This section will sharpen students "research knowledge," rather than having them answer simple "recall questions" such as "What are the levels of federal court?" Students will be presented with true-to-life fact patterns so that they can see that the research they perform in the profession will affect real people every day.

■ SPECIAL AND UNIQUE PEDAGOGICAL FEATURES

I have added some unique features to this book that will enhance the experience in this course for both student and instructor.

- Prior to actually learning how to research the sources of law in print and online, the student will first build a foundation, including the basic elements of legal research. The student will be "introduced" to each working component of the legal research process. By introducing those concepts early, students will recognize and understand them later and throughout the book. The student can therefore concentrate solely on learning each source of law and the quickest and most efficient way to research each source in print and online.

- Typically, the duties of paralegals include researching the law in the state in which they work. A paralegal is less likely to be responsible for researching federal law on a daily basis in a typical legal environment. However, many textbooks teach the federal research methods in detail, only to "wrap-up" the chapter by including the counterpart state sources of research in one or two paragraphs. Many instructors and students, including my own, have expressed concern over this issue. Although each state is different, the **basic fundamentals** of how to find, read, and analyze a source of law can be applied to the law in *any* state. This book provides equal emphasis on the fundamentals of researching federal and state resources.

- Cases and statutes are the most important and widely used sources of law. Therefore, cases and statutes are broken down into two chapters each. In the first chapter, the student is instructed on the basic information of each source, including publication and how to read and analyze that source. Thereafter, in the follow-up chapter, the student will learn solely how to locate that source in print and online in a step-by-step example. Although cases and statutes are different and unique, students will be shown that both sources of law include many of the same aspects and can be researched in the same manner.

- In order to further assist students and instructors, I have demonstrated, through the use of screenshots, how to navigate a search on both *Lexis Advance* and *WestlawNext* **within each chapter** rather than confine computer-aided research to one chapter. Therefore, the student can follow the textbook instruction outside of class at any time to become truly proficient on either or both systems. In addition, instruction on how to utilize a digest, as well as how to utilize the "word search" index method in print and online is included **within each chapter** so that students can actually "see" how to utilize these sources together in a typical research assignment.

- While everyone is aware of the popular online databases of *Westlaw (WestlawNext)* and *Lexis (Lexis Advance)*, the student will be introduced to many less expensive, educational, and *free* legal online databases that are gaining momentum in the legal field. Although not everything can be accessed through these sites, basic utilization can cut client costs dramatically. Therefore, students need to know that these options are available to them in practice.

The chapters are presented in understandable terms, with charts, graphs, and visual aids where appropriate. This not only breaks up the text, but also reinforces the print material. Many additional features are also provided in various chapters, including,

- *Practice Tips* – these include important information relevant to the section where they are found, which provide useful tips for the classroom and the office;
- *Side Notes* – these include material relevant to the section where they are found, which provide an interesting fact or point of interest;
- *Ethics Reminders* – these include important information reminding students of the paralegal's ethical duties concerning legal research and writing during their employment.

A CASE STUDY APPROACH

In order to reinforce the material learned throughout the textbook, I have also created a new and unique approach to learning the material through the use of the "Comprehensive Case Study." The case study demonstrates the *process* of legal research by using a practical situation that a paralegal could encounter in the profession. The case study is a cumulative exercise that utilizes all the skills and knowledge presented throughout the entire book. Upon completion, the student can use the case study not only as a professional-quality writing sample, but they can also submit a practical research assignment to any prospective employer. Many of my former students who secured employment as paralegals told me that the prospective employer was impressed with the quality and content of their research and writing samples from my course.

In *Part I* of the case study, the student will be introduced to a fictional client in need of legal advice. Students will read the facts and begin to formulate the unique issues in the case with their instructor as they would with their supervising attorney. In *Part II*, students will search the various sources of law, in print and online, and locate, read, and understand the law that addresses the issues presented in the case study. In *Part III*, students will organize their findings by reading cases and statutes and formulating the rule of law. Thereafter, students will outline and draft a research memorandum that will answer all the legal issues raised in the case study. Lastly, in *Part IV* of the case study, student will send legal correspondence to the appropriate parties in the case. For even more practice, an additional case study is included at the end of the book.

INSTRUCTOR SUPPLEMENTS

Instructor's Manual with Test Bank

Includes content outlines for classroom discussion, teaching suggestions, and answers to selected end-of-chapter questions from the text. This also contains a Word document version of the test bank.

TestGen

This computerized test generation system gives you maximum flexibility in creating and administering tests on paper, electronically, or online. It provides state-of-the-art features for viewing and editing test bank questions, dragging a selected question into a test you are creating, and printing sleek, formatted tests in a variety of layouts. Select test items from test banks included with TestGen for quick test creation, or write your own questions from scratch. TestGen's random generator provides the option to display different text or calculated number values each time questions are used.

PowerPoint Presentations

Presentations offer clear, straightforward outlines and notes to use for class lectures or study materials. Photos, illustrations, charts, and tables from the book are included in the presentations when applicable.

To access supplementary materials online, instructors need to request an instructor access code. Go to **www.pearsonhighered.com/irc**, to register for an instructor access code. Within 48 hours after registering, you will receive a confirming e-mail, including an instructor access code. Once you have received your code, go to the site and log on for full instructions on downloading the materials you wish to use.

Pearson Online Course Solutions

Legal Research and Writing is supported by online course solutions that include interactive learning modules, a variety of assessment tools, and current event features. Go to **www.pearsonhighered.com** or contact your local representative for the latest information.

Alternate Versions

eBooks

This text is also available in multiple eBook formats. These are an exciting new choice for students looking to save money. As an alternative to purchasing the printed textbook, students can purchase an electronic version of the same content. With an eTextbook, students can search the text, make notes online, print out reading assignments that incorporate lecture notes, and bookmark important passages for later review. For more information, visit your favorite online eBook reseller or **www.mypearsonstore.com**.

To the instructors who teach this important course, I hope this instructional book assists in your ability to teach this material in a more clear and effective manner. To the students learning from this text, be patient in developing these skills and always ask questions in class, as well as during your legal employment. Keep this book as guide throughout your legal career. I wish the best of luck to each and every one of you.

Robert P. O'Neill Jr.

ACKNOWLEDGMENTS

I would like to acknowledge all of the individuals whose assistance and encouragement was invaluable in the creation and development of this textbook. First, I would like to thank Dr. Julia Hall. She not only offered me my first teaching position to create and instruct legal research and writing courses at Drexel University, but after many discussions on the subject, it was she who persuaded me to author my own textbook, for which I am forever grateful—thank you for everything.

Thanks to my Executive Editor, Gary Bauer for taking a chance on a first-time author and believing in me and in this book. Thank you for your guidance, assistance, insight, and patience with me over the past couple of years in bringing this project to completion. Thanks to the entire management and production team at Pearson, and also many thanks to Shylaja Gattupalli and the team at SPI Global, for all their hard work on this project.

Thanks to my development editor Elisa Rogers, for the development of this textbook and her input in preparing this project for production.

Thanks to Tausha Major, Vice-President of the Philadelphia Association of Paralegals, for taking the time during her busy schedule to discuss the research and writing skills an entry-level paralegal must possess entering the legal profession. Your insight was very helpful—thank you.

Thanks to the attorneys whom I worked for in Pittsburgh while in law school who first taught me the basics of legal research and writing, especially William Walls, my supervisor, mentor, and friend, who not only gave me a job, but an opportunity, so thank you. Thanks also to Dan Dietrick, Estelle Kokalas, and all of the attorneys at the firm for trusting me with your research and writing.

Thanks to the judges in the Philadelphia courts where I further strengthened my research and writing skills during my judicial clerkships.

Thanks also to the many paralegals in the profession who also imparted their knowledge of their research and writing tasks, which has undoubtedly made this a better textbook. They include my good friend and former coworker Brian Shipley, and also Tina Paluti, an exceptional paralegal and not only a good friend to me but also to my sister during her recovery, so thank you. Thanks also to Karla Dublin, David Evans, and my cousin Michelle Marano for all their knowledge, advice, and encouragement during the beginning stages of this project.

Thanks to everyone for all their help at the Jenkins Law Library in Philadelphia (the nation's first law library). I obtained much of my print material from those shelves. I will miss the quiet afternoons spent surrounded not only by the multitude of books, but also its history as well. Thanks also to the librarians at the Drexel University Law Library, especially Peter Egler, John Cannon, and Stephanie Huffnagle for allowing my paralegal students to use the law library for class and for retrieving research required for this textbook.

Thanks to all my former students at Drexel in my legal research and writing courses who truly made me a better professor. Thank you all for your input and feedback from a student's perspective, which was invaluable to me. I want to specifically thank my assistant Alisa Melekhina for her tireless efforts in assisting me research and edit. She provided valuable input for much of the book. I want to also thank my former student and good friend Shawn Hendricks for his time, effort, and valuable insight in assisting me with this project from the beginning.

Thanks to Mary Dilenschneider, Director of Segment Management for LexisNexis, for all her efforts to make certain I had everything and anything I needed from Lexis to incorporate into this text—thank you very much. I want to also thank Karen Henry at Thomson Reuters for her diligent efforts to ensure I had the necessary Westlaw material for my book as well. I must also thank Anne Barnard, Copyright Editor and New Media Counsel for Thomson Reuters, for reviewing and granting permissions on the numerous Westlaw online screenshots and scanned book references used in this textbook, and thanks as well to Allison Manchester and the entire Lexis permissions team for their guidance and assistance for all the Lexis Advance screenshots used in this book. Thanks to Frear Simons, Product Planner at LexisNexis who granted my permission requests and granted the use of their material for this textbook.

A special thanks to my family, including my parents and sisters for their unwavering confidence in me and their continuous support during this project, and thanks to my grandparents (some of whom are no longer with us but supported and encouraged me from the beginning). As I worked on this project, I will never forget my grandmother's continuous inquiry: "Are you done yet?" Thank you also to all my extended family and friends for their support along this journey. As you all know, it was an extremely rough road getting here, but I did it, so thank you.

I want to also thank all of the instructors and their students who will read and learn from this textbook. This book was written for you—I hope it serves you well.

Lastly, many thanks to the reviewers who, after careful review of my manuscript, offered many helpful comments and suggestions on how to make the book the best it can be. Thank you to the following: Carina Aguirre, Platt College/Everest College; Brian Craig, Globe University/Minnesota School of Business; Steve Dayton, Fullerton College; Teri D. Fields, Clayton State University; Deborah Hoffman, Columbus State Community College; Lisa Robinson, Central Carolina Community College; and Sonia Toson, Kennesaw State University.

ABOUT THE AUTHOR

ROBERT P. O'NEILL JR. is a lawyer and professor who began his legal career at the District Attorney's Office in Philadelphia, starting as a volunteer and later employed as a paralegal in various units within the office. Thereafter, he accepted an invitation to study law at Duquesne University in Pittsburgh were he earned his Juris Doctorate. While enrolled in his legal studies, he utilized and sharpened his research and writing skills as the senior law clerk at a large defense litigation firm. There, he performed legal research on complex issues on a daily basis and wrote numerous defense briefs and memorandums for multiple attorneys in the areas of workers' compensation, federal civil rights, municipal law, and personal injury law.

He later returned to Philadelphia and became an adjunct professor of paralegal and pre-law studies at Drexel University. He created and taught Legal Research and Writing and Advanced Legal Research and Writing, as well as assisted in restructuring the Paralegal Studies Minor Program. During that time, he also served as a judicial clerk in the First Judicial District of Pennsylvania, where he has clerked in the homicide, felony, and family courts. He has engaged in hundreds of hours of legal research and drafted more than 80 judicial opinions to the Superior Court of Pennsylvania, as well as three death penalty opinions to the Supreme Court of Pennsylvania. He also has mentored numerous undergraduate and law school interns providing instruction in legal research and writing.

SOURCES OF LAW

RESEARCH

ISSUES

COURT SYSTEM

The Basics of Legal Research | CHAPTER 1

In this chapter, you will see what legal research entails and its importance in the legal profession. Strong research and writing skills plus drive, motivation, and hard work will make you a highly marketable paralegal. You will also learn about the American legal system and its importance in legal research. Lastly, you will need a complete understanding of the federal and state court system to build your foundation in legal research.

■ WHAT IS LEGAL RESEARCH?

What is research? You have undoubtedly heard of the process of conducting "research" within many different fields and professions. Many individuals, such as doctors, scientists, actors, historians, politicians, engineers, archeologists, and lawyers, all routinely engage in research to assist them in furthering their knowledge and production in their particular field or profession. Most importantly, research *provides answers*. Research involves the *careful process of collecting and gathering information about a particular subject and then applying that information to problems and issues to be resolved*. This is true in the legal profession, and it is one of the most important skills that a paralegal can possess.

So what is *legal* research? Simply defined, **legal research** is the search for law in order to address and solve your legal question. Typically, you conduct research to find out how other courts have decided cases with fact patterns similar to your case. As a paralegal, it will be your job to search the law and obtain the necessary information for your supervising attorney to use to take appropriate action in the case.

LEARNING OBJECTIVE 1
Describe what legal research is and its importance in the legal profession.

legal research
legal research is the search for law that can be applied to a set of facts in order to address/solve a legal issue.

SIDE NOTE

Many successful individuals in various fields place heavy emphasis on the importance of research in their work, such as doctors, writers, actors, physicists, and rocket scientists, just to name a few. Astronaut and Professor Neil Armstrong once stated, "Research is creating new knowledge." This is true in the legal field. Each time you perform a legal research assignment, you are creating new knowledge, not only for yourself but for the many others who will learn from it.

Legal research is not conducted in a single action. In its broadest sense, legal research, like all research, is a *process*. Even after you understand the research process, the individual parts can and will vary with each project. For instance, if you do not understand the topic you are researching, your research process will begin differently than if you know exactly what you are looking for in the law library or online. Therefore, the goal of this textbook is to learn the basic skills of legal research. With that foundation, you will be able to apply your knowledge to research and answer or address *any* legal topic, question, or issue presented to you.

Suppose you have just begun your legal career as a paralegal. The following basic scenario might occur in any legal office. Your supervising attorney calls you into his office for an assignment during your first week of employment.

> "I just met with a client who is very upset. A large branch broke off a tree rooted in the public sidewalk next to the client's home. The branch fell onto the client's property. It demolished the client's backyard shed and the huge branch is still lying on his property. I want you to research this issue and tell me if it is the responsibility of the city or the client to keep the tree trimmed. Also, is the city responsible for the shed damage and removing the tree limb from the property? Have a short memo to me by 2 p.m. tomorrow."

He wants an answer by 2 p.m. tomorrow—so where do you begin? Do you use the law books or can the information be found on the Internet? Which law controls the situation? Does this concern state or local law? Has this issue been researched before? No need to worry—once you understand *how* to research, you will be able to determine what type of law controls the situation and where to look for it. By the end of this book, the above hypothetical will be easy to resolve.

The process of legal research begins with asking the right questions so you will know *where* to look to find the answer—that's the key to beginning any research project. By knowing the right issue, you will not waste any time performing the research. Albert Einstein said, "If I had an hour to solve a problem, I'd spend 55 minutes thinking about the problem and 5 minutes thinking about the solution." Once you have the right issue in mind, you should then take the time to carefully perform the research needed to answer or at least address that issue. Lastly, after you have completed the research, you should be in a position to read, understand, and apply the research findings to the issue at hand. Even if your supervising attorney asks you to simply find out how many days he has to file a motion, you are engaging in a research process. You have to know what type of motion he is talking about and where to find it in the rules, and then you must read, understand, and interpret the rule in order to explain it to the attorney.

In this book, you will learn the basics of legal research. Do not worry about the particulars—that will come later. Right now, concentrate on building a solid foundation that you can apply to any research task. To use an applicable analogy, let's say you want to become a professional tennis player. Although you will face many different opponents during your career, some great and some mediocre, you must learn the basics of the sport and perfect your skills. Then you can apply the skills learned and compete against anyone you encounter. Review the components of the legal research process in Figure 1-1.

It is good to understand that there are no "typical" research assignments, as they can range from very simple to very complex. For example, you may be asked to research the elements of negligence in the case of an elderly woman who slipped and fell in her local grocery store, or to locate the exceptions to a breach

Figure 1-1 The Process of Legal Research

Ask the right questions and know the issue(s). → Search and locate the law. → Read, understand, and apply the law to the issue(s).

of contract in a multimillion dollar real estate transaction. These assignments can be performed by conducting research in a particular area of law. On the other hand, rather than being asked to perform extensive research, you may be asked to answer a legal question for your supervising attorney. For example, "How many days does a defendant have to respond to a complaint?" "How many strikes is a defense attorney permitted during jury selection in a homicide trial?" Finding these answers will hopefully require only a review of the rules of court. Again, the issues will vary, but the basic skills needed for successful research are the same. It does not matter how simple or complicated the issue is; it matters that you know how and where to find the answers. In this book, you will learn what the sources of law are and how you can find them quickly and efficiently.

Legal research can be conducted anytime before, during, or after a trial. For example, your supervising attorney may need you to research the law so she can file an appropriate pretrial motion before the court. You will learn that your research skills can also be used during trial. For example, your supervising attorney may need you to find reviews of the medical expert witness the attorney intends to use during trial. Even after a verdict is rendered, you may have to research the law addressing various appellate issues so that your attorney can file an appeal, which is why it is so important for you, as a paralegal, to learn and understand how to become a proficient legal researcher. In addition, you will see in later chapters that a good researcher must be proficient in searching legal *and* nonlegal sources to find the answers needed.

The Comprehensive Case Study is included in this book so that you can *see* the process of legal research. As you learn the material in each section of the book, you will apply that knowledge to the case study hypothetical. Make certain you understand a particular topic completely before moving on to the next section.

Take your time to read the material in this book carefully. Ask questions on anything you do not completely understand, as legal research skills will "build" upon the knowledge you gain throughout the course.

You will undoubtedly learn about legal ethics in another course during your paralegal studies. However, it is important to understand that paralegals cannot engage in the practice of law and have an ethical duty to conduct their legal research accurately, efficiently, and proficiently. Attorneys must follow strict ethical rules, and they must ensure that the paralegals working under them are competent to perform any task, including legal research and writing. If a paralegal fails to conduct a research and writing assignment adequately on behalf of the client, their supervising attorney may lose the case and may even be subjected to malpractice.

Always remember to perform any research and writing assignment with professionalism. Perform each assignment as if you are conducting the research and resolving the legal issues for *your own* case. Think of how you would want your legal team working for you.

■ INTRODUCTION TO THE UNITED STATES LEGAL SYSTEM

LEARNING OBJECTIVE 2
Explain how the multibranches of the United States government system create the sources of law used in legal research.

Although you may have already covered the following material in another paralegal course or during high school history classes, we will review it here from another perspective—how the US legal system and its branches of government "create" the sources of law used in legal research.

Federal Government

federalism
A system of government in which entities such as states, share power with a national government.

The United States of America is a federal constitutional republic including fifty states and a federal district. The principle that defines the relationship between a national level government and a separate state level of government is called **federalism**. This principle delegates the federal government to control all federal matters and the states to retain control over all state affairs, while other powers are shared between them. As such, the United States functions as a multitiered system of government. Essentially, this means that the nation is comprised of one federal government, fifty individual state governments, and many lower-level governmental bodies, including cities, counties, districts, and townships. Under the federal government, the United States consists of three separate and unique branches of government. These branches are identified and described in the first three sections, or "articles" of the **US Constitution**, which is the main originating source from which *all* other sources of legal research are derived. You will learn that the US Constitution establishes the "law of the land," meaning nothing defeats the rights established in this document over 200 years ago.

US constitution
The document that established America's national government, and the foundation for all the sources of legal research.

legislative branch
The branch of government that creates law though the enactment of statutes.

The **legislative branch** (Article I) is comprised of two chambers of Congress—the House of Representatives and the Senate. The main duty of this branch is to enact law. Legislative bills (proposed laws) are introduced by these two chambers and signed into law (statutes) or vetoed by the president. It is within this branch of government where *statutes* are created. A statute, which you will learn below, is enacted written law (e.g., The Americans with Disabilities Act) created by a legislative body.

executive branch
The branch of government that enforces the laws passed by the legislature and interpreted by the courts, as well as oversee many administrative agencies that enact regulatory law.

The **executive branch** (Article II) carries out the laws enacted by Congress and is headed by the President, whose main powers include the power to enter into treaties or executive agreements with other nations, issue executive orders, appoint or remove cabinet members and officials, and act as the commander-in-chief of the military forces. The main duty of this branch is to maintain and enforce the daily management of the federal government. This branch can also enact another primary source of law, *administrative regulations*, which are created by specialized administrative agencies, such as the Food and Drug Administration.

judicial branch
The branch of government that interprets, through case law, the laws created by the other branches of government.

The **judicial branch** (Article III) is headed by United States Supreme Court (USSC) which oversee the federal courts, and is divided into a multitiered court system. The courts have the capacity to interpret and invalidate the laws passed by the legislative branch and draft their legal analysis and conclusions in the form of *case opinions*. You will learn that cases are the most abundant of all legal sources of research.

State Government

Each of the 50 states also has a multibranch structure similar to its federal counterpart. Each individual state constitution has an executive, legislative, and judicial branch with functions similar to those of the federal branches. The legislative branch introduces proposed laws generated by the state legislature that can be signed into statutory law or vetoed by the governor. The executive branch is headed by the governor and enforces the laws of the state. Each state's supreme court, the highest court in the state, oversees the state court structure. Because all of the primary sources of research, including constitutions, statutes, regulations, and cases, are also created and utilized on the state level, you will need to know whether your legal issue falls under federal or state law.

In the federal and state government structures, each branch of government overlaps the other branches and can monitor each other in a system of checks and balances to ensure that any one branch does not yield too much power, as is demonstrated in Figure 1-2. Therefore, the legal sources of research can also overlap. For example, the legislative branch makes the laws but the executive branch can veto them, and although the legislative branch makes the laws, the judicial branch can invalidate them as unconstitutional.

Although the federal and state governments control areas of power specific and unique to their system of government, there are many areas where both systems *share* the same powers. The state and federal systems each have a constitution that establishes certain rights and each can define crimes, enact civil law, and establish courts.

Figure 1-2 The Over-lapping Branches of Government

■ THE FEDERAL AND STATE COURT STRUCTURE

Before you learn the structure of the federal and state court system, it is important to understand the two basic levels of court—*trial* and *appellate*.

Levels of Court: Trial and Appellate

A court is the institution created to settle legal disputes through a process called trial. The **trial court** level is where evidence is admitted into the record by means of testimony and exhibits. The main purpose of the trial, in civil and criminal cases, is for evidence to be admitted into the record and for the fact finder (a judge or paneled jury) to deliberate and render a verdict.

Following trial, the party who lost at trial will most likely appeal the decision of the judge or jury. The main purpose of an **appellate court** is to *review* the decision of the trial court to see if any legal errors were made, such as imposing an improper sentence. The appellate court cannot hear any witness testimony or admit any evidence into the record. If the trial court record is proper, and the law was followed, the verdict will be affirmed. Conversely, if the court determines that the verdict was improper, it will be reversed. However, if any legal errors are discovered that do not disturb the verdict, the appellate court will remand or send the case back to the trial court to rectify the error, such as ordering the judge to resentence a defendant.

LEARNING OBJECTIVE 3
Describe the federal and state court structure.

trial court
The place where cases are heard for the first time where both parties admit evidence into the record and a verdict is rendered by a judge or jury.

appellate court
The place where cases are only reviewed for any possible errors of law made at the trial level.

The Federal Court System

The following is a breakdown of the three levels of federal court as well as the requirement for bringing a case into federal court.

United States District Courts

In the federal system, the trial court level is called the **United States District Court**. In this court, 650 judges in 95 courts across the country hear disputes concerning federal law. As you can see in Figure 1-3, the number of courts within each state is based upon the size of the state and population. There is at least one federal court located in each state.

So, what types of cases can be heard in federal court? Although properly filing a case in federal court is the job of your supervising attorney, you should become familiar with this information in order to distinguish federal issues from state issues. A federal court can only hear a case if jurisdiction is proper in that court.

US district court
The general trial courts of the federal court system.

Figure 1-3 The US District Courts within Each State

Number of District Courts	States Included
States with four district courts	California, New York, Texas
States with three district courts	Alabama, Florida, Georgia, Illinois, Louisiana, North Carolina, Oklahoma, Pennsylvania, Tennessee
States with two district courts	Arkansas, Indiana, Iowa, Michigan, Mississippi, Missouri, Ohio, Virginia, Washington, West Virginia, Wisconsin
States with one district court	Alaska, Arizona, Colorado, Connecticut, Delaware, District of Columbia, Hawaii, Idaho, Kansas, Maine, Maryland, Massachusetts, Minnesota, Montana, Nebraska, Nevada, New Hampshire, New Jersey, New Mexico, North Dakota, Oregon, Rhode Island, South Carolina, South Dakota, Utah, Vermont, Wyoming, Guam, Puerto Rico, Virgin Islands, US Court of Appeals, Federal Circuit

federal question
The authority of the federal courts to hear a case under a claim arising from the US Constitution or federal statute.

federal diversity
The authority of the federal courts to hear a case where the amount in controversy exceeds $75,000 and no plaintiff can share residency in the same state with any defendant in the case.

Federal jurisdiction can be achieved in one of two ways: by a **federal question**, where jurisdiction is met because the United States is a party in the case; or by a federal issue, such as that involving federal bankruptcy or federal copyright infringement. A federal question can also include any right enumerated in the US Constitution or in a federal statute, such as a federal employee filing an age discrimination suit against an employer.

Federal jurisdiction can also be achieved through **federal diversity**, meaning that jurisdiction is not determined by the *issues* in the case but by the *status of the parties*. However, two elements must be fulfilled: each party in the case must be residents of different states (complete diversity) and the amount in controversy in the case must *exceed* $75,000. For example, Jimmy, who lives in Georgia, and Johnny, who lives in Texas, are involved in a contract dispute for $83,221.88. This case could be heard in federal court, as federal diversity jurisdiction is complete because Jimmy and Johnny are residents of different states and the amount in controversy *exceeds* $75,000.

In criminal matters, the federal district courts have jurisdiction over any federal crime that occurs within the US borders, including federal prisons, courthouses, federally insured banks, or post offices. Federal crimes include a violation of a criminal law; any crime where the defendant crosses state boundaries, such as kidnapping; or any criminal "activity" that crosses state lines, such as mail fraud, Internet scams, or crimes occurring on domestic flights or on vessels in US waters. If a defendant has committed a federal crime, he will be tried in a federal court in the state in which the crime was committed (Article III, §2), or, if the crime spanned multiple states, the defendant can be tried in any of the states involved.

Even if a case is improperly filed in federal court, remedies do exist. If a case is filed in federal court but the court does not have jurisdiction (federal question or diversity) to hear the case, it must be remanded (returned) to the state court. On the other hand, if a case is originally filed by a plaintiff in state court and a federal court has jurisdiction, the defendant may remove the case to the federal courts.

In addition to the 94 US District Courts, there are many other federal trial courts that hear specific federal claims and issues.

United States Court of Appeals (Circuit Courts)

US court of appeals
The intermediate appellate court of the federal court system.

After a federal district court renders a verdict, the losing party may file an appeal with the federal intermediate appellate court, or the **US Court of Appeals**. These courts, consisting of 167 judges covering 12 courts, hear appeals based on decisions from the federal district courts. The United States Courts of Appeals are

Figure 1-4 The Circuit Courts of the United States Court of Appeals

Circuit	Main Office	States Included in the Circuit
First Circuit	Boston, Massachusetts	Maine, Massachusetts, New Hampshire, Puerto Rico, Rhode Island
Second Circuit	New York, New York	Connecticut, New York, Vermont
Third Circuit	Philadelphia, Pennsylvania	Delaware, New Jersey, Pennsylvania, US Virgin Islands
Fourth Circuit	Richmond, Virginia	Maryland, North Carolina, South Carolina, Virginia, West Virginia
Fifth Circuit	Houston, Texas	Canal Zone, Louisiana, Mississippi, Texas
Sixth Circuit	Cincinnati, Ohio	Kentucky, Michigan, Ohio, Tennessee
Seventh Circuit	Chicago, Illinois	Illinois, Indiana, Wisconsin
Eighth Circuit	St. Paul, Minnesota	Arkansas, Iowa, Minnesota, Missouri, Nebraska, North Dakota, South Dakota
Ninth Circuit	San Francisco, California	Alaska, Arizona, California, Guam, Hawaii, Idaho, Montana, Nevada, Oregon, Washington
Tenth Circuit	Denver, Colorado	Colorado, Kansas, New Mexico, Oklahoma, Utah, Wyoming
Eleventh Circuit	Atlanta, Georgia	Alabama, Florida, Georgia
DC Circuit	Washington, DC	Washington, DC
Federal Circuit	Washington, DC	Washington, DC

divided into 12 circuit courts across the country, as shown in Figure 1-4. Each circuit is comprised of three to four states which are divided within their geographical area. These courts are limited to reviewing the federal trial decisions.

United States Supreme Court

The highest federal court, as well as the highest court in the country, is the **United States Supreme Court (USSC)**, which was established by the United States Constitution and includes nine justices who hear federal *and* state cases. The USSC is unique because it acts as both a trial *and* an appellate court!

The USSC acts as a trial court involving controversies between two or more states. For example, if New Jersey sues New York over the use of a landfill on the border of the two states, the dispute could be heard in the Supreme Court. The USSC can also hear cases involving ambassadors or other public officials of foreign locations or cases between the United States and a particular state—for example, if California sues the federal government over federal money to build highways. The Court can also hear actions by citizens of different states (Article III, §2).

The USSC also acts as an appellate court of review. A party can have a case heard by filing a **writ of certiorari** concerning a case that was decided in the US Court of Appeals, or from the highest appellate court of any state, *if* it involves a federal constitutional issue or a federal statute. Such a *writ* is a Latin term that simply means the party "seeks review." However, filing this writ is no guarantee the appeal will be heard, as the USSC uses discretion in the cases it decides to hear. In any given year, the USSC may hear only about 50–80 cases of the more than 10,000 cases it is asked to review. The Court will usually choose cases that have a profound impact on the nation, such as a right to free speech, a privacy issue, a case involving the federal government taking private lands, or a criminal search and seizure issue.

The United States District Courts, the intermediate United States Court of Appeals, and the United States Supreme Court are referred to as "constitutional" courts as they were created under *Article III* of the US Constitution.

US supreme court
The highest level appellate court of the federal system and the court of last resort for any state court system.

writ of certiorari
An order issued by a higher court in order to review the decision of a lower court.

Figure 1-5 The Federal Court Structure

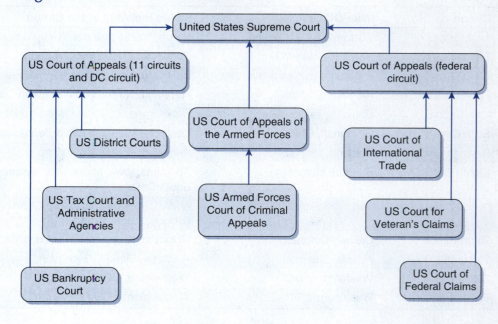

Any additional federal courts shown in Figure 1-5 are referred to as "legislative" or "specialized" courts, created under *Article I* of the US Constitution. They are courts that are not within the judicial branch of government but equally important and hear disputes and appeals concerning specific issues. For example, the US Court of Appeals of the Armed Forces hear all final appeals for *all* branches of the military; the US Tax Court issues decisions concerning any federally related tax claim/issue; the US Court of International Trade handles all claims involving the handling/shipping of international goods and border protection; the US Court of Veteran's Claims handles matters specifically affecting military veterans, mostly benefit and disability claims; the US Court of Federal Claims includes all cases filed by US citizens where the United States is a defendant; and the US Bankruptcy Court handles all claims relating to any of the bankruptcy chapters that are decided.

Review Figure 1-5 to see how those courts are arranged within the federal system and their route of appeal to the United States Supreme Court.

SIDE NOTE

When the USSC denies a *writ of certiorari*, it is not affirming the decision of the lower appellate court. Rather, with thousands of appeals filed each year, the denial only means that the Court has decided not to hear the case and nothing more.

The State Court System

The following is a breakdown of the three levels of the state court system, as well as the requirement for bringing a case into state court.

Based on the federal model, every state, and the District of Columbia, has developed its own court system structure. The general hierarchical levels are similar to their federal counterparts: the base structure includes a trial level, an intermediate appellate court, and a high state court. Some states have different names for the different court levels, but the basic overall structure is the same.

State Trial Court

Most state court systems have established a first-level trial court. Many states also have an even lower-level court that hears summary offenses and traffic violations. Similar to the federal district courts, the state trial courts conduct trials and admit evidence and testimony into the record. There are separate but equal trial-level courts for civil, criminal, and family law matters. Some smaller states and their surrounding counties may hear civil, criminal, and family law matters all in the same trial court.

So, what type of cases can be heard in state court? Similar to the federal trial courts, each state court must have proper jurisdiction to hear the case. Depending on the population of the state, city, and county you work in, the trial-level court may be different. Many courts of general jurisdiction hear civil and criminal cases separately. For example, a civil court may hear cases concerning negligence, medical malpractice, contracts, defamation, privacy, and products liability. In addition, some states have specialty courts that only hear certain types of claims, such as domestic/family law cases, or landlord/tenant disputes. Some states have small claims courts, meaning they only have jurisdiction to hear cases in dispute under $5,000. These various types of courts maintain the court system and prevent any one court from becoming overburdened.

In criminal matters, the jurisdiction of state trial courts will depend on the court structure in your state. Certain courts will only hear minor offenses or misdemeanor crimes such as simple assault, vandalism, forgery, or retail theft. Other courts only hear major offenses such as robbery, burglary, arson, rape, and homicide. Unlike federal jurisdiction, when a state crime is committed, the trial must be held in the particular city or county where the crime occurred. For example, a trial for a murder committed in San Francisco will be held in that city. The trial could *not* be held in San Diego, even though both cities are located within the state of California.

State Intermediate Appellate Court

Similar to the federal system, the losing party at the trial most likely will appeal to the state intermediate appellate court. This second-tier court (first appellate level) is similar to its federal counterpart. At this level, jurisdiction is limited: the court reviews only the decisions of the lower-level state courts and cannot hear disputes. However, not every state has an intermediate appellate court. These states include Delaware, Maine, Montana, Nevada, New Hampshire, North Dakota, Rhode Island, South Dakota, Vermont, West Virginia, and Wyoming. For those states, direct appeals must be heard by the highest state appellate court (the court of last resort) under what is called **mandatory review**. In the states that do have an intermediate appellate court, appeals heard by the state supreme court are heard by discretion.

Some states with intermediate appellate courts have two courts. For example, Alabama has an intermediate appellate court for civil matters and one for criminal matters, and Pennsylvania also has two intermediate courts. In addition, Texas and Oklahoma have two state supreme courts, one criminal and one civil.

mandatory review
A review of a direct appeal by the highest state appellate court in a state system that does not have an intermediate appellate court.

Highest State Appellate Court

The highest level state court, the court of last resort, reviews trial records and renders decisions in a way similar to that of the United States Supreme Court. The highest state courts hear cases based on appeal from the lower-level appellate court or by discretion, other than the states that have no intermediate appellate court. In most states, death penalty convictions bypass the intermediate state court and are reviewed by the highest state court under mandatory review to ensure that no errors occurred before affirming a sentence of death. As a last resort, if a party loses an appeal at the highest state appellate court, they can file a writ with the United States Supreme Court.

As you can see in Figure 1-6, most states are similarly arranged according to that hierarchy. Your instructor will review the court system in *your* particular state. You should also know in which federal circuit your state is located (see Figure 1-4), as this will be very important when you learn from which circuits you can conduct federal research.

Every state has established a website that includes all court docket information, recently published case law from the courts in that state, as well as useful contact phone numbers and room numbers of court personnel. Many states also permit electronic filing (e-file) of court documents. Most websites, even governmental addresses, were never intended to be permanent. How many times have you entered an Internet address only to see an ERROR MESSAGE on the screen? Unfortunately, Internet addresses change or move continuously. Therefore, this book will not provide numerous charts of the web addresses for state and federal information that may become outdated by the time this book is published; rather, you will find any legal website you need to resource by using your own personal online searching techniques.

Figure 1-6 A Typical State Court Structure

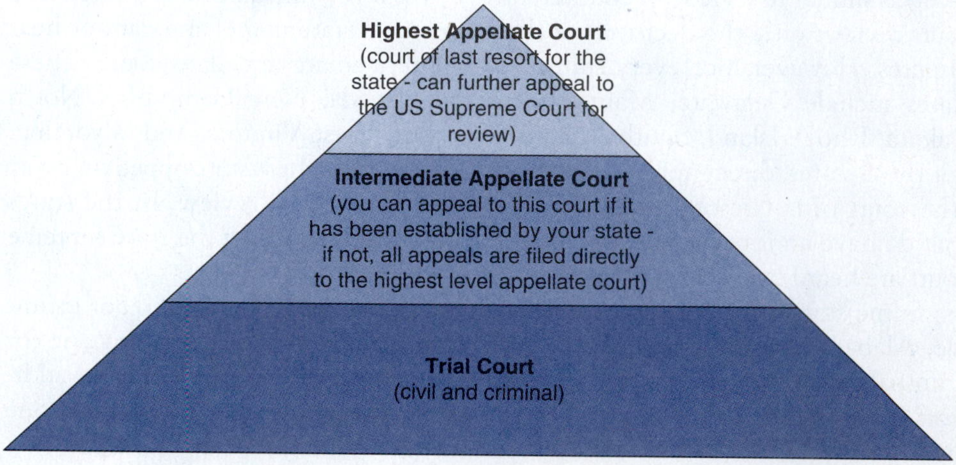

Highest Appellate Court
(court of last resort for the state – can further appeal to the US Supreme Court for review)

Intermediate Appellate Court
(you can appeal to this court if it has been established by your state – if not, all appeals are filed directly to the highest level appellate court)

Trial Court
(civil and criminal)

Figure 1-7 A Results Page from a Google Search

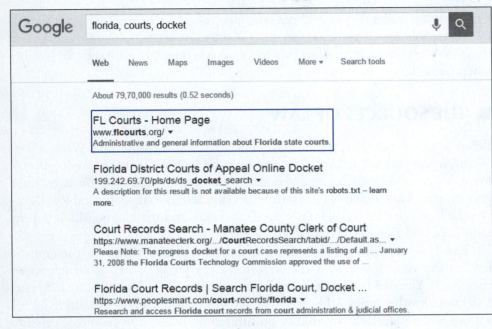

Source: https://www.google.com

For example, if you wanted to look up the website for the Florida court system, simply enter the terms: FLORIDA, COURTS, DOCKET, into any search engine. As shown in Figure 1-7, the first result is the website to the *Florida State Courts*, along with websites for the *Florida Court Records* and other helpful and useful sites that you may not have even known existed. Remember to use your Internet search skills to find many legal resources.

Federal and State Issues Combined

We have discussed which cases can be heard exclusively in federal court and which in state court. However, what if your supervising attorney is addressing an issue that is *both* federal and state in nature? As a legal researcher, you will need to understand this concept.

In the interest of judicial economy, your supervising attorney is not required to file a case in both federal *and* state court. Doing so would drain taxpayer dollars and unnecessarily clog the court dockets. Judicial economy ensures that taxpayer dollars are not wasted and utilizes the court resources in a single trial only where the evidence is admitted into the record in front of one jury. State courts can hear federal issues, and vice versa. If you have a case that involves a federal and state issue, your supervising attorney will most likely file in state court. The state trial judge will apply state law for the state issue and apply federal law for the federal issue. This is referred to as **concurrent jurisdiction**.

For example, say the parents of a potential client come to your firm and say that their son was stopped at a sobriety checkpoint last Saturday night. Although he was not arrested for driving under the influence (DUI), his car was searched and he was arrested for carrying a loaded firearm. Now, there is a state law violation (the state crime of carrying an unlicensed firearm) and a federal issue (probable cause for search and seizure under the Fourth Amendment). The case would be filed and heard in a state court, where the judge would apply *state law* for the gun violation and apply *federal law* for the search and seizure issue. If the son lost

concurrent jurisdiction
Jurisdiction that exists where two or more courts from different systems simultaneously have jurisdiction over a case.

his case at the highest state level, he could appeal to the United States Supreme Court, as the search and seizure is a federal issue.

These are issues that should not concern you—your supervising attorney will be responsible for them. However, it is good to at least know and understand these concepts so that you can provide as much research assistance as possible when needed.

■ THE SOURCES OF LAW

law
The system of rules that govern and maintain order within a society.

Before searching the law, you need to know *what* you are searching. What is law? We all live by rules. Children follow rules made by their parents, employees follow rules created by their employer, and citizens follow the rules made by their government. **Law** includes an extensive set of rules, federal, state, and local, created by legislative bodies, administrative agencies, and the courts, which govern individual and group behavior in our society.

Law holds the answers to our legal questions. Think of law as the equivalent to the rules found in a rulebook for a particular sport, or an employee handbook. You need to know the rules in order to succeed—law is no different. Law provides the "rules" of how we should conduct ourselves in society for all actions we are legally permitted or prohibited from doing in public or private. However, unlike learning the rules for a sport or a new job, the law is vast, and it is impossible to know and understand each and every law on a state or federal level. However, a good legal researcher will at least know *how* and *where* to look them up.

Law is continually changing and adapting to the needs of society. Just look at the news to see how many states continually change, supplement, or modify certain laws, such as privacy rights, physician-assisted suicide, or same-sex marriage. Law is flexible because it is continually growing and redefining itself, which is what makes it so dynamic. The law must maintain flexibility in order to be effective in adapting to social and economic changes in society. Thus, a paralegal must master the skills of legal research as the law is continually changing on a yearly, monthly, weekly, or even daily basis. A good researcher will know that a law enacted last year may have been amended or repealed this year. As the law changes and evolves, so does legal research. Law touches on almost every aspect of our society, so a working knowledge of the legal system is a powerful thing.

The rules that make up the law are designed, among other things, to keep the peace, punish the wrongdoers, promote social justice, ensure individual freedom, and protect us all from any potential wrongdoings involving civil or criminal law. For instance, contract law is supposed to govern the actions equally and fairly, whether between a conductor and a passenger over a forty-dollar train ticket or between two corporations engaged in a ten million dollar contract dispute. In addition, criminal law seeks to protect the victims of crime, yet also ensures that the criminal defendant is provided with a fair trial.

Types of Law: Civil and Criminal

Law is divided into civil and criminal. Civil law involves disputes between two parties, a plaintiff and a defendant. The plaintiff brings legal action against the defendant who has harmed them (physically, economically, or emotionally).

The typical remedy sought is compensation (money damages). On the other hand, criminal law involves the federal, state, or county government prosecuting a criminal defendant. The typical remedy sought is imprisonment. Within civil and criminal law, you could be asked to research either substantive or procedural issues, so it is good to know the difference.

In civil law, **substantive issues** define the rights and duties of citizens within society, which include *personal injury, workers' compensation, medical malpractice, contracts, employment law,* and *landlord/tenant disputes,* among others. Therefore, you could be asked to research what a plaintiff needs to prove in initiating a medical malpractice lawsuit or to check the state statutory codes to determine a specific claim against a landlord. In criminal law, substantive issues define the crimes themselves, including *forgery, homicide, identity theft, burglary, drug offenses, retail theft,* and *conspiracy.* If you work for a criminal defense attorney, you may be asked to look up a specific crime in the state's crime code or locate the elements for burglary so that your supervising attorney can prepare for his defense.

On the other hand, **procedural issues** govern the *rules* set in that area of law that must be followed. For example, in civil law, you could be asked to research the *procedure for filing a civil lawsuit* or *how to join an additional defendant in your lawsuit,* or *how to file a pretrial motion.* In criminal law, important procedural issues need to be researched, as they are continually being challenged in the courts, including *a defendant's Miranda rights (the right to remain silent), treatment during detention and interrogation of a defendant,* and *search and seizure issues.* You may be called upon to research substantive and procedural issues in a civil or criminal case at any time, so it is good to know this information.

Review Figure 1-8 to understand all the primary legal distinctions between civil and criminal cases.

In any civil or criminal case, there will be multiple substantive and procedural issues to be researched and resolved. Again, before you begin researching material, you have to know all the basic concepts and fundamentals so that you can later concentrate solely on learning the most productive and efficient way to conduct your legal research.

substantive issues
Issues that concern the rights and obligations of individuals, including what is permitted and prohibited in various areas of the law.

procedural issues
Issues that govern civil and criminal proceedings to ensure a fair application of due process.

Figure 1-8 The Main Distinctions between Civil and Criminal Law

Criminal Law	Distinction	Civil Law
To rehabilitate the offender and protect society	**Purpose/Objective**	To protect the rights of individuals and resolve disputes
Federal, state or local government (Prosecution) vs. Defendant (Accused)	**Parties**	Plaintiff (one who initiates the lawsuit) vs. Defendant (one who defends the lawsuit)
Beyond a reasonable doubt (100%)	**Burden of Proof**	A preponderance of the evidence (51% or greater)
Guilty	**Legal Finding**	Liable
Fines; imprisonment; death (only in capital homicide cases)	**Penalty**	Injunction (to prohibit someone from continuing an action); restitution; damages (compensatory or/and punitive)
Plea agreement (open or negotiated)	**Alternatives to Trial**	Settlement; mediation; arbitration

Primary Sources

Law, also referred to as legal authority, is divided into primary and secondary sources of law.

primary sources
Refers to the direct sources of law, including constitutions, statutes, regulations, cases, and court rules.

The **primary sources**, those that you will use in conducting your legal research, include *constitutions*, *statutes*, *treaties*, *regulations*, *cases*, as well as *rules of court*. These sources include law created by constitution, legislative or executive body, or the courts. It is these sources that you research to resolve your legal issues.

In Chapters 4 through 8, you will learn where the primary sources of law are located in print and online and how to read and understand each source of law.

The primary sources of law are arranged in order of priority, according to the legal weight they carry. This hierarchy, as seen in Figure 1-9, is arranged from the highest to the lowest authority.

Within the federal and each state jurisdiction, the constitution is the highest form of enacted primary authority, followed by statutory and regulatory law, which is also enacted law. Enacted law is a body of law that a government has implemented, such as constitutions, statutes, and regulations. On the other hand, case law is the lowest form of primary law, which is adjudicated by the judicial system (i.e., the courts), which applies and interprets the enacted laws.

constitution
A document that establishes the framework for a state or nation.

The first source of primary law is the constitution, which is the highest form of state and federal law. A **constitution** is a document that establishes the framework for a nation or an individual state. Our federal constitution is the highest law in the nation. It is the document established by our founding fathers and guarantees each citizen certain basic rights that cannot be abridged by any other federal laws. In essence, the US Constitution is the highest form of primary authority because all other laws are measured against it. For example, if Congress creates a law that proves controversial, the federal courts will hear the case to determine if the law is "constitutional"; that is, the court decides if the newly enacted law violates any of the rights enumerated in the Constitution. The US Constitution includes seven articles and twenty-seven amendments. The first ten amendments are known as the Bill of Rights, which include our basic rights, including freedom of speech and the right to bear arms. In addition, the US Constitution establishes the legislative, executive, and judicial branches, which is the basic framework of the federal government.

Although each state has established its own constitution which mirrors the rights afforded in the federal Constitution, the US Constitution supersedes any state constitution. Importantly, although these individual state constitutions can offer *more* protection than found in the US Constitution, they cannot afford *less* protection that what is found in the federal version. Similar to the federal Constitution, each state constitution has established three branches of government, and the state courts will hear cases that possibly violate the laws of their state constitution.

The US Constitution can be found in print at any library and online at **www.constitutionus.com**. In addition, if needed, a simple "Google" search will yield hundreds of sources for the actual text and explanation of the federal constitution. Similar to the federal document, the individual state constitutions can be located online and on every state government website. Federal and state constitutions can also be accessed through *WestlawNext* and *Lexis Advance*.

Figure 1-9 The Hierarchy of Primary Law

United States Constitution
Federal Statutes, Treaties, Court Rules
Federal Regulations
Federal Case Law
State Constitutions
State Statutes and Court Rules
State Regulations
State Case Law

Rarely will you refer directly to the federal or state constitution in your research. In the event that you do reference a law found in the US Constitution, you will learn that there is always a case opinion that interprets and explains that law and that it provides more information than the particular constitutional amendment. For this reason, paralegals usually do not cite the US Constitution, or their state constitution, in their legal research assignment.

By reading through the US Constitution and the constitution of your state, you will see the similarities and differences between them.

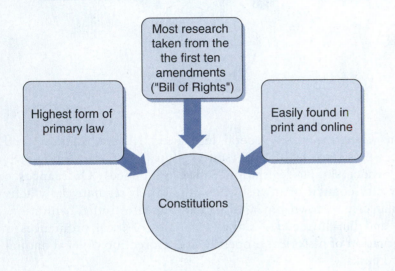

Another primary source of law that is rarely, if ever, used in legal research by a paralegal, are **treaties**. The treaty power (Article. II, §2) is equal to the US Constitution as the supreme law of the land. The President may enter into treaties (contracts) with foreign governments, but the treaty requires ratification by a two-thirds Senate vote. Thereafter, these treaties become enforceable law. For example, in 2013, the United States and Mexico entered into a treaty to share water from the Colorado River to avoid a potential drought in both countries. Treaties can be found online at **www.congress.gov** (which has replaced www. THOMAS.gov). In addition, **executive orders** are similar in that they are legally binding orders given by the President. They do not require congressional approval but carry the same weight as legislation. For example, in 2013, the President executed an order making adjustments to certain rates of pay for federal workers. Executive orders can be found online at the Federal Register at **www. archives.gov/federal-register**.

treaty
A formal written agreement between countries.

executive order
A rule or order issued by the President having the force of law.

The next level of primary law is called statutory law. **Statutes** establish the conduct that permits or prohibits behavior of its citizens. Statutes cover criminal and civil law and are compiled by topic and organized into a *code*. As you learned earlier in this chapter, the legislative branch of government enacts legislation that becomes statutory law.

statute
A formal written law enacted by a legislative body.

Federal statutes cover many aspects of criminal and civil federal law. For example, if you need to know what constitutes copyright infringement, you can refer to the federal statute that governs it. Other examples include federal antitrust, bankruptcy, or environmental and consumer protection laws. Each state legislature passes statutory law in the same manner as the federal government. Unlike federal statutory law, which covers the entire nation, the statutory code of each state is only applicable to that particular state. Examples include tort, criminal, and workers' compensation laws, as well as laws that govern corporations within the state or professions that require state licensure, such as chiropractors.

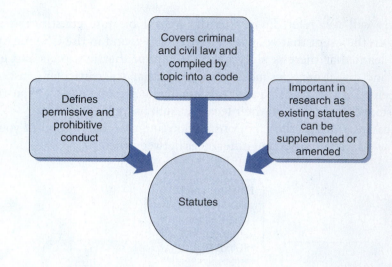

Just as Congress passes federal legislation (federal statutes) and state legislatures pass state legislation (state statutes), local government has the power to enact similar legislation called ordinances. **Ordinances** can be passed by city council or township boards, which regulate daily activity in a particular city or township. Ordinances regulate traffic, sanitation, snow removal, and building codes. Other examples of local ordinances include the preservation of historical properties and protection of local natural landscapes and parks.

ordinances
Laws enacted by a local governmental body that regulate daily citizen activity.

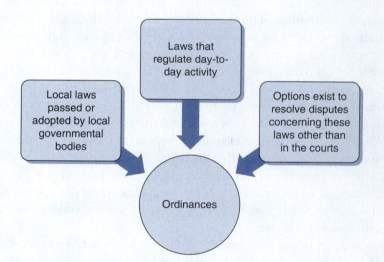

regulations
Rules enacted, monitored, and adjudicated by administrative agencies.

The next level of authority below statutes is administrative law (regulations). Federal **regulations** are laws created and passed by specialized agencies. These agencies are created by Congress and are categorized as executive and independent. The agencies are composed of experts in particular fields who create these specialized laws rather than members of Congress who do not possess the expertise. Administrative agencies are unique in that they act like their own legislature by enacting certain rules and regulations but also act as their own judiciary by enforcing those same rules and regulations. For example, if you fail to file taxes, the Internal Revenue Service (IRS) has the power *itself* to collect that money and impose any penalties.

Other examples of specialized agencies include the Federal Drug Administration (FDA), Occupational Safety and Health Administration (OSHA), Federal Communications Commission (FCC), and Equal Employment Opportunity Commission (EEOC).

Similar to its federal counterpart, each state can pass their own administrative regulations which fall under the leadership of the state governor. An example is the requirement in many states to file both federal *and* state taxes each year. Other examples include milk that is pasteurized and sold in the state and the use of pesticides by a farmer in a particular state.

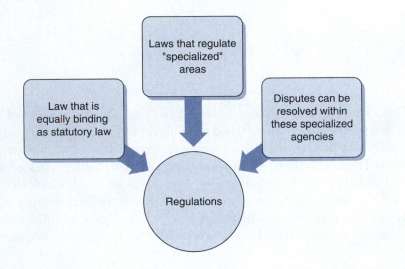

The last main source of primary law, but also the most abundant, is **case law**. Courts interpret the rules created by the legislative and executive branches of government and affirm/reverse/remand trial verdicts in the form of *judicial opinions*. Courts have the power to interpret, invalidate, or create law. Therefore, courts can also be considered independent sources of law.

In the federal system, Article III of the US Constitution established the Supreme Court and authorized Congress to pass laws establishing a system of lower federal courts. The United States Supreme Court is the highest court in the land, and its decisions are binding on every court in the country. Federal and state appellate court decisions are compiled into reports and are binding only in their particular jurisdiction (circuit/state). Appellate judges create "rules of law" that can supplement existing law (statutes). For example, the typical criminal statute for first-degree murder states that murder must be committed with premeditation. However, an appellate court may hold that inflicting a wound on a "vital part" of the victim's body can also be considered an element of first-degree murder. In civil law, the elements of negligence cannot be found in any statute; rather, it is a cause of action developed by the courts.

Case law, or "judge-made" law, is based on the *common law system*, which is a system created by judges who apply and interpret the law on a case-by-case basis to resolve a specific dispute. In order to decide an individual case, the court will look to earlier case decisions involving similar facts and issues rendered by a prior court. A common law system is a legal system that *strengthens* its common law by using legal *precedent*, or past court decisions that bind future decisions. The idea is simple—once a court has made and announced a principle of law, parties in a lawsuit should be able to rely on that principle to argue future cases. You will learn more about this concept later in the book.

case law
The body of law created by judicial decisions.

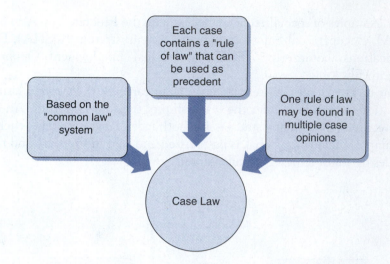

rules of practice
The rules of court and evidence that must be followed during the litigation of a case.

There are other primary sources of law. Examples include the **Rules of Practice**, which include the Rules of Court, and the Rules of Evidence. Rules of court are just that—rules that need to be followed during the pretrial, trial, and posttrial stages of litigation. These federal and state rules directly regulate the legal procedure in the criminal and civil courts, including how evidence is admitted, where to file a trial brief and the number of preemptory challenges (strikes) each attorney is allowed during jury selection. Any violation of the rules, regardless of intent, could result in case dismissal. A lawyer must know the rules in order to engage in litigation.

Secondary Sources

secondary sources
The sources that explain, interpret, comment, and direct researchers to the primary sources of law.

In contrast, secondary sources of law offer commentary and/or discussion on the primary sources of law and *cannot* be used as legal authority. The **secondary sources** help to explain the primary sources. They are very helpful in assisting, instructing, directing, and commenting on the primary sources of law. These sources can be broken down into two categories, including reference sources used to learn about a particular topic/subject of law and secondary practice sources, which are used in daily legal practice. Figure 1-10 includes the secondary sources of law.

Mandatory and Persuasive Authority

The primary sources are compiled on a federal, state, and local level—that is a large amount of authority from which to conduct your research! Fortunately, you are restricted in the sources you can research, in that you can only research authority within *your jurisdiction*, the geographic area designated by the courts.

LEARNING OBJECTIVE 5
Describe the difference between mandatory and persuasive authority.

For example, law is considered **mandatory** or **binding** if it is the "controlling" law within that jurisdiction. Therefore, when the Mississippi appellate courts issue a case opinion, it is considered mandatory/binding authority for all the lower courts in Mississippi *only*. A researcher working in Texas cannot use case law from Mississippi. The state constitution of Maryland governs *only* the citizens of Maryland and not the citizens of Georgia or Arizona.

mandatory/binding law
Law that must be followed within a particular jurisdiction.

If you are researching an issue concerning *state* law, you are bound by not only the primary sources of law within that particular state, but also the law handed down by the United States Supreme Court as it is the law of the land. However, if you are researching an issue concerning *federal* law, you are bound by the primary sources of law *only* within the federal circuit in which you work as well as those of the United States Supreme Court. It is important to know *all*

Figure 1-10 Secondary Sources of Authority

Secondary Sources Used as Reference	Description
Legal Encyclopedias	Multivolume set; broad overview of a topic/subject in federal and state law; cites primary sources; excellent to help "learn" a topic prior to research
American Law Reports (ALR)	Multivolume set; publishes selected appellate court cases from across the nation; offers objective yet greater detail than the legal encyclopedias
Restatements of law	Provides a "restatement" of the common law in understandable terms; provides many examples to demonstrate a point of law
Treatises	Provides good information, but focuses on one particular or specific area of law rather than many areas of law found in a legal encyclopedia or ALR
Looseleaf services	Provides information forms on "specialized" areas of law, including consumer credit guide and state tax guide, among others
Legal periodicals	Includes bar association material, law reviews, and legal newspapers that focus on "hot issues" in the law
Legal dictionary	Legal dictionaries are helpful in learning new legal terms while reading a case or beginning a research project; a legal thesaurus is beneficial when writing legal memorandums
Secondary Sources Used in Daily Practice	**Description**
Form books	These forms are used in practice, typically involving contracts, wills, or leases as "guides" to make certain that no important information was missed or omitted or the actual forms are used in these areas of law
Jury instructions	Jury instructions break the law down into elements that the jury can understand in order to effectively deliberate

the states included in your circuit so you can research federal *case law* from any of those states (see Figure 1-4).

Only mandatory/binding law can be used as legal authority. Therefore, **persuasive law** is found *outside* your particular jurisdiction and therefore cannot be used as legal authority in your research. If you were to research an issue that you discover has not yet been addressed or decided in your jurisdiction, but it has been decided in another jurisdiction, your attorney can request the law to be adopted by the courts within your jurisdiction. However, that does not mean that the law suddenly becomes mandatory authority within your jurisdiction; rather, it applies *only* to that particular case.

persuasive law
Law found outside a particular jurisdiction that a court may consider, but can only be used as precedent if adopted by a court.

Knowing your state and federal jurisdiction is crucial to becoming an effective legal researcher. Your instructor will address your specific jurisdiction, which you can later insert in Appendix B called "My Law." There you will fill in the citation and jurisdictional information for the state in which you will be employed as an easy and quick reference guide in practice.

SIDE NOTE

In 2009, in a criminal trial in Philadelphia, a trial judge defended her decision to reopen trial proceedings after jury deliberations had begun due to the defense admitting false evidence into the record. No case law in Pennsylvania existed that addressed this issue, yet multiple states across the country issued decisions that defended the judge's actions. In her opinion, the judge cited every state that addressed that issue and asked the Pennsylvania appellate court to adopt the holdings of the other states. They did—the conviction and sentence was affirmed.

Chapter Checklist ✔

- Remember that legal research is a process.

- The research process includes searching and locating the law, reading, understanding, and analyzing the law, and applying the law to your legal issue.

- Your research assignments will vary greatly, but the basic process will remain consistent. Learn the basics and you can research any type of assignment.

- Paralegal certification is voluntary in almost every state, and it gives you the competitive edge in seeking an entry-level paralegal position and helps to prepare you to "hit the ground running" within the legal field.

- The American legal system establishes, through the branches of government, the sources of law used in legal research.

- There are two levels of court: trial and appellate. The federal and state court structures are similar. Both consist of a trial court of general jurisdiction, an intermediate appellate court, and a court of last resort.

- Remember that only certain types of cases can be heard in federal and state trial court.

- Know the federal and state jurisdiction of the state in which you are employed.

- Know that many "specialized" federal courts hear certain and unique disputes.

- The state court system is similar to its federal counterpart, although a few states do not have an intermediate appellate court. For those states, all appeals are directed to the state's highest appellate court.

- There may be instances where federal and state claims/issues may overlap. Your supervising attorney will discuss with you how to proceed and which law to research.

- Remember that you can find many federal and state government websites by conducting a simple Internet search.

- You may be called upon to research substantive or procedural issues, or both, within civil or criminal law—know the difference.

- The primary sources of law include *constitutions, statutes, regulations,* and *cases* on both the state and federal level. These are the areas of law from which you will conduct your research.

- The numerous secondary sources are broken down into two categories, including *reference, and practice.* These sources are not used as legal authority but provide commentary and discussion on the law.

- Remember that you can only utilize authority within your particular federal or state jurisdiction.

KEY TERMS

Legal research   3
Federalism   6
US Constitution   6
Legislative branch   6
Executive branch   6
Judicial branch   6
Trial court   7
Appellate court   7
US District Court   7
Federal question   8
Federal diversity   8

US Court of Appeals   8
US Supreme Court   9
Writ of certiorari   9
Mandatory review   11
Concurrent jurisdiction   13
Law   14
Substantive issues   15
Procedural issues   15
Primary sources   16
Constitution   16
Treaty   17

Executive order   17
Statute   17
Ordinances   18
Regulations   18
Case law   19
Rules of Practice   20
Secondary sources   20
Mandatory/binding law   20
Persuasive law   21

CRITICAL THINKING AND APPLICATION

1. In this chapter, you learned about the federal and state court systems. Your instructor reviewed the federal and state court structure in your jurisdiction. Therefore, before learning how to conduct legal research, it is best to know and understand from *where* you are conducting that research. Under the guidance of your instructor, go to Appendix B and fill in the appropriate information under "Part II—Jurisdictional Guide." You can use the guide during your coursework as well as in practice.

   a. In Appendix B, list the federal court of appeals within your circuit in the chart provided. List every state within that circuit. It is from these courts and the decisions of the United States Supreme Court that you will conduct your federal appellate research.

   b. In addition, list the intermediate appellate court of your state (if applicable) as well as the highest state appellate court. It is from these courts that you will conduct your state appellate research.

2. Conduct an online search using any search engine (Google, Bing, Ask) to find your state's court website. Navigate these sites and become familiar with them.

   a. Are there different websites for different courts? If so, what are they?

   b. What is the content included on these websites?

3. You are a paralegal working in New Jersey. Your supervising attorney is licensed to practice in New Jersey, Pennsylvania, and New York. You are conducting research for an upcoming case filed in New Jersey, and you found a case decision handed down by the Pennsylvania Supreme Court that directly relates to the issue you are researching. Can you use that case decision in your research? Why or why not? Explain.

   a. If you cannot use that case, would there be a circumstance when you could use that case decision in your research?

4. Suppose you work for a federal defense attorney in the Seventh Circuit, and she needs you to conduct some legal research concerning the defense of an alleged charge of an internet scam filed in federal court in the state of Illinois. The states included in that circuit are Illinois, Indiana, and Wisconsin. From which state within the Seventh Circuit can you research federal case law to assist your attorney in defending this charge?

LEARNING OBJECTIVES

After completion of this chapter, you should be able to

1. Explain how to formulate and develop an issue.

2. Understand the two methods of legal research.

3. Explain how to conduct the citation and word search methods of research.

4. Understand why validation is important in the research process.

5. Understand what citation is and why it is important to correctly and properly identify your research findings.

METHODS

LEGAL QUESTIONS

CITATION

VALIDATION

The Five Components of Legal Research

Prior to beginning any type of legal research assignment, steps must be taken to ensure that your actual research venture is a productive one. You will learn that because the law is so vast, you need to have a specific starting point before conducting any research in print or online. Also in this chapter, you will be introduced to the components of the legal research process which you will utilize each time you perform a legal research assignment.

■ FORMULATING AND DEVELOPING THE ISSUE

In conducting any type of research assignment, you will utilize each of the components introduced in this chapter. The sole purpose of this chapter is to briefly introduce you to these main components. The idea is that you will be able to later recognize certain names/concepts as you learn the main components of the book. Therefore, you will not become overwhelmed by learning all this information at one time. Legal research and writing is comprised of many individual parts, many of which overlap and work together, so it's best to establish a solid foundation by seeing how all those parts work together before engaging in the research process.

LEARNING OBJECTIVE 1
Explain how to formulate and develop an issue.

Defining the Issues

An **issue** is a legal question that needs to be researched and resolved. By researching and resolving the legal issue(s) in the case, your supervising attorney can determine whether to take any legal action for the client. The legal issue provides the foundation, and is the map, for your legal research. For example, suppose a client walks into your office and tells your attorney that his grandfather, who was very wealthy, died last week. During the reading of the grandfather's will, it was determined that everything be left to the client's brother, leaving the client with nothing. The client said that his grandfather recently amended his will before he died, but also claims that the grandfather was not of sound mind. The client feels that his brother influenced the grandfather to amend the will. The client needs legal assistance to fight for his share of the estate.

issue
The Issue is the legal question that needs to be answered.

If the above facts are true, what questions should you be developing in your mind? Prior to conducting any research in this case, you should ask yourself the following questions:

1. Could the grandfather legally amend his will if he was not of sound mind?
2. If the brother unduly influenced the grandfather to change the will, does that make the will invalid?
3. If the will is invalid, what happens to the estate?

As you can see, asking questions and discussing the case can formulate new issues. Furthermore, even after you begin your research, new issues may form that will need to be addressed as well.

As soon as you receive your research assignment, you have to make certain you know *exactly* what you are looking for before running off to the library or turning on the laptop. This requires patience. If you remember anything from this chapter, it should be this: as you conduct your legal research, make sure you *answer the issue*. This is because the law is so vast that if you do not know what you are looking for, you could spend countless hours (and run up the client's bill) looking for the incorrect law.

You will find in practice that in some cases the issues will have to be formulated with your attorney, and, in some cases, the issues can be created on your own when the attorney provides only a broad and general issue to be reseached. For example, in a complex medical malpractice case, your attorney will tell you exactly what areas on which to concentrate, including the doctor's negligent actions or possible omission to act, any possible third-party actions, or any action comitted by the patient that contributes to the injury such as not taking prescribed medication. On the other hand, if a client is injured after slipping and falling in a supermarket because the manager forgot to place mats at the door on a rainy day, you could determine that the main issue is whether the supermarket manager could be liable for the customer's injury for not laying a mat at the door. In both instances, the main claim is *negligence*, however, both are quite different cases, and the issues for each are different as well.

If you ever become overwhelmed in forming an issue, just think of the *Who*, *What*, *Where*, *When*, *How*, and *Why* questions you need answered? A review of the facts will help in answering those questions as you will see below.

However you receive your research assignment, be sure to always *ask questions* if you are uncertain as to any part of your assignment. Take the time in the beginning to be certain about your task rather than spending countless hours researching the incorrect issue. Asking questions is never a sign of weakness or unintelligence, but rather demonstrates the wisdom to know the task is unclear and that you are willing to rectify any confusion or uncertainty.

Knowing the Facts

fact
A true piece of information that is indisputable.

This brings us to the next relevant point. To fully understand the issue to be researched, you need to know the facts in the case. A **fact** is an action or event that has already happened and is distinguishable from something perceived or assumed. For example, it is a fact that you were late for class today because you overslept, or it is a fact that your phone will not power on because you forgot to charge the battery last night. In the law, the issues in the case are born out of the facts, so without them, it is hard to narrow and specify the issues. It is important to always discuss the facts of the case with the attorney so you that you clearly understand what you need to research. After receiving an assignment, if you find yourself thinking or asking your attorney any *why, when,* or *how* questions, then you know you do not have all the facts.

Making sure you are in possession of *all* the facts is important, *even after you know the issue(s),* because new issues may arise during your research. For example, suppose your supervising attorney tells you he or she just had a meeting with a potential client whose wife sustained a medical injury by their family doctor. The attorney tells you that he has never represented a plaintiff in a medical injury case and tells you to research what an injured party (plaintiff) needs to prove to bring legal action in a medical malpractice case.

However, as you research the law, additional questions are generated in your mind based on your research. For instance, what was the alleged injury committed by the doctor? Was it a direct action performed by the doctor or an omission to act by the doctor? Was it an action by the doctor himself, or did the doctor direct a third party, such as a nurse or resident, to perform the action that caused harm? Did the patient contribute to the injury by not taking her prescribed medication or by not following the doctor's orders? Etc., etc . . .

As you can see, you should know all those facts *before* beginning your research. Such facts could have been easily obtained from the attorney/client. By knowing the important facts that support the issue, you know exactly what to look for. You do not have to guess or make the mistake of handing the attorney *everything* included in the realm of medical malpractice. Even if all the facts were not made known to you, or questions arise as you research your issue, you can always talk with the attorney, or refer to the case file and attorney notes to extract what you need. Lastly, with permission of the attorney, you can always call the client to ascertain any facts you may need.

Ethics Reminder

One of the ethical rules a paralegal must follow is the duty to research effectively. Meaning you need to be fully informed of the issues to be addressed and always research them with diligence and professionalism.

LEARNING OBJECTIVE 2
Understand the two methods of legal research.

Remember the importance of beginning your search by knowing the issue(s) and the facts of the case. In Part One of the textbook Comprehensive Case Study, you will learn to develop legal issues based on a set of hypothetical facts.

■ METHODS OF RESEARCH: PRINT AND ONLINE

Once you have received your research assignment, obtained all the facts, and formulated the issue(s), you are ready to begin the research process. There are two unique yet equally important methods by which to conduct your research: the **print method** and the **online method**.

Years ago, individuals researching the law were confined within the walls of the law library to conduct their research. Today, the law library is still a good resource for conducting legal research but the scope has reached far beyond the walls of the law library, as online legal databases are steadily growing and gaining momentum in the legal field.

print method
A method of research utilizing sets of hardbound and softbound books that are shelved in a law library.

online method
A method of research utilizing subscription, government, educational, and free online resources that can be accessed from any computer or hand held mobile device.

Print Resources

Legal research is first and foremost a "hands-on" skill. That is why, even with the emergence of online legal databases, the law library is still used by legal professionals as a valuable resource, and is the best environment to conduct hands-on research. That is why it is best to know the location and physical layout of the closest law library. During your paralegal studies, you will undoubtedly utilize the law library in your area.

In addition, many cities and counties maintain a law library that is open to the public or may charge a nominal fee for a membership. A list of local law libraries can be found at *The American Association of Law Libraries* at **www.aallnet.org.** Also, many courthouses shelve sources of legal research, but the printed material may not be as up-to-date as a law school library, and these libraries may restrict access to attorneys and judges, so be sure to check out the rules at your local courthouse. Lastly, many mid-size to large law firms maintain their own law library. Purchasing sets of statutes and case reports is expensive, but having the print materials lowers research costs because attorneys and staff can first utilize these books to search a point of law rather than running up the client's bill by using subscription online services, which are expensive.

Knowing the physical layout of the law library is just as important as knowing the location of the law library itself. As you walk through the front doors you will be greeted by the staff at the reference desk, which functions as a typical reference desk found in any library. The law library director and staff will provide assistance and help you with whatever you need, except for performing your research of course! At the reference desk, be sure to ask for a copy of a map/layout of the library, which denotes the different areas of law and where they are located in the library. Be sure to also inquire as to the Internet policy and Wi-Fi use. Lastly, if you prefer to study alone without interruption, or with a study group, ask if you are required to sign up for a study room in advance. Most law libraries have numerous open tables and private cubicles in which to study as well.

As you walk through the law library during a class tour or on your own, you will undoubtedly see numerous shelves with hundreds of books. These shelves are referred to as *stacks*, which are home to sets of legal sources of law. For example, all of the state statutes in your state are comprised of a set, as well as a set of federal regulations in another location. Each set, as you will learn, is comprised of numerous volumes, as well as an index at the end of each set to help you navigate through the volumes within the set. If you ever need help locating a certain set of legal resources, be sure to ask the library staff at the reference desk. In addition, most law schools offer "virtual law libraries" on their university website, meaning that you can view the physical layout of the library using a 360-degree virtual tour.

Conducting legal research in the law library is truly a hands-on experience. Unlike opening numerous documents online that are all confined to a single screen, researching in the library allows you to "see" the research process at work as you pull the books from the stacks and fan through the actual pages. Be sure to visit and spend some time there.

Online Resources

Although the law library is great legal resource, the legal profession is making some major technological advances to ensure legal research is quick and efficient. Today, legal authority can be obtained online through many online subscription as well as many governmental, educational, and free online databases.

PRACTICE TIP

Remember to follow proper library etiquette while conducting your research. Do not write in, highlight, or fold any pages in any law book, as those books are very expensive. In addition, be certain to learn and follow the library's procedure on re-shelving law books.

WestlawNext and Lexis Advance

Although many up-and-coming legal research databases are growing, *Westlaw* and *Lexis* continue to offer the most comprehensive legal research databases. Both of these industry giants provide extensive federal and state sources of law—among many others—but they are both expensive. Your accessibility and usage will depend on the type of firm/government office where you are employed. Below you will be briefly introduced to the main legal online databases, which you will learn in more detail throughout the book.

In keeping up with its competition, both *Westlaw Classic* (now *WestlawNext*) and *Lexis Nexis* (now *Lexis Advance*) have recently reorganized their entire online databases. Both companies realized the need for change in order to adapt to ever-growing technological changes in our society. Some firms/offices may still subscribe to the older version of both *Westlaw* and *Lexis*, but these older versions are being phased out to make room for newer versions.

The greatest benefit of utilizing either *WestlawNext* or *Lexis Advance* is the ability to research and access thousands of documents not only from your own state, but from any state and federal jurisdiction in the country without leaving your desk. In addition, all the information you find will be the most current and up-to-date. However, if we remove the rose-colored glasses for a moment, we also see that the major disadvantage of both these systems is cost. Both system subscriptions are very costly and most of the cost eventually falls to the client. If your law firm/office subscribes to either system, you may be restricted with your use. Thus, two things are certain: (1) you must learn to navigate both/either system quickly and efficiently, and (2) this is why most firms/offices have in-house law libraries of the basic state and federal primary source material. If you do utilize *Westlaw* or *Lexis*, you may incur costs of several hundred dollars for a basic search.

Both **WestlawNext** and **Lexis Advance** offer essentially the same access to hundreds of thousands of cases, as well as statutes, regulations, constitutions, law articles, and restatements of the law from every state and federal jurisdiction. Please review Figure 2-1 and Figure 2-2 for a look at the homepage for both

westlawnext and lexis advance The two primary online paid subscription legal databases that provide up-to-date information on various primary and secondary sources of law.

Figure 2-1 The Homepage for *WestlawNext*

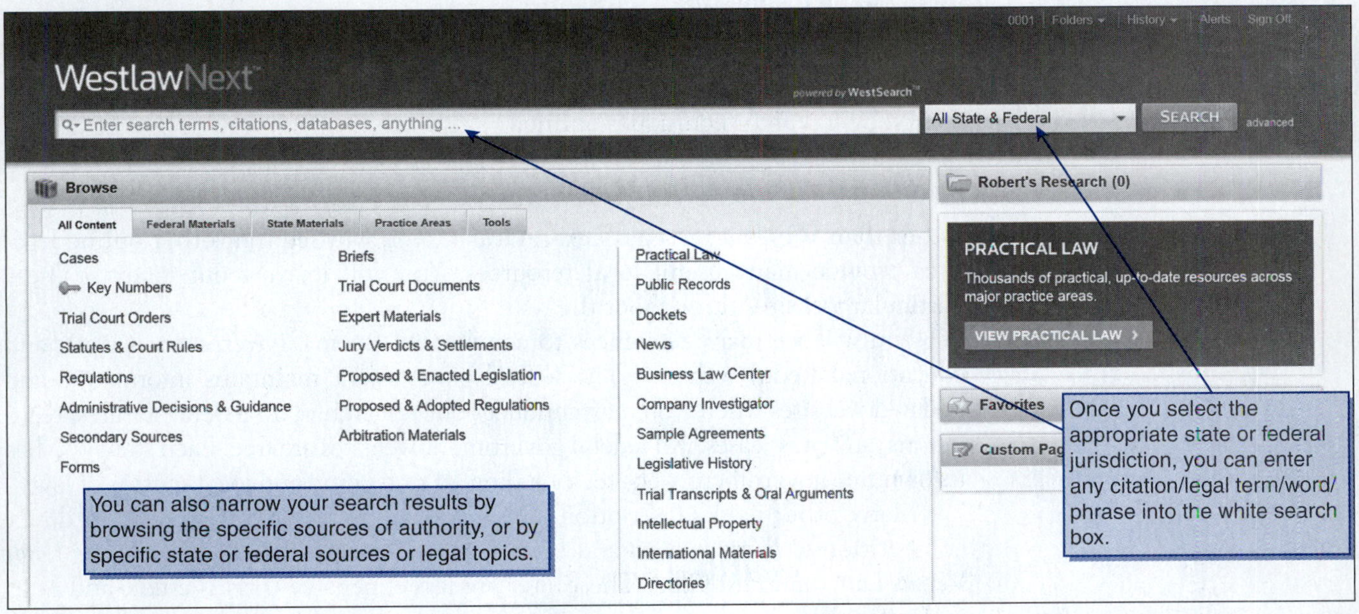

Source: Reprinted with permission of Thomson Reuters: the homepage for WestlawNext.

Figure 2-2 The Homepage for *Lexis Advance*

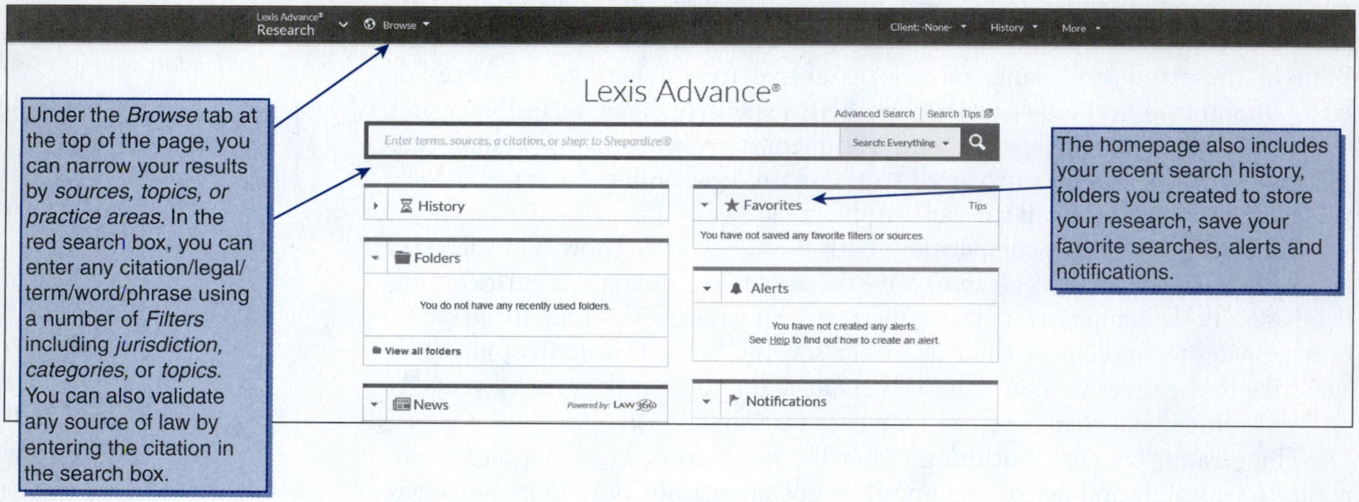

Under the *Browse* tab at the top of the page, you can narrow your results by *sources, topics, or practice areas*. In the red search box, you can enter any citation/legal/term/word/phrase using a number of *Filters* including *jurisdiction, categories,* or *topics.* You can also validate any source of law by entering the citation in the search box.

The homepage also includes your recent search history, folders you created to store your research, save your favorite searches, alerts and notifications.

Source: Reprinted with the permission of LexisNexis.

systems. You can search both databases by citation or word search method as well as determine if the law you have found is still "good law."

The *WestlawNext* homepage can be accessed at **www.next.westlaw.com**, and the *Lexis Advance* homepage can be accessed at **www.signin.lexisnexis.com**.

It is important to note that in this textbook, you will learn the **basics** of how to search for various sources of primary and secondary sources. Your instructor, or a representative from either company, will instruct you further and in greater detail. However, if you follow the step-by-step instructions in this book, you will become at least proficient in conducting a basic search and will become familiar navigating both systems, which you can make known to your potential employer during interview for a paralegal position.

As you learn each system, a good rule to remember is that when you are given a *specific* issue, or a case or statute, to research, especially with a citation, either online system is the best and most efficient way to research. However, if you are beginning a *general* search, you should use the printed material and free online sources first. You can always refer to the subscription sites after you have a good grasp on what are searching. *WestlawNext* and *Lexis Advance* are expensive, so remember that time is money. You will be taught how to conduct the most *quick* and *efficient* search techniques online.

Additional Online Research Sources

Other than *WestlawNext* and *Lexis Advance*, you will see that other online legal sites provide many useful legal resources. You will learn about many of these particular websites throughout the text.

You will see many references to commercial (.com), government (.gov), and educational (.edu) websites. The federal government maintains informative and updated websites where you may conduct your research of all federal statutes, regulations, and most cases. All federal government websites are free. Each state also has its own free government website, including all state, city, and local sources of law.

Many other paid subscription sites continue to emerge each year in direct competition to *WestlawNext* and *Lexis Advance,* such as *Loislaw, Bloomberg Law, Versus Law,* and *Fast Case.* These sites are less expensive than *Westlaw* and *Lexis* and offer some of the same sources for yearly, monthly, and even daily rates. Another website, *Findlaw,* essentially has two websites within one—a "consumer" webpage, which introduces and teaches users aspects of law for nonlegal professionals. The site offers many blogs and instructional videos to learn about the law or to find a legal professional in one's jurisdiction. The "legal professional" webpage (both are interchangeable with a link on the homepage) offers actual legal research sources and directories to locate expert witnesses, legal news, and blogs. The website *Google Scholar* is also growing in the legal field by providing many case opinions within federal and individual state jurisdictions.

Many law schools have a website dedicated solely to legal research through their law library which you will see throughout this book. These sites also maintain their own databases or provide direct links to other free sources of law, such as *Cornell University's Legal Information Institute (LII)*. Many other colleges and universities maintain similar sites, such as *Washburn University* and *Georgetown University*.

Lastly, you will be amazed to learn that you can find any state or federal websites simply by conducting a basic Internet search utilizing any search engine (*Google, Chrome, Bing, Ask, Safari,* or *Firefox*). As you recall from Chapter 1, rather than providing you with various charts, including the websites of the 50 states concerning state or federal authority, where appropriate, you will be shown throughout this text how to conduct a simple Internet search to find any state or federal website you need, providing that the information has been published online.

PRACTICE TIP

You will see that in researching any primary or secondary source in print, every set of books has an index at the end of the multiple volumes. Once you learn and understand how to use a particular index, and retrieve the information you need from it, then you can easily navigate the volumes to find the law. Online searches also have a similar search option format in that most of your searches begin with a main search box on the homepage or from a main tab on the homepage. Do not be overwhelmed by believing that you need to learn multiple research techniques for each source of law in print and online—you do not. Once you have the basics mastered (the index and word search method) you will be able to engage in any type of research with confidence and ease.

Which Is Better—Print or Online Research?

You will learn how to conduct your research using both sources, but which is better?

The Pros and Cons of Print Research:

- The obvious advantage to using print sources is cost. You can search the print sources in your law library for as long as you want, for free. The printed pocket parts and supplemental and cummulative pamphlets do a good job of keeping you updated as well. As many students agree, athough we are advancing quickly through a new technologoical era, nothing equates pulling an index from the shelf, searching for a citation, then physically fanning through the pages of the volumes to find what you need and to "see" the legal process at work. This is especially true for statutes and cases and annotated material that can be numerous in length. It is easier to open a few books than to have multiple screens open at once and reading small print. In addition, it is easier to use the word search method, using the print code rather than online, which can generate thousands of results at one time. Lastly, it is much easier to conduct a general word search in print than online, which can yield hundreds if not thousands of results if not properly done.

■ One main disadvantage of reseaching the print material is the "currency" of the material. All supplemental updates do a good job of keeping you current. However, an online subscription to *WestlawNext* or *Lexis Advance* will note changes on a daily basis. This can also be resolved by checking the currency of a statute online on your state's governmental website. Another disadvantage of using print material is that you must physically go to the library—although a little exercise is always a good thing! Once there, you must find what you need, copy it, and take it home for review. However, most libraries today have scanners, and you can easily and conveniently scan any print page to an e-mail account or USB. There is no need to leave the library with tons of paper.

The Pros and Cons of Online Research:

■ An obvious advantage of using an online service to search for statutes is quick and efficient service from anywhere with just a click of a mouse or a tap on your tablet. Another advantage of online research (especially *WestlawNext* and *Lexis Advance*) is that both services offer the full text of any case or statute plus full annotated material, and the results will be the most current.

■ A disadvantage of researching online using a free online service other than *WestlawNext, Lexis Advance* or a government website is the danger that the information is incorrect or outdated. For primary sources of law, make sure the website is a legitimate and trusted source. Another disadvantage to using an online provider is that it can become frustrating and tiresome on the eyes to open numerous windows or to switch between multiple screens to search for what you need, especially for a novice researcher conducting a word search. You should be careful conducting a general word search until you have mastered the searching techniques. General searches can yield thousands of unnecessary and unwanted results, which will take much longer to read through, as opposed to flipping quickly through printed pages.

As you can see, it weighs out equally. That is why even though legal online research is quickly expanding, *for the beginning researcher*, a *combination* of print and online searches still works best. If after a while you feel comfortable in searching solely online, then go for it. As long as books are still being printed, the best method for researching the law is to perfom the search in print, gather what you need, then make sure the law is still good online and find any updated material. This is the most efficient method for a researcher who is new to legal research. It also allows you to see the legal process and to be most efficient and effective using both methods.

As you become more familiar with conducting research, you can decide which sources are best and most efficient for you to use in your research.

LEARNING OBJECTIVE 3
Explain how to conduct the citation and word search methods of research.

■ RESEARCH STRATEGIES: THE CITATION AND THE WORD SEARCH METHOD

You will learn that after you have formulated your issue and decided on whether to use the print or online method, or a combination of both, your actual search will depend on the information you possess to conduct your search. There are two methods used to conduct legal research: the citation and the word search format.

The Citation Method

citation method
One of the main research strategies that uses citations to locate a primary or secondary source of law in print and online.

Whether conducting research in print or online, the **citation method** is the quickest and easiest form of research. A citation, is simply a specific and unique identifier for every primary source of law. A legal citation includes a combination of abbreviated letters and numbers. Typically, the numbers denote volume and page numbers, and the letters denote abbreviations of the names of the set of books where the law can be found. By providing the citation for a particular source into a legal document, readers can (on their own) locate and find the source as needed.

In print, because a citation specifically identifies a legal source, *no research is necessary*. A researcher can use a citation to go directly to the set of books located in the law library stacks, pull the appropriate volume, and turn to the appropriate page where the source of law is found. For example, if you were asked to determine if wheelchair access ramps are required for a client building a new casino, you would locate the **Americans with Disabilities Act** (ADA). If you were given its citation, **42 U.S.C.§12101**, you would know that you could go to the United States Code (USC) in the law library, go to volume 42, pull that volume and "fan through" the pages until you find section 12101 in the upper right-hand corner of the page.

When researching online using *WestlawNext*, *Lexis Advance*, or any other online legal database, there is an option to "search by citation," which immediately retrieves the source for the citation you entered. For example, you would enter **42 U.S.C.§12101,** which would pull up the federal statute.

However, you will see that on most occasions, it is rare that you will possess the actual citation for the law you need. Most research is conducted using an actual "word search" method though the use of an index.

The Word Search Method

The **word search method** is the more typical format for conducting research. When supervising attorneys give you a research assignment, they will not likely possess the citation for any particular primary source of law. However, as you will see, this is why it is sometimes beneficial to consult the *secondary sources* of law, not only to become educated on an unfamiliar area of law, but also to obtain any citations provided in those materials. In this case, you could find what you need using the easier citation method.

In conducting an actual research assignment, you may be asked, "See if any cases exist where the claimant in a workers' compensation case received benefits after suffering a heatstroke when he was ordered by his employer to paint the outside of a building when the temperature was 103 degrees." You will learn in this book that with that information, no matter how specific and complete the issue is, you cannot simply go to the library stacks or click on your laptop and find the answers to these inquiries. Rather, you must "search" for these answers.

When utilizing the word search method in *print*, you will learn that the print index is the tool to use to find what law you need. Every set of books that contains the legal sources you need includes a separate index at the end of the set. You then take that citation and locate it within the actual volumes of books within the set, which is easy—the more difficult part is the index search.

For example, if your supervising attorney asked you to research the licensing requirements in your state for massage therapists, you would look up such terms as, *license* or *therapist* to find what you need. Massage therapist should fall under a subtopic. You will learn to use "key" words to quickly find what you need.

However, when searching that same information using a legal *online* database such as *WestlawNext*, *Lexis Advance*, and others, you want to use more *specific* terms, rather than general terms. You will see that when conducting word searches online, you can utilize either the **Boolean search** or **Natural Language search**. The Boolean search uses various "terms and connectors," (and, or, but not) and a Natural Language search uses, well, natural language (criminal conspiracy, drugs, shooting, murder).

word search method
One of the main research strategies that uses an index or digest to locate a primary or secondary source of law in print and online.

boolean search
The process of combining words and phrases to narrow a search through the use of quotations and conjunctives such as AND, OR, and NOT.

natural language search
The process of using everyday language to conduct a general search.

You will learn the various Boolean terms and connectors used on *West-lawNext* and *Lexis Advance*, with many examples. Again, for now, just know that sources of law can be found by citation or a word search in print or online.

You should know that no one strategy exists or is required for conducting legal research. Therefore, you are not locked into any particular process to complete your assignment. The process of legal research is not so much about following and applying a particular formula as it is about learning the basic search methods and techniques. Supervising attorneys will not supervise each and every step in completing your research; they just want it completed on time—how you finish and complete that task is up to you. This is why it is imperative to learn the basic fundamentals of research.

■ VALIDATING AND UPDATING THE RESEARCH

LEARNING OBJECTIVE 4
Understand why validation is important in the research process.

After formulating your issue, deciding on a search method, and conducting your research by the citation or word search method, you must validate your findings. When drafting a brief, memorandum, or any legal document, the reader will assume that any and all law cited within the document is "good law." This means simply that, especially in case law research, millions of cases exist, and, over time, many of those cases are overturned, reversed, or repealed. When that happens, the case is no longer good law, and it cannot be used as precedent. The same holds true for a particular statute that may be deemed unconstitutional by a state or federal court. If you do not validate your sources and use bad law, your supervising attorney's case can be thrown out of court, which can also embarrass and negatively impact the professional reputation of the firm or office in which you are employed. When you validate your research findings, you also determine if the law you found is the most current. A case from 1983 in a legal document looks good, but a case from 2010 that states the same rule of law looks better because it denotes that the issue in question was more recently decided.

So, you will learn that for every source of law you locate in print or online, you must validate that source to ensure that it has not been overturned, reversed, or ruled unconstitutional. The two industry-leading validation services are *KeyCite* (found online through *WestlawNext*) and *Shepard's* (found in print and online through *Lexis Advance*).

Print Sources

Citators originated as a print resource. The case reporters containing cases would be accompanied with separate print citators, which included a state and regional version. To validate a case, the researcher would have to look at both print citators. Today, there is only one print source to validate your legal findings and that is the *Shepard's* citator, published by *Lexis*. This citator, which has been in publication for many years, was the *only* method to validate the law prior to online legal databases. Although somewhat archaic, the print citator is rarely, if ever, used and many law libraries have discontinued it. You will find that even if you do not subscribe to either *Westlaw* or *Lexis*, many law libraries will permit you, for a nominal fee, to access *Westlaw* or *Lexis* solely to validate and update your research.

You will also learn that all print resources continually update their material. Prior to a new hardcover volume being released, the commercial publisher will release softbound supplements and **pocket parts** located in the back cover "pocket" of each volume that provide updates of the material in the volume every

pocket part
A thin pamphlet located inside the back cover of a hardbound volume within a set that is reviewed to ensure the law within that volume is current.

few months. These pocket parts should always be reviewed for any recent changes in the law within a particular section/topic.

Online Sources

As mentioned, both *Westlaw* **KeyCite** and *Lexis* **Shepard's** offer online validation services through their online website. Each is easy to use by entering a citation into the search box on the homepage of both systems, or by viewing the validating information from the document itself. Both *WestlawNext* and *Lexis Advance* utilize a key/legend that includes different "symbols" denoting whether a case or statute is deemed "good law" by indicating any positive, neutral, or negative treatment. You will learn and understand how to validate particular sources throughout the book where appropriate. For now, know that they exist.

While *KeyCite* and *Shepard's* are the most popular and widely used citators, other legal online databases offer similar versions that are not yet at the level of *KeyCite* or *Shepard's* citators but are slowly gaining momentum in the field. For example, *Bloomberg Law*, *Loislaw*, *Fastcase*, *Casemaker*, and *Versus Law* all have online validation systems, some of which provide the basic validation requirements.

You will see the importance of these validation indictors, as well as all of the above components described in this chapter throughout the book.

Cite-Checking

Another important feature concerning citation is the use of cite-checking. You will learn how to cite-check in Chapter 15, but it is good to introduce the topic to you. It is important to know and to understand how to validate your research because you will undoubtedly utilize that skill in other ways as well. As a paralegal, you will be given a brief or some type of legal argument drafted by your supervising attorney that will include multiple citations to legal authority. In addition, you will also receive briefs and other legal documents from opposing counsel or other third parties asserting arguments, which will also include multiple citations of authority. In both instances, you will need to **cite-check** by scanning those documents to make certain that the law is still good, or that a particular statute has not been overturned or a particular case was not reversed and remanded. The skill of cite-checking is a very important paralegal skill.

■ CITATION: IDENTIFYING THE RESEARCH

Once you have formulated your issue, determined which method of research to utilize, conducted your citation or word search, and validated your findings, you must "cite" your legal results properly into your legal correspondence to your attorney. You will learn throughout this book that every primary source of law, including cases, statutes, regulations, or constitutions, whether state or federal, are given a unique identifier from which to distinguish it from all other sources of authority. Every source of law that you use in a memorandum, brief, complaint, or any legal document must be identified with a citation. Simply put, the **citation** identifies your law.

A citation is like a fingerprint for a source of law and no two sources have the same citation. A legal citation serves many purposes, and knowing the correct citation is crucial in legal research for two important reasons: (1) the reader knows immediately that the point of law cited is from a reliable legal source and not just legal argument or opinion of the author, (2) the reader, if needed, can easily locate and/or verify the point of law. For example, say you included the following citation sentence in a memorandum to your supervising attorney: *First degree murder includes the premeditated and intentional killing of another human person.* **18 Pa.C.S.§2502**. People who read that sentence would know that if they went to volume 18, section 2502 of the Pennsylvania criminal statutes, they would find that specific law. You will see throughout the book that each source of law has a unique but similar format. Once you know the citation format for a statute, you will know the format for *all* statutes, and once you know the citation format for a case, you will know how to cite *all* cases, etc.

Legal practitioners rely on citation manuals to help guide them in properly citing their law. The two main published manuals used today include The *Bluebook* and The *ALWD* Manual.

The *Bluebook*

bluebook
A citation manual that can be accessed in print and online, including numerous rules and examples of legal citation style.

In your research and writing course, as well as in practice, the citation reference book most widely used is *The Bluebook: A Uniform System of Citation*. The **Bluebook** is compiled and updated by the editors of the Columbia, Harvard, Yale, and University of Pennsylvania Law Review. As of 2015, the *Bluebook* is in its twentieth edition.

The *Bluebook* can be found in print in any law bookstore. As you can see in Figure 2-3, the book can also be accessed online at **www.legalbluebook.com** for a subscription price for one year and can be accessed from your mobile devices. It can also be ordered in print from the website for the same price. Since it is the first and oldest citation manual, the *Bluebook* is most widely used in the legal field as well as

Figure 2-3 The *Bluebook* Online

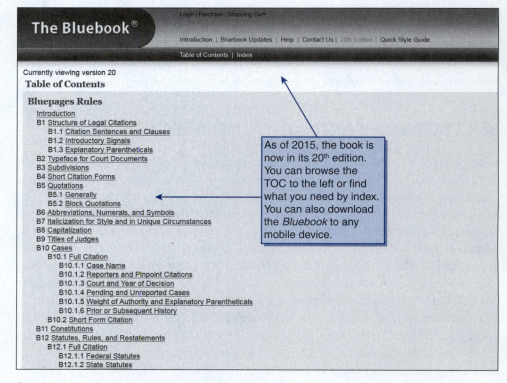

Source: https://www.legalbluebook.com. Used with permission.

in your legal research course. Your instructor, however, will inform you on which format to use. If ever in doubt, refer to the *Bluebook* as the default in your legal writing.

You will see that the *Bluebook* is organized into multiple sections. First, a comprehensive Table of Contents organizes all the citation material. Second, the book is further organized into the rules themselves. Nearly every rule is accompanied by examples to demonstrate the proper citation.

The last section of the *Bluebook* includes actual blue pages of material, including all federal, individual state, and foreign citation formats for every primary and secondary source of law. In print, if you ever need to locate a particular citation format, use the *Bluebook* Index in the back of the book. Online, the *Bluebook* website has many helpful and specific online tutorials. In addition, as you learn the citation for each source throughout the book, you can fill in the correct citation formats in your particular state and federal jurisdiction in a feature called "My Law" found in Appendix B at the end of this textbook.

Similar to any other legal source, the *Bluebook* also updates and supplements its material. You can find any and all updates as well as useful tips on the *Bluebook* website.

The *ALWD* Citation Manual

Although the *Bluebook* is most widely used, citation instruction can also be found in a more recently published book by the **Association of Legal Writing Directors (ALWD)**, which is a nonprofit professional association that includes directors of many law school research and writing programs. Whereas the *Bluebook* contains the actual citation method, this book is an alternative to the *Bluebook* and is more of a "restatement" of the citations drafted by professionals for professionals.

Similar to the *Bluebook*, the ALWD includes a detailed Table of Contents and individual chapters denoting various rules of citation.

association of legal writing directors (ALWD)
A printed citation manual, including numerous rules of legal citation style.

Figure 2-4 The *ALWD* Online

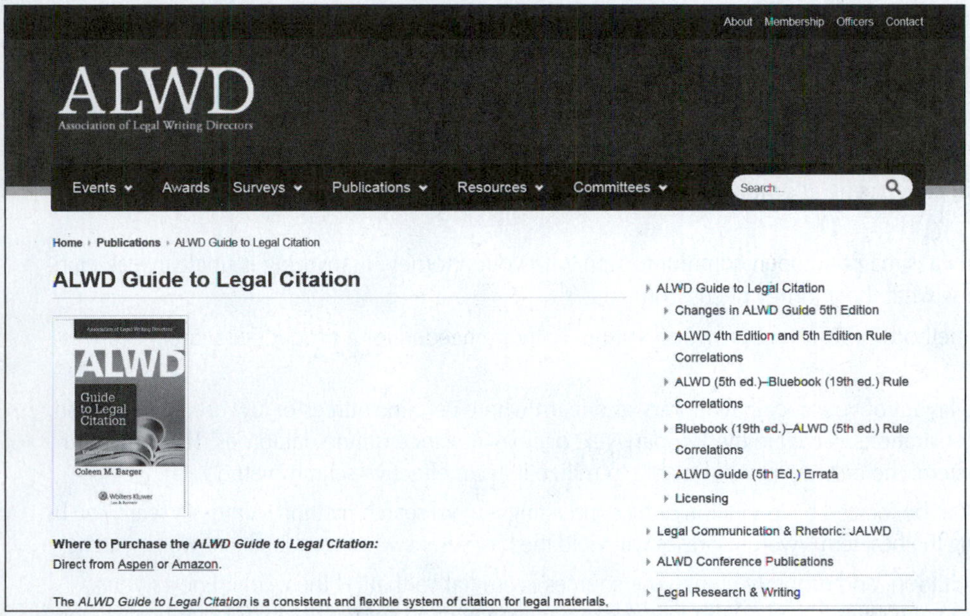

Source: http://www.alwd.org. Used with permission of the Association of Legal Writing Directors.

This publication, in its fifth edition as of 2014, provides many easy-to-follow examples in its "Fast Format" feature. This book is *not* available to view online, but as you can see in Figure 2-4, it can be purchased online at the *ALWD* website at **www.alwd.org**. Similar to the *Bluebook*, all updates to the *ALWD* manual can be found on its website.

In school, your instructor will determine which book will be referenced. In practice, it will depend on the office you work in or which citation rules your courts follow. More often than not, the *Bluebook* is the best resource for citation, but it is best to know that both citation resources exist.

As you learn each source of law in the next section, you will also learn the proper *Bluebook* and *ALWD* format for each source of law where appropriate.

Cornell's Legal Information Institute (LII)

The Legal Information Institute (LII) is a good research source located on the Internet at **www.law.cornell.edu/citation**. The site was recently updated in 2014 and provides clear and accurate citation formats for all state and federal sources presented in the proper *Bluebook* and *ALWD* formats. The citation formats provided by the LII are available in three e-book formats wherein the content can be viewed as (1) a PDF file that can be printed as a whole or in individual sections, (2) a version designed for Kindle (Amazon), and (3) a version designed for Nook (Barnes and Noble). Best of all, all three formats can be viewed for free. This site also offers online tutorials in citing the primary sources of law.

The Cornell website is a good online resource for not only including the proper federal and state citation formats, but also for any doubt as to the *difference* between a particular *Bluebook* or *ALWD* citation format.

You will learn the importance of legal citation throughout this text. It is not difficult to understand and is a necessary component in your research.

Chapter Checklist ✔

- There are essentially five main "components" included in legal research: *formulating the issue, deciding which method of research to use; using either a citation or word search strategy; properly citing your authority;* and *validating your findings*.

- It is important to make certain you are researching the correct issue. Know exactly what is expected of you, and answer the issue completely.

- Be mindful that although you are given a particular issue to address and answer, other issues may arise during the research process. Talk with your supervising attorney to determine whether to address or disregard those additional issues.

- During the research process, always maintain open communication with your attorney. If anything is unclear seek clarification. Do not assume or guess what the attorney needs from you.

- Remember that you have two methods of research: print *and* online. Both are needed for a productive search. Learn to use them together.

- It is best to know the complete layout of your local law library and learn where certain sources of law are located. Also, following your classroom demonstrations, navigate the *WestlawNext* or *Lexis Advance* online databases. The more you become familiar with either system, the better you will be able to utilize it as an effective search method.

- Remember that legal authority can be located by its citation or by conducting a word search method. Although searching by citation is easy, only by choosing the best terms/words/phrases will yield the best results when conducting a word search.

- Every source of law is given a citation, and properly citing your sources is crucial so that (1) the reader knows your points of law are derived from a valid source, and (2) the reader can access any cited source of law for clarification, or to read the source in full.

- Learn to cite-check every legal document not only to ensure that the documents contain good law but also to improve your speed and efficiency in performing such a task.

- Lastly, make certain to validate and update your sources to ensure they are still "good law." Every print volume has a pocket part and/or supplement. Online, if you have access to *WestlawNext,* then you also have access to *KeyCite.* If you have access to *Lexis Advance,* then you also have access to *Shepard's* as well.

KEY TERMS

Issue   25

Fact   26

Print Method Research   27

Online Method Research   27

WestlawNext   29

Lexis Advance   29

Citation Method search   32

Word Search Method   33

Boolean Search   33

Natural Language Search   33

Pocket Parts   34

KeyCite   35

Shepard's   35

Cite-Check   35

Citation   35

Bluebook   36

Association of Legal Writing Directors (ALWD)   37

CRITICAL THINKING AND APPLICATION

1. Visit your local law library and find out the following information:

   a. Know the physical layout of the library, including where each source of state and federal law are located.

   b. What are the hours of the library during the week and on weekends?

   c. Where are the state materials of your jurisdiction located?

   d. Where are the federal materials located?

   e. Where are the study rooms? What is the policy for securing and using them?

   f. What is the Internet policy? Does the library offer free Wi-Fi? If so, save your own data usage and obtain the library Internet username and password.

   g. Does the library offer classes for conducting library research?

   h. What is the re-shelving policy?

   i. Can you take any material out on loan?

2. Think about formulating issues. Without knowing how to conduct any legal research at this point, just answer the following to begin to "think" in terms of forming issues.

   a. If a client has been charged with the crime of, among other things, possession of an instrument of crime (PIC) for using a curtain rod in an attack on another, what would be the issue that needs to be resolved in determining whether the client can be convicted of the crime of PIC?

   b. A client wants to sue the local township after he refused to allow the township workers to dig up the concrete sidewalk along his home, which he just had recently replaced, to lay new fiber optic cable in the ground. The township is only permitted by law to dig on township property, not private property. Before your supervising attorney decides whether to file suit, what would be the issue that needs to be resolved in determining whether the client can be compensated for the destruction of the concrete sidewalk?

   c. Suppose your supervising attorney spoke with a potential client regarding a will. The client's mother recently passed and the will leaves all of the mother's assets to be divided between her two children, one of which is the client, and the other is the client's sister. The assets include a home ($100,000) and a car ($3,000). However, the mother also had a bank account of $50,000 in which she recently signed the client as co-owner of the account. Only the mother and client have access to the bank account as joint owners. The client stated that her sister says she is entitled to receive $76,500 of the entire estate. What would be the issue that needs to be resolved in determining whether the client's sister is correct?

COMPREHENSIVE CASE STUDY
Part I   The Facts and Issues

"Tell me and I forget. Teach me and I remember. Involve me and I learn." –

Benjamin Franklin

OVERVIEW:

Your instructors can *tell* you how to research an issue, or they can even *show* you how to conduct research, but you will not truly understand the process until you *engage* in the process yourself. Welcome to the Comprehensive Case Study. The goal of this assignment is to ensure that you are proficient in utilizing the skills demonstrated throughout this text. If you can complete this case study and understand all the multiple components involved, then you should be able to perform a basic legal research and writing assignment for your supervising attorney in practice. We learn by doing—it's as simple as that. The case study includes a practical situation you could encounter in the legal field as a paralegal.

Think of this as an actual assignment with the student playing the role of the paralegal, and your instructor playing the role of the supervising attorney. The following four part case study walks you through the "steps" for completing the assignment. In Part I of the case study you will be introduced to a hypothetical fact pattern as well as to the issues that need to be addressed and answered that you will discuss and formulate with your instructor. In Part II, you will utilize those sources in print and online to answer the issues presented. In Part III, you will gather, organize, and outline your findings to draft a legal memorandum, addressing each issue in detail and providing the legal answers for each and present them in a quality professional document. Lastly, in Part IV, you will draft letters to the appropriate parties in the case.

■ INTRODUCTION

You are employed as a paralegal in a law firm in the city in which you live. One day, a potential client, Lena Mitchell, walks into the office and asks to speak with your supervising attorney. After an initial meeting, your supervising attorney calls you into the office (*always make certain you have a pen and legal pad anytime your supervising attorney calls you in for a discussion*). The attorney relates the basic points of the meeting and tells you s/he will later assist you in formulating the issues to be researched. Please read the facts for the case study below.

■ THE FACTS

Lena A. Mitchell (age 39) has been employed for four years (over 1,000 hours) as a Human Resource Manager in a federal office in your state. Her office employs more than 60 people on a full-time basis. Lena is recently divorced and has one child, Max (8). Lena and Max now live with her father, Peter (70). Two months ago, Peter was diagnosed with early stages of dementia, which is the gradual deterioration of mental function. The condition disrupts concentration, memory, and judgment, affecting a person's ability to perform normal daily activities. Lena's family doctor referred Lena to a specialist who explained that since her father is in the early stages of the condition, he can stay at home, but must be looked after and taken for cognitive training and treatments every Monday, Wednesday, and Friday under the doctor's supervision. The treatments will improve his symptoms and slow the progression of the disease. If the condition worsens, he will have to eventually be admitted to a treatment facility. Because Lena is paying for Max's tuition and after-school day care, she cannot afford to hire a nurse to stay with Peter every other day.

On January 20, 20__, Lena informed her supervisor of the above facts and requested off every Monday, Wednesday, and Friday beginning the following month on February 12, 20__. Lena also informed her staff of the situation and told them that on those three days each week, she would be available to handle all the day-to-day functions through her e-mail and voicemail. Lena transformed her father's study into a functional home office with everything she utilized in the office, including a webcam to take part in meetings and handle any problems or emergencies in the office. The leave of absence will last 3 months, at which time the doctor will re-evaluate Peter's progress.

Lena's supervisor permitted her to take the time off as requested, but is not pleased with the arrangement, as she is a vital member of the office. He demanded medical certification stating her father's condition and course of treatment. Further, Lena's supervisor told her that while she can have the time off, she is to use all her allotted sick time. Once that time is used up, he informed Lena that she will not get paid. Lastly, in a move that prompted Lena to come to your office, following a week into her father's treatments, her supervisor removed her from her managerial position and placed her in an alternative staff position in human resources. Lena is qualified for the new position, and it better accommodates her reoccurring periods of leave, but the position pays $550 less per month and she lost her managerial title. Lena informed her supervisor that she is entitled to her original pay and title. Lena's supervisor told her that he hired someone to fill her position.

Before you read further, it is important to note that the laws protecting workers in this type of situation are, like many laws, grounded in federal *and* state law. The federal government will not enforce the state laws and the states will not enforce the federal laws. In this case, you will only be researching the FEDERAL LAW applicable to this situation.

■ THE ISSUES

As you learned in Chapter 2, it is not only crucial to develop the issue(s) in the case, but to develop the *correct* issues. Your attorney will likely give you the issue(s) she or he wants you to research. If attorneys are knowledgeable in the area of law practiced, or specialize in an area of law, they will tell you directly what to research. If attorneys are unfamiliar in a particular area of law, they probably will at least guide you in the direction of where to begin, or they may even give you particular words/terms/phrases that will be helpful in your research. Remember that as you conduct your research for one issue, other issues may also present themselves that may also need to be researched. If so, you will have to regroup with your attorney and alter the research plan if necessary.

You arrive at work the day after Lena Mitchell's visit and you find the following e-mail in your inbox.

> Good morning,
> When I get back from court today, hopefully around 3:30, please stop by my office. Let's discuss the issues I want you to begin researching for the client. I need to know if any legal remedies are available to her, which will depend on what you find out for me. I told Ms. Mitchell that we would do some research and get back to her next week to discuss her options. I'll call or text you from court if I need anything - thanks.

Review the concept of issue formulation found in Chapter 2 if needed. What do *you* think are the possible legal issues to be researched in the Lena Mitchell case? Even though you may not know anything about the area of law that concerns the client's situation, what questions need to be answered in order address/answer/resolve the legal issues? What is the first obvious question to be addressed? What other questions do you want and need answered after reading the facts? Remember to separate the facts from the legally significant facts.

You will develop and formulate the issues with your instructor during class. Make sure you ask questions and participate—be involved in the process. Become comfortable engaging in discussion with your instructor, as you will need to do so with your supervising atttorney. You can fill in the questions you need answered below. Once you are equipped with the information you need, and have the issues formulated, you will later research the law to address and answer those issues.

To help guide you through your research, if you choose, take your legal pad and draw up a quick research "guide" to ensure that you stay on track with your research assignment. The information in the guide should be short and direct to the point. You want to at least include: *client name; quick set of facts; the main issue(s); any key words/terms/phrases needed to begin your research; the immediate plan for where you are beginning the research; and the time you are allowed to spend on the assignment.*

Look at the research worksheet below concerning the Lena Mitchell case. Please fill in the issues (questions) you have formulated with your instructor.

Research Assignment

Lena Mitchell—client

Legally Significant Facts—client needs time off (3 days a week) from her federal position to care for her sick father—time off could be around 6 months - told by manager she has to use all her sick/vacation time—needs medical documentation—***removed from her position that pays much less and lost her title.*** Is there any legal remedy?

Issues

1. _____

2. _____

3. _____

4. _____

5. _____

Key Terms _____

_____

Research Plan _____

_____

Timetable—*Always inquire as to the "timeframe" for completion in order to allow you adequate time to fully finish the assignment!

This quick reference guide is not meant to be a perfectly organized articulate document. It is just a quick helpful guide written by you, and only for you. It will list all the important elements you need before you head out to the library. As you can see above, you have everything you need (on one piece of paper) to confidently begin your research. However, do not run off to the law library just yet.

At this point, you have the facts, and you have filled in the issues you will use to begin your research into your research guide. After completing the next section of the text, you will be able to fill in more of the above worksheet, including the key words/terms/phrases, as well as an actual research plan in order to complete the worksheet.

In Part Two of the Comprehensive Case Study, you will utilize the primary and secondary sources of law and actually begin researching Lena Mitchell's issues.

LEARNING OBJECTIVES

After completion of this chapter, you should be able to

1. Define what a secondary source is and its importance in legal research.

2. Explain which secondary sources are used as references and how and where to locate each in print and online.

3. Explain which secondary sources are used in practice and how and where to locate each in print and online.

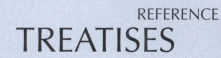

ENCYCLOPEDIA

REFERENCE

TREATISES

RESTATEMENTS

Secondary Sources of Research

CHAPTER 3

The sources of legal research are divided into primary and secondary material. Although the secondary sources of research are not binding authority like the primary sources, they can still be very helpful to you in your legal research.

A researcher can "learn" about an unfamiliar area of law, as well as be directed to many valuable primary sources of law used during the research process. In addition, secondary sources can also be used in everyday practice, such as formbooks and jury instructions.

■ AN INTRODUCTION TO THE SECONDARY SOURCES

Your supervising attorney asks you to perform some research concerning the following issue: whether a witness at a coroner's inquest may be represented by legal counsel? You may not even know what an inquest is, let alone the procedural aspects of one. So, before running off and searching the hundreds of cases, statutes, regulations, constitutions, and local and municipal laws, wouldn't it be nice to be able to familiarize yourself and learn a little about this issue *prior* to researching it? Well you can—that is the purpose of the secondary sources of law.

It is important to understand that **secondary sources** are not binding authority, as they are not the law. Therefore, they should never be substituted or take the place of any primary authority, although you will see that some secondary sources can in fact be used in research to *support* and/or strengthen your argument using the primary sources of law. Therefore, these sources can never be the only foundation for any legal argument. Rather, they are informative sources written by lawyers, scholars, and legal experts who offer analysis and commentary on the law. Therefore, the secondary sources will always be viewed in terms of their academic authority and not their legal authority. However, as you will see in this chapter, they can prove very helpful to you.

Secondary sources of authority are helpful in that they:

- Introduce new concepts and legal terminology so you can gain a better understanding of the law, as they analyze and interpret the legal topic in understandable language; and
- Provide key legal terminology for an index or digest search in print or online; and
- Direct you to the primary sources of law through the use of numerous citations and annotated material, thus, saving valuable research time.

LEARNING OBJECTIVE 1
Define what a secondary source is and its importance in legal research.

secondary sources
A source that is not the law itself, but provides commentary and explanation on the law, as well as provides direction, through citation, to the primary sources of law.

In this chapter, you will learn the various types of secondary sources, where you can find them in print and online, as well as how to cite them. Remember that one of the main purposes of these sources is to direct you to the relevant cases, statutes, and regulations you need. In practice, the secondary sources themselves are rarely, if ever, cited and/or used in legal documents filed with the court, and if they are, the courts are not obligated to consider them. However, if you cannot find the primary law you need, it does not exist (out-of-print), or you simply want to *support* the legal argument you have developed, you may include them in your legal document.

■ SECONDARY SOURCES USED AS REFERENCES

Secondary sources as references are the most widely used prior to when a researcher begins a research assignment. These sources help not only to educate the researcher on an unfamiliar or unknown area or topic of law, but also to help narrow your focus, which can prove helpful before searching the numerous primary sources. For example, suppose your supervising attorney gives you an assignment in which he needs to know if a claim of medical malpractice includes a situation when a doctor fails to diagnose a life threatening condition. By reading the secondary sources concerning this issue, you would learn that medical malpractice involves many elements and can be applied in many different circumstances. Therefore, the secondary sources can at least define, describe, and explain what the law is as well as provide and direct you to some helpful citations to the primary sources of law within your jurisdiction.

As you read the secondary reference sources, remember that the goal is to *educate* you on a particular topic of law, and to *direct* you to the law.

Legal Encyclopedias

One type of secondary source is the legal encyclopedia. Many years ago, prior to the Internet, people referred to print encyclopedias, such as the *Encyclopedia Britannica*, to learn information about a general topic. However, those books lacked sufficient content and the volumes were seldom updated. Similarly, legal researchers utilize what are referred to as "legal" encyclopedias in order to learn about a general topic of American law. These print encyclopedias cover a wide range of broad legal topics arranged alphabetically, written in general easy-to-understand language, and are updated. Within each discussion on a particular topic, numerous footnotes provide useful annotated material directing you to primary sources of law concerning that particular topic. These sources cover numerous jurisdictions of federal and state law. There are two main legal encyclopedias: **American Jurisprudence 2d** and **Corpus Juris Secundum**. Your local law library may have either or both sets on the shelves, so it is good to know and understand the features for both. Both sets are easy to navigate to find what you need.

Similarities Between the Am. Jur. 2d and the C.J.S.

Both the *American Jurisprudence 2d* (Am. Jur. 2d) and the *Corpus Juris Secundum* (C.J.S.) have more than 400 legal topics arranged alphabetically. Both sets include multiple hardbound volumes (the Am. Jur. 2d covers are green and the C.J.S. is blue), and both have multiple softbound indexes located at the end of each set. Although both sets essentially cover the same material, differences do exist between them. Navigating through each is relatively easy, as they both employ two methods of searching for information: the index method or the topic method.

LEARNING OBJECTIVE 2
Explain which secondary sources are used as references and how and where to locate each in print and online.

american jurisprudence 2d
A legal encyclopedia containing easy-to-read explanations of legal topics, including numerous citations to relevant cases, statutes, and references to American Law Report (ALR) annotations.

corpus juris secundum
A legal encyclopedia containing easy-to-read explanations of easy-to-understand legal topics, including numerous citations to cases, statutes, and relevant West topics and key numbers.

The Index Method.   Follow the steps for the index method below.

STEP 1:   In searching through either encyclopedia, begin by searching the multiple softbound general indexes located at the end of the set, which are updated and republished every year. The references in the index correlate to specific legal topics (headings) within the encyclopedia. Think of the terms/words/phrases relative to the information you need and look up those terms/words/phrases in the index. For example, if you needed to learn about renter's responsibilities, you would look up the words RENT and/or LANDLORD in the index to eventually find the heading "Landlord/Tenant." This is also referred to as the "descriptive word method." Every legal topic listed also includes multiple and specific subtopics below it. When you find the subtopic you need, you will see a *topic name abbreviation* and *section number* next to it in bold. This is the information you use to locate the topic within the encyclopedia set. You will notice that engraved on the spine of each volume within both encyclopedias is a "topic name range," such as *Patents to Products Liability*. If there are many subtopics under one heading, such as *Banking*, it will fill the entire volume, or multiple volumes.

As you can see in Figure 3-1, suppose you needed to learn about the causation element in asbestos products cases in the Am. Jur. 2d? Under the heading of *Products Liability*, you find *proximate cause* under *Asbestos*. You see that this topic is found in the volume titled **ProductsLi §72 to 74**, which you would see engraved on the spine of that volume.

Likewise, as you can see in Figure 3-2, suppose you needed to determine if an individual can file a workers' compensation claim after suffering heatstroke while working as a commercial painter when the outside temperature was 97 degrees in the C.J.S. Under the heading

Figure 3-1 The General Index for Am. Jur. 2d

AMERICAN JURISPRUDENCE 2d

PRODUCTS LIABILITY—*continued*
Ancient documents, hearsay evidence,
  ProductsLi § 1680
Animals, drugs, **ProductsLi § 280**
Answers, **ProductsLi § 1558**
Appeal and review
  excessive or inadequate damages,
    ProductsLi § 1774
  punitive damages, **ProductsLi § 1861,
    1862**
  warranty, notice of breach of,
    ProductsLi § 819
Appointment of legal guardian for mentally
  incompetent plaintiff, tolling of limitations
  period, **ProductsLi § 1481**
Apportionment of damages
  attorney's fees and costs, **ProductsLi
    § 1869**
  concurrent causes, **ProductsLi § 46, 47**
  design defects, enhanced injuries,
    ProductsLi § 940
  market-share alternate liability,
    ProductsLi § 205, 206
  market-share liability, **ProductsLi § 189**
  risk contribution, **ProductsLi §-201**
Approval. Consent and approval, below
Armed forces personnel, third-party benefi-
  ciaries under Uniform Commercial Code
  § 2-318, **ProductsLi § 707**
Asbestos
  alternative liability, **ProductsLi § 171**
  market-share liability, **ProductsLi § 195**
  mental or emotional injury, **ProductsLi
    § 1789, 1790**
  proximate cause, **ProductsLi § 72 to 74**

PRODUCTS LIABILITY—*continued*
Assumption of risk—*continued*
  experience with product, **ProductsLi
    § 1257**
  express and implied assumption of risk,
    ProductsLi § 1245
  firefighter's rule, **ProductsLi § 1271,
    1272**
  foreseeability, **ProductsLi § 1260**
  government contractor defense,
    ProductsLi § 1354
  inevitable risk of harm, **ProductsLi
    § 1280**
  instructions to jury, **ProductsLi § 1268**
  intoxication, **ProductsLi § 1278**
  knowledge, **ProductsLi § 1253 to 1258**
  knowledge and appreciation of danger,
    ProductsLi § 1253 to 1258
  limbs, extension into product,
    ProductsLi § 1270
  misrepresentation, **ProductsLi § 846**
  misuse, relationship to, **ProductsLi
    § 1242, 1284**
  Model Uniform Product Liability Act,
    ProductsLi § 1264
  negligence actions, **ProductsLi § 1261**
  notice or knowledge, **ProductsLi § 1253
    to 1258**
  obviousness of danger, **ProductsLi
    § 1259**
  primary and secondary assumption of
    risk, **ProductsLi § 1246**
  proximate cause, relationship to,
    ProductsLi § 1240
  questions of law and fact, **ProductsLi
    § 1243**

PRODUCTS LIABILITY—*continued*
Assumption of risk—*continued*
  warnings or instructions, compliance or
    noncompliance with, **ProductsLi
    § 1273**
  warranty actions, **ProductsLi § 1263**
Attorney's fees and costs
  generally, **ProductsLi § 1864 to 1888**
  amount of award, **ProductsLi § 1886 to
    1888**
  apportionment, **ProductsLi § 1869**
  bad faith, **ProductsLi § 1870, 1871**
  compromise and settlement proposal
    amount exceeding verdict amount,
    recovery by defendant, **ProductsLi
    § 1868**
  defendant, recovery by, **ProductsLi
    § 1868**
  indemnity, below
  mediation evaluation amount exceeding
    verdict amount, recovery by
    defendant, **ProductsLi § 1868**
  party, recovery by, **ProductsLi § 1864
    to 1871**
  prevailing party, recovery by,
    ProductsLi § 1865 to 1867
  statute, decision or agreement, necessity
    of, **ProductsLi § 1864**
Auctioneers, parties liable, **ProductsLi § 90**
Authentication, documentary evidence,
  ProductsLi § 1704
Automobiles and highway traffic
  air bags, res ipsa loquitur, **ProductsLi
    § 500**
  assumption of risk, driving at excessive
    speeds, **ProductsLi § 1278**

Source: Reprinted with permission of Thomson Reuters, American Jurisprudence 2d, 2014 General Index, (P-R), Page 236.

Figure 3-2 The General Index for C.J.S.

```
WOR

WORKERS' COMPENSATION—continued          WORKERS' COMPENSATION—continued
Acts of God—continued                     Administrative boards or commissions—continued
    cold and wet, below                       jurisdiction—continued
    floods, Workers § 513                           determination of jurisdictional facts, Workers § 919
    freezing, Workers § 514                         insurance, Workers § 769, 770
    frostbite, Workers § 514                        presumptions and burden of proof, Workers § 814
    heat injuries, Workers § 388, 515           laboratories, regulation of, Workers § 819
    hurricanes, Workers § 512                   liability of members, Workers § 834
    lightning, injuries from, Workers § 396, 513   medical boards, Workers § 819, 820
    rainstorms, Workers § 513                   membership. Officers or members, below in this group
    sunstroke, Workers § 388, 515               notice, excuses for want or defect in, Workers § 973
    tornadoes, Workers § 512                    number of members required for action, Workers § 831
    windstorms, Workers § 512                   officers or members
Actual notice or knowledge                          generally, Workers § 830 to 839
    actions for compensation, Workers § 965 to 968  appointment, Workers § 835, 836
    subsequent injury funds, Workers § 1599         changes in membership, Workers § 832
Actual physical harm, necessity of, Workers § 341, 342; 1746  confirmation of appointment, Workers § 836
Additional parties. New parties, below              conflicts of interest, Workers § 833
Additions to wages, Workers § 602 to 609            disqualification of members, Workers § 833
Adjournments, Workers § 1167                        grounds for removal, Workers § 838
Administration of state or national fund, Workers § 746   number of members required for action, Workers § 831
Administration of statutes, Workers § 56            personal liability of members, Workers § 834
Administrative boards or commissions                recusal of members, Workers § 833
    generally, Workers § 809 to 839                 removal, Workers § 837, 838
    actions for compensation, Workers § 903         vacancies, Workers § 839
    appeal and review, below                    personal liability of members, Workers § 834
    appointment of members, Workers § 835, 836  pharmacies, regulation of, Workers § 819
    arbitration committee or board, Workers § 1005  physical examinations, Workers § 994
    assistants, Workers § 817, 818              physicians and surgeons, regulation of, Workers § 819
    attorneys, discipline of, Workers § 827     powers and duties, Workers § 815 to 829
    burden of proof, jurisdiction, Workers § 814  presumptions and burden of proof, jurisdiction, Workers
    capacity to sue and be sued, Workers § 816       § 814
    changes in membership, Workers § 832        quasi-judicial nature, Workers § 810
    confirmation of appointment of members, Workers § 836  quorum, Workers § 831
```

Source: Reprinted with permission of Thomson Reuters, Corpus Juris Secundum (CJS), 2014 General Index (R-Z), Page 730.

of "Workers Compensation," you find hundreds of subtopics related to this heading. You see that this topic is found under *Acts of God* in the volume titled **Workers §388, 515,** which you would see engraved on the spine of that volume. Notice that under that main heading, *heat injuries* and *sunstroke* are listed. Both are included in the same section.

STEP 2: In either encyclopedia, once you have the topic name and section number, the rest is easy. Go to the corresponding volume within each set. As you fan through the pages, the section number in bold will appear at the top right corner of each page. Once you have found your particular legal topic, each encyclopedia states a brief definition or general statement describing or defining that source in general terms. This provides a good overview of your topic. Below that heading, you will find more outlined material that discusses and expands on the information even further as you can see in Figure 3-3 and Figure 3-4. Do not forget to check the back insert (if any) of the volume you are using to see if the particular section you are viewing has been recently updated. You do this by checking the inside back cover of the volume you are using. Sitting in a "pocket" in the back cover, is a thin pamphlet called a pocket part, which lists all the newest updated additions relevant to that particular volume since the last time that hardbound volume was printed. This check only takes a minute or so but is very important in a print search, as the law you are viewing may have been recently amended or supplemented.

STEP 3: As you read the discussion section of your topic, you will see that almost every sentence ends with a **footnote**. Those footnotes refer to valuable annotated material, and are one of the main reasons why you search the secondary sources. Each footnote directs you to a particular source of primary authority relevant to your particular topic. Always read the footnotes to determine if a case or statute may be of use to you. Also note that included in both sets are many cross-references to other sections within that same encyclopedia as well as to other secondary sources.

If you notice in Figure 3-3, the Am. Jur. 2d first provides helpful research references with the *West Key Numbers*, and other secondary

Figure 3-3 Search Result for Section 73 in the Am. Jur. 2d

PRODUCTS LIABILITY   **§ 73**

able and may float in the air, it is possible that even those who do not come into direct physical contact with asbestos products may suffer from asbestos poisoning.[4] Second, due to the microscopic size of asbestos fibers, asbestos cannot always be seen drifting in the air or entering a plaintiff's body. The small size of these fibers also means that asbestos fibers from different sources are generally indistinguishable from one another, even when removed from a plaintiff's body and examined through a microscope.[5] Third, asbestos injuries take extended period of time to manifest itself. A plaintiff exposed to asbestos fibers often does not know exactly when or how he or she was injured and therefore is unable to describe the circumstances of such injury occurred. In addition, even when a plaintiff can narrow the circumstances of exposure to a single event or location, the extended passage of time between exposure and manifestation means that witnesses are no longer readily available and the memories of those who are available have become unreliable. Due to these unique problems, plaintiffs have had to rely heavily upon circumstantial evidence in order to show causation.[7]

> *The information provided is very helpful and easy to read and understand. Remember that you read a legal encyclopedia to "learn" about a topic. Many footnotes to cases are provided. As you can see, practice tips and observations are included where appropriate.*

◆ **Practice Tip:** Plaintiffs who claim they were injured from inhaling asbestos dust do not have to produce evidence that they would have avoided exposure had they been warned of the risk, where the manufacturer fails to produce evidence bearing on the plaintiffs' knowledge of the risk of injury posed by inhalation of asbestos dust.[8]

◆ **Observation:** It has been noted that any time a person who has been exposed to asbestos in the workplace subsequently is found to have cancer, there will be a reasonable medical probability that the asbestos exposure caused the cancer. However, this statistical correlation standing alone, in the absence of any medical evidence of asbestos fibers in the cancer victim's body, does not give rise to liability.[9]

---

§ 73   Asbestos cases—Proving exposure

Research References
West's Key Number Digest, Products Liability ☞201, 349, 369, 390

A plaintiff in a products liability case must present evidence justify-

---

[4]Thacker v. UNR Industries, Inc., 151 Ill. 2d 343, 177 Ill. Dec. 379, 603 N.E.2d 449 (1992).

[5]Thacker v. UNR Industries, Inc., 151 Ill. 2d 343, 177 Ill. Dec. 379, 603 N.E.2d 449 (1992).

[6]Thacker v. UNR Industries, Inc., 151 Ill. 2d 343, 177 Ill. Dec. 379, 603 N.E.2d 449 (1992).

[7]Thacker v. UNR Industries, Inc., 151 Ill. 2d 343, 177 Ill. Dec. 379, 603 N.E.2d 449 (1992).

[8]Coward v. Owens-Corning Fiberglas Corp., 1999 PA Super 82, 729 A.2d 614 (1999).

[9]Norman v. National Gypsum Co., 739 F. Supp. 1137 (E.D. Tenn. 1990).

117

---

sources. As you can see, the topic explanations are written in understandable language. Footnotes to cases that have ruled on this topic are arranged according to jurisdiction. Many additional research sources are also at your disposal so you may conduct further research on the topic.

As you can see, in Figure 3-4, in the C.J.S., the subtopic entry first provides a research reference with *West Key Numbers*. Also, the topic provides a quick summary of the law, followed by an explanation written in understandable language, as well as multiple footnotes to cases that have ruled on this topic, which are arranged according to jurisdiction.

STEP 4: After reading about your particular topic, be sure to make sure the material concerning your topic is the most recent printed version. Make sure to check the pocket part for any updates.

Take note that within any print set, if a particular topic or section has been updated with a large amount of material and becomes "too thick" to be a pocket part, an individual softbound supplement pamphlet may be printed and placed in between the corresponding hardbound volumes on the shelf until a new volume can be printed.

Figure 3-4 Search Result for "Sunstroke" in the C.J.S.

§ 514 CORPUS JURIS SECUNDUM

and that the employee's risk is no greater than that of the coemployees, is not a defense in a workers' compensation proceeding.[2]

§ 515 Sunstroke, heatstroke, or heat prostration

Research References

West's Key Number Digest, Workers' Compensation ⟹642

Heat exhaustion, sunstroke, heatstroke, or heat prostration caused by an employee's usual conditions of employment are within the coverage afforded by a workers' compensation act if the employee is subject to risks in excess of those of the general public.

Heat exhaustion, sunstroke, heatstroke, or heat prostration caused by an employee's usual conditions of employment are within the coverage afforded by the workers' compensation act if the employee is subject to risks in excess of those of the general public.[1] The requirement that a compensable injury arise out of and in the course of the employment is met where the employment exposes a worker to a special risk from heatstroke or sunstroke, and the employee suffers death or disability from a heatstroke or sunstroke.[2] If the exposure results in the employee's death from heatstroke, compensation will not be denied on the ground that the worker does not die immediately.[3]

The heat exhaustion of an employee wh[...]ter hazard[...]ed to the pub[...]ed in the cou[...]was not compensable.

The *West* Key Number #642. This number can be used to find this topic in any *West* publication in print or online.

j. Miscellaneous Causes, Circumstances, and Conditions of Injury

vicinity was subjected, and therefore, his injuries were compensable.[1]

Ill.—American Freight Forwarding Corp. Yale Transp. Division v. Industrial Commission, 31 Ill. 2d 293, 201 N.E.2d 399 (1964).

[2]Neb.—Mead v. Missouri Val. Grain, Inc., 178 Neb. 553, 134 N.W.2d 243 (1965).

[Section 515]

[1]Ariz.—Aquino v. Industrial Commission, 8 Ariz. App. 444, 447 P.2d 259 (1968).

truck, was subject to greater hazard of heat exhaustion than applied to the general public.[1]

[1]Tex.—Texas Employers' Ins. Ass'n v. Rogers, 487 S.W.2d 807 (Tex. Civ. App. Eastland 1972).

Stroke from heat and heavy lifting

An employee's heatstroke while on the job was a sudden change in body attributable to lifting heavy materials in hot and humid conditions over a short period of time rather than a gradually occurring degenerative condition that would not qualify for workers' compensation.

Source: Reprinted with permission of Thomson Reuters, CJS, Volume 99 section 515, Page 576.

PRACTICE TIP

Some, if not many of the primary sources of law cited in the legal encyclopedia footnotes can be quite old. However, it is important to know that just because a case was decided 20 years ago, it is not "bad law." If you find a case that stands for the law you need, and that case has not been overturned, it is still considered "good law" and should be used. However, it is good practice to use the most recent law if possible. You will learn that many older decisions may also lead you to a newer more recent case that states the same legal principle. You will learn about the importance of updating case law in Chapter 7.

STEP 5: Once you have learned about your topic, with some possible citations in hand, go to those primary sources of law and retrieve them. You will learn in later chapters how to use the citations to find relevant primary authority.

The Topic Method. When using either encyclopedia set, the topic method is easy to use. Because the individual volumes in each set are arranged alphabetically by topic range, you can simply scan the volumes for the one that *should* include what you need. At the beginning of each volume, an index, for that particular volume, includes the scope of the information in that volume.

Differences Between the Am. Jur. 2d and the C.J.S.

Before beginning a search, it is important to know there are differences between these sets that you should be aware. Knowing these differences will help you determine which encyclopedia is best for you.

1. While both encyclopedias include state and federal sources on a national level, Am. Jur. 2d focuses more on federal law, particularly statutory law, whereas C.J.S. divides state and federal coverage more equally.
2. The explanation and coverage of legal topics in Am. Jur. 2d are shorter and to the point, whereas the explanations in C.J.S. are longer, more in-depth, and more comprehensive.
3. The citations included in the footnotes include mostly statutory law found in Am. Jur. 2d, whereas the citations found in C.J.S. consist mostly of case law.
4. Am. Jur. 2d is more "selective" in its use of footnotes than C.J.S. Am. Jur. 2d provides citations for the cases that the publishers determine are most important, whereas C.J.S. is more liberal and generous with its use of annotated material.
5. If you need help deciphering the topic abbreviations in the index, a *Table of Abbreviations* in the Am. Jur. 2d set will help, located at the front of each volume. A *Desk Book* is also located at the end of the set, which includes a topic list. The C.J.S. lists its topics in each volume on the first page.
6. Am. Jur. 2d also has published a *Table of Statutes*. This supplement, located at the end of the set, can be helpful if you *already have* a federal citation. This supplement has a list of numerous citations with the appropriate corresponding legal topic and section number within the set. This can be helpful if you have a case or statute that you need explained for you. C.J.S. does not have this volume. Instead, it does publish a supplemental multi-volume entitled *Table of Cases*, which operates in the same fashion.

7. Am. Jur. 2d also has also printed a hardbound supplement (or three-ring binder) called the *New Topic Service*, which does not update any information within the existing encyclopedia, but updates *new topics* within the law. For example, suppose the encyclopedia included a topic concerning "Police Surveillance." Suppose under that particular topic, various surveillance methods were listed, including the use of wiretapping and GPS systems. However, after all the updated supplements were printed, a new surveillance method was introduced into the law, for example, the use of drones hovering over your home! That would be considered a new topic and would be included within the *New Topic Service* supplement. The C.J.S. does not have this volume.

8. The Am. Jur. 2d set also provides cross-references to another secondary source, the *American Law Reports* (ALR), which the C.J.S. does not.

9. When searching in print, be sure to scan all the indexes for both sets. If either publisher decides to publish a new type of supplemental booklet, just read and navigate it the same as you would any of the supplements mentioned above, as all are easy to use.

west key number system
A system created by West where each legal issue and topic found in a case published by West is summarized in a headnote and assigned a specific and unique Topic and Key Number.

One similar and useful feature that both encyclopedias have in common includes yet another method of research—the Digest System, also referred to as the **West Key Number System**. A digest is not considered a primary or secondary source, but a "finding tool." Simply stated, a digest includes a set of printed books, similar to the legal encyclopedias, which include multiple volumes and indexes. Within the index, topic words and terms are given a "key number," similar to the section number used in the legal encyclopedias, that can be used to find the law you seek within the volumes in the set. The unique feature of the digest is that *West* has incorporated its "key number" system into all of its publications and online sources. This means that the key number given to each topic is the same number recognized in any source that utilizes the *West* key number system, including the legal encyclopedias. Please refer to Chapter 7 for a complete and detailed step-by-step explanation on how to use the digest system.

Am. Jur. 2d and C.J.S. Online

Unfortunately, neither legal encyclopedia can be accessed online for free which is a good reason to know how to navigate the print sources. However, if you have a subscription, you can access Am. Jur. 2d through *WestlawNext* and *Lexis Advance*. You can only access the C.J.S. through *WestlawNext*. Once you become familiar with the print set, an advantage of using the online version is that any and all citations to primary authority are in hyperlink form and are just a click away from accessing that source.

WESTLAWNEXT: type in the phrase: AMERICAN JURISPRUDENCE 2D into the top search box. Before you can even finish typing, a drop-down of suggestions will include: *American Jurisprudence 2d* (choose if you are using the "topic method") and *American Jurisprudence 2d General Index* (choose if you are using the "index method"). You can begin searching as you would the print version. Similarly, to access the other encyclopedia, type the phrase: CORPUS JURIS SECUNDUM into the top search box. Again, before you can finish typing, a drop-down of suggestions will include: *Corpus Juris Secundum* (choose if you are using the "topic method") and *Corpus Juris Secundum Index* (choose if you are using the "index method"). Begin searching as you would the print version. As you can see in Figure 3-5, an entry concerning the topic of "Adoption" was found on *WestlawNext*. Notice that this general topic is identified as *West* Key Number #4, meaning that key number can be used to find that topic within any *West* publication.

LEXIS ADVANCE: type in the term: AMERICAN JURISPRUDENCE 2D into the top search box. You can also run a search from the same search box by first clicking on **Filter** and choose **Secondary Sources**. Thereafter, type: AM. JUR. 2D, ASBESTOS, PRODUCTS LIABILITY into the search box and select **Search**. Note that you must narrow your search by including the ***particular*** secondary source (Am Jur 2d) with your search terms—if not, the search will retrieve thousands of entries where asbestos topics occur in ***every*** secondary source available. As you can see in Figure 3-6, the search result page will list results in the order of the most highlighted terms that you entered in your search. It is more than likely that the first result will be the best result to begin reading.

Of course, if you already have a citation from either encyclopedia, you can simply enter it into the search box on either *WestlawNext* or *Lexis Advance* to retrieve it.

Figure 3-5 An Entry in the Am. Jur. on *WestlawNext*

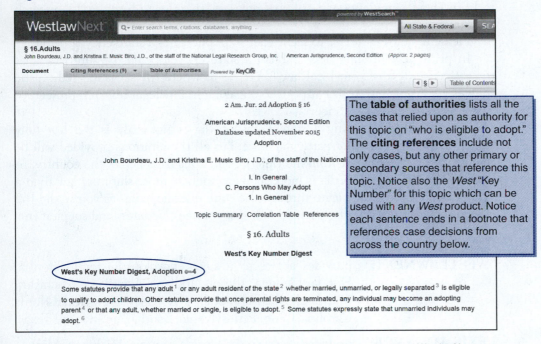

Source: Reprinted with permission of Thomson Reuters, 2 Am. Jur. 2d Adoption section 16 on WestlawNext.

Figure 3-6 Am. Jur. 2d on Lexis Advance

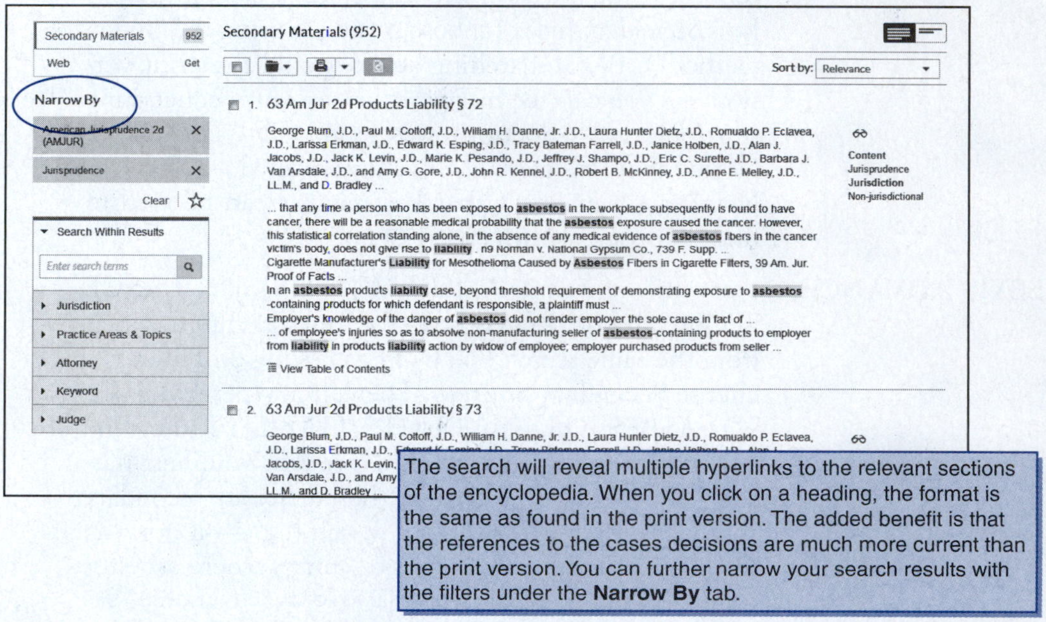

The search will reveal multiple hyperlinks to the relevant sections of the encyclopedia. When you click on a heading, the format is the same as found in the print version. The added benefit is that the references to the cases decisions are much more current than the print version. You can further narrow your search results with the filters under the **Narrow By** tab.

Source: Reproduced with the permission of LexisNexis.

State Legal Encyclopedias

Although the Am. Jur. 2d and C.J.S. provides national coverage, nearly half the states have published their own legal encyclopedias. These state publications are very useful, as they only include coverage of many legal topics specific to your state. State encyclopedias are a great starting point for many entry-level paralegals to learn about many civil and criminal areas of law prior to beginning a research assignment.

Please review Figure 3-7 to see if your state publishes a state encyclopedia.

In print, if your state does publish a state encyclopedia, be sure to ask at the reference desk of your local law library as to where the set is located on the shelves, and be sure to utilize it prior to engaging in any legal research project for your instructor and in practice.

An advantage to using a state encyclopedia is not only is the law fully explained pursuant to your particular state, but all the citations provided will be that of your state, and not from multiple jurisdictions from across the country. In addition, a state encyclopedia is more likely to include more statutory law than a federal encyclopedia. Navigate through the state encyclopedias as you would the federal sets, as they will also include indexes, volumes, updates, and supplements within each set.

WESTLAWNEXT: provides access to a state encyclopedia for California, Florida, Georgia, Illinois, Indiana, Louisiana, Michigan, Maryland, Massachusetts, New Jersey, New York, North Carolina, Ohio, Pennsylvania, South Carolina, and Texas.

LEXIS ADVANCE: provides access to the Florida, Illinois, Michigan, Minnesota, New York, Ohio, Pennsylvania, Tennessee, Texas, and Virginia and West Virginia state encyclopedias.

Figure 3-7 States with a Published Legal Encyclopedia

State	Legal Encyclopedia Name and Location
California	California Jurisprudence 3d (in print and on *Westlaw*); Summary of California Law (in print)
Colorado	Colorado Law Annotated 2d (in print)
Florida	Florida Jurisprudence 2d (in print and on *Lexis* and *Westlaw*)
Georgia	Georgia Jurisprudence (in print and on *Westlaw*)
Illinois	Illinois Law and Practice (in print and on *Lexis* and *Westlaw*)
Indiana	Indiana Law Encyclopedia (in print and on *Westlaw*)
Louisiana	Louisiana Civil Law Treatise (in print and on *Westlaw*)
Maryland	Maryland Law Encyclopedia (in print and on *Westlaw*)
Massachusetts	Massachusetts Practice (in print and on *Westlaw*)
Michigan	Michigan Law Encyclopedia (in print and on *Westlaw/ Lexis*)
Minnesota	Dunnell Minnesota Digest (online on *Lexis* only)
Mississippi	Encyclopedia of Mississippi Law; Summary of Mississippi Law (in print)
New Hampshire	New Hampshire Practice (in print)
New Jersey	New Jersey Practice (in print and on *Westlaw*)
New York	New York Jurisprudence 2d (in print and on *Westlaw* and *Lexis*)
North Carolina	Strong's North Carolina Index (in print and *Westlaw*)
Ohio	Ohio Jurisprudence 3d (in print and on *Westlaw* and *Lexis*)
Pennsylvania	Pennsylvania Law Encyclopedia (in print and on *Westlaw* and *Lexis*)
South Carolina	South Carolina Jurisprudence (in print and on *Westlaw*)
Tennessee	Tennessee Jurisprudence (in print and on *Lexis*)
Texas	Texas Jurisprudence 3d (in print and on *Lexis* and *Westlaw*)
Virginia / West Virginia	Michie's Jurisprudence of Virginia and West Virginia (in print and on *Lexis*)
Wisconsin	Wisconsin does not publish a legal encyclopedia. The *Wisconsin Practice Series* covers several legal topics in relation to Wisconsin law.

Citing Legal Encyclopedias

After each description of secondary authority, the proper format will be given in accordance with *Bluebook* and *ALWD*. Remember that a citation consists of "elements," just like the law. The following citation formats for legal encyclopedias according to *Bluebook* (Rule 15.8) and *ALWD* (Rule 26) are as follows:

Am. Jur. 2d (*Bluebook* and ALWD)
CITATION: 75 Am. Jur. 2d *Trespass* § 53 (1991).
CITATION ELEMENTS:

75	The volume
Am. Jur. 2d	The encyclopedia set
Trespass	The topic name
§ 53	The section number
(1991)	The date of publication

Remember that for each of the secondary sources of law, when you include the date in the citation, it is to refer to the "publication date" of the source you found it in. It is not the date of when the secondary source itself was written.

C.J.S. (*Bluebook* and *ALWD*):
CITATION: 11 C.J.S. *Bonds* § 21, at 65 (1998).
CITATION ELEMENTS:

11	The volume
C.J.S.	The encyclopedia set
Bonds	The topic name
§ 21	The section number
at 65	The particular page where the information was found
(1998)	The date of publication

Both *Bluebook* and *ALWD* state that when using these citations in the practice of law (e.g., motions, briefs, etc.) the topic name is to be *italicized*. In addition, for either citation, if you are citing the main volume and the pocket part, the "date of book" section would read as: (1991 & Supp. 2010)—the "Supp. 2010" means that you also looked up the topic in the 1991 set *and* in the 2010 pocket part as well. If you are **only** citing to the pocket part, that same date section would read (Supp. 2010).

American Law Reports

The **American Law Reports (ALR)** is another multivolume print set that provides detailed analysis of specific legal issues in the form of numerous articles/summaries called *annotations*, which outline areas of law that are frequently changing and evolving. These annotations consist of small abstracts or summaries of individual cases. The ALR provides a complete list of every case from every jurisdiction that discusses it. The more recent annotations provide references to other research sources. The ALR provides greater detail on a topic than the legal encyclopedias, without much analysis or commentary.

american law reports
A multi-volume set that provides detailed analysis, through the use of case summaries, on specific legal topics and issues.

Searching the ALR

The ALR, similar to the legal encyclopedias, includes many hardbound multivolumes (the covers are tan in color) and multiple indexes used to navigate the set. Searching the ALR for the information you need is easy. The ALR has been published in eight series, dating back to 1919 (ALR through ALR 6th, plus ALR Federal and Federal 2d). Up to and including ALR 3rd, the contents of the set included references to both state and federal material. Due to a heavier volume of cases over the years, subsequent sets, beginning with ALR 4th, moved the federal cases to ALR Federal. In navigating through the ALR, you can employ either the index method or the digest method.

The Index Method.   Follow the steps for the index method below.

STEP 1:   Consider all the pertinent keywords for the topic you want to search. Thereafter, begin by looking through the six-volume *ALR Index* at the end of the set that includes federal topics. You can also save some time and narrow your search to federal law by reading through the orange-colored *ALR Quick Index*, which only includes annotations in the *Federal and Federal 2d* series, arranged in alphabetical order from A-Z. Remember that the Index is updated by pocket parts in the back of the Index—check it out! Also, an *Annotation History Table* appears in the last volume of the ALR Index to determine if the annotation you have found within the index has been recently superseded.

For example, suppose your supervising attorney needs to know if a federal law exists concerning the issue of whether a legally blind tenant can keep a seeing-eye dog in an apartment complex that does not allow pets. As shown in Figure 3-8, if you looked under landlord/tenant law, you would see under the multiple subtopics, that under the letter "D," you find that an entry exists for dogs as assistance animals under the federal Fair Housing Act.

If you look carefully, under the main heading of *Landlord and Tenant*, an entry also exists under *Dogs* and under the *Fair Housing Act* under the same heading.

After you locate what you want to look up and read, each subtopic includes a **first number** (volume number in the set), **the abbreviation ALR** (and the number in the series such as ALR 3d, 4th, etc), and a **second number** (the **page number in that volume**, which you will see below why that is so unique). For example, (8 ALR4th 324) means the legal topic can be found in volume 8 of the 4th series of the ALR, on **page 324**.

Figure 3-8 The ALR Federal Quick Index

LANDLORD AND TENANT

Advertisements, validity, construction, and application of § 804(c) of Civil Rights Act of 1968 (42 U.S.C.A. § 3604(c)) prohibiting discriminatory notice, statement, or advertisement with respect to rental of dwelling, **142 ALR Fed 1**

Animals, assistance animals qualifying as reasonable accommodation under Fair Housing Act 42 U.S.C.A. § 3604(f), **66 ALR Fed 2d 209**

Antitrust violations, standing of lessor under percentage lease to sue for treble damages under § 4 of Clayton Act (15 U.S.C.A. § 15) for antitrust violations decreasing profits or gross receipts, **27 ALR Fed 866**

Assignments, what is "shopping center" within meaning of Bankruptcy Code provision governing assumption and assignment of debtor's leases by bankruptcy trustee (11 U.S.C.A. § 365(b)(3)), **117 ALR Fed 321**

Assistance animals qualifying as reasonable accommodation under Fair Housing Act 42 U.S.C.A. § 3604(f), **66 ALR Fed 2d 209**

Attachment or garnishment, modern views as to validity, under federal constitution, of state prejudgment attachment, garnishment, and replevin procedures, distraint procedures under landlords' or innkeepers' lien statutes, and like procedures authorizing summary seizure of property, **18 ALR Fed 223**

Bankruptcy

  good faith purchaser or lessee, construction and application of 11 U.S.C.A. § 363(m), protecting good faith purchaser or lessee under Bankruptcy Code — status as "good faith" purchaser or lessee, **51 ALR Fed 2d 471**

  limitation of lessors' claims for damages, construction and application of Bankruptcy Code provision limiting lessors' claims for damages resulting from termination of real property leases, 11

LANDLORD AND TENANT—Cont'd

Developer or agent, who is developer or agent within meaning of § 1402(5), (6) of the Interstate Land Sales Full Disclosure Act (15 U.S.C.A. § 1701(5), (6)), **49 ALR Fed 781**

Dogs, assistance animals qualifying as reasonable accommodation under Fair Housing Act 42 U.S.C.A. § 3604(f), **66 ALR Fed 2d 209**

Drugs and narcotics, validity, construction, and application of federal "crack-house statute" criminalizing maintaining place for purpose of making, distributing, or using controlled drugs (21 U.S.C.A. § 856), **116 ALR Fed 345**

Due process

  government housing, tenants' rights, under due process clause federal constitution, to notice and hearing prior to imposition of higher rent or additional service charges for government-owned or government-subsidized housing, **28 ALR Fed 739**

  low-income housing, due process rights of applicants for low income housing assistance benefits under § 8 of Housing Act of 1937, as amended (42 U.S.C.A. § 1437f), **66 ALR Fed 721**

Ejectment, Eviction, and Ouster (this index)

Fair Housing Act

  advertisement or notice, validity, construction, and application of § 804(c) of Civil Rights Act of 1968 (Fair Housing Act) (42 U.S.C.A. § 3604(c)) prohibiting discriminatory notice, statement, or advertisement with respect to sale or rental of dwelling, **142 ALR Fed 1**

  assistance animals qualifying as reasonable accommodation under Fair Housing Act 42 U.S.C.A. § 3604(f), **66 ALR Fed 2d 209**

  disability discrimination, construction and applica-

Source: Reprinted with permission of Thomson Reuters, American Law Reports (ALR), 2014 Federal Quick Index (A-Z) "Landlord/Tenant", Page 871.

STEP 2: Now that you are equipped with the ALR citation, go to the appropriate volume and page number to find the discussion on your legal topic. Unlike the spine of each volume on a legal encyclopedia, the spine on the ALR only includes the volume number and the name of the ALR series. When you go to the particular volume you need, refer to the **Summary of Contents** at the beginning of each volume. As you can see in Figure 3-9, the ALR volumes are complied quite differently from many other print sources in that the topic of law you want to read is found by *page number*, and NOT by sequential *section number*. Please do not fan through the pages looking, in this example, in section 209—there is none; only page 209. It is published this way because as you will see, each entry concerning a topic is quite detailed and extensive—so much so that, as seen in Figure 3-9, the topic of assistance animals covers 30 pages of material! It would take too many volumes of books to organize the topics by section number.

As you can see, Figure 3-10, provides a snapshot of the first page of a typical ALR annotation. The different sections of the annotation

Figure 3-9 The Summary of Contents in the ALR

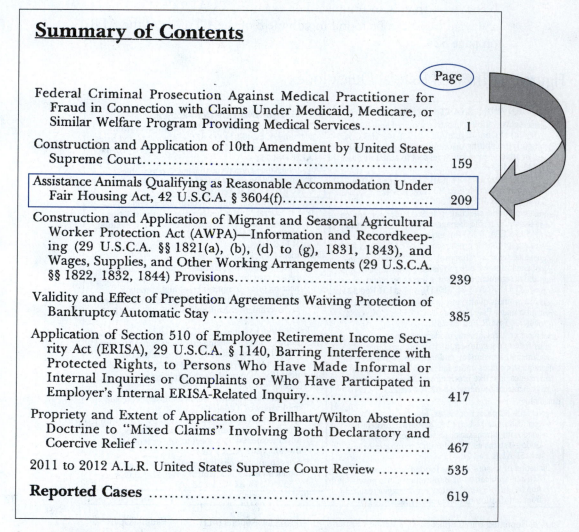

Summary of Contents

Source: Reprinted with permission of Thomson Reuters, ALR, Volume 66 ALR Fed 2d 209 "Summary of Contents", Page xiii.

Figure 3-10 A Section of the Annotation for Service Animals in the ALR

66 A.L.R. Fed. 2d FAIR HOUSING ACT-SERVICE ANIMALS § 2
66 A.L.R. Fed. 2d 209

West Virginia

Kenna Homes Co-op. Corp., In re, 210 W. Va. 380, 557 S.E.2d 787 (2001) — §§ 4, 8

I. PRELIMINARY MATTERS

§ 1 Scope

This annotation[1] collects and discusses the state and federal cases in which the courts have considered whether and under what circumstances permitting individuals[2] to keep animals[3] on the premises for purpose of assisting the individual with daily living constituted a "reasonable accommodation" of the individual's "handicap"[4] as required by the Fair Housing Act of 1968, as amended (42 U.S.C.A. § 3604(f)(3)(B)).[5]

Some opinions discussed in this annotation may be restricted by court rule as to publication and citation in briefs; readers are cautioned to check each case for restrictions. A number of jurisdictions may have rules, regulations, constitutional provisions, or legislative enactments directly bearing upon this subject. These provisions are discussed herein only to the extent and in the form that they are reflected in the court opinions that fall within the scope of this annotation. The reader is consequently advised to consult the appropriate statutory or regulatory compilations to ascertain the current status of all statutes discussed herein.

§ 2 Summary and comment

The Fair Housing Act makes it unlawful to "discriminate in the sale or rental, or to otherwise make unavailable or deny, a dwelling to any . . .

1. This annotation supersedes §§ 49[a] and 49[b] of the annotation, Construction and Application of sec. 804(f) of Fair Housing Act (42 U.S.C.A. sec. 3604(f)), Prohibiting Discrimination in Housing Because of

2. The scope extends to all tenants statutory coverage includes occupants cooperatives.

Once you find the appropriate topic within the volume, a specific index, the statutory text of the subject of the law you are reading about, and a table of case law decisions, arranged by jurisdiction, all precede the actual discussion of the main topic – in this case, "the use of assistance dogs under the Fair Housing Act."

3. The scope of the annotation considers cases involving claims as to any domestic or wild land animal, or fish or birds, and regardless of whether the animals were formally trained as long as the plaintiff claims the animal as a reasonable accommodation to a disability.

4. The term "handicap" is used in this article in place of the more common locution "disability" in accord with the language of the statute.

5. Hereinafter referred to as the FHA.

217

Source: Reprinted with permission of Thomson Reuters, ALR, Volume 66 ALR Fed 2d 209, Page 217.

include the title/author; the "scope statement" (usually consists of one paragraph summarizing the contents of the annotation); the **table of contents** (provides the location within that particular annotation of specific legal issues); the **research references** (contains references to *West's* key numbers, ALR citations, legal encyclopedias, and relevant websites if applicable); a **subject index** (to help you really narrow your search and locate information within that particular annotation); a **table of cases**, laws and rules (provides citations for primary law arranged by state jurisdiction alphabetically); and the statutory text, which includes the language of the actual statute or source of primary law.

STEP 3: Once you have secured the information you need, be sure to check the pocket part at the back of the volume you are using for any recent updates on the topic you are reading. Pocket parts are located only in the ALR 3d through 6th series, ALR Fed and the ALR Index. If you need an update for an earlier set in the series, refer to the *Blue Book of Supplemental Decisions* (not to be confused with the *Bluebook* of citation) or the *Later Case Service*, both found at the end of the volume set. The citations in the pocket part correspond with the exact citation for you topic. The newer cases within the pocket parts are briefly summarized for you. If a case looks promising in addressing your legal issue, be sure to write it down, including the names of the parties in the case and the full numeric citation so you can retrieve it and read it later. You will learn case citations and how to locate case law, in detail, in Chapter 7.

STEP 4: Once you have learned about your topic, with some possible citations in hand, go to those primary sources of law and retrieve them. You will learn how to actually look up each primary source of law in subsequent chapters.

The Digest Method. As mentioned above in discussing the legal encyclopedias, the ALR has its own *ALR Digest*, which can be used as another searching method. The Digest only corresponds to ALR 3rd, 4th, and 5th. The ALR Digest is organized and operates like any other digest concerning its topics and sections. However, keep in mind that it may not be the best decision to begin with the ALR Digest unless you already have a *West* "key number." The digest is not of much use if you are searching by "topic." You will be better served by searching the ALR **Index**, rather than the ALR Digest. Please see Chapter 7 for a detailed step-by-step instruction on how to navigate a digest, as well as to learn the importance of the West Key Number system.

Additional ALR Indexes. Lastly, you can also search the contents of the ALR with two other indexes. First, if you already have a case citation, you can read through the *ALR Federal Table of Cases* (for federal cases), or the *ALR 5th and 6th Table of Cases* (for state cases). There is no table of cases for ALR series 1-4. If you find your case, you will be directed within the ALR set for further discussion of that particular legal topic/issue. If you do not see your case, this means the case is not the "most significant" as deemed by the publisher in that area of law. In addition, if you already have a statute, regulation, or legal rule you can search through the *ALR Table of Laws, Rules, and Regulations* in the same manner as the table of cases. The table of laws is contained in its own volume at the end of the set.

ALR Online

Similar to the legal encyclopedias, the ALR **cannot** be located online for free, which is a good reason to know how to navigate the print source. The ALR can, however, be located both on *WestlawNext* and on *Lexis Advance*.

WESTLAWNEXT: click on **Secondary Sources** on the home screen. Next, the first secondary source listed under **Type** is the ALR. On that screen, numerous general topics are listed. In addition, hyperlinks are available for *American Law Reports Digest,* and *American Law Reports Index.* Each topic under the index will state when that material was last updated, which is usually weekly. You can also begin to type: AMERICAN LAW REPORTS into the search box, which will drop down suggestions, including the ALR. As you can see in Figure 3-11, it may be wise to search the ALR Index, as merely clicking on a topic will only provide the most recently published articles. The *Westlaw* database is the most comprehensive online source because *West* publishes the print version.

LEXIS ADVANCE: in the main search box, using the example above concerning service animals, type: ASSISTANCE DOGS, FAIR HOUSING ACT then filter by selecting **Secondary Materials**. Once it generates the results, you can still narrow those search results by selecting **ALR** under **Sources**, and by **Jurisdiction**, if needed. Lastly, you can further narrow the results by **Keyword**, such as "dog" or "tenant" as you can see in Figure 3-12.

Figure 3-11 The A.L.R. on *WestlawNext*

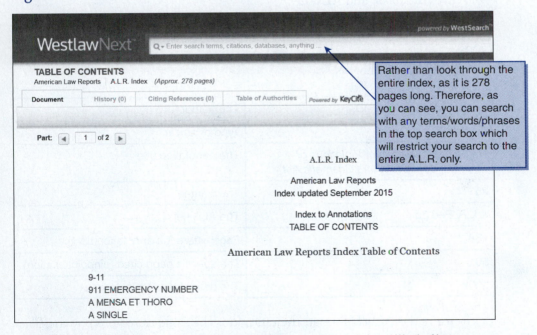

Source: Reprinted with permission of Thomson Reuters, American Law Reports Index on WestlawNext.

Figure 3-12 Accessing the A.L.R. on *Lexis Advance*

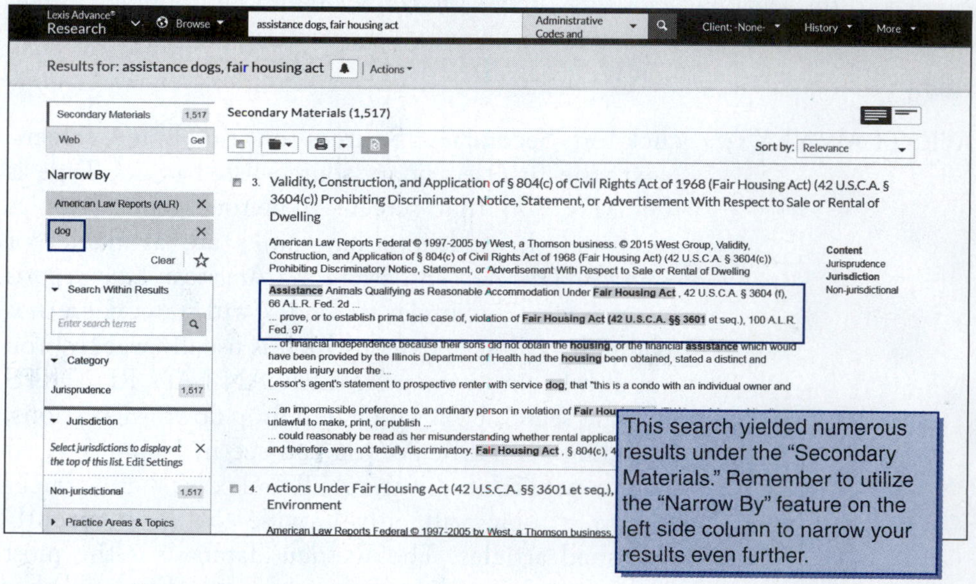

Source: Reprinted with the permission of LexisNexis.

Also, with either *WestlawNext* or *Lexis Advance*, you can always insert an ALR citation directly into either main search box.

Citing the ALR

The proper citation formats for the ALR, according to *Bluebook* (Rule 16.6) and *ALWD* (Rule 24) are as follows:

ALR (*Bluebook* and *ALWD*)

CITATION: Deborah F. Buckman, JD., Annotation, *Remedies Available for Violations of Federal Food, Drug, and Cosmetic Act*, 25 A.L.R. Fed 2d 488, 501 (2008).

CITATION ELEMENTS:

Deborah F. Buckman, JD.	The author
Annotation	Type of article
Remedies Available for Violations of Federal Food, Drug, and Cosmetic Act	The annotation title
25	The volume
A.L.R. Fed 2d	The ALR set
488	Page where the annotation begins
501	The specific page cited (pinpoint citation)
2008	The date of publication

In using the *ALWD* format, the citation is the same as required by the *Bluebook*, with one exception: the word "Annotation" is **not** used in the *ALWD* citation. Therefore, the title of the annotation would begin immediately following the comma that follows "JD."

Restatements of Law

Many years ago, a group of professors, lawyers, and judges created the American Law Institute (ALI). The goal of the ALI is to be "the leading independent organization in the United States producing scholarly work to clarify, modernize, and otherwise improve the law." In response to the rapidly increasing number of case decisions being published across the country, the members of the ALI essentially "restated" the law found in case decisions in order to present the law in a clear and understandable format. **Restatements of Law** have been published by the ALI in the following areas with the number of series published on that restatement.

- Agency (1st, 2nd, and 3rd)
- Concise Restatements
- Conflicts of Law (1st, 2nd)
- Contracts (1st, 2nd)
- Employment Law (1st, 2nd)
- Foreign Relations Law of the United States (2nd, 3rd)
- International Commercial Arbitration (2nd)
- Judgments (1st, 2nd)
- Law Governing Lawyers (3rd)
- Property (Landlord/Tenant; Mortgages; Servitudes; Wills) (1st)
- Restitution and Unjust Enrichment (3rd)
- Security (out of print—only online at *WestlawNext* and *Lexis Advance*)
- Suretyship and Guaranty (3rd)
- Torts (Economic Harm; Physical and Emotional Harm; Products Liability) (1st, 2nd)
- Trusts (1st, 2nd, 3rd)
- Unfair Competition (1st, 2nd, 3rd)

restatements of law
A set of treatises on various legal subjects, prepared by the American Law Institute, that synthesize and clarify principles of common law through the use of easy-to-understand examples.

The ALI restates the American common law, and the institute often looks to the rules found in the *majority* of the jurisdictions across the country and restates them. Therefore, they are not jurisdiction specific. In addition to restating the law, the published volumes also include commentary on the particular law as well as summaries of cases applying and interpreting the law. It is important to note that the restatements can be used as a back-up to strengthen your primary sources of law, as they do not only provide commentary or explanation of the law, but also are a "restatement" of the law. You will notice that appellate courts will sometimes (if appropriate) cite to the restatements in their opinions to make a point or strengthen their holding.

Searching the Restatements

Each restatement consists of approximately two to five volumes. In navigating through the restatements, most of the volumes will include a *Table of Contents* at the front of the volume and a detailed **Index** located at the end of each volume. The contents are organized into **chapters - titles - sections**. Each section includes a number and a brief explanation/summary of the particular law in bold. The law is typically broken down into "elements" for a clearer understanding of the law. After explaining the law, the **Comment** section explains each element in further detail, and the **Illustrations** section provides clear examples so that the researcher can "see" the law utilized in practical situations. The restatements are updated by an **Appendix** which contains summaries of cases in section number order of the restatement.

Restatements Online

Unfortunately, the restatements *cannot* be located online for free, which is a good reason to know how to navigate the print source. The restatements can, however, be located on *WestlawNext* and on *Lexis Advance*.

Figure 3-13 The Restatements of Law on *WestlawNext*

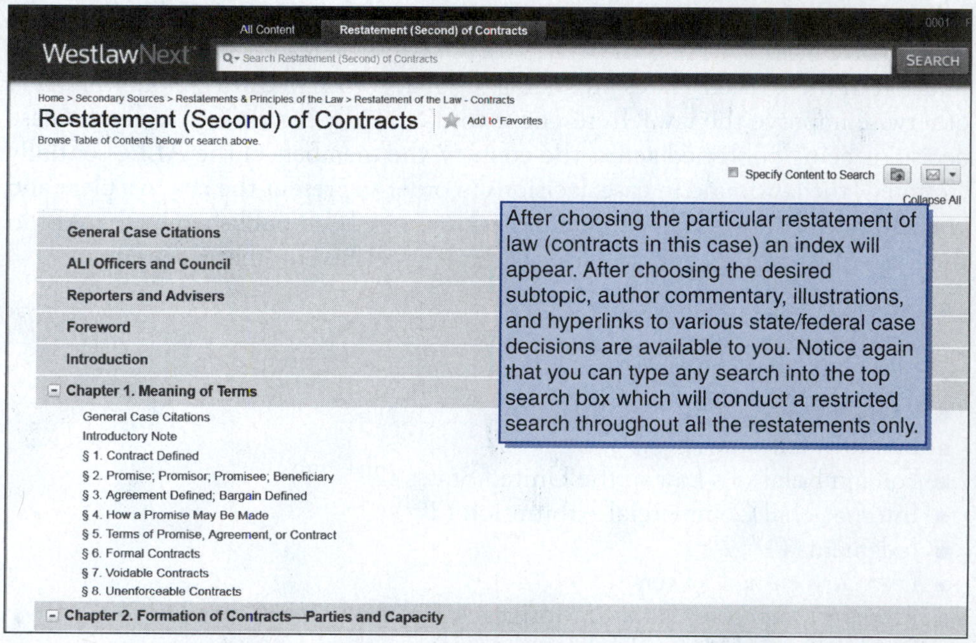

Source: Reprinted with permission of Thomson Reuters, Restatement (Second) of Contracts on WestlawNext.

WESTLAWNEXT: on the home screen, click on **Secondary Sources**. Next, the first secondary source listed under **Type** is the *Restatements and Principles of Law*. On that screen, multiple restatement topics are listed. As you can see in Figure 3-13, clicking on any restatement topic will take you directly to the table of contents for that topic where you can break down each restatement into its multiple chapters and subtopics for viewing. After the *Illustration* section of each topic, case citations are listed by jurisdiction to narrow the search to your own jurisdiction. You can also access the restatements by typing: RESTATEMENTS into the search box, which will dropdown suggestions, including the every restatement topic.

LEXIS ADVANCE: similar to the other secondary sources above, begin any search by typing in any search terms into the search box, such as: ASSAULT AND BATTERY, THIRD PERSON, and use the filter for **Secondary Sources** and any specific **Jurisdiction** as well. Once the results are generated, you can further narrow your search results by selecting *Restatements*. Narrow the results further by utilizing the multiple filters as seen in Figure 3-14.

You can also access information concerning the restatements online at **www.ali.org**. If your supervising attorney specializes in a particular area of law, such as property, contracts, or torts, it may be worthwhile to have those volumes in the office.

Figure 3-14 The Restatements of Law on *Lexis Advance*

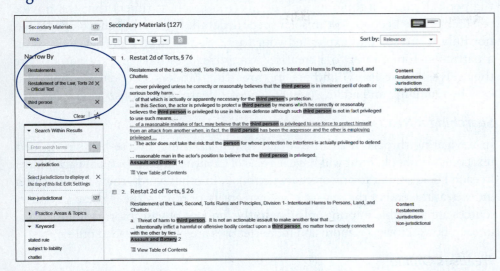

Source: Reprinted with the permission of LexisNexis.

Citing Restatements

The proper citation formats for the Restatements of Law according to *Bluebook* (Rule 12.8) and *ALWD* (Rule 27) are as follows:

> **Restatements of Law (*Bluebook* and ALWD)**
> CITATION: Restatement (Second) of Contracts § 41 (1995).
> CITATION ELEMENTS:

Restatement (Second) of Contracts	The name of the particular restatement
§ 41	The section number
(1995)	The date of publication

The citation for the ALWD is the same, with a minor exception—the restatement name "*Restatement (Second) of Contracts*" is *italicized*.

Treatises

Legal encyclopedias and the ALR cover a broad range of topics; however, **treatises** are "scholarly works" that can be found in single book or multivolume sets. The word "treatise" implies comprehensive coverage on a single topic of law. Some of the more popular treatises that have been in publication over the years include, *Contracts (Murray; Corbin; Farnsworth)*; *Evidence (McCormick; Wigmore)*; *Criminal Law (LaFave and Scott)*; *Bankruptcy (Herzog)*; *Torts (Prosser)*; and *Federal Practice and Procedure (Wright and Miller)*. Many newer treatises are also emerging in the legal field, including topics on *Animal Law*; *E-Commerce*, and *Internet Law*. Many law students utilize treatises in order to understand or master a specific legal topic such as contracts or criminal law; these treatises are called *hornbooks* and *nutshells*, which are small paperback books, usually found in a law school bookstore.

Primarily used to delve deeper into a particular topic of study, treatises can be found on the shelves of many law offices. If not, be sure to stop by the reference desk of your local law library. The librarian should have a list of the treatises on the shelf, as each law library will shelve different treatises.

Finding what you need to read will not prove difficult because unlike other secondary sources, a treatise is written almost like a textbook so it is easy to

treatise
An academic or scholarly work on one specific topic or subject found in a single or multi-volume set.

find what you are looking for. However, a downside to reading a treatise is that the book discusses a topic in such detail (too much at times) that the novice researcher may become lost in such specific detail. If the legal encyclopedia has not fully addressed and explained your topic, or you need a deeper analysis on a particular topic, refer to a treatise. Many treatises have pocket parts or are themselves "loose leafs," and are in three-ring binders so updating the law is easy by removing and adding papers. You will learn about loose leafs below.

Searching a Treatise

In navigating through a treatise, whether you are using a loose-leaf binder, or a textbook/hornbook, most will have a *Table of Contents* and an *Index* in each binder in each book, similar to any ordinary textbook. In other words, there are no master indexes at the end of the set—it is its own entity or unit. Most of these secondary sources are available in print only due to the amount of vast information included in each book. However, more and more treatises are being uploaded online.

Treatises Online

Similar to the other secondary sources discussed, treatises are *not* available online for free. As mentioned above, certain treatises may be available in your law firm's law library or at your local law library. However, this secondary source can be found on *WestlawNext* and on *Lexis Advance*.

WESTLAWNEXT: type the word: TREATISES in the main search box and *Texts & Treatises* will appear as an option, in which you can choose what you need by **Topic** or by **State**. Using Ohio as an example in Figure 3-15, you can also access *Texts & Treatises* first under **Secondary Sources** under the **Browse** tab on the homepage, then the Ohio Texts and Treatises under the state of Ohio sources.

LEXIS ADVANCE: type in any search terms into the search box, such as: RULES OF EVIDENCE, HEARSAY and use the filter for **Secondary Sources** and any specific **Jurisdiction,** such as Florida. Once the results are generated, you can further narrow your search results by selecting a filter under **Sources** as you can see in Figure 3-16.

Figure 3-15 Treatises on *WestlawNext*

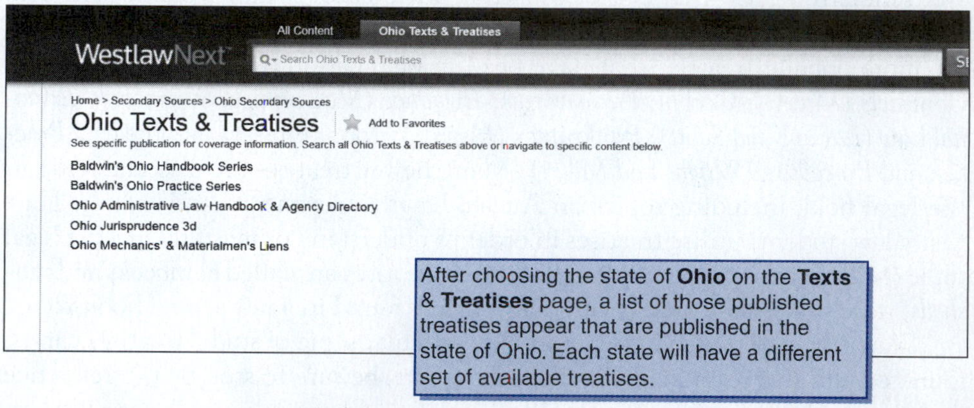

Source: Reprinted with permission of Thomson Reuters, Result page for state secondary sources on WestlawNext.

Figure 3-16 Treatises on *Lexis Advance*

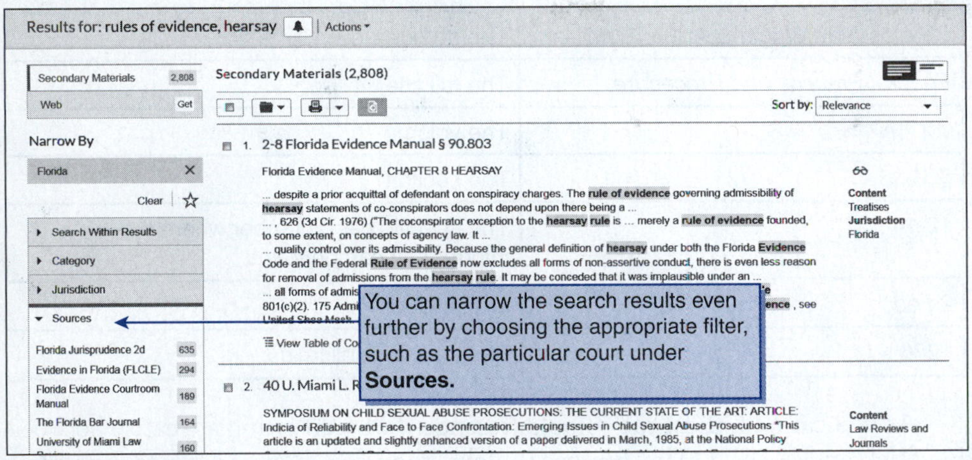

Source: Reprinted with the permission of LexisNexis.

Citing Treatises

The proper citation formats for treatise material according to *Bluebook* (Rule 15) and *ALWD* (Rule 22) are as follows:

Treatises (*Bluebook*)

CITATION: 4 Charles Alan Wright & Arthur R. Miller, *Federal Practice and Procedure* § 1006, at 12-14 (2d ed. 1987).

CITATION ELEMENTS:

4	The volume number
Charles Alan Wright & Arthur R. Miller	The author(s) full name
Federal Practice and Procedure	The full title
§ 1006	The section number
at 12-14	The specific page number where the information can be found
2d ed.	The edition
1987	The date of publication

If there are more than two authors, list all the names, or you can state the first author's name, followed by "et al." Also, if there is only one edition, only include the date of publication.

Treatises (*ALWD*)

CITATION: Charles Alan Wright & Arthur R. Miller, *Federal Practice and Procedure* vol. 4A, § 1006, 12-14 (2d ed. 1986).

CITATION ELEMENTS:

Charles Alan Wright & Arthur R. Miller	The author(s) full name
Federal Practice and Procedure	The full title
vol. 4A	The volume
§ 1006	The section
12-14	The specific page number where the information can be found
2d ed.	The edition
1986	The date of publication

As you can see, there are some differences between citing a treatise between *Bluebook* and *ALWD*. The *Bluebook* allows the use of "et al." for two or more authors, whereas the *ALWD* requires its use for three or more authors. When citing under *ALWD* requirements, the volume number is placed *after* the title of the treatise. Also, the "at" is not used preceding the page numbers.

Legal Dictionary and Thesaurus

legal dictionary
A dictionary similar in format and organization of a typical dictionary, but different in content, including numerous legal words, terms, and phrases.

Another good source of secondary authority is the **legal dictionary**. You will not find any deep analysis of any particular legal topic or issue, but what you will get is a legal *term/word/phrase* defined for you. Having a legal dictionary is extremely helpful for a novice researcher who is just learning about a topic in a secondary source of law. Even though a secondary source will help explain a legal topic for you, it will not explain and define each and every word for you. That is where the legal dictionary can be of good use. In addition, when you are actually reading the law itself, including a statute, regulation, or especially a case opinion, you will undoubtedly encounter a legal term/word/phrase unfamiliar to you. It is important that you should never, ever, guess or assume a legal word you do not know. Keeping a legal dictionary with you will not only help you to define unfamiliar words, it will also help to expand your own legal vocabulary.

Legal dictionaries can be found in print, including *Black's Law Dictionary*, which includes more than 45,000 terms (in its 10th edition as of 2015), and the *Bouvier Law Dictionary* (which also publishes a "compact" edition and "quick reference" edition). Both of these publications can be purchased on Amazon and on Barnes and Noble (Nook). In addition, there are many free and low-cost law dictionary apps for your smart phone and tablet.

Many legal dictionaries can also be found online for free, which you should bookmark on your computer for quick and easy access if you are reading a case or statute or drafting a brief. These websites including the following:

- **www.legal-dictionary.thefreedictionary.com**
- **www.thelawdictionary.org** (*Black's* Online Dictionary)
- **www.dictionary.findlaw.com**

legal thesaurus
A resource including thousands of synonyms of many common legal words, terms, and phrases.

Similarly, every paralegal should also have the latest edition of a **legal thesaurus** to utilize when engaged in any type of legal writing. Rather than using the same legal term repeatedly throughout a memo, use the legal thesaurus. A good choice is *Burton's Legal Thesaurus* (in its 5th edition as of 2014). This paperback edition includes more than 10,000 synonyms specifically related to the legal profession and can be purchased on Amazon.

Citing a Legal Dictionary

The proper citation formats for a legal dictionary according to *Bluebook* (Rule 15.8) and *ALWD* (Rule 25) are as follows:

The Legal Dictionary (*Bluebook*)
CITATION: *Black's Law Dictionary* 387 (9th ed. 2009).
CITATION ELEMENTS:

Black's Law Dictionary	The dictionary name
387	The page the entry was found
8th ed.	The edition of the book
2004	The date published

The Legal Dictionary (*ALWD*)
CITATION: *Black's Law Dictionary* 387 (Bryan A. Garner, 9th ed., West 2009).
CITATION ELEMENTS:

Black's Law Dictionary	The dictionary name
Bryan A. Garner	The author
9th ed.	The edition of the book
West	The publisher
2009	The date published

As you can see, *ALWD* requires the author's name, as well as the publisher's name of the dictionary.

Loose-leaf Services

Loose-leaf services are yet another source of secondary material that not only educate you on a specific legal topic, but also provide primary source material. This secondary source, also referred to as "subject-matter research," brings together the most important information on one particular legal topic. You will immediately notice this secondary source in the law library by its use of large three-ring binders, rather than a hardbound print set. These sources are good to research because contained in one binder are multiple primary and secondary sources cited for one topic such as tax or labor law.

The major loose-leaf publishers are the *Bureau of National Affairs (BNA)*, the *Commerce Clearing House (CCH)*, *Lexis Legal/Matthew Bender*, and the *Research Institute of America (RIA)*.

PRACTICE TIP

As of 2015, *Black's Law Dictionary* is now available on *WestlawNext*. It can be accessed from the main search page (type "Black's") by selecting the dictionary from the drop-down menu. Similarly, *Ballentine's Law Dictionary* is available on *Lexis Advance* and can be found under the *Secondary Sources* filter. However, many quality free online sources exist to define a legal word for you. Whichever legal dictionary you decide to use, make sure you have quick and easy access to it when needed.

---

loose-leaf services
A research source, contained in large three-ring binders, that include the results of various sources of information on one particular legal topic.

There are two types of loose-leaf material:

- *Interfiled Loose-leaf Service*—this type of service includes numerous individual pages filled in a loose-leaf binder (hence the name). Therefore, pages within the binder can be easily removed or added, which allows for quick and efficient updating, sometimes weekly, rather than waiting for a new hardcover volume to be printed like the other secondary sources; and
- *Newsletter-Style Loose-leaf Service*—this type of service includes softbound pamphlet newsletters that are issued periodically and also filled in a binder. However, the new releases do NOT replace any already existing pages. This type of service usually includes a cumulative index.

These resources cover many legal topics that are continually in flux and changing frequently, especially tax law. The primary material included is either summarized or presented in full text. These sources also provide great explanatory text. Similar to the treatises, be sure to check with your law librarian as to which looseleaf materials are shelved in your law library. Of particular interest, loose-leaf materials can include the decisions and advisory opinions within the realm of regulatory law (Chapter 8), which may not appear in any other publication.

Searching a Loose-leaf Binder

Each binder will be easily recognizable as to the subject included within that particular binder. Once you find the binder set you need, follow the steps below.

STEP 1: Go to the first binder in the set and open to the beginning section entitled *How to Use this Service or Overview*. These brief but helpful guidelines describe the contents, methods of access, and any special services that the set may contain. Also, if you law library has it, ask for the *Legal Looseleafs in Print* to determine what loose-leaf resources are available in the law library.

STEP 2: Reference the general index to find the direction you need. Depending on the loose-leaf service, some binders provide references to page numbers and others refer to section or paragraph numbers. Note that there are different binders referred to as "current binders" and "transfer binders." The current binders include the most current and updated material, whereas the transfer binders include the material that has been replaced and removed for the current binders, but still may be of interest to the researcher.

STEP 3: Once you find the section you need, read the text of the primary material, such as the cases, rules, and any secondary source material. Please note that since these loose-leaf services include many primary *and* secondary sources, make certain you know the difference between the two sources if you intend to cite a particular source within a memorandum.

STEP 4: As always, be sure to update and validate the material in the binder under the *Current Materials* section. For any citations to the primary sources you find, you will need to ensure they are still valid. You will learn later how to *Shepardize* and *KeyCite* those sources to ensure the law is still valid.

Loose-leaf Material Online

Some loose-leaf material is available by the publisher through CD format at many law libraries. To save on printing costs, many loose-leaf publishers are transferring material online through a paid subscription service. Many law libraries offer a library membership (usually discounted for students/paralegals), which will provide you access to these loose-leaf services through the law library computers. Be sure to inquire as to this service. Searching this secondary source online is easier than navigating the print material, as you can easily enter search terms rather than search the print index. In addition, many law schools have online databases including many of the loose-leaf services. A few of these materials can also be accessed on *WestlawNext* and *Lexis Advance*.

Citing Loose-leaf Material

The proper citation formats for loose-leaf materials according to *Bluebook* (Rule 19) and *ALWD* (Rule 28) are as follows:

Loose-leaf Materials (*Bluebook* and ALWD)
CITATION: 1 Bus. Franchise Guide (CCH) ¶ 3202 (Aug. 8, 1988).
CITATION ELEMENTS:

1	The volume
Bus. Franchise Guide	The title of the service
(CCH)	The publisher (Commerce Clearing House)
¶ 3202	The section/topic/subdivision
Aug. 8, 1988	The date of publication

For the name of the "title of the service," be sure to review *Bluebook Table T.15* for the appropriate use of abbreviations. The citation format for loose-leaf services includes the same requirements under the *ALWD*.

Additional Secondary Resources

Lastly, there are other secondary sources available that do not possess the voluminous resources as the publications above. Rather, these publications, called legal publications, focus primarily on the discussion of many current legal topics, trends, and issues.

Legal publications fall into three categories:

- Law School Publications;
- Bar Association Publications;
- Legal Newspapers

Unlike the other above-mentioned secondary sources, legal periodicals do not delve deeply into any particular topic or subject. Rather, think of a legal periodical as the "daily news" in the legal world. This source presents brief discussion and commentary on the trending and newly emerging topics in the field, as well as explanation on recent high-level court decisions and newly enacted statutes and regulations.

1. ***Law School Publications***—The main source under this category is the Law Review, which is a scholarly publication published quarterly by every law school and can be authored by judges, lawyers, and law students. A law review

publication includes four to six articles concerning hot topics or newly emerging issues in the law. Not only are these articles good for a discussion of a legal topic, but also throughout each article, nearly every sentence ends with a footnote, directing the reader to multiple sources of primary authority.

Many law schools also publish many additional legal periodicals and journals, also written by law students, including business, environmental, international, or ethics journals. Any law review or journal published by a law school will be listed on that law school's website. Both *WestlawNext* and *Lexis Advance* publish law reviews and journals which are both categorized by jurisdiction. Both can be accessed under secondary sources.

2. *Bar Association Publications*—In addition to the American Bar Association, each state also has a local bar association. Attorneys must be a member of that state's local bar in order to practice law in the state. In addition to the national publication of the ABA Journal published by the American Bar Association, every local chapter also publishes a state bar journal, which includes any and all recent updates and changes to the local rules or laws within that particular jurisdiction. Each state journal will typically include the state name in the title, such as the *California Lawyer*, or *Pennsylvania Lawyer*. They can usually be found in most law firms.

3. *Legal Newspapers*—Many lawyers also subscribe to a daily legal newspaper. These newspapers, such as *The Legal Intelligencer*, look like and are arranged similar to a local newspaper. These publications are another quick and efficient way to stay on top of the latest topics and news in the legal profession.

So with all these choices, how do you quickly know the best and most efficient secondary source you need prior to beginning your research assignment? In deciding which source would be most beneficial to you, please review the chart in Figure 3-17 for a quick breakdown of the purpose of each source and when to use it.

Many legal publications are available in your local law library. For instance, legal books/binders/pamphlets have been published on topics such as *police civil liberty*, *hazardous waste litigation*, *auto design liability*, and *hotel law*, just to name a few. If you get the opportunity, please make a visit to the local law library and walk through the stacks to see what miscellaneous sources are available.

Figure 3-17 A Summary of Secondary Sources

What Do You Need?	Secondary Source
A source that includes a broad range of topics across multiple jurisdictions in order to "learn" about the law. For any state law research, this is the best source to use, especially if your state publishes one.	*Legal Encyclopedias
A source including topics slightly more detailed and more specific than an encyclopedia and does not include legal analysis or discussion of policy issues.	*A.L.R.
An in-depth scholarly source that includes more specific legal topics in greater detail.	*Treatise; *Law Reviews
An in-depth scholarly source that also provides many detailed illustrations and examples of that particular law and can be used as a good support for the primary sources of law.	*Restatements of Law
A source that includes a quick and brief definition of a legal word/term/phrase to understand its meaning in its proper context.	Legal Dictionary
A source that provides objective commentary on new emerging topics within the law as well as pending lawsuits and appeals.	Legal Periodicals

*These sources also provide citations to relevant primary material (cases, statutes, regulations).

◼ SECONDARY SOURCES USED IN PRACTICE

In addition to the secondary sources described above, there are two additional sources that are used more in the practice of law than for reference alone; these include Formbooks and Jury Instructions.

Formbooks in Print and Online

During the entire litigation process, many standard and routine forms must be filed with the court, such as motions, discovery issues, or a request for a DNA paternity test during a custody dispute. Attorneys and paralegals do not create these routine forms again and again for each case. Instead, **formbooks** are multivolume sets that include hundreds of sample forms and templates to be used in the practice of law and are required in most state and federal jurisdictions. These forms are considered standard in the profession. There are two types of formbooks:

- *Forms of Pleading and Practice*—these forms include documents filed in the courts, including complaints and answers, motions, consent to adopt, etc.
- *Forms of Transaction*—these forms include documents not filed with the courts, but they can be enforceable within the courts, including wills, an apartment or business lease, a basic contract, etc.

The idea for a formbook is simple—once you locate the form that is needed, the paralegal needs only to review and update the form for any changes, fill in the blanks with the client's information, and file it with the court. As you will see in practice, no matter what type of law firm you work in, the attorney's staff will already have most, if not every, forms on file that are used in that office or firm.

Not only can you find many forms and legal templates, but you may also find many helpful trial and litigation assistance with trial procedures. You may find the more popular and widely used formbooks below in your local law library.

- *American Jurisprudence Pleading and Practice Forms*—these formbooks include more than 25,000 forms all relating to the most basic forms used in litigation, including complaints and answers, motions, orders, etc.
- *American Jurisprudence Legal Forms 2d*—these formbooks include more than 50 volumes arranged alphabetically of standard forms for contracts, leases, etc.
- *American Jurisprudence Trials*—set includes "practice" trials, including examples of direct and cross-examination, among other trial procedures.
- *Bender's Federal Practice Forms*—these formbooks include a multivolume set that contain hundreds of federal civil and criminal forms.
- *West's Legal Forms 3d*—these formbooks include a multivolume set used in the general practice of everyday law.
- *West Trial Practice Series*—includes many works concerning various stages of the litigation process, including "how to prepare a witness for trial," "trial communication skills," "questioning techniques and practice," among others.
- *Bender's Forms on Discovery*—these formbooks include a full set of 17 volumes dedicated solely to the various types of discovery exchanged during pre-trial.

Figure 3-18, demonstrates a petition to enforce a living will, taken from the *West's Legal Form's* publication found in the "Elder Law" volume of the set. As you can see, many of these forms are standard (boilerplate), and the client's specific information just needs to be inserted in the appropriate spaces.

LEARNING OBJECTIVE 3
Explain which secondary sources are used in practice and how and where to locate each in print and online.

formbooks
Multi-volume books that include hundreds of templates for various legal documents, such as wills, leases, complaints, and various motions.

Figure 3-18 A Standard "Petition to Enforce a Living Will"

§ 8.60 Petition to Enforce Living Will

IN THE *[name of court]*

IN RE: MATTER OF HEALTH CARE OF MILDRED SICK

Surrogate Court

Case No. ______________

Drawer ______________

Petition to Enforce Living Will

NOW COMES, SIDNEY SICK, who respectively alleges and petitions the court as follows:

1. I am the sole child of MILDRED SICK and I reside at *[address]*.

2. MILDRED SICK is age 98, resides at *[name and address of nursing home]*, North Carolina under treatment by her physician, DONALD DOCTOR ("DOCTOR") and currently is a patient at ___ Hospital in ______(city) ______(state).

3. MILDRED SICK was admitted to said hospital on March 14, 2004, suffering from congestive heart failure, emphysema, dementia and arthritis.

4. I am informed that MILDRED SICK slipped into a vegetative state on March 15, 2004 and has remained in said status to this day.

5. The prospects of MILDRED SICK's recovery and passage to competent abilities and/or interaction to her environment are nil.

6. On February 16, 2001 MILDRED SICK made and executed an Advance Health Care Directive attached hereto and made a part hereof, naming petitioner as her health care proxy and health care attorney in fact.

7. She now is on life support systems including feeding tubes, heart/lung machine and oxygen mask.

8. I gave a copy of the said Advance Health Care Directive to

Source: Reprinted with permission of Thomson Reuters, West's Legal Form Books, Volume 18A; "Elder Law", Page 526.

Many states have *practice books*, which are typically a single volume book that not only provide samples of typical forms used within the law, but also provides an explanation of the law used in those forms as well as references to other sources of law.

Similar to many of the other secondary sources of law, formbooks include an index, as well as multiple volumes that include the forms. So how do you find the form you need? The lead formbook will likely have directions on how to use the set of books. If not, go to the index and determine which descriptive words will guide you to the correct form/template.

As you will see, many online businesses also offer downloads of many popular forms for a fee. Always be cautious when downloading any material from the Internet with which you are unfamiliar—especially on a work computer. Other websites, such as **www.findlaw.com** also provide access to many legal forms. If you have a subscription, you can also access many of these standard forms from *WestlawNext*.

WESTLAWNEXT: on the homepage, under the **All Content** tab, you will see **Forms** as the last option. Once you click on that, the page provides options for obtaining various forms by state, by topic, and by publication, including **Westlaw eforms**, which include numerous standard forms in every state and federal jurisdiction. Just choose **Westlaw eforms** under **Publications** then choose your jurisdiction, such as Pennsylvania. Thereafter, you can enter any search term into the top search box, such as: PLAINTIFF INTERROGATORIES, MOTOR VEHICLE ACCIDENT. As you can see in Figure 3-19, you can easily access the standard form in PDF format, which can be completed and saved.

Some of these forms can also be accessed on *Lexis Advance*.

LEXIS ADVANCE: on the homepage, if you type in the term: DISCOVERY, multiple formbooks such as the *Bender* or *Arkfeld* series appear in the drop-down menu as an option, where you can view the *Table of Contents*, as shown in Figure 3-20. You can scan the series or conduct a search within any of the formbooks.

However, in whatever law firm you are employed, it is likely that any and all forms your supervising attorney needs will already be on the firm's computer network.

Ethics Reminder

Keep in mind that even if your supervising attorney allows you to "fill-in" any forms to be filed with the court, be sure to show it to the attorney for review, approval, and signature. If not, it could be considered engaging in the unauthorized practice of law.

Figure 3-19 A Standard PDF Form for Plaintiff's Interrogatories

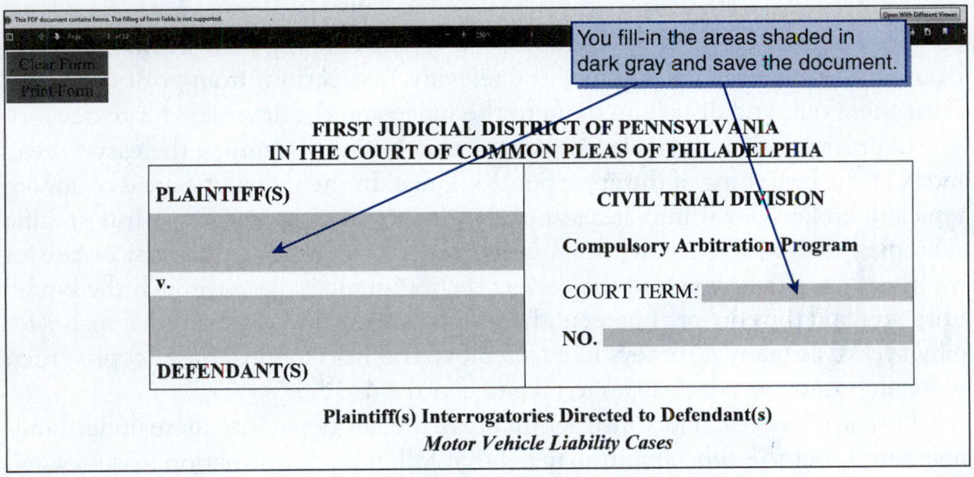

FIRST JUDICIAL DISTRICT OF PENNSYLVANIA
IN THE COURT OF COMMON PLEAS OF PHILADELPHIA

PLAINTIFF(S)	**CIVIL TRIAL DIVISION**
	Compulsory Arbitration Program
v.	COURT TERM:
	NO.
DEFENDANT(S)	

Plaintiff(s) Interrogatories Directed to Defendant(s)
Motor Vehicle Liability Cases

Source: Reprinted with permission of Thomson Reuters, West's Interrogatory PDF Legal Form on WestlawNext.

Figure 3-20 Options for Rules of Discovery on *Lexis Advance*

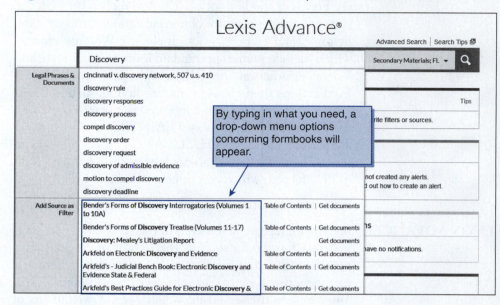

Source: Reprinted with the permission of LexisNexis.

Jury Instructions in Print and Online

Another secondary source used in the daily practice of law is **jury instructions**, which are a very important aspect of trial. Prior to the end of trial, the judge and all the attorneys will review the jury instructions relevant to that case that will be presented to the jury prior to deliberation. The jury instructions guide the jury on the law that is to be applied to the facts of the case in order to reach a verdict. For example, in a negligence case, the instructions will specifically enumerate each element of the cause of action that the plaintiff needs to prove to be successful against the defendant.

As you can see in Figure 3-21, jury instructions are not created by the judge during each trial; rather, they are "fill-in-the-blank" documents, similar to formbooks. The judge and the attorneys will typically amend or supplement, and even redact (remove) portions of the jury instructions that do not apply to the case. The jury instructions are printed and bound in two binders—one for criminal and one for civil cases (the instructions are also available online through your local bar association). Once the judge and attorneys decide on what instructions will be used, the paralegal will retrieve the relevant instructions from print or online, print them out, and distribute them to the judge and the attorneys for review.

In order to find a particular jury instruction begin by scanning the easy-to-read index at the beginning of the appropriate volume. In the index, the areas of law are typically broken down into *chapters* or *sections*. Each chapter/section lists specific subtopics, each with their own section number, as well as the latest revision date for each section. When you find the correct section number, page through the binder until you find the correct chapter and section number. The binder format makes for easy access, as many attorneys like to remove the instructions, make copies, then write any comments or changes to take to court.

Not only does each jury instruction break the law down into more understandable terms, but the **subcommittee notes** that follow each instruction discusses and explains the relevant law the jury is to be instructed on as well as many references of citations to relevant primary authority. In that sense, jury instructions are a

Figure 3-21 A Section of the Pennsylvania Civil Jury Instructions

13.40 (Civ)   **NEGLIGENT CONDUCT CAUSING ONLY EMOTIONAL DISTRESS**

[First Alternative—Emotional injury—zone of danger:]

[name of plaintiff] claims that *[name of defendant]*'s negligent conduct caused [him] [her] to suffer emotional distress.

In order to receive compensation for emotional distress, *[name of plaintiff]* must prove *all* of the following:

1.   *[name of defendant]* was negligent;

2.   *[name of defendant]*'s negligence placed *[name of plaintiff]* in danger of physical impact or injury; and

3.   *[name of plaintiff]* suffered emotional distress as a result of *[name of defendant]*'s negligent conduct.

[Second Alternative—Emotional injury with physical symptoms—not in zone of danger—injury to close family member:]

[name of plaintiff] claims that [he] [she] was near the scene of *[insert type of event]* and witnessed injury to *[insert name of close family member]*, which caused *[name of plaintiff]* to suffer emotional distress.

In order to receive compensation for emotional distress, *[name of plaintiff]* must prove *all* of the following:

1.   *[name of defendant]* was negligent;

2.   *[name of defendant]*'s negligence caused [injury] [harm] to *[insert name of close family member]*;

3.   *[name of plaintiff]* witnessed *[name of defendant]*'s negligent conduct;

4.   *[name of plaintiff]* suffered emotional distress as a result of witnessing *[name of defendant]*'s negligent conduct; and

5.   *[name of plaintiff]* suffered physical symptoms as a result of this emotional distress. Physical symptoms of emotional distress include, but are not limited to, [continued nausea, headaches, hysterical attacks, insomnia, severe depression, nightmares, nervousness, stress or anxiety, *[add other applicable symptoms in case]*].

*Renumbered (former 13.260).

Source: Selected materials from Pennsylvania Suggested Standard Civil Jury Instructions, Fourth Edition with 2015 Supplement. Reprinted with permission. This book (6770-3) can be ordered by contacting the Pennsylvania Bar Institute, 5080 Ritter Road, Mechanissburg, PA 17055, 800-932-4637. www.pbi.org.

good place to look prior to your research to see the law broken down into elements and helpful citations to the law that may address and even answer your legal issue.

The law office you work in should already have the state jury instructions in print and on CD. State jury instructions can also be found online through the state's bar association and on CD at your local law library. The local bar association also sells the print and online versions. Like any other authority, the jury instructions are revised and updated periodically. Be sure to check with the bar association in your state for any updates or changes prior to the release of a new edition.

Citing Jury Instructions

There will be occasions when your supervising attorney will need the citations for proposed jury instructions to be submitted to the court during trial, or to use in an appellate brief. Almost every state has compiled an official (model or pattern) set of civil and criminal jury instructions. Most states post their jury instructions, with citation format, online, or with the local bar association. Citation format can also be found in the first volume of jury instructions in print.

Although many of these secondary sources can be accessed online, be sure to at least become familiar with how the sets operate by navigating the print sources first. The secondary sources described in this chapter can be quite helpful in educating and directing you to what you need—take advantage of them.

Chapter Checklist ✓

- Secondary sources of law, although not law themselves, are extremely helpful for the paralegal prior to enagaging in the research process.
- Remember that secondary sources do three important things: they introduce new concepts and legal terminology so you can gain a better understanding of the law as they analyze and interpret the legal topic in understandable language; they provide key legal terminology for an index or digest search in print or online; and they direct you to the primary sources of law through the use of numerous citations and annotated material, thus, saving valuable research time.
- The secondary sources in print are set up in a similar way as the primary sources—the index system. Use the descriptive word method to find the relevant index term and corresponding number and locate that information within the numerous volumes in the set.
- There are two federal legal encyclopedias, as well as many state versions. Use these sources to learn about a particular legal topic in its broadest sense, as well as its multiple subtopics.
- Although they are similar in content and format, be sure to read the differences between the AmJur 2d and the CJS prior to utilizing either source as both have different helpful indexes.
- If your state does publish a state encyclopedia, use it prior to beginning your research! It is an invaluable tool to begin your search.
- The ALR is similar to the legal encyclopedias, but the coverage is more specific, and tends to include many topics concerning developing areas of law.
- If you need examples and illustrations demonstrating how a law is applied, then use the Restatements of Law. This source breaks the law down into easy-to-understand elements.
- Remember to only use a treatise or loose-leaf service if you need extensive and deep detail on one particualr subject. Be careful that you do not lose focus as to what you researching.
- As you are reading a statute, regualtion, or especially a case opinion, never underestimate the value of having a legal dictionary on hand. Never guess or assume the meaning of any legal term/word/phrase that you do not understand.
- The legal periodicals, with the exception of the law reviews, are published only to keep the legal field updated on the current cases or legal news on a daily basis. They have no real research value.
- Many of these sources can be accessed online as well; just follow the directions for each source within this chapter.

KEY TERMS

CRITICAL THINKING AND APPLICATION

Please read each question and follow the directions.

1. Locate the Am. Jur. 2d in your law library. Your supervising attorney has asked you to determine whether children (minors) can bring a cause of action against their parents for committing a tort against them.

   a. What terms/words did you use to begin an index search?

   b. Describe your research trail in locating this topic?

   c. In what volume and section is this topic located?

   d. Are there instances when a child can sue a parent for committing a tort? When? How? Under what circumstances?

   e. Do any citations to relevant case law (or any primary authority) exist within your jurisdiction? If so, what?

2. Locate the C.J.S. in your law library. Your supervising attorney has asked you to determine what a "warranty of habitability" is concerning a landlord's duty to his tenant.

   a. What terms/words did you use to begin an index search?

   b. Describe your research trail in locating this topic?

   c. In what volume and section is this topic located?

   d. What is a warranty of habitabiltiy?

   e. Does a landlord violate this warranty if the apartment he rents is infested with carpenter ants? Why or why not?

   f. Do any citations to relevant case law (or any primary authority) exist within your jurisdiction? If so, what?

   g. Which defect would fall under the protection of a warranty of habitability: a broken ceiling fan in the middle of the summer, or a broken furnace in the middle of the winter? Why?

   h. Which defect would fall under the protection of a warranty of habitability: a hole in the roof of a dwelling, or a hole in the first floor living room ceiling in a two-story dwelling? Why?

3. Locate the A.L.R. in your law library. Your supervising attoney has asked you to determine whether a plaintiff can bring cause of action against a hospital and/or doctor for emotional distress after the plaintiff's loved one died in the hospital due to the negligence of the hosptial and/or doctor. This is a *state* issue.

   a. What terms/words did you use to begin an index search?

   b. Describe your research trail in locating this topic?

   c. In what volume and page is this topic located?

   d. Can a plaintiff can bring cause of action against a hospital and/or doctor for emotional distress after the plaintiff's loved one died in the hospital due to the negligence of the hosptial and/or doctor?

   e. Do any citations to relevant case law (or any primary authority) exist within your jurisdiction? If so, what?

4. Read the three passages below. Do you know the meaning of the terms in **bold**? If not, look them up in a *legal dictionary*. Thereafter, explain to your instructor, in class, the meaning of the terms within the context of the passage. If you cannot find any of these terms in a legal dictionary, where would you look to find their meaning?

a. " . . . in essence, the defendant has not made clear which if any of the following catagories his actions fall under, including that of a **licensee**, an **invitee**, or a **traspasser**. The defendant has not addressed that issue, but rather argued that due to his age, the **attractive nusiance doctrine** should apply to this case."

b. " . . . the plaintiff argued that the city electrical company did not have permission to build a electrical transformer box in the back of his property. The city argued that they had an **easement** to access the plaintiff's property. In addition, the defense argued that the case was moot in that the city was in the process of seizing the property, where the transformer sits, by **eminent domain**."

c. " . . . at the end of hearing the judge awarded the mother sole physical custody of the child, but also ordered that both parents would share **legal custody** of the child. Further, Mr. Peters was **adjudicated** as the biological father following genetic testing."

5. Obtain a copy of a law review publication from a law school within your state, in print or online. Read through it and become familiar with its format and its use of footnotes. Discuss an article of interest in class. Why was it written? What is the importance of the topic?

6. Read through any periodical (newspaper, magazine, or online publication) and find a recent story in the news concerning either a controversial law, or analysis and/or discssion of a new case decision handed down in your state. Explain to the class what the article is about and why you feel it was important enough to be published in the paper.

LEARNING OBJECTIVES

After completion of this chapter, you should be able to

1. Identify and understand the individual components of a statute.

2. Describe the three stages of statutory publication.

3. Explain how to conduct a legislative history in print and online.

4. Describe and illustrate how to read and understand the language contained in a statute.

LEGISLATIVE

SLIP LAW

ORDINANCE

CODE

The Basics of Statutory Law | CHAPTER 4

Most research performed by a paralegal in a typical law office will include statutes, case law, or a combination of both. In this chapter, you will learn the basics of statutory law, including how statutes are organized and published in print and online. Most importantly, you will learn how to read and analyze a statute—an invaluable skill. It is important not only to learn how to locate a statute, but also to understand how it addresses and answers your legal issue.

■ INTRODUCTION TO STATUTORY RESEARCH

A **statute** is a written law that was passed by a governmental legislative body that regulates our day-to-day life. Those written laws govern the actions that are permitted or prohibited in society. What are the rules that govern federal bankruptcy or copyright law? What are the elements for the crime of kidnapping in Florida, or Illinois, or California? What if you need to calculate veterans' benefits for a potential client? These questions, as well as a majority of other legal issues, can be answered or at least addressed in statutory law. Statutory law is typically the first source of primary law a researcher will look at to see if a written law exists that addresses a legal issue.

Statutes are created on a federal, state, and local level. For instance, federal statutes regulate and enforce the laws of bankruptcy, and state laws regulate and enforce state DUI laws. Statutory law enacted by local governing bodies include cities, counties, townships, and districts. State legislatures have given these "sub-level" government levels the ability to enact ordinances. **Ordinances** are very similar to statutes, but they regulate everyday local rules such as zoning, traffic, and sanitation regulations. For example, a local ordinance could mandate where a resident can install a satellite cable dish as to preserve the aesthetic appeal of the city's neighborhoods, or it can determine which items can be discarded for recycling.

statute
A law passed by a federal or state legislative body.

ordinance
A piece of legislation, similar to a statute, created by a local governmental body or municipal authority.

Adapting to the Needs of Society

Although statutes are drafted carefully over time to ensure their longevity, any statute has the possibility of being amended, supplemented, or even overturned over time. The written law must maintain some level of flexibility in order to adapt to the continual changes or needs of society.

For example, prior to 1994, 21 states enacted laws requiring all convicted sexual offenders to register with state law enforcement upon their release from prison. During this time, such a law did not exist in New Jersey when young

Megan Kanka was murdered by a convicted sex offender who lived across the street from Megan's family. At that time, the *federal* government previously passed legislation that required convicted sexual offenders to register with law enforcement following their release from prison, probation, or parole, but the law did not provide for notice to the residents of a community where a convicted sexual offender may reside upon release from prison. Megan's parents, along with a multitude of supporters, persuaded the New Jersey state legislature to pass a law that would provide greater protection to children from these offenders. In only three months, a new bill was passed. The new law included the registration requirement and, more importantly, public notification of the address of any convicted sexual offender. Thereafter, Congress amended its law to include both provisions of the new "Megan's Law" and withheld federal funding to any state that did not adopt the new law. Today, most states have adopted "Megan's Law," including limited or active public notification requirements.

If you pick up any newspaper or turn on the television, you will undoubtedly see laws being amended or supplemented by Congress or your state legislature in response to some event. This is why it is crucial as a researcher to always locate the most recent and updated law, as statutes can be amended, supplemented, or overturned at any time.

SIDE NOTE

Many statutes are created and supplemented each year. In 2013, the Pennsylvania state legislature *amended* its child labor laws to extend the same protection to child actors who appear in television reality programs as to those children on movie sets. The law was passed following the long hours of continuous filming of the reality program "Jon & Kate Plus 8." Also that same year, the state legislature *created* a law to permit victims of crime and their families to speak to the members of the PA Board of Probation and Parole prior to any decision on whether to release a prisoner on parole.

■ HOW TO IDENTIFY THE PARTS OF A STATUTE IN PRINT

LEARNING OBJECTIVE 1
Identify and understand the individual components of a statute.

At first glance, a statute may appear difficult or confusing to read only because you are not familiar with reading that type of legal material on a daily basis. However, the more statutes you read, the easier they will be to understand and comprehend. Similar to learning case briefs, you have to first learn and understand the individual parts that make up a statute. Only then can you learn how to read and understand the language in a statute.

Statutes that are published in print will typically include the following basic elements: *body of the statute; historical & statutory notes; library references; research references; definitions; sub-statutes;* and *notes of decisions*.

In Figure 4-1, please review the sample statute and corresponding descriptions of each component of a statute that follow. Do not worry about how to locate a statute, or how to read or understand the statute here. You will learn all that information later. You are learning in steps. In this section, just know and understand the individual parts.

At the top of the first page of your particular statute, you will see the statute name. Here, it is the **Junkyard and Automotive Recycler Screening Law.**

Figure 4-1 Pennsylvania Statute in Print

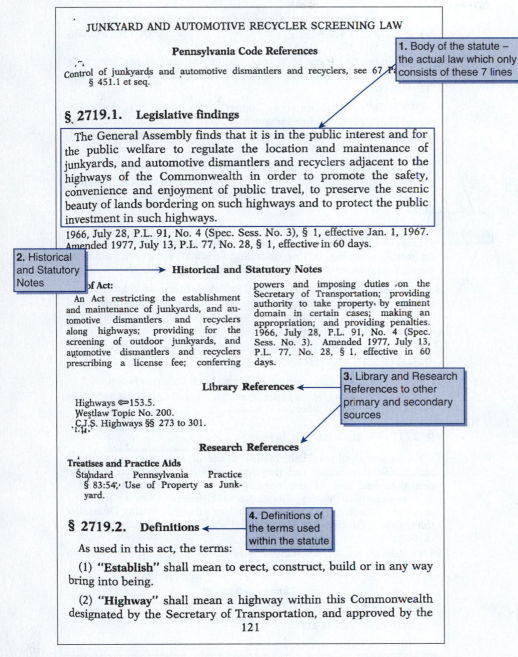

JUNKYARD AND AUTOMOTIVE RECYCLER SCREENING LAW

Pennsylvania Code References

Control of junkyards and automotive dismantlers and recyclers, see 67 P̲a̲
§ 451.1 et seq.

> **1. Body of the statute –** the actual law which only consists of these 7 lines

§ 2719.1.   Legislative findings

> The General Assembly finds that it is in the public interest and for the public welfare to regulate the location and maintenance of junkyards, and automotive dismantlers and recyclers adjacent to the highways of the Commonwealth in order to promote the safety, convenience and enjoyment of public travel, to preserve the scenic beauty of lands bordering on such highways and to protect the public investment in such highways.

1966, July 28, P.L. 91, No. 4 (Spec. Sess. No. 3), § 1, effective Jan. 1, 1967. Amended 1977, July 13, P.L. 77, No. 28, § 1, effective in 60 days.

> **2. Historical and Statutory Notes**

Historical and Statutory Notes

of Act:
An Act restricting the establishment and maintenance of junkyards, and automotive dismantlers and recyclers along highways; providing for the screening of outdoor junkyards, and automotive dismantlers and recyclers prescribing a license fee; conferring

powers and imposing duties ,on the Secretary of Transportation; providing authority to take property, by eminent domain in certain cases; making an appropriation; and providing penalties. 1966, July 28, P.L. 91, No. 4 (Spec. Sess. No. 3). Amended 1977, July 13, P.L. 77, No. 28, § 1, effective in 60 days.

> **3. Library and Research References** to other primary and secondary sources

Library References

Highways ⚖153.5.
Westlaw Topic No. 200.
C.J.S. Highways §§ 273 to 301.

Research References

Treatises and Practice Aids
Standard   Pennsylvania   Practice
§ 83:54; Use of Property as Junk-yard.

> **4. Definitions** of the terms used within the statute

§ 2719.2.   Definitions

As used in this act, the terms:

(1) "**Establish**" shall mean to erect, construct, build or in any way bring into being.

(2) "**Highway**" shall mean a highway within this Commonwealth designated by the Secretary of Transportation, and approved by the

121

Source: Reprinted with permission of Thomson Reuters, Title 36, section 2719.1; 2719.2; 2719.3; 2719.4.

1. **Body of the Statute**—You can typically identify the actual text of the statute by its title and numerical identifier in bold, which immediately precedes the text or body of the particular statute. In this case, it is *§2719.1 Legislative Findings*. The body of the statute includes the law itself. Here, the state legislature created this statute in the interest of the welfare of the public to regulate the location of junkyards within the state in order to preserve the scenic beauty of the public roads and the safety and enjoyment of public travel. In other words, in the state of Pennsylvania, junkyards, garbage dumps, and landfills are necessary, but they are not to be seen or interfere with any public state highway. Please note that any text following a particular section number in bold was written and passed by the legislature. Anything else is *annotated material*, which is added historical and

Figure 4-1 Continued

---

36 P.S. § 2719.2 `[5. Citation]` **PUBLIC ROADS**

United States Secretary of Transportation, as part of the Interstate System or primary system; pursuant to Title 23, United States Code, "Highways."

(3) **"Junk"** shall mean scrap copper, brass, rope, rags, batteries, paper, trash, rubber debris, waste, iron, steel, and other old or scrap ferrous or non-ferrous material, including wrecked, scrapped, ruined, dismantled or junked motor vehicles or parts thereof.

(4) **"Junkyard"** shall mean any outdoor establishment or place of business which is maintained, used or operated for storing, keeping, buying or selling junk, and the term shall include garbage dumps and sanitary fills.

`[Definitions continued...]` (4.1) **"Automotive dismantler and recycler"** shall mean any establishment or place of business which is maintained, used or operated for storing, keeping, buying or selling wrecked, scrapped, ruined or dismantled motor vehicles, or motor vehicle parts, or both.

(5) **"Scrap metal processing facility"** shall mean an establishment having facilities for processing iron, steel or non-ferrous scrap metal and whose principal product is scrap iron, steel or non-ferrous scrap for sale for remelting purposes only.

(6) **"Visible"** shall mean capable of being seen by a person of normal visual acuity traversing the highway.

(7) **"Secretary"** shall mean the Secretary of Transportation.

1966, July 28, P.L. 91, No. 4 (Spec. Sess. No. 3), § 2. Amended 1977, July 13, P.L. 77, No. 28, § 1, effective in 60 days.

§ 2719.3. Restrictions; license `[6. Sub-section of the main statute]`

No person shall establish, maintain, use or operate a junkyard, or automotive dismantler and recycler any portion of which is within one thousand feet of the nearest edge of the right-of-way of a highway, without having obtained a valid license therefor from the secretary. Each license shall be valid for one year ending December thirty-first. The fee for each license shall be one hundred dollars ($100).

1966, July 28, P.L. 91, No. 4 (Spec. Sess. No. 3), § 3. Amended 1977, July 13, P.L. 77, No. 28, § 1, effective in 60 days.

Library References

Highways ⬥153.5.	C.J.S. Highways §§ 273 to 301.
Licenses ⬥16(11).	C.J.S. Licenses § 55.
Westlaw Topic Nos. 200, 238.	

---

reference material added by the publisher of the code, not the legislature. As you read the remainder of this section, all annotated material will be denoted with the (*) symbol to help you learn and understand the difference.

2. ***Historical and Statutory Notes***—This section is important as it usually describes the reason for the law as well as the legislative history of the law. This includes the original bill number and any amendments to it over the years.

3. ***Library and Research References***—*Library References* inform you as to where this particular statute can be found in other sections of the statutory code as well as in any other secondary sources of law. Here, because the publisher is *West*, you can see that the added term "Highways" under the *Key Number* system is provided so that you can find reference to this statute in any *West* published legal authority. You can also find reference to this statute in the legal encyclopedia

Figure 4-1 Continued

JUNKYARD SCREENING   **36 P.S. § 2719.4**

Notes of Decisions

Construction and application 1
Right to file petition 2

---

1. Construction and application

Junkyard Act, which contains no clear language showing overriding intent and limits eminent domain powers to then-existing junkyards, does not demonstrate that legislature intended to preempt local zoning ordinances as to future junkyards. Washington Tp. v. Com., Dept. of Transp., 421 A.2d 859, 54 Pa.Cmwlth. 431, Cmwlth.1980, affirmed 425 A.2d 1107, 493 Pa. 246. Zoning And Planning ⇔ 1033

Department of transportation did not transgress bounds of its statutory powers by conditioning issuance of license under Junkyard Act solely upon compliance with provisions of that statute. Washington Tp. v. Com., Dept. of Transp., 421 A.2d 859, 54 Pa.Cmwlth. 431, Cmwlth. 1980, affirmed 425 A.2d 1107, 493 Pa. 246. Licenses ⇔ 25

Recipient of license under Junkyard Act is not thereby relieved of his obligation to comply with municipal zoning. Washington Tp. v. Com., Dept. of Transp., 421 A.2d 859, 54 Pa.Cmwlth. 431, Cmwlth. 1980, affirmed 425 A.2d 1107, 493 Pa. 246. Zoning And Planning ⇔ 1033

The action of the [...] land in encroaching [...] defendants' land for [...] automobiles as part [...] ation could establish [...] id nonconforming [...] zoning ordinance and this section. Com. v. Cossell, 17 Pa. D. & C.3d 250 (1980). Zoning And Planning ⇔ 1300

7. Notes of Decisions which are case summaries directly concerning the statute which are arranged by topic

2. Right to file petition

Township had right to file petition to review issuance of automotive dismantler and recycler license by department of transportation for site within its corporate limits, since issue of its standing could not be determined until decision had been reached on the merits. Washington Tp. v. Com., Dept. of Transp., 421 A.2d 859, 54 Pa.Cmwlth. 431, Cmwlth. 1980, affirmed 425 A.2d 1107, 493 Pa. 246. Licenses ⇔ 22

C.J.S. in section §§ 273 to 301. On the other hand, **Research References** also provide similar and useful information to other secondary sources of law.

4. **Definitions**—This section was added by the legislature and not considered annotated material. How do you know? Because it is language that is preceded by a section number in bold denoting it as part of the statute. This section, typical in many statutes, is drafted by the legislature for individuals to fully and clearly understand the actual meaning of the statute. In other words, if a word within the statute appears vague, or you assume its meaning, the definition section will clarify it for you. For example, according to definition #4, a junkyard, according to this statute refers also to garbage dumps and sanitary fills; something one would not have assumed when reading this statute.

5. **Citation**—The citation is the identifier for how to retrieve and identify the statute.

6. **Statute Sub-Section**—Almost every statute has multiple subsections that are identified by a section number in bold. These subsections include information related to the main statute. For example, if a statute denotes the elements for the crime of arson, the subsection will state the possible penalties.

7. ***Notes of Decisions**—This section is important in that *West* has found all cases within your jurisdiction that have dealt with this statute. These case summaries are quite helpful in helping you understand how the statute applies by how the courts interpreted it. Also, the publisher has provided the case citation for you to find and read the entire case as well as the *West* "key number."

This format is basically universal for all statutes in any state. Although some degrees of variation will exist, the overall content will be the same.

■ STATUTE PUBLICATION

Statutes are created through a careful legislative process, which basically follows the same procedure within federal and state governments.

The Legislative Process: A Brief Look

LEARNING OBJECTIVE 2
Describe the three stages of statutory publication.

bill
A proposed law.

How is statutory law created? Whether on the state or federal level, a statute is created from a governmental legislative body. It is good to have a brief understanding of *how* a statute is created, as you may be called upon to locate a certain law at any time through its evolution.

In its simplest terms, the process begins when a sponsor introduces a **bill** (a proposed law), which is given a numerical identifier and introduced to the state or federal legislative body. On the state level, every state, with the exception of Nebraska, is comprised of a bicameral congress, meaning each congress includes two governmental bodies: a house of representatives and a senate. The names of these two chambers may differ from state to state, but the legislative duties are the same. As you know, on the federal level, Congress is comprised of the House of Representatives and the Senate.

Once the bill, which can include a proposal for a *new* law or *amendment* to a current law, has been introduced into either chamber, the bill is carefully and closely analyzed, scrutinized, and debated. Bills are identified by a letter/number combination denoting where the bill originated. For instance, a state bill could be originated in the house (**H23**) or senate (**S102**). On the federal level, each bill is denoted as either (**HR432**) or (**S177**). Amendments to the bill can be made prior to any vote taken by committee. Once both governmental bodies individually approve the bill, it is sent to the governor (state level) or the president (federal level) who can either sign the bill into law (typically required within 10 days) or veto it. The bill can also pass by a majority vote (2/3) of both chambers or by the governor's inaction to sign the bill into law within the 10 days at the state or federal level. The bill then becomes a slip law, and is then later organized and compiled into a set of books called session laws (state level) or Statutes at Large (federal level). These session laws are eventually compiled into state and federal statutory codes.

On a local government level, including counties, districts, boroughs, or townships, legislative enactment is similar to that of the state and federal process. However, because those local laws (ordinances) affect only a small locality, they are usually not submitted to a standing committee, but they must only meet the approval of the local legislative delegation. Ordinances do not become part of the official state code, but they are compiled into local township or county codes, which regulate such items as removal of weeds on residential property to controlling barking dogs in the middle of the night.

Although a statute becomes law as soon as it is enacted into law, make sure to carefully read the law as some civil and many criminal statutes will state that the particular law will not take effect until 30, 60, or 90 days from passage of the bill. This is to allow people to become aware of the new law prior to it going into effect. It is important to tell your supervising attorney this during your research.

The Stages of Statutory Publication

Every law enacted passes through three stages of publication: slip laws, session laws, and codes.

Slip Laws

The **slip law** is the first print version of a newly enacted or amended law. As you can see in Figure 4-2, state and federal slip laws can be designated as *public* or *private*. Nearly all statutes you will research are public and are designated as such: **Pub.L. 107-007.** This abbreviation denotes the statute as **public law** (Pub .L.), the (107) stands for the 107th session of Congress, and the (007) stands for the actual bill number. Each slip law is numbered sequentially in the order that it is

slip law
The first print version of a newly enacted or amended law.

public law
Enacted laws that affect all citizens.

Figure 4-2 Sample of a Public and Private Slip Law

Public Law 109–8
109th Congress

An Act

To amend title 11 of the United States Code, and for other purposes.

Apr. 20, 2005
[S. 256]

Be it enacted by the Senate and House of Representatives of the United States of America in Congress assembled,

SECTION 1. SHORT TITLE; REFERENCES; TABLE OF CONTENTS.

(a) SHORT TITLE.—This Act may be cited as the "Bankruptcy Abuse Prevention and Consumer Protection Act of 2005".

(b) TABLE OF CONTENTS.—The table of contents for this Act is as follows:

Bankruptcy Abuse Prevention and Consumer Protection Act of 2005.
11 USC 101 note.

Sec. 1. Short title; references; table of contents.

TITLE I—NEEDS-BASED BANKRUPTCY

Sec. 101. Conversion.
Sec. 102. Dismissal or conversion.
Sec. 103. Sense of Congress and study.
Sec. 104. Notice of alternatives.
Sec. 105. Debtor financial management training test program.
Sec. 106. Credit counseling.
Sec. 107. Schedules of reasonable and necessary expenses.

> Notice the law identified by the "public law number" of Pub.L. 109-8. This law was the eighth passed during the 109th Congress on April 20, 2005. You can also see that the bill was originated in the Senate (S256).

Private Law 112–1
112th Congress

An Act

For the relief of Sopuruchi Chukwueke.

Dec. 28, 2012
[S. 285]

Be it enacted by the Senate and House of Representatives of the United States of America in Congress assembled,

SECTION 1. ADJUSTMENT OF STATUS.

(a) IN GENERAL.—Notwithstanding any other provision of law, for the purposes of the Immigration and Nationality Act (8 U.S.C. 1101 et seq.), Sopuruchi Chukwueke shall be deemed to have been lawfully admitted to, and remained in, the United States, and shall be eligible for adjustment of status to that of an alien lawfully admitted for permanent residence under section 245 of the Immigration and Nationality Act (8 U.S.C. 1255) upon filing an application for such adjustment of status.

(b) APPLICATION AND PAYMENT OF FEES.—Subsection (a) shall apply only if the application for adjustment of status is filed with appropriate fees not later than 2 years after the date of the enactment of this Act.

(c) REDUCTION OF IMMIGRANT VISA NUMBERS.—Upon the granting of permanent resident status to Sopuruchi Chukwueke, the Secretary of State shall instruct the proper officer to reduce by 1, during the current or next following fiscal year, the total number of immigrant visas that are made available to natives of the country of the birth of Sopuruchi Chukwueke under section 202(a)(2) of the Immigration and Nationality Act (8 U.S.C. 1152(a)(2)).

> Notice the law identified by the "private law number" of Pvt.L. 112-1. This law was the first, and possibly only, bill passed during the 112th Congress on December 28, 2012. You can also see that the bill was originated in the Senate (S285).

Source: http://www.gpo.gov/fdsys and https://www.congress.gov

passed within a particular congressional session, meaning this bill was the 7th law passed during that session.

On the other hand, statutes can also be enacted as private, but it is rare. **Private law** affects a minority of the population, or even small groups of people facing similar issues, such as deportation or immigration issues. Some private laws are even passed into law for a single individual and are designated as such: **Pvt.L. 107-008,** meaning this law was passed immediately after the public law above, as denoted by the citation.

Statutes can also be designated as **permanent law** or **temporary law.** Mostly all statutes are permanent, considering the time and effort taken to enact a law. Those laws remain in effect until they are possibly amended, supplemented, or repealed at a later time. Temporary statutes have a certain "expiration date" due to the temporary nature that addresses an immediate issue or situation, such as an individual deportation.

Slip laws are published in print and online. However, they are easiest to access online in state or federal format. You can locate the most current state slip laws from any state with a simple Internet search. Like you have already learned, if you need to see the language in a newly passed law in Idaho, you simply enter the terms: IDAHO, SLIP LAWS, 2013, to access the Idaho Legislative government website. There, as for any state, you can access the most current and newly passed state laws, as you can see in Figure 4-3.

The main online source for locating federal slip laws is the US Government Printing Office (GPO) at **www.gpo.gov/fdsys.** There you can find any newly enacted or recently amended federal statutory law by congressional session as well as by public and private laws. You can also access federal slip laws from The Library

private law
Enacted laws that affect a minority of the population or only one person.

permanent law
An enacted law intended to remain unchanged for an indefinite period of time.

temporary law
An enacted law with a specific expiration date.

Figure 4-3 Google Search Result Page for Idaho Slip Laws

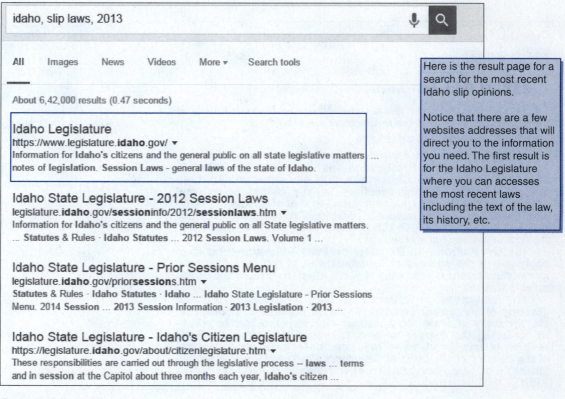

Source: https://www.google.com

of Congress where you can browse all the newly enacted federal laws by congressional session or by bill number from the House or the Senate at **www.Congress.gov**. Summaries are included for all slip laws from 1973 and full text of the laws from 1989. Many law libraries also shelve state and federal slip laws in print if they are a governmental depository, which is defined as a library that carries many federal government publications, such as slip laws, that other law libraries would not carry. Ask your law librarian if your library is a governmental depository.

As you know, a bill can propose a **new** law or **amend** an existing law. In amending a law, the state or federal legislature will post the slip law complete with all the crossing out (text deleted) or underscoring (text added) that occurred during the debate of the bill prior to enactment into law so that citizens can view the changes made to the law.

For example, consider if a state legislature sought to amend an existing law defining which type of "motor vehicles" are permitted on state highways. This law was proposed after numerous casualties were recorded on the state highways by individuals riding small motorized bikes which are deemed unsafe for highway and interstate travel.

A portion of the proposed bill and/or slip law could be stated as follows:

> " . . . (2) Motorcycle: defined as a vehicle for state and highway travel, which includes a seat for the rider, two handlebars, and two wheels, as well as including at least a two-stroke or four-stroke internal combustion engine, ~~as well as any vehicle that satisfies those requirements~~, <u>excluding any type of moped or "converted" motorbike, or any vehicle not including the above-mentioned parts and engine</u> . . .

You will see this in the initial drafting of any "amended" legislation. Any words/terms/phrases that have the strikethough feature are *eliminated* from the new law, and any words/terms/phrases that are underlined are *added* to the new law.

Remember that a newly enacted law becomes binding authority the moment it is signed into law. What happens when your supervising attorney requires a new law that has not yet been compiled, organized, and published, even in any supplemental material? You know where to find it, but how do you cite it? You will see that every law falls under a particular name or title. Therefore, follow the formats below. At the least, make certain you include the full public or private law number, as it is the only numerical identifier attached to the new law. If the law does not have an actual title, you can simply use "Act of 2012, Pub. L. No . . . "

The American Taxpayer Relief Act of 2012, Pub. L. No. 112–240.

For a law that was recently **amended**, a statute will *already exist* in electronic and even print publication. In those situations, you cite the newly amended law as follows.

27 U.S.C. §1129 (1998), *amended by* **27 U.S.C. §1129(e) (2003).**

Va. Code Ann. §22.1-254.1 *amended by* **§22.1-254.1B (2012).**

As you can see, the first portion of the citation is the official statutory code citation, which you learn below. The second part of the citation is the newly amended portion, which includes sections 1129(e) and 254.1B above, as well as the *date of amendment*, **NOT** the date the original law was enacted.

Session Laws

session laws
A collection of all the slip laws following a state legislative session that are edited and published in a series of bound volumes. In the federal legislature, these are referred to as the Statutes at Large.

At the conclusion of a state or federal congressional session, the slip laws are accumulated, corrected, and published in a series of bound volumes referred to as the **session laws**, which are either published by each state (*Laws of Ohio, Laws of Texas*) or by the federal government (*Statutes at Large*). Each session law is published in the order of its enactment. The version of the session law and the version of the original slip law are identical. The only difference is the publication format. An index is typically used to locate a law, but you have to know the number of the congressional session to use it.

The session laws are actually the most authoritative form of the law, meaning that any mistakes found in the slip law are corrected by the time the session law is printed, and if there is any discrepancy in the statutory code, it is the session law that controls. Viewing the session laws are helpful if a researcher is required to compile a legislative history, as you will see below.

Most law libraries have the session laws of each state as well as all federal laws. The state session laws for your state are most likely in print form shelved in your law library next to the statutory code. Also, "recent" session laws can also be located on *WestlawNext* and *Lexis Advance*. In addition, conduct an Internet search for your state, as many session laws are also found on state legislative government websites. On the federal level, the *Statutes at Large* can be located in print at government depository law libraries, as well as online at the GPO website, including volumes 2003 through 2008 as well as *WestlawNext* and *Lexis Advance*.

If you need to cite a federal session law, use the format below. For any state session laws, your instructor will provide the proper format. The *Bluebook* also addresses this situation (Rule 12.4, as well as the blue pages for each state at the end of the book), and the ALWD (Rule 14.6–14.8).

> **Act of Nov. 25, 2002, Pub. L. No. 107–296, 116 Stat. 2135.**

Whether it is a federal or state statute, it is advised *not* to cite to a session law if an official/unofficial version (statute) of the law exists and can therefore be cited in a more universal citation format. The only time it is advised to cite a session law is if you need it to cite in a brief or legal document and the enactment of the law is very recent, and is not yet included in a printed code, online, or in an updated supplement, and the session law is the *only* available source of the newly *enacted* law. For newly *amended* law, follow the format in the slip law citations above. Please review Figure 4-4 for a good example of the various citation formats within one public law.

Statutory Codes

statutory codes
The final stage of statutory publication when all of the session laws, and Statutes at Large, are compiled and organized into permanent titles and sections in a hardbound print set and online.

The final stage of statutory law publication is referred to as codification, meaning that all the session laws are eventually organized into **statutory codes** which are topical arrangements of all the permanent laws within a state or federal jurisdiction. Note that the difference in locating a codified statute and a slip/session

Figure 4-4 Example of a Session Law Compiled in the Statutes at Large

PUBLIC LAW 104–134—APR. 26, 1996   110 STAT. 1321–358

CHAPTER 10

DEBT COLLECTION IMPROVEMENTS

SEC. 31001. DEBT COLLECTION IMPROVEMENT ACT OF 1996.

(a)(1) This section may be cited as the "Debt Collection Improvement Act of 1996".

(2)(A) IN GENERAL.—The provisions of this section and the amendments made by this section shall take effect on the date of the enactment of this Act.

(B) OFFSETS FROM SOCIAL SECURITY PAYMENTS, ETC.— Subparagraph (A) of section 3716(c)(3) of title 31, United States Code (as added by subsection (d)(2) of this section), shall apply only to payments made after the date which is 4 months after the date of the enactment of this Act.

(b) The purposes of this section are the following:

(1) To maximize collections of delinquent debts owed to the Government by ensuring quick action to enforce recovery of debts and the use of all appropriate collection tools.

(2) To minimize the costs of debt collection by consolidating related functions and activities and utilizing interagency teams.

(3) To reduce losses arising from debt management activities by requiring proper screening of potential borrowers, aggressive monitoring of all accounts, and sharing of information within and among Federal agencies.

(4) To ensure that the public is fully informed of the Federal Government's debt collection policies and that debtors are cog-

Marginal notes: Debt Collection Improvement Act of 1996. 31 USC 3701 note. Effective date. 31 USC 3322 note. Applicability. 31 USC 3716 note.

31 USC 3701 note.

Callout box: Notice the public law number (104-134) for the federal "Debt Collection Improvement Act," as well as the designated citation (**110 Stat. 1321–358**) for the Statutes at Large volume set, as well as where this law will fit into the U.S. Code.

Source: http://www.dol.gov

law is how you search for it. The slip and session laws are located by their *date of passage* according to their *numerical identifier*, but the statutory code is organized by the *index system*. Each state and federal statutory code is broken down and arranged into "titles" that makes locating a law much easier.

It is from the statutory codes where you will conduct most of your research. That is why, in the next chapter, you will see, step-by-step, where state, local, and federal laws are located in print and online, and how to use the statutory index and word search method to find them.

■ HOW TO CONDUCT THE LEGISLATIVE HISTORY OF A LAW

Even *before* a bill is passed into law, you may be asked by your supervising attorney to track or monitor the status of a proposed law of interest that could affect a case. For example, if your attorney learns that the state legislature is in the process of amending the elements of the crime of self-defense based on a recent high-profile crime, he may ask you to "monitor" the progress of the bill.

In addition, you may also have to review the **legislative history** of a law to determine the statute's meaning or *legislative intent* more clearly. For example, in drafting a new law, the legislature passed a new law prohibiting "persons of importance" from doing X, but who is a "person of importance" in reference to that particular law? Are police officers included? What about firemen? How about any state official or even the mayor? A detailed legislative history will provide all the congressional and committee action, including the debates from which you could determine the legislative intent of the bill.

LEARNING OBJECTIVE 3
Know how to conduct a legislative history in print and online.

legislative history
A term referring to the documents produced by a legislative body as a bill is introduced and debated, used to determine the legislative intent or clarification of a law.

Specifically, the legislative history will include the transcripts of the debates and hearings as well as the reports and different versions of a particular bill. The main sources of the legislative history of a bill include:

- **Congressional Bills** - a bill may undergo multiple changes before becoming a law, so by reading all the versions, you may be able to determine the legislative intent;
- **Committee Hearings** – these hearing transcripts include the debates concerning a particular bill;
- **Committee Reports** – these reports contain the actual text of a bill;
- **Congressional Debates** – these include all the transcripts of the debates arguing for or against the bill and the reasoning for those debates.

If you do need to conduct a legislative history, there are a few steps to take and a few good resources from which to obtain the information.

STEP 1: The key to a legislative search is to know the public law number (Pub. L.) This is the number assigned to the bill prior to its enactment into law. Remember to read the public law number as follows: Pub. L. 101–88. This means this was the 88th bill enacted by the 101st Congress.

STEP 2: Once you have the necessary public law number, there are a number of sources from which you can obtain the information you need.

Print (State):

1. If you look to the hardbound codified statutes in your state, references to the creation, amendment, or supplementation of that law will be found in the annotated codes listed at the end of each statute. There you will find the original public law number for each law that originated as a bill. At the end of a particular statute, information may also include any legislative notes that also briefly explain some of the legislative history of the law.
2. Check with your local law library to see what is available for you to view. In most instances, a local law library will not carry committee notes or reports. However, you can obtain the phone/fax number of your state legislature from the library reference desk. These reports should be in a House or Senate "archives" facility. The staff should be able to assist you in viewing/copying what you may need. Many law libraries should carry the debates and remarks concerning a particular bill, which will be published in the state's legislative journals. Again, seek assistance with these journals from the reference desk.
3. Remember that any debates or hearings concerning a particular bill are always open to the public. If you know when a bill will be argued and/or debated, it is much easier to hear the arguments and discussions live than to read about them. Again, call your state's legislative personnel for a schedule of upcoming legislative debates.

Online (State):

1. Every state has a legislative website. Again, rather than provide information that could soon be outdated, use your Internet searching skills. For example, type in any search engine, [YOUR STATE], LEGISLATURE, BILLS—that's all.

Each state website has options on the homepage for how to easily and quickly obtain the legislative history or to track the current status of a bill on the legislative floor.

2. Almost all local law libraries have a step-by-step format for how to conduct a legislative history within that particular state, which is a great reference and resource because "links" to online versions of sources to conduct a legislative search are also likely provided.

Print (Federal):

1. The **United States Code Congressional and Administrative News (U.S.C.C.A.N.)** is a *West* Group monthly publication that collects selected congressional materials for publication in a single resource for later inclusion into a hardbound volume set. This publication provides excellent information concerning the purpose of the legislation. These sets are found in all law libraries.

2. The **Congressional Information Service (C.I.S.)** is a *Lexis* publication and also is published in monthly pamphlets, which eventually are bound in a printed set. This set includes a comprehensive index and provides excellent coverage of any bill to compile a complete legislative history.

3. The **Congressional Index** is a loose-leaf service (no hardbound binding; material is complied into large ring binders for easily adding new material). It provides an index of various bills organized by **subject**, **sponsor**, **actions taken**, and **companion bills**.

Online (Federal):

1. **www.congress.gov** - (enter the bill number or word/phrase on the home screen).

2. **www.gpo.gov/fdsys** - (click on a number of hyperlinks on the left-hand column of the home screen, including *congressional bills*, *congressional hearings*, *congressional records*, and *congressional reports*).

Figure 4-5 Legislative History Search on WestlawNext and Lexis Advance

WestlawNext	On the homepage, choose *Statutes and Court Rules*. In the right-hand column, choose *Legislative History*. There, you have the choice of **Federal** (legislative histories of the US Code and the Congressional Record), **State: Jurisdiction** (legislative history search by state name using a Boolean or Natural Language search), and **State: Type** (Committee Notes, Hearing Transcripts).
Lexis Advance	On the top of the homepage, choose *Browse*, then *Category*, and under *Sources*, choose *Statutes and Legislation*. In the left-hand column, choose *Legislative Histories* under *Category*. There, you can scroll through the choices of numerous legislative histories by federal (C.I.S.) or state name. Once you find the appropriate jurisdiction, you have the option of: (1) **get docs**, or (2) **add source as a filter**.

Figure 4-6 The Main Page for Congress.gov

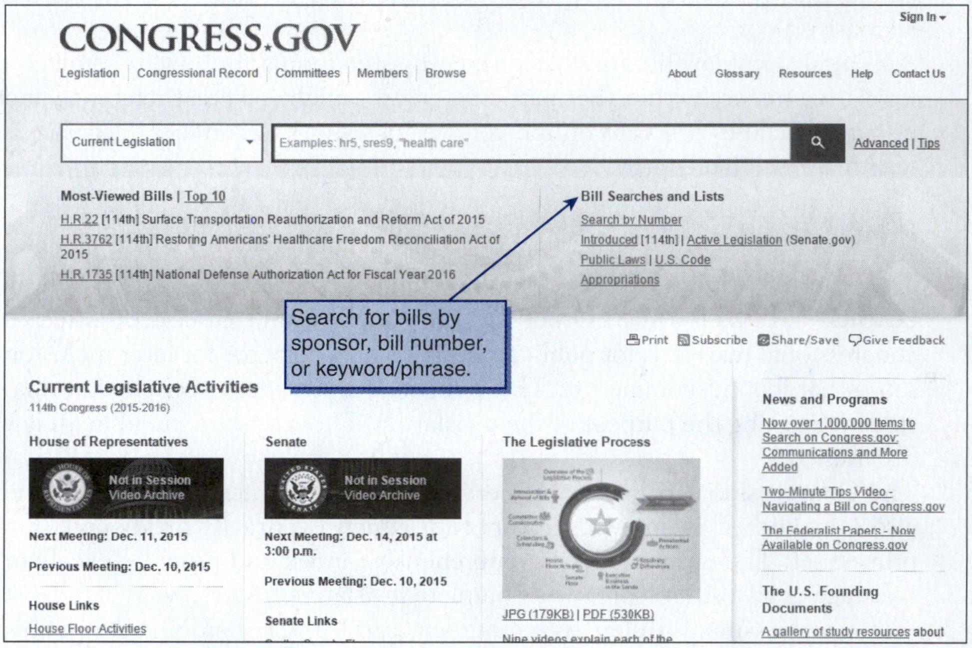

Source: https://www.congress.gov

If you have a subscription to either *WestlawNext* or *Lexis Advance*, you can also access state or federal legislative history information, as you can see in Figure 4-5. However, even if you do have a subscription to either database, there are many ways, as you have just learned, in print and online, that can be accessed for free.

For example, as you can see in Figure 4-6, you can track any federal bills and legislation at the new **www.congress.gov**, which replaces www.THOMAS.gov.

Also, as you can see in Figure 4-7, the Government Printing Office (GPO) is the official website for all federal congressional and legislative content.

An important point to note is that legislative histories are **not** considered primary law. They are secondary sources of law because, like all secondary sources, they provide the material to interpret statutes—a primary source of law.

It is rare you would need to conduct a legislative history, but if you do, how do you cite it? The *Bluebook* (Rule 13.2) and the *ALWD Manual* (Rule 15) address the citation format for state and federal legislative histories. Unlike the primary sources of law, it is best to look at your particular state legislative website, or your instructor will show you the proper legislative history format for your state. Similarly, for the citation of any federal legislative history, the *Bluebook* provides excellent examples for each particular legislative history format, including histories from federal committee hearings, legislative sessions, and debates. Also, keep in mind that the Legal Information Institute at Cornell not only has examples of many types of citation formats but also provides any differences between the *Bluebook* and *ALWD* format for any source.

In summary, remember that the initial and most recent version of a newly enacted or amended law is found within the slip opinion online. Session laws are helpful to use when you are conducting the legislative history of a law. Lastly, statutory codes are the most used and researched version of a law, particularly the annotated version, which provide numerous case opinions that explain and interpret the statutory law.

Figure 4-7 The Main Page for the FDsys

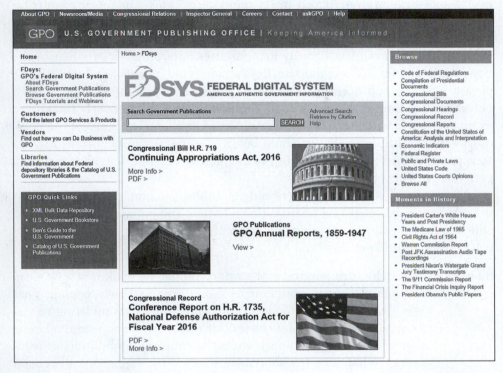

Source: http://www.gpo.gov/fdsys/

■ HOW TO READ A STATUTE

Now that you know and understand the various parts of a statute, you will learn the most important part—how to "read" one. Anyone can learn how to find a statute. However, after studying this chapter, you will be able to *read* and *understand* the meaning of a statute to see if it answers or at least addresses your legal issue.

Statutes are written with great care over time to ensure that the statute is written in unambiguous language. The idea is that statutes should be written so that everyone can understand its meaning, as well as know and understand what activity contained in the statute is permitted or prohibited. We all follow this same idea in our daily lives. For instance, suppose you came home and found a Post-it™ note on the refrigerator.

You are painting on Saturday and it is your job to purchase the items below. From which Post-it™ note would you feel most confident in buying the correct supplies?

LEARNING OBJECTIVE 4
Know how to read and understand the language contained in a statute.

> Hi! - We are staining the deck today, so be sure to pick up 2 wide brushes for the floor and 2 thin brushes for the rails, and make sure the stain is walnut (water-resistant).
> Thanks – See you later!

> Hi! - We are staining the deck today, so be sure to pick up brushes and deck stain.
> Thanks – See you later!

Similar to the Post-it notes above, it is important that statutory language not be *too vague* or *overly broad* in its application. This is more of a constitutional issue, but it is important to note that a statute must permit, prohibit, or regulate **specific** behavior. For example, a statute that states, "Citizens are prohibited from acting in a rowdy manner after 9pm on any city street in the downtown district." What did the legislature mean by the word *rowdy*? The phrase is vague and does not clearly define what is permitted or prohibited behavior. On the other hand, a statute should also not be overly broad. For example, if a particular criminal statute prohibits the carrying of "dangerous weapons" into a baseball stadium before a game, it can be assumed that a weapon is defined as any knife, gun, bomb, and so on. But does that include a penknife on a keychain?

Many statutes are easy to understand and others are more difficult. However, in knowing the basics, it may take a little bit of time and patience, but you will be able to read any statute concerning any topic. Just follow these basic steps, which will become second nature to you.

STEP 1: When locating any type of statute, similar to briefing a case, read through the entire statute at least one time without stopping. That way the statute will not seem overwhelming or intimidating to you because now you have a general idea of what the statute is addressing—that is, what actions is the act permitting, prohibiting, or regulating. What does the short title state? What is the overall general area of law?

STEP 2: Once you have read the statute overall at least once, if you have any uncertainty as to any of the words/terms/phrases, it would be a good time to read through the definition section, if there is one. Read **all** the definitions. For instance, even if you happen to see the word "structure" in the definitions section, do not assume you know what a structure is. The question you should ask yourself is how is a "structure" defined in *this particular statute?* If it is a criminal statute defining burglary, in addition to a residence or business, a structure could also be defined as a garage, an outhouse, or even a doghouse. Consider the example below of a statute that regulates how junkyards are to be maintained in the state.

You may be familiar with the term "junkyard" and know that it is typically a place where scrap metal or junk cars are stored and dismantled, which is true. However, back in Figure 4-1, as you read the definition of "junkyard" *in that particular statute,* would you know that it included "garbage dumps" and "sanitary landfills?"

STEP 3: Now return to the body of the statute and read it again, carefully. Make sure you read every word. Do not skip any words. It is best to have a legal dictionary to define any legal words/terms/phrases you do not know that are not included in the definitions section.

statutory elements
The individual and specific conditions that must be satisfied in order to bring a successful cause of action in criminal and civil law.

STEP 4: Nearly all statutes are broken down into **statutory elements**, meaning each element needs to be satisfied, or there are *conditions* concerning the elements. Read each element carefully. Consider the following example of a federal statute. In order for a state to receive federal funding for the public education of children with disabilities, certain elements must be met, or satisfied.

(1) Free appropriate public education
(A) In general
A free appropriate public education is available to all children with disabilities residing in the State between the ages of 3 and 21, inclusive, including children with disabilities who have been suspended or expelled from school.
(B) Limitation
The obligation to make a free appropriate public education available to all children with disabilities does not apply with respect to children—
(i) aged 3 through 5 and 18 through 21 in a State to the extent that its application to those children would be inconsistent with State law or practice, or the order of any court, respecting the provision of public education to children in those age ranges; and
(ii) aged 18 through 21 to the extent that State law does not require that special education and related services under this subchapter be provided to children with disabilities who, in the educational placement prior to their incarceration in an adult correctional facility–
(I) were not actually identified as being a child with a disability under section **1401** of this title; or
(II) did not have an individualized education program under this subchapter.

Notice that in the example above, Section A grants that a public education is available to all children with disabilities residing in the State between the ages of 3 and 21. However, in Section B of the statute, there are certain limitations. In other words, a state has to satisfy all of the elements in order to receive the federal funding. Most statutes consist of similar "elements" that need to be satisfied in order to apply to your particular legal issue.

As you are reading the statute, pay particular attention to terms you know and understand but that are extremely important, including important words such as *must, except, shall, any,* or *may*. For example, suppose your supervising attorney needs to determine if a client can become a licensed massage therapist in the state if she has been previously been convicted of a felony. If you see the word "must," then you know the client ***must*** take some action before applying for licensure. If you find the word "may," that could mean that the client can eventually become licensed providing some action is taken. Similarly, if you see the word "never" or "cannot" then you know the client may be searching for a new profession.

In addition, notice the circled words in the example above. Remember the conjunctives "*if, and, or,* and *but*" you learned in grade school? You need to know, understand, and apply them here, as they are also very important. Notice that under Section B, subsection (i) must be satisfied, and either sub-subsections (I) or (II) must be satisfied under subsection (ii). Confused? Don't be, it's easy. You just have to read the conjunctives carefully.

Consider another example of a criminal statute defining arson demonstrating this point:

(A) Arson Statute—A person commits a felony of the second degree if he intentionally starts a fire or causes an explosion, or if he aids, counsels, pays or agrees to pay another to cause a fire or explosion, whether on his own property or on that of another, and if:

   (1) the act destroys or damages a building or unoccupied structure of another; or

> **(2)** the act recklessly places an inhabited building or occupied structure of another in danger of damage or destruction; **or**
>
> **(3)** the defendant commits the act with intent of damaging or destroying any property, whether his own or of another, solely to collect the insurance for such loss.

Suppose your supervising attorney tells you that her client, Jason, owned a local bar down by the river. Jason was behind in his rent and could no longer afford to pay his bills so he decided to burn down the bar in the hope of collecting the insurance money on the property. He asked his best friend, Peter, to set fire to the bar on the 4th of July. Jason's plan was to close the bar for the night so everyone, including himself, could attend a firework display a few miles from the bar. Once he secured his alibi, Jason promised Peter $5,000 from the insurance check to commit the crime. On the night of the 4th, Peter left a burning cigarette lying next to a couple of old rags behind the bar and left out the back door. The fire spread quickly, and within two hours, the structure was burnt to the ground. No witnesses saw anyone enter or leave the bar that evening. Peter, feeling guilty about what he did, went to the local police station and told them the entire plan.

Question—According to the criminal statute of State X, can Jason be charged with arson? Remember Jason didn't burn down the bar, and he was nowhere near the scene of the crime.

Let's break it down. After carefully reading the criminal statute, you should have answered the question in the following manner.

Answer—Although Jason did not actually burn down the bar himself, nor was he even present at the scene, Jason **can** be charged and convicted of arson endangering property. According to the above statute, a person can be convicted of a crime if they intentionally start a fire **or** if they aid, counsel, pay **or** *agree to pay another to cause a fire*. Jason agreed to pay Peter $5,000 to burn down his bar, thus satisfying this element.

The analysis is not complete. Notice that after you read (A), the conjunctive **and** follows, meaning that you need at least **one** of the three elements that follow. Notice that you only need **one** of the three remaining elements as each is separated by the word **or**.

The first element does not apply as the facts state that Jason owns the bar. Next, the second element does not apply as the facts do not state that anyone was in the bar while it burned, nor were there any surrounding or attached buildings or structures near the bar while it burned. However, the facts *do* state that Jason's intent to burn the bar down was to collect the insurance money, thus satisfying the third element. According to the above statute, Jason White can be charged and convicted of arson endangering property, a felony of the second degree. Do you see how the pieces fit together like a puzzle? You must read statutes carefully and be mindful of the conjunctive terms: *and – or – if – but*.

STEP 5: At this point, you should clearly understand the meaning of the statute and be able to determine whether the written law applies to your legal issue. If you still need clarification, or you need to determine *how* the statute applies to similar fact patterns, read the very helpful annotated case summaries that follow the full text of the statute, and, of course, read the full text of the case opinion if necessary.

In reading any state, local, or federal statute, always remember to read it carefully, as statutes are written very specifically. It may take some time, but soon you will be able to easily read *and* understand any statute.

Statutory Construction

Statutes and cases work well together during your legal research. If you read a statute and do not understand its meaning, or even if you do, a good case discussing that statute can easily clarify and help you to further understand the statutory meaning. The courts will analyze any ambiguous terms by reference to the rest of the language in the statute. If the statute is challenged, the courts may look to the legislative intent and the intended purpose of the statute. This is referred to as **statutory construction**. The legislatures enact the law, and the courts attempt to interpret the law.

statutory construction
The process of determining the actual meaning of a statute so that a court can apply the law correctly.

For example, in a trial court in Maryland in 2006, two female defendants were convicted of the crime of "reckless endangerment" of a child after they ingested cocaine while pregnant. The criminal statute defined reckless endangerment as when a person recklessly engages in conduct that creates a substantial risk of death or serious physical injury *to another*. The appellate court had to consider the question of whether ingesting cocaine while pregnant constituted the crime of reckless endangerment *to another; that is, an unborn person*. It concluded that the answer involved construing that statute and that when it did, it could not find that the state legislature intended that the crime be applied to prenatal drug ingestion by a pregnant woman. The convictions were reversed.

Reading statutes and cases together provides a clear understanding of the meaning of a particular statute. That is why it is best to read the case summaries within the statutory codes. When reading both sources, you can then assert a particular point of law *and* state that a particular court decided a case in a certain manner by applying the statutory language to a particular set of facts. You will learn this concept in Chapter 10 when you learn the concept of legal analysis concerning statutes and cases.

Statutory law encompasses numerous rules of law that govern our society. Most legal issues can be resolved by referring to the rule of law located in the federal or state codes. By knowing where to locate statutory law, as well as understanding how to read and analyze the law, you will undoubtedly become a great asset to your supervising attorney. Now that you have learned the important basics of statutory law, in the next chapter, you will learn, in detail, where statutes are found in print and online, and how to locate them in print and online.

Chapter Checklist ✔

- Remember that law can be passed by a state, federal, or local legislative governmental body.
- You learned that statutory law is drafted slowly and carefully to ensure its longevity, but many laws are amended or repealed. Law must be flexible and adaptable to the ever-changing needs of society.
- You learned all the individual components that make up a statute. Make certain you know and understand each component, as each is important.
- You learned how a bill becomes a law, as well as the three stages of statutory publication.
- Remember that new laws can be public (most) or private, and permanent (most) or temporary (certain expiration date).
- Also remember that when reading a *newly enacted law* read the words carefully as each word was included for a specific reason; whereas on the other hand, when reading a *newly amended law*, any language with a strikethrough has been deleted from the law and any language underlined has been added to the law.

- You can conduct a legislative history when the meaning of a statute is in question or if you need to track or monitor a pending bill. Many free online sources can assist you in conducting a legislative search, and you can consult with a reference law librarian when conducting such research in print.

- Read statutes with precision and care. Follow the steps given to you within the chapter, which will soon become second nature to you. Like anything else, the more statutes you read, the easier it will be to understand them.

- When reading statutes, be mindful of any "conjunctives" and "conditional" words within the text.

- When conducting your research, remember to also locate any case law that addresses your particular statute, as it is an invaluable resource to use cases and statutes together.

KEY TERMS

Statute 83	Private law 90	Legislative history 93
Ordinance 83	Permanent law 90	Statutory elements 98
Bill 88	Temporary law 90	Statutory construction 101
Slip law 89	Session law 92	
Public law 89	Statutory Codes 92	

CRITICAL THINKING AND APPLICATION

1. During the semester, read the news in print and online and locate a story concerning the enactment of a newly enacted or recently amended law at the state or federal level.

   a. What is the new or amended law?

   b. How would you describe the new law to someone?

   c. Why was the law created?

   d. What does the law specifically permit or prohibit?

2. Statutes are identified by their numerical citation during the many stages of publication. Match the numeric citation with its identifier:

1. 107 STAT. 1001-198	**A.** Bill that was introduced in the House of Representatives.
2. S102	**B.** A Statute-at-Large session law enacted by the 107th Congress
3. Pvt. L. 108-112	**C.** Public law number 3 enacted by the 110th Congress
4. 28 U.S.C. §1187 (2008), amended by 28 U.S.C. §1187(f) (2010)	**D.** The newly enacted law recognized by name as the 121st law enacted at by the 110th Congress
5. Pub. L. 110-003	**E.** Bill that was introduced in the Senate.
6. HR119	**F.** Private law number 112 enacted by the 108th Congress
7. The American Banking Act of 2013, Pub. L. No. 110–121	**G.** A newly amended law consisting of the addition of subsection (f).

3. Go online and locate your state government's legislative website. Read over and navigate through the homepage. Look at the most recently enacted laws. Determine how you can be updated on recent developments of the newly enacted and amended laws in your state.

4. Go online and conduct the following legislative histories:

   a. As of 2013, every state has enacted post-conviction DNA testing laws. Conduct a legislative history search for the post-conviction DNA testing laws in your state.

      i. Explain to your classmates and your instructor the history of the law.

      ii. What was the date of enactment?

iii. How long did it take for the bill to become law? Why?

iv. Has the law in your state been recently amended? If so, why?

5. Search the federal databases to locate the legislative history of the "Stolen Valor Act of 2013."

a. In which Congress did this bill become law?

b. What was the bill identifier and which chamber of Congress initiated the bill?

c. What was the date of enactment?

d. Is this a newly enacted law or a recently amended law?

e. If recently amended, what was struck and/or added?

6. In the hypothetical below, you are given a fact pattern and five (5) criminal statutes. This is what is referred to as a closed hypothetical, meaning the law has already been provided for you. This exercise is solely designed for you to be able to effectively read, understand, and apply statutory law to a given set of facts. Carefully read the facts below. The fact pattern concerns a *state* issue and lists numerous state criminal statutes.

a. After reading the fact pattern and the statutes that follow, for which, if any, of these crimes *could* Sherry be charged with and why? Explain your answer(s).

Brad (25), a third-year student at a local law school met and began to date Sherry (27), who was employed for two years at the law school and worked in the main administration office. One day, Brad received a call from one of the premiere law firms in the city. Brad had applied to the firm six months prior hoping to secure a first-year associate position starting at $120,000 a year. The law firm, however, told Brad during his interview that it would need to see his last semester grades in order to make a decision. Brad knew that his grades would not be released for another two weeks, but he knew he needed access to them for a chance to be hired at the firm.

After the interview, Brad asked the law school to provide him a copy of his grades, but the Dean refused stating that Brad could not receive his grades prior to the official release date for any reason. Brad knew that Sherry had access to all law student information on the computer, so he asked Sherry if she would access his grades. Sherry was shocked at the request and hesitated, knowing that she could risk losing her job if she accessed Brad's grades without permission or authorization.

As an administrator, Sherry had online access to each student's e-mail, home address, emergency contact, class roster, class rank, and grades, but for security purposes, she was prohibited from accessing any student's information without obtaining authorized permission from the Dean. Sherry knew that if Brad could secure employment at the firm, they could have enough money to move in together, so she agreed to the plan. The next morning, Sherry was first to arrive at 8:30 and went straight to her desk. She entered her password and pulled up Brad's grades for the last semester. Sherry printed the grades and closed out of the program. All of the other employees arrived at 9:00 and were not aware of Sherry's actions.

At the end of the day, a technical employee informed the Dean that someone from Sherry's computer accessed the grades of Brad Carson, ID 123-456 and printed the information at 8:43a.m. The Dean remembered refusing to give Brad his grades and called Sherry into his office. After a few moments, Sherry told the Dean what she did, and she was suspended without pay.

(12 A.B.C. § 105.1): Definitions–For purposes of this subsection, a person is "*without authority*" when (i) the person has no right or permission of the owner to use a computer, or the person is permitted to use a computer but exceeds that right or permission.

For purposes of the subsection, the phrase "*downloads confidential data*" refers to the offender transferring (not printing) information or data electronically from a main computer system to another computer system or to an external device, such as a USB device.

For purposes of this subsection, the phrase "*temporarily or permanently remove computer data*" refers to when the offender electronically or by other means, extracts, copies, or views any unauthorized information or data.

(12 A.B.C. § 100.2): Unauthorized Use of a Computer or Device–A person commits the offense of unlawful use of a computer if he or she knowingly and without authority: (1) accesses, alters, edits, damages or destroys any computer, computer system, computer network, computer software, or any part thereof with the intent to interrupt its normal functioning; or (2) accesses, alters, edits or interferes with any unauthorized information or data concerning any computer, system, computer network, computer software, or any part thereof; or (3) intentionally or knowingly and without authority gives or publishes a password, identifying code, personal identification number or other confidential information about a computer system, computer network, or computer software device to another.

(12 A.B.C. § 104.4): Unauthorized Duplication of Information–A person commits this offense if he or she makes, or causes to be made, an unauthorized copy, in any form, including but not limited to any printed or electronic form of computer information or data, computer programs or computer software produced by a computer program or network.

(12 A.B.C. § 101.2): Computer Theft– A person commits an offense if he or she accesses any data, without authority, from a computer, computer system or computer network, and downloads confidential data or information to any other internal or external computer source or device without authority.

(12 A.B.C. § 102.3): Computer Trespass– A person commits the offense of computer trespass if he or she knowingly and without authority uses a computer or computer network with the intent to (1) temporarily or permanently remove computer data, computer programs or computer software from a computer or computer network; or (2) alter or erase any computer data, computer programs or computer software.

(12 A.B.C. § 103.4): Computer Service Disruption–A person commits this offense if he or she knowingly engages in a plan to disrupt service or distribute a virus into any computer, computer system, or computer program or network that is designed to impede, block or deny the access of information in such computer network.

7. Jack McMullin (47) has arrived at your supervising attorney's office and needs advice. Jack is a licensed chiropractor in Philadelphia, PA. Jack is going through a divorce and has also recently learned that his mother has terminal cancer. Jack is extremely stressed and he has begun drinking before work to calm his nerves before seeing his patients. Someone informed the state board that someone smelled alcohol on Jack's breath and that lately he seemed distracted at work. The state has issued notice to Jack that his license has been temporarily suspended. In any event, let the lawyer handle the law and the legal argument for Jack. The attorney needs you to give him the correct legal information on how to proceed. Carefully review the state code below then answer the following questions:

a. Is Jack's behavior at work reason, according to the statute, for which Jack could have his license suspended? Why or why not? Explain.

b. Can the State Licensing Board issue the suspension immediately with a hearing?

c. Jack told the attorney he received the notice of the order of suspension in the mail. Your supervising attorney wants to know what happens next. Be specific, as your attorney needs to know exactly how to proceed and trusts you to provide the correct information. Explain in your own words.

§ 625.506. Refusal, suspension or revocation of license

(a) Reasons enumerated.—The board may refuse to issue a license or may suspend or revoke a license for any of the following reasons:

(1) Failing to demonstrate the qualifications or standards for a license contained in this act or regulations of the board.

(2) Making misleading, deceptive, untrue or fraudulent representations in the practice of chiropractic.

(3) Practicing fraud or deceit in obtaining a license to practice chiropractic.

(4) Displaying gross incompetence, negligence or misconduct in carrying on the practice of chiropractic.

(5) Submitting a false or deceptive biennial registration to the board.

(6) Being convicted of a felony, a misdemeanor in the practice of chiropractic, or receiving probation without verdict, disposition in lieu of trial or an Accelerated Rehabilitative Disposition in the disposition of felony charges, in the courts of this Commonwealth, a Federal court, or a court of any other state, territory, possession or country.

(7) Having a license to practice chiropractic suspended, revoked or refused or receiving other disciplinary action by the proper chiropractic licensing authority of another state, territory, possession or country.

(8) Being unable to practice chiropractic with reasonable skill and safety to patients by reason of illness, drunkenness, excessive use of drugs, narcotics, chemicals or any other type of material, or as a result of any mental or physical condition. In enforcing this paragraph, the board shall, upon probable cause, have authority to compel a chiropractor to submit to a mental or physical examination by physicians approved by the board. Failure of a chiropractor to submit to such examination when directed by the board, unless such failure is due to circumstances beyond his control, shall constitute an admission of the allegations against him, consequent upon which a default and final order may be entered without the taking of testimony or presentation of evidence. A chiropractor affected under this paragraph shall at reasonable intervals be afforded an opportunity to demonstrate that he can resume a competent practice of chiropractic with reasonable skill and safety to patients.

199

Source: Used with permission of Thomson Reuters.

(9) Violating a lawful regulation promulgated by the board or violating a lawful order of the board previously entered in a disciplinary proceeding.

(10) Knowingly aiding, assisting, procuring or advising any unlicensed person to practice chiropractic contrary to this act or regulations of the board.

(11) Committing immoral or unprofessional conduct. Unprofessional conduct shall include any departure from, or failure to conform to, the standards of acceptable and prevailing chiropractic practice. Actual injury to a patient need not be established.

(12) Soliciting any engagement to perform professional services by any direct, in-person or uninvited soliciting through the use of coercion, duress, compulsion, intimidation, threats, overreaching or harassing conduct.

(13) Failing to perform any statutory obligation placed upon a licensed chiropractor.

(14) Intentionally submitting to any third-party payor a claim for a service or treatment which was not actually provided to a patient.

(15) Failing to maintain chronological documentation or patient care in accordance with regulations prescribed by the board.

(16) Making representations that chiropractic treatment will cure cancer or an infectious or communicable disease.

(17) Holding himself out as a specialist unless he possesses a postgraduate certification in that specialty.

(18) Unconditionally guaranteeing that a cure will result from the performance of chiropractic treatment.

(19) Failing to refer a patient to a licensed practitioner of another branch of the healing arts for consultation or treatment when a diagnosis of such patient indicates that such a referral is appropriate.

(b) Discretion of board.—When the board finds that the license of any person may be refused, revoked or suspended under the terms of subsection (a), the board may:

(1) Deny the application for a license.

(2) Administer a public reprimand.

(3) Revoke, suspend, limit or otherwise restrict a license as determined by the board. Unless ordered to do so by a court, the board shall not reinstate the license of a person to practice chiropractic which has been revoked, and such person shall be required to apply for a license after a five-year period in accordance with

200

section 501 [1] if he desires to practice at any time after such revocation.

(4) Require a licensee to submit to the care, counseling or treatment of a physician or physicians designated by the board.

(5) Suspend enforcement of its findings thereof and place a licensee on probation with the right to vacate the probationary order for noncompliance.

(6) Restore a suspended license to practice chiropractic and impose any disciplinary or corrective measure which it might originally have imposed.

(c) Procedure.—All actions of the board shall be taken subject to the right of notice, hearing and adjudication and the right of appeal therefrom in accordance with Title 2 of the Pennsylvania Consolidated Statutes (relating to administrative law and procedure).

(d) Temporary suspension.—The board shall temporarily suspend a license under circumstances as determined by the board to be an immediate and clear danger to the public health or safety. The board shall issue an order to that effect without a hearing, but upon due notice to the licensee concerned at his last known address, which shall include a written statement of all allegations against the licensee. The provisions of subsection (c) shall not apply to temporary suspension. The board shall thereupon commence formal action to suspend, revoke or restrict the license of the person concerned as otherwise provided for in this act. All actions shall be taken promptly and without delay. Within 30 days following the issuance of an order temporarily suspending a license, the board shall conduct, or cause to be conducted, a preliminary hearing to determine that there is a prima facie case supporting the suspension. The licensee whose license has been temporarily suspended may be present at the preliminary hearing and may be represented by counsel, cross-examine witnesses, inspect physical evidence, call witnesses, offer evidence and testimony and make a record of the proceedings. If it is determined that there is not a prima facie case, the suspended license shall be immediately restored. The temporary suspension shall remain in effect until vacated by the board, but in no event longer than 180 days.

(e) Automatic suspension.—A license issued under this act shall automatically be suspended upon the legal commitment of a licensee to an institution because of mental incompetency from any cause upon filing with the board a certified copy of such commitment; conviction of a felony under the act of April 14, 1972 (P.L. 233, No. 64), known as The Controlled Substance, Drug, Device and Cosmetic Act; [2] or conviction of an offense under the laws of another jurisdic-

201

Source: Purdon's Pennsylvania Statutes, Title 63, section 625.506, Pages 199–201.

LEARNING OBJECTIVES

After completion of this chapter, you should be able to

1. Explain where statutes are located in print.

2. Describe the process of how to locate a statute in print.

3. Demonstrate how to search for statutes online using Westlaw and Lexis.

4. Identify the free online sources available to search for a statute.

5. Explain where to locate local laws in print and online.

STATUTES

ANNOTATED

TITLE SEARCH

DESCRIPTIVE INDEX

How to Search for a Statute | CHAPTER 5

As you will see, locating statutes from the various codes is similar to locating cases in the print and online reporters. Statutes can be located by their citation and by a word search using the index method.

■ STATE AND FEDERAL STATUTES IN PRINT

As you learned in Chapter 2, all sources of primary law, including statutes, can be found in print and online. Once you learn *where* and *how* statutes are found, you should be able to find any state, federal, or local law you need at any time. In this section, through the use of examples, you will learn where statutes are located in the library and how to navigate the books to retrieve the statutes you need. Thereafter, you will see how to locate state and federal statutory laws online.

Statutory Codes: Publication and Citation

Before you can locate the statutes you need in your research, you need to know the different hardbound sets of books where those statutes are located. Statutes are printed in *official* and *unofficial* sets.

LEARNING OBJECTIVE 1
Explain where statutes are located in print.

State Codes

During your employment as a paralegal, you will frequently research state codes. After a state legislature enacts a law, it is first published as a slip law, then a session law. Thereafter, each state has compiled a state code that includes all the civil and criminal law enacted in that state. However, although unique, the *format* of each state code is very similar, meaning that once you understand the code of your state, you should be able to easily research the code of any state.

Statutory codes are found in the law library and are printed in "official" or "unofficial" publications. Any publication printed by a governmental entity is considered official, whereas any publication by a commercial publisher, such as *West* or *Lexis,* is considered an unofficial or "annotated" version. Also, the official codes *only* include the actual text of the statutes, and nothing more.

The unofficial versions include the full text of the statute *plus* helpful annotated material, including:

- **Legislative information** (following the text of the statute, any amendments or supplements to the law will be noted by date);
- **Historical / statutory notes and references** (this information provides the basic reason for the creation of the statute and will likely list the "public law" number);
- **Library / research references** (this information is provided by citation so that you can quickly refer to other primary and secondary sources to help explain or understand the statute);
- **Case summaries** (following each section of a statute, numerous case summaries also help to explain or interpret the language in a statute).

Not all states have an "official" statutory code. Most states print an unofficial or *annotated* code that they *refer* to as their "official" code. *Lexis* prints the code for some states, and *West* publishes the code of other states.

In the law libraries of your state, the statutory code will be easily distinguishable on the shelves. Each **state statutory code** includes an extensive hardbound volume set with the volume numbers, code range, and/or topic names engraved on the spine of each volume/title. Each set will also have a general index at the end of the set (hardbound or softbound booklet) in order to navigate through the actual volumes/titles themselves. The individual laws of your state may be divided into *sections, parts, articles,* or *chapters.*

Differences among the state codes are minor, including the color of the books in the set, or the number of volumes or indexes in the set. For example, Washington has compiled 91 titles in its code, yet Delaware only has 31 titles, and most states fall in between those numbers. This is not to indicate that the statutes of one state are more important than another because one state has more titles. Each state has enacted statutory laws that address certain industrial needs unique to that state. For instance, because many companies are incorporated in Delaware, which is known for its tax benefits, the code in that state includes the "Delaware General Corporation Law," which specifically governs corporate law in that state, which you will not find in any other code. Also, because horses are a major part of the industry in Kentucky, you will find specific and unique laws concerning the "Kentucky Horse Racing Commission," as well as extensive laws governing the sale and purchase of horses (equestrian law) that you will not find in any other state code.

In addition, if your state legislature prints and binds the session laws of your state, these will be shelved next to the statutory code and are also easily distinguishable by its cover.

Review the chart below in Figure 5-1 to learn the name of the state code within your jurisdiction, and highlight it.

state statutory code
The official state publication of all the statutory laws of each state.

SIDE NOTE

Many archaic and outrageous laws remain a part of many state statutory codes today. For example, in one state, you can be fined for engaging in a duel as a means to settling a dispute! In another state, it is illegal to operate a horse-drawn carriage without a horse! Many of these states utilize legal volunteers to browse through their state codes each year to find such laws, which are later considered by the state legislature for abolishment.

Figure 5-1 State Statutory Code Names

State	The Official Statutory Code Name
Alabama	Code of Alabama
Alaska	Alaska Statutes
Arizona	Arizona Revised Statutes
Arkansas	Arkansas Code of 1987 Annotated
California	California Codes
Colorado	Colorado Revised Statutes
Connecticut	The General Statutes of Connecticut
Delaware	Delaware Code Annotated
Florida	The Florida Statutes
Georgia	The Official Code of Georgia Annotated
Hawaii	Hawaii Revised Statutes
Idaho	Idaho Code
Illinois	Illinois Compiled Statutes
Indiana	The Indiana Code
Iowa	The Iowa Code and (Iowa Acts)
Kansas	Kansas Statutes
Kentucky	Kentucky Revised Statutes
Louisiana	West's Louisiana Statutes Annotated
Maine	Maine Revised Statutes and (Laws of Maine)
Maryland	The Annotated Code of Maryland; (The Annotated Code); (The Maryland Code)
Massachusetts	Massachusetts General Laws
Michigan	Michigan Compiled Laws
Minnesota	Minnesota Statutes and (Laws of Minnesota)
Mississippi	Mississippi Code of 1972
Missouri	Missouri Revised Statutes
Montana	Montana Code Annotated
Nebraska	Revised Statutes Nebraska
Nevada	Nevada Revised Statutes with Annotations
New Hampshire	New Hampshire Revised Statutes Annotated
New Jersey	New Jersey Statutes Annotated
New Mexico	New Mexico Statutes Annotated
New York	New York Statutes
North Carolina	General Statutes of North Carolina
North Dakota	North Dakota Century Code
Ohio	Ohio Revised Code Annotated
Oklahoma	Oklahoma Statutes (Official and Annotated)
Oregon	Oregon Revised Statutes
Pennsylvania	Pennsylvania Consolidated Statutes
Rhode Island	Rhode Island General Laws
South Carolina	Code of Laws South Carolina
South Dakota	South Dakota Codified Laws
Tennessee	Tennessee Code Annotated
Texas	Vernon's Texas Codes Annotated / Vernon's Texas Revised Civil Annotated
Utah	Utah Code Annotated

Figure 5-1 Continued

State	The Official Statutory Code Name
Vermont	Vermont Statutes Annotated
Virginia	Code of Virginia
Washington	Revised Code of Washington
West Virginia	West Virginia Code; Michie's West Virginia Code Annotated
Wisconsin	Wisconsin Statutes and Annotations
Wyoming	Wyoming Statutes Annotated

PRACTICE TIP

Inserting the proper state citations in Appendix B will prove beneficial in that you will be able to recognize a statute citation, which is very important prior to learning how to locate statutes in print and online.

On a class tour, or on your own, go to your law library and locate your state code in the stacks. Know its location and the number of volumes/titles and indexes. Also, pick out a volume, any volume, and thumb through the pages just to see how the statutes are organized to get a feel for the code—something you cannot do online.

State Statutory Citation. Every state statutory citation includes the volume number, the name of the particular code, the section number, as well as the date of the published edition you are using. The format is similar when citing federal statutes, as you will see below.

Rule 12 and Table 1 of the *Bluebook* dictate how to cite a state statute, as well as Rule 14 in the ALWD manual. Cornell's Legal Information Institute (LII) has created an online chart that includes the citation of every state in official/unofficial format, as well as any differences between the *Bluebook* and *ALWD* formats. The chart also includes hyperlinks to numerous examples of how to cite statutory law within a legal document. This resource can be found at **www.law.cornell. edu/citation**. Your instructor will also review, in detail, the specifics of statutory citation in your state. Once you have learned how to cite statutes in your state, be sure to complete that information in the "My Law" section in Appendix B.

Please review the different state statutes below in Figure 5-2.

Figure 5-2 Examples of Annotated Statutory Codes

TRIAL BEFORE JURY Art. 36.22
Ch. 36

Art. 36.215. **Recording of Jury Deliberations**

A person may not use any device to produce or make an audio, visual, or audio-visual broadcast, recording, or photograph of a jury while the jury is deliberating.

Added by Acts 2003, 78th Leg., ch. 54, § 1, eff. Sept. 1, 2003.

Historical and Statutory Notes

Section 3(b) of Acts 2003, 78th Leg., ch. 54, provides:

"(b) The change in law made by this Act applies only to a trial commenced on or after September 1, 2003. A trial commenced before September 1, 2003, is covered by the law in effect when the trial commenced, and the former law is continued in effect for that purpose."

Library References

Criminal Law ☞857(1).
Westlaw Topic No. 110.
C.J.S. Criminal Law § 1372.

Research References

Encyclopedias
TX Jur. 3d Criminal Law § 3328, Generally; Persons Present.
TX Jur. 3d Criminal Law § 3336, Generally; Exhibits.
TX Jur. 3d Trial § 111, Generally; Manner of Reaching Agreement.
TX Jur. 3d Trial § 122, Materials Permitted Generally; Purpose.

Treatises and Practice Aids
McCormick, Blackwell & Blackwell, 7A Tex. Prac. Series § 67.1, Commentary -- Trial Jury.
McCormick, Blackwell & Blackwell, 7A Tex. Prac. Series § 89.42, Petition for Writ of Mandamus.

This is a Texas statute. Note the details of the legislative amendments, as well as the library and research references in this annotated code.

*Notice that whether your state's code is comprised of articles, chapters, sections, or titles, the numerical identifier of the statute you are viewing will always be found in **bold** in the upper right-hand corner of the page.*

Sources: Reprinted with permission of Thomson Reuters, Michigan Compiled Laws Annotated, Section 409.103, Page 305 and Vernon's Texas Statutes Annotated – Code of Criminal Procedure, Article 36.215 and Article 36.22, Page 269.

Figure 5-2   Continued

This is a Michigan statute. Note the definitions section that defines certain terms used within the language of this particular statute, as well as case summaries that explain and/or interpret this particular section of the statute.

YOUTH EMPLOYMENT STANDARDS ACT   **409.103**

Historical and Statutory Notes

Source:
P.A.1978, No. 90, § 2, Eff. June 1.
C.L.1970, § 409.102.

The 1996 amendment rewrote this section which prior thereto read:

"As used in this act:

"(a) 'Employ' means engage, permit, or allow to work,

"(b) 'Employer' means a person, firm, or corporation which employs a minor, and includes the state or a political subdivision of the state, an agency or instrumentality of the state, and an agent of an employer.

"(c) 'Issuing officer' means a superintendent of a school district or intermediate school dis-

trict or a person whom the superintendent authorizes in writing to act on behalf of the superintendent.

"(d) 'Minor' means a person under 18 years of age.

"(e) 'Rule' means a rule promulgated pursuant to Act No. 306 of the Public Acts of 1969, as amended, being sections 24.201 to 24.315 of the Michigan Compiled Laws."

Prior Laws:

P.A.1947, No. 157, § 29.
C.L.1948, § 409.29.
C.L.1970, § 409.29.

Notes of Decisions

Employ   1

1. Employ

The word "employment", as used in § 408.60 (repealed) governing child labor, was not in-

tended to apply to vocational training of boy committed to Boys' Vocational School. Cadeau v. Boys' Vocational School (1960) 103 N.W.2d 443, 359 Mich. 598.

The Federal Code

Federal statutes are laws enacted and amended by the United States Congress during each congressional session. Congress keeps busy enacting and amending new law each year. For example, in 2013, the 112th Congress created more than 230 new public statutes, and 1 private statute. Similar to the state statutes, the final stop for federal statutory law is codification. The U.S. Code is a formal compilation of all the federal civil and criminal laws of the United States. The code includes the law followed by judges and lawyers each day in federal court.

As you can see in Figure 5-3, the **United States Code** (U.S.C.) is the "official" federal code and is organized into 52 titles. The current federal code was published in 1926, and subsequent editions have been published every six years since 1934. Each title includes a very broad area of law. For example, Title 39 includes *everything* concerning the federal postal service, including designated postal roads, mail delivery, postal offices, employee rules and benefits, mail violations, and so on.

New laws do not always create new titles; they are simply added into the appropriate category. However, new titles can still be created if needed. For example, **Title 51** of the USC, entitled **National and Commercial Space Programs**, is the compilation of all general laws concerning the space program. The President approved and signed PL111-314 (H.R. 3237) into law on December 18, 2010. More recently, in 2012, all the provisions included in Titles 2 and 42 concerning voting rights were collected, organized, and transferred into **Title 52 – Voting and Elections**. No new statutory language was added. The information was only compiled into a new title.

The federal code is also published in not one, but *two* annotated versions. These two "annotated" or "unofficial" versions of the statutory code are available from *Lexis* (U.S.C.S.) and *West* (U.S.C.A.) publishing companies. They are called unofficial because only the "official" code has been approved by the U.S. government. However, the annotated versions by *Lexis* and *West* are *identical* to the federal version. The annotated codes are favored over the official version due to the added annotated material. Another benefit is that *Lexis* and *West* update

united states code
The official federal statutory code printed and published by the U.S. government.

Figure 5-3 The Titles of the United States Code

1. General Provisions
2. The Congress
3. The President
4. Flag and Seal, Seat of Government and the States
5. Government Organization and Employees
6. Surety Bonds
7. Agriculture
8. Aliens and Nationality
9. Arbitration
10. Armed Forces
11. Bankruptcy
12. Banks and Banking
13. Census
14. Coast Guard
15. Commerce and Trade
16. Conservation
17. Copyrights
18. Crimes and Criminal Procedure
19. Customs Duties
20. Education
21. Food and Drugs
22. Foreign Relations and Intercourse
23. Highways
24. Hospitals and Asylums
25. Indians
26. Internal Revenue Code

27. Intoxicating Liquors
28. Judiciary and Judicial Procedure
29. Labor
30. Mineral Lands and Mining
31. Money and Finance
32. National Guard
33. Navigation and Navigational Waters
34. Navy (repealed – now in Title 10)
35. Patents
36. Patriotic Societies and Observances
37. Pay and Allowances of the Uniform Services
38. Veteran's Benefits
39. Postal Service
40. Public Buildings, Property and Works
41. Public Contracts
42. The Public Health and Welfare
43. Public Lands
44. Public Printing and Documents
45. Railroads
46. Shipping
47. Telegraphs, Telephones, and Radiotelegraphs
48. Territories and Insular Possessions
49. Transportation
50. War and National Defense
51. National and Commercial Space Programs
52. Voting and Elections

the code more frequently than the printed supplement of the government code in print and online. The full title of the *West* version is United States Code Annotated (U.S.C.A.) This set is bound in a maroon hardcover. The full title of the *Lexis* version is United States Code Service, Lawyers Edition (U.S.C.S.) This set is bound in a black hardcover. Your law library will most likely shelve one but not both versions.

Other than their name and distinguishing book color, both annotated versions include the same 52 titles as the official code and include the same indexes at the end of the volume set. As you review the chart in Figure 5-4, note the similarities and differences concerning the annotated material included in each of the commercial versions of the federal code.

Federal Statutory Citation. Your instructor will guide you on citing a statute in your state. As for the federal code, since there is only one universal code, the format is standard for all federal statutes. A researcher can tell which code is being used simply by looking at the "abbreviation" of the code.

When viewing the entire "set" of the code on the bookshelf, you will notice that each book binding has the name of the edition, the volume number, the numerical section range, and the topic name included in that volume. This is how you can find the statute you need without the index. The format is standard

Figure 5-4 Similar and Different Annotated Features of *Lexis* and *West*

Statutory Code Name	Historical Notes	Library References	Cross-References	Case Summaries
Lexis (U.S.C.S.)	Yes. This code provides the "*History, Ancillary Laws and Directives*," meaning that it provides the history and legislative information of the statute.	Yes. This code provides the "*Research References*," meaning it provides all the secondary source information pertaining to the statute.	Yes. Both commercial codes provide federal statutory citations within the set that mention or reference the statute you are reading.	Yes. Both commercial codes provide case summaries that interpret or explain the statute in the context of a court case. However, if you see a case of interest, be mindful to look up the case in full and read it. The case summaries in the code are written by the commercial publisher and not the court that issued the opinion.
West (U.S.C.A.)	Yes. This code provides the "*Historical and Revision Notes*," meaning it provides the public law number and all the legislative history and amendments to the statute.	Yes. This code provides the "*Library References*," meaning that it provides the secondary sources such as the federal rules and regulations that refer to your statute.		

for all federal statutes. The following is a breakdown of the federal statute **5 U.S.C.A. §522 (2010)**.

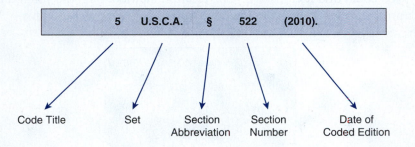

The basic federal statute citation is composed of three main parts: the title number, the set from which the citation was obtained, and the section number. The first number **5** identifies **Title 5 Government Organization**, taken from the main titles of the code. The citation was taken from the annotated code as denoted by the **U.S.C.A.** The number **522** defines the actual location of the statute in the particular volume being used. The statutes are listed numerically in each volume/title. The section is always preceded by the section abbreviation symbol.

The **date** closes the citation. It is good practice to insert the date when citing a statute so that the intended audience knows that you are using the most recent version of the code. When writing the statute citation, it is very important to always use the date from the *published edition* you are using. Do **not** use the date when the actual statute was *enacted*.

For example, if you were to cite the federal statute for the *Americans with Disabilities Act* that was passed into law in **1990**, but you are using the most current version of the government code from **2010**, the citation would look like this:

Correct	**42 U.S.C. §12101 (2010)** - *Bluebook and ALWD*
Incorrect	**42 U.S.C. §12101 (1990)**

If you obtain your statute from an annotated version, *Bluebook* and *ALWD* require a parenthetical giving the year *and* publishers name. For example:

West Publishing (in print)	**42 U.S.C.A. §12101 (West 2010)** – *Bluebook and ALWD*
Lexis Publishing (in print)	**42 U.S.C.S. §12101 (LexisNexis 2010)** – *Bluebook* **42 U.S.C.S. §12101 (Lexis 2010)** – *ALWD*

Search Approach: The Citation and Index Methods

LEARNING OBJECTIVE 2
Describe the process of how to locate a statute in print.

Up to this point, you know what a statute is, the various parts, and where they are located in print. Now, you will see, in a detailed step-by-step process, *how* to locate statutory law in print.

Similar to locating case opinions, statutes can be located using two basic methods: (1) the citation method and (2) the word search method.

The Citation Method

citation method
The method used to locate a statute when the citation is known.

Of the two methods to locate a state or federal statute, the **citation method** is the easiest. If your attorney needed to review a statute quickly before running off to court, you could find it easily using the citation method. Suppose you return from lunch and find the following Post-it™ note on your computer monitor

> Hi! - Please pull this statute and copy it. I need to read it before I go to court today.
> Thanks!!   18 USCA §122

Is there enough information here to find it quickly and easily? Yes. Remember that by looking at the code abbreviation, you can determine what type of statute you need to find. For instance, in the note above, you know that you are being asked to locate a federal statute, which is denoted by the "U.S.C.A." abbreviation. Once there, you would go to volume/title 18 and flip through the pages until you find section 122 in the upper right-hand corner.

Whenever you see citation that includes (USC, USCA, or USCS) you know it is a federal statute. You can also determine where a statute is from anywhere in the country. If you saw **Ark. Code §4-1-101**, you would know to look in the Arkansas state statutes by the abbreviation **Ark.**, or if you saw **Fla. Stat. Ann. §775.13,** you would know to look in the Florida state code by the abbreviation **Fla.**, and so on. Once you know how to cite your own state's code, you will be able to easily distinguish between any state and the federal code.

The Word Search Method

Because statutes are published in the official and unofficial sets by title and section number, they are easy to locate by citation, but not by utilizing a general word search. Whether searching the official or annotated codes, a researcher, who does not possess the citation, must utilize the index via the **word search method**.

How do you use the index? Each state and all the versions of the federal code utilize the index system. As you look upon the entire state or federal code on the shelf in the library, every set, similar to the case reporter system, will consist of multiple volumes followed by a number of indexes at the end. Each volume includes the volume number, the section range, and most have the title of the statute, all engraved on the book's spine. And of course, the *General Index* can be found at the end of any printed set, state or federal, as your guide. Think of the index as your "GPS" system in finding what you need within the volumes. Once you become more comfortable using a particular code, you will be able to just scan the titles, but for now, the index is a much more specific and detailed method. As you can see in Figure 5-5, both the state and federal codes have similar indexes to utilize, depending on what information you possess.

Finding the Correct Words/Terms/Phrases. Now you know the different indexes at your disposal, but how do you know what words/terms/phrases to use when searching the index?

Generating search terms for statutory law is easier than searching for case opinions using a word search. Similar to searching for case opinions think of the key terms that describe your legal issue. For example, as shown in Figure 5-6, if you need to find the law concerning the licensing reinstatement requirements for a chiropractor in your state, you would use the **descriptive word index (DWI)** and look up the words LICENSE or CHIROPRACTOR to begin your search. Think of using the index just like you would use the index in this book, or any of your academic textbooks. Suppose you are taking a class concerning contract law and you need to look up what constitutes a valid acceptance for a contract. In the index of the textbook, you would look up the words ACCEPTANCE, or OFFER, both of which would direct you to the correct section of the textbook. You use the same approach with the index in the statutory code. You will see this put into practice.

Remember to always have *Black's Law Dictionary* and *Burton's Legal Thesaurus* with you in case you need to use another term/word/phrase in your search.

Notice in Figure 5-6 that if you look up the issue of *chiropractor reinstatement*, you see the *first* entry noted in this section as **Chiropractors, Generally, 63 P.S. §625.101 et seq.** (If you pulled the volume from the shelf, the cover

word search method
The method used to locate a statute when the citation is not known and a search is conducted using key terms, words, and phrases through the use of an index.

descriptive word index
The main index including numerous general legal terms and topics directing the researcher to the relevant section number of the statutory code.

Figure 5-5 Indexes Included in State and Federal Codes

Statutory Code	Descriptive Word Index (DWI)	Popular Name Index (PNI)	Title/Topic
State and Federal Annotated Code	In the annotated code, the DWI is a soft-cover multivolume general index arranged and broken down alphabetically by topic and subtopic.	In the annotated code, the PNI allows you to locate a statute by its name given by the legislature that enacted it, such as, *Megan's Law, The Freedom of Information Act,* or *The Americans with Disabilities Act.*	In the annotated code, the title/topic method can be used after you become familiar with the titles and can locate a statute merely by scanning the volume's spines.

Figure 5-6 The DWI Index

CHILDRENS' MEDICAL ASSISTANCE
Definitions, childrens health care, 62 P.S. § 5001.103

CHILDRENS TRUST FUND
Generally, 11 P.S. § 2231 et seq.
Tax refunds, contributions, checkoff, 72 P.S. § 7315.10

CHIMNEYS
Cities of third class, 53 P.S. § 37411

CHIROPODISTS
Podiatrists, generally, this index

CHIROPODY
Podiatrists, generally, this index

CHIROPRACTIC BOARD
Generally, 63 P.S. § 625.301 et seq.
Approval, chiropractic colleges, 63 P.S. § 625.303
Certificates and certification, 63 P.S. § 625.304
Civil penalties, 63 P.S. § 625.703
Colleges and universities, approval, 63 P.S. § 625.303
Compensation and salaries, 63 P.S. § 625.301
Discipline, 63 P.S. §§ 625.302, 625.506
Education, standards, 63 P.S. § 625.303
Examiners and examinations, 63 P.S. § 625.304
    Professional testing organizations, 63 P.S. § 625.502
Fees, 63 P.S. § 1401-205
Fines and penalties, civil penalties, 63 P.S. § 625.703
Grandfather rights, 63 P.S. § 625.1102
Hearings, 63 P.S. § 625.302
Investigations and investigators, 63 P.S. § 625.302
Licenses and permits, 63 P.S. § 625.304
Meetings, 63 P.S. § 625.301
Powers and duties, 63 P.S. § 625.302
Quorum, 63 P.S. § 625.301
Rates and charges, fees, 63 P.S.

CHIROPRACTIC BOARD—Cont'd
Terms of office, 63 P.S. §§ 625.301, 625.1102
Tests, professional testing organizations, 63 P.S. § 625.502
Training, 63 P.S. § 625.301
    Accreditation, 63 P.S. § 625.303
Treatment, alcoholics and intoxicated persons, drugs and medicine, 63 P.S. § 625.509

CHIROPRACTIC PRACTICE ACT
Generally, 63 P.S. § 625.101 et seq.

CHIROPRACTORS
Generally, 63 P.S. § 625.101 et seq.
Abuse of children, persons required to report, 23 Pa.C.S.A. §§ 6311, 6311.1
Accident and health insurance, licensed personnel, reimbursement, 40 P.S. § 1511
Accreditation, chiropractic colleges, 63 P.S. § 625.303
Adjunctive procedures, 63 P.S. § 625.304
    Definitions, 63 P.S. § 625.102
Advertisements,
    Discipline, 63 P.S. § 625.506
    False advertisements, 63 P.S. § 625.702
AIDS, confidentiality of information, 35 P.S. § 7601 et seq.
Alcoholics and intoxicated persons,
    Discipline, 63 P.S. § 625.506
Reinstatement of license, 63 P.S. § 625.527
Treatment programs, 63 P.S. § 625.509
Application of law, 35 P.S. § 7601 et seq.; 63 P.S. § 625.526
Licenses and permits, grandfather rights, 63 P.S. § 625.1103
Occupational therapists, 63 P.S. § 1519
Professional health service plan corporations, 40 Pa.C.S.A. § 6302
Repeals, 63 P.S. § 625.1106
Rules and regulations, grandfather rights, 63 P.S. § 625.1104

Suppose you needed to look up information for a client, licensed as a chiropractor, who is seeking reinstatement of his license following conviction of a felony. You would begin with the general term CHIROPRACTOR. As you can see, everything that the profession entails is addressed in the code. Here, "reinstatement of license" is specifically enumerated in its own section – 63 P.S. §625.527.

Look at all the other legal aspects addressed that concern the profession as well.

Source: Reprinted with permission of Thomson Reuters, Purdon's Pennsylvania Consolidated Statutes, 2015 General Index (A-D), Page 613.

would read, "Professions and Occupations, §§456.01 to 1800). You will see many index entries with this language, and when you see it you know you have succeeded in your search. Here is how you read it: the word *"Generally"* is defined as the section of the code that includes most of the relevant information for that subject/title. This means that the main title and all the subtitles for "chiropractor" are located in Title 63 of the Pennsylvania state code. In addition, "et seq.," is a Latin phrase that is defined as, "and the following," meaning that the main title (63 P.S. *§625.101*) is continued through all the subsections that follow, as shown in Figure 5-6. For example, if you needed information concerning chiropractors that falsely advertise, you would find it under *§625*.702, or if you needed to research chiropractor accreditation, you would find it under *§625*.303, and so on. Notice that under the main title of CHIROPRACTORS, you see many different subtitles directly relating to that main title from which to choose.

Notice also in Figure 5-6 that some of the subtitles under "chiropractor" are listed with different titles. For example, any issues concerning *accident and health insurance* falls under title 40, not title 63. This is also common and basically means that there are some issues concerning chiropractors that fall under and are addressed in other sections of the code. Remember the example of the textbook index? Suppose in your contract law textbook you look in the back index under *offer*. You may see the following:

Contract -

Offer . . . . pgs., 3, 18, 47, 98, 112, 226

That means that the term "offer" can be found on all the above pages within the textbook. The information is not restricted to one chapter; the statutory code works the same way.

Finding State Statutes

Now that you understand all the basics and fundamentals of statutory law, you should be feeling fairly confident to conduct a statutory search. Now, you will see, step-by-step, how to look through the state and federal statutes to answer a legal issue given to you. Please follow the steps below to "see" the process.

Suppose you work as a paralegal in Philadelphia, Pennsylvania, and your supervising attorney calls you into her office (don't forget the pen and legal pad!). The attorney works as a solo practitioner and specializes in family law. The attorney's client is a grandfather who is seeking custody of his granddaughter. The attorney needs you to look up when and how grandparents can file for custody rights.

> Every state in the country recognizes custodial rights for grandparents in family law. After learning how to navigate the statutory code in this example, conduct the same steps in your particular state utilizing your state's code.

Before going to the library, remember you must formulate the relevant "key words" to navigate through the statutory code smoothly. Remember, similar to the case digests, take a few minutes to generate the relevant terms needed to conduct a proper search. In this example, you may want to begin with the general terms of CHILD, CUSTODY, or GRANDPARENTS. A good rule to remember when searching the index in any print source is to begin with the "broad general" terms, then narrow your search terms to find particularly what you need.

Remember that whatever you state you work in, the code and indexes will be similarly arranged. As mentioned above, there are a few ways to navigate through the indexes.

STEP 1:   Search the DWI Index using the above terms for the information you need. If you began your search under the main topic "CHILDREN," you will find numerous subtopics; one of those being "CHILDREN AND MINORS." As you can see in Figure 5-7, under the subtopic CHILDREN AND MINORS, you find the sub-subtopic "***Grandparents and grandchildren, generally, this index.***"

Whenever you see this type of entry, the index is telling you to look in the general alphabetical listing of the subject preceding the phrase "*generally this index.*" In other words, in this example, the index is telling you to look under "G" for GRANDPARENTS or GRAND-CHILDREN for the topic you need, rather than looking under "C" for CHILDREN. Remember the saying, "If at first you don't

Figure 5-7 Sub-Topics for a Search for Children

CHILDREN

CHILDREN AND MINORS—Cont'd.
Foreign countries—Cont'd
 Custody, ante
 Exemptions, labor and employment, **43 P.S. § 40.5**
Foreign states,
 Abused children, referrals, **23 Pa.C.S.A. § 6334**
 Custody, ante
Forfeitures, crimes and offenses, sexting, **18 Pa.C.S.A. § 6321**
Forms,
 Abused children, ante
 Custody, ante
 Licenses and permits, labor and employ-ment, **43 P.S. § 40.9**
 Pleadings, captions, **Pa.R.C.P. No. 1930.1**
Formula, medical food insurance, **40 P.S. § 3901 et seq.**
Foster Care, generally, this index
Fraud, identity and identification, crimes and offenses, tobacco and tobacco products, **18 Pa.C.S.A. § 6305**
Full age attainment, **23 Pa.C.S.A. § 5101**
Full faith and credit, custody, **23 Pa.C.S.A. § 5453**
Funds,
 Child passenger protection, **75 Pa.C.S.A. § 4581 et seq.**
 Child passenger restraint fund, **75 Pa.C.S.A. § 4582**
  Application of law, **42 Pa.C.S.A. § 3733**
 Childrens advocacy centers, **71 P.S. § 614.3a**

CHILDREN AND MINORS—Cont'd
Good faith—Cont'd
 Custody, sanctions, **23 Pa.C.S.A. § 5339**
Graduating seniors, secondary schools, lists, military recruitment, **51 P.S. § 20221 et seq.**
Grandfather rights,
 Handicapped persons, early intervention services, **11 P.S. § 875–502**
 Industrial county homes, **11 P.S. § 304**
Grandparents and Grandchildren, gener-ally, this index
Group, definitions, medical care and treatment, **40 P.S. § 991.2303**
Group accident and health insurance, dependents of employees or members, **40 P.S. § 756.2**
Group homes, family preservation program, **62 P.S. § 2171 et seq.**
Guardian Ad Litem, generally, this index
Guardian and Ward, generally, this index
Hague Convention, custody, **23 Pa.C.S.A. § 5441 et seq.**
Handicapped persons, **16 P.S. § 2168**
 Adoption, **62 P.S. § 771 et seq.**
 Adoption Opportunities Act, hard to place children, **62 P.S. § 771 et seq.**
 Blind and visually impaired persons, education, preferences and priori-ties, **24 P.S. § 2602**
 Commitment, care and treatment, **11 P.S. §§ 871, 872**
 County care or employment, **16 P.S. § 2160 et seq.**

Source: Reprinted with permission of Thomson Reuters, Purdon's Pennsylvania Consolidated Statutes, 2015 General Index (A–D), Page 598.

succeed, try, try again." As you can see in Figure 5-8, after looking up GRANDPARENTS AND GRANDCHILDREN, you find the sub-topic of *"Custody, standing, 23 Pa.C.S.A. §§5324, 5325."* If you were unsure of the term "standing," you would need to look it up in your legal dictionary. Please do not guess at terms with which you are unfamiliar. After looking up the word, you would have learned that *standing* refers to the right of an individual to bring a case to court. In other words, they have a legal right to assert a cause of action in court. Therefore, that section looks good.

STEP 2: As you can see, you now have a statute citation (23 Pa.C.S.A. §5324). You can leave the index and go to the volumes in the set.

STEP 3: You would go directly to *Title 23* in the code: *Domestic Relations, §§4101-6100* (§5324 falls between §4101-6100). As you can see in Figure 5-9, you find the statute stating when the custodial rights of a grandparent may be asserted.

Figure 5-8 Sub-Topics for a Search under GRANDPARENTS

GRANDFATHER

GRANDFATHER RIGHTS—Cont'd

School Taxes, this index

Secured transactions, statutes, amendments, 13 Pa.C.S.A. §§ 9705 et seq., 9805 et seq.

Self service storage facilities, 73 P.S. § 1917

Sewers and sewer systems;
  Boroughs, opening, 8 Pa.C.S.A. § 2013
  Operators, certificates and certification, 63 P.S. § 1013

Social workers, titles, abbreviations, crimes and offenses, 63 P.S. § 1920

Streets and alleys, boroughs, laying out, 8 Pa.C.S.A. § 1721.2

Surviving spouses, senior citizens rebate and assistance, repeal of statutes, 53 P.S. § 6926.5006

Tax collection, qualified tax collectors, 72 P.S. § 5511.4a

Taxation, senior citizens rebate and assistance, repeal of statutes, 53 P.S. § 6926.5006

Telecommunications, local exchange telecommunications companies, competitive services, 66 Pa.C.S.A. § 3013

Tourists and tourism, agents and agencies, grants, 73 P.S. § 410.8

Water pollution, 35 P.S. § 691,701

Water Supply, this index

GRANDPARENTS AND GRANDCHILDREN

Custody, standing, 23 Pa.C.S.A. §§ 5324, 5325

Realty transfer tax, 53 P.S. § 6924.301.1

Scotland School for Veterans Children,

GRANTS—Cont'd

Agricultural land conservation assistance program, 3 P.S. § 1207.3

Agricultural Products, this index

Agriculture, this index

Airports, local real estate tax reimbursements, 74 Pa.C.S.A. § 6122

Aliens, labor and employment, crimes and offenses, 43 P.S. § 166.1 et seq.

Allegheny regional asset district, 16 P.S. § 6112-B

Alternative fuels incentive fund, 73 P.S. § 1647.3

Ambulances, volunteers, 72 P.S. § 1799-E; 35 Pa.C.S.A. § 7801 et seq.

Anatomical gifts, governor Robert P. Casey Memorial organ and tissue donation awareness trust fund, 20 Pa.C.S.A. § 8622

Animal byproduct management technology, 3 P.S. § 2007

Animal health and diagnostic commission, powers and duties, 3 P.S. § 430.5

Animal research, diagnosis, control and prevention, 3 P.S. § 430.7

Annual announcement, higher education assistance grants, 24 P.S. § 5152.1

Appalachian local development districts, rural marketing plans, 73 P.S. § 392.303

Application of law, commonwealth procurement, 62 Pa.C.S.A. § 102

Applications;
  Community based health care, 35 P.S. §§ 10227.112, 10227.113
  Opportunity grants, 12 Pa.C.S.A. § 2104 et seq.

Source: Reprinted with permission of Thomson Reuters, Purdon's Pennsylvania Consolidated Statutes, 2015 General Index (E-O), Page 376.

STEP 4: Remember how to *read* a statute. Pay close attention to words such as "must," "shall," "always," and "never," and the conjunctives "and," "or," "but," and "if." In reading this statute, you can inform your supervising attorney that a grandparent has standing to file for custody who is not considered in *loco parentis* to the child. What does that mean? Remember that statutes have a "definition" section. If it does not, or a term is not listed, consult a legal dictionary. After looking it up, you learn that the term is Latin for "in place of the parent." The term refers to when an individual assumes parental status of a child without formally adopting that child. As you can see, under (3), the grandparent must prove to the court that his relationship with the child began either with the consent of the parent, or by court order, and that he/she assumes, or is willing to assume, responsibility for the child. Thereafter, when either subsection (A), (B), or (C) is satisfied under section (iii), all the elements of the statute are satisfied.

Figure 5-9 23 Pa.C.S.A. §5324 of the Pennsylvania Annotated Code

DOMESTIC RELATIONS
23 Pa.C.S.A. §·5324

but devoid of any viable findings of fact, a best interest of the child analysis, or conclusions of law; Superior Court was without authority to make credibility determinations or finding of facts necessary for requisite analysis. T.B. v. L.R.M., 874 A.2d 34, Super.2005, reargument denied, appeal denied 890 A.2d 1060, 586 Pa. 729. Parent And Child ⚭ 244; Parent And Child ⚭ 246

The scope of review applied by an appellate court to a child custody order is of the broadest type; the appellate court is not bound by the deductions or inferences made by the trial court from its findings of fact, nor must the reviewing court accept a finding that is not supported by competent evidence; however, this broad scope of review does not vest an appellate court with the duty or privilege of making its own independent determination. T.B. v. L.R.M., 786 A.2d 913, 567 Pa. 222, Sup. 2001. Child Custody ⚭ 915; Child Custody ⚭ 916; Child Custody ⚭ 919; Child Custody ⚭ 922(1)

An appellate court may not interfere with the trial court's factual conclusions unless they are unreasonable in view of the trial court's factual findings and thus represent an abuse of discretion. T.B. v. L.R.M., 786 A.2d 913, 567 Pa. 222, Sup. 2001. Appeal And Error ⚭ 996

Once determination is made that party has standing to seek visitation, Superior Court will review decision under abuse of discretion or error of law standard. MacDonald v. Quaglia, 658 A.2d 1343, 442

Pa.Super. 149, Super.1995. Child Custody ⚭ 921(3)

Scope of review for visitation order is same as that for custody order, paramount concern is for best interest of child. MacDonald v. Quaglia, 658 A.2d 1343, 442 Pa.Super. 149, Super.1995. Child Custody ⚭ 914

When reviewing visitation orders, appellate courts are not bound by trial court's deductions, inferences, and interpretations of evidence, but matters of credibility are solely within trial court's discretion as only trial judge can observe demeanor and assess trustworthiness. In Interest of C.F., 647 A.2d 253, 436 Pa.Super. 83, Super.1994. Child Custody ⚭ 922(4)

Appellate courts, in reviewing visitation orders, are not bound by trial court's deductions, inferences and interpretations of evidence, but can exercise independent judgment to consider merits of case and to provide order that is correct and just. Bucci v. Bucci, 506 A.2d 438, 351 Pa.Super. 457, Super.1986. Child Custody ⚭ 914

Order dismissing divorced husband's petition for visitation rights with child who was born four months after separation of husband and wife who testified that she had not engaged in sexual intercourse with husband for 38 months prior to birth of child and that husband was not father of child was affirmed. Burrell v. Burrell, 247 A.2d 476, 213 Pa.Super. 249, Super.1968. Child Custody ⚭ 182

> Hold the book and fan through the pages until you see 23 Pa.C.S.A. §5324 in the upper right-hand corner.

> Case summaries from the previous section of the statute.

§ 5324. **Standing for any form of physical custody or legal custody**

The following individuals may file an action under this chapter for any form of physical custody or legal custody:

(1) A parent of the child.

(2) A person who stands in loco parentis to the child.

(3) A grandparent of the child who is not in loco parentis to the child:

(i) whose relationship with the child began either with the consent of a parent of the child or under a court order;

(ii) who assumes or is willing to assume responsibility for the child; and

(iii) when one of the following conditions is met:

(A) the child has been determined to be a dependent child under 42 Pa.C.S. Ch. 63 (relating to juvenile matters);

(B) the child is substantially at risk due to parental abuse, neglect, drug or alcohol abuse or incapacity; or

(C) the child has, for a period of at least 12 consecutive months, resided with the grandparent, excluding brief temporary absences of the child from the home, and is removed from the home by the parents,

> The section heading - §5324 describes, in detail, when a grandparent has standing to file a custody claim.

Source: Reprinted with permission of Thomson Reuters, Title 23, 2015 Pocket Part, Page 129.

case summaries
A section of annotated material following the text of a statute included to explain and interpret that statute through brief summaries of case opinions relevant to that statute.

Keep in mind that statutes and cases not only work well together but also are used together to strengthen your legal argument. As you can see in Figure 5-10, **case summaries**, which are arranged by topic, can be found following statute *23 Pa.C.S.A. §5324*. These summaries help interpret and explain this particular section of the statute.

Figure 5-10 Case Summaries: 23 Pa.C.S.A. §5324

23 Pa.C.S.A. § 5324
Note 3

DOMESTIC RELATIONS

though she had physical possession of children and discharged duties as to children's day-to-day needs, it did not follow that she was in loco parentis or had undertaken rights and responsibilities that existed between parent and child. In re N.S., 845 A.2d 884, Super.2004. Adoption ⟜ 4; Child Custody ⟜ 274; Infants ⟜ 1775; Parent And Child ⟜ 382

Former husband stood in loco parentis to former wife's son, and thus, had legal standing to seek visitation; for a period of approximately three years, parties lived together as a family unit, son referred to former husband as his "dad" and was treated by former husband's extended family as their own, former husband maintained regular contact with son for three years following parties' separation, and to the extent mother argued that son no longer wished to visit former husband, factor was not relevant to determination of whether former husband stood in loco parentis. Liebner v. Simcox, 834 A.2d 606, Super.2003. Child Custody ⟜ 409

The term "prima facie right to custody" means only that the party has a colorable claim to custody of the child; the existence of such a colorable claim to custody outside of any statutory right grants standing only where the third party has established in loco parentis status. K.B. II v. C.B.F., 833 A.2d 767, Super.2003, appeal granted in part 842 A.2d 917, 577 Pa. 135, appeal dismissed as improvidently granted 885 A.2d 983, 584 Pa. 538. Child Custody ⟜ 409

For the purpose of a child custody dispute, the phrase in loco parentis refers to a person who puts oneself in the situation of a lawful parent by assuming the obligations incident to the parental relationship without going through the formality of a legal adoption. T.B. v. L.R.M., 786 A.2d 913, 567 Pa. 222, Sup.2001. Child Custody ⟜ 22

Evidence supported finding that lesbian former partner stood in loco parentis to child, and thus possessed standing to bring an action against biological mother for visitation with child; former partner and biological mother shared day-to-day child rearing responsibilities, they owned a house together, they took family vacations together with child, and when biological mother was away from home former partner had exclusive responsibility for child. T.B. v. L.R.M., 786 A.2d 913, 567 Pa. 222, Sup.2001. Child Custody ⟜ 409

Lesbian former partner possessed standing to bring action against biological mother for visitation with child, even though the

child custody statutes did not encompass former partners of biological parents; former partner invoked the doctrine of in loco parentis to establish standing, and child custody statutes did not reference the doctrine of in loco parentis or preclude in loco parentis standing. T.B. v. L.R.M., 786 A.2d 913, 567 Pa. 222, Sup.2001. Child Custody ⟜ 409

Inability of lesbian former partner to legally adopt child of biological mother, her former partner, did not bar former partner's litigation for partial custody and visitation with child; nature of relationship between former partner and biological mother had no legal significance to determination that former partner stood in loco parentis to child. T.B. v. L.R.M., 786 A.2d 913, 567 Pa. 222, Sup.2001. Child Custody ⟜ 409

Evidence was insufficient to establish that lesbian former partner merely acted as a caretaker for child, rather than standing in loco parentis to child, for the purpose of child custody litigation; record established that former partner and biological mother lived with child as a family unit, and that former partner acted as a co-parent with biological mother. T.B. v. L.R.M., 786 A.2d 913, 567 Pa. 222, Sup.2001. Child Custody ⟜ 468

4. Grandparents

Grandparents of grandchild, determined to be dependant under state statute, did not have standing to seek custody or visitation under Pennsylvania Grandparents' Visitation Act; grandparents had not filed petition required by Act or assumed responsibility for granddaughter during eight months period she lived with them. Gordon v. Lowell, E.D.Pa.2000, 95 F.Supp.2d 264. Child Custody ⟜ 409

Non-biological and non-adoptive grandparents, who took care of biological mother pursuant to custody agreement with her parent, stood in loco parentis to biological mother, and therefore, they were the parents of mother and the "grandparents" of mother's child for purposes of grandparent visitation statute, and, as such, grandparents had standing to file a petition seeking visitation with their grandchild. Peters v. Costello, 891 A.2d 705, 586 Pa. 102, Sup. 2005. Child Custody ⟜ 283; Child Custody ⟜ 409

Paternal grandparents had standing under grandparent visitation statute to seek full custody of child, even though there had been no prior determination of mother's unfitness or dependency of child. K.B. II v. C.B.F., 833 A.2d 767, Su-

All the case summaries are organized and arranged by specific topic/subject.

Notice that each case summary provides the case citation **and** the *West* Key Number for the case digests.

Source: Reprinted with permission of Thomson Reuters, Title 23, 2015 Pocket Part, Page 130.

annotated material
Supplemental material added to statutory publications that include references and citations to numerous primary and secondary sources of law relevant to a particular statute.

In Figure 5-11, the **annotated material** provides you with many references to other helpful and useful sources of law. This is helpful in that you could provide your supervising attorney with a few cases (or at least one) with similar facts as your situation that discusses statute *23 Pa.C.S.A. §5324*.

As you can see, it is not difficult to navigate the statutory indexes to find what you need. The part that will involve the most practice is using the right terms when using the DWI index to obtain the correct citation. Notice that in

Figure 5-11 23 Pa.C.S.A. §5324 – Annotated Material

23 Pa.C.S.A. § 5324   DOMESTIC RELATIONS

"in which case the action must be filed within six months after the removal of the child from the home.

2010, Nov. 23, P.L. 1106, No. 112, § 2, effective in 60 days [Jan. 24, 2011].

Historical and Statutory Notes

Act 2010–112 legislation

Section 4 of 2010, Nov. 23, P.L. 1106, No. 112, effective in 60 days [Jan. 24, 2011], provides that "[a] proceeding under the former provisions of 23 Pa.C.S. Ch. 53 [23 Pa.C.S.A. §§ 5301 to 5315] which was commenced before the effective date of this section shall be governed by the law in

effect at the time the proceeding was initiated."

Prior Laws:

1981, Nov. 5, P.L. 322, No. 115, § (P.S. § 1014).

1985, Oct. 30, P.L. 264, No. 66, § Pa.C.S.A. § 5313).

1996, Oct. 16, P.L. 706, No. 124, §

Cross References

Award of custody, see 23 Pa.C.S.A. § 5323.

Complaint, pleading requirements, see Pa.R.C.P. No. 1915.3.

Dependency matters, motion to intervene, see Pa.R.J.C.P. No. 1133.

Effect of adoption, see 23 Pa § 5326.

Standing for partial physical custo supervised physical custody, see C.S.A. § 5325.

Library References

Child Custody ☞276, 278, 282, 409.
Westlaw Topic No. 76D.
C.J.S. Parent and Child § 97.

Research References

Encyclopedias

Summary Pa. Jur. 2d Family Law § 9:9, Who May Adopt—Relatives.

Summary Pa. Jur. 2d Family Law § 9:42, Effect of Decree; Finality and Conclusiveness.

Summary Pa. Jur. 2d Family Law § 10:101, Other Relatives.

Summary Pa. Jur. 2d Family Law § 10:104, Rights Upon Death of Parent.

Summary Pa. Jur. 2d Family Law § 10:105, Rights Upon Divorce or Separation.

Summary Pa. Jur. 2d Family Law

Treatises and Practice Aids

Goodrich-Amram 2d Rule 1915.15, Form of Complaint. Caption. Order. Petition to Modify a Custody Order.

Standard Pennsylvania Practice § 126:1010, Complaint.

Standard Pennsylvania Practice § 126:1011, Complaint—Form of Complaint.

Standard Pennsylvania Practice § 126:1102, Standing.

Standard Pennsylvania Practice § 126:1118, When Grandparents May Petition for Legal or Physical Custody.

Standard Pennsylvania Practice

> Notice all of the annotated material following the statute, including cross-references to other applicable sections of the code; library references including relevant *Westlaw* Key Numbers, and research references, including numerous legal encyclopedia citations, in order to learn more about the topic of grandparents filing for custody rights.

Source: Reprinted with permission of Thomson Reuters, Title 23, 2015 Pocket Part, Page 132.

this situation, the **Popular Name Index** would not prove helpful concerning the custody issue, as it is not known by a popular name. In addition, once you become familiar and comfortable with using the index, you could have used the topic method and determined that this custody issue would have fallen under *Title 23* – "Domestic Relations."

popular name index
The index used when a statute is referred to and known by its popular name, such as the Americans with Disabilities Act, or the Freedom of Information Act.

Finding Federal Statutes

The process for finding federal statutes is very similar if not the same as locating state statutes. Follow the steps below in locating a particular federal statute from the U.S.C.A.

Suppose you are employed as a paralegal in the state in which you live. Your supervising attorney needs specific information from the federal Freedom of Information Act.

STEP 1: In utilizing the DWI, you would of course begin searching under the word FREEDOM. As you can see in Figure 5-12, the statute can be found "generally" at *5 §552*. In other words, it is found in *Title 5, section 552*.

Figure 5-12 The Freedom of Information Act Found in the DWI Index

FREE	900
FREE PRODUCTS Social Security Administration, 42 § 1320b–10 **FREE PUBLIC LIBRARY** Surplus property, disposal, 40 § 557 **FREE SERVICES** Social Security Administration, 42 § 1320b–10 **FREE TERRITORY OF DANZIG** War claims, 50 App. § 2017 **FREE TRADE** Exports and Imports, this index **FREE TRADE ZONE ACT** Generally, 19 § 81a et seq. **FREEDMEN'S BUREAU** Records and recordation, preservation, 44 §§ 101 nt, 2910 **FREEDMEN'S BUREAU RECORDS PRESERVATION ACT OF 2000** Generally, 44 §§ 101 nt, 2910 **FREEDMEN'S HOSPITAL** Howard University, 5 App. 1 RPN IV of 1940; 20 § 124 **FREEDOM** See, also, Liberty, generally, this index Cold War, commemoration, 10 § 113 nt Cuba, assistance, 22 § 6061 et seq.	**FREEDOM OF ACCESS TO CLINIC ENTRANCES ACT OF 1994** See Popular Name Table **FREEDOM OF ASSEMBLY AND PETI- TION** Generally, U.S. Const. Am. I **FREEDOM OF CONSCIENCE** National cemeteries, protection, 38 § 2404 **FREEDOM OF INFORMATION** Generally, 5 § 552 Air pollution, off site consequence analy- sis, 42 § 7412 Armed Forces, this index Attorneys, fees, 5 § 552 Board of Governors of the Federal Re- serve System, exemptions, studies, 12 § 248 Central Intelligence Agency, 50 § 3141 Claims, United States, 31 §§ 3729, 3733 Commodity exchanges, exemptions, whistleblowing, studies, 7 § 26 Copyrights, Code of Federal Regulations, (Title 17, Appendix), 37 CFR § 203.1 et seq. Costs, 5 § 552 Critical infrastructure information, 6 § 133 National security, 10 § 130e Definitions, 5 § 552 nt Democracy Corps, Independent States of the Former Soviet Union, aid, 22 § 5841

Although many sub-sections are listed concerning the FOIA, you only need the "general" title.

STEP 2: In this instance, you could also utilize the federal *Popular Name Index* since the statute is also known by its "popular name," as shown in Figure 5-13.

Many federal statutes are known by their "popular names" because federal laws affect all citizens, and most laws need to be clearly identifiable. For instance, it is easily understandable to hear on the evening news that Congress is currently debating portions of the *Freedom of Information Act* that may affect millions of Americans, rather than hearing Congress is debating portions of **Title 5, section 522** of the federal code. Other examples include the *Americans with Disabilities Act*, the *Espionage Act*, the *Patriot Act*, and the *Act to Combat International Terrorism*.

STEP 3: Now that you have the citation, you pull the appropriate volume/title (5) from the shelf and fan through the pages until reaching the appropriate section (552), as you can see in Figure 5-14.

Most federal statutes can be quite long and wordy! However, you read a federal statute the same way you read a state statute—carefully. Remember to read all the elements and make sure each is satisfied. Also, pay particular attention to cross-referenced material.

More than likely, your local law library will *not* shelve the official U.S. Code. Rather, depending on cost and availability, the library will shelve *either* the U.S.C.A. or the U.S.C.S., but not both.

Figure 5-13 The FIOA Found in the Popular Name Index

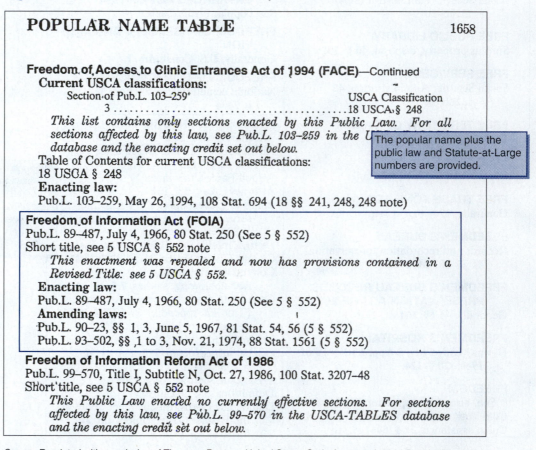

POPULAR NAME TABLE 1658

Freedom of Access to Clinic Entrances Act of 1994 (FACE)—Continued
 Current USCA classifications:
  Section of Pub.L. 103–259ˈ USCA Classification
  3 ....18 USCA § 248
   This list contains only sections enacted by this Public Law. For all sections affected by this law, see Pub.L. 103–259 in the U[SCA-TABLES] database and the enacting credit set out below.
 Table of Contents for current USCA classifications:
 18 USCA § 248
 Enacting law:
 Pub.L. 103–259, May 26, 1994, 108 Stat. 694 (18 §§ 241, 248, 248 note)

The popular name plus the public law and Statute-at-Large numbers are provided.

Freedom of Information Act (FOIA)
Pub.L. 89–487, July 4, 1966, 80 Stat. 250 (See 5 § 552)
Short title, see 5 USCA § 552 note
 This enactment was repealed and now has provisions contained in a Revised Title: see 5 USCA § 552.
 Enacting law:
 Pub.L. 89–487, July 4, 1966, 80 Stat. 250 (See 5 § 552)
 Amending laws:
 Pub.L. 90–23, §§ 1, 3, June 5, 1967, 81 Stat. 54, 56 (5 § 552)
 Pub.L. 93–502, §§ 1 to 3, Nov. 21, 1974, 88 Stat. 1561 (5 § 552)

Freedom of Information Reform Act of 1986
Pub.L. 99–570, Title I, Subtitle N, Oct. 27, 1986, 100 Stat. 3207–48
Short title, see 5 USCA § 552 note
 This Public Law enacted no currently effective sections. For sections affected by this law, see Pub.L. 99–570 in the USCA-TABLES database and the enacting credit set out below.

Figure 5-14 The FIOA Found in the Federal Code

Ch. 5   ADMINISTRATIVE PROCEDURE   **5 § 552**

40.   Ex parte communication

Congress enacted provisions of this subchapter and chapter 7 of this title, prohibiting ex parte communication to ensure that agency decisions required to be made on a public record are not influenced by private, off-the-record communications from those personally interested in the outcome. Raz Inland Navigation Co., Inc. v. I.C.C., C.A.9 1980, 625 F.2d 258. Administrative Law And Procedure ⇨ 473

> The initial part of the statute enumerates which specific items must be made available to the public upon request of each "agency."

§ 552.   Public information; agency rules, opinions, orders, records, and proceedings

(a) Each agency shall make available to the public information as follows:

(1) Each agency shall separately state and currently publish in the Federal Register for the guidance of the public—

(A) descriptions of its central and field organization and the established places at which, the employees (and in the case of a uniformed service, the members) from whom, and the methods whereby, the public may obtain information, make submittals or requests, or obtain decisions;

(B) statements of the general course and method by which its functions are channeled and determined, including the nature and requirements of all formal and informal procedures available;

(C) rules of procedure, descriptions of forms available or the places at which forms may be obtained, and instructions as to the scope and contents of all papers, reports, or examinations;

(D) substantive rules of general applicability adopted as authorized by law, and statements of general policy or interpretations of general applicability formulated and adopted by the agency; and

(E) each amendment, revision, or repeal of the foregoing.

> As you are reading the statute, you should be thinking, "What do they mean by the word agency? What constitutes an "agency?" Don't forget to review the *definitions* section prior to the actual statute. There, the word will be defined as it was intended within the "context of *that* statute."

Source: Reprinted with permission of Thomson Reuters, United States Code Annotated, Title 5; Section 552, Page 151.

Similar to the state annotated code, the federal annotated code includes numerous supplemental materials in addition to the full text of the law. These annotations are especially helpful in understanding the law because the federal statutes, as mentioned, can be long, tedious, and at times more difficult to understand than state statutes. The federal annotated materials include cross-references to other statutes in the code that include or mention the statute you are reading, as well as many research and library sources directing you to many secondary sources to help you understand the statute you are reading. Lastly, and most importantly, do not forget to read the case summaries concerning the statute, which will interpret and explain the language of the statute with the court's reasoning and decision.

Remember that a topic search can also be utilized once you become familiar with the code itself. The federal titles are quite broad and general (see Figure 5-2), but in time, you should know which statutes should fall under which titles.

Again, once you become familiar with how to read a statute and understand its components, you should be able to read, understand, and interpret *any* statute.

Updating and Validating State and Federal Statutes

In print, state and federal statutes are updated the same as case reporters, as pocket parts. The **pocket part** is the thin loose-leaf pamphlet inserted into the back of each volume/title within the code. If a certain section of the statutory code has been updated, it will be reflected in the pocket part. Illustrated in Figure 5-15, after enough amendments and additions to the law have been compiled, a softbound **cumulative supplement** will be printed and inserted within the set until the new hardbound volume is printed.

If no pocket part exists, then one was not needed. A slip of paper should read: THIS VOLUME CONTAINS NO POCKET PART, or some similar language to inform you that the pocket part was not removed or lost. Pocket parts are typically updated *annually*.

If you are researching a statute in printed form, it is *crucial* to check the pocket part for updates. If the statute you seek has been changed and you are not aware, then the research findings you provide to your supervising attorney will be invalid. In Figure 5-16, the pocket part for the FOIA states the changes and amendments to ***Title 5, section 552***.

So how important is it to always check the pocket parts? Consider the following example. Suppose a potential client, Mark, arrives at your office and asks to speak with your supervising attorney who works in criminal defense. Mark tells

pocket part
A thin pamphlet located inside the back cover of hardbound reference books which are consulted to ensure a particular law is the most current.

cumulative supplement
A softbound pamphlet including all the current updates found in a particular volume that is placed within the set as a placeholder until a new hardbound updated volume is printed.

Figure 5-15 Pocket-Part and Cumulative Supplement in a State Code

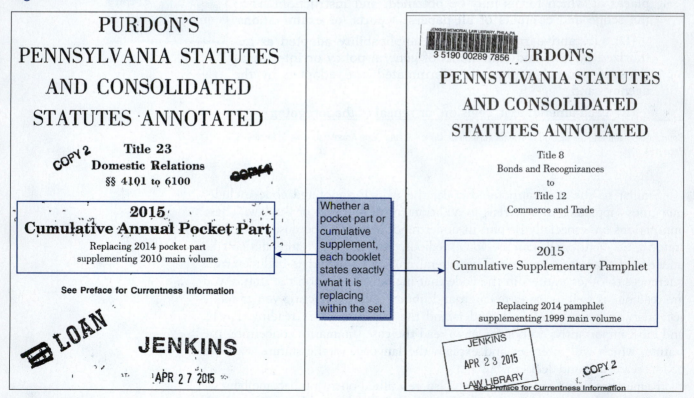

Source: Reprinted with permission of Thomson Reuters, Purdon's Pennsylvania Statutes Title 23 – 2015 Pocket Part & Purdon's Pennsylvania Statutes Title 8 – 2015 Cumulative Supplementary Pamphlet – the front cover page for both booklets.

Figure 5-16 The FOIA in the Pocket Part Supplement

whether an asylee who had been involved in terrorism-related activities was entitled to adjustment of status under exemption process, there was no indication that government officials' deliberative process in asylee's case was a sham, and government had a strong interest in completing exemption process in terrorism-related cases with great care. Irshad v. Johnson, C.A.8 (Neb.) 2014, 754 F.3d 604, rehearing and in part to PHA's failure to comply with HUD's repeated requests for legal opinion from state attorney general certifying its exclusive jurisdiction, there was no statutory duty that HUD could have been ordered to perform, and PHA failed to plausibly allege that HUD's inaction had same impact as actual denial. Lauderhill Housing Authority v. Donovan, D.D.C.2011, 818 F.Supp.2d 185. Landlord And Tenant ⚷ 2066

§ 552. Public information; agency rules, opinions, orders, records, and proceedings

(a) Each agency shall make available to the public information as follows:

[See main volume for text of (1) to (3)]

(4)(A)(i) In order to carry out the provisions of this section, each agency shall promulgate regulations, pursuant to notice and receipt of public comment, specifying the schedule of fees applicable to the processing of requests under this section and establishing procedures and guidelines for determining when such fees should be waived or reduced. Such schedule shall conform to the guidelines which shall be promulgated, pursuant to notice and receipt of public comment, by the Director of the Office of Management and Budget and which shall provide for a uniform schedule of fees for all agencies.

(ii) Such agency regulations shall provide th

34

The updated material for the statute is included, which describes where in the original statute the new amended information is to be inserted. Notice in this example of the FOIA, the new section (4)(A)(i) is to follow the existing sections of text 1-3.

Source: Reprinted with permission of Thomson Reuters, United States Code Annotated, 2015 Supplement Pamphlet, Page 34.

the attorney that his son, David (37) is currently being held for trial in a minimal security federal detention center. Mark's younger son, William (23) was also arrested after attempting to smuggle a cell phone to his brother on his last visit. William was arrested for "providing contraband in prison," a federal criminal offense.

Prior to going to court and informing the client and his father, your supervising attorney needs you to look up this crime in the federal code and asks you to research the possible penalties. Suppose, the latest printed version of the code found in the law library was the 2006 version. You find and read the following statute, ***18 U.S.C.A. §1791***:

§1791(d) . . . As used in this section, (1) the term "prohibited object" means:

(A) A firearm or destructive device . . .
(B) Marijuana or a controlled substance . . .
(C) A narcotic drug . . .
(D) A controlled substance other than referred to in (B) or (C) . . .
(E) Any United States or foreign currency . . .
(F) Any other object that threatens the order, discipline, or security of a prison . . .

You would tell your supervising attorney that a "cell phone" is not listed as a particular prohibited object, and the defense attorney could therefore argue that the possession of the phone falls under section (F), which only carries a maximum sentence of six months imprisonment.

However, if you would have looked at the pocket part (updated 2010) you would find that this section of the statute was amended to include the following in bold italics:

> **§1791(d)** . . . As used in this section, (1) the term "prohibited object" means:
>
> **(A)** A firearm or destructive device . . .
> **(B)** Marijuana or a controlled substance . . .
> **(C)** A narcotic drug . . .
> **(D)** A controlled substance other than referred to in (B) or (C) . . .
> **(E)** Any United States or foreign currency . . .
> **(F)** *A phone or other device used by a user of commercial mobile service* . . . .
> **(G)** Any other object that threatens the order, discipline, or security of a prison . . .

As you can see, in 2010, the federal statute was amended with the content in bold italics. This was an actual amendment to the law due to the high number of cell phones attempted to be smuggled or confiscated in many federal prisons. So today, not only is the phone listed as a particular prohibited object, but it also carries a maximum sentence of one year imprisonment. This information completely changes the research results. Your supervising attorney, and the client, would need this information *prior* to arguing the case in court, and your attorney would be arguing incorrect and outdated law if you did not read the supplemental pocket part.

You may be asking yourself, "What if an existing law is amended or even repealed *between* the printing of the pocket parts or cumulative updates?" Since it is very difficult to stay up-to-date in print, there are many online sources that do provide up-to-date material.

Concerning updating and validating state statutory law online, each state legislative website will state the currency of a statutory law, meaning any changes or amendments to any current law for the latest session. In addition, if any law was repealed, that information will also be stated. This information can usually be found on the homepage concerning statutory law and is typically updated at the end of a congressional session.

As you can see in Figure 5-17, the Legal Information Institute (LII) at Cornell also provides direct links to each state's main legislative website as well as current and pending bills in that state's legislature.

In addition, when you search for a statute on *WestlawNext* and *Lexis Advance*, as you will see, each statute will have the date in parenthesis to demonstrate the currency of the law. Remember that when you cite a statute, you cite the most updated and current date of the code, *not* the date that the statute was originally enacted.

Concerning updating and validating federal statutory law online, if you have a *Lexis Advance* or *WestlawNext* subscription, you have instant access to the latest sections of the code. If you do not have a subscription to either, Cornell's LLI website does a good job at alerting you to any pending updates on the particular section you accessed through the site. Also, the *Office of the Law Revision Counsel (LRC)* maintains its own website solely to keep you updated as to any changes in the federal code, which can be found at **www.uscode.house.gov**. As shown in Figure 5-18, the classification tables are frequently updated (it is a federal government website) and are easy to use; the site includes easy to follow directions on how to navigate the tables.

Figure 5-17 Cornell's Use of Pending Alerts in the Federal Code

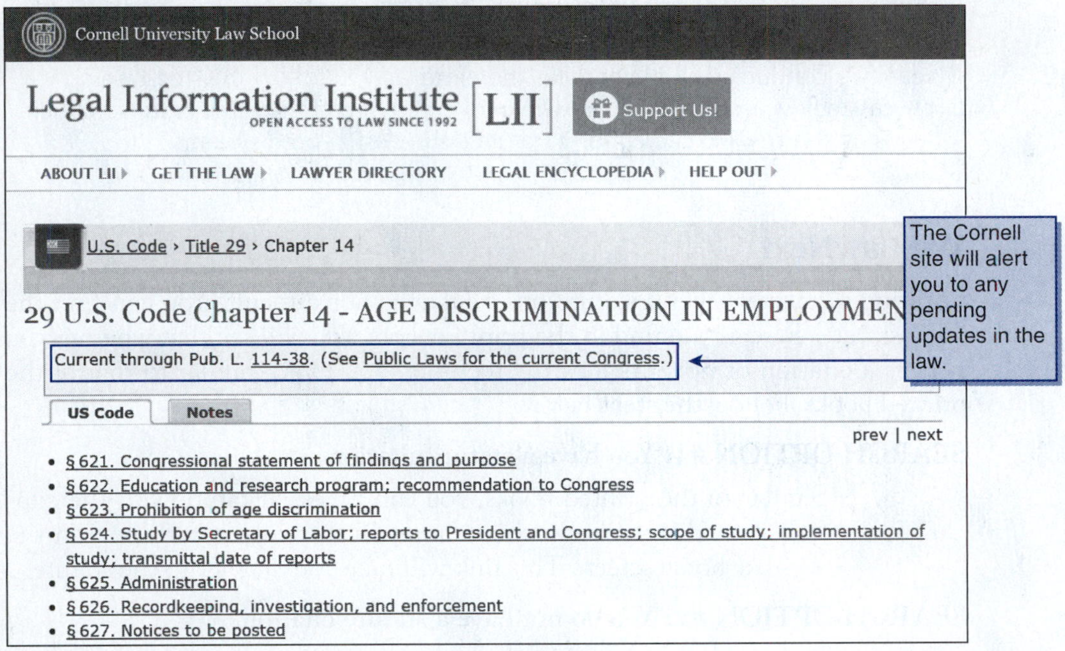

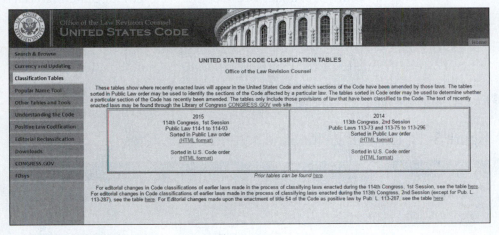

Source: Courtesy of Cornell University Law School. Used with permission.

Figure 5-18 The US Code Classification Tables

Source: http://uscode.house.gov

■ STATE AND FEDERAL STATUTES ONLINE

Aside from the print sources, you can also find nearly every state and federal statute online. In this section, you will learn how to locate statutes through *WestlawNext* and *Lexis Advance*. However, many paralegals do not always have immediate access to either of those services or are restricted with their use. For those situations, you will also learn about all the paid subscription services that are considerably less expensive as well as many free government and educational websites that publish statutory authority.

In this section, using the same "grandparent custody" example that you learned researching the printed code, you will be shown step-by-step, using both online systems, how to retrieve the relevant statute you need.

LEARNING OBJECTIVE 3
Demonstrate how to search for statutes online using Westlaw and Lexis.

WestlawNext and *Lexis Advance* update their systems daily. Therefore, both systems continually add, delete, and amend its material and content. A search conducted today on either system may yield different results when the same search is conducted at a later date. Therefore, as you follow the step-by-step process below, do not focus on whether you arrived at the same *results*. Rather, focus on the *steps* to search for a statute online using both systems.

WestlawNext

Locating a state or federal statute on *Westlaw* is not difficult. You can find the same statutes here as you find in the print version. You will see that whether you possess a citation or not, the locating techniques are very similar to that of the printed books. Follow the steps below.

SEARCH OPTION #1: You have a statute citation.

> Similar to the printed books, you can access a statute with the citation immediately. Enter the citation in the main search box on the *Westlaw* home screen. This link will take you directly to the statute.

SEARCH OPTION #2: You do not have a statute citation.

> Similar to the printed books, if you do not have the statute citation, you will need to take just a few more steps to get it. This is where you would need to generate your word search method.

On the *Westlaw* homepage, under **Browse**, there are tabs for **State Materials** or **Federal Materials**. For *state* statutes, choose the **State** tab and all 50 state names will appear. As you can see in Figure 5-19, Pennsylvania was chosen.

On the state homepage, you can search for *any* state content using the white search box or navigate using the tabs below the white search box. In Figure 5-20, you can access the state statutes by title from this page. This format is the same for *every* state.

Figure 5-19 Result Page for State and Federal Statutes

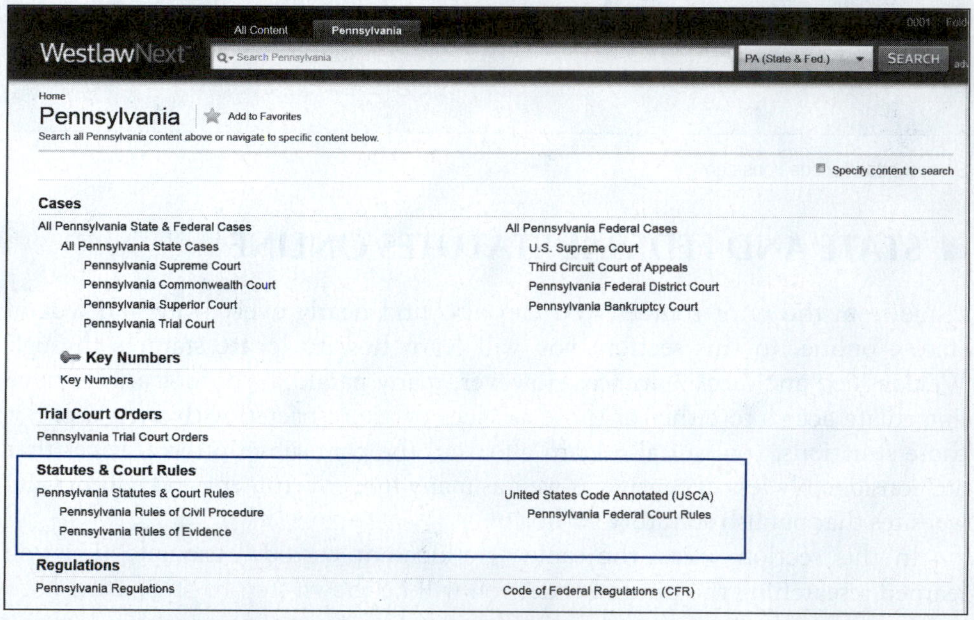

Source: Reprinted with permission of Thomson Reuters. State search result on WestlawNext.

Figure 5-20 Result Page for State and Federal Statutes

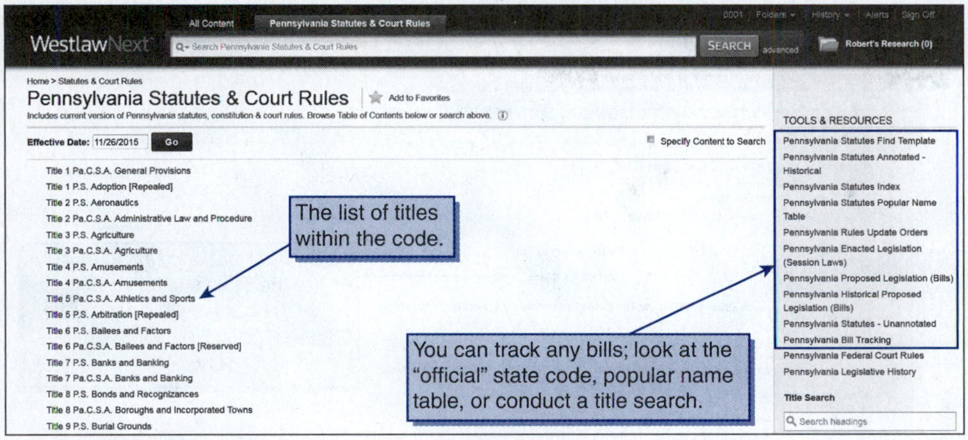

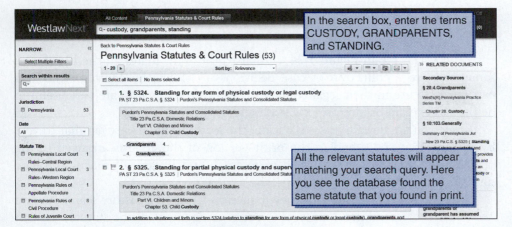

Source: Reprinted with permission of Thomson Reuters. State statute result on WestlawNext.

Remember the hypothetical problem when you searched the print sources concerning the issue of a grandparent having standing to file for custody? Just like with searching cases in print and online, the process is the same. Use the same word search technique you used in print as online by typing: CUSTODY, GRANDPARENTS, and STANDING into the search box, as you see in Figure 5-21.

As shown in Figure 5-22, after you conduct the search and choose the best search result, click on it. This will open the actual statute. It may look different than the print version, but the content is the same.

Similar to the print version, you can see all the annotated sources listed in Figure 5-23. The advantage to viewing a statute on either *WestlawNext* or *Lexis Advance* is that every annotated source listed can be viewed in a single click.

Figure 5-21 Result Page for State Statute Word Search

Source: Reprinted with permission of Thomson Reuters. Statute search results on WestlawNext.

Figure 5-22 Pennsylvania Statute 23 Pa.C.S.A. §5324

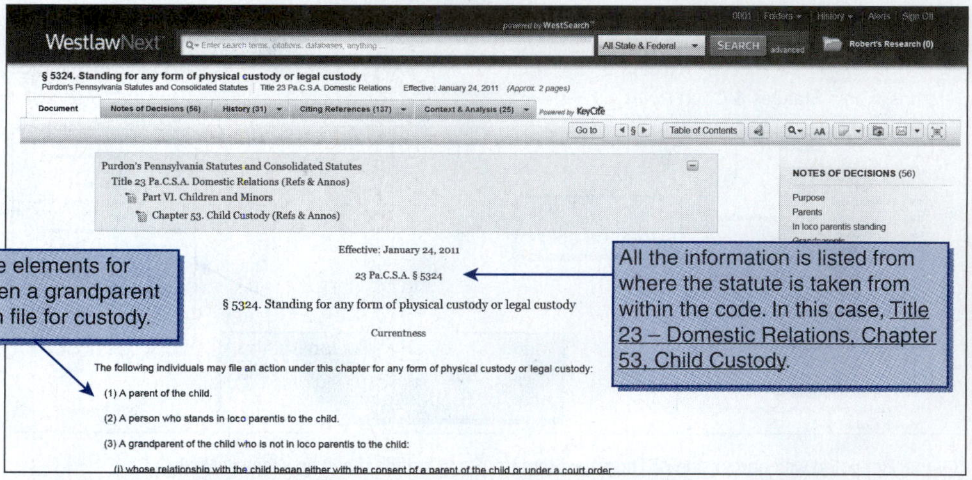

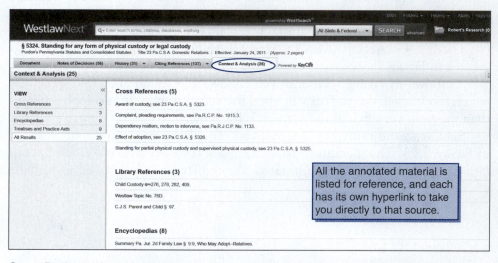

The elements for when a grandparent can file for custody.

All the information is listed from where the statute is taken from within the code. In this case, Title 23 – Domestic Relations, Chapter 53, Child Custody.

Source: Reprinted with permission of Thomson Reuters. Statute 23 Pa.C.S.A. section 5324 on WestlawNext.

Figure 5-23 23 Pa.C.S.A. §5324 - Annotated Material

All the annotated material is listed for reference, and each has its own hyperlink to take you directly to that source.

Source: Reprinted with permission of Thomson Reuters. Statute 23 Pa.C.S.A. section 5324 annotated material on WestlawNext.

As you can see in Figure 5-24, similar to the print material, the list of case summaries are a collection of case decisions in which the court utilized that particular statute in their legal analysis. These case summaries are very useful in helping to explain or interpret the statute for you.

Once you are directed to the statute, the format will be very familiar to you. Everything that you found in the print version of the code is arranged in the same format on *WestlawNext*, such as research and library references and case summaries.

Also, if your supervising attorney requests a legislative history search, or you need to find some information from a recent amendment to the statute, you can conduct a full legislative history search by selecting the **History** tab as you can see in Figure 5-25.

Figure 5-24 23 Pa.C.S.A. §5324 – Case Summary Material

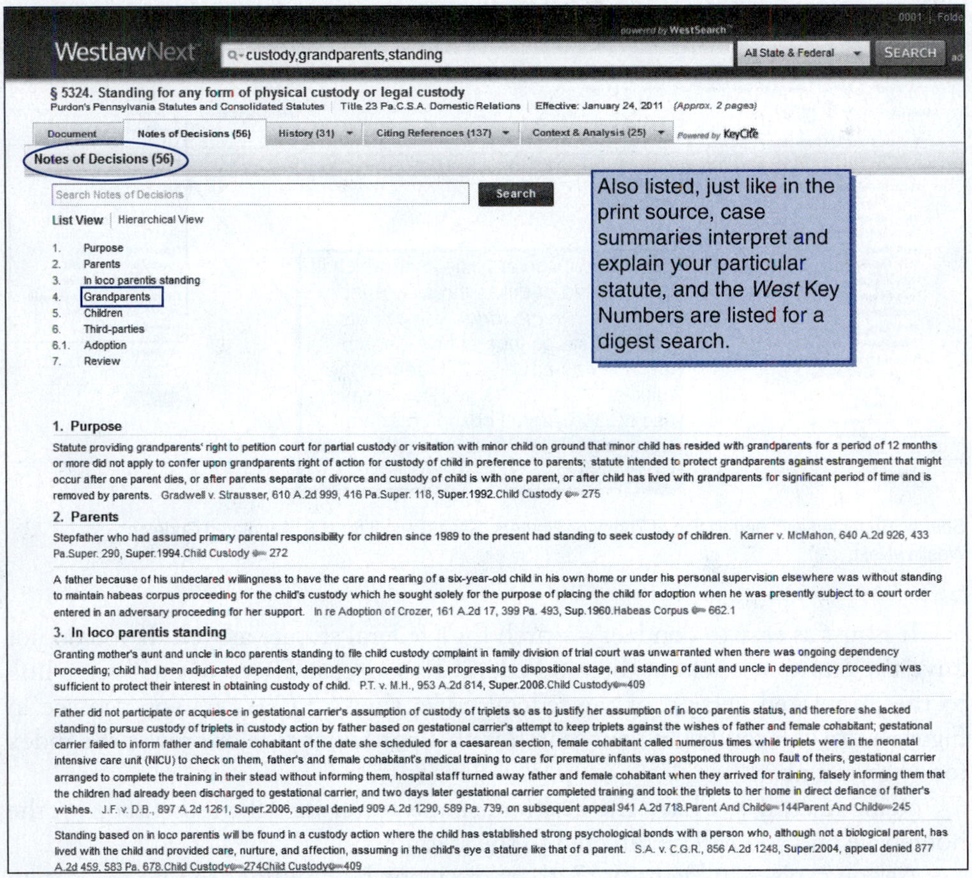

WestlawNext custody,grandparents,standing | All State & Federal | SEARCH

§ 5324. Standing for any form of physical custody or legal custody
Purdon's Pennsylvania Statutes and Consolidated Statutes | Title 23 Pa.C.S.A. Domestic Relations | Effective: January 24, 2011 *(Approx. 2 pages)*

Document | Notes of Decisions (56) | History (31) | Citing References (137) | Context & Analysis (25) | Powered by KeyCite

Notes of Decisions (56)

Search Notes of Decisions | Search

List View | Hierarchical View

1. Purpose
2. Parents
3. In loco parentis standing
4. Grandparents
5. Children
6. Third-parties
6.1. Adoption
7. Review

Also listed, just like in the print source, case summaries interpret and explain your particular statute, and the *West* Key Numbers are listed for a digest search.

1. Purpose

Statute providing grandparents' right to petition court for partial custody or visitation with minor child on ground that minor child has resided with grandparents for a period of 12 months or more did not apply to confer upon grandparents right of action for custody of child in preference to parents; statute intended to protect grandparents against estrangement that might occur after one parent dies, or after parents separate or divorce and custody of child is with one parent, or after child has lived with grandparents for significant period of time and is removed by parents. Gradwell v. Strausser, 610 A.2d 999, 416 Pa.Super. 118, Super.1992.Child Custody 275

2. Parents

Stepfather who had assumed primary parental responsibility for children since 1989 to the present had standing to seek custody of children. Karner v. McMahon, 640 A.2d 926, 433 Pa.Super. 290, Super.1994.Child Custody 272

A father because of his undeclared willingness to have the care and rearing of a six-year-old child in his own home or under his personal supervision elsewhere was without standing to maintain habeas corpus proceeding for the child's custody which he sought solely for the purpose of placing the child for adoption when he was presently subject to a court order entered in an adversary proceeding for her support. In re Adoption of Crozer, 161 A.2d 17, 399 Pa. 493, Sup.1960.Habeas Corpus 662.1

3. In loco parentis standing

Granting mother's aunt and uncle in loco parentis standing to file child custody complaint in family division of trial court was unwarranted when there was ongoing dependency proceeding; child had been adjudicated dependent, dependency proceeding was progressing to dispositional stage, and standing of aunt and uncle in dependency proceeding was sufficient to protect their interest in obtaining custody of child. P.T. v. M.H., 953 A.2d 814, Super.2008.Child Custody 409

Father did not participate or acquiesce in gestational carrier's assumption of custody of triplets so as to justify her assumption of in loco parentis status, and therefore she lacked standing to pursue custody of triplets in custody action by father based on gestational carrier's attempt to keep triplets against the wishes of father and female cohabitant; gestational carrier failed to inform father and female cohabitant of the date she scheduled for a caesarean section, female cohabitant called numerous times while triplets were in the neonatal intensive care unit (NICU) to check on them, father's and female cohabitant's medical training to care for premature infants was postponed through no fault of theirs, gestational carrier arranged to complete the training in their stead without informing them, hospital staff turned away father and female cohabitant when they arrived for training, falsely informing them that the children had already been discharged to gestational carrier, and two days later gestational carrier completed training and took the triplets to her home in direct defiance of father's wishes. J.F. v. D.B., 897 A.2d 1261, Super.2006, appeal denied 909 A.2d 1290, 589 Pa. 739, on subsequent appeal 941 A.2d 718.Parent And Child 144Parent And Child 245

Standing based on in loco parentis will be found in a custody action where the child has established strong psychological bonds with a person who, although not a biological parent, has lived with the child and provided care, nurture, and affection, assuming in the child's eye a stature like that of a parent. S.A. v. C.G.R., 856 A.2d 1248, Super.2004, appeal denied 877 A.2d 459, 583 Pa. 678.Child Custody 274Child Custody 409

Source: Reprinted with permission of Thomson Reuters. Statute 23 Pa.C.S.A. section 5324 case summaries on WestlawNext.

Figure 5-25 23 Pa.C.S.A. §5324 – Legislative History

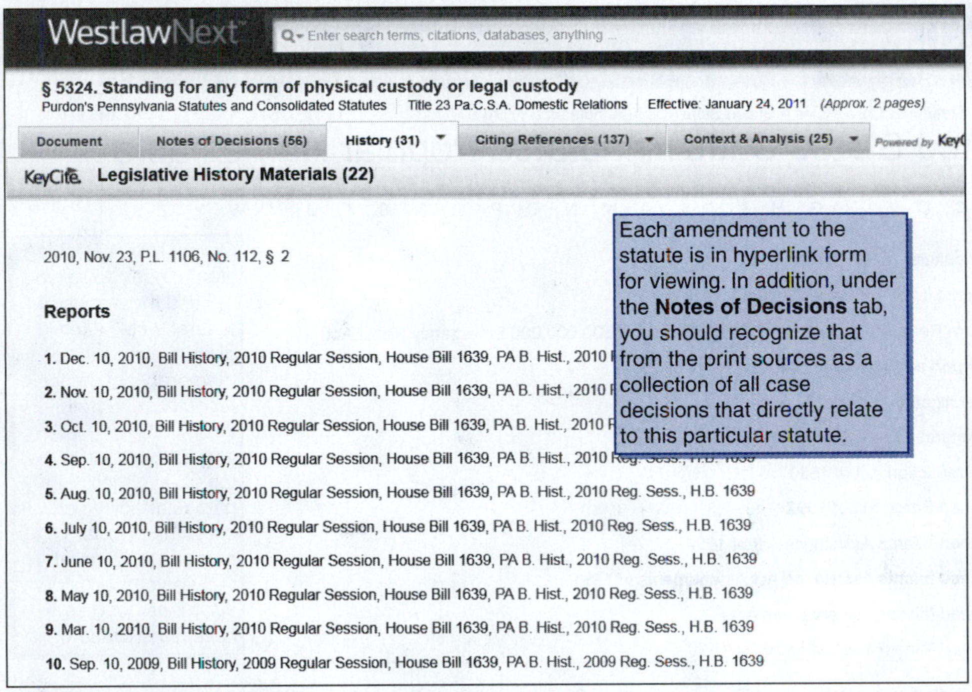

WestlawNext Enter search terms, citations, databases, anything ...

§ 5324. Standing for any form of physical custody or legal custody
Purdon's Pennsylvania Statutes and Consolidated Statutes | Title 23 Pa.C.S.A. Domestic Relations | Effective: January 24, 2011 *(Approx. 2 pages)*

Document | Notes of Decisions (56) | History (31) | Citing References (137) | Context & Analysis (25) | Powered by KeyCite

KeyCite **Legislative History Materials (22)**

2010, Nov. 23, P.L. 1106, No. 112, § 2

Each amendment to the statute is in hyperlink form for viewing. In addition, under the **Notes of Decisions** tab, you should recognize that from the print sources as a collection of all case decisions that directly relate to this particular statute.

Reports

1. Dec. 10, 2010, Bill History, 2010 Regular Session, House Bill 1639, PA B. Hist., 2010
2. Nov. 10, 2010, Bill History, 2010 Regular Session, House Bill 1639, PA B. Hist., 2010
3. Oct. 10, 2010, Bill History, 2010 Regular Session, House Bill 1639, PA B. Hist., 2010
4. Sep. 10, 2010, Bill History, 2010 Regular Session, House Bill 1639, PA B. Hist., 2010
5. Aug. 10, 2010, Bill History, 2010 Regular Session, House Bill 1639, PA B. Hist., 2010 Reg. Sess., H.B. 1639
6. July 10, 2010, Bill History, 2010 Regular Session, House Bill 1639, PA B. Hist., 2010 Reg. Sess., H.B. 1639
7. June 10, 2010, Bill History, 2010 Regular Session, House Bill 1639, PA B. Hist., 2010 Reg. Sess., H.B. 1639
8. May 10, 2010, Bill History, 2010 Regular Session, House Bill 1639, PA B. Hist., 2010 Reg. Sess., H.B. 1639
9. Mar. 10, 2010, Bill History, 2010 Regular Session, House Bill 1639, PA B. Hist., 2010 Reg. Sess., H.B. 1639
10. Sep. 10, 2009, Bill History, 2009 Regular Session, House Bill 1639, PA B. Hist., 2009 Reg. Sess., H.B. 1639

Source: Reprinted with permission of Thomson Reuters. Statute 23 Pa.C.S.A. section 5324 legislative history on WestlawNext.

Figure 5-26 The Main Search Page for the Federal Annotated Code

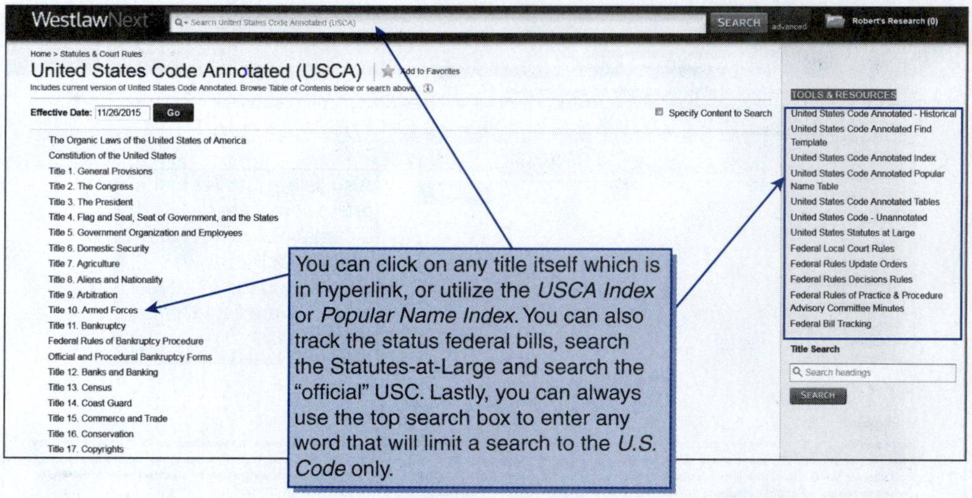

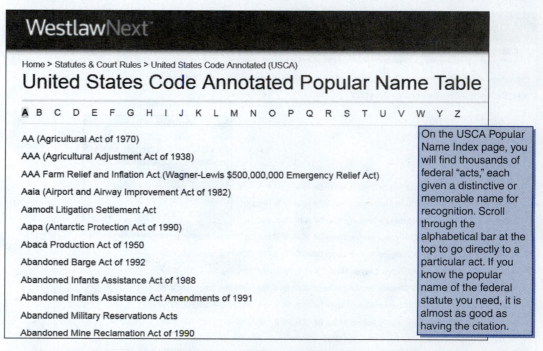

Source: Reprinted with permission of Thomson Reuters. Search result for U.S. Annotated Code on WestlawNext.

It is just as easy to conduct a search for a federal statute as well. If you do not have the citation, click on the tab **Federal Resources.** There you will see a link to the annotated version of the federal code, the U.S.C.A. As you can see in Figure 5-26, you can begin your search with a particular title or browse the index for what you need.

Remember, if you have the citation, simply enter into the search box on the homepage and you will be directed to the statute.

As you can see in Figure 5-27, there are many helpful links to find the statute you need, especially the *Popular Name Index*.

Figure 5-27 The Popular Name Index Page for the Federal Annotated Code

Source: Reprinted with permission of Thomson Reuters. Search result for U.S.C.A. Popular Name Table on WestlawNext.

Now, after following that online tutorial, and provided you have a subscription, conduct your own search to find the statute that allows a grandparent to file for custody using the *WestlawNext* system.

Make sure you use this system regularly on your own to locate statutory law. Become comfortable and get a feel for navigating the website so that you become more proficient in your searches. Remember that the great advantage to using any *West* product is the "Key Number System," which can be used with any print or online *West* product.

Lexis Advance

Locating a state or federal statute on *Lexis Advance* is easy. *Lexis* recently upgraded its database and developed a quicker, more efficient and user-friendly way to search. Follow the steps below.

SEARCH OPTION #1: You have a statute citation.

Similar to the printed books, you can access a statute with the citation immediately. If you have the citation, enter it in the main search box on the *Lexis Advance* home page. This link will take you directly to the statute.

SEARCH OPTION #2: You do not have a statute citation.

Similar to printed books, if you do not have the statute citation, you will need to take just a few more steps to get it. This is where you would need to generate your word search method.

On the *Lexis Advance* home page, under the **Browse** tab at the top of the page, select **Sources,** which you can filter by choosing **Statutes and Legislation.** As you can see in Figure 5-28, the statutory and legislative material for all 50 states will appear.

You can either choose your state jurisdiction from the alphabet bar across the top of the page or by the **Jurisdiction** tab under **Narrow By.** You will have then narrowed your results to the maximum. Only all of the statutory and legislative material particular to your state should appear. As you can see in Figure 5-29, by choosing the statutory code of your state, an automatic table of contents (TOC) will appear. If you know the title you need, you can keep breaking down the title

Figure 5-28 All State Statutory Resources

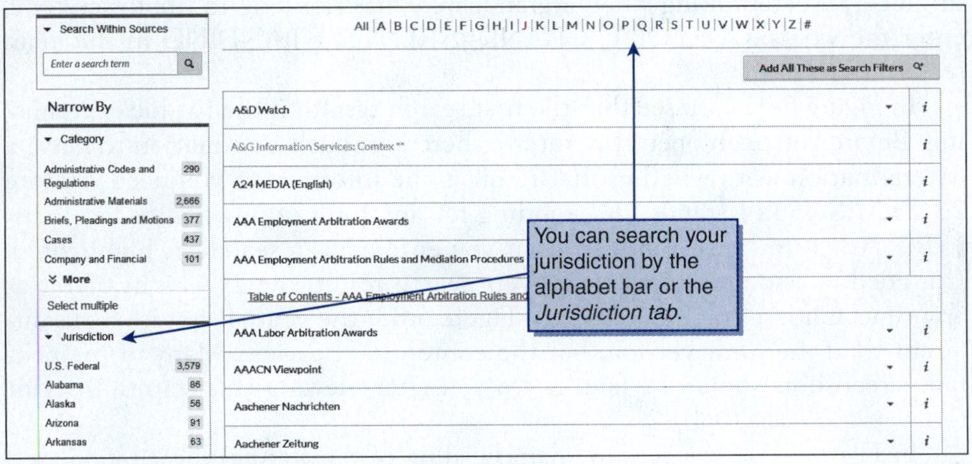

Source: Reprinted with the permission of LexisNexis.

Figure 5-29 The TOC for the Statutory Code

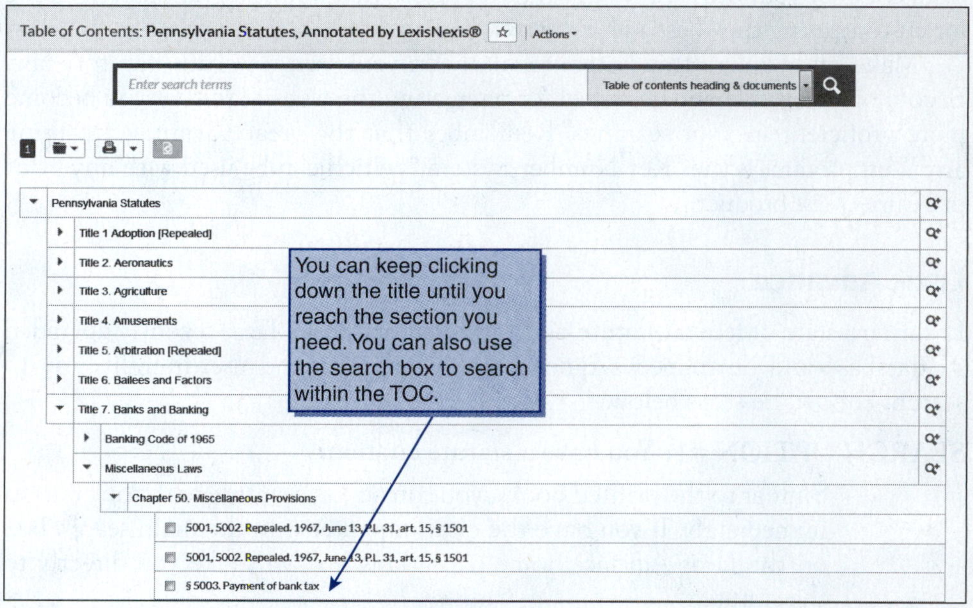

Table of Contents: Pennsylvania Statutes, Annotated by LexisNexis® ☆ | Actions ▾

Enter search terms | Table of contents heading & documents ▾ | 🔍

Pennsylvania Statutes

- Title 1. Adoption [Repealed]
- Title 2. Aeronautics
- Title 3. Agriculture
- Title 4. Amusements
- Title 5. Arbitration [Repealed]
- Title 6. Bailees and Factors
- Title 7. Banks and Banking
  - Banking Code of 1965
  - Miscellaneous Laws
    - Chapter 50. Miscellaneous Provisions
      - 5001, 5002. Repealed. 1967, June 13, P.L. 31, art. 15, § 1501
      - 5001, 5002. Repealed. 1967, June 13, P.L. 31, art. 15, § 1501
      - § 5003. Payment of bank tax

> You can keep clicking down the title until you reach the section you need. You can also use the search box to search within the TOC.

Source: Reprinted with the permission of LexisNexis.

into particular articles and sections. Note that you cannot open any of the main titles or chapters as a hyperlink—only the specific sections.

Alternatively, as you can see in Figure 5-30, you can also access a state statute from the main search box found on the home page by typing in the words: (YOUR STATE) STATUTES. A drop-down option will include your state's statutory name. Now you have created a filter in the main search box on the homepage. Now you can enter any relevant search terms/words to find what you need.

Do you recall the hypothetical problem from when you researched print sources concerning the issue of a grandparent having standing to file for custody? Similar to searching for statutes in print using the "word search" technique, you can utilize the same search online, as you can see in Figure 5-31. For instance, in determining when a grandparent has standing to file for custody, enter the words: CUSTODY, GRANDPARENTS, STANDING in the main search box.

In Figure 5-32, you see that the first search result on the list looks promising. Before you even open the statute, there is enough information to make a determination as to whether that result is the information you need. Statute **23 Pa.C.S.§5324** stands for "standing for any form of physical or legal custody." Any term or search word that you entered as a search, is highlighted. It is good to also note that under every search result, the TOC is available at any time. Choose the first result. In Figure 5-33, the acutual statute looks different than the print version, but the content is the same. Many of the next few screenshots should be familiar to you after viewing this statute in print form.

In Figure 5-32, you see the main heading of the statute, the citation, and the "research trail" of how you arrived at this point. Each part of that research

Figure 5-30 Accessing a Statute Search from the Homepage

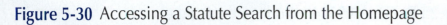

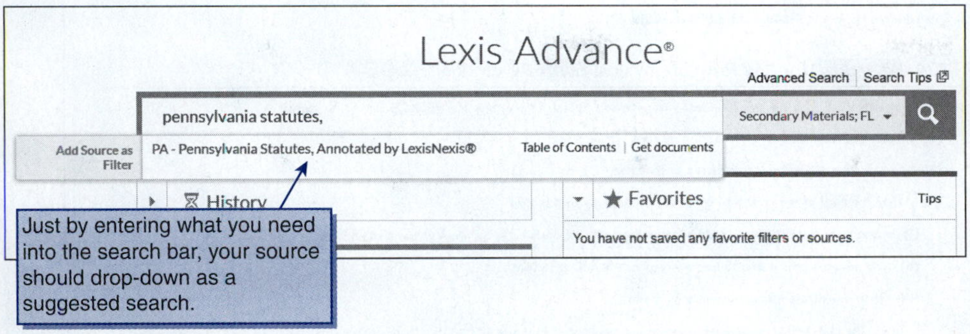

Source: Reprinted with the permission of LexisNexis.

Figure 5-31 The Search Results Page

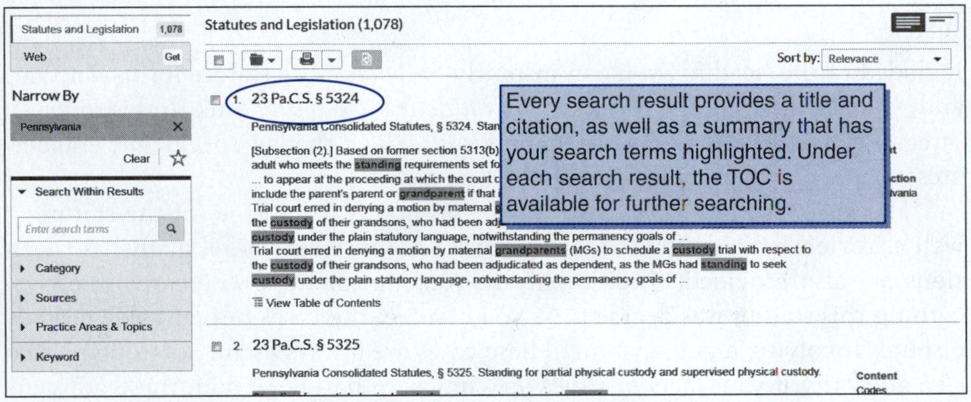

Source: Reprinted with the permission of LexisNexis.

Figure 5-32 Pennsylvania Statute 23 Pa.C.S.A §5324

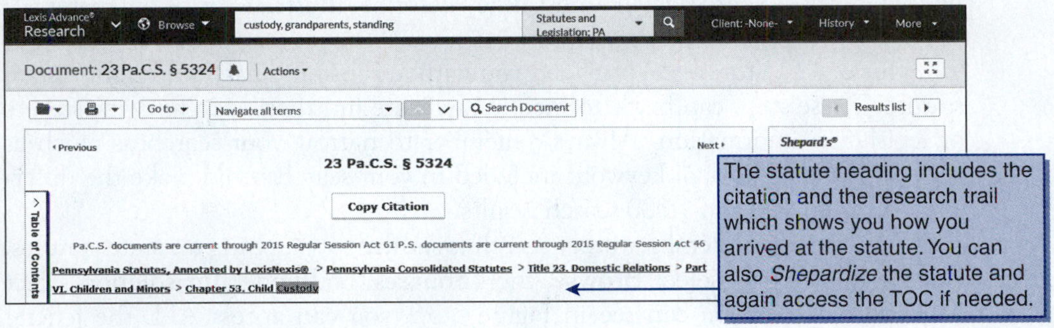

Source: Reprinted with the permission of LexisNexis.

trail is its own hyperlink that you can go to at any time. Think of the hyperlink research trail as the search you would have to conduct with the index in the print version. Here, you arrived at this statute as follows: Pa. Consolidated Statutes *» Title 23, Domestic Relations » Part VI, Children and Minors » Chapter 53, Child Custody*. Now you have all the identifying information you need. Also

Figure 5-33 23 Pa.C.S.A §5324 – Body of the Statute

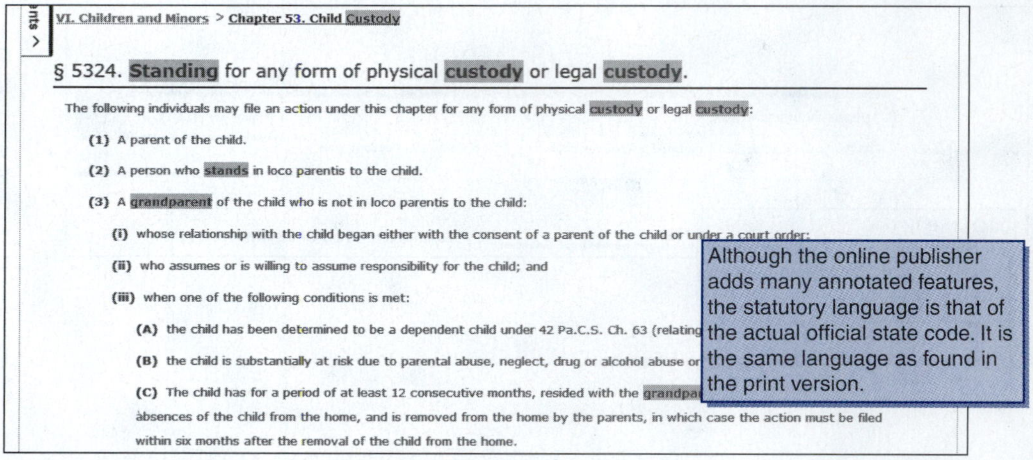

Source: Reprinted with the permission of LexisNexis.

included in the heading, you can instantly *Shepardize* the statute for its currency and validation by clicking on the "*Shepardize this document*" link. In Figure 5-33, directly below the heading is the statute itself. Here, the law specifically enumerates when a grandparent can petition for custody.

The page also has a link where you can access the history of the statute as well as review many annotations. Demonstrated in Figure 5-34, many case decisions are also provided, specific only to your jurisdiction, where an issue concerning this statute was decided. As you can see, the cases here involve custody disputes involving a grandparent. These cases are always useful as strong persuasive authority if your facts or issues are similar in nature. Again, these are same case annotations you would find in the print version.

In Figure 5-35, the various research resources concerning that statute can be accessed as well. Many of these sources are secondary sources of law. In this example, many treatises and legal forms are shown. Remember that you would only want to choose an annotation that has many of your search terms highlighted, as those sources would most likley describe, illustrate, or be of greater use to you.

This quick tutorial has provided you with a quick and easy search for a state statute. These steps can be performed in any state jurisdiction to find any statute or legislative information. Always remember to narrow your search as much as possible. One additional keyword included in your search could make the difference between 100 and 1,000 search results.

Conducting a federal statutory search is similar to searching for state statutes. On the home page, select **Browse**, then **Sources,** and under **Jurisdiction** select **U.S. Federal**. As you can see in Figure 5-36, you can access ALL the federal sources of law. You can narrow those results by selecting **Statutes and Legislation** under **Category**. You can also access the alphabet bar across the top of the page if you know the first letter of the topic you are seeking. In Figure 5-37, once you choose federal statutory authority, you find the *U.S. Code*, the *Popular Names Table*, and the *Statutes at Large*. You can choose either the Code to browse the titles, or search alphabetically by popular name.

Figure 5-34 23 Pa.C.S.A §5324 – Annotated Material

12. Permanent legal custody order did not prohibit a parent from later seeking primary custody because neither the Pennsylvania Juvenile Act, 42 Pa.C.S. § 6301 et seq., nor the federal Adoption and Safe Families Act of 1997, 42 U.S.C.S. §§ 671 — 675, prohibited the parent from petitioning to regain custody of their child. In re S.H., 2013 PA Super 165, 71 A.3d 973, 2013 Pa. Super. LEXIS 1611 (Pa. Super. Ct. 2013).

13. Even if a mother could successfully challenge a father's status, the father had standing to pursue custody because he was listed as father on the child's birth certificate, and he provided support, cared for, and loved the child; the father testified that he changed the child's diapers, fed, clothed, played, and generally took care of all the child's needs, and the child called the father "daddy." Roberts v. Nafus, 2013 Pa. Dist. & Cnty. Dec. LEXIS 400 (Pa. County Ct. 2013).

14. Boyfriend, who had lived with the adoptive mother prior to her adoption of the children, lacked standing to seek custody of the children where the boyfriend ultimately sought to assert custody based upon his relationship with the children prior to their adoption. E.T.S. v. S.L.H., 2012 PA Super 207, 54 A.3d 880, 2012 Pa. Super. LEXIS 2526 (Pa. Super. Ct. 2012).

15. 23 Pa.C.S. § 5326 terminates all custody rights granted under 23 Pa.C.S. § 5324, without regard as to whether the person seeking to assert those rights is a grandparent, in the situation where the child is adopted by an individual other than a stepparent, grandparent, or great-grandparent. E.T.S. v. S.L.H., 2012 PA Super 207, 54 A.3d 880, 2012 Pa. Super. LEXIS 2526 (Pa. Super. Ct. 2012).

16. Trial court erred under Pa. R. Civ. P. 1028(a)(4) when it failed to grant a father's preliminary objection to a grandmother's assertion of standing and request for custody of the parties' child, as the grandmother failed to sufficiently plead that she was entitled to fully custody pursuant to former 23 Pa.C.S. § 5313 (now at 23 Pa.C.S. § 5324). R.M. v. J.S., 2011 PA Super 98, 20 A.3d 496, 2011 Pa. Super. LEXIS 601 (Pa. Super. Ct. 2011).

☞ Family Law: Parental Duties & Rights: In Loco Parentis

17. Trial court misapplied the law in finding that the grandmother stood in loco parentis to the child and therefore had standing to pursue the child custody action because the grandmother's efforts to assist the mother and the child in leaving her home were strongly inconsistent with an assumption of full parental responsibility, and the periods of co-residence were more consistent with the grandmother assisting the mother and the child in a time of need than with the grandmother's informal adoption of the child. D.G. v. D.B., 2014 PA Super 93, 91 A.3d 706, 2014 Pa. Super. LEXIS 235 (Pa. Super. Ct. 2014).

> The annotated material is abundant and directly relevant to your particular statute at hand. The cases are updated weekly.

Source: Reprinted with the permission of LexisNexis.

Figure 5-35 23 Pa.C.S.A §5324 – Annotated Material

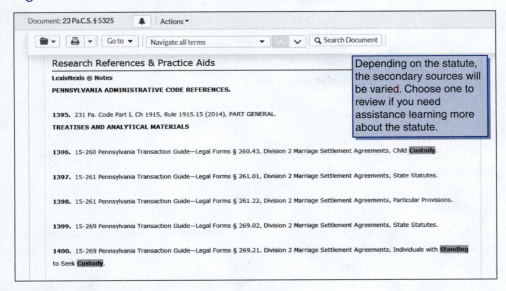

> Depending on the statute, the secondary sources will be varied. Choose one to review if you need assistance learning more about the statute.

Source: Reprinted with the permission of LexisNexis.

Figure 5-36 The Results Page for U.S. Federal Sources of Law

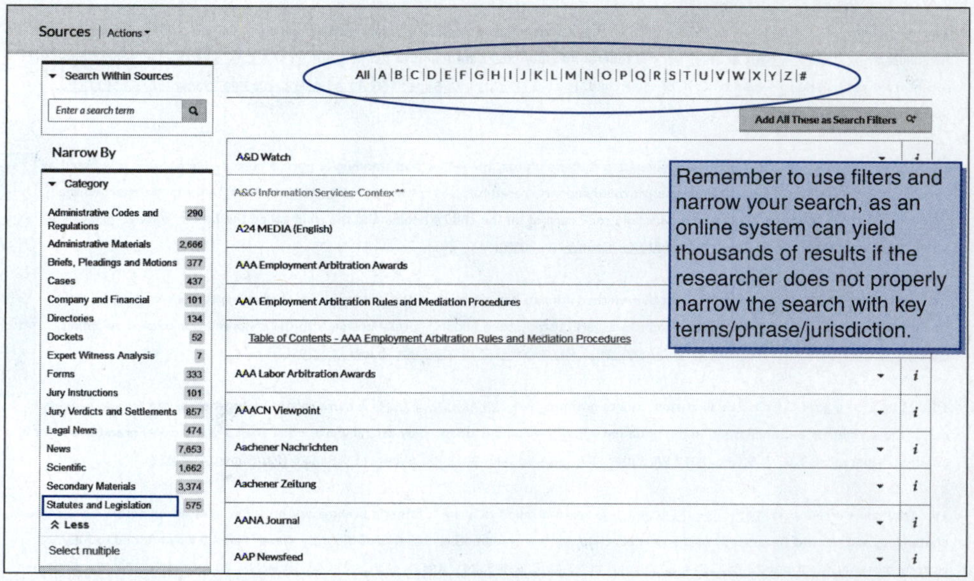

Source: Reprinted with the permission of LexisNexis.

Figure 5-37 Search Results for U.S. Code

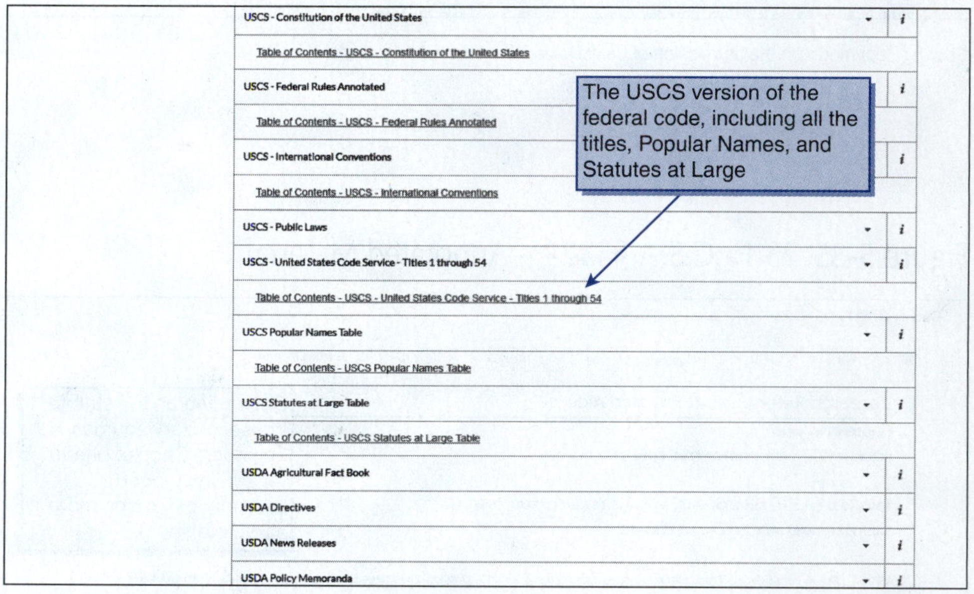

Source: Reprinted with the permission of LexisNexis.

As you can see in Figure 5-38, unlike state statutes, many federal laws are known by their popular name, such as the *Americans with Disabilities Act*, the *Freedom of Information Act*, or *the Patriot Act*.

Lastly, in Figure 5-39, if you search the federal code by title, once you find what you need, you can break it down into subtitles, chapters, and sections.

Figure 5-38 Search Results for Popular Name Index

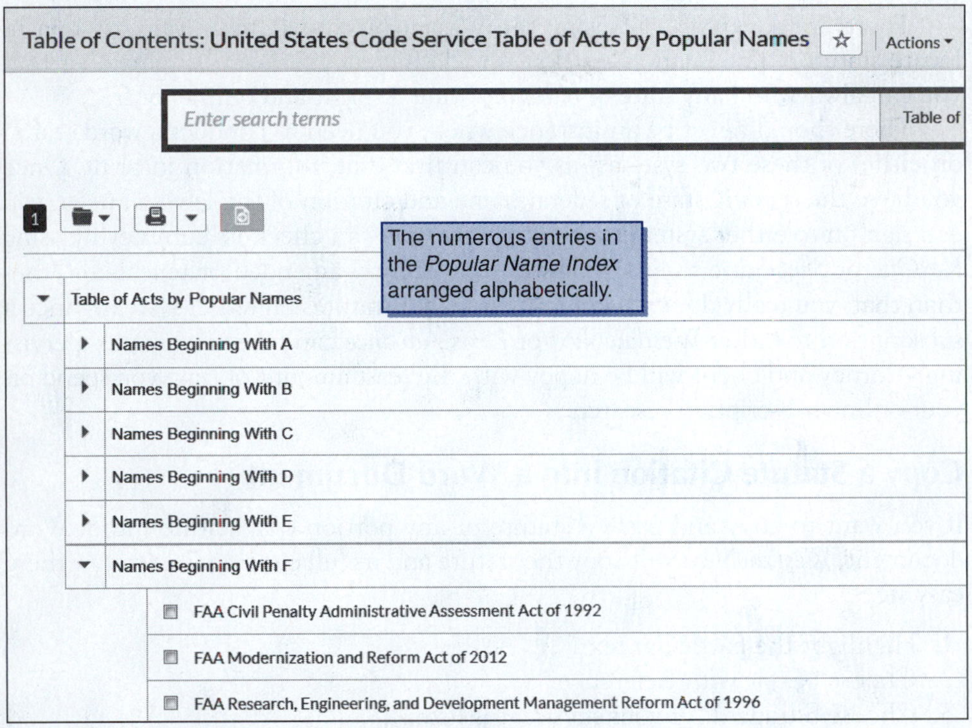

| Table of Contents: United States Code Service Table of Acts by Popular Names ☆ | Actions ▾ |

Enter search terms Table of

1 ▾ ▾ ⊡

The numerous entries in the *Popular Name Index* arranged alphabetically.

▾ Table of Acts by Popular Names

▸ Names Beginning With A

▸ Names Beginning With B

▸ Names Beginning With C

▸ Names Beginning With D

▸ Names Beginning With E

▾ Names Beginning With F

☐ FAA Civil Penalty Administrative Assessment Act of 1992

☐ FAA Modernization and Reform Act of 2012

☐ FAA Research, Engineering, and Development Management Reform Act of 1996

Source: Reprinted with the permission of LexisNexis.

Figure 5-39 The U.S. Code Organized by Title

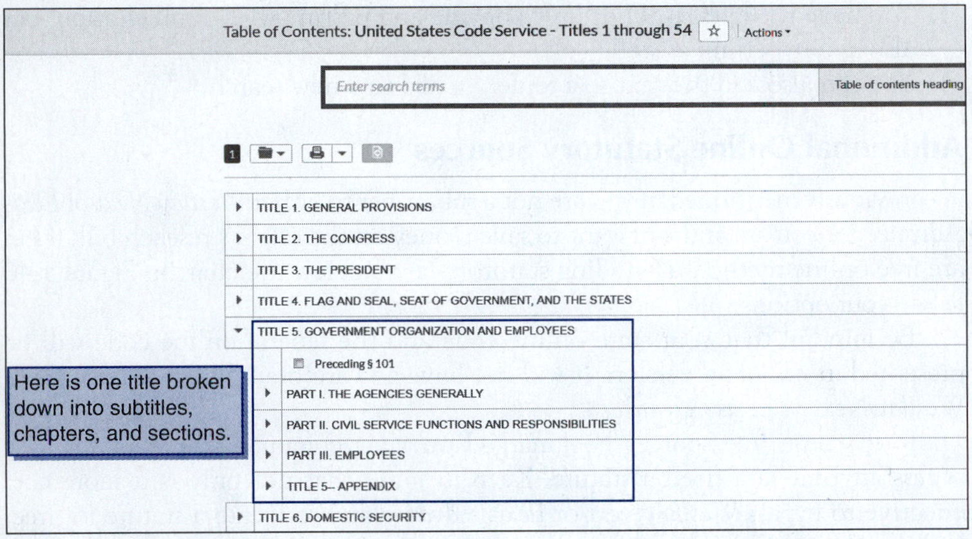

Table of Contents: United States Code Service - Titles 1 through 54 ☆ Actions ▾

Enter search terms Table of contents heading

1 ▾ ▾ ⊡

▸ TITLE 1. GENERAL PROVISIONS

▸ TITLE 2. THE CONGRESS

▸ TITLE 3. THE PRESIDENT

▸ TITLE 4. FLAG AND SEAL, SEAT OF GOVERNMENT, AND THE STATES

▾ TITLE 5. GOVERNMENT ORGANIZATION AND EMPLOYEES

☐ Preceding § 101

▸ PART I. THE AGENCIES GENERALLY

Here is one title broken down into subtitles, chapters, and sections.

▸ PART II. CIVIL SERVICE FUNCTIONS AND RESPONSIBILITIES

▸ PART III. EMPLOYEES

▸ TITLE 5– APPENDIX

▸ TITLE 6. DOMESTIC SECURITY

Source: Reprinted with the permission of LexisNexis.

Similar to the state statutes, you can only click on the actual sections, which contain the actual federal law.

There are advantages to using the *WestlawNext* or *Lexis Advance* system to locate statutory law, such as quickness and efficiency. However, remember that you can always find any state or federal statute in print and online for free.

There should never be an instance where you need to conduct a word search on either of these two systems, as you can find that information in print. Once you have the specific state or federal name and citation of the law you need, you can sign on to either system to read the law. You can check its currency by using *KeyCite* or *Shepardize* to ensure it was not recently amended or repealed. Other than that, you really do not need to "search" for statutes on either system. Since a subscription to either *WestlawNext* or *Lexis Advance* can be costly, your supervising attorney and client will be happy with the least amount of time you spend on your online subscription research.

Copy a Statute Citation into a Word Document

If you want to copy and paste a statute or any portion of a statute into a Word document, *WestlawNext* will copy the statute and its full citation. Just follow these easy steps:

1. Highlight the particular text.
2. Choose "Copy with Reference."
3. Choose Standard (or your state if it is listed).
4. Paste into your Word document.

The highlighted portion will appear in the Word text and will automatically include proper citation.

If you are drafting a legal memorandum or simply writing a quick e-mail to your supervising attorney concerning a case or statute you located, it is always best to have the full citation for future reference. *Lexis Advance* also has a cut-and-paste with full citation feature. Just follow these easy steps:

1. Highlight the particular text.
2. A box will pop up stating "Copy Selected Text to Clipboard."
3. You have the option of not only copying and pasting with a full citation, but also as a hyperlink as well.
4. You can also add the text to a folder, or add to a new search.

Additional Online Statutory Sources

LEARNING OBJECTIVE 4
Identify the free online sources available to search for a statute.

As previously mentioned, if you are not a subscriber to either *WestlawNext* or *Lexis Advance*, or you are and you want to save money on the client's reseach bill, there are free online methods to finding statutory law. Review the chart in Figure 5-40 to see your options.

Be mindful that your state online code and the federal online code will be presented in its *official* version. It will not have any annotated material similar to *WestlawNext* or *Lexis Advance*.

Keep these free sources bookmarked on your computer or tablet for easy access anytime you need a statute. Keep in mind that not only is it more cost effective to bypass *WestlawNext* or *Lexis Advance* and to locate a statute for free, but also there will be occasions when *Westlaw* or *Lexis* will be temporarily down and you cannot sit and wait until it comes back online. You will need to know where you can obtain statutes elsewhere.

Figure 5-40 Free Online Resources for Statutory Law

Jurisdiction	Online Resource
State	*Cornell* has statutory information on all 50 states at [**law.cornell.edu**];
	Findlaw provides links to every state legislative website at [**findlaw.com**];
	Georgetown University also provides clear and easy to find links to every state's legal resources at [**law.georgetown.edu**].
	Washburn University provides full legislative and statutory law information for every state at [**washlaw.edu**]; and
	Google Search will provide a search result that will include the web address for your particular state statutory code at [**google.com**].
Federal	*U.S. House of Representatives* provides access to the official federal code at [**uscode.house.gov**];
	U.S. Government Printing Office (GPO) website also provides access to the federal code at [**gpo.gov**]; and
	Cornell has the complete federal code at [**law.cornell.edu**].

◼ LOCAL LAWS IN PRINT AND ONLINE

Although most of your time will be spent locating state statutes, and occasionally a federal statute, it is very important that you also know how to access the *local* laws of your particular city, county, township, or bourough. Local laws are referred to as **ordinances** and govern and regulate the everyday activities of local citizens. For instance, the local governing board or council can pass an ordinance prohibiting you from placing your trash on the sidewalk no earlier than 24 hours before trash pickup. Ordinances also cover areas of local concern such as rent control, building standards, business licenses, parking, and public health and safety.

Rather than legislative debate, before an ordinance is passed, the township or city may hold town meetings to allow citizens to voice their concerns or approval of a pending ordinance. Once passed, the ordinace is enforced by the local police and courts.

You may be asked to locate these local laws in preparation for litigation so you need to know where they are located in your state. For instance, your supervising attorney may have to litigate a case concerning the death of a child who was struck by a vehicle going 35 mph on a street with a 15-mph posted speed limit. It was determined that the speed limit sign was obstructed by hanging trees. Therefore, you would be asked to reseach the local township ordinances to determine who is responsible for keeping the trees trimmed and the signage clear from obstruction so that the correct party can be held accountable.

The local laws of your state can be located in print in your local law library. These laws will be shelved next to the statutory code. Each local law library has a "home section" of all the case reporters, digests, codes, and local laws of that particular state. In addition, these laws will also be found at the city clerk's office of your particular township or county.

LEARNING OBJECTIVE 5
Explain where to locate local laws in print and online.

ordinances
Laws that are created by local governing boards that affect everyday activities such as trash collection, parking, and property rentals.

These ordinances can also be accessed online for free at **www.statelocalgov.net**. There, links are provided for every branch of local government for every county in every state. This is an invaluable website for the information listed—be sure to bookmark it. In addition, local laws can be accessed through **www.municode.com**. This website, however, does charge a yearly subscription fee to access the information.

Chapter Checklist ✔

- Remember that state statutes are published in an official and unofficial print version that can be found in your local law library.

- The annotated versions are much more helpful in that they provide *cross references* to other statutes within the code, *library references* to other sources of primary and secondary law within the library, and of course *case summaries* for each particular section or part of a statute that explains and interprets that statute.

- Although each state has a different and unique name for its statutory code, and color of the books may be different, every state code's format is the similar, meaning that each code consists of numerous volumes within the set and multiple indexes at the end of the set to guide you through the sets.

- The federal code also consists of an official code, but unlike the state codes, both *Lexis* and *West* publish an unofficial code, which are similar to the format of the state codes.

- Both federal annotated codes provide similar supplemental material; however, they have different naming conventions.

- Your instructor (and the *Bluebook*) will tell you how to cite the statutes of your state, as each has a different format. Federal citation, as you learned, has a universal format.

- Remember to cite a statute with the most current date of the amended code and not the date the statute was originally enacted.

- Similar to case opinions, statutes can be searched by either the "citation" or "word search" method. The statutory indexes include the *descriptive word index,* the *popular name index,* and the *title/topic* search.

- Approach each state statutory research assignment the same as the hypothetical explained to you in this chapter concerning when a grandparent has standing to file for custody. Keep searching the index until you find what you need.

- When you find your statute, read it carefully. Be mindful of each element.

- Remember to search for a federal statute the same way as a state statute. However, utilizing the *Popular Name Index* may be as good as having the statute citation, as thousands of federal laws are designated with a popular name.

- In print, the statutes are updated with pocket parts, as well as supplemental and cumulative booklets. Online, many state and federal websites provide the "currency" of statutes as well.

- Other than *WestlawNext* and *Lexis Advance,* there are other free websites from which to obtain state, federal, and local laws—utilize them!

KEY TERMS

state statutory code 110	descriptive word index	popular name index 125
United States code 113	(DWI) 117	pocket parts 128
citation method 116	case summaries 122	cumulative supplement 128
word search method 117	annotated material 124	ordinances 145

CRITICAL THINKING AND APPLICATION

1. You work as a paralegal in the law office of a solo practitioner in the state in which you live. A potential client enters your office. You conduct the interview. The client, Marisa (45), tells you that two weeks prior, her neighbor poured a new concrete driveway alongside his home. Thereafter, the neighbor put up stakes with "caution tape" surrounding the driveway. The next day, Marisa's son, James (10), intentionally rode his bicycle through the wet concrete up and down the driveway. It is estimated that the repairs to the driveway will cost $3,500. The neighbor is furious and told Marisa that she is paying the bill. Marisa has come to your office to see if she is liable for the actions of her child. You discuss the facts with your attorney and she asks you to research the issue.

Every state has some version of a "parental responsibility law" which holds parents responsible for property damage and/or personal injury resulting from intentional or willful acts of their underage children. Such statutory liability may have certain conditions and dollar limits attached to it.

   a. Research the statutory code in *your state*, **in print**, for the tort liability of a parent. If Marisa walked into your office, can she be held liable for her son's actions in your state? Why or why not? Explain.

   b. What is the dollar limit of parental liability in *your state* under this statute?

   c. Is the applicable statute in *your state* confined to liability of property damage or personal injury only? Explain.

2. Susan (26) was shopping at the local mall. After she made her purchase at the department store counter, unbeknownst to her, she dropped her credit card on the floor. Michael (42) saw this and quickly picked up the card behind her. As Susan was walking away, Michael wrote down Susan's name, card number and security number off the back of the card. Afterwards, he ran up and tapped Susan on the shoulder. Michael handed her back the card telling her she dropped it. Susan was relieved and thanked him. Thereafter, Michael made over $8,000 in purchases online using Susan's credit card information. Susan did not become aware of the purchases until her statement came in the mail.

Every state has some version of an "identity theft" statute. Identify theft occurs when someone uses another individual's personal information, like a person's name, Social Security number, or credit card number or other financial information, without permission, to commit fraud or other crimes.

   a. Research the statutory code in *your state,* **in print**, for the criminal liability for identity theft. Can Michael be charged with this crime? What facts support your answer?

   b. If you had to explain it to your attorney, what are the possible penalties for this crime?

   c. Does your statute state anything concerning restitution (financial reimbursement)?

3. Ronald "Buck" Buchanan (46) works at the World Fitness Gym in Los Angeles, California. Buck was a semi-professional surfer and marathon runner, and won many competitions. At 38, he retired from competition, and was employed at World Fitness as a "competition trainer." Today, Buck surfs for recreation on occasion and runs in 5k marathons to keep in shape. The gym currently employs twenty-eight employees, and the manager, Doug Williams (33), hired Buck to train clients outside the gym and "in the field" to prepare them for competition. Buck takes clients to the ocean in Malibu and conducts surfing classes three days a week. In addition, Buck trains clients on outdoor trails to train the runners for marathons, which also includes diet, weight training, and cardio fitness. Along with his regular salary of 43,000 a year, Buck also makes a percentage profit from his outdoor classes, which pays an additional 6,500 a year. Recently, Doug hired additional trainers for the gym, all between the ages of 20-30. He placed an ad in the local paper (to run for six weeks) attempting to entice new young trainers by stating, " . . . only the young and physically fit need apply for the demanding position as a fitness trainer." Many similar style gyms and fitness centers have opened all over the area, which copied Doug's outdoor training classes for running and surfing. Doug has decided that for World Gym to compete with all the new fitness centers, he needs to start fresh with younger "competition trainers" who currently train themselves. Doug is afraid that with all the new changes, Buck will not be

able to keep up with the other new younger trainers. However, he is doing just fine. Buck's client base is 8% less than the other trainer's classes, but Buck's clients "seek him out and like his training methods and experience from his years of competition."

Doug calls Buck into his office and tells him that his client base is dropping. Doug told Buck that he feels that Buck will be better suited "inside the gym" and assist client members with basic cardio and weight training. Doug terminated Buck's outdoor classes, and reduced his schedule to part-time work, which also reduced his salary to $29,000 a year. Doug made these changes in the hope Buck will eventually quit and leave the gym on his own, in the hope of avoiding any lawsuit.

Buck has come to your law office and said that he feels he was demoted due to his age. Buck said that it would be difficult to live on the reduced salary and wants to know if anything can be done to help him. Your supervising attorney asks you to look up the *federal* statute in the US Code (annotated) in *print* for "age discrimination."

a. Your supervising attorney, a new associate, calls you into her office and tells you that she is worried because she thinks the only way you can bring an age discrimination suit is if you were *fired* due to your age or were *refused employment* due to your age. Buck is still employed at the gym. Can he bring suit against Doug according to the statute and facts presented? If so, under which section?

b. What facts support Doug's alleged discrimination against Buck to satisfy the statute?

c. Other than alleged discrimination against Buck, has Doug committed any other unlawful acts according to the statute? Explain.

4. Abe, (32), recently lost his job as a parking attendant at a hospital after failing a drug test for the third time. The hospital issued Abe his last check and instructed him not to return to the premises. After a month or so, Abe's money ran out and he had no savings to withdraw from to live. Abe could not find employment and his friends would not lend him any money.

One day, Abe decided he would rob the federal credit union located in his township, about two (2) miles away. He drove to the office multiple times and watched how many customers would enter and exit each day. He even went inside a few times to look around and ask questions about accounts to see if the office had any security guards and/or cameras.

Last week, Abe decided he would rob the local credit union. He loaded his 9mm handgun and stuffed a thin duffle bag underneath his jacket, and drove to the office early in the morning. Abe walked in, but immediately panicked. He ran to the counter and grabbed money from the teller's window. When the manager approached and told Abe that he called police, Abe pulled out his gun and pointed it at the manger and told him to get on the ground. He then turned the gun on the teller and told her to fill his bag. Abe heard police sirens in the distance, and ran out the door without the bag, and took only the money he grabbed off the counter. The police arrived, and after a short chase, Abe was eventually apprehended and arrested.

It was determined that since the credit union is charted by the federal government, and that one federal employee is always on the premises to oversee the daily operation of the office, Abe has been handed over to the federal assistant prosecutor on federal charges. Abe was apprehended with only $675 in cash taken from the credit union.

You work for a federal defense attorney who has agreed to take Abe's case, but needs you to perform some research prior to trial. Find the following federal crimes in the US Code in *print* (annotated) and answer the following issues.

a. Can Abe be convicted of robbery according to the federal criminal statute? Explain.

b. Can Abe be convicted of possession of a firearm in a federal facility according to the federal criminal statute? Explain.

c. Taking into consideration all of the above facts, what is the possible sentence Abe could face according to the federal criminal statute? Why?

5. Consumers are protected under federal and state lemon laws. Find the applicable lemon law *online* in *your state*. Read and summarize the law. How would you describe the law to your supervising attorney if requested?

6. A potential client, Roger (37), enters your office and asks to speak with your supervising attorney. Roger stated that he had an appointment with an agent to rent a low-income apartment dwelling that receives loans and contributions from the federal government. Roger brought his brother, Nathan (28), to the appointment. Nathan is physically

healthy and able but suffers from a traumatic brain injury due to an accident. He requires Roger's continual care and supervision. After meeting Nathan, the agent said that Roger could rent the apartment, but not Nathan, as the apartment facilities could not accommodate "someone like Nathan." Roger feels he was discriminated against, and wants the apartment for both he and his brother.

a. Look up the "Fair Housing" act in the federal statutes *online* which your attorney says can be found under title 42. First, you must see if Roger's situation qualifies under the act. Under section 3603, does the apartment complex "qualify" under the fair housing act? Why?

b. Does Nathan's condition fit within the definition of "handicapped" according to the definitions found under section 3602? Why?

c. Under section 3604, does Roger's situation qualify under "discrimination in the sale or rental of housing?" Why? Explain.

7. Your supervising attorney is representing a client who has been arrested and charged with "interstate domestic violence," a federal offense. The client, Jason (37), was married for eight years to Elizabeth (35), and the couple resided in Chicago, Illinois. Jason fell in love with an associate at work and wanted to divorce Elizabeth. However, Elizabeth refused divorce and said they would "work things out." Jason agreed to reconcile and to discontinue seeing the associate at work. Jason planned a trip with his wife to upstate New York; however, Jason secretly planned to kill her and collect on her insurance policy. During a mountain bike ride, Jason ran Elizabeth's bike off a cliff. However, as Jason ran back to the lodge to explain what happened concerning the "accident," Elizabeth survived. She walked back to the lodge and informed the authorities as to what really happened. Jason was arrested, and Elizabeth was taken to the hospital. Due to the fall, Elizabeth's leg had to be amputated due to medical complications.

a. Find this crime *online* in federal statutory law. After a careful reading of the statute, can Jason be charged with the federal crime of "interstate domestic violence?" Explain. Why or why not.

b. If he can be charged, considering the facts presented, what is the possible penalty Jason faces for this crime? Explain.

LEARNING OBJECTIVES

After completion of this chapter, you should be able to

1. Understand the concepts of common law and legal precedent.

2. Identify the parts of a case opinion.

3. Understand the difference between published and unpublished opinions.

4. Explain the three stages of case publication.

5. Understand the difference between mandatory and persuasive law.

6. Demonstrate how to brief a case.

REPORTER

JURISDICTION

CASE BRIEFING

PRECEDENT

The Basics of Case Law

CHAPTER **6**

Most research performed by a paralegal will include mainly statutes, case law, or a combination of both. In this chapter, you will learn to know to understand this important and abundant source of law. You will further become proficient in case briefing, which is an invaluable skill to possess as a legal researcher.

■ INTRODUCTION TO CASE LAW RESEARCH

The American legal system is based upon the **common law** system, which is the body of law generated by the courts, rather than from legislatures. Case law is the collective term for the individual opinions written by judges within the state and federal court system. Those written opinions, also called cases or decisions, create the body of law in a particular state or federal jurisdiction. Whether in a civil or criminal court, or state or federal court, case research is utilized on a daily basis. Hundreds of thousands of case decisions are handed down across the country each year.

So what is case law research? Consider these two examples. Suppose your supervising attorney tells you he is meeting a new client who claims he slipped on ice in front of a supermarket. Before discussing any options or legal strategy with the client, the attorney instructs you to find recently decided state cases where a plaintiff sued a supermarket or business that failed to clear the walkways and parking lot of ice and snow. The idea is to see how those cases were decided. Those cases you find will prove to be a good indicator of how the court will rule in the current case. In another example, suppose you worked as a paralegal for a criminal defense attorney who is filing an appeal on behalf of his client who was recently convicted of criminal trespass. The attorney argued that the defendant broke into the victim's house to escape a blizzard after his car broke down in the middle of the winter. In order to draft the appeal, your supervising attorney may need you to research past criminal cases to see if any court had overturned a criminal trespass conviction due to an emergency or necessity. If so, there is a good chance that the client's conviction would be overturned or the client would receive a new trial.

In the common law system, nearly every written opinion becomes part of the large body of case law that can be used for future decisions—this concept is known as creating **legal precedent**. Applying legal precedent means that as each court issues a decision, it is adding to the collection of available cases that can be

LEARNING OBJECTIVE 1
Understand the concepts of common law and legal precedent.

common law
Case law or precedent that is created by judges and the courts rather than by statute.

legal precedent
In a common law system, a legal case that establishes a principle or rule of law that other courts look to when deciding similar cases.

researched within the realm of case law. This means, as in the examples above, that once a court issues an opinion announcing a rule of law that case can be followed by all the courts of equal and lower jurisdiction in all future cases that are similar in nature. This concept attempts to ensure that all parties in all cases will be treated with consistency and fairness in the court system.

To understand the concept of legal precedent more clearly, consider the following example: Philip and Davidson are neighbors. Davidson empties his above-ground pool and releases 5,000 gallons of water onto his property. Davidson could not control the flow of water, which washed onto Philip's property destroying his new fence and flooding his property. Philip (the plaintiff) sues Davidson (the defendant) in court for the damage to his property. How is this issue resolved? After hearing argument from both sides, the judge looks to the appellate cases in her jurisdiction in order to decide how to render her decision. The judge's law clerk finds the case of *Jones v. Brown*, reviewed by an appellate court in the same jurisdiction.

> **1998:** In the case of *Jones v. Brown,* the plaintiff (Jones) sued the defendant (Brown) after Brown blasted rocks onto Jones' property while clearing a rock bed near his property. The debris caused damage to Jones' roof, and he sued for the cost to repair it. The court ruled that Brown was at fault and ordered Brown to pay damages to Jones' property. The rule of law used in that case held that - when one "causes" a "physical invasion" onto another's property, that person has committed a tort and is liable for any damage caused due to his actions.

Therefore, the judge in the present case could use the *Jones* case as precedent and find in favor of Philip and order Davidson to pay damages for the loss of his property. By using the *Jones* case to guide her, the judge reinforces her decision by using precedent within her jurisdiction in order to rule in favor of the plaintiff. As you can see in Figure 6-1, now both the *Philip* and *Jones* case decisions can be used as precedent.

This is basically how trial judges, appellate judges, attorneys, and paralegals conduct case law research. With all the case decisions being handed down within

Figure 6-1 The How Precedent is Created

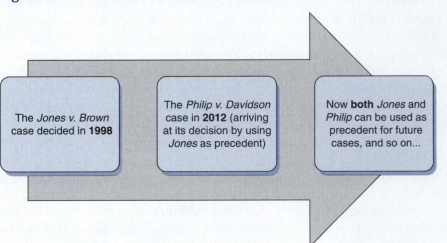

The *Jones v. Brown* case decided in **1998**

The *Philip v. Davidson* case in **2012** (arriving at its decision by using *Jones* as precedent)

Now **both** *Jones* and *Philip* can be used as precedent for future cases, and so on...

the legal profession, not only is case law the most abundant of the primary sources, but all primary sources "return" to case law. Whether you are reading a statute, regulation, or even a constitution, at least one case likely exists that has resolved an issue pertaining to that particular statute, regulation, or constitution.

In this chapter, you will see what a published opinion looks like and learn the individual parts that make up an opinion. You will then see how those opinions are compiled and published for public use. You will see that although case law is made up of numerous opinions within the state and federal court system, you are restricted to only researching cases within your particular jurisdiction—which, as you will see, is a good thing. Using the concepts of mandatory and persuasive authority, you will know from which particular courts and jurisdictions you can search case law. After learning the basics, you will learn how to read and brief a judicial opinion in order to assist your supervising attorney in addressing and solving legal issues.

■ HOW TO IDENTIFY THE PARTS OF AN OPINION

The United States is comprised of 50 individual state court systems and one federal court system. If you recall, most states and the federal system are comprised of three levels of court (trial, intermediate appellate, and the highest appellate court). Judges from any of those courts can write and issue a written opinion, but only specific opinions are used in legal case law research.

Before you learn the basic parts that make up an opinion, it is important to know that there are two *types* of opinions issued by the state and federal courts, as there are two levels of court—trial and appellate. When two parties engage in a legal dispute in court, the party who loses the case will likely appeal the decision. If so, the **trial court** will issue an opinion stating the reasoning behind the verdict. Thereafter, the **appellate court** will review the trial court record to make certain that no legal errors were made during trial. The appellate court will also review the case to make certain no misapplication of the law was applied in the trial court opinion. The appellate court will then issue its own opinion, including a brief procedural history of the case, the facts, the rule of law used in the decision, and a holding.

After appellate court review, it is the appellate decisions that are used in legal research, not the trial opinions, as they are not typically used in research. There are very good reasons for this. First, state trial court opinions are usually not published or reported in most states. This is because, across the country, countless trial court decisions are decided in the state courts each year. Many trial verdicts consist of only minor disputes, such as a California court deciding a retail theft case, or a Florida court deciding whether to award custody to a parent, or a Michigan court deciding a negligence lawsuit between neighbors. All of these decisions have no real legal value to anyone other than the litigants themselves. Hundreds of similar cases are decided in the state courts every day. It would be impossible to compile and publish every trial opinion from every state each year. Second, trial court opinions have not yet been reviewed by a higher appellate court. Therefore, legal errors may exist, or the trial judge may have applied the law improperly, and you would not want to use such a case as precedent in your research.

Why do you need to know this? Because you will see trial and appellate case decisions in your research and you need to know and understand the difference. For instance, *West* publishes *both* trial and appellate opinions in print and online. You will learn how to distinguish between the two types simply by their

LEARNING OBJECTIVE 2
Identify the parts of a case opinion.

trial court
A court of law where both parties present evidence and a verdict is rendered.

appellate court
A court having jurisdiction to review the decision of a lower court.

citation, as many students frequently cite trial court opinions in error. However, as you will see later, federal trial opinions *are* published and printed in a reporter since there are far fewer federal trial decisions handed down each year than from all the states combined. Either way, there are many appellate cases to utilize in your case law research, and in comparison, only a small percentage of trial court opinions are even published, but it is important to know the difference. Unless otherwise noted, all discussions of case law in this chapter will concern appellate cases only.

The Elements of an Opinion

After an appellate court reviews the entire trial court record and renders a decision, it will issue its written opinion. The court opinion basically tells the "story" of the case, and is the written record of a case from trial through appeal. An opinion is made up of various parts, each of which you need to recognize and understand. All written opinions follow the following format in state and federal court.

Cases that are published in print will typically include the following basic elements: *case name, docket number, court deciding the case, date of the court decision, procedural history and case summary, headnotes, attorneys involved in the case, judge authoring the opinion, the full text of the majority opinion*, and any possible *concurring/dissenting opinions*.

In Figure 6-2, review the sample opinion and corresponding descriptions of each component of an opinion that follow. Do not worry about reading or understanding the opinion. For now, just become familiar with the individual parts of the opinion.

case caption

The information included at the beginning of case opinion, including the case name, deciding court, and date of decision.

1. **Case Caption** - At the top of each opinion, the *Case Name*, *Deciding Court*, and *Date of Decision* are referred to collectively as the **case caption**.

   - **Case Name – The case name identifies the case by the two (or more) parties involved in the case. However, there are some deviations in the party names.**

     - The first name, before the "versus" symbol, will always be the party *bringing* the lawsuit. Typically, this party will be identified as the *plaintiff*. The second name, following the "versus" symbol, will be the party *defending* the lawsuit, and will typically be identified as the *defendant*, such as in the case of Peterson (plaintiff) v. Davidson (defendant). You may also see a case where the two parties are identified as *appellant*, the party who lost the case at the trial level and is bringing the appeal, and the *appellee*, who won the case at the trial level and is now defending the appeal. You will see that for individual plaintiffs, only the last name is used in the case name, whereas if a company or corporation is a party in the lawsuit, the entire name is used, such as in the case of *Comcast Corporation v. Behrend*.

     - If you see the following case name, *In re Brown.*, that is Latin for "regarding," and denotes that the lawsuit is not adversarial in nature, but rather a **singular** party seeking legal relief. Typically, this is used concerning an individual filing for bankruptcy. You may also see a deviation of this case name when the case involves a juvenile or minor, such as in the case of, *In the Interest of B.G.* Due to the status as a minor, the party is only identified by initials to protect the party's identity. You will typically see this type of case name in family law or criminal law case opinions in juvenile court.

Figure 6-2 *Northwest Medical Center v. W.C.A.B*

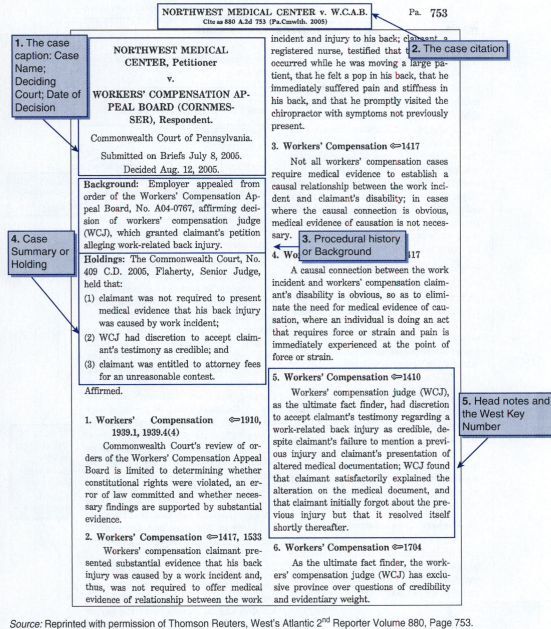

- If you see the following case names, **Commonwealth** v. *Jones*; **State** v. *Andrews*, **People** v. *Williams*, or **U.S.A.** v. *Hendricks*, they are all criminal cases where the state or federal government is bringing a lawsuit against a defendant.

- **Deciding Court** – The court that decided the case and wrote the opinion you are reading will also be included in the main case caption. Once you are familiar with the trial and appellate court names in your state, you will know immediately which court wrote the opinion.

- **Date of the Decision** – If you only see one date listed, it is the date the case was decided and the opinion written. Many times, you may see two or more dates, including *date filed, date argued,* and *date of decision*—all of which are self-explanatory. The important date to know is the "date of decision."

Figure 6-2 Continued

6. Panel of judges deciding the case

---

754 Pa.   **880 ATLANTIC REPORTER, 2d SERIES**

7. Workers' Compensation ☞1981

Workers' compensation claimant who prevailed on claim for back injury was entitled to attorney fees for an unreasonable contest by employer, although employer argued that claimant presented no medical evidence to support his claim and that his credibility was at issue; claimant was not required to present medical evidence of causation of his injury, and employer produced no evidence that claimant's injury was not work-related, but supplied only a medical report stating that there were ongoing uncertainties regarding causation. 77 P.S. § 996.

8. Workers' Compensation ☞1981

Under workers' compensation statute governing contested cases, when a claimant prevails in a litigated case, the workers' compensation judge (WCJ) must assess attorney fees against the employer unless the employer satisfies its burden of establishing a reasonable basis for the contest. 77 P.S. § 996.

9. Workers' Compensation ☞1981

Absent some evidence to contradict or challenge a workers' compensation claimant's allegations that he suffered a work-related injury, a bald credibility challenge to an unwitnessed work-related injury is insufficient to show a reasonable contest, as required to avoid assessment of attorney fees against employer. 77 P.S. § 996.

10. Workers' Compensation ☞1001

Where a workers' compensation claimant's medical bills have not been submitted in the proper form, the remedy is to remand the matter to the workers' compensation judge (WCJ).

---

6. The names of counsel

Richard E. Bordonaro, Erie, for petitioner.

No appearance entered on behalf of respondent.

BEFORE: McGINLEY, J., LEAVITT, J., and FLAHERTY, Senior Judge.

OPINION BY Senior Judge FLAHERTY.

6. Judge who authored the opinion

Northwest Medical Center (Employer) petitions for review from an order of the Workers' Compensation Appeal Board (Board) which affirmed the decision of a Workers' Compensation Judge (WCJ) granting the claim petition filed by Kenton Cornmesser (Claimant). We affirm.

Claimant worked as a registered nurse for Employer. Claimant filed a claim petition alleging he sustained a work-related injury on March 21, 2001. At the WCJ's hearing, Claimant testified that he was moving a large patient on Monday, March 21, 2001, when he felt something pop in his back and mentioned it to his co-worker. Although Claimant's back was stiff and he felt pain, he continued his shift. The next morning, which was Claimant's scheduled day off, Claimant awoke with a lot of back pain, which was made worse when he moved. Claimant noted that on Wednesday, the pain continued to increase so he called his chiropractor. By Friday, the earliest the chiropractor could see him, Claimant was having difficulty getting into a chair, walking and also had pain down his leg. Claimant had another chiropractic treatment on Saturday, and also received some herbal non-prescription muscle relaxants.

Claimant reported for work Saturday evening and requested light duty work because of the pain. Claimant completed his shift and on Sunday spent the day on the couch because of the pain. Claimant had pain so severe on Monday that he could not move. On Tuesday, Claimant's doctor phoned a prescription for muscle

7. Body of the opinion which continues until the court's holding.

---

case citation
The unique identifier of a case opinion in order to locate it in print and online.

procedural history
Information that provides the background information, including verdicts, motions, and filings in the case.

2. **Case Citation** – You will learn about case citation in the next chapter. For now, just know that the **case citation** is the universal "identifier" for how to locate this case opinion in print or online.

3. **Procedural History/Background** – The **procedural history** can easily be identified because it tells the reader "where" the case has been up to this point and "why" it is being decided in the current court. This section may also be titled "Background." Also found in the "Background/Holdings" section is the *docket number*, which is the numerical identifier for the court issuing the opinion. It is not to be confused with the case citation. As you now know, each level of court, trial and appellate, identifies cases with their

Figure 6-2 Continued

756 Pa.   **880 ATLANTIC REPORTER, 2d SERIES**

cal evidence supplied by Claimant refers to an injury date of March 13, 2001, rather than March 21, 2001, the date Claimant maintains he felt a pop in his back. Additionally, Employer maintains that Claimant's testimony was inconsistent as to a previous injury and that he supplied altered medical documentation.

[6] We observe that the WCJ, however, explained in his decision that he accepted Claimant's explanation with regard to the above, namely that Claimant initially forgot about the previous injury but that it resolved itself shortly thereafter, and that there may have been a typographical error in the medical report. In addition, the WCJ found that Claimant had satisfactorily explained the change made on a medical form. As the ultimate fact finder, the WCJ has exclusive province over questions of credibility and evidentiary weight, *Williams v. Workers' Compensation Appeal Board (USX Corporation–Fairless Works),* 862 A.2d 137 (Pa.Cmwlth.2004) and, as such, was free to accept as credible the testimony of Claimant.

[7, 8] Next, Employer argues that the WCJ erred in awarding counsel fees for an unreasonable contest. In accordance with Section 440 of the Workers' Compensation Act, Act of June 2, 1915, P.L. 736, *as amended,* 77 P.S. § 996, when a claimant prevails in a litigated case, the WCJ must assess attorney's fees against the employer unless the employer satisfies its burden of establishing a reasonable basis for the contest. *Bell's Repair Service v. Workers' Compensation Appeal Board (Murphy, Jr.),* 850 A.2d 49 (Pa.Cmwlth.2004). Here, Employer argues that attorney's fees should not have been awarded because Claimant presented no medical evidence to support his claim and Claimant's credibility was at issue.

[9] As previously stated, however, where as here, a causal connection is obvious, medical testimony is not necessary to establish a connection between the work incident and the disability. *Kensington.* Although Employer argues that Claimant's injury was not work-related, Employer produced no evidence to this effect. The medical report introduced by Employer merely stated that there were ongoing uncertainties regarding the issue of causation. As stated in *Bell's Repair,* absent some evidence to contradict or challenge the claimant's allegations that he suffered a work-related injury, a bald credibility challenge to an unwitnessed work-related injury is insufficient to show a reasonable contest.

[10] Finally, Employer alleges that it was error when the Board, in its remand order permitted Claimant to introduce reasonable and necessary medical bills in accordance with the Act which were causally related to the work injury. Where, as here, medical bills have not been submitted in the proper form, the remedy is to remand the matter to the WCJ. *AT & T v. Workers' Compensation Appeal Board (DiNapoli),* 728 A.2d 381 (Pa.Cmwlth. 1999). As such, the Board's remand order to the WCJ was proper. *Westinghouse Electric Corporation/CBS v. Workers' Compensation Appeal Board (Burger),* 838 A.2d 831 (Pa.Cmwlth.2003).

In accordance with the above, the decision of the Board is affirmed.

ORDER

Now, August 12, 2005, the order of the Workers' Compensation Appeal Board, in the above-captioned matter, is affirmed.

> **8.** The Holding and Order of the court

> In the printed reporter, when you see the *West* "key symbol," you have reached the end of the opinion.

own docket number to keep track of all *their* cases. This is more efficient and effective than filing five different cases with the name "Smith" as the defendant. As a paralegal, if you ever need to locate a case brief or memorandum filed by your supervising attorney from the court clerk, you would give them the docket number, not the case name.

4. **Case Summary/Holding** - You will learn in this chapter that cases are printed in official and unofficial publications. The unofficial commercial publishers

case summary
A section of the case opinion that includes a quick summary of the holding in the case.

add some very helpful annotated material to the print opinion for ease of understanding, which you will NOT find in the official publications. One of these helpful annotations is the **case summary**, which is NOT written by the court, but by the commercial publisher. This information briefly summarizes the case and allows the researcher to determine if the entire case is worth reading to address your legal issue.

5. **Headnotes (West Key Number)** – Simply defined, a **headnote** consists of a short paragraph of a few sentences written by the commercial publisher (not the court) and listed by number before the opinion that serves as an "index" of each point of law the court used or referenced in the opinion. Each numbered headnote directly corresponds with that same number directly inserted into the opinion. You can **NEVER** cite directly to a headnote, as they are not written by the court. Many times, the headnote itself does not match the language in the opinion because headnotes are "summaries" of the rule of law analyzed within the opinion. If you determine that the case can address/answer your issue, always read the entire opinion. In addition, next to each numbered headnote, you will see a topic heading and **key number**. That number is part of the *West* key number system. You will learn the importance of that number in the next chapter.

6. **Attorneys and Judges** – The opinion will also state the names of the attorneys (counsel) for each party in the case. Also, all the names of each judge on the panel who decided the opinion and the judge who wrote (authored) the opinion will immediately precede the full text of the opinion itself. Even though an appellate case is decided a panel of judges, only one of those judges will be designated to author the opinion.

7. **Body of the Opinion** – After learning all the important information concerning the case opinion itself, and if the researcher determines after reading the case summary and headnotes that the case is useful, the researcher can read the full text opinion, which includes the legal issue(s) or legal questions to be resolved, and the court's *analysis* of the facts of the case with the rule of law utilized by the court in answering/addressing those issues. The full opinion is called the **majority opinion**, because it was written by a majority number of the members of the appellate court. As you can see in Figure 6-2, each new paragraph within the body of the opinion is numbered for ease of reference.

8. **Holding/Order of the Court** – The holding is the final component of the full text opinion and is always located at the end of the majority opinion. The holding is also known as the *disposition* of the court. Also included in the holding is the final *order* (instructions) if any, to the lower court. For example, you may see three possible holdings, including *affirmed* (meaning that the decision of the appellate court is in agreement with the lower court and no further action is necessary), *reversed* (meaning the appellate court reversed the decision of the lower court and no further action is necessary), or *remanded* (meaning that the case is being sent back down to the lower court to correct a legal error). It is important to read the holding to know where the case stands in the courts and if it can be used as legal precedent. For example, if the case was reversed or remanded, it could not be utilized as legal precedent because it would have been overturned or sent back to the lower court.

Also included in a case opinion are the concurring and dissenting opinions. The concurring/dissenting opinion will always follow the majority opinion and

headnote
A section of a case opinion including specific points of law not written by the court, but rather by a commercial publisher.

key number
A specific numerical identifier next to each headnote that correlates to a particular topic that can be found in any West publication using that key number.

majority opinion
The holding in the case written by a majority of the court that can be used as precedent.

may or may not appear after the decision in all cases, as they are optional at the discretion of the court. A **concurring opinion** will be written by another judge(s) on the appellate panel who *agrees* with the majority opinion, but for a *different reason*. In addition, a **dissenting opinion** can also be written by another judge(s) on the appellate court that *disagrees* with the majority opinion and states their reasons. ***Neither the concurring nor dissenting opinion are part of the majority opinion and as such, cannot be used a precedential authority***. You may also see the term **plurality opinion**, which means that the majority of the court could not agree collectively on a majority decision. This type of opinion does resolve the legal dispute between the two parties involved, but it is a weak opinion to rely on as precedential authority due to the lack of majority vote.

A **memorandum opinion**, as you can see in Figure 6-3, is very brief and only states the ruling of the court but without any analysis. For example, you may see pages in the printed reporters of multiple case headings and one- or two-sentence rulings on one page. These are memorandum opinions that usually state that the appeal to the appellate court was accepted or denied, or a judgment was affirmed

concurring opinion
An opinion written by a minority of the court who agree with the majority opinion but for a different reason, which cannot be used as precedent.

dissenting opinion
An opinion written by a minority of the court who disagree with the majority opinion, which cannot be used as precedent.

plurality opinion
An opinion written without a majority vote that resolves the legal dispute and cannot be used as precedent.

memorandum opinion
A brief opinion by a court that announces its decision without a formal opinion, which cannot be used as precedent.

Figure 6-3 Example of Memorandum Opinions in Print

724 Conn. 23 ATLANTIC REPORTER, 3d SERIES

1

301 Conn. 929

Margaret CULVER

v.

Michael CULVER.

Supreme Court of Connecticut.

Decided June 30, 2011.

Karen L. Dowd and Brendon P. Levesque, Hartford, in support of the petition.

Samuel V. Schoonmaker IV and Wendy Dunne DiChristina, in opposition.

The defendant's petition for certification for appeal from the Appellate Court, 127 Conn.App. 236, 17 A.3d 1048, is denied.

KEY NUMBER SYSTEM

2

301 Conn. 929

STATE of Connecticut

v.

Alex MITCHELL.

Supreme Court of Connecticut.

3

301 Conn. 929

Leyla MIRJAVADI et al.

v.

Anthony VAKILZADEH et al.

Supreme Court of Connecticut.

Decided June 30, 2011.

Lloyd D. Pedersen, Hartford, in support of the petition.

Brenden P. Leydon, Stamford, in opposition.

The defendant Maria Varone's petition for certification for appeal from the Appellate Court, 128 Conn.App. 61, 18 A.3d 591, is granted, limited to the following issue:

"Did the Appellate Court properly determine that several of the facts found by the trial court were clearly erroneous, and, therefore, the judgment in favor of the defendant must be reversed?"

ROGERS, C.J., did not participate in the consideration of or decision on this petition.

KEY NUMBER SYSTEM

Source: Reprinted with permission of Thomson Reuters, West's Atlantic 3rd Reporter Volume 23, Page 724.

without an opinion. *WestlawNext* and *Lexis Advance* also post memorandum opinions, which you can tell immediately, as the full case caption will be displayed, but the full text of the opinion will not. These opinions have no precedential value in legal research, as they do not analyze any legal issues.

At the end of this chapter, you will learn how to "brief" a case opinion, which includes reading a summarizing the information in the case. For now, just know and understand the multiple parts that make up an opinion and be able to identify them.

■ CASE PUBLICATION

LEARNING OBJECTIVE 3
Understand the difference between published and unpublished opinions.

published opinion
An opinion that is officially designated to be used as precedent.

unpublished opinion
An opinion that is deemed not to have legal value and cannot be used as precedent.

You now know what an opinion is and its various parts—that's a good start. Now, you will see how and where those opinions are published for public use.

Published and Unpublished Opinions

An opinion is deemed a **published opinion** when it is designated to be used as legal precedent. Although many opinions are decided in state and federal courts, it is important to know that not all opinions are published. It is the collection of "published opinions" from which a researcher in that state can conduct case law research. Even before an appellate court writes an opinion, it makes the decision of whether the opinion merits the badge of "published." Many states have different factors that go into the determination of whether an opinion should be published, including whether the opinion establishes a new rule of law, or whether the case concerns an issue of widespread public legal interest. Besides occupying too much shelf space in the library, opinions are deemed **unpublished opinions** if they do not advance the law, meaning that the decision does not possess any legal value. Remember the examples above of the California court deciding a case concerning a retail theft and the Florida court deciding a standard custody case. Hundreds of the same types of cases are decided each day in each state. When a court selects certain cases to be published, it helps to narrow the research possibilities to specific areas/topics of law, rather than publishing a multitude of cases that merely reiterate countless existing opinions.

In the majority of the *state appellate courts*, the vast number of "unpublished" or "non-precedential decisions" *cannot* be utilized in research according the rules of court in that state. This, however, has produced a heated debate among legal experts who have argued that it is unconstitutional to allow each state to arbitrarily determine which opinions to publish, as many legally relevant unpublished opinions, not recognized as precedent, may include valuable and important points of law. However, just because an opinion cannot be used as precedent does not mean it serves no purpose. An unpublished opinion, or even trial opinion, can be used as a guide to point you in the right direction for precedential cases you need to address to answer your legal issue, which you will see how to do later. An unpublished decision is not bad law; it was simply not chosen, for a number of reasons, to be designated as legal precedent.

Today, with the Internet slowly but steadily gaining momentum in the legal profession, many published AND unpublished opinions are being posted on state and federal court websites. Because of this, the term "unpublished" is losing its meaning, which is why you will see many opinions online marked "non-precedential," meaning they have no precedential value. As you can see in Figure 6-4, the "non-precedential" opinion from the Pennsylvania appellate court is clearly noted to the

Figure 6-4 Non-Precedential State Opinions Online

J-S01045-13

NON-PRECEDENTIAL DECISION - SEE SUPERIOR COURT I.O.P. 65.37

IN RE: ADOPTION OF R.C., A MINOR	IN THE SUPERIOR COURT OF PENNSYLVANIA
APPEAL OF: R.C., FATHER	

Appellant

> Notice this opinion has been deemed "non-precedential" on the Pennsylvania state court website to inform the researcher that the opinion cannot be used as legal precedent.

Appeal from the Decree
in the Court of Common
Domestic Relations at No. 27 OCA 2012

BEFORE: BENDER, LAZARUS and COLVILLE*, JJ.

MEMORANDUM BY COLVILLE, J.:   Filed: February 20, 2013

R.C. ("Father") appeals from the decree in the Court of Common Pleas

Source: http://www.pacourts.us

researcher. Many other states similarly make this notation on their unpublished opinions as well.

In addition, on *Lexis Advance* and *WestlawNext*, any case you retrieve that is unpublished, will state such information in the case caption, as you can see in Figure 6-5 and Figure 6-6. In addition, any case found on either database with only a *LEXIS* or *WESTLAW* citation, will also be an unpublished opinion.

In the **federal appellate** courts, approximately 80% of the appellate decisions are unpublished. However, contrary to the state appellate courts, the federal courts recently permitted the citation of unpublished opinions. That is because there are fewer federal cases than state cases handed down each year. On January 26, 2006, the Federal Rules of Appellate Procedure were amended to add **Rule 32.1,** which prohibited courts from restricting attorneys from citing unpublished federal judicial opinions issued *after* January 1, 2007. In recent years, the commercial publisher, *West*, began publishing a collection of these unpublished opinions. In addition, in accordance with the **E-Government Act of 2002**, all federal court opinions, precedential and non-precedential, were made available on the Internet for viewing. Only time will tell if the states will follow, as many are currently petitioning their state supreme courts to permit the use of unpublished opinions as precedent.

In the **United States Supreme Court**, *all* opinions are published and *must* be used as precedent, as those opinions establish the "law of the land" that every lower court, state and federal, is required to follow as precedent. As you will see in the next chapter, all of these opinions are quite easy to access at any time through multiple print and online sources.

There are ways to distinguish between a published and unpublished opinion, and it is important to know the difference between them. Your instructor will inform you as to the rules concerning the use of unpublished non-precedential appellate cases in your particular state.

Figure 6-5 Non-Precedential State Opinions on *Lexis Advance*

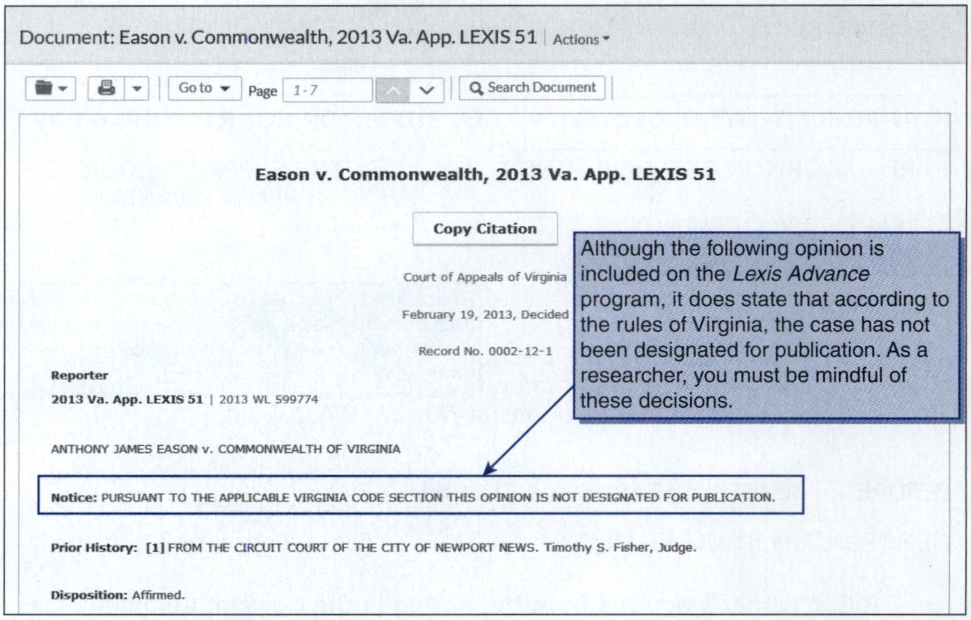

Document: Eason v. Commonwealth, 2013 Va. App. LEXIS 51 | Actions
Go to
Page 1-7
Search Document
Eason v. Commonwealth, 2013 Va. App. LEXIS 51
Copy Citation
Court of Appeals of Virginia
February 19, 2013, Decided
Record No. 0002-12-1
Reporter
2013 Va. App. LEXIS 51 | 2013 WL 599774
ANTHONY JAMES EASON v. COMMONWEALTH OF VIRGINIA
Notice: PURSUANT TO THE APPLICABLE VIRGINIA CODE SECTION THIS OPINION IS NOT DESIGNATED FOR PUBLICATION.
Prior History: [1] FROM THE CIRCUIT COURT OF THE CITY OF NEWPORT NEWS. Timothy S. Fisher, Judge.
Disposition: Affirmed.
Although the following opinion is included on the Lexis Advance program, it does state that according to the rules of Virginia, the case has not been designated for publication. As a researcher, you must be mindful of these decisions.

Source: Reprinted with the permission of LexisNexis.

Figure 6-6 Non-Precedential State Opinions on *WestlawNext*

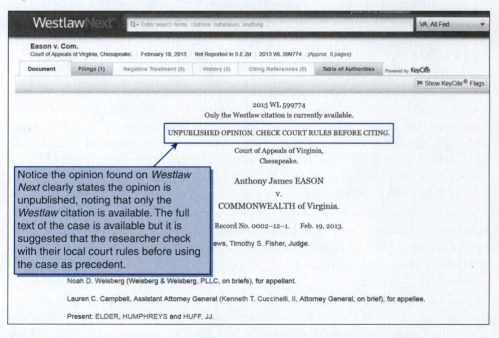

WestlawNext
Enter search terms, citations, databases, anything ...
VA, All Fed.
Eason v. Com.
Court of Appeals of Virginia, Chesapeake. | February 19, 2013 | Not Reported in S.E.2d | 2013 WL 599774 | (Approx. 5 pages)
Document | Filings (1) | Negative Treatment (0) | History (0) | Citing References (0) | Table of Authorities
Powered by KeyCite
Show KeyCite® Flags
2013 WL 599774
Only the Westlaw citation is currently available.
UNPUBLISHED OPINION. CHECK COURT RULES BEFORE CITING.
Court of Appeals of Virginia,
Chesapeake.
Anthony James EASON
v.
COMMONWEALTH of Virginia.
Record No. 0002–12–1. | Feb. 19, 2013.
ews, Timothy S. Fisher, Judge.
Noah D. Weisberg (Weisberg & Weisberg, PLLC, on briefs), for appellant.
Lauren C. Campbell, Assistant Attorney General (Kenneth T. Cuccinelli, II, Attorney General, on brief), for appellee.
Present: ELDER, HUMPHREYS and HUFF, JJ.
Notice the opinion found on Westlaw Next clearly states the opinion is unpublished, noting that only the Westlaw citation is available. The full text of the case is available but it is suggested that the researcher check with their local court rules before using the case as precedent.

Source: Reprinted with permission of Thomson Reuters, Unpublished opinion 2013 WL 599774 on WestlawNext.

The Stages of Case Publication

All state, federal, and US Supreme Court case opinions generally develop through three stages of publication: slip opinions (individual loose leaf opinion), advance sheets (multiple opinions compiled in a softbound booklet), and reporters (multiple opinions compiled in a hardbound book). Each form of publication is important to know and to understand, as you may need to retrieve an opinion during any of those stages of publication.

Slip Opinions

The initial appellate opinion written by the court is called a **bench opinion**. The first printed version available to the public is called the **slip opinion**. These loose-leaf opinions are important in that if the opinion is never officially published in a reporter, the slip opinion is the only printed record of the case. Slip opinions are typically available on the court website the same day the case was decided. The slip opinion includes the actual text of the opinion, but does not include any editorial features or enhancements such as headnotes or case summaries as in Figure 6-1. The slip opinion may also include a case syllabus, which is a brief summary of the case immediately preceding the text of the opinion, but is not part of the case itself and has no precedential value. A slip opinion will include, *the case name, the docket number, date the opinion was written, the author of the opinion, the majority opinion,* and *any concurring or dissenting opinions.*

Similar to a *slip law,* which is considered official law even before it is compiled and bound into a statutory code, a *slip opinion* is also official law before it is compiled and bound into a state reporter. The reasoning for both is simple—once law has been created, it would be illogical to wait to cite a case prior to it being published in a hardbound volume. Therefore, as you can see in Figure 6-7, a slip opinion has many numeric identifiers from which to identify the case decision before it is officially published. However, there typically is no need to immediately access an appellate slip opinion unless your supervising attorney requests one. Any rule of law discussed within those opinions has likely been addressed in many prior opinions that can easily be accessed in print and online.

You will learn later in this chapter the importance of retrieving slip opinions from the US Supreme Court. When those opinions are released, they immediately become binding precedent for every federal, state, and local court in the land. Immediate access to these opinions is crucial, and access can be gained usually within a few hours of release.

In reality, the only reason you may be called upon to retrieve a state or federal slip opinion for your supervising attorney is if the case has established a new rule of law, or the facts of the case are very similar to your own case. But be careful in that a newly decided case will most likely be appealed. Remember, you can appeal an intermediate decision to the supreme or highest court in the state, as well as up to the US Supreme Court. So, if your attorney does need a slip opinion, it needs to be cited as such. You may also need to keep track of the appellate *process* of that slip opinion, as it may very well be traveling upwards through the appellate courts. You need to make sure the case is not overturned on appeal. That's why US Supreme Court opinions are considered precedent upon release, as no higher court of appeal exists.

LEARNING OBJECTIVE 4
Explain the three stages of case publication.

bench opinion
The actual opinion written by a trial judge or appellate court.

slip opinion
The first printed version of an opinion available for public view.

PRACTICE TIP

If you check the judicial court website of your state, you can receive "electronic notification" of newly released appellate opinions with a subscription to the court. Typically, one person in the firm, usually a paralegal or law clerk, will receive these notifications and distribute the cases of importance to the firm or law office. This is quite helpful in that you can also receive any court news or updates on any case law. Talk with someone in your firm or law office and be sure to utilize this great resource.

Figure 6-7 An Example of an Online Slip Opinion

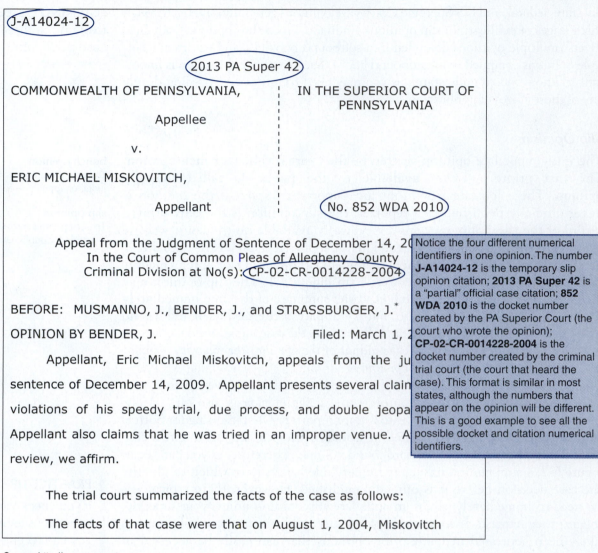

Source: http://www.pacourts.us

Locating Slip Opinions

Although you can request a copy of a slip opinion at the courthouse, many, if not all, slip opinions can be located online through the state or federal court website. As you learned in Chapter 2, you can search the Internet for your particular state judicial website. For instance, if you insert the words: NEW JERSEY, APPELLATE COURT, OPINIONS into a web browser, you see the search result page in Figure 6-8.

Other than conducting your own search, you can also visit **wwwncsc.org** for a complete list of every state and direct links to each state's judicial website. Be sure to bookmark the website on your computer. If the judicial website happens to move for any reason, you will know how to find it. In addition, *Lexis Advance* and *WestlawNext* typically post opinions the date of release. However, without a citation, it may be more difficult to search for your case on either of those databases. A search of your state's judicial website would be quicker and more efficient.

Figure 6-8 An Example of a Search Result Page on Google

Source: https://www.google.com

If you recall learning in Chapter 2, every primary source of law requires a citation for identification. What if your supervising attorney needed a slip opinion from a *state* appellate court to use for an upcoming case? You already know where you can locate the opinion. But how would you cite it since it has yet to be published and bound into a reporter? Both the *Bluebook*, (Rule 10.8.1) and the *ALWD Manual*, (Rule 12.18) address this situation. Basically, to cite a slip opinion the information should include *the case name, the slip opinion number, the court issuing the opinion, and the full date it was decided.*

Refer back to Figure 6-7 and notice the multiple numerical identifiers listed on the opinion. The **CP-02-CR-0014228-2004** number would not be used to cite the slip opinion, as it is the TRIAL COURT docket number for that court only. The **852 WDA 2010** number would not be used to cite the slip opinion, as it is the SUPERIOR COURT docket number for that court only. The **2013 PA Super 42** number is an "incomplete" official citation, meaning the court knows the case will end up in volume 42 of the hardbound reporter, but the citation is incomplete because it has not yet been designated a page number to complete the citation. Therefore, the number at the top of the opinion is the temporary slip opinion citation, as you can see below.

> **Commonwealth v. Miskovitch, No. J-A14024-12 (March 1, 2013)**

Remember that the trial court, intermediate appellate court, and the highest state appellate court all issue a different case number for the same case. This is to keep and maintain their *own* court docket, but all are easily identifiable on the cover of the particular opinion.

If your supervising attorney needed to locate a slip opinion from a *federal* appellate court, it can also be obtained easily from the federal judicial website in your state. Again, any federal judicial website can be located by conducting a simple Internet search. For example, if you work as a paralegal in Rhode Island and your attorney needed a slip opinion from a case decided last week. In any basic search engine you can enter the terms, RHODE ISLAND, FEDERAL, JUDICIAL APPELLATE COURTS to locate the federal appellate court opinions in that state. Also, if you go to **www.uscourts.gov**. This government site provides direct links to every state and federal judicial website. Once you enter the website, you can search the latest slip opinions by *case number, short title, date published,* or *recently published.* Keep in mind that all federal appellate courts are organized into circuits. So you would have to know that Rhode Island is in the First Circuit.

When citing a newly decided federal slip opinion, it is important to include the full case name, date, and circuit court. Remember, it is crucial to include the docket number in the citation, as the case has yet to be given a full page and volume number citation. The *Bluebook* (Rule 10.8.1) and the *AWLD* (Rule 12.2) address the citation of federal slip opinions. When you find the case you need, it would be cited as the following.

> ### Paolino v. JF Realty, LLC, No. 12-2031 (1st Cir. Mar. 13, 2013)

However, be certain you know how the particular circuit court in which you will be working cites federal slip opinions, as the format may be different in the federal courts of each state. Again, this is a basic format. Your instructor will review the proper citation formats for slip opinions in your jurisdiction.

Advance Sheets

advance sheets
The collection of numerous slip opinions that are arranged in a softbound booklet.

After multiple slip opinions are released in any given jurisdiction, they are gathered and compiled into **advance sheets**, which are distributed in a softbound booklet. The importance of this stage is that publishers review the slip opinion in detail and correct any typographical errors. The advance sheets include the same content as the slip opinion with one exception—the publisher includes the headnotes that summarize the points of law addressed in the opinion, as well as many other editorial enhancements, which is why they are more desirable to the researcher than the slip opinion version (See Figure 6-1). The advance sheets are placed directly within the set of hardbound reporters and act as a "placeholder" for the soon to be published hardbound volume. If you wanted to cite any opinion found in an advance sheet, the page numbers would be consistent with the hardbound reporter, which will later replace the advance sheet.

Advance sheets are typically published a week or so after a set of slip opinions are issued and are published about 50 times each year. After the publisher mails the advance sheets to law libraries and law firms, a designated librarian or paralegal in the library or firm will shelve the advance sheets in between the specific volumes of the hardbound reporters. In the event there *is* an error found between the slip opinion and advance sheets, it is the advance sheet that should be followed.

Citation of a case found in an advance sheet is the same as locating it in a case reporter, which you will see below.

Case Law Reporters

reporters
A collection of numerous advance sheets that are arranged in a hardbound print set.

Once enough advance sheets have been collected to fill an entire volume, the appellate opinions are compiled into a hardbound set. These **reporters**, published in chronological order, are the *final* publication for appellate opinions. Each set of reporters are subdivided into different series that cover different time periods.

An "official" publication is any printing by a *governmental* entity. Any opinions published by the federal or a state government is considered an official publication, or report, and is designated by the name CASE REPORT. On the other hand, any publication printed by a *commercial* publisher, such as *Thomson Reuters/West*, is considered an "unofficial" reporter and is designated by the name CASE REPORTER. An official version is no more superior then an unofficial version, as they contain the same cases. In the event there is a discrepancy or error in an opinion, it is the official version that should be followed.

■ RESEARCHING CASE LAW BY JURISDICTION

Earlier in this text, you were first introduced to the concept of jurisdiction. Jurisdiction can mean that (1) a court needs both subject matter and personal jurisdiction in order to hear a case, and (2) the jurisdiction of the state and federal trial and appellate courts are limited to either general, limited, or special jurisdiction. For example, trial courts are considered courts of general jurisdiction because they only have to assert jurisdiction over a party, such as a defendant in a criminal case or a civil party in a contract dispute. The courts of limited jurisdiction derive their power from an issuing authority such as the United States Constitution, and can only perform the functions given to it, such as appellate review. Lastly, courts of special jurisdiction can hear only certain types of cases such as juvenile court or bankruptcy court.

> **LEARNING OBJECTIVE 5**
> Understand the difference between mandatory and persuasive law.

Jurisdiction also dictates from *where* you can research the law. Let's begin with a simple concept. Suppose you were given a research assignment concerning state law. Appellate courts render decisions every day in all 50 states. That's an immense amount of case law research! So imagine the task before you if jurisdiction was not relevant and you had to search the law in every state for authority to answer or address your legal issue. Well, don't worry—you don't have to.

A particular authority is considered **mandatory/binding law** if it is the "controlling law" within that particular jurisdiction. In other words, it is the authority you are obligated to follow. For example, when the intermediate appellate court of Mississippi renders a case decision, it is only mandatory authority upon every trial court in Mississippi. Appellate decisions generated by a particular state court are only considered mandatory authority for *that particular state*. On the other hand, an authority is considered **persuasive law** when it is authority "outside" your particular jurisdiction. Using the example above, if you worked as a paralegal in Mississippi, you could use any of those appellate decisions in your research, but you could not research any appellate decisions from Texas or Georgia, as they are not within your jurisdiction.

mandatory/binding law
Legal authority that is the controlling law within a particular jurisdiction.

persuasive law
Legal authority outside a particular jurisdiction that a court may consider, but can only be used as precedent if adopted by a court.

The same concept holds true for the federal system. Remember the "circuit court system" you learned earlier? If you were conducting research for federal case law, you would not review the federal appellate decisions from every circuit court in the country. Rather, you are restricted to researching the cases *within your particular federal circuit*. This includes the federal appellate decisions from *each state* included in that circuit. For example, if you are a paralegal conducting research for a federal issue in New York, you can also search the appellate decisions from Connecticut and Vermont, which are all included in the Second Circuit. Determining jurisdiction for the US Supreme Court is easy, as every state and federal court can research any opinion from this Court. This is true because each decision establishes precedent for every lower court in the country.

You will understand the differences between mandatory and persuasive authority more as you begin to research the sources of law from your jurisdiction.

Be sure to read and understand the information found in Figure 6-9 to remember the differences between mandatory and persuasive authority.

The following examples should help you understand case law jurisdiction. In order to answer the following questions, you need to have a good understanding of the circuit and state court geographic boundaries of the state and federal courts.

QUESTION: If you were a paralegal working in the state of Texas, what three types of federal and state authority would you be limited to in conducting your research?

ANSWER: Any and all appellate Texas state law, the federal decisions of the 5th Circuit, and the US Supreme Court.

In contrast, persuasive authority is authority **not** contained within your jurisdiction and **cannot** be used as relevant authority. For example, if you were a paralegal in New Jersey and were researching state law, you could **not** research authority from the Pennsylvania courts—only New Jersey.

QUESTION: When *would* it be proper for that New Jersey paralegal to search for Pennsylvania law?

ANSWER: If the paralegal was researching federal law since both New Jersey and Pennsylvania are in the same 3rd Circuit.

Figure 6-9 How to Distinguish Mandatory from Persuasive Case Law Authority

Type of Authority	Mandatory (Binding)	Persuasive
United States Supreme Court Case Law	Case law from the US Supreme Court is mandatory authority and binding on every state and federal jurisdiction in the country on matters of federal law.	Never persuasive.
Federal Appellate Case Law	Case law from the federal appellate courts is mandatory authority on federal district courts and all lower courts **within each circuit**. (*research can be conducted from ANY of the states included in that particular circuit*)	Case law is considered persuasive authority only **outside** your particular circuit.
State Appellate Case Law (highest state court level)	Case law from a state supreme (highest) court on that state's laws is mandatory for all lower courts in *that particular state* (*these decisions are also binding on federal courts that interpret state law under diversity jurisdiction*)	Case law is considered persuasive authority only **outside** your state.
State Appellate Case Law (intermediate state court level)	Case law from a state intermediate appellate court is mandatory for all lower trial courts in *that particular state*.	Case law is considered persuasive authority only **outside** your state.
Federal district courts and State trial court opinions	Trial court opinions should not be used as precedent or utilized in legal research, as they have not been reviewed by an appellate court and are mostly unpublished cases.	

One more . . .

QUESTION: Suppose you are a paralegal working in Ohio and you are asked to research all *state* law to answer a legal issue? From what courts could you conduct your research?

ANSWER: Any case law from the Ohio state appellate courts (the Ohio Supreme Court and the Ohio Court of Appeals), and the US Supreme Court (if applicable).

Once you know your particular jurisdiction you will know exactly from where you can conduct your research. Your instructor will review your particular state and federal jurisdiction. Be certain to look at Appendix B. There you will find a helpful feature entitled "My Law" where you can fill in your state and federal jurisdictional and citation requirements for all the sources of law. Once you complete the information in the chart, you have a handy guide in class, as well as during your legal employment.

■ CASE BRIEFING

Now that you know and understand the various parts of a court opinion, you will now learn how to read and brief an opinion. Similar to researching any other source of law, a good researcher needs to effectively read, interpret, and analyze a case opinion in order to detemine if the case can be utilized in reserch. The basic idea of case briefing is that you are summarizing a 5- to 15-page case opinion into a 1- to 2-page brief. A **case brief** saves you time later if you need to refer to the case. Rather than reading the 15-page opinion again, which you may have forgotten, you can quickly scan the case brief to determine all the crucial points of law used in the decision, the issues raised, and the important facts.

Many attorneys assign case briefing to their paralegals. Some law firms/offices with an exclusive practice, such as in workers' compensation or real estate law, will have their paralegal brief all the new case opinions concerning the new and upcoming issues in that area of law and file it in a binder, folder, or firm database. Thereafter, any attorney or paralegal in the firm/office can quickly and easily access the new case decisions and keep abreast in that area of law in order to serve their clients to the best of their ability without having to read through countless opinions. Briefing cases is also helpful in assisting your supervising attorney construct an argument to assert or defend a motion before or during trial, or on appeal. Lastly, briefing is also necessary for you to effectivley draft a quality legal memorandum, which you will learn later. You can only draft a quality memorandum by including the correct case opinions into the analysis.

Briefing cases is not the same as just "reading" a case. It is also unlike reading a newspaper, magazine article, or even a book. Rather, learning how to read will take time, but its rewards will pay off during your entire legal career. As you read the opinion, it may include many legal terms/phrases/words with which you are unfamilar. For this reason, it is best to always have a legal dictionary with you while reading an opinion. Never guess at any legal term/phrase/word, as it may prove crucial to understanding the case. The more cases you brief, the easier it will become. By learning this new skill, you will raise the bar of your legal skills considerably, so let's get started.

LEARNING OBJECTIVE 6
Demonstrate how to brief a case.

case brief
A condensed and concise outlined summary of a court opinion.

The Components of a Case Brief

The brief condenses and summarizes key information in the opinion in a clear and condensed format.

A quality brief will include the following components: *case name, procedural history, issue, holding, facts, analysis/reasoning,* and *disposition*.

As with any topic in legal research and writing, it is best to demonstrate the steps of case briefing with an example. Before you begin, remember the various components of a case opinion that you learned earlier in this chapter. If not, please refer back to Figure 6-1 to refresh your memory.

In Figure 6-10, you see the sample case of *Commonwealth v. Williams*. Remember, any time you see *Commonwealth, State,* or *People,* in a case heading, you know it is a criminal case. This case is very easy and straightforward to understand—a great case for a beginner to learn the art of case briefing. However, be mindful that this case was taken from the print sources. If you located this case using *WestlawNext* or *Lexis Advance,* the format and information would be presented in a slightly different format. You will see an example of a case found on both online systems in the next chapter. Here, just learn to identify the important facts, issues, reasoning, and holding—all of which are universal in print and online format.

Figure 6-10 *Commonwealth v. Williams*

when Father offered to release the escrowed funds in return for a reduction in his past and future support payments. She could take the escrowed funds and receive something, or refuse to take the escrowed funds and receive nothing. The terms of the agreement were unreasonably favorable to Father who stood to gain a substantial reduction in his obligation to Mother in return for which Mother received nothing more than that to which she had been previously entitled. *See Miesen, supra.* Because Mother had no meaningful choice and the agreement was unreasonably favorable to Father, the agreement is unenforceable as unconscionable. *See Wagner, supra.*

[15] ¶ 21 Further, at the time of the alleged agreement Mother did not have an immediate alternative remedy. Father had already been ordered to pay support in a specific amount, which he consistently refused to pay. The only avenue left to

marital property, [Mother] was (at least in part) paying [Father's] support obligation for him. Thus at the time of equitable distribution, this matter must be addressed and [Fa-

forceable on grounds of public policy, lack of adequate consideration, and contractual injustice. Accordingly, we affirm the court's decision to deny Father's petition for specific performance.

¶ 23 Order affirmed.

○W○E○S○T KEY NUMBER SYSTEM

COMMONWEALTH of Pennsylvania, Appellee,

v.

Henry WILLIAMS, Appellant.

Superior Court of Pennsylvania.

Submitted Feb. 12, 2002.

Filed Sept. 20, 2002.

Defendant was convicted after a bench trial in the Court of Common Pleas,

ther] may be charged with receipt of [some of] these funds even though [Mother] actually received them." *See* Trial Court Opinion at 2 n. 1.

Source: Reprinted with permission of Thomson Reuters, West's Atlantic 2nd Reporter Volume 808, Page 213.

Figure 6-10 Continued

Philadelphia County, Criminal Division, No. 0006-0790 1/1, Fitzgerald, J., of possession with intent to deliver a controlled substance, possession of a controlled substance, and possession of an instrument of crime. Defendant appealed. The Superior Court, No. 1290 EDA 2001, Beck, J., held that use of walkie-talkie to facilitate drug sales did not constitute possession of an instrument of crime.

Affirmed in part and reversed in part.

1. Criminal Law ⬤⟿878(4)

Evidence is not insufficient to prove a crime merely because the verdict is inconsistent with a verdict on another charge.

2. Controlled Substances ⬤⟿42

Defendant's use of a walkie-talkie to direct various persons into a nearby house to facilitate drug sales did not transform the walkie-talkie into an instrument of crime for purposes of possession of an instrument of crime statute; statute was not intended to include as instruments of crime equipment not used in the crime itself, but used only to facilitate the crime. 18 Pa.C.S.A. § 907(d)(1, 2).

Troy H. Wilson, Philadelphia, for appellant.

Catherine L. Marshall, Asst. Dist. Atty., Philadelphia, for Com., appellee.

Before FORD ELLIOTT, JOYCE and BECK, JJ.

OPINION BY BECK, J.

¶ 1 Appellant Henry Williams, convicted in a bench trial of possession with intent to deliver a controlled substance, possession of a controlled substance, and possession of an instrument of crime (PIC), brings this timely direct appeal from judgment of sentence. On April 12, 2001, the court of common pleas, Philadelphia County, sentenced appellant to a mandatory term of imprisonment of one to two years. He now raises six issues relating to the sufficiency and weight of the evidence and trial court error. After review of the record and the briefs of the parties, we affirm judgment of sentence on the basis of the excellent and thorough opinion of the Honorable James J. Fitzgerald, III for all issues except one.

¶ 2 For the reasons that follow, we find that the trial court erred in convicting appellant for PIC. We conclude that the Commonwealth failed to prove that the walkie-talkie, or hand-held radio, used by appellant was an instrument of crime as defined in the statute.

¶ 3 The statute at issue, 18 Pa.C.S.A. § 907(d)(1), (2), Possessing instruments of crime, defines an instrument of crime as (1) "anything specially made or specially adapted for criminal use" or (2) "anything used for criminal purposes and possessed by the actor under circumstances not manifestly appropriate for lawful uses it may have."

¶ 4 Appellant was using a walkie-talkie during the time he was under surveillance. He stood on the street, spoke into the walkie-talkie, and directed various persons into a nearby house on Turner Street in Philadelphia. A confidential informant effected a drug sale after he was directed into the house by appellant, who was using the walkie-talkie.

[1] ¶ 5 The question is whether there was sufficient evidence to convict appellant of PIC based on his use of the walkie-talkie. Appellant argues that the Commonwealth failed to prove *mens rea* in the use of the walkie-talkie and that the walkie-talkie was not specially adapted to a

Figure 6-10 Continued

COM. v. SMITH   Pa. **215**
Cite as 808 A.2d 215 (Pa.Super. 2002)

criminal use. He also asserts that since he was acquitted of the underlying conspiracy charge, he was not using the walkie-talkie for criminal purposes.[1]

¶6 On the other hand the Commonwealth argues that appellant's criminal intent may be inferred from circumstances surrounding possession. *Commonwealth v. Andrews,* 564 Pa. 321, 768 A.2d 309 (2001). The Commonwealth's main argument that the walkie-talkie is an instrument of crime relies on *Commonwealth v. Vida,* 715 A.2d 1180 (Pa.Super.1998); *appeal denied,* 558 Pa. 608, 736 A.2d 604 (1999). In that case we held that a paint stick is an instrument of crime when wielded by a graffiti artist to commit criminal mischief.

¶7 The concurrence in *Vida* expressed reservations about the Superior Court's broad reading of the statute. The concurrence worried that the PIC statute in the future might be interpreted to include a telephone used to harass someone, or a megaphone used to incite a riot, as instruments of crime.

[2] ¶8 While recognizing that appellant's walkie-talkie, under the circumstances, facilitated the illicit drug sales, we distinguish its use from the paint stick in *Vida,* where the stick itself was the instrument whereby the criminal mischief (graffiti) was committed. Instantly, the walkie-talkie was used during the course of the drug sales, as a truck might be used in the course of a theft to transport stolen property, to help carry out the criminal offense. We hold that the mere use of an item to facilitate a crime does not transform the item into an instrument of crime for purposes of the PIC statute.

¶9 While appellant's use of the walkie-talkie facilitated the narcotics sales, we conclude that the statute was not intended to include as instruments of crime equipment not used in the crime itself, but used only to facilitate the crime.

¶10 Judgment of sentence affirmed in part on the basis of the trial court's opinion, and reversed in part as to the crime of PIC. Matter remanded for re-sentencing in light of our decision on the PIC charge. Jurisdiction relinquished.

COMMONWEALTH of Pennsylvania, Appellee,

v.

Rene C. SMITH, Appellant.

Superior Court of Pennsylvania.

Argued June 19, 2002.
Filed Sept. 23, 2002.

Defendant was convicted after jury trial in the Court of Common Pleas, McKean County, Criminal Division, No. 99 Criminal 1997, Cleland, J., of homicide by vehicle while driving under the influence, homicide by vehicle, two counts driving under the influence of alcohol, driving on roadways laned for traffic, and careless driving. Defendant appealed. The Superior

---

1. Appellant incorrectly asserts that he was charged only with possessing a weapon. He was in fact charged with both PIC, § 907(a), *and* possessing a firearm or other weapon, § 907(b). Only § 907(a) is at issue here. We agree with the Commonwealth that it is irrel-

evant that appellant was acquitted of conspiracy, since evidence is not insufficient to prove a crime merely because the verdict is inconsistent with a verdict on another charge. *Commonwealth v. Coon,* 695 A.2d 794 (Pa.Super.1997).

Before you learn the different parts of a case brief using the opinion found in Figure 6-10, please read the opinion once to yourself to get an idea of the facts, issues, and content presented in the case. Thereafter, please follow the steps that follow as you learn how to create each part of the brief.

1. **Case Name** – The case heading basically includes the **parties** involved in the case and the **citation**. This information is included so that readers can locate the opinion themselves by the case name and/or the citation. In this example, the full citation for *Commonwealth v. Williams* is 2002 PA Super 299; 808 A.2d 213. You will learn about case citation in the next chapter. It is important to include the case citation in the brief for identification purposes. There is no need to include the names of counsel or the judge who wrote the opinion in the brief.

2. **Procedural History** – The procedural history is important as it lets the reader know how the case arrived at the current court. It is important to note if the case was previously appealed and the disposition of that appeal. This information, as shown in Figure 6-11, can be summed up in a few sentences.

3. **Issue(s)** – This brings us to the next important, and probably most important, component of a case brief—the issue to be answered. Simply put, the issue is the *question* that the court needs to answer. In other words, "Why is the case before them?" The question may be easy to determine, or you may have the read the entire opinion to determine it. For example, in this case, as you can see in Paragraph #6 of the opinion, the court states, "*The question is whether there was sufficient evidence to convict appellant of PIC based on his use of the walkie-talkie.*" It is also good practice to add relevant facts to the issue as well. For instance, as you can see in Figure 6-12, the issue could be stated as, "*The issue is whether appellant can be convicted of possessing an instrument of crime for his use of a walkie-talkie to effectuate a drug deal?*" The more facts you incorporate, the easy it will be to (1) answer the issue, and (2) easier for the reader to understand the case. Suppose you stated "*Whether the appellant could be convicted of PIC.*" That is not a clear issue. You will learn to "develop" your issues over time. Keep in mind that the court may have multiple issues to resolve. If so, you would list each issue and answer each separately.

issue
The most important component of a case brief. It is the question that the court must address and answer.

Figure 6-11 *Commonwealth v. Williams* – Caption and Procedural History

---

Case Brief

CRIMINAL LAW - Possession of an Instrument of Crime (PIC)

Commonwealth v. Williams
2002 PA Super 299; 808 A.2d 213 (Pa. Super. 2002)

Procedural History:
Following his conviction of multiple drug offenses, Appellant sought to appeal those convictions and sentence in the Court of Common Pleas criminal trial court in Philadelphia County. This is the defendant's first appeal before the Pennsylvania Superior Court.

Figure 6-12 *Commonwealth v. Williams* – Issues

Case Brief

CRIMINAL LAW - Possession of an Instrument of Crime (PIC)
Commonwealth v. Williams
2002 PA Super 299; 808 A.2d 213 (Pa. Super. 2002)

Procedural History:
Following his conviction of multiple drug offenses, Appellant sought to appeal those convictions and sentence in the Court of Common Pleas criminal trial court in Philadelphia County. This is the defendant's first appeal before the Pennsylvania Superior Court.

Issue:
Whether Appellant can be convicted of possessing an instrument of crime for his use of a walkie-talkie to effectuate a drug deal?

---

facts
A true piece of information that is indisputable.

legally significant facts
The facts that can determine the outcome of a case by satisfying the specific elements of a civil or criminal cause of action.

analysis/reasoning
Using a combination of the law and facts of the case, the court answers the issue presented and explains the reasoning for its decision.

4. **Holding** – The holding is quite short, and briefly answers the question (issue) presented, although it should not include a mere yes/no answer. The holding will "mirror" the issue presented for clarification for the reader with a few facts for clarification, but will not include any legal authority as you can see in Figure 6-13.

5. **Facts** – There is a difference between "**facts**" and "**legally significant facts**." Consider this example: If an attorney files suit against a supermarket on behalf of his client following a slip, fall, and injury, the client would need to prove that the store owner knew of a spill on the floor caused by an employee, but did not clean it up. As a result, the client was injured. The owner's omission to act would result in the client sustaining an injury. Therefore, when the attorney questions his client, the following facts are revealed: (1) she went to the market to purchase soda, chips, and chicken for a barbeque, (2) the weather outside that day was sunny, 84 degrees, and the conditions were clear, (3) as she turned down aisle #4 she slipped on some liquid, and (4) she fell backwards onto her lower back, injuring it severely. Now, do *all* these facts contribute to establishing a case for negligence? No. The only facts of any *legal significance* are #3 and #4. It is completely irrelevant *why* she went to the market. Also, it does not matter what the weather conditions were *outside* the market that day. In addition, writing out the facts in chronological order makes it easier for the reader to understand the "story" you are presenting. Remember that the legally significant facts directly relate to the question at hand. Ask yourself, do these facts need to be known in order to answer the issue presented? Look at the facts section in Figure 6-14 to see how only the legally significant facts are used.

6. **Analysis/Reasoning** – Up to this point in the brief, if readers wanted to quickly ascertain what the case is about, they could easily and quickly read the case name, procedural history, issue, holding, and possibly the facts to understand the case. If readers wanted/needed a deeper analysis of how/why the court ruled the way it did, then they could read the "analysis/reasoning" section of the brief. The rule of law is not only important because it *answers*

Figure 6-13 *Commonwealth v. Williams* – Holding

Case Brief

CRIMINAL LAW - Possession of an Instrument of Crime (PIC)
Commonwealth v. Williams
2002 PA Super 299; 808 A.2d 213 (Pa. Super. 2002)

Procedural History:
Following his conviction of multiple drug offenses, Appellant sought to appeal those convictions and sentence in the Court of Common Pleas criminal trial court in Philadelphia County. This is the defendant's first appeal before the Pennsylvania Superior Court.

Issue:
Can a defendant be convicted of possessing an instrument of crime for the mere possession and use of a walkie-talkie to effectuate a drug deal?

Holding:
No, a defendant cannot be convicted of possessing an instrument of crime for the mere possession and use of a walkie-talkie to effectuate a drug deal as he used it to direct individuals into a nearby drug house.

Figure 6-14 *Commonwealth v. Williams* – Facts

Case Brief

CRIMINAL LAW - Possession of an Instrument of Crime (PIC)
Commonwealth v. Williams
2002 PA Super 299; 808 A.2d 213 (Pa. Super. 2002)

Procedural History:
Following his conviction of multiple drug offenses, Appellant sought to appeal those convictions and sentence in the Court of Common Pleas criminal trial court in Philadelphia County. This is the defendant's first appeal before the Pennsylvania Superior Court.

Issue:
Can a defendant be convicted of possessing an instrument of crime for his use of a walkie-talkie to effectuate a drug deal?

Holding:
No, a defendant cannot be convicted of possessing an instrument of crime for the mere possession and use of a walkie-talkie to effectuate a drug deal as he stood on a corner directing persons into a suspected drug house after utilizing the walkie-talkie.

Facts:
Appellant communicated into a walkie-talkie while he stood on a street corner near a suspected drug house which was under surveillance by the police. After talking into the walkie-talkie, Appellant would direct certain persons into the suspected drug house. A confidential informant working for the police entered into a drug sale after he was directed into the house by Appellant after communicating into the walkie-talkie.

the issue presented, but also because it explains *why* they ruled as they did, as you can see in Figure 6-15.

The court cannot create its own logic in resolving the issue; rather, it must base its decision in *legal precedent*. The court can also reference what is referred to as the *black letter law*, meaning the court cites the actual language found in any primary source of law such as a statute or regulation. In this example, the court looked to the criminal statutes and past cases to determine if the elements of "possession of an instrument of crime" could be applied to the use of a walkie-talkie used in a drug deal.

In reading the opinion, do you see how the court combines the rule of law with the facts of the case? This is how the court performs its analysis/reasoning. When in doubt as to how to craft the analysis section, remember the formula.

THE FORMULA FOR A CASE BRIEF ANALYSIS

LAW + FACTS = ANALYSIS

7. **Disposition** – The disposition, while brief, is important as it informs the reader of the *subsequent history* of the case. The disposition is the "order" of the appellate court. Meaning that either the case was affirmed, or reversed/remanded back to the lower court, as you can see in Figure 6-16.

In Figure 6-17 you have a complete case brief. As you can see, you have taken a full three-page opinion and condensed and summarized its most important elements into a single page. Now, if you were to refer to this case at a later date, perhaps in drafting your legal research memo, you would not have to read the case in its entirety; only the case brief. As you will improve your reading ability and speed over time, you will not likely follow this format. However, get into the habit of learning and understanding the basics of case briefing before adopting your own particular style.

Try to brief another case for good practice. Read the following case in Figure 6-18 below. Thereafter, rather than writing out the brief, *discuss* as a class

Figure 6-15 *Commonwealth v. Williams* – Analysis/Reasoning

Analysis/Reasoning:
In Pennsylvania, the crime of "possessing an instrument of crime" is established when the defendant is in possession of (1) anything specially made or adapted for criminal use, or (2) anything used for criminal purposes and possessed by the actor under circumstances not appropriate for its lawful use. **18 Pa.C.S.A.§907**. Here, the court reviewed the case of **Commonwealth v. Vida, 715 A.2d 1180 (Pa. Super. 1998)**, in which they held that a paint-stick can be considered an instrument of crime when wielded by a graffiti artist to commit criminal mischief. However, the court found that the use of the walkie-talkie to effectuate a drug deal is <u>not</u> similar to the holding in *Vida*, and therefore does not fall under section (1) of the statute. Under section (2) of the statute, the court reasoned that if someone can be convicted of using a walkie-talkie as an instrument of crime, then someone could be convicted of PIC for using a telephone to harass someone, or through the use of someone using a megaphone to incite a riot. The court does not seem to want to travel down that "slippery slope." The court held that the use of a walkie-talkie in this situation is similar to that of a criminal merely using a truck to transport stolen property, as the truck itself would not be considered an instrument of crime. Although the walkie-talkie was used *during* the crime, it was not *itself* an instrument of crime.

Some case briefs do not include the citation to the authority used by the court, and only "summarizes" the rule of law used. This is unwise because the rule is necessary so that the reader can see what specific wording in the law supported the court's decision. In addition, the reader has no citation reference to validate or locate the law themselves if needed.

Figure 6-16 *Commonwealth v. Williams* – Disposition

Analysis/Reasoning:

In Pennsylvania, the crime of "possessing an instrument of crime" is established when the defendant is in possession of (1) anything specially made or adapted for criminal use, or (2) anything used for criminal purposes and possessed by the actor under circumstances not appropriate for its lawful use. *18 Pa.C.S.A. §907*. Here, the court reviewed the case of *Commonwealth v. Vida*, 715 A.2d 1180 (Pa. Super. 1998), in which they held that a paint-stick *can* be considered an instrument of crime when wielded by a graffiti artist to commit criminal mischief. However, the court found that the use of the walkie-talkie to effectuate a drug deal is *not* similar to the holding in *Vida*, and therefore does not fall under section (1) of the statute. Under section (2) of the statute, the court reasoned that if someone can be convicted of using a walkie-talkie as an instrument of crime, then someone could be convicted of PIC for using a telephone to harass someone, or through the use of someone using a megaphone to incite a riot. The court does not seem to want to travel down that "slippery slope." The court held that the use of a walkie-talkie in this situation is similar to that of a criminal merely using a truck to transport stolen property, as the truck itself would not be considered an instrument of crime. Although the walkie-talkie was used *during* the crime, it was not *itself* an instrument of crime.

Disposition:

The judgment of sentence was *afffirmed* as to Appellant's drug convictions, but *reversed* as to his conviction for PIC. The matter was further *remanded* back to the lower trial court for Appellant's re-sentencing.

PRACTICE TIP

Once you become proficient and very comfortable briefing cases, there is an alternative method to writing them out called "book briefing." After reading the full opinion, go back and assign highlighter colors to the most important sections of the brief. For example, GREEN for the legally significant facts, BLUE for the issue(s), YELLOW for the analysis and reasoning of the court, and ORANGE for the disposition. In addition, you can make various notes in the margins in shorthand. Whatever colors or shorthand symbols you use, make sure you use them every time to maintain consistency and familiarity.

the different components of the case brief so that everyone learns how to construct each part of the brief together.

The following are some tips to use in your case briefing.

■ Construct short, clear and concise sentences. Remember to use proper punctuation. However, if your instructor/supervising attorney permits, use bullets for the procedural history, facts, and rule of law.

■ Do not copy the opinion word-for-word, or cut-and-paste large chunks of information. Case briefing forces you to read and digest large amounts of information to be able to condense and summarize the information. Furthermore, do not quote large amounts of text extracted from the opinion.

■ Transfer the information in the opinion and do not add any opinions, personal feelings, or commentary in the brief.

■ Do not use or rely on "commercial briefs" which are written by publishing companies and are sometimes used by law students. First, they are not always accurate or correct, and second, the only way you will understand a case opinion is to read one in its entirety yourself.

Until you are more comfortable reading and briefing cases on your own, brief the case together in class with your fellow students discussing each part of the case brief. This will make certain that everyone is on the same page. Your instructor may also provide you with an opinion to brief together in class. Can you answer the following questions to detemine if you are properly extracting the correct information from the opinion? In briefing a case opinion, be sure to answer the following:

1. Briefly, what is the procedural history of the case?
2. Briefly, what were the legally significant facts of the case?
3. What was the issue(s) in the case? Explain.
4. What rule(s) of law did the appellate court use to arrive at its decision to address and answer the issue? Explain.
5. What was the disposition?

Always remember the basic components of a brief and extract the correct information. Remember also to always have a legal dictionary with you for those unfamilar terms.

Figure 6-17 *Commonwealth v. Williams* – Full Case Brief

CRIMINAL LAW – Possession of an Instrument of Crime (PIC)

Commonwealth v. Williams
2002 PA Super 299; 808 A.2d 213 (Pa. Super. 2002)

Procedural History:
Following his conviction of multiple drug offenses, Appellant sought to appeal those convictions and sentence in the Court of Common Pleas criminal trial court in Philadelphia County. This is the defendant's first appeal before the Pennsylvania Superior Court.

Issue:
Can a defendant be convicted of possessing an instrument of crime for his use of a walkie-talkie to effectuate a drug deal?

Holding:
No, a defendant cannot be convicted of possessing an instrument of crime for the mere possession and use of a walkie-talkie to effectuate a drug deal as he stood on a corner directing persons into a suspected drug house after utilizing the walkie-talkie.

Facts:
Appellant communicated into a walkie-talkie while he stood on a street corner near a suspected drug house which was under surveillance by the police. After communicating into the walkie-talkie, Appellant would direct certain persons into the suspected drug house. A confidential informant working for the police entered into a drug sale after he was directed into the house by Appellant after communicating into the walkie-talkie.

Analysis/Reasoning:
In Pennsylvania, the crime of "possessing an instrument of crime" is established when the defendant is in possession of (1) anything specially made or adapted for criminal use, or (2) anything used for criminal purposes and possessed by the actor under circumstances not appropriate for its lawful use. *18 Pa.C.S.A. §907*. Here, the court reviewed the case of *Commonwealth v. Vida*, 715 A.2d 1180 (Pa. Super. 1998), in which they held that a paint-stick *can* be considered an instrument of crime when wielded by a graffiti artist to commit criminal mischief. However, the court found that the use of the walkie-talkie to effectuate a drug deal is *not* similar to the holding in *Vida*, and therefore does not fall under section (1) of the statute. Under section (2) of the statute, the court reasoned that if someone can be convicted of using a walkie-talkie as an instrument of crime, then someone could be convicted of PIC for using a telephone to harass someone, or through the use of someone using a megaphone to incite a riot. The court does not seem to want to travel down that "slippery slope." The court held that the use of a walkie-talkie in this situation is similar to that of a criminal merely using a truck to transport stolen property, as the truck itself would not be considered an instrument of crime. Although the walkie-talkie was used *during* the crime, it was not *itself* an instrument of crime.

Disposition:
The judgment of sentence was ***afffirmed*** as to Appellant's drug convictions, but ***reversed*** as to his conviction for PIC. The matter was further ***remanded*** to the trial court for resentencing.

Figure 6-18 *Schnitzer v. Unemployment Compensation Board of Review*

deadline in Section 8(c), with or without the omitted phrase. At the very least, the difference between subsections (a) and (c) should have prompted further inquiry. The official text of the Assessment Law, *i.e.,* the pamphlet law, might have been consulted. Tenet's counsel might have inquired with the Board whether the Bucks County Commissioners had exercised their authority under Section 8(a)(2) of the Assessment Law. He did neither. This failure cannot be termed, as Tenet argues, a non-negligent omission and, thus, the extraordinary circumstances needed for a *nunc pro tunc* appeal cannot be found here.[15]

This is a close case. Had Section 8 of the Assessment Law been incorrect in its entirety in *Purdon's,* the result might have been different. It is routine for lawyers in Pennsylvania to rely upon *Purdon's,* as opposed to the pamphlet laws, but there are times this routine must be broken. *Purdon's* is not legal evidence of the official version of Pennsylvania's pamphlet laws.

For these reasons, we affirm the trial court.

ORDER

AND NOW, this 10th day of August, 2005, the order the Court of Common Pleas of Bucks County dated June 8, 2004, in the above-captioned matter is hereby affirmed.

---

15. Tenet argues that fairness requires its appeal to proceed because it was only three weeks late and was filed as soon as Tenet learned of the error. As held in *Bass* and *Cook,* prompt action by a litigant or his lawyer is needed in order for an appeal *nunc pro*

Allan B. **SCHNITZER,** Petitioner

v.

UNEMPLOYMENT COMPENSATION BOARD OF REVIEW, Respondent.

Commonwealth Court of Pennsylvania.

Submitted on Briefs July 1, 2005.

Decided Aug. 10, 2005.

Background: Unemployment compensation claimant petitioned for review of an order of the Unemployment Compensation Board of Review which reversed the determination of a referee and determined that claimant was ineligible for benefits.

Holding: The Commonwealth Court, No. 559 C.D. 2005, Flaherty, Senior Judge, held that claimant's conduct in lying to employer about having loaded gun at work constituted act of wanton or willful disregard of employer's interest, and disregard of behavior which employer had right to expect.

Affirmed.

1. Unemployment Compensation ⚖472, 486, 491(1)

In reviewing unemployment compensation case, Commonwealth Court's review is limited to determining whether constitutional rights were violated, errors of law were committed, or essential findings of fact are supported by substantial evidence.

2. Unemployment Compensation ⚖68

Fact that employer did not have policy that prohibited bringing guns to work,

tunc to be allowed, and we agree that Tenet's action was prompt. However, it must first be found that the failure to file untimely was non-negligent; that condition precedent was not found here.

Figure 6-18 Continued

SCHNITZER v. UNEMPLOYMENT COMP. BD. OF REV.   Pa.   **729**
Cite as 880 A.2d 728 (Pa.Cmwlth. 2005)

and lying about having guns at work, did not preclude finding that unemployment compensation claimant's conduct in lying to employer about having loaded gun at work constituted act of wanton or willful disregard of employer's interest, and disregard of behavior which employer had right to expect, as would disqualify claimant from receiving unemployment compensation benefits. 43 P.S. § 802(e).

3. Unemployment Compensation ⊙83

Unemployment compensation claimant's conduct in lying to employer about having loaded gun at work constituted act of wanton or willful disregard of employer's interest, and disregard of behavior which employer had right to expect, and thus claimant was not eligible for unemployment compensation benefits. 43 P.S. § 802(e).

4. Unemployment Compensation ⊙286

In unemployment compensation case, Unemployment Compensation Board of Review is ultimate fact finder, and is empowered to resolve conflicts in evidence and to determine credibility of witnesses.

Allan B. Schnitzer, petitioner, pro se.

No appearance entered on behalf of respondent.

BEFORE: McGINLEY, J., LEAVITT, J., and FLAHERTY, Senior Judge.

OPINION BY Senior Judge FLAHERTY.

Allan B. Schnitzer (Claimant) petitions for review from an order of the Unemployment Compensation Board of Review

(Board) which reversed the determination of a referee and determined that Claimant was ineligible for benefits due to his willful misconduct.[1] We affirm.

Claimant worked for Cardiac Telecom (Employer) from March 14, 1998 until his discharge on October 19, 2004. Claimant's request for unemployment benefits was denied and Claimant appealed the determination. After a hearing, at which Claimant and Employer's representative testified along with a co-worker, the referee concluded that Claimant did not engage in willful misconduct and granted his petition for benefits.

Employer appealed to the Board which made the following relevant findings of fact:

2. The claimant is licensed to carry a gun and, on a number of occasions, has reported to work with the concealed weapon, a Glock 9 millimeter.

3. The claimant works at a facility that monitors the hearts of patients all over the country in a central processing lab.

4. Shortly prior to the claimant's discharge, a co-worker complained about the claimant having a gun with him at the work place.

5. The employer questioned the claimant regarding whether he had ever brought a gun to work. In response, the claimant stated that he had only brought unloaded weapons in order to show them to co-workers who had asked to see them. The claimant admitted that, on one occasion, he unintentionally wore a weapon to work and, upon realizing this, returned it to his car.

1. Section 402(e) of the Unemployment Compensation Law (Law), Act of December 5, 1936, Second Ex.Sess., (1937), *as amended*, 43 P.S. § 802(e) provides that an employee

shall be ineligible for benefits for any week in which the employee's unemployment is due to discharge from work due to his willful misconduct.

Figure 6-18 Continued

6. Contrary to what he told the employer during the investigation, the claimant did bring loaded guns to work.

7. The employer discharged the claimant for bringing a gun to work and for lying during the investigation about not bringing loaded weapons into the work place.

[1] Based on the above, the Board determined that during Employer's investigation with respect to guns at the work place, Claimant denied having loaded weapons at work. However, Employer's investigation revealed that Claimant did bring a loaded gun to work. Claimant's conduct in lying about bringing loaded guns to the work place during Employer's investigation constituted a disregard of the standards of behavior which the employer had a right to expect and as such, the Board denied Claimant benefits. This appeal followed.[2]

[2] Claimant initially argues that there was no policy prohibiting guns at the work place. In *Bolden v. Chartiers Valley School District*, 869 A.2d 1134 (Pa.Cmwlth. 2005), a bus supervisor employed by the district inadvertently brought a gun to school and was disciplined by the school district. The bus supervisor claimed that the district did not have a formal policy prohibiting such inadvertent conduct. This court, relying on an unemployment case wherein the employer also did not have a formal policy prohibiting certain conduct, stated:

> There is no requirement that a school district have a policy specifically prohibiting every circumstance that could result in discipline. Indeed, where common sense dictates that certain actions are grounds for discipline, we have held

in other contexts that there need not be a policy prohibiting such conduct.... *See, e.g. Denardis v. Unemployment Compensation Board of Review*, 76 Pa. Cmwlth. 212, 463 A.2d 116 (1983) (employer need not have a policy prohibiting the use of company property for personal use because no such policy is necessary for an employee to understand the wrongfulness of that conduct). The same logic applies here.

Here, although there was no policy prohibiting guns at work and then lying about it, such a policy was not necessarily needed and in addition, we note that Claimant was not fired for violating a policy. Rather, Claimant was fired for bringing a loaded gun to work and lying to Employer about it during Employer's investigation.

[3, 4] As to the investigation, at which time Claimant was warned that he would be fired if he lied, Claimant maintains that he did not lie. In addressing this argument, we note that the Board is the ultimate fact finder, is empowered to resolve conflicts in the evidence and to determine the credibility of witnesses. *Goppman v. Unemployment Compensation Board of Review*, 845 A.2d 946 (Pa.Cmwlth.2004).

According to Employer's witness, when interviewed, Claimant denied having a loaded gun at work. Employer's investigation, however, revealed that Claimant did bring a gun to work with a clip. Specifically, a co-worker testified that a couple of times Claimant brought guns to the workplace and then removed the clip before handing it to him. After the co-worker examined it, Claimant returned the

---

2. Our review is limited to determining whether constitutional rights were violated, errors of law were committed, or essential findings of fact are supported by substantial evidence.

Lee Hospital v. Unemployment Compensation Board of Review, 161 Pa.Cmwlth. 464, 637 A.2d 695 (1994).

Figure 6-18 Continued

SEPTA v. TRANSPORT WORKERS UNION   Pa. **731**

Cite as 880 A.2d 731 (Pa.Cmwlth. 2005)

gun to his holster.[3] In addition, it was reported that Claimant also cleaned his gun at work. Although Claimant maintains that he did not lie, the Board credited the testimony of Employer's witness that Claimant stated during the investigation that he never had a loaded gun at work when, in fact, he did. Such activity of lying to Employer about having a loaded gun at work constitutes an act of wanton or willful disregard of Employer's interest and a disregard of behavior which Employer has a right to expect.

In accordance with the above, the decision of the Board is affirmed.

ORDER

Now, August 10, 2005, the decision of the Unemployment Compensation Board of Review, in the above-captioned matter, is affirmed.

**SOUTHEASTERN PENNSYLVANIA
TRANSPORTATION AUTHORITY,
Appellant**

v.

**TRANSPORT WORKERS UNION
OF AMERICA, LOCAL 290.**

tion Authority to discharge employee, who brought union grievance following discharge. The Court of Common Pleas, Philadelphia County, No. 1066 September Term 2004, Carrafiello, J., affirmed, and Transportation Authority appealed.

Holdings: The Commonwealth Court, No. 2766 C.D. 2004, Flaherty, Senior Judge, held that:

(1) issue of whether employee could be discharged for just cause was properly before arbitrator, and

(2) reinstatement deprived Transportation Authority of ability to discharge essential function of providing safe and reliable bus transportation and thus was not rationally derived from Memorandum of Understanding.

Reversed.

1. Labor and Employment ⚷1592

Under the essence test to determine if an arbitrator's award pursuant to a union grievance draws its essence from a collective bargaining agreement and is therefore final, the court first determines if the issue as properly defined is within the terms of the collective bargaining agreement; if the issue is embraced by the agreement, and thus, appropriately before the arbitrator, the arbitrator's award will be upheld if the arbitrator's interpretation can rationally be derived from the collective bargaining agreement.

For better practice, each time you visit the law library, take a classmate. Randomly choose a short opinion from the reporters and read it. You can discuss the case together to ensure you are extracting the correct information. In addition, anytime you are on *WestlawNext* or *Lexis Advance*, pull up an opinion and see if you can determine the issue presented, the legal facts, and the analysis/reasoning of the court.

Chapter Checklist ✔

- Case law research is based on the common law system, where law is created by the courts, and not by constitutions, statutes, or regulations. It is the only source of primary authority originated in the judicial branch of government.

- Judges from all across the country issue hundreds of thousands of opinions each year, creating a vast amount of case law based upon the concept of legal precedent, which is the foundation for legal research.

- Judges from trial and appellate courts write opinions, but only appellate opinions are used in legal research.

- Simply stated, and opinion tells the "story" of a particular case, and includes multiple and important components.

- Remember that not all cases are published, or possess "precedential value." Be certain to determine the laws in your state concerning the use of unpublished opinions. Most, if not all, opinions, in print and online, denote whether or not the case was published by the court to be used as precedential authority.

- A state or federal case opinion evolves through three stages of publication. A case is deemed as having precedential authority the moment it is issued by the court. Most if not all slip opinions can be accessed online through the appropriate state/federal judicial website.

- It is good practice to become familiar with and understand any and all numerical indicators listed on a case opinion. Know the difference between the various docket numbers.

- Remember that as a researcher you are restricted in locating case law within the state and federal jurisdiction in which you are employed. Know your particular state and federal jurisdiction and be sure to complete the information in "My Law" located in Appendix B of this text.

- Know and understand the various important components of a case brief. Remember that the purpose of briefing a case includes summarizing an entire case into a single page of information. Remember also the "tips" you learned as you brief, and, above all, be patient. The more cases you brief, the easier it will become and it will increase your marketability in the legal profession.

KEY TERMS

CRITICAL THINKING AND APPLICATION

1. Knowing each part/component of a case opinion is important in order to read, brief, and analyze it. Match the name of each part/component of the opinion with its corresponding language found within the opinion itself.

   _____ Case Name

   _____ Issue

   _____ Facts

   _____ Rule

   _____ Holding

   _____ Procedural History

   A) "this case is appealed from the trial court of Monroe County."

   B) "On May 1, 2009, the defendant mailed the documents to the plaintiff, which included the contract in question."

   C) "We must decide whether or not proper notice was given to the plaintiff according to the 30 day rule."

   D) "*Section 12 A.B.C. §123* states that legal documents are properly "sent" and/or "mailed" according to the law when the document is time-stamped at the post-office."

   E) "Lewis v. Jenkins, 123 P.2d 456 (Az. 2010)"

   F) "the case is reversed and remanded for re- sentencing."

2. Your instructor will give you one civil and one criminal case to brief from your jurisdiction. Take time to carefully read, understand, and brief the cases. Thereafter, take turns in class analyzing the case and discussing the individual parts.

LEARNING OBJECTIVES

After completion of this chapter, you should be able to

1. Explain where cases are located in print.

2. Explain the process for how to locate a case in print.

3. Understand how to utilize the digest system in print.

4. Describe how to search for cases online using Westlaw and Lexis.

5. Explain how to validate a case using KeyCite and Shepard's online.

6. Identify the additional subscription and free online sources available to search for a case.

7. Describe how to search for United States Supreme Court cases.

CASE LAW

DIGEST
PARALLEL CITATION

OPINION

How to Search for a Case

In the previous chapter, you learned the basics of case law, including what case is, how and where case laws are published, and how to read and brief one. In this chapter, you will now learn where cases are found in print and online in an easy step-by-step format.

■ STATE AND FEDERAL CASES IN PRINT

As you have learned earlier in the textbook, all primary sources of law can be found in print and online. Because case law is the most abundant of these sources, state and federal opinions occupy many shelves in the law library. Once you understand *where* and *how* case opinions are found in print, you will discover that you can find any state or federal case you need in your research. In this section, you will learn where the opinions are complied in the library and how to navigate the books to retrieve the cases you need. Thereafter, you will learn, through specific and detailed examples, how to find a state and federal case opinion in print and online.

LEARNING OBJECTIVE 1
Explain where cases are located in print.

Case Reporters: Publication and Citation

Before you can find the cases you need to conduct your research, you need to know the different hardbound sets of books wherein the cases are located. Cases are published in both an official and unofficial printed set.

Official Reports

Any publication printed by a governmental entity, or any commercial publisher commissioned by a governmental entity to print a case report is considered an **official report** publication.

State Cases. Many, but not all states publish an official report set. The series of official state reports include all the supreme (highest appellate level) court opinions. Many states that have an intermediate appellate court publish a separate series only for those opinions. Some states publish one series including both appellate levels. Usually, you can tell an official version because of its title, which includes the state name, such as *The Pennsylvania State Reports*. Review Figure 7-1 to see which states publish an official state report.

official report
Any publication printed and published by an official governmental body, or by a commercial publisher (West) that is commissioned by a governmental body.

Figure 7-1 States with Official State Reports

Arizona	Massachusetts	Ohio
Arkansas	Michigan	Oregon
California	Montana	Pennsylvania
Connecticut	Nebraska	South Carolina
Georgia	Nevada	Vermont
Hawaii	New Hampshire	Virginia
Idaho	New Jersey	Washington
Illinois	New Mexico	West Virginia
Kansas	New York	Wisconsin
Maryland	North Carolina	

All the cases published in an official report are also published in the unofficial commercial version. For this reason, as you can see in the chart above, some states do NOT publish an official set. In particular, some states have discontinued their official version of intermediate appellate opinions, but still publish an official report for the highest state appellate court decisions. Furthermore, although not used in appellate research, some states also publish their *trial court* decisions in a report or specialized publication.

In a typical official state report set, all the cases reported by that state's appellate courts are arranged in chronological order. In these official sets, no index exists—you need to possess the citation of the particular case in order to find it. However, if you know the case name, an alphabetical index is included at the beginning of each volume along with the page where the case begins. A commercial publisher that is commissioned by the state to publish an official report will include the headnotes that you first learned about in Chapter 3. However, any set printed by the state government itself will not include headnotes or an index. Either way, and because these sets do not include an index, it is best to locate opinions in an official report using a "finding tool," which you will learn later.

How is a case cited in an official reporter? When an opinion makes it to its final publication in a reporter, the citations are similar to home addresses. Just as John Smith resides at 1234 Main Street, thousands of case opinions are assigned by a "home address" directing you to the shelf where it "resides" in the library. No two citations are the same. It is important to note that once an opinion is printed in the advance sheets, it is given its official citation, which will be the same citation as in the print reporter. The only difference is the publisher must wait until enough advance sheets fill one hardbound volume in the set of reporters. So you can use the citation in the advance sheet, as it is an official citation.

A basic case citation found in an official reporter includes the following information: (1) the names of both opposing parties separated by the "versus" abbreviation and ends with a comma; (2) the first number in the citation denotes the number of the volume in the set where the case is found within the set; (3) the abbreviation that identifies the official reporter, which will always be the particular state abbreviation; (4) the second number in the citation that denotes the page number of the volume where the text of the opinion begins; and (5) the parenthetical, which includes the date of the decision. Consider the following case citation, *Welsh v. Bulger*, 548 Pa. 504 (1997) found in the official **Pennsylvania State Reports**.

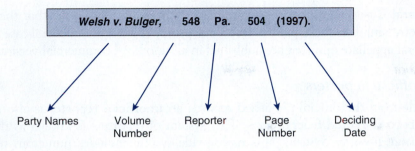

As you can see, the party names in the case are **Welsh and Bulger**. The case can be found in **volume 548** of the *Pennsylvania State Reports*. The case begins on **page 504** of the reporter, and was decided by the *Pennsylvania Supreme Court* in **1997**. You will learn the state abbreviations for each appellate court in your state from your instructor, the *Bluebook* (Rule 10.1) and the *ALWD Manual* (Rule 2; Appendix 4).

The abbreviation for the official set will always be the state abbreviation. It is universally understood that the case was cited from the official report.

Let's add a step. Suppose, using the same case, you saw this citation:

Welsh v. Bulger, 548 Pa. 504, 510 (1997).

Notice the number 510. You will often see this citation format in briefs and legal memorandums. It is called a **pinpoint citation** (also called a "jumpcite" or "pincite" citation). Very simply, a pinpoint citation directs the reader to a *specific page within the text of the opinion*. For example, this pinpoint citation is directing you to a specific point of law in the opinion, found on page 510, even though the actual opinion begins on page 504. No comma is placed after the pinpoint number. You will see how to utilize pinpoint citations when you learn how to cite authority within a memorandum in Chapter 12.

Many case opinions can be located in an official and unofficial set. For those cases that can be found in both, the case is referred to as having a **parallel citation**. This means that the same case has two distinct citations for each reported set in which they are located. If the rules in your jurisdiction require you to include this parallel citation, you must do so. As you can see from using the *Welsh* case, the official citation always precedes the unofficial citation and the two are separated by a comma. Notice the state abbreviation does not need to be inserted in the ending parenthetical, as it is included in the official citation. This citation informs the reader that the case can be found in both the hardbound report and reporter.

pinpoint citation
A citation that includes an additional number other than the standard volume number and page number, which directs the reader to a specific page within the case opinion.

parallel citation
A case that has two different and distinct citations where the case can be found in different reporters.

Welsh v. Bulger, 548 Pa. 504, 698 A.2d 581 (Pa. 1997).

Federal Cases. During a tour of the law library, you will notice that the federal government does NOT publish an official print publication for federal case law. All federal appellate opinions are published in an unofficial commercial version only.

Unofficial Reporters

unofficial reporter
A reporter that is printed and published by a commercial publisher (West) and not an governmental body.

Aside from the official published reports, an **unofficial reporter** is also in print for both state and federal cases. This system of reporters is known as the *West National Reporter System*. This nationwide system includes numerous reporters published exclusively by *West*. This system of books includes state and federal opinions compiled in their own respective sets. Below you will see how this national reporter system organizes and prints its state and federal versions.

State Cases. As you can see in Figure 7-2, the *West* regional reporter system organizes all state appellate opinions into seven regional reporters, which include multiple states in each reporter. This organization is not strictly geographical in nature. Each regional reporter, however, does attempt to configure the states in proximity to other states in the reporter.

PRACTICE TIP

Unlike the federal circuits which include multiple states from which you can retrieve federal cases, that is not true of the state reporters. You can retrieve binding authority from your state only. The multiple state opinions found in the print reporters are for organizational purpose only.

In addition to these reporters, three additional reporters also exist. Due to the high number of case opinions issued in the populous states of California, Illinois, and New York, these states also have an additional reporter for included supreme and intermediate level opinions, which include *The California Reporter* (Cal.Rptr. / 2nd / 3rd), the *Illinois Decisions* (Ill. Dec.) and *The New York Supplement* (N.Y.S. / 2nd). If you plan to work as a paralegal in any of these three states, make certain you know these reporters exist.

If you notice under the heading of "abbreviations" in the above chart, each reporter has published at least two "series" of books. This means that opinions compiled in the *Atlantic Reporter* began with an initial set of books denoted by the abbreviation of "**A.**" Thereafter, once that series reached a sufficient number of volumes (usually 999) a new set was created and denoted with an "A.2d,"

Figure 7-2 The *West* National State Reporter System

Name of Reporter	Reporter Abbreviation	States Included
Atlantic Reporter	A. / A.2d / A.3d	Includes the supreme and intermediate court opinions of *Connecticut, Delaware, DC, Maine, Maryland, New Hampshire, New Jersey, Pennsylvania, Rhode Island, Vermont*
Northeastern Reporter	N.E. / N.E.2d	Includes the Court of Appeals opinions of *New York,* and the supreme and intermediate court opinions of *Illinois, Indiana, Massachusetts, Ohio*
Northwestern Reporter	N.W. / N.W.2d	Includes the supreme and intermediate court opinions of *Michigan, Minnesota, Nebraska, North Dakota, South Dakota, Wisconsin*
Pacific Reporter	P. / P.2d / P.3d	Includes the supreme and intermediate court opinions of *Alaska, Arizona, California, Colorado, Hawaii, Idaho, Kansas, Montana, Nevada, New Mexico, Oklahoma, Oregon, Utah, Washington, Wyoming*
Southeastern Reporter	S.E. / S.E.2d	Includes the supreme and intermediate court opinions of *Georgia, North Carolina, South Carolina, Virginia, West Virginia*
Southwestern Reporter	S.W. / S.W.2d / S.W.3d	Includes the supreme and intermediate court opinions of *Arkansas, Kentucky, Missouri, Tennessee, Texas*
Southern Reporter	So. / So.2d / So.3d	Includes the supreme and intermediate court opinions of *Alabama, Florida, Louisiana, Mississippi*

meaning the *second series* of the reporter. Once that was filled then the *third* series was begun denoted as "A.3d," and so on. The series and volume number is clearly printed on the spine of each book in the series.

As you can see in Figure 7-3, the official reports include only the full text of the opinion. The *West* reporters also include the entire full text opinion. But unlike those reports, the *West* version does include headnotes. Using the same case example found in Figure 7-3, you can see in Figure 7-4 that the print versions utilize a cross-referencing technique called "star paging."

West also publishes what are called the **offprint reporters**. These reporters contain only the opinions of *individual* states but *with the same page numbers as in the regional reporter*. This allows libraries and law firms to purchase volumes containing cases for their *own state* while still utilizing the pagination of the regional reporter system. This is also cost efficient by freeing up valuable shelf space in the library.

How is a state case cited in a *West* reporter? Cases cited in a *West* state reporter are similar to that of a state official report. However, it is the abbreviation of the reporter set and information in the ending parenthetical that is different. For example, look at the *Welsh* case again below. This time, it is in the regional reporter citation format.

offprint reporters
A West reporter that reprints individual state court opinions from the regional reporter, but retains the regional reporter citations.

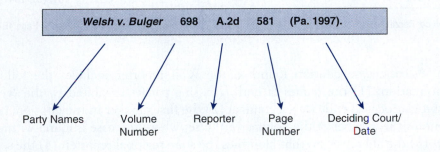

| Party Names | Volume Number | Reporter | Page Number | Deciding Court/ Date |

Figure 7-3 A Case Opinion in the *Atlantic Reporter*

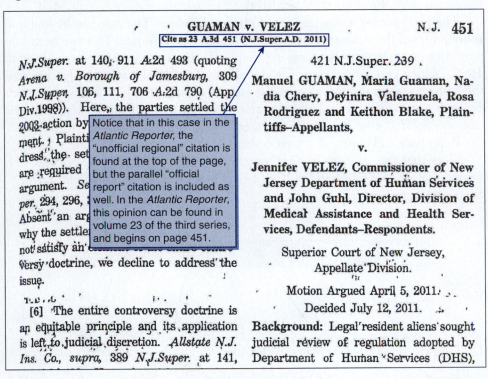

Source: Reprinted with permission of Thomson Reuters, West's Atlantic 3rd Reporter Volume 23, Page 451.

Figure 7-4 An Example of Star Paging

> **GUAMAN v. VELEZ**   N. J.   **457**
> Cite as 23 A.3d 451 (N.J.Super.A.D. 2011)
>
> In 1968, New Jersey elected to partici-   non-citizen's access to federally-subsidized
> pate in the Medicaid program by enacting   medical benefits. A.B. v. Div. of Med.
> the " 'New Jersey Medical Assistance   Assistance & Health Serv., N.J.Su-
> Health Services Act,' " N.J.S.A. 30:4D   (N.J.Super.A.D.),
> to–19.5; administered by DHS through   386
> Division. N.J.S.A. 30:4D–3(c) and 30:4   purpose
> 4. The program enables the State: illegal
> [T]o provide medical assistance, insofar   ity of
> as practicable, on behalf of pers
> whose resources are determined to   aliens
> inadequate to enable them to sec   quali-
> quality medical care at their own   ty to
> pense, and to enable the State, with   de-
> the limits of funds available for   sig-
> fiscal year for such purposes, to ob   and
> all benefits for medical assistance pro-   other specified categories of lawfully-pres-
> vided by the Federal Social Security   ent aliens. 8 U.S.C.A. §§ 1612(b), 1641(b).

*Within the same opinion found in Figure 7-3 above, notice the numbers 249 inserted within the body of the opinion. This is what is referred to as "**star paging**." If you are required to cite cases using a parallel citation and do not have access to the official report in print, West has cross-referenced the official page numbers of the official report directly into the text of the commercial print set for ease of reference. This cross-referencing is known as "star paging" because online West denotes star paging with a star or asterisk (*). In print, as you can see here, West identifies the star paging with an inverted "T" symbol. The pinpoint cites correlate directly with the official citation, 421 N.J. Super. 239.*

Source: Reprinted with permission of Thomson Reuters, West's Atlantic 3rd Reporter Volume 23, Page 457.

A basic case citation found in the *West* reporter includes the following information: (1) the names of both opposing parties separated by the "versus" abbreviation and ends with a comma; (2) the first number in the citation, which denotes the number of the volume in the set where the case is found within the set; (3) the abbreviation that identifies the state regional reporter; (4) the second number in the citation, which denotes the page number of the volume where the text of the opinion begins; and (5) the parenthetical, which includes the abbreviation of the court that decided the case and the date of the decision.

The party names in the case are **Welsh and Bulger**. The case can be found in **volume 698** of the **Atlantic Regional Reporter, Second Series**. The case begins on **page 581** of the reporter, and was decided by the **Pennsylvania Supreme Court** in **1997**. Notice two differences. First, the abbreviation of the reporter denotes that the case was taken from a regional reporter, as opposed to an official state report. Second, because the reporter abbreviation does not indicate from which state the case was decided, that information is inserted in the ending parenthetical.

Refer back to Figure 7-3. What is the "regional reporter" citation?

Note that this citation "format" can be used in ANY state for ANY reporter. For example, a case found in the Pacific Reporter from an Arizona court would be cited as follows:

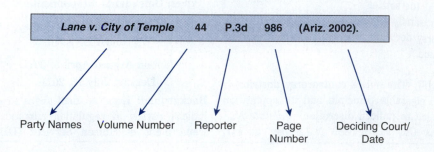

Figure 7-5 Examples of State Citations in Official and Unofficial Reporters

State	Intermediate State Appellate Court Citation (regional reporter)	State Supreme Court Citation (state official report)
Georgia	*Hendley v. Evans,* 734 S.E.2d 548 (Ga. Ct. App. 2012)	*Manzano v. The State,* 290 Ga. 892 (2012)
Texas	*Ford Motor Company v. Miles,* 141 S.W.3d 309 (Tex. Civ. App. - Dallas 2004)	*Holland v. Wal-Mart Stores,* 1 S.W. 3d 91 (Tex. 1999) ◄
Oregon	*Lowe v. Philip Morris USA,* 142 P.3d 1079 (Ore. App. 2006)	*Alto v. State Fire Marshall,* 319 Or. 382 (1994)

Texas does not print an official report, so a legal researcher in Texas would cite to the commercial regional reporter.

The format, for any state case in any reporter, will be the same. Only the information within the citation will obviously vary from state to state.

Below are some examples of different state appellate opinions from the official report and regional reporters of three states below. As you can see in Figure 7-5, they all follow the same basic format.

If your state does not publish an official report set, do not feel that you are missing out on valuable research information. Both the official and commercial publications include the same cases. Although both sets are similar in nature, there are two advantages to utilizing case law in the commercial set. The *West* version updates its print material more quickly and contains valuable annotations (headnotes/summaries) not included in the official case report.

Federal Cases. *West* compiles all federal trial and appellate opinions in the unofficial *West National Reporter System.* As you can see below, the federal reporters are much more extensive than their counterpart regional state reporters.

- Unlike the state court system, *West* does publish federal *trial* court decisions in the district courts. *The Federal Supplement* first series (F.Supp.) includes 999 volumes and includes trial opinions from 1933 to1998. Opinions are included from the US District Courts and US Customs Courts. The Federal Supplement is currently in its second series (F.Supp.2d) and includes the trial decisions from 1998 to the present. Opinions are included from US District Courts, the US Court of Federal Claims, and the US Court of International Trade.
- *The Federal Rules Decisions Reporter* (F.R.D.) included in the *West* reporter system publishes decisions of the federal *trial* courts, specifically those involving the Federal Rules of Civil, Criminal, and Appellate Procedure, and the Federal Rules of Evidence not published in the Federal Supplement. The publication includes cases that have defined, explained, or interpreted various federal rules.
- *The Federal Reporter* publishes all federal *appellate* decisions beginning from 1880 forward. The original Federal Reporter (F.) includes 300 volumes and includes case decisions from 1880 to 1924. The cases included are compiled from US Commerce Court, Court of Appeals for D.C., the US Court of Claims, the US Circuit Courts, and the US District Courts. *The Federal Reporter Second Series* (F.2d) includes 999 volumes and includes case decisions from 1924 to 1993. The cases included are compiled from the same courts as in the original reporter. *The Federal Reporter Third Series* (F.3d) currently includes 600 volumes and includes case

decisions from 1993 to the present. The only cases included in this series are compiled from the US Court of Federal Claims and the US Court of Appeals.

- *The Federal Appendix* (Fed. Appx.), published by *West* beginning in 2001, includes all the "non-precedential" opinions of the federal appellate courts. Almost every circuit court around the country submits these non-precedential decisions for inclusion in the federal appendix. As you will recall at the beginning of this chapter, you learned that the federal rules were recently amended to permit attorneys to cite all published and un-published *federal* case opinions in their research.

Just as you learned earlier in the book that many "specialized" courts are included in the structure of the federal court system, and *West* also publishes reporter sets from these specialized courts. The main reporters are as follows.

- *West's Federal Bankruptcy Reporter* publishes selected opinions that are decided exclusively by the US Bankruptcy Courts (trial and appellate level). This set also publishes federal bankruptcy appeals decided by the US District Courts, the US Courts of Appeal, and the US Supreme Court.
- *West's Veteran's Appeals Reporter* publishes all case opinions for veteran's claims issued by the US Court of Appeals, the Federal Circuit, and the US Supreme Court.
- *West's Military Justice Reporter* publishes all case opinions from the US Court of Military Appeals, and the Court of Military Review for all the federal armed forces.
- *West's Federal Claims Reporter* publishes decisions from the US Courts of Federal Claims, which can include cases where citizens file suits or are involved in suits directly with a federal entity. For example, citizens who suffered physical harm/injury from childhood vaccinations can file claims against the federal government under the "National Vaccine Injury Compensation Program." Cases are also included from the US Court of Appeals, Federal Circuit Courts, and the US Supreme Court.

The federal reporters are compiled and arranged similar to the state reporters. There are no indexes, and the cases can be retrieved only by citation. These cases can also be retrieved by the use of finding tools.

How is a federal appellate case cited in the *West* reporter? Cases cited in a *West* federal reporter are cited similar to those state cases found in the *West* reporter but, again, the distinction is in the reporter abbreviation and ending parenthetical. Consider the example below.

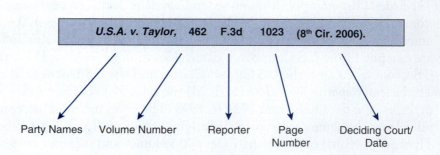

As you can see, the party names in the case are the **United States Government** and **Taylor**. The case can be found in **volume 462** of the **Federal Reporter, Third Series.** In the reporter, the case begins on **page 1023** and was decided by the **Eighth Circuit** in **2006.** Understand that a federal citation will state the circuit court, but it does **not** tell you the state within that circuit that decided the case. This citation example was an appeal from a federal district court in Rhode Island, but this is irrelevant for the citation. That is because, as you may recall, multiple states are included within a particular circuit, and any state within a particular circuit is considered mandatory/binding authority. In a state citation, the *state* appellate court is required in the ending parenthetical, but in a federal citation, only the *circuit* court is required.

However, if you are citing a federal *trial* court decision, then the format does change and the state in which the district court is physically located must be included. As you may recall in an earlier chapter, the federal courts sit in singular or multiple federal districts in each state across the country. Each district is divided into *east*, *west*, *north*, *south*, *middle* or *central*, and a federal trial decision must be cited as such. Please review Figure 7-6 which identifies each state's federal districts.

Figure 7-6 The Federal Districts of Each State

State	Districts and Citation Abbreviation	Circuit
Alabama	Middle, Northern, Southern (Ala.)	11th Circuit
Arkansas	Eastern, Western (Ark.)	8th Circuit
California	Central, Eastern, Northern, Southern (Cal.)	9th Circuit
Florida	Middle, Northern, Southern (Fla.)	11th Circuit
Georgia	Middle, Northern, Southern (Ga.)	11th Circuit
Illinois	Central, Northern, Southern (Ill.)	7th Circuit
Indiana	Northern, Southern (Ind.)	7th Circuit
Iowa	Northern, Southern (Iowa)	8th Circuit
Kentucky	Eastern, Western (Ky.)	6th Circuit
Louisiana	Eastern, Middle, Western (La.)	5th Circuit
Michigan	Eastern, Western (Mich.)	6th Circuit
Mississippi	Northern, Southern (Miss.)	5th Circuit
Missouri	Eastern, Western (Mo.)	8th Circuit
New York	Eastern, Northern, Southern, Western (N.Y.)	2nd Circuit
North Carolina	Eastern, Middle, Western (N.C.)	4th Circuit
Ohio	Northern, Southern (Ohio)	6th Circuit
Oklahoma	Eastern, Northern, Western (Okla.)	10th Circuit
Pennsylvania	Eastern, Middle, Western (Pa.)	3rd Circuit
Tennessee	Eastern, Middle, Western (Tenn.)	6th Circuit
Texas	Eastern, Northern, Southern, Western (Tex.)	5th Circuit
Virginia	Eastern, Western (Va.)	4th Circuit
Washington	Eastern, Western (Wash.)	9th Circuit
West Virginia	Northern, Southern (W.Va.)	4th Circuit
Wisconsin	Eastern, Western (Wis.)	7th Circuit

The following states have only **one** federal district. The federal courts in these states are abbreviated in case citations as (D.): Alaska, Arizona, Colorado, Connecticut, Delaware, D.C., Hawaii, Idaho, Kansas, Maine, Maryland, Massachusetts, Minnesota, Montana, Nebraska, Nevada, New Hampshire, New Jersey, New Mexico, North Dakota, Oregon, Rhode Island, South Carolina, South Dakota, Utah, Vermont, Wyoming, US Court of Appeals, Federal Circuit.

For example, a federal *trial* court opinion from a district court would look like the following: This case was decided in the **Eastern District Court of North Carolina** in **2006**. The case can be found in the **Federal Supplement, second edition**, in **volume 410**, and the case begins on **page 432**.

> *Lewis v. Microsoft Corporation,* **410 F. Supp. 2d 432 (E.D.N.C. 2006)**

Because no official federal reporter exists, there is no need for parallel citation strings. Remember what you learned under state citations concerning pinpoint citations, which are utilized in federal case citations as well.

Search Approach: The Citation and Digest Methods

LEARNING OBJECTIVE 2
Explain the process for how to locate a case in print.

Up to this point, you have learned much concerning case law research. You now know what an opinion is and its various components. You also know the three stages of case publication and where state and federal case law is located in print. That's a good start. Now you will learn the basic methods for how to search for a particular opinion in the law library.

There are two basic methods used to locate a state or federal case in print: (1) the citation method and (2) the word search method.

The Citation Method

Of the two main methods to find a case, the easiest way is the citation method. Now that you know how to read a case citation, you can quickly and easily locate any state opinion in print. Suppose your supervising attorney was about to begin a big trial, but she needs to quickly read a case before heading out the door to go to court. When you arrive in the morning, you find the following Post-it™ note on your computer monitor:

> Hi! - Please pull this case and copy it. I need to read it before I go to court today. Thanks!   1 A.3d 965

Where do you look to find this case? Is this enough information? It is. Remember, you look at the court abbreviation to know which court decided the case *and* from which reporter it can be found in. Here, by looking at the citation, you would know to go to the *Atlantic Reporter* in the stacks in the library. Notice that the case is in volume one of the new third series. You pull the volume and fan through the pages until you come to page 965. The citation also works when locating federal case law the same way.

Having the citation to a case is a very direct and easy way to locate a case in the reporter, rather than searching by topic or subject. Other than your attorney or another legal staff member handing you a citation for a case, there are other instances in which to use a citation to retrieve a case. One way is to read the case abstracts at the end of a statute. When reading through a statute, you can find a multitude of case abstracts or case summaries that directly relate that part or section of a statute. The case summaries interpret or explain cases that have been litigated concerning that particular statute.

In addition, many secondary sources, which you will learn about later, will provide case citations in the annotated material. These are found in legal encyclopedias, among others. This is why you learned early in this chapter that all other sources of law "return" to case law. Remember, for any source of law, there is likely a case that has described, explained, or interpreted that particular source of law.

The Word Search Method

Because cases are published in the official and unofficial sets chronologically, you can easily find a case by its citation. However, it is impossible to conduct a "search" of any of the cases in the reported set. In response, *West* created the *American Digest System*. The researcher can use this vast system of books to search legal topics using an index to locate the cases needed in the reporters. You will likely conduct a good deal of your research utilizing the topic/subject method. Digests are not considered primary or even secondary law, but are referred to as a *finding tool*. Therefore, the digest itself, or any information found in a digest, can never be cited as authority.

So what is the Digest System? Simply stated, a **digest** is a set of hardbound books including numerous volumes and indexes. You use the various indexes to locate the legal topic/subject you are searching. Once found, each topic/subject is assigned a specific and unique *West* **Key Number**, which can be used in any print or online *West* publication. You use that topic/subject and key number to find the corresponding volume in the set. Within that particular volume, you will find numerous case summaries with their citations that correspond directly to your specific topic/subject. If after reading the case summary, it is of interest to you, you can take the citation and find the full opinion in a print reporter or online.

On the *state* level, *West* prints a state and regional digest. These state digests are easily identifiable by their name, such as *West's Florida Digest*, or *West's California Digest*. Each state digest includes an index system for all the cases within that particular state. The regional digests are also easily identifiable, as they mirror the *West Reporters*. For instance, the *West's Pacific Digest* indexes cases from all the states included in *West's Pacific Reporter*, and *West's Atlantic Digest* indexes cases from all the states contained in the *Atlantic Reporter*, and so on. *West* publishes digests for 47 states and the District of Columbia. Individual state digests are NOT published for Delaware, Nevada, or Utah. In those states, you must utilize the *Atlantic Regional Digest* (Delaware), and the *Pacific Regional Digest* (Nevada, Utah). In addition, *West* does NOT publish a regional digest for the *North Eastern*, *South Western*, or *Southern Reporters*. For those regional jurisdictions, you must utilize the individual state digest.

On the *federal* level, the *West Federal Practice Digest Series* indexes all reported federal case law, including US Supreme Court cases. Speaking of which, *West* also publishes the *Supreme Court Digest* that includes an index system containing opinions exclusively from the US Supreme Court, which you see later in this chapter.

For an even broader search, *West* created a digest on a *national* level. The *West General Digest* compiles only the *headnotes* from *every* case opinion published each month from the *entire* National Reporter System into a softbound pamphlet. These headnotes are arranged alphabetically by topic name along with each corresponding headnote. The monthly soft pamphlets are subsequently arranged and complied into a hardbound book. *West* compiles enough books to make up a *Decennial Digest*, which is complied and published as a volume set every **10 years**. As of 2013, the last Decennial Digest is the **Eleventh Decennial, Part II,** including the headnotes from all the cases compiled between 2001 and 2005. The current General Digest includes the headnotes of the cases from 2005 to the present. Therefore, if you have a particular headnote and key number, you can locate **every** case decided from the early 1600s to the present that discussed that particular headnote—now that's a broad search! You will not typically need to reference this particular digest, as the state and regional are more than adequate, but it is good practice to know it exists. Review Figure 7-7 for a complete list of the available *West* digests found in print.

So how does a researcher use the digest system? When you approach a state, regional, or federal digest, they are all compiled and organized the same way. Similar to many of the print resources, the first 80 to 100 volumes in the set are engraved with a range of specific subjects and their abbreviations on the spine of each volume ("Divorce;" "Workers Compensation"). At the end of each set, you will find multiple indexes to help you navigate through the volumes.

There are a few methods to utilize while navigating through a digest.

descriptive word index
An index that directs you to topics of law and their key numbers through the use of 'descriptive' words.

■ The most effective navigating tool is the **Descriptive Word Index (DWI).** In order to use the DWI, you need to have a general word or phrase in mind such as "landlord" or "contract." Once you find it in the index, the topic will have an accompanying "key number," which literally is the "key" to finding the topic you need within the digest. The researcher will then go to that appropriate volume within the set. As you can see in Figure 7-8, a distinguishing feature of the digest is that in the beginning pages of any particular volume, a very detailed index of subtopics will be listed that are specific to

Figure 7-7 A Summary of West's State, Regional, Federal, and General Digests

Description	State Digest	State Regional Digest	Federal Digest	General Digest
Types of case summaries included	Includes case summaries (abstracts) from the trial and appellate state and federal court decisions within that *state*.	Includes case summaries from only the state courts within a particular *region* (the same states found in a particular regional reporter).	Includes case summaries from the federal court system, including all federal trial and appellate courts.	Includes all the head notes from **every** case in the National Reporter System.
Types of digests included	*West* publishes state digests for all states, **excluding** *Delaware, Nevada,* and *Utah.* Some state digests have multiple series, and some are combined, including the *Virginia Digest* which includes the cases from Virginia and West Virginia, as well as the *Dakota Digest* which includes the cases from North and South Dakota.	*West* **only** publishes an *Atlantic, North Western, Pacific,* and *South Eastern* digest; it does **not** publish a *North Eastern, Southern,* or *South Western* digest.	Includes the Federal Practice Digest, currently in its 5th edition. *West* also publishes separate digests for numerous *specialized* federal courts.	Includes **every** digest in the National Reporter System, which is subsequently compiled every ten years into a Decennial Digest.

Figure 7-8 The Main Topic and Subtopics of Workers' Compensation

62A Pa D 2d—29

WORKERS' COMPENSATION

VIII. INJURIES FOR WHICH COMPENSATION MAY BE HAD.—Continued.

(E) DEFENSES AGAINST CLAIMS FOR COMPENSATION; MISCON-
DUCT OF EMPLOYEE.—Continued.

774. Serious and willful misconduct in general.
    —— In general.
    —— Meaning of terms in general.
    —— Particular acts constituting misconduct.
Willful or culpable negligence, serious neglect, or recklessness.
Violation of statutory or other regulations in general.
    —— In general.
    —— Failure to obtain license.
    —— Excessive speed.
    —— Unlighted vehicle.
    —— Violation of traffic regulations.
    —— Violation of mining regulations.
786. Violation of rules, orders, or warnings.
787. —— In general.
788. —— Making and enforcement of rules and orders in general.
789. —— Employee's knowledge and understanding of rules and or-
        ders.
790. —— Failure to enforce rules or orders.
791. —— Acts prohibited in general.
792. —— Place of work.
793. —— Manner of doing work.
794. —— Doing prohibited work.
795. —— Use of vehicles, and modes of transportation.
796. —— Operation and use of elevators.
797. Failure to use safety devices.
798. Intoxication.
799. Injury intentional on part of employee.
800. Injury caused by employee's assault or willful intention to injure
        another.

IX. AMOUNT AND PERIOD OF COMPENSATION.

(A) BASIS FOR DETERMINATION OF AMOUNT.
    ☞801. In general.
    810. Earnings or wages in general.
    811. Average earnings.
    812. Daily wages.
    813. Weekly wages; number of days included.
    814. Choice between methods of computation.
    815. Computation of earnings or wages.
    816. —— In general.
    817. —— Length of time in employment prior to injury.
    818. —— Wages of employee of same class.
    819. —— Employment and rate of wages when injured.
    820. —— Just and fair mode of computation.

> The citation is found in the upper left hand side of each page, which includes the volume, set, and page number.
>
> This page is found at the beginning of the volume for "Workers' Compensation."

> As you can see, the general main topic in the specific volume of this state digest is WORKERS COMPENSATION. Below that main title is a comprehensive list of DEFENSES against a claim of workers' compensation; specifically, misconduct of the employee which causes an injury.

Source: Reprinted with permission of Thomson Reuters, West's Pennsylvania Digest 2nd, Volume 62A, Page 29.

that volume only. All the key numbers are listed in bold at the top right-hand corner of each page of the volume. Therefore, researchers need only to fan through the pages until they see their key number. After finding the particular topic and key number you need within the volume, you will find numerous case abstracts (summaries). These are very similar to the case summaries you will find within an *annotated* statutory code. As you can see in Figure 7-9, each case summary highlights a specific point(s) of law concerning your specific topic. Each summary also provides the full case citation, so when researchers find a case that promising, they can write down the citation and find the full text opinion in either the corresponding reporter or on

Figure 7-9 Case Summaries for Defenses against Workers Compensation Claims

⚷798 WORKERS' COMPENSATION 62A Pa D 2d—504

For later cases, see same Topic and Key Number in Pocket Part

⚷798. Intoxication.
Library references
C.J.S. Workmen's Compensation §§ 247, 263.

Pa.Super. 2008. In cases where an employee is killed or injured when driving while intoxicated, when attempting to show that the employee is not entitled to workers' compensation benefits the employer must establish that the employee's intoxication is the cause of the accident; otherwise, the employee is entitled to benefits. 77 P.S. § 431.
Employers Mut. Cas. Co. v. Boiler Erection and Repair Co., 964 A.2d 381, reargument denied, appeal denied Kerr v. Boiler Erection and Repair Co., Inc., 983 A.2d 729.

The fact an employee was over the legal limit for blood alcohol content (BAC), by itself, does not prove that intoxication was the factual cause of the accident, for purposes of determining whether an employee is not entitled to recover workers' compensation benefits. 77 P.S. § 431.
Employers Mut. Cas. Co. v. Boiler Erection and Repair Co., 964 A.2d 381, reargument denied, appeal denied Kerr v. Boiler Erection and Repair Co., Inc., 983 A.2d 729.

Pa.Super. 1943. Orderly's willful violation of hospital rule prohibiting drinking while on duty did not bar compensation for his death, where evidence did not establish intoxication in any degree as the cause of injuries which resulted in his

intoxication in a public place. 47 **P.S.** § 722; 77 P.S. § 411.
Hopwood v. City of Pittsburgh, **33** A.2d 658, 152...

Hospital order... prohibiting drinking... in itself amount to... employment", parti... tendent of nurses ha... dition allowed him... spite thereof. 77 P....
Hopwood v. C... A.2d 658, 152...

Pa.Cmwlth. 20... able to present evidence that a **workers'** compensation claimant's voluntary intoxication was the cause in fact of his injury, no benefits will be awarded. 77 **P.S.** § 431.
YDC New Castle-PA DPW v. W.C.A.B. (Hedland), 950 A.2d 1107.

Pa.Cmwlth. 2003. By using **the** phrase "but for" in section of Workers' Compensation Act providing that no compensation will be paid if an employee's injuries would not... the employee's in... sembly meant that... claiming an empl... affirmative defens... similar to a plaint... tion by establishing that intoxication **was** the cause in fact of an injury, **without** regard to proof that the intoxication **was** the proximate cause of or a substantial factor in causing the injury. 77 P.S. § 431.

> If you look back to Figure 7-8, one of the defenses against claims for workers compensation is intoxication (key number 798). Under that sub-topic, numerous case summaries from state courts specifically address this issue. If a case appears to be of interest, you can copy the citation and locate the case to read it in its entirety.

> As you can see, the summaries not only include case citations but statutory citations as well, where applicable.

Source: Reprinted with permission of Thomson Reuters, West's Pennsylvania Digest 2nd, Volume 62A, Page 504.

an online database. Remember, the information written in the digest, including the summaries, was written by the publisher, not the court. Therefore, you can *never* cite or rely solely on the information in the digest. You must locate and read the full text opinion in its entirety. Remember that a digest is neither a primary nor a secondary source of law, but is only a finding tool.

words and phrases index
An index that alphabetically lists legal words and phrases that have been defined within case opinions and includes the head notes and citations of the cases in which those definitions appear.

table of cases
A digest index that provides the full case citation for hundreds of cases listed alphabetically by case name only.

- Case summaries can also be found using the **Words and Phrases Index**. This index identifies specific words and phrases to find case citations within the digest and includes full citations to cases that have defined or utilized certain legal terms and/or phrases. This index is not as effective as the descriptive word index. However, just know it exists and that it is a search option.

- The **Table of Cases**, also found at the end of set, can be useful to the researcher who has the full case name but not the numeric citation. The table of cases lists all the cases in the digest in alphabetical order, with the case citation, as well as any rules of law used in the case.

- You can also use the **Topic Method**. In other words, if you are feeling adventurous, go directly to the volume you need, as the topics are printed on the spine of each book. Believe it or not, the digests are so well organized that you can find what you need by going directly to the appropriate volume in set. On the beginning pages of each volume, prior to each volume index, is a list including more than 400 "general topics" that are included in the set from (1) **A**bandoned & Lost Property to (414) **Z**oning and Planning. These are arranged in alphabetical order, similar to the print encyclopedia sets. By scanning that outline, researchers can find exactly what they need to search the case summaries.

- A researcher can also use the **One Good Case Method**. Do you remember the headnotes found at the beginning of a case opinion? As you may recall in Chapter 6, Figure 6-2, each headnote preceding an opinion includes a topic of law and key number assigned to each headnote. One huge benefit of the *West* digest system is that all the key numbers are universal and can be used with **any** digest published by *West*. For example, if your supervising attorney or another paralegal gave you a case from which to begin your research, you could use the key numbers in the headnotes to navigate the digest to find other case summaries to read.

topic method
A method of locating legal topics and key numbers solely by general topic located alphabetically on the spine of each volume of the digest.

one good case method
A search for relevant cases solely from the head notes of one specific case rather than by conducting a random search using word or topic indexes.

Finding the Correct Words/Term/Phrase. So how do you know what legal terms/words/phrases to use when using the index? It is important, when conducting a search in print, to begin with the correct BROAD GENERAL legal term/phrase.

When generating your search terms in print (and especially online) it is best to have a legal thesaurus on hand in the beginning to help you develop those legal terms. One very useful website is **www.thesaurus.com**. In print, *Burton's Legal Thesaurus,* which includes more than 8,000 legal terms, including thousands of synonyms and definitions, is an excellent resource to help find the correct terms to conduct a search and can be purchased on Amazon.

So, when searching the digest in print, always begin your search with a BROAD GENERAL topic, and utilize a legal thesaurus if necessary. As you will see in conducting word searches with *WestlawNext* and *Lexis Advance*, the opposite is true in that the more *specific* you are in your word search, the narrower and more relevant your results because computer generated word searches can yield hundreds if not thousands of search results when using broad and general words.

The best and most effective way to learn anything is through the use of an example. In the next two sections, you will see how to navigate a state and federal digest using a specific topic. Please follow the steps and look at each screenshot so that you will be able recognize the parts of the digest and its index in the law library.

Finding State Cases

You now know and understand *where* state cases are located in print and more importantly *how* you find those cases in print. Follow the steps below so you can "walk" through the process of utilizing the state digest in order to find the legal authority you need to address and answer the hypothetical example below.

Suppose you work as a paralegal in Philadelphia, Pennsylvania and your supervising attorney calls you into his office (*remember to bring your pen and legal pad!*). The attorney just got off the phone with a client whose son attends college in the city. The client's son recently signed a lease for a one-bedroom apartment. The client told the attorney that a 4-inch wide hole in the apartment roof leaks into the bedroom; the living room ceiling fan is broken and hanging by a wire;

the toilet in the bathroom continually leaks onto the floor; there is no hot water in the apartment; and the kitchen has grease stains on the wall. Lastly, the client's son was recently at the doctor's office being treated for bed bug bites from the mattress in the apartment! The client told your attorney that he advised his son to hold back any payment of rent until all the problems were fixed. The landlord was notified two weeks ago as to the problems, yet none of the issues have been addressed or resolved. However, the landlord told the client's son to pay this month's rent or move out. The client needs advice on how to proceed.

Your supervising attorney knows that even if omitted from the lease, some type of warranty exists and passes from the landlord to the tenant. The attorney is not certain, but he believes the warranty implies that the landlord must make certain that the premises are at the very least habitable and suitable for the tenant to live in the dwelling. The attorney needs you to research what the warranty is and what is covered under such a warranty. In addition, what are the recourses, if any, available to the client and his son.

> Every state in the country recognizes this type of implied warranty in a land-lord/tenant agreement. After seeing how to navigate the digest in this example, conduct the same steps in your particular state or regional digest.

Before going to the library, remember you must formulate the relevant words/terms/phrases to navigate through the digest more smoothly. Prior to beginning any type of research in books or online it's good practice to take five minutes and pinpoint the specific legal words, terms, and phrases concerning the legal issue. Remember the explanation of how to conduct a word search in print above. You always begin with the BROAD GENERAL topic. In this case, what would that be? If you said the overall general topic is "landlord and tenant," then you are correct. The attorney also gave you some helpful terms including, "warranty," "habitable," and "suitable for living."

The digest used in this example will be the *West Atlantic Digest, 2d.* Although you may be in a different state, remember that the **books** and **process** are **similar**. If you recall, there are a few possible ways to navigate through the digests.

STEP 1: Pull the DWI and look for "landlord and tenant." As you can see in Figure 7-10, all the subtopics are organized alphabetically. Using your search terms, as you thumb through the various subtopics under "landlord and tenant," you find two that look very promising: HABITABILITY and IMPLIED covenants. It is also good that both have been assigned the same key number, which, in this case, is **Land & Ten #125**. Now you have a key number from which to search the volumes of the index.

If you were not this fortunate, then at times you just have to "adjust" your search terms, meaning that if your first or second term doesn't work, you try the third, then the fourth, until you find what you need. However, once you have you main broad topic, then if you cannot think of a subtopic, just read through all the subtopics until you find what you need. As you can see, the subtopics are very specific, so there is a good chance you will find what you need.

STEP 2: As you can see in Figure 7-11, now that you have **Key Number #125**, go to the corresponding volume within the set. Remember that all the abbreviations of the topics within a specific volume are engraved on the spine. In this example, you go to **Volume 20A (Land & Ten #1-168)**. This means that all landlord and tenant subtopics with key numbers ranging from 1-168 are included in that volume.

Figure 7-10 The Index Page for Landlord/Tenant and Various Subtopics

LANDLORD 36 Atl D 2d–368

References are to Digest Topics and Key Numbers

LANDLORD AND TENANT—Cont'd

FRAUDS, statute of. See heading **FRAUDS, STATUTE OF, LEASES.**

GAMING,
- Lease of house or place for gaming, criminal law, **Gaming ⊂= 76**
- Validity of lease, legality, **Land & Ten ⊂= 29(3)**

GARNISHMENT of leased property, **Garn ⊂= 28**

GAS and oil leases. See heading **OIL AND GAS, LEASES.**

GENERAL and special laws. See heading **SPECIAL AND GENERAL LAWS, LANDLORD** and tenant.

GOOD faith of landlord,
- Suspension or restriction of eviction remedies. See subheading SUSPENSION or restriction of eviction remedies, Good faith of landlord, under this heading.

GOODS,
- Rent, medium of payment, **Land & Ten ⊂= 215**

GRASS,
- Injuries to premises by third parties, **Land & Ten ⊂= 142(2)**

GUARANTY of lease, **Guar ⊂= 36(8)**

GUARDIAN'S lease of ward's property,
- Generally, **Guard & W ⊂= 44**
- Mentally ill persons, **Mental H ⊂= 274**
- Under order of court,
  - Generally, **Guard & W ⊂= 113**
  - Determination as to necessity, **Guard & W ⊂= 89**

GUESTS, injuries to, **Land & Ten ⊂= 167(8)**

HABITABILITY, warranty of, **Land & Ten ⊂= 125(1)**

HEALTH, rent liability,
- Effect of unhealthy premises, **Land & Ten**

LANDLORD AND TENANT—Cont'd
HOLDING over—Cont'd
Extension of term—Cont'd
- Election by landlord, **Land & Ten ⊂= 90(5)**
- Notice, option to extend, **Land & Ten ⊂= 90(6)**
- Option to extend, **Land & Ten ⊂= 90(6)**
- Term, **Land & Ten ⊂= 90(3)**
- What constitutes holding over, **Land & Ten ⊂= 90(4)**

Month to month tenancies, creation of,
- Holding over after expiration of term, **Land & Ten ⊂= 115(3)**

Notice, option to extend or renew lease, **Land & Ten ⊂= 90(6)**

Option to extend or renew lease, **Land & Ten ⊂= 90(6)**

Renewal of lease,
- Generally, **Land & Ten ⊂= 90(1)**
- Conditions, **Land & Ten ⊂= 90(2)**
- Election by landlord, **Land & Ten ⊂= 90(5)**
- Notice, option to renew, **Land & Ten ⊂= 90(6)**
- Option to renew, **Land & Ten ⊂= 90(6)**
- Term, **Land & Ten ⊂= 90(3)**
- What constitutes holding over, **Land & Ten ⊂= 90(4)**

Rent liability,
- Generally, **Land & Ten ⊂= 196**
- Amount, **Land & Ten ⊂= 200.9**

Tenancy at sufferance, creation of,
- Holding over after expiration of term, **Land & Ten ⊂= 119(2)**

Tenancy at will, creation of,
- Holding over after expiration of term, **Land & Ten ⊂= 118(4)**

Term, extension or renewal of lease, **Land & Ten ⊂= 90(3)**

Year to year tenancies, creation of,
- Holding over after expiration of term, **Land & Ten ⊂= 114(3)**

HUSBAND and wife,

Source: Reprinted with permission of Thomson Reuters, West's Atlantic Digest 2nd, Descriptive Word Index (H-LH), Page 368.

STEP 3: Go through the pages of that volume until you arrive at 125. Please note that the pages are ***not*** in numerical order, but organized by "key number" in the upper right-hand corner. As you can see in Figure 7-12, you arrive at the page for ***landlord and tenant, key number #125***.

So what is a case summary and how do you read one? A **case summary** is a summary consisting of a small paragraph (3-5 sentences) briefly describing the rule of law or holding in that particular case. Enough information is provided to inform you as to whether the case summary describes the issue or rule of law you are seeking.

case summary
A brief case summary describing the main rule of law included in a particular case opinion.

Please note that if you are using a *state* digest, every entry will be binding authority, as they include case summaries only from your state. However, if you are using a *regional* digest, multiple states are included. So under each subtopic, you have to find *your* state's summaries, which are all in bold and arranged by state alphabetically. Each case summary for each state is organized in descending order from the highest court in the state to the lowest trial court.

Figure 7-11 The Index Page for Landlord/Tenant and Various Subtopics

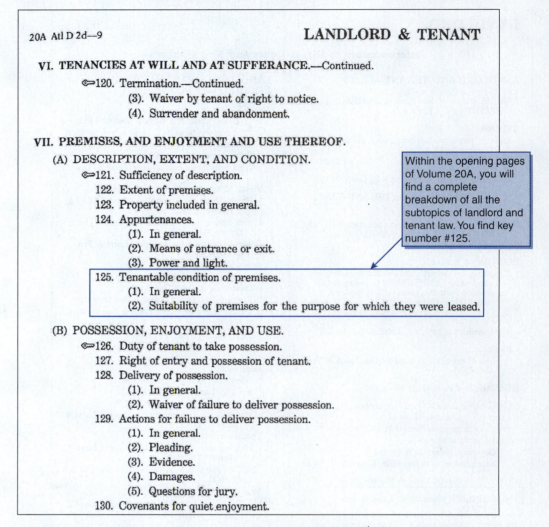

20A Atl D 2d—9

LANDLORD & TENANT

VI. TENANCIES AT WILL AND AT SUFFERANCE.—Continued.

   120. Termination.—Continued.
      (3). Waiver by tenant of right to notice.
      (4). Surrender and abandonment.

VII. PREMISES, AND ENJOYMENT AND USE THEREOF.

  (A) DESCRIPTION, EXTENT, AND CONDITION.
     121. Sufficiency of description.
     122. Extent of premises.
     123. Property included in general.
     124. Appurtenances.
       (1). In general.
       (2). Means of entrance or exit.
       (3). Power and light.
     125. Tenantable condition of premises.
       (1). In general.
       (2). Suitability of premises for the purpose for which they were leased.

  (B) POSSESSION, ENJOYMENT, AND USE.
     126. Duty of tenant to take possession.
     127. Right of entry and possession of tenant.
     128. Delivery of possession.
       (1). In general.
       (2). Waiver of failure to deliver possession.
     129. Actions for failure to deliver possession.
       (1). In general.
       (2). Pleading.
       (3). Evidence.
       (4). Damages.
       (5). Questions for jury.
     130. Covenants for quiet enjoyment.

Callout: Within the opening pages of Volume 20A, you will find a complete breakdown of all the subtopics of landlord and tenant law. You find key number #125.

Source: Reprinted with permission of Thomson Reuters, West's Atlantic Digest 2nd, Volume 20A Index, Page 9.

For each case summary listed, the court name and year the case was decided will be in bold. Thereafter, the case summary will state a brief point or rule of law taken from the full length opinion itself. Each case will also have its parallel citation listed as well.

As you can see in Figure 7-12, if more than one point or rule of law is used or mentioned within a single case, that case will be listed more than once. This is true in the example here, as the *Pugh v. Holmes* case looks like it may help to address your issue.

STEP 4: Browse the case summaries to determine which, if any, could be of good use to you. In this case, just from reading the case summaries, you can determine that:

- All residential leases contain a warranty of habitability;
- The warranty is applicable both at the beginning of the lease and throughout its duration;
- At a minimum, the warranty means the premises are safe and sanitary, although there is no duty on the landlord to make an aesthetically pleasing dwelling;

Figure 7-12 The "Results" Page for Landlord and Tenant #125

20A Atl D 2d—327   **LANDLORD & TENANT**   ⊙—125(1)

For references to other topics, see Descriptive-Word Index

dispossess suit but also in an action for rent itself.

> Berzito v. Gambino, 274 A.2d 865, 114 N.J.Super. 124, reversed 291 A.2d 577, 119 N.J.Super. 332, certification granted 299 A.2d 65, 62 N.J. 67, reversed 308 A.2d 17, 63 N.J. 460, reinstated as amended 308 A.2d 17, 63 N.J. 460.

Fact that tenant continued to pay weekly rent in full for a period of almost a year in a half did not constitute a waiver of landlord's breach of express warranty of habitability, where tenant, with no husband and thus solely respo̶n̶s̶i̶b̶l̶e̶ ̶f̶o̶r̶ ̶w̶e̶l̶f̶a̶r̶e̶ ̶o̶f̶ ̶h̶e̶r̶ child, went along w̶i̶t̶h̶ ̶p̶r̶o̶p̶o̶s̶a̶l̶ ̶t̶h̶a̶t̶ ̶landlord would perfo̶r̶m̶ ̶n̶e̶c̶e̶s̶s̶a̶r̶y̶ ̶w̶o̶r̶k̶ to make an issue a̶b̶o̶u̶t̶ ̶d̶e̶f̶e̶c̶t̶i̶v̶e̶ ̶c̶o̶n̶dition, ten-ant's i̶n̶t̶e̶n̶t̶ ̶t̶o̶ ̶w̶a̶i̶v̶e̶ ̶h̶a̶d̶ ̶been clearly estab̶l̶i̶s̶h̶e̶d̶ ̶a̶n̶d̶ ̶w̶a̶i̶v̶e̶r̶ ̶would not be held t̶o̶ ̶h̶a̶v̶e̶ ̶o̶c̶c̶u̶r̶r̶e̶d̶.

> B̶e̶r̶z̶i̶t̶o̶ ̶v̶.̶ ̶G̶a̶m̶b̶i̶n̶o̶,̶ ̶2̶7̶4̶ l 865, 114 ̶N̶.̶J̶.̶S̶u̶p̶e̶r̶.̶ ̶1̶2̶4̶,̶ ̶r̶e̶v̶e̶r̶s̶e̶d̶ A.2d 577, ̶1̶1̶9̶ ̶N̶.̶J̶.̶S̶u̶p̶e̶r̶.̶ ̶3̶3̶2̶,̶ ̶ion granted ̶2̶9̶9̶ ̶A̶.̶2̶d̶ ̶6̶5̶,̶ ̶6̶2̶ ̶N̶.̶J̶.̶ ̶6̶7̶,̶ ̶versed 308 A.2d 17, 63 N.J. 460, reinstated as amended 308 A.2d 17, 63 N.J. 460.

[Annotation box overlapping text:] Each "case summary" under that specific subtopic will state a significant point or rule of law used in that case relating specifically to the subtopic. The case of Pugh v. Holmes looks like it addresses the issues in the textbook hypothetical.

Where landlord breached his express warranty of habitability, there was a partial failure of consideration, and tenant was entitled to recover loss of her bargain, that is, difference between value of premises in their actual condition and rent paid.

> Berzito v. Gambino, 274 A.2d 865, 114 N.J.Super. 124, reversed 291 A.2d 577, 119 N.J.Super. 332, certification granted 299 A.2d 65, 62 N.J. 67, reversed 308 A.2d 17, 63 N.J. 460, reinstated as amended 308 A.2d 17, 63 N.J. 460.

N.J.Dist.Ct. 1970. Failure of landlord in multistoried apartment building to supply heat, hot water, garbage disposal, or elevator service is breach of implied "covenant of habitability" and will be considered in diminution of rent;

the beginning of a lease and throughout its duration.

> Pugh v. Holmes, 405 A.2d 897, 486 Pa. 272.

At a minimum, the implied warranty of habitability in a residential lease means that the premises must be safe and sanitary; however, there is no obligation on the part of the landlord to supply a perfect or aesthetically pleasing dwelling.

> Pugh v. Holmes, 405 A.2d 897, 486 Pa. 272.

To establish a breach of the implied warranty of habitability, a tenant must prove that he or she gave notice to the landlord of the defect or condition, that the landlord had a reasonable opportunity to make the necessary repairs and that the landlord failed to do so.

> Pugh v. Holmes, 405 A.2d 897, 486 Pa. 272.

Proof that local housing codes were violated is not necessary to establish a breach of the implied warranty of habitability.

> Pugh v. Holmes, 405 A.2d 897, 486 Pa. 272.

> If established, conditions including a leaky roof, lack of hot water, leaking toilet and pipes, cockroach infestation and hazardous floors and steps could justify a finding by the trier of fact that the warranty of habitability implied in a residential lease had been breached.
>
> Pugh v. Holmes, 405 A.2d 897, 486 Pa. 272.

Pa. 1967. Landlord does not warrant that leased premises are in tenantable condition.

> Smith v. M.P.W. Realty Co., 225 A.2d 227, 423 Pa. 536.

Pa. 1962. Provisions of Philadelphia Housing Code were not incorporated in lease as terms and conditions thereof, and alleged breach of Code did not give rise to action in assumpsit by injured tenant against landlord for breach of those provisions.

> Kearse v. Spaulding, 176 A.2d 450, 406 Pa. 140.

Source: Reprinted with permission of Thomson Reuters, West's Atlantic Digest 2nd, Volume 20A, Page 327.

- To establish the breach, the tenant must give the landlord warning of the defect and that the landlord has a reasonable amount of time to correct the problem;
- Defects such as a leaky roof, lack of hot water, leaking toilet and pipes, cockroach infestation, and hazardous floors and steps could justify a finding that the warranty was breached.

That's not a bad start only by reading the case summaries. Now that you have a good case as a starting point, you can locate it in print or online.

Lastly, when you have the citation for the *Pugh* case, you can locate it online (which you will learn later) or in the print reporter, as you can see in Figure 7-13. Remember that *every* key number can be used universally for any state, regional, or federal digest, as well as the headnotes found in each opinion.

Figure 7-13 *Pugh v. Holmes* – Headnotes *(Atlantic Reporter)*

PUGH v. HOLMES   Pa. **1235**
Cite as, Pa.Super., 384 A.2d 1234

1. Landlord and Tenant ⟞125(1)

Principle of caveat emptor, or caveat tenant, is no longer applicable to residential leases and an implied warranty of habitability is now applicable to all such leases.

2. Landlord and Tenant ⟞187(1)

A tenant's obligation under a residential lease to pay rent and landlord's obligation to maintain habitable premises are mutually dependent with a material breach of one of obligations relieving obligation of other so long as breach continues, inasmuch as all residential leases, be they written or oral, periodic or at will, are to be controlled by principles of contract law.

3. Landlord and Tenant ⟞125(1)

The implied warranty of habitability in residential leases is designed to insure that a landlord will provide facilities and services...

(Notice how the "key number" 125(1) found in the West *digest is the same number found in the above headnote found in this case opinion,* Pugh v. Holmes. *Remember that the key number system works with any* West *publication.)*

4. Landlord and Tenant ⟞125(1)

Under implied warranty of habitability

leases, defect must be of a nature and kind which will render premises unsafe, or unsanitary and thus unfit for living therein.

8. Landlord and Tenant ⟞125(1)

Among those factors to be considered by trier of fact on a case by case basis in determining whether a breach of implied warranty of habitability in residential lease is material are: (1) whether condition violates a housing law, regulation or ordinance; (2) nature and seriousness of defect; (3) effect of defect on safety and sanitation; (4) length of time for which condition has persisted, and (5) age of structure.

9. Landlord and Tenant ⟞187(1), 284(1)

Tenant may assert a breach of implied warranty of habitability in residential lease as a defense against a landlord's action for possession or for unpaid rent.

... and Tenant ⟞223(7), 284(2)

...may assert breach of implied warranty of habitability in residential lease as a counterclaim and seek reimbursement...

Source: Reprinted with permission of Thomson Reuters, West's Atlantic 2nd Reporter Volume 384, Page 1235.

Validating and Updating the Digest Research

After you find a case name and citation from the digest, you must validate it to ensure the case is still good law. Many case summaries you will find in the digests are older cases, many of which provide excellent points of law, but may also have been overturned. You will learn later in this chapter how to validate your case findings online. For now, just now that you must validate the law.

Also, in the back inside cover of each volume, a pocket part should be inserted. Pocket parts are included when material in the digest is updated. As you can see in Figure 7-14, the pocket part looks the same as the pages in the volume itself, but they are not bound within the volume. If many cases have been added in a particular volume, a separate softbound white pamphlet will be included directly in between the corresponding volumes on the shelf until a new hardbound volume can be added. In addition, *West* also publishes a thicker white cumulative pamphlet that is a *yearly* update including **every** updated topic within the **entire** digest. This is located at the end of the digest.

Before conducting your assignment, you did not know what a warranty of habitability was, or maybe that it even existed, but now you are equipped to answer the issues raised by your supervising attorney. It would be wise to research more cases, or to see if more recent cases exist that state the same point of law, but at least now you have a good foundation to address and answer the issue.

The DWI is the most efficient index to utilize, but remember that there are other indexes. The *Words and Phrases* index is sufficient, but it does not offer as many specific subtopics of information as does the DWI.

Figure 7-14 The Pocket Part of Volume 20A

20A Atl D 2d—43   **LANDLORD & TENANT**   ☞130(.5)

dentally during incidental research. 9 V.S.A. §§ 4451 et seq., 4458(a).—Willard v. Parsons Hill Partnership, 882 A.2d 1213, 178 Vt. 300, 2005 VT 69.

Landlord's failure to comply with applicable housing code regulations can result in a breach of the warranty of habitability.—Id.

Potential availability of common law or statutory tort remedies for personal injuries suffered by tenants before they discovered toxic contamination of their water supply, a condition theretofore known to landlord for some fourteen years, were not a sufficient substitute for and did not preclude a common law action for breach of implied warranty of habitability, which sounded in contract and, as such, was a different remedy for a different wrong. 9 V.S.A. § 4457.—Id.

☞**125(2). Suitability of premises for the purpose for which they were leased.**

N.H. 2009. Evidence failed to establish that property with leaking roof was not safe or unsuitable for its intended use as clothing store and that landlord was liable to tenant; tenant's renovations initially resulted in severe and numerous leaks, subsequent repairs lessened the number and severity of the leaks, and the leaks required employees to move racks of clothing, cover them with plastic, use barrels to catch the drips, and restrict customer access to some areas.—South Willow Properties, LLC v. Burlington Coat Factory of New Hampshire, LLC, 986 A.2d 506, 159 N.H. 494.

(B) POSSESSION, ENJOYMENT, AND USE.

☞**127. Right of entry and possession of tenant.**

Conn.App. 2013. Distinguishing characteristic of a lease is the surrender of possession by the landlord to the tenant so that he may occupy the

ed lease was not entitled to key, as though lease were still alive, and, after brief, reasonable period of time in which tenant had right to retrieve her belongings, she stood in no stronger relationship to landlord than a trespasser. Restatement (Second) of Property § 14.7.—Id.

Me. 2007. A tenant who has a lease is entitled to possession and exclusive occupancy of the premises, but a licensee merely has a contract for use without a transfer in an interest in land.—Benham v. Morton & Furbish Agency, 929 A.2d 471, 2007 ME 83.

Me. 2002. A tenant ga[n]trol of an area through a[ ]ment.—Chiu v. City of P[ ]2002 ME 8.

Md. 2012. Tenant pro[ ]a property has a right of [ ]landlord; it follows that [ ]who has succeeded to the [ ]would have no right of immediate possession as against a tenant legally in possession of the property. West's Ann.Md.Code, Real Property, § 7-105.6.—Curtis v. U.S. Bank Nat. Ass'n, 50 A.3d 558, 427 Md. 526.

N.J.Super.A.D. 2013. A tenant enjoys the exclusive right to privacy within his or her leasehold during the tenancy, subject to a landlord's qualified right to enter the unit for repairs, inspections, or other similar purposes upon proper notice. N.J.A.C. 5:10–5.1(c).—State v. Wright, 71 A.3d 212, 431 N.J.Super. 558.

☞**130. Covenants for quiet enjoyment.**
See ☞130(.5).

☞**130(.5). In general.**
Conn.App. 2009. Under landlord-tenant law, it is the right of a tenant to enforce a "covenant of quiet enjoyment," which assures that the lessee shall have legal quiet and peaceable possession

> Because this is the "Atlantic" Digest, all of the pocket part entries are listed by state under each corresponding "key number" within the digest itself.

Source: Reprinted with permission of Thomson Reuters, West's Atlantic Digest 2nd, Volume 20A Pocket Part, Page 39.

Using the digest to find cases supporting the point of law needed or addressing your issue is an invaluable resource. With just two or three easy steps, and use of some good search terms, you can build a great starting point for your research. Now, go to the law library and conduct that same search using the digest in your jurisdiction. Take a classmate.

Finding Federal Cases

You can navigate the federal digests similarly. Follow the steps below that will walk you through the process of utilizing the federal digest to find the legal authority you need to address and answer the hypothetical example below. You can either read the following example or take this text with you to the library to become better acquainted with the federal set.

Suppose you work as a paralegal and your supervising attorney tells you that a federal grand jury has been convened for one of his clients. The attorney is unfamiliar with all the legal aspects of a grand jury proceeding and needs you to conduct research to answer the following question: What is the attorney's role, if any, during the grand jury proceeding of the client?

Remember to begin with the BROAD GENERAL topic. What is the large general topic here? It would be GRAND JURY. The attorney also gave you some helpful terms including, "attorney's role," and "grand jury proceeding."

The digest used in this example will be the *West Federal Practice Digest, 4th*. If you recall, there are a few possible ways to navigate through the digests.

STEP 1: Follow the same steps similar to the state digest search. Search the DWI index for the main topic of GRAND JURY. As you can see in Figure 7-15, under the topic of GRAND JURY, there are two possibilities:

- "ATTORNEYS, general, Participation in proceedings, key number Gr Jury #34" and
- "COUNSEL, Presence during proceedings, Gr Jury #35.

Figure 7-15 The DWI Index for the Topic of GRAND JURY

GRAIN
98 F P D 4th

References are to Digest Topics and Key Numbers

GRAIN ELEVATORS

See also heading **WAREHOUSEMEN**, generally.

EMINENT domain, grain elevators as public use, Em Dom ☞ 38

GRAMMAR

MISTAKES,
   Contracts, **Contracts** ☞ 157
   Indictment and information, **Ind & Inf** ☞ 79
   Pleading, **Plead** ☞ 30
   Statutes, **Statut** ☞ 200
   Verdict, **Crim Law** ☞ 875(3)

WILLS,
   See heading **WILLS, GRAMMATICAL** mistakes

GRAMMAR SCHOOLS

See heading **SCHOOLS AND SCHOOL DISTRICTS**, generally.

GRAND JURY

ACCUSATIONS,
   Powers and duties, **Gr Jury** ☞ 26

ACCUSED,
   Examination, **Gr Jury** ☞ 37
   Presence during proceedings, **Gr Jury** ☞ 35

ADJOURNMENTS, **Gr Jury** ☞ 31

APPORTIONMENT of jurors, **Gr Jury** ☞ 4

ARREST of judgment. See heading **ARREST OF JUDGMENT**, GRAND jury.

ATTENDANCE of jurors, **Gr Jury** ☞ 13

ATTORNEY and client,
   Adverse or pecuniary interest, **Atty & C** ☞ 21.5(7)

ATTORNEYS general,
   Participation in proceedings, **Gr Jury** ☞ 34

GRAND JURY—Cont'd
CHALLENGES—Cont'd

   Individual jurors, **Gr Jury** ☞ 18

CHARGE to jury, **Gr Jury** ☞ 23

COMMUNITY representation, **Gr Jury** ☞ 2.5
   Foreperson, **Gr Jury** ☞ 21

COMPENSATION of jurors, **Gr Jury** ☞ 14

COMPETENCY of jurors, **Gr Jury** ☞ 15

CONSTITUTION of jury, **Gr Jury** ☞ 2.5

CONSTITUTIONAL law,
   Generally, **Gr Jury** ☞ 2
   Due process, **Const Law** ☞ 265
   Equal protection. See subheading **EQUAL PROTECTION** under this heading.

CONTEMPT,
   Interference, **Gr Jury** ☞ 44
   Refusal to testify or produce evidence,
      Generally, **Gr Jury** ☞ 36.5(1)
      Purging contempt, **Gr Jury** ☞ 36.5(2)
   Secrecy requirements,
      Violation, **Gr Jury** ☞ 41.60
   Witnesses, **Gr Jury** ☞ 36.5

COUNSEL,
   Presence during proceedings, **Gr Jury** ☞ 35
   Witnesses,
      Right to counsel, **Gr Jury** ☞ 35

CREDIBILITY,
   Witnesses,
      Testimony before grand jury, **Witn** ☞ 379(9)

DECLARATIONS by third persons, **Crim Law** ☞ 417(3)

DEFECTS,
   Grounds,
      Plea in abatement, **Crim Law** ☞ 278(2), 280(2)

DESCRIPTION of grand jury in caption of indictment, **Ind & Inf** ☞ 25

Source: Reprinted with permission of Thomson Reuters, West's Federal Practice Digest 4th, Descriptive Word Index Volume 98, Page 548.

If you do find more than one key number in your search, make sure you check them all out just to make certain you have exhausted all possibilities. In this example, both look promising.

STEP 2:   Now you go to the volumes in the set and find, *Grand Jury, Volume 58.*

STEP 3:   Once you find the appropriate volume, go through the pages until you find **Grand Jury #34-35**. There, as you can see in Figure 7-16, you find that **key number #34** denotes cases that include **Presence of accused or counsel**.

Similar to the state digest, these cases would build a solid foundation from which to continue your research. The other index methods utilized in the state digests are also available in the federal digests. Also similar to the state digests, *West* publishes white softbound pamphlets that are inserted between the volumes of cumulative updates, as well as an overall cumulative update of the entire digest each *year* that is found at the end of the set.

Lastly, don't forget to check the pocket part of the volume you are reading to see if any other new case summaries were added to your topic section.

Utilizing the state or federal digest is a free and efficient way to conduct your research. After you learn how to conduct online research below, you will see how the print and online sources can be used together.

■ STATE AND FEDERAL CASES ONLINE

Aside from the print sources, you can also find most state and federal case law online. In this section, you will learn how to locate case law through the paid subscription services such as *WestlawNext* and *Lexis Advance*. However, many paralegals do not always have immediate access to either of those services, or are restricted with their use. For those situations, you will also learn about all the paid subscription services that are considerably less expensive, as well as many free government and educational websites that publish case law authority.

In this section, you will learn the basics of case research through the use *WestlawNext* and *Lexis Advance*. Using the same landlord/tenant example that

> **LEARNING OBJECTIVE 4**
> Describe how to search for cases online using Westlaw and Lexis.

Figure 7-16 The "Results" Page for Grand Jury

> Government's referring to uncharged offenses and conduct and allegedly making misstatements in describing charges contained in indictment were not sufficient to warrant finding of misconduct or to justify dismissal of indictment.
> U.S. v. Fisher, 692 F.Supp. 495, appeal dismissed 871 F.2d 444.
>
> Key number #35 denotes the "presence of accused or counsel."
>
> and not disclose subpoena were not prosecutorial misconduct resulting in interference in pending criminal case, where purpose of subpoena was to investigate charges other than those for which defendants had been indicted, rather than to harass and intimidate potential witnesses and supporters of defendants, and letter

> ⌨ **35. Presence of accused or counsel.**
> **Library references**
> C.J.S. Grand Juries §§ 99–101, 166, 170.
>
> **C.A.8 (Ark.) 1996.** Counsel's presence inside grand jury room was not constitutionally required to protect right to counsel of witness, who was found in civil contempt after refusing to answer grand jury's questions, as Sixth Amendment does not apply to witness's grand jury testimony and counsel was available for consultations outside grand jury room. U.S.C.A. Const.Amend. 6; Fed.Rules Cr.Proc. Rule 6(d), 18 U.S.C.A.
> In re Grand Jury Subpoena, 97 F.3d 1090.
>
> **C.A.9 (Cal.) 2003.** A witness must face a prosecutor's questions in federal grand jury

Source: Reprinted with permission of Thomson Reuters, West's Federal Practice Digest 4th, Volume 58, Page 614.

you researched in print, you will be shown step-by-step of how to retrieve cases addressing that same issue.

> *WestlawNext* and *Lexis Advance* update their systems daily. Therefore, both systems continually add, delete, and amend its material and content. A search conducted today on either system may yield different results when the same search is conducted at a later date. Therefore, as you follow the step-by-step process below, do not focus on whether you arrived at the same ***results***. Rather, focus on the ***steps*** to search for a case online using both systems.

WestlawNext

Locating a state or federal case on *Westlaw* is not difficult. You can find the same cases here as you can in the print version. You will see that whether you possess a citation or not, the locating techniques are very similar to that of the printed books. Please follow the steps below.

SEARCH OPTION #1: You have a case citation.

Similar to the printed books, you can access a case with the citation immediately. Enter the citation in the main search box on the *Westlaw* home screen. This link will take you directly to the case opinion.

SEARCH OPTION #2: You do not have a case citation.

Similar to the printed books, if you do not have the case citation, you will need to take just a few more steps to get it. This is where you would need to generate your "word search" method.

Also similar to the printed books, if you do not have the case citation, you will need to take a few steps before finding the case you need. This is where you will need to generate your online "word search."

On the *WestlawNext* home page, under **Browse**, there are options for **State** or **Federal** materials. For ***state*** case law, choose the **State** tab and all 50 state names will appear. Choose your state.

Figure 7-17 Results Page for State Cases

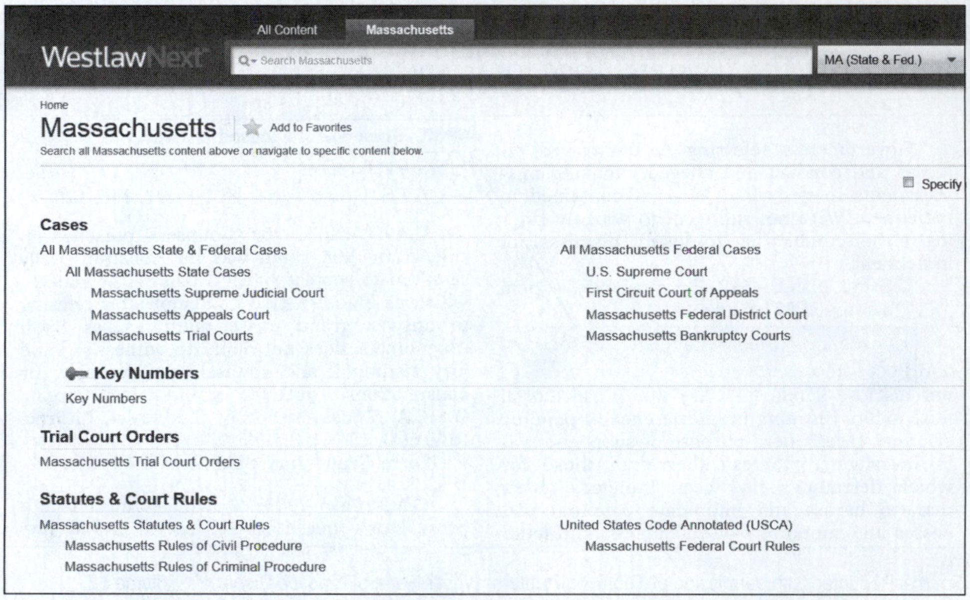

Source: Reprinted with permission of Thomson Reuters, State search result on WestlawNext.

As you can see in Figure 7-17, on the home page of your particular state, you can search for *any* state content using the main search box or navigate using any of the specific content on the screen below the search box, which includes all *cases, statutes, court rules, regulations, administrative decisions,* and *trial court orders* for that state (**this format is the same for every state**).

The search box now states "search Massachusetts." You can also save this page as a "favorite" by clicking the, **Add to Favorites**, under the main search box. It would be wise to do this if you work in a particular state and frequently utilize case law from that state.

The **Cases** category includes all state *and* federal case law in that state (remember federal courts sit in one or more districts in a state). For instance, for whatever state you choose, you will have options for *all state cases, the state supreme or highest state appellate court, the intermediate appellate court,* and *the state trial courts.*

For *federal* case law, you have two options. On the *Westlaw* home page, under **Browse**, choose **Federal Materials**. You will see options for *all federal cases* and each of the *11 circuit courts,* plus the *D.C. and Federal Circuits.* Alternatively, on the home page of any **state** you choose, as in Figure 7-18, options also include *all federal cases in that state, US Supreme Court, appeals for that particular circuit and case from the federal district courts* of that state.

Conducting a Word Search on WestlawNext

"Choose your words carefully . . . " You have undoubtedly heard this saying before, but it has never been truer than when generating your legal search terms online. It is very important, when conducting a word search, to utilize the correct words/terms/phrases to ensure a successful and productive search. If not, the search could be frustrating because you may not find what you are looking for, you may miss something completely, or worst of all you may generate a search including more than 10,000 results! Generating a good word search online is not

Figure 7-18 Results Page for Federal Cases

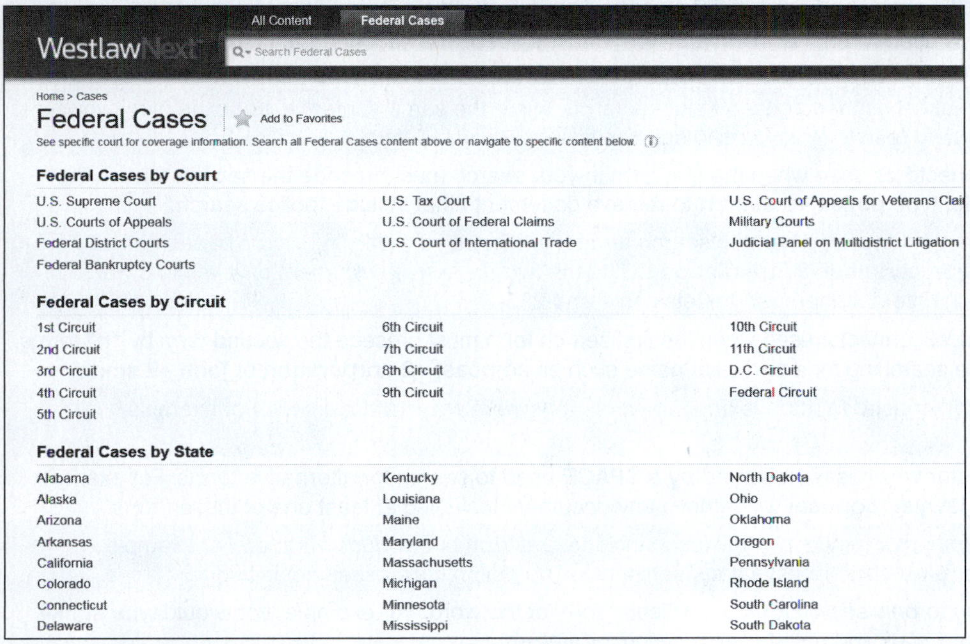

Source: Reprinted with permission of Thomson Reuters, Federal courts result on WestlawNext.

something you will immediately master, as many seasoned researchers occasionally must use a few different search terms before achieving their desired results.

This is why *WestlawNext* has created its own "language," including certain terms and connectors to assist in your online search. Also, remember to keep your print or online legal dictionary and thesaurus with you to assist in your case law search.

As you learned in the print digests, the index is broken down into different levels of legal words/terms where you begin your search with general topics and end with more specific topics. Here, the opposite is true. Suppose you had to research what needs to be proven to establish the liability of a surgeon who amputates the wrong limb on a patient during surgery. If you inserted the search words: MALPRACTICE, DOCTOR, SURGERY, you would generate thousands of results because the words/terms/phrases are so general and broad, and those words are included in thousands of cases. The computer database would find *every* case that includes those broad general terms.

You need to know *how* to properly use/insert the correct terms to generate a productive and effective search. Most online search databases recognize two types of search techniques: **Boolean searches** and **Natural Language searches**. First, a Boolean search retrieves information based upon the *relationship* among words in a particular search. This type of search is also referred to as a **Terms and Connectors (T&C) search**, meaning you use helpful terms and connectors along with the words to maximize your results to only the most relevant. Review Figure 7-19 for a list of all the *Westlaw* T&C commands.

boolean search
A search that uses operators such as AND, OR, and NOT to combine or limit words within your search.

natural language search
A search that uses everyday language to create various search terms.

Figure 7-19 Common Terms and Connectors on *WestlawNext*

Term/ Connector	Command
!	This is a root expander to search for words with multiple endings. For example, type **object!** to retrieve any document including the words, *object, objected, objection,* and *objecting*.
*****	This is a universal (wildcard) character that acts as any type of character. For example, type **jur*r** to retrieve *jury* and *juror*. Also, type **withdr*w** to retrieve withdraw and withdrew. You can also specify the *length* of a word using the universal character. For example, the word **object*** would retrieve *object, objects, objected, objective, objection,* and *objecting*.
/p	This is a grammatical connector used to search for terms that must appear in the same paragraph. For example, typing **hearsay /p police officer** will retrieve documents where those terms are found in the same paragraph.
+p	This similar character is used when the first search term must *precede* the second term in the paragraph. For example, typing in **Miranda +p interrogation** to retrieve documents including both terms in the same paragraph.
/s	This is another grammatical connector used to locate terms within the same sentence. For example, if you type **design /s defect** will yield results of any document discussing a design defect.
+s	This grammatical connector is used when the first term in your search must precede the second term in the sentence. For example, type **police +s search** to retrieve documents that include "police search."
/n	This is a numerical connector used when the search terms must be used within "n" words of each other. For example, you would type **personal /3 jurisdiction** to find the two terms in a document only within 3 words of each other. You can choose a number range between 1 and 255.
+n	This is another numerical connector used when the first search term must precede the second term by "n" terms. For example, if you are searching for a particular name such as **comcast +2 corporation** or **john +2 smith**.
&	This is the AND connector used to retrieve *any* two words *anywhere* within a document. For example, **narcotics & warrant**.
(_)	This is the "or" connector which is represented **by a SPACE** used to search for alternative terms. For example, the search **attorney_lawyer_counsel** will retrieve any document including at least one of these terms.
%	This is the "but not" connector for when you want to include one term but *exclude* another. For example, **medical malpractice % nurse** to retrieve documents including malpractice cases not including nurses.
#	This connector is used to *only* search for that particular *form* of the word. For example, you would type **stalk#** to only retrieve the word *stalk* and not *stalker, stalking,* or *stalked*.

These terms and connectors may initially seem confusing or difficult to understand, but after using them with some frequency, they will become easier to use. Keep in mind that the following symbols ALONE DO NOT trigger a Boolean search: the ampersand (&), the space symbol (_), quotation marks (" "), or the hyphen (-). For a Boolean search to be conducted, you must use them in conjunction with any of the terms and connectors in Figure 7-19.

However, if you cannot find what you need from a traditional T&C search, click on **Advance Search** next to the main orange **Search** button to the right of the main search box. A new search box will appear on the screen. Click on **Jurisdiction** if you wish to change it. Type in your terms in the appropriate text boxes. You can choose from (1) *All these terms*, (2) *Any of these terms*, or (3) *This exact phrase*. You can also enter terms into a search box to exclude documents that do not include certain words/terms/phrases you enter. The advance search helps to narrow your results even further while conducting your search.

A Natural Language search means just that—it's a search that does not utilize terms or connectors but rather natural everyday language. For example, you can either:

1. Enter any combination of legal words/terms/phrases such as DEFENDANT, CRIME, CONSPIRACY, DRUGS, and SHOOTING. If you want to include a particular or specific phrase, then you must include it in quotes such as "MEDICAL MALPRACTICE." If you did not place the phrase in quotes, then the database would search for each case that deals with malpractice, including engineers, architects, pharmacists, attorneys, and so on. The search would also search the thousands of cases that even mention the word "medical."

2. You can also enter an actual question or phase, such as: DOES A WITNESS WHO IS CALLED TO A CORONER'S INQUEST HAVE THE RIGHT TO COUNSEL?

In conducting a natural language search (and for a terms/connectors search) be sure to utilize the legal dictionary and thesaurus to assist in your search. It can provide a helpful reminder to use the terms "youth" and "juvenile" in addition to the word "child." In addition, you can use the terms "attorney" and "counsel" in addition to the word "lawyer."

As you can see, it is important to utilize the proper word search methods in an online database. Only with practice will you become better at searching online.

After you choose either a state or federal case law option, you can enter any words/terms/phrases you want into the main search box. Let us continue with the same landlord/tenant example you conducted in the print sources. Remember that the client's son rented an apartment with many structural defects. Your supervising attorney wants you to research if any implied warranties exist and if the client's son has any recourse under the law to enforce the repair of the apartment. Either you could begin a T&C search including such terms as: WARRANT! +P HABITAB! & LANDLORD/10 SAFE, or you could try: LANDLORD/5 "WARRANTY OF HABITABILITY" SAFE PREMISES. There is no set T&C search. Remember, it's up to you to use whatever combination of search terms works best, which may take a few attempts. You could also conduct a natural language search including such terms as: LANDLORD, TENANT, LEASE, "WARRANTY OF HABITABILITY", SAFE, RENT.

For this example, in the **Jurisdiction** box next to the main search box, make certain your chosen jurisdiction is "Pennsylvania" and insert: WARRANT! +P HABITAB! & LANDLORD /10 SAFE into the main search box (after you conduct this search to learn the steps, be certain to conduct the same search within your jurisdiction).

PRACTICE TIP

Suppose you were asked to conduct a search for the elements of negligence concerning a client who crashed into a neighbor's garage after taking his eyes off the road to change the radio station. In using a Boolean search, you could craft your terms in this manner: negligen! /p automobile_car, or you could enter negligen! /p liability & property damage. There is no strict rule or specific formula that you must adhere by. The terms and connectors are "tools" to assist in your search—how you use them is up to you. You could alter and modify the terms to achieve the desired result. Keep practicing . . .

If you notice, after you select the **Search** button, the general search results page will include "previews" of the top *cases*, *statutes*, *regulations*, and so on. Click on **See All Cases**. The top result, as you can see in Figure 7-20, is the *McIntyre* case. Once you click on that case, the full opinion will appear, as shown in Figure 7-21.

Figure 7-20 Search Results Page on *Westlaw Next*

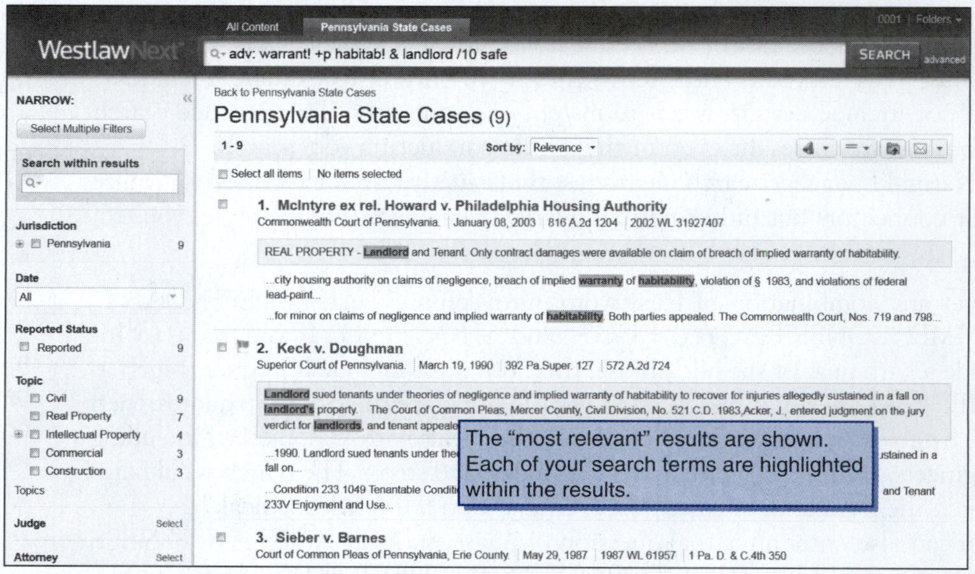

Source: Reprinted with permission of Thomson Reuters, Case search results on WestlawNext.

Figure 7-21 The *McIntyre* Case on *WestlawNext*

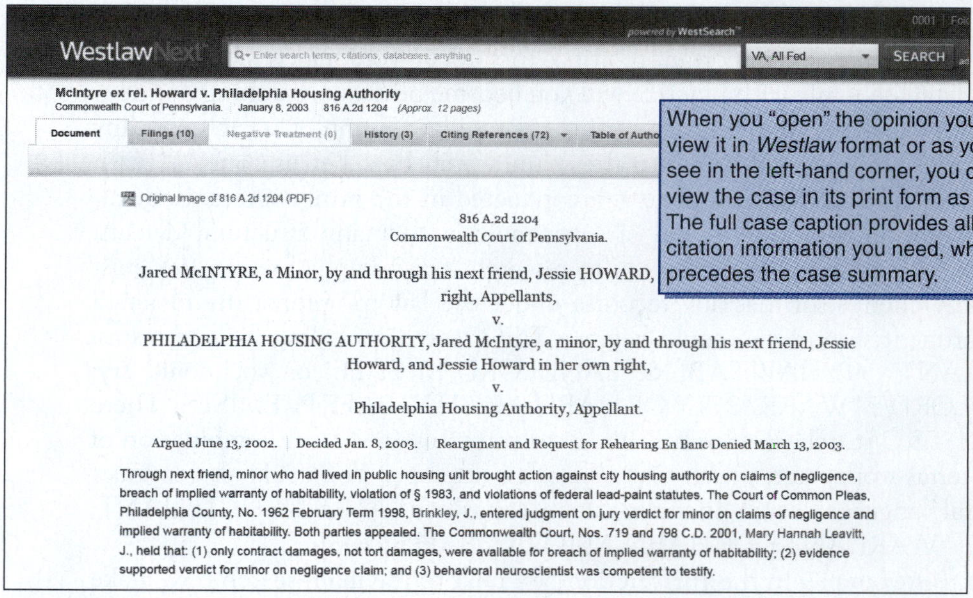

Source: Reprinted with permission of Thomson Reuters, Case 816 A.2d 1204 caption on WestlawNext.

As you can see in Figure 7-22, if you choose the first case on the search results page, the actual opinion is similar to how you have seen opinions in print materials. Following the case summary, each headnote found within the opinion is listed at the beginning of the opinion. In addition to reading the headnotes in the case to understand the rule of law, you can also utilize the headnotes as a way of conducting an online digest search. *WestlawNext* does not provide direct access to any digest, but as you can see in Figure 7-22, the "key symbol" in head-note #3, is informing you that "Landlord and Tenant" is a digest topic name. Clicking on that key symbol will take you to that topic. In addition, if you select the hyperlink **2 Cases that cite this headnote**, that will take you to other case decisions that used that exact headnote. This is a way to perform a type of online digest search on *WestlawNext*. So not only are online case headnotes helpful for the case you are reading, but helpful to conduct more detailed and more narrow searches.

By reading the first few **headnotes**, you can see that the opinion itself might be worth reading to extract the rule of law you need from the case, even if the facts do not line up, and that is ok. Remember, it will be rare that you find a case that includes the exact facts, issues, and rule of law as your case. Instead, you are looking for issues and rules of law where you can find them. You will learn how to conduct different types of legal authority in Chapter 10.

As you can see in Figure 7-23, if you see a headnote of interest, you can click on the number of the headnote in the square, which will take you directly to where that headnote begins within the text of the opinion, rather than searching each page. This is very helpful, especially in a 30-page opinion.

After you read through the body of the opinion, it ends with the conclusion and order (disposition) of the court, followed by any **footnotes** cited within the opinion. Almost every footnote that describes or cites authority is presented as

headnotes
A specific rule or point of law included at the beginning of a commercially published case opinion which directs you to that rule or point of law within the body of the opinion.

footnotes
Used in opinions and written by the court that credit any sources of material borrowed or summarized within the opinion.

Figure 7-22 Headnotes on *WestlawNext*

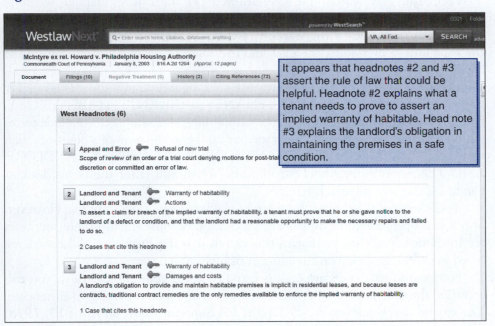

Source: Reprinted with permission of Thomson Reuters, Case 816 A.2d 1204 headnotes on WestlawNext.

Figure 7-23 The Body of the Opinion on *WestlawNext*

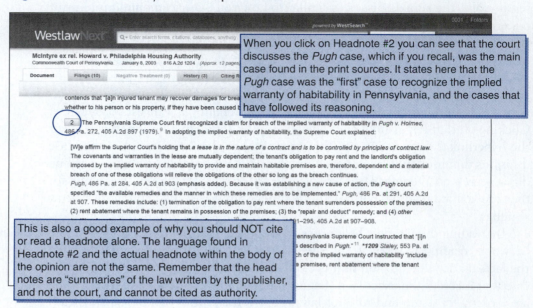

Source: Reprinted with permission of Thomson Reuters, Case 816 A.2d 1204 opinion on WestlawNext.

a hyperlink taking you immediately to that source. One of the great benefits of online research that obviously cannot be conducted in a book is hyperlinks! For example, you see that within this opinion, the *Pugh* case is cited and you want to read it. There is no search involved. Just click on the blue hyperlink, as well as that of any other case cited within the opinion that is of interest to you. You can always hit the back button to take you back to your original screen.

From this easy search you have learned (1) there is an implied warranty between the landlord and tenant, (2) it is called a warranty of habitability, (3) there are remedies if the warranty is breached. As noted, you can research the issue further by reading the *Pugh* and the *Staley v. Bouril* case cited within the *McIntyre* opinion.

Perhaps you wanted to conduct a natural language search for this issue. Try inserting the terms: LANDLORD, TENANT, WARRANTY, HABITABILITY, SAFE, PREMISES. Remember that a natural language search can include terms without the use of terms and connectors, or can be in the form of a question, such as: DOES AN IMPLIED WARRANTY EXIST BETWEEN A LANDLORD AND TENANT IN A RENTAL LEASE? When you enter the terms, look at Figure 7-24 to see the search results.

You can see this particular search yielded over 7,000 results. However, only a small percentage of those results are cases. Because the most relevant cases are listed first, you can see that in this search it is the *Pugh* case. All results are listed by relevance based on the number of highlighted terms.

Notice also that the *Pugh* case is listed twice. If you look carefully, you can ascertain the difference between the two opinions without opening up either case. The second case result was decided in the **PA Superior Court on April 13, 1978**. The first case result for the *Pugh* case was decided in the **PA Supreme Court on July 6, 1979**. This means that the case was appealed in the PA Supreme court,

Figure 7-24 A Natural Language Search on *WestlawNext*

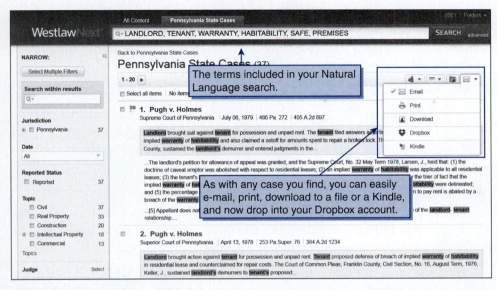

Source: Reprinted with permission of Thomson Reuters, Natural language search results on WestlawNext.

Figure 7-25 An Advanced Search on *WestlawNext*

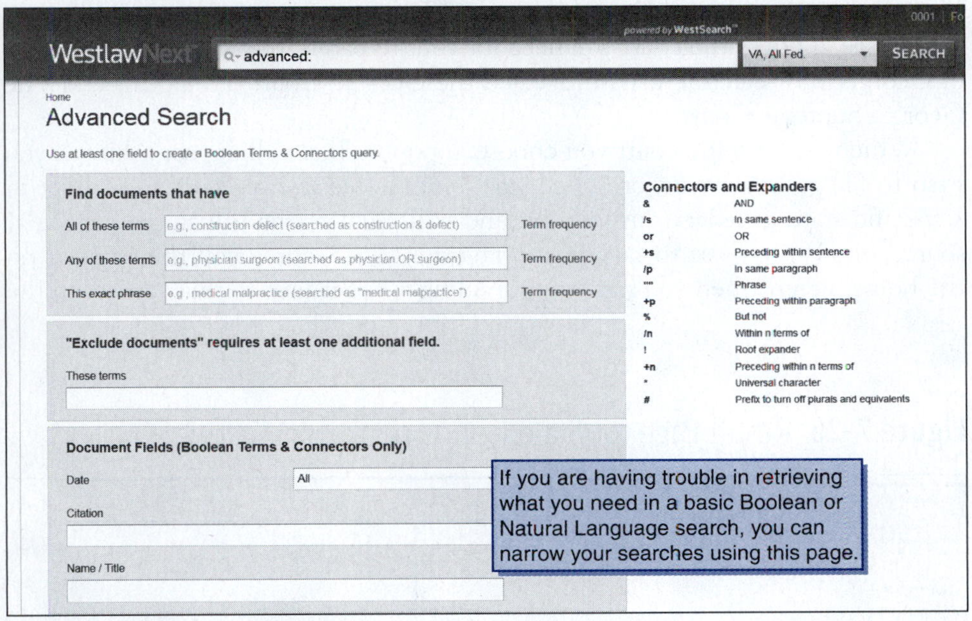

Source: Reprinted with permission of Thomson Reuters, Advance search on WestlawNext.

the state's highest state court. From what you now know about the hierarchy of the court system, it would be best to read the PA Supreme Court case, as it is the decision of the highest state court (this is true in any state).

As you can see in Figure 7-25, you can also conduct an advanced search by clicking on the **Advanced** button next to the main **Search** box. This feature helps you to narrow your searches by guiding you in utilizing the terms and expanders.

If you have access to *WestlawNext* in your course, navigate the site outside of class. After conducting a print search, conduct the same search on *WestlawNext* to see the similarities in the searches. Remember it is good to be proficient in both methods of research.

Lexis Advance

Locating a state or federal case on *Lexis Advance* is also easy. You can find the same cases here as you can in the print version. You will see that whether you possess a citation or not, the locating techniques are very similar to that of the printed books. Please follow the steps below.

SEARCH OPTION #1: You have a case citation.

Similar to the printed books, you can access a case with the citation immediately. Enter the citation in the main search box on the *Lexis Advance* home screen. This link will take you directly to the case opinion.

SEARCH OPTION #2: You do not have a case citation.

Similar to the printed books, if you do not have the case citation, you will need to take just a few more steps to get it. This is where you would need to generate your "word search" method.

For **state** cases, on the home page click on the **Browse** tab found at the top of the home screen. On the next screen, choose **Sources,** then select **Categories,** then select **Cases.** As you can see in Figure 7-26, you can select your state juris- diction by selecting the letter of your state at the top alphabet bar. For instance, click on the "**M**" to access the courts of Massachusetts, Montana, Missouri, Maryland, and so on. Click on the letter "**T**" to access the courts of Texas or Tennessee. Choose the court you need for your research. In Figure 7-26, the state of Georgia was selected, which revealed the Georgia Court of Appeals and The Georgia Supreme Court.

Whichever specific court you choose, a pop-up box will appear asking if you wish to (1) *get documents*, or (2) *add the source to the search filter*. If you work in a specific state or federal jurisdiction and will regularly be utilizing a particular source, you can choose to save it as a favorite. That source will then appear on the home screen when you sign on, providing a direct link to that source. In the

Figure 7-26 Result Page for State Courts on *Lexis Advance*

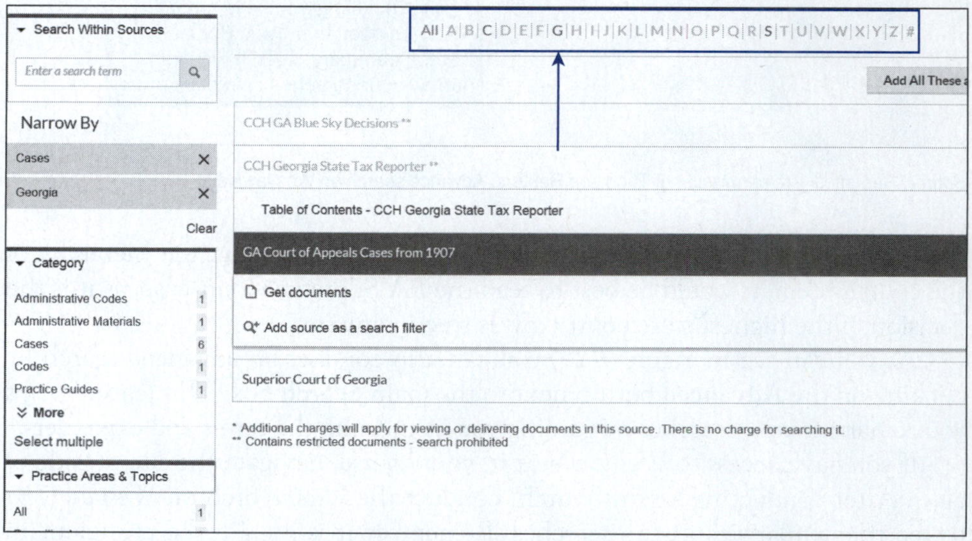

Source: Reprinted with permission of LexisNexis.

Figure 7-27 Search Results Page for the GA Supreme Court

Source Results: GA Supreme Court Cases from 1846	Actions ▾	

Cases 10,000+ | Cases (10,000+)

Narrow By | Sort by: Date (newest - oldest) ▾

Cases ✕ | ☐ 1. Anderson v. S. Home Care Servs., 2015 Ga. LEXIS 906
Clear ☆

▾ Search Within Results | **Jurisdiction** Georgia **Court** Supreme Court **Date** Nov 23, 2015

Enter search terms 🔍

▸ Court

▸ Timeline | ☐ 2. Harper v. State, 20...

▾ Publication Status | **Jurisdiction** Georgia **Court** Supreme Court **Date** Nov 23, 2015

Reported 70,145
Unreported 15,946

▾ Practice Areas & Topics

Civil Procedure | ☐ 3. Metro Atlanta Task Force for the Homeless v. Cmty. Trust, 2015 Ga. LEXIS 905
Criminal Law & Procedure

> Remember the difference between using a "published" (reported) and "unpublished" (unreported) opinion as authority. This search result has separated them for you.

Source: Reprinted with the permission of LexisNexis.

search box at the top of the home page, you will now see that you have made a filter, which will be designated in red. If you choose to *get documents*, a source results page will appear as you can see in Figure 7-27. As you can see, the search has revealed 10,000+ results, as every case decision, published and unpublished is included. Not to worry, as you can utilize the numerous filters to narrow your search to what you need.

For *federal* cases, under the **Browse** tab, you can choose **Sources,** then choose **Jurisdiction**, then choose **U.S. Federal.** Once on that page, every federal source will be listed. As you can see in Figure 7-28, under **Category,** you can choose **Cases** to narrow your search. On that page, you will find all federal courts, including all circuit courts.

Figure 7-28 Result Page for Federal Courts on *Lexis Advance*

2nd Circuit - US Bankruptcy Cases	▾	*i*
2nd Circuit - US Court of Appeals Cases	▾	*i*
2nd Circuit - US District Court Cases	▾	*i*
3rd Circuit - US Bankruptcy Cases	▾	*i*
3rd Circuit - US Court of Appeals Cases	▾	*i*
3rd Circuit - US District Court Cases	▾	*i*
📄 Get documents		*i*
Q⁺ Add source as a search filter		*i*
4th Circuit - US Bankruptcy Cases	▾	*i*
4th Circuit - US Court of Appeals Cases	▾	*i*
4th Circuit - US District Court Cases	▾	*i*
4Wheel Drive **		*i*
5th Circuit - US Bankruptcy Cases	▾	*i*

> Once you choose your court, and prior to searching the documents, you can add that court as a permanent filter if this is the particular jurisdiction in which you will regularly be conducting your research.

Source: Reprinted with the permission of LexisNexis.

Conducting a Word Search on Lexis Advance

Conducting a word search on *Lexis Advanced* is a detailed process that does take time to master after much practice. It is very important to utilize the correct words/terms/phrases to ensure you are constructing an effective and productive word search. Remember that case law is the most abundant of the primary sources. Therefore, if you do not generate the correct word search you need, you could end up with thousands of unnecessary and useless cases for your research. When you are monitored by your law firm (or worse, the client) time is of the essence and you cannot run up a client's bill conducting random searches, or reading through 3,000 possible cases because your search terms were too broad and general. This is why you always have the printed digests and reporters available, which is why you can always search the print sources first (which are easier to utilize) and then validate the results online, which you will learn later.

You can conduct a word search on *Lexis Advance* using terms and connectors (Boolean search) and by natural language. Unlike the print sources, where you begin with a broad general term that eventually leads you to more specific subjects, you have to generate a more specific search in order to effectively narrow your results.

Remember that a Boolean search retrieves information based on the *relationship* among words in a particular search. *Lexis Advance* uses terms and connectors but they are different from *Westlaw*. Review Figure 7-29 to learn the particular terms and connectors utilized in a *Lexis* terms and connectors search.

You can also conduct a natural language search on *Lexis Advance*. Remember, as you learned above, the natural language search does **not** utilize any terms or connectors. Rather, you can enter a series of words/terms/phrases. For example, you can enter the words: EASEMENT PROPERTY, NEIGHBOR, "RIGHT OF WAY." Remember to insert any specific phrase within quotation marks to ensure the entire phrase is searched. If not, the database will search for each term *separately*. You can also enter a question or statement. For example, you can enter "MUST THE PLAINTIFF PROVE A PHYSICAL INJURY FOR THE DEFENDANT TO BE LIABLE FOR NEGLIGENCE?" Be sure to keep your online or print versions of the latest legal dictionary and thesaurus to assist in your word search. Also remember to use different variations of words, such as "culpable," "liable," "guilty," "responsible."

Now that you know and understand the different types of word searches and how to utilize them, continue the steps below to learn how to retrieve case law on *Lexis Advance*.

Whether you choose a state or federal case law opinion, you can enter legal words/terms/phrases into the red search box. Let's use the same research problem that was utilized in the print digest so that you can see the similarities and differences between the research sources. Remember the client whose son rented an apartment with numerous structural defects and damage? If you recall, in that situation, you were asked to research if an implied warranty exists that ensures a landlord will make the premises safe and habitable for the tenant. If so, what is that warranty and what does it cover in the lease? In conducting a word search on an online database, you must first generate the words/terms/phrases that address the situation. Here, those words would be: LANLORD, TENANT, WARRANTY, HABITABLE, SAFE, PREMISES. Second, you can use those terms as is and run a natural language search, or rewrite the terms in a terms and connectors language search. Here, you can try: LANDLORD /5 "WARRANTY

Figure 7-29 Common Terms and Connectors on *Lexis Advanced*

Term/Connector	Command
(!) (*)	These are root expanders used to search for words with multiple endings. Both symbols can only be used at the *end* of a word. For example, type **acqui!** to retrieve any document including the words, *acquire, acquisition,* or *acquiring.* *There must be at least three characters prior to the use of either symbol.
?	This character also replaces characters *anywhere* in a word. For example, type **wom?n** to retrieve *woman* and *women.*
w/para	This is a grammatical connector used to search for terms that must appear in the same paragraph, or within 50 words. For example, typing **mobile phone w/para child** will yield results including the words "child" and "mobile phone" in the same paragraph.
pre/n	This term/connector is used when the first search term must *precede* the second term by not more than "**n**" words. For example, typing **digital pre/3 television** will retrieve documents including both terms within 3 words of each other in the same paragraph.
(/n) (w/n)	Both of these grammatical connectors are used to locate terms within "**n**" words of each other. For example, **fiduciary duty /10 breach of each other.**
w/sent	This grammatical connector is used when your terms occur within the same sentence, or within 15 words or each other. For example, **negligence w/sent breach.**
w/seg	This grammatical connector is used to include words appearing within the same *segment.* This includes headline, body of the document, or within 100 words.
near/n	This grammatical connector includes words simply "near each other" anywhere in the document.
onear/n	This grammatical connector is used to include words where the first word precedes the second by not more than "**n**" words. For example, **fiduciary duty near/10 breach.**
and	This connector simply searches for both terms separated by the "and" connector. For example, type **budget and deficit** to locate the terms together.
and not	This is the "but not" connector for when you want to include one term but *exclude* another. For example, use **conspiracy and not drugs** to locate cases discussing conspiracy cases but those that do not include drugs.
or	This connector is used to include one or more words in a search. For example, use **ship or vessel or boat** will locate any of the 3 terms.

OF HABITABILITY" SAFE PREMISES. Click the **Search** button. Figure 7-30 illustrates the result of your search.

The search page will yield hundreds of results from numerous legal sources and jurisdictions. Make certain you always utilize the multiple filter tabs on the left-hand side of the page. The most important filters in this case would be **Cases** and **Jurisdiction**, which in this case is *Pennsylvania.* As you can see in Figure 7-30, when you use the correct terms and connectors and utilize the most efficient filters, you arrive at *one* case in this jurisdiction—*McIntyre v. Philadelphia Housing Authority,* 816 A.2d 1204.

However, do not expect this type of good luck for every search! If your search yields only one result, it is worth checking out to see if (1) the case addresses/answers your issue, or (2) the case points or leads you to another positive result.

If you want to view and read a case, click on the case name. The full text of the opinion will appear. As you can see in Figure 7-31, you should recognize the separate and individual parts that make up the opinion. By clicking on the "**Jump To**" tab at the top of the page, you can go directly to any section of the opinion, or directly to any of the terms/words used in your search within the opinion. For example, in Figure 7-32, you could "jump to" the headnotes to scan the law that was used in the opinion before actually reading it. In addition, you learned how

Figure 7-30 A Word Search Result Page

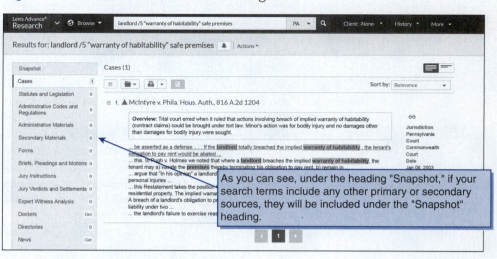

Source: Reprinted with the permission of LexisNexis.

Figure 7-31 *McIntyre v. Phila. Hous. Auth. – Heading and Caption*

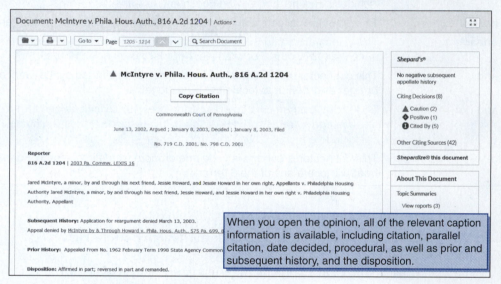

Source: Reprinted with the permission of LexisNexis.

to utilize the print digest to assist you in locating case decisions. *Lexis Advance,* similar to *WestlawNext,* does not provide direct access to an online version of a digest. However, if you see in Figure 7-32, if you click on the hyperlink **Implied Warranties** next to **Contracts Law,** that will take you to additional search results for an implied warranty of habitability within the topic of contract law. Also in Figure 7-32, if you were to click on the hyperlink **Shepardize – Narrow by this Headnote,** that will take you to a number of cases that used that exact same headnote. This is a way where you can perform a type of online digest search on *Lexis Advance.* Similar to *WestlawNext,* the case headnotes found within these online

Figure 7-32 *McIntyre v. Phila. Hous. Auth. – Headnotes*

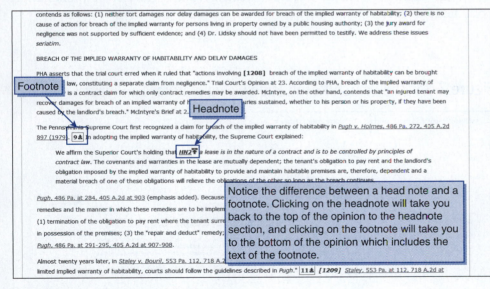

Source: Reprinted with the permission of LexisNexis.

databases are not only helpful for the case you are reading, but helpful to conduct more detailed and more narrow searches.

As shown in Figure 7-33, the parts of the opinion that you see are formatted similarly as you would find in an annotated print version. The look of the online version is different, but the content is the same. The main advantage to using an online legal search database is the hyperlinks! When you access the opinion, you will be able to see all of the hyperlinks within the opinion that can take you to immediate relevant information with one click. Most importantly,

Figure 7-33 *McIntyre v. Phila. Hous. Auth. – Body of the Opinion*

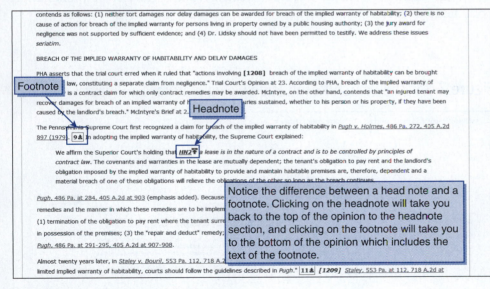

Source: Reprinted with the permission of LexisNexis.

at the beginning of the opinion, you can browse the headnotes to see if any are of interest. If so, click on the headnote number which will take you directly to where that headnote is discussed within the opinion. Remember, it is never wise to quote from a headnote so always click on it to read how it is presented and discussed within the opinion.

Further, any and all cases or any authority discussed by the court within the opinion will also have their hyperlinks to take you right to that source. As you can see in Figure 7-33, the *McIntyre* decision quotes the *Pugh* case, which is what was included in the print digest (and the *WestlawNext* online search) concerning this issue. Because the court in *McIntyre* presents the *Pugh* case with such high regard, you can click on the hyperlink within the *McIntyre* opinion to read about it. You can do this with any case opinion you find, as that is a great advantage to either of these online sources. Do not limit yourself to one to two cases. Keep clicking on cases in the hyperlinks to see which case is most beneficial to your research.

Just to demonstrate the difference between a terms/connectors search and a natural language search, if you were to enter the original terms: LANDLORD, TENANT, WARRANTY, HABITABLE, SAFE as you can see in Figure 7-34, you get a very different result—7,000 results to be exact. Even though the *Pugh* case is listed first, it is important to take the time to think and generate the terms you will use in your word search. Make up searches on your own to master using the terms and connectors.

Lexis Advance has an advanced search option. In the main search box at the top of the page click on **Filter.** Then, click on **Advanced Search**. As you can see in Figure 7-35, you will find the options of search terms, in which you can enter your search terms then click on a variety of commands. In addition, you can choose from a number of terms and connectors, and *Shepard's* Citation Service—all of which you can add to your search as a new filter.

If you have access to *Lexis Advance* in your course, navigate the site outside of class. After conducting a print search, conduct the same search on *Lexis Advance* to see the similarities in the searches. Remember it is good to be proficient in both methods of research.

Figure 7-34 The Search Result Page Using Natural Language

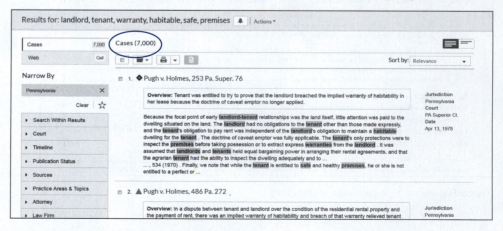

Source: Reprinted with the permission of LexisNexis.

Figure 7-35 The Advanced Search Option on *Lexis Advance*

Search within entire document for...

Terms

Search within document *segments/fields* for...

Note: While these segments apply to the majority of documents, they may not apply to all documents.

Party Name

> If you are having trouble in retrieving what you need in a basic Boolean or Natural Language search, you can narrow your searches using a more detailed search by using the **Advanced Search** key.

Court

Date

All available dates

Date values will not appear in the search box query but will be added to your search.   date format

Number

Citation

Use Connectors

" "	Exact phrase
and	2 or more words anywhere in the document (alternative: &)
or	1 or both terms or phrases
and not	Exclude documents containing the word or phrase
/n	First word within "n" words of the second (alternative: w/n or near/n)
!	Word variations using this as the root word (alternative: *)

View all connectors and commands

Segment Examples

Source: Reprinted with the permission of LexisNexis.

Copy a Case Citation into a Word Document

If you want to copy-and-paste a case or any portion of a case into a Word document, *WestlawNext* will copy the statute and its full citation. Just follow these easy steps:

1. Highlight the particular text;
2. Choose "Copy with Reference;"
3. Choose Standard (or your state if it is listed);
4. Paste into your Word document.

The highlighted portion will appear in the Word text and will automatically include proper citation.

If you are drafting a legal memorandum or simply writing a quick e-mail to your supervising attorney concerning a case or statute you located, it is always best to have the full citation for future reference. *Lexis Advance* also has a cut-and-paste with full citation feature. Just follow these easy steps:

1. Highlight the particular text;
2. A box will appear stating "Copy Selected Text to Clipboard;"
3. You have the option of not only copying and pasting with a full citation, but also as a hyperlink as well;
4. You can also add the text to a folder or add to a new search.

So how do you cite an opinion taken from *WestlawNext* or *Lexis Advance* that does not yet have a designated full print citation?

Notice how the *Bluebook* (Rule18) addresses this citation format.

Missouri v. McNeeley, 2013 WL 1628934

Notice how the *ALWD Manual* (Rule 12) addresses the same citation.

> ### *Missouri v. McNeeley*, 2013 U.S. LEXIS 3160

For a more detailed explanation for how to cite case law in your state, be certain to review your *Bluebook* citation manual (in print or online), specifically (Rule 10) for all case law citation. Also, (Rule 12) covers basic case law citation for the *ALWD Manual*. Lastly, don't forget the Cornell Legal Information Institute (LII) website for information on state jurisdiction citation, which also includes many examples. The online manual can be downloaded into PDF format, as well as onto a Kindle (Amazon) or Nook (Barnes and Noble) for free. Some states also post a citation manual on its judicial website, which includes the proper citation format for all primary and secondary authority in the state.

PRACTICE TIP

Suppose you work as a paralegal in a law office that has a paid subscription to *Lexis Advance* only. You receive a brief or court document from opposing counsel and your supervising attorney wants you to validate the cases to make sure they are still good law. You find many "new" case decisions with only the *Westlaw* citation. How can you verify the law? *Lexis* has developed software that allows the researcher to insert the *Westlaw citation* into the *Lexis* search box, which will recognize and convert the *Westlaw* citation to the *Lexis* system in order to locate the opinion.

■ SEARCHING CASE VALIDATION: *KEYCITE* AND *SHEPARD'S*

LEARNING OBJECTIVE 5
Explain how to validate a case using KeyCite and Shepard's online.

Although *WestlawNext* and *Lexis Advance* provide the most updated case law material online, the single most unique and outstanding feature in both is the ability to validate your findings, or in other words, determine if the case(s) you choose are still "good law." This undoubtedly is an extremely important feature to both databases, as you want to make certain that the cases you choose to include in a legal memorandum or any legal document have not been overruled or overturned by an appellate court. Therefore, it is imperative to "validate" your case results *before* utilizing it as precedential authority. The validation "tool" that is used to determine if a case is still good law is a **citator**. The most well-known citator known in the legal field is *Lexis' Shepard's* citatory, which can be used in print (as you will see below) and online through *Lexis*.

citator
A tool that allows a researcher to track the history of a case and the treatment of a case to determine if it is good law.

Print Source: *Shepard's*

Most, if not all, law libraries today do **not** shelve *Shepard's* in print for two reasons. First, the print version is not as current as the online versions of *Shepard's* and *KeyCite*. Second, the online version is much easier to use. If you do not subscribe to either *WestlawNext* or *Lexis Advance*, you can subscribe to your local library's use of either online legal for a fee much less expensive than a paying for a full subscription.

Although it is possible to validate other sources of primary law, no other source depends on validation more than case law. This is because, as you know, case law is the most abundant of the primary sources, and case authority is overturned and reversed more than any other source of law. Every case you research and decide to use as authority needs to be validated to ensure you are using good law.

Online Source: *Shepard's*

The online citator for *Lexis Advance* is also called **Shepard's**. You can validate your case law quickly and easily with this citator system in one of two ways.

- If you already have the citation, on the home page, you can type (**shep: 816 A.2d 1204**) into the main search box followed by the citation you want to *Shepardize* as you can see in Figure 7-36.

As you can see in Figure 7-37, in entering the citation for the *McIntyre* case, you see there is no negative appellate history.

If you look to Figure 7-38, *Lexis Advance* utilizes a legend to describe each type of validation "indicator" it uses for each case, all of which are self-explanatory. As a good rule of thumb, if your case has been labeled with the red stop sign or the exclamation signal in a circle, read the validation page and see why it was overruled, reversed, remanded , or deemed unconstitutional or void. If your case has been labeled with any of the other remaining labels, your case can be used as precedent, but if the indicator is orange or yellow, check to see why the case

Shepard's
The online citator found on Lexis Advance that provides information and treatment of the primary and secondary sources of law.

Figure 7-36 Using the Search Box as a Citator on *Lexis Advance*

Lexis Advance®

Advanced Search | Search Tips

shep: 816 A.2d 1204   Search: Everything ▾ 🔍

Source: Reprinted with the permission of LexisNexis.

Figure 7-37 The Validation Page on *Lexis Advance*

Shepard's®: ▲ McIntyre v. Phila. Hous. Auth., 816 A.2d 1204   Parallel Citations ▾   🔔   Actions ▾

Appellate History   Appellate History (2)   List   Map

▲ Citing Decisions   No negative subsequent appellate history

Other Citing Sources

Table of Authorities   After you have determined that your case
                                                                    has no negative subsequent appellate
                                                                    history, you can see what other more
                              ☐ 1.   ♀ *Citation you Shepardized*™   recent case opinions exist that stands for
                                    McIntyre v. Phila. Hous. Auth. ▲ the same rule of law or issue by clicking
                                    816 A.2d 1204, 2003 Pa. Commw. LEXIS 16   on **Citing Decisions**. You can also click
                                    Show in map   on **Other Citing Sources** to see how the
                                                                    secondary sources have addressed this
                                                                    issue as well.
                              Subsequent

                              ☐ 2.   ■ Appeal denied by:

Source: Reprinted with the permission of LexisNexis.

Figure 7-38 The Validation Legend on *Lexis Advance*

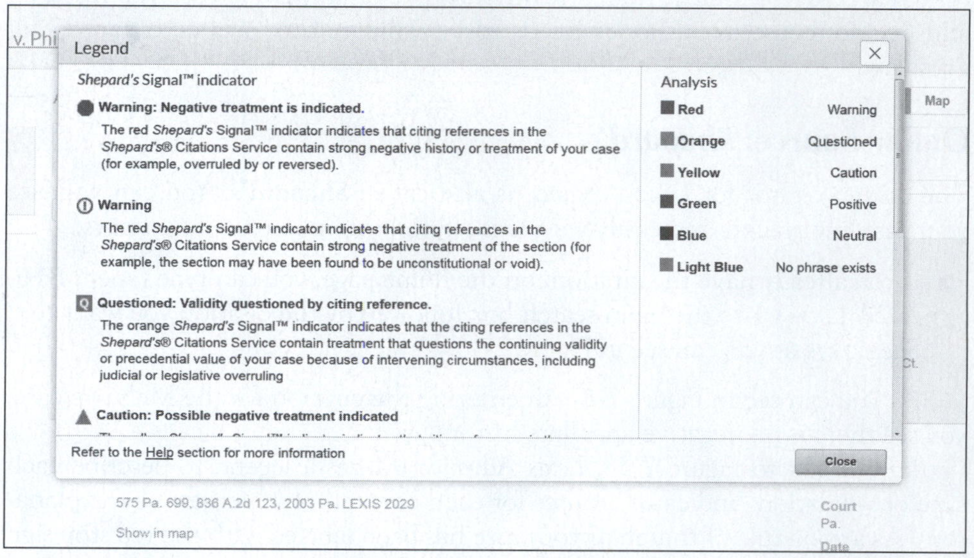

Source: Reprinted with the permission of LexisNexis.

was questioned or cautioned. Even if a case had been questioned by a court this does not mean it was reversed or overturned, and it may be used as authority. A court may question one particular issue or finding that does not render the entire opinion void.

In addition, under the **Depth of Discussion**, the more of the four blocks that are filled, the more a particular case mirrors the case you are *Shepardizing*. Any case that is labeled **Analyzed** or **Discussed** is worth your time to read in its entirety to see how that court rendered its decision concerning your issue.

If you do not have a case citation to enter on the home page to *Shepardize*, you can always *Shepardize **any*** case opinion you are viewing or reading. Please refer back to Figure 7-31. In the right-hand corner, you can see the appellate history and have the option to *Shepardize* the case. Click on **Shepardize This Document**, and it will take you to the screen as displayed in Figure 7-37.

The *Shepard's* validation service from *Lexis Advance* allows you to conduct the validation process quickly and efficiently. Once you know and understand the keys and legends used by the online system, you can validate any case anytime with ease.

Online Source: *KeyCite*

KeyCite
The online citator found on WestlawNext that provides information and treatment of the primary and secondary sources of law.

The online citator for *Westlaw Next* is also called **KeyCite**. You can validate your case law quickly and easily with this citator system in one of two ways.

- If you already have the citation, on the home page, you can insert the either **(keycite 816 A.2d 1204)** or **(kc 816 A.2d 1204)** into the main search box, then select **Search**, as you can see in Figure 7-39, the result will take you directly to the case validation page.

As you can see in Figure 7-40, you can view any **Filings** in the case such as motions or briefs. You can also determine if the case has any **Negative Treatment** such as being overturned for any reason. In the **History** tab, the appeal process of the case you are viewing (*McIntyre*) is demonstrated. In the **Citing References**

Figure 7-39 Using the Search Box as a Citator on *WestlawNext*

Source: Reprinted with permission of Thomson Reuters, Main search box on WestlawNext.

Figure 7-40 The Validation Screen for *McIntyre* on *WestlawNext*

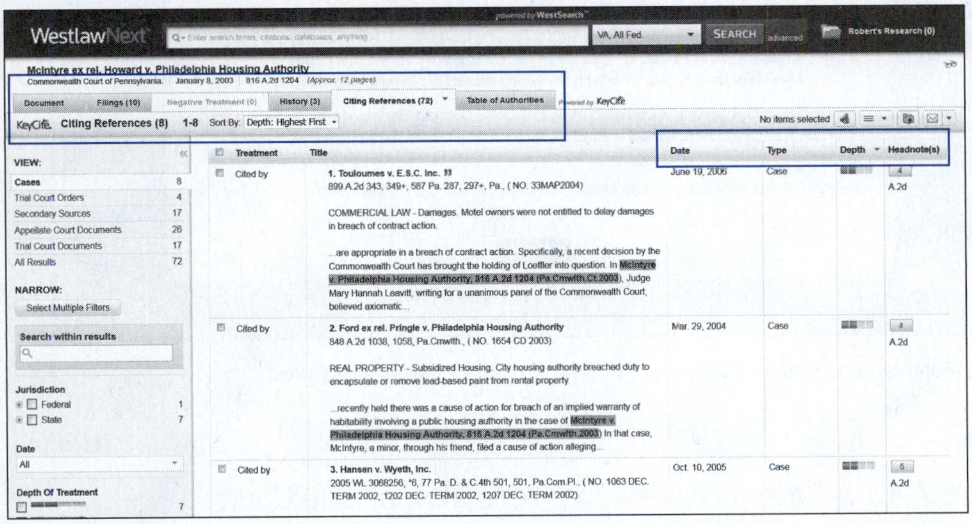

Source: Reprinted with permission of Thomson Reuters, Case 816 A.2d 1204 validation results on WestlawNext.

tab, any and all sources of law are listed that cite to your case. You can narrow the results through the use of the filters under **View**. Lastly, the **Table of Authorities** is a list of the cases relied upon as authority by the document you are viewing.

In addition, the four-block bars indicate the **Depth** of coverage of your case to make browsing easier and more efficient. Also, if you hold your cursor over a **Headnote**, a textbox will appear, and you can read the text from that headnote without having to go the actual source.

WestlawNext also utilizes the *KeyCite* flag validation system. When you conduct any case law search on *WestlawNext*, cases found to have negative treatment or cases that have even been overturned are indicated through the use of color-coded flags, as you can see in Figure 7-41.

A case opinion with no flag is an indicator that the case is good law. If, during your search, you see a yellow flag next to a case name (anywhere on the system) this indicates that the case has *some* negative treatment associated with it. This does not indicate that the case is bad law. Rather, review the appellate history to see why some later courts decided not to follow the reasoning of your case. A red flag, however, is a strong indicator that the case is no longer good law, for at least one point of law. Recently, the blue-striped flag was added, which indicates that the case has been appealed to the US Court of Appeals or the US Supreme Court, as you can see in Figure 7-42. The striped flag is considered "neutral," as a final decision has yet to be made in the case. When a final decision is reached and all appeals are exhausted, the blue-striped flag will be dropped.

Figure 7-41 The *KeyCite* Legend on *WestlawNext*

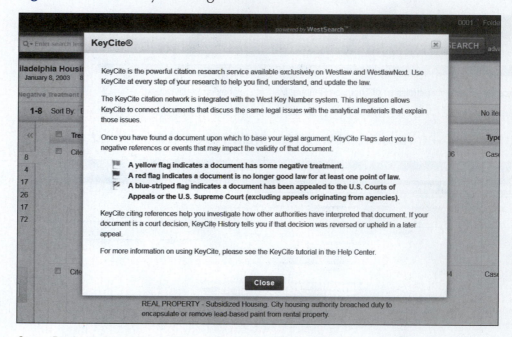

Source: Reprinted with permission of Thomson Reuters, KeyCite legend on WestlawNext.

Figure 7-42 A Case on Appeal to a Federal Appellate Court

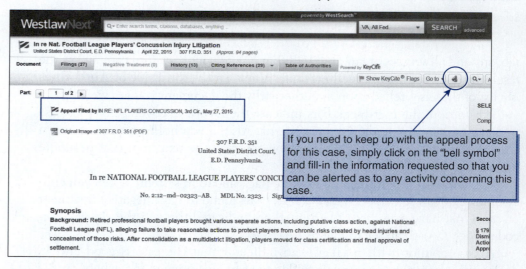

Source: Reprinted with permission of Thomson Reuters, Case 2015 WL 1822254 on WestlawNext.

Also recently added, *WestlawNext* implemented its *KeyCite* flag indicator system into the body of each opinion you read. As you can see in Figure 7-43, you have the option of showing or hiding the *KeyCite* flags within the case opinion. Now, if you see a case of interest within the case decision you are reading, rather than click on the hyperlink to validate it, each case is validated already. In addition, if you hold the cursor over a flag a text box will pop up indicating the positive or negative appellate treatment.

Figure 7-43 The *KeyCite* Flag Indicator System within an Opinion

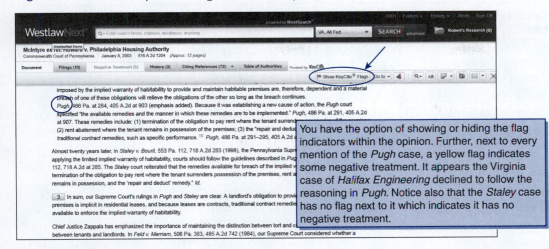

Source: Reprinted with permission of Thomson Reuters, Case 816 A.2d 1204 KeyCite indicators on WestlawNext.

In using either online version of *Shepard's* or *Keycite*, you will receive the most up-to-date case validation available. So, which one is better? Both offer many great and similar features that are easy to adapt and use. Basically, it may very well come down to your personal preference or learning the system that your instructor/employer provides for you.

As a practicing paralegal, you will undoubtedly utilize either *WestlawNext* or *Lexis Advance*. Some large law firms have subscriptions to both. Also, many law libraries will charge a nominal fee to utilize the *Shepard's* or *KeyCite* systems. That is why it is important to understand how to utilize both online databases. Remember to utilize the numerous online guide sheets and video tutorials offered online by both companies with assistance in validating case law.

However, if you work for a small firm that does not subscribe to either *WestlawNext* or *Lexis Advance*, or you are limited to usage, there are many other subscription databases that also provide case law materials at an equal or reduced cost. In addition, many free sites also provide many state and federal cases as well.

■ ADDITIONAL ONLINE CASE LAW SOURCES

The online subscription services in Figure 7-44 are "alternatives" to *WestlawNext* and *Lexis Advanced*.

In addition to the five top competitors to *WestlawNext* and *Lexis Advance* mentioned above, many other online start-up companies are trying to compete with the top competitors. If you find an online legal research company that is considerably cheaper, make sure it at least provides the following top five features before handing over your credit card:

- **Cost:** Does the company offer a "free trial" to navigate the website to see if you can navigate easily? Only the companies confident in their product will make such an offer. If you are going to pay, are you locked into an annual subscription, or does the company offer a low-cost tiered plan?
- **Tutorials:** Does the company provide online tutorials and demonstrations that instruct the researcher in locating authority? This is very important

LEARNING OBJECTIVE 6
Identify the additional subscription and free online sources available to search for a case.

Figure 7-44 Alternative Subscription Online Services

Online Service	Coverage of Case Law	Types of Case Law Searches	Validation Service?	Pricing Plan?
Bloomberg Law	All state and federal coverage similar in content to *Westlaw* and *Lexis*.	Boolean, natural language, and citation.	Yes. *B-Cite*, which is similar to *KeyCite* and *Shepard's*.	No. Flat-fee monthly pricing, which is comparable to *Westlaw* and *Lexis*.
LoisLaw	Under a specific plan, you can access all the primary law (including cases) on the federal level and one state.	Boolean and citation.	Yes. *GlobalCite*, which not only validates but also retrieves other authority that cited your case.	Yes. 2-day, 7-day, or 31-day pass, as well as 1-year access.
FastCase	Federal and state case law from all 50 states.	Boolean, natural language, and citation.	Yes. *Authority Check*, which determines if a case is good by listing all the cases that cited your case.	Yes. Monthly and yearly plans.
Casemaker	Most state and federal appellate cases.	Syntax (Boolean), phrase (natural language), or citation search.	Yes. *CaseCheck+*, which validates individual cases, and *CiteCheck*, which validates all the cited authority in an entire legal document.	Yes. A basic monthly plan, or an advanced plan that includes access to both validation services.
Versus Law	The standard plan offers limited case law research. The premium plan offers more case law and access to validation service.	Keyword (Boolean), field search, and citation.	Yes. *V-Cite*, which can determine the validity of the cited case.	Yes. Three pricing plans including standard, premium, and professional.

*Note that each online service that provides a Boolean search has generated its own list of "terms and connectors" that can be found on its website. Each company also provides online research guides or links for research tutorials.

especially for a system that you are unfamiliar with and did not utilize in your legal education. In addition, does the company provide a toll-free number to call for assistance?

- **Validation:** While it may be difficult to match the reliability of *KeyCite* or *Shepard's*, many companies today offer some type of citator service. As you know, this is not just important but is also crucial in deciding which authority to utilize. Make sure you see if the company describes the citator service on its website. If so, how does it work?

- **Coverage:** While many online companies state that they have state and federal authority in their database, to what extent is the coverage included? In discussing federal case law, does the website include only opinions from the USSC, or all the federal circuit and appeals courts as well? What about state law, can you access every state or only your particular state where you work? As for a particular span of time, most companies should publish opinions that go back at least 50 years. It is not necessary to include cases earlier than that in the database.

- **User Friendly:** We seem to use that term a lot lately, but it does apply here. Does the company you are seeking provide results in an easy-to-read and easy-to-understand format, or is all the information confusingly crammed onto a single page?

Figure 7-45 Alternative Free Online Services

Online Service	Coverage of Case Law	Types of Case Law Searches
The Cornell Legal Information Institute (LII)	All federal circuit court and US Court of Appeals opinions and US Courts of Special Jurisdiction. Most appellate case opinions of all 50 states.	Many, if not most, opinions can be searched by direct links to that particular jurisdiction's website; therefore, search options vary by jurisdiction.
Findlaw	Most case law from the federal appellate courts, federal specialized courts, and appellate courts of all 50 states. Search by "party name," docket number," or "court."	Search by "party name," docket number," or "court."
Google Scholar	Most federal US Court of Appeals, US District Courts and all state appellate courts.	Natural language and citation.
Justia	Most case law from the federal appellate courts and all 50 state courts.	Natural language and citation.
Public Library of Law (*powered by Fastcase*)	Most case law from the US Court of Appeals and all 50 state courts (only case results from 1997 to the present).	Natural language and citation.

As mentioned previously, many large firms allow their paralegals access to both *WestlawNext* and *Lexis Advance*, or at least one of them. For mid-sized, to smaller and solo firms, they may subscribe to either one, but may restrict your access, or they may encourage staff to utilize the print authority and use either database solely for validation. If you are restricted in your use in *Westlaw* or *Lexis* and do not want to spend money for another paid online subscription service, there are also some free alternatives for you to consider.

Although you can access *most*, but certainly not *all* case law online for free, remember that aside from *Shepard's* in print, there is no free validation service online. Please review Figure 7-45 to learn the best free governmental and educational sites for accessing case law, *excluding* opinions from the US Supreme Court, which are discussed in the next section.

In addition to the above paid and free sites in the two charts above, there is also a federal governmental website to consider. The Public Access to Court Electronic Records (PACER) website located at **www.pacer.gov** is a national index for most federal district, bankruptcy, and appellate courts. The service is free to register and to use the service but you are charged a nominal fee for any printed copies of any documents.

As you can see, if you cannot access either *WestlawNext* and *Lexis Advance* there are alternatives. However, if you do not have access to either *Westlaw* or *Lexis*, or your firm or its clients limit your research time, check out the options above for a good backup if needed.

■ UNITED STATES SUPREME COURT OPINIONS

Although the case decisions handed down by the US Supreme Court (USSC) are considered "federal" in nature, they are not published in print with the federal court appellate opinions. Rather, the USSC opinions are categorized and compiled separately due to the importance of this high Court and the law generated by its decisions.

LEARNING OBJECTIVE 7
Describe how to search for United States Supreme Court cases.

Where to Find USSC Cases in Print

Similar to state and federal opinions, the USSC case decisions are first published in print as a slip opinion, then as an advance sheet, and, finally, as a report or reporter in a hardbound set. USSC cases are the only cases published in *three* different print publications, including:

- **United States Reports** (U.S.) – the official government version
- **Supreme Court Reporter** (S.Ct.) – the unofficial commercial version by *West*
- **United States Supreme Court Reports, Lawyer's Edition** (L.Ed.) – the unofficial commercial lawyer's edition by Lawyer's Cooperative Publishing Co.

Although the decisions of the USSC are found in three different sets, it is more than likely that your firm/office will purchase and utilize only one. A good law library will have all three sets. The same opinions are included in each set; however, they are printed by different publishers. You will see the three distinct sets listed below along with their citation format.

United States Reports (U.S.)

The *United States Reports* is published by the Government Printing Office (GPO) and includes all the full-text opinions issued by the USSC, arranged in chronological order. These cases date from 1790 to the present. These official reports include all the cases, orders, and rulings of the Court. The latest published *United States Reports* as of January 2013, was Volume 552, which was published in July 2012. Because this is an official report, there are no headnotes and no pocket parts included, only the full text of each opinion.

The *United States Reports* is the offical print set for USSC case opinions. As such, you will typically see the citation to this particular set most often. For example, using the infamous USSC landmark decision, *Texas v. Johnson*, the citation to the *United States Reports* is as follows.

> *Texas v. Johnson,* 491 U.S. 397 (1989).

You do not include any reference to the USSC in the ending parenthetical. It is universally understood that this case is from the USSC by the abbreviation U.S., as it is the only court that uses that abbreviation.

Supreme Court Reporter (S. Ct.)

This unofficial commercial print set is published by *West*, and also arranges the cases in chronological order. This set is very helpful in that it includes the most updated information and useful annotated material, including a synopsis and headnotes for each case. The set also includes a table of cases reported and statutes construed. As with the state and federal reporters, the headnotes found in each case are connected directly to the topic/subtopic tables in the *US Supreme Court Digest*, which you will see below.

In citing this set, using the same USSC case as above, the citation would look like the following. As you can see again, no abbreviations are included in the parenthetical as the abbreviations for the USSC are unique and no other state or federal court uses them.

> *Texas v. Johnson,* 109 S. Ct. 2533 (1989).

U.S. Supreme Court Reports, Lawyers' Edition (L. Ed.)

This second unofficial commercial print set is published by *Lexis Law Publishers*. Again, the cases are printed in chronological order with the advance sheets as current as one to two weeks following decision. Unique researching features include annotation references and briefs of counsel. As with any commercial publication, each case contains summaries and headnotes. The citation for this print set is as follows.

> ***Texas v. Johnson,*** **105 L. Ed. 2d 342 (1989).**

When a USSC case opinion is cited, you will often see that it includes the full ***parallel string citation***. Remember that the official cite always precedes the two unofficial cites. The citation format would like the following:

> ***Texas v. Johnson,*** **491 U.S. 397, 109 S. Ct. 2533, 105 L. Ed. 2d 342 (1989).**

How to Find USSC Cases in Print

Similar to the state and federal reporters, there are two main ways in which to locate USSC opinions in print: the citation method and the subject/topic method using a digest.

The Citation Method

You know that in a case citation the first number is always the *volume number* and the second number is always the *page number*. As you can see from the three different citation formats for each of the three reporters above, you will know which print set to look at just by seeing either (U.S.), (S. Ct.), or (L. Ed).

The Word Search Method

Because the unofficial print set of USSC opinions are arranged chronologically, and not by subject, the digest provides access to any reported case using the key number system similar to the state and federal digest system.

The main digest is called the *United States Supreme Court Digest*, and is arranged alphabetically by subject. If you remember, the Descriptive Word Index (DWI) assists you in locating the cases you need by topic and subtopic. You use the DWI to locate the topic you need, which will list the "key number" for locating the appropriate case summaries, as well as case headnotes within those cases. Again, just apply the ***same*** method you utilized for both the state and federal digest.

If you know the case name but *do not* have any of the three possible citations, you can use the **Table of Cases** at the end of the set. This table will provide the appropriate citation for your case. In addition, if you only have the ***name of the defendant*** in the case, the citations listed by defendant are incorporated into the alphabetic listing of cases.

As mentioned, *Lexis* also prints an unofficial reporter. The *U.S. Supreme Court Digest, Lawyers' Edition* is also shelved with the USSC reporters. Since there is no "key number" system to use, the cases are arranged ***alphabetically by subject***, which is a different format from the *West* digest. This set is seldom used, as the *West* digest key number system is more effective and efficient. Overall, this digest has a structure and organization similar to the *United States Supreme Court Digest*.

Updating

As with any printed set, each volume, where needed, includes a pocket part to determine if any more recent cases exist under the topic you are searching. In addition, you also are now aware that you can utilize the legal online databases as well to validate using citators.

Where to Find USSC Cases Online

There are many online resources from which to retrieve USSC opinions. Furthermore, unlike state and federal cases, you can access almost any USSC opinion for free using a multitude of sites, as you will see below.

www.supremecourtus.gov. First and foremost, the official government website of the US Supreme Court provides access to all Court cases dating back to 1991. On the right-hand side of the home page, you will see a list for the most *Recent Decisions* handed down in the past month of the current term, which typically runs from October to October. On the left-hand side of the home page, when you click on *Opinions* a choice of selections are offered. The following selections list USSC cases by case name, docket number, and date of decision. Since not many opinions are decided in a given term, it is not difficult to scroll through a particular term to locate the case you need.

- The first option includes the *Latest Slip Opinions*. There you will find a chart including all the latest opinions for that particular term; or
- You can select the *Term Opinions Relating to Orders*. These decisions include those written by an individual justice to comment on the summary disposition of cases by court order; for example, an opinion defending the Court's ruling of denial of a writ of certiorari. These opinions are posted throughout the remainder of the current term; or
- You can search by the *Term In-Chambers Opinions*. These opinions are also written by an individual justice ruling on an immediate appeal, such as a stay or an injunction; or
- You can also retrieve the *Sliplists,* which include all cases from the 2007 term to the present. These opinions are listed by their official "open-ended" citation. Like any collection of slip opinions, once an opinion is given its full official citation and compiled into a hardbound print reporter, the slip opinion is eliminated from the website. When you click on a volume, all the opinions included are listed with a brief and helpful case summary for each case; or
- Lastly, you can click on the *Bound Volumes* selection to view all the Court's past opinions from 1991 to the present (beginning with volumes 502 forward). However, the website cautions the researcher in downloading an entire bound volume, as each file is very large. You may wish to save it to a USB first, as you are not downloading only the case you seek, but *every* decision published in a particular volume.

As mentioned previously, unlike the state or federal courts, accessing a slip opinion from the USSC is very important because a decision handed down by the highest court in the land *instantly* becomes binding precedent on *every* state and federal court in the country. This is because no other appellate court exists in which to file an appeal once a case has been decided in the US Supreme Court (the exception being if the Court remands the case back to the state or federal government). One drawback from accessing a slip opinion, or any opinion from the USSC website, is that unlike the state and federal opinions found in the

Figure 7-46 *Williams v. Illinois – Syllabus*

(Slip Opinion)   OCTOBER TERM, 2011   1

Syllabus

NOTE: Where it is feasible, a syllabus (headnote) will be released, as is being done in connection with this case, at the time the opinion is issued. The syllabus constitutes no part of the opinion of the Court but has been prepared by the Reporter of Decisions for the convenience of the reader. See *United States* v. *Detroit Timber & Lumber Co.,* 200 U. S. 321, 337.

SUPREME COURT OF THE UNITED STATES

> The syllabus is **not** to be cited or used as precedent since it is not part of the *official* opinion by the court.

Syllabus

WILLIAMS *v.* ILLINOIS

CERTIORARI TO THE SUPREME COURT OF ILLINOIS

No. 10–8505.   Argued December 6, 2011—Decided June 18, 2012

At petitioner's bench trial for rape, Sandra Lambatos, a forensic specialist at the Illinois State Police lab, testified that she matched a DNA profile produced by an outside laboratory, Cellmark, to a profile

---

Source: http://www.supremecourt.gov/opinions/11pdf/10-8505.pdf

commercial hardbound reporters, every opinion found on the USSC official website lacks any annotated material, such as case summaries or helpful headnotes. Each case only provides the official text of the opinion.

So what's included in a USSC opinion on the official website? Each opinion will begin with a syllabus, which precedes the opinion as you can see in Figure 7-46. Note that the syllabus is **not** part of the opinion and has no precedential value. The syllabus only provides a brief summary and holding in the case, as some Supreme Court opinions can be well over 30 to 50 pages in length. As you can see in Figure 7-47 the actual opinion follows the syllabus.

Notice in Figure 7-47, the opinion is missing the important "page number" to complete the citation. This is known as an "open-ended citation." This means that because the case was recently issued, it has not yet been designated a full citation. The open-ended citation only has a designated volume number. The case recitation is not complete until it receives a designated page number in that volume, which closes the citation. These opinions can be cited in this manner as official citations. This is because since there are so few opinions issued by this Court in comparison to state and federal decisions, it takes much longer to fill a hardbound volume in an offiical report or commerical reporter. A slip opinion is binding, precedential law, and this open-ended citation can be used only with US Supreme Court opinions.

So, just how important is a USSC slip opinion? Consider the following fact pattern. Your supervising attorney is currently defending a juvenile charged with first-degree murder. The prosecution is seeking the death penalty. Jury selection has recently concluded and the trial begins tomorrow. As your attorney is driving

Figure 7-47 *Williams v. Illinois – Official Opinion*

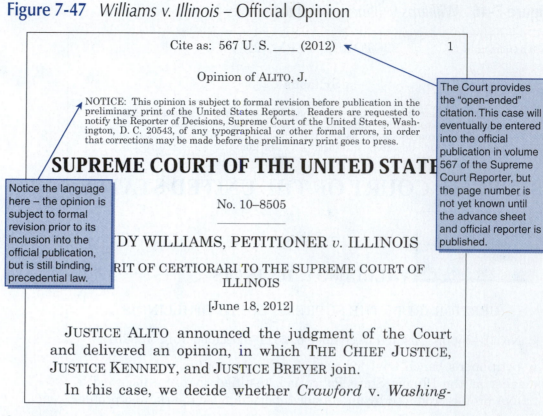

Cite as: 567 U. S. ____ (2012)   1

Opinion of ALITO, J.

> NOTICE: This opinion is subject to formal revision before publication in the preliminary print of the United States Reports. Readers are requested to notify the Reporter of Decisions, Supreme Court of the United States, Washington, D. C. 20543, of any typographical or other formal errors, in order that corrections may be made before the preliminary print goes to press.

SUPREME COURT OF THE UNITED STATE

No. 10–8505

DY WILLIAMS, PETITIONER *v.* ILLINOIS

RIT OF CERTIORARI TO THE SUPREME COURT OF ILLINOIS

[June 18, 2012]

JUSTICE ALITO announced the judgment of the Court and delivered an opinion, in which THE CHIEF JUSTICE, JUSTICE KENNEDY, and JUSTICE BREYER join.

In this case, we decide whether *Crawford* v. *Washing-*

Notice the language here – the opinion is subject to formal revision prior to its inclusion into the official publication, but is still binding, precedential law.

The Court provides the "open-ended" citation. This case will eventually be entered into the official publication in volume 567 of the Supreme Court Reporter, but the page number is not yet known until the advance sheet and official reporter is published.

Source: http://www.supremecourt.gov/opinions/11pdf/10-8505.pdf

into work, he hears on the radio that the US Supreme Court handed down a decision the day before holding that it is cruel and unusual punishment for any juvenile defendant who committed a capital offense to be subject to the death penalty. Your supervising attorney calls you on your way to work. He tells you about the case, and asks you to find it, read it, print it out, and to meet him at the courthouse—all before your morning coffee. The attorney didn't hear the full case name, but he knows one of the parties is *Roper*. The attorney must present the case to the court today before the beginning of trial.

So where do you find it? In this situation, you can access the official Supreme Court website and click on the most recent opinions. As you can see in Figure 7-48, you find the case, *Roper v. Simmons* under the "most recent decisions" tab.

You easily find the opinion, print it out, and bring it to court. Your supervising attorney makes an argument to the trial judge that it is unconstitutional to sentence a minor to death under the facts of the above case. The prosecution and trial court judge agree. For the record, the case would be cited as *Roper v. Simmons*, 543 U.S. ____ (2005).

That is how you locate and cite a US Supreme Court slip opinion. This situation not only demonstrates how to retrieve and cite a newly issued USSC opinion, but it is a situation that actually occurred during a first-degree death penalty case in Philadelphia in 2005. It is always good to be on alert and to be informed, as a single case can change the national landscape of the law overnight. Cable news stations, as well as many newspapers, keep the nation up-to-date on current issues/cases before the US Supreme Court. As a paralegal, you should always keep abreast of the current news in print or online, and bookmark the official government website to keep on top of the cases decided during the current term of the court.

Figure 7-48 *Roper v. Simmons* - Open-Ended Citation

Cite as: 543 U. S. ____ (2005) 1

Opinion of the Court

NOTICE: This opinion is subject to formal revision before publication in the preliminary print of the United States Reports. Readers are requested to notify the Reporter of Decisions, Supreme Court of the United States, Washington, D. C. 20543, of any typographical or other formal errors, in order that corrections may be made before the preliminary print goes to press.

SUPREME COURT OF THE UNITED STATES

No. 03–633

DONALD P. ROPER, SUPERINTENDENT, POTOSI CORRECTIONAL CENTER, PETITIONER *v.* CHRISTOPHER SIMMONS

Source: http://www.supremecourt.gov/opinions/04pdf/03-633.pdf

WestlawNext and Lexis Advance

By now, you know how to search for case law using either *Lexis Advance* or *WestlawNext*. Searching for a USSC on either system is straightforward and similar to locating a state or federal case.

WESTLAWNEXT: access USSC opinions by choosing the **United States Supreme Court** from the **Jurisdiction** drop-down tab next to the main search box, as you can see in Figure 7-49. Thereafter, you can conduct a case search similar to searching for a state or federal opinion.

Figure 7-49 A USSC Case Search on *WestlawNext*

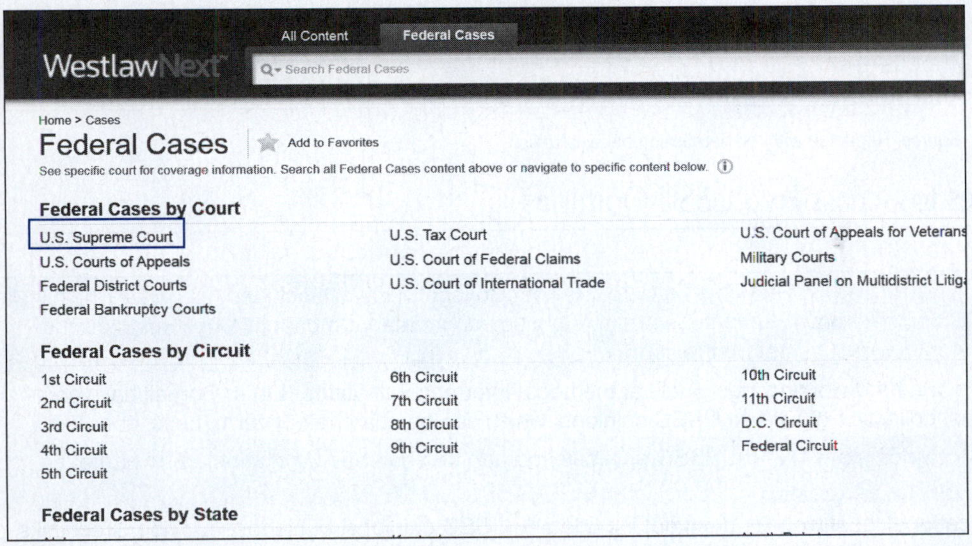

Source: Reprinted with permission of Thomson Reuters, Results for United States Supreme Court on WestlawNext.

LEXIS ADVANCE: from the home page, choose **Browse** from the top of the page. Then, choose **Sources**, then **Jurisdiction**, then **U.S. Federal**, as you can see in Figure 7-50. When you get to the results page, click on the "**U**" in the top alphabet bar and scroll down until you reach the **U.S. Supreme Court Cases, Lawyer's Edition,** the same as the Lawyer's Edition in print, as *Lexis* is the same publisher.

WestlawNext and *Lexis Advance* both offer quick and easy access for US Supreme Court decisions. However, if you are monitored or have restricted use of either of these databases at work, you can access any of the free sites listed in Figure 7-51 without a paid subscription.

As a last resort, you can also locate and retrieve *some* US Supreme Court cases simply on the Internet. If you are unsure which sites to visit, you can conduct a search using an Internet search engine. This, however, is only useful for

Figure 7-50 A USSC Case Search on *Lexis Advance*

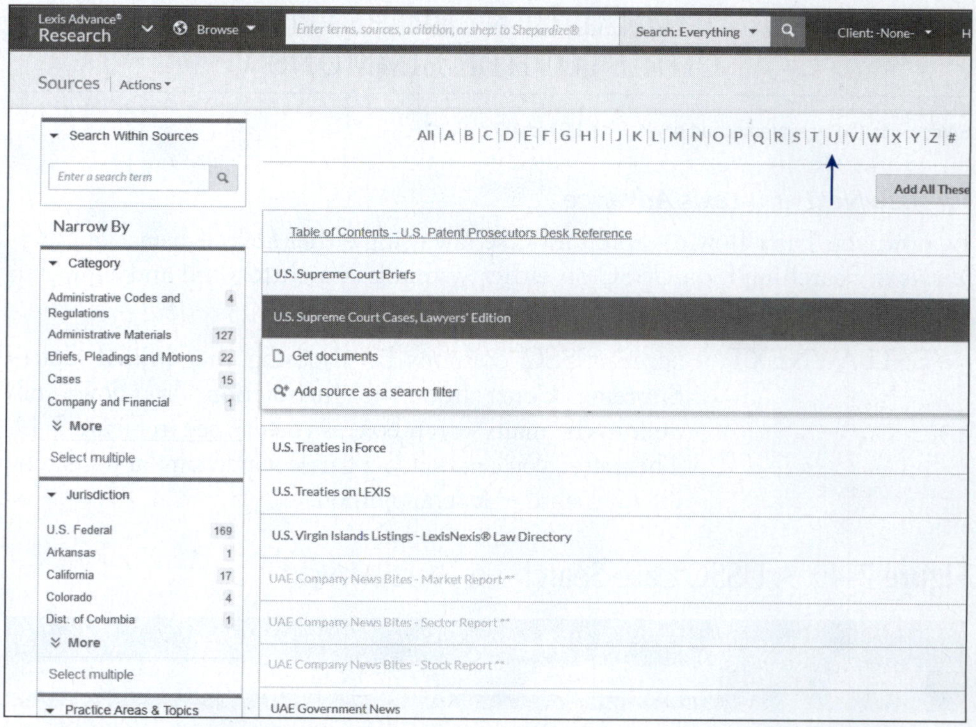

Source: Reprinted with the permission of LexisNexis.

Figure 7-51 Online Websites to Access Free USSC Opinions

Website	Content
www.Oyez.org	This is a great website created by the Chicago-Kent College of Law. It includes not only every full-text USSC opinion from 1792 to the present, but also commentary on past and upcoming discussions on hot-topic issues before the court.
www.Law.cornell.edu	As always, the hard working individuals at the Legal Information Institute (LII) at Cornell have compiled a vast collection of full-text USSC opinions, which can be searched by term, topic, or author.
www.Findlaw.com	This site includes many full-text USSC opinions that can be searched by citation, party name, or calendar year.
www.Washlaw.edu	This educational legal website does not include any USSC opinions, but it does provide direct links to the *Cornell* site, the official USSC website, and *Findlaw* where you can access opinions as well as USSC briefs.
www.Law.justia.com	This site provides all USSC opinions in full text since 1790.

any landmark decision such as *Roe v. Wade* or *Bush v. Gore.* By inserting only the case name into a search engine, numerous results are provided. You should be able to access a full opinion. Other "hits" may briefly describe the case, its history, or legal commentary on the case.

You should now feel confident in searching for any state, federal, or US Supreme Court case in print and online. When conducting a word search in print, remember to begin with general basic words/terms/phrases to narrow your findings to locate the headings, topics, and subtopics you need. Conversely, when searching for cases online using *WestlawNext* or *Lexis Advance*, make certain to be as specific as you can using your search words/terms/phrases because using general basic words will yield hundreds if not thousands of unwanted results. Learn to use the terms and connectors specific to each online system to assist you, and always utilize the numerous filters within each system to make your search as quick and efficient as possible.

Chapter Checklist ✓

- State case law can be located in official and unofficial print sources. Know the print resources available in your state to access case law in print.
- As you learned in step-by-step detail, utilizing the state and regional digests is very helpful in generating many case summaries that can then be located, read, and briefed in print and/or online.
- Federal case law can also be located in unofficial (*West*) reporters, but official federal print reporters are not published.
- As you also learned in step-by-step detail, utilizing the federal digests is very helpful in generating case summaries that can then be located, read, and briefed in print and/or online.
- In utilizing either state or federal digests, remember to begin with broad general topics and the digest will direct you to more specific subtopics until you find your desired point of law.
- You also learned, in detail, how to use the online subscription services of *Westlaw Next* and *Lexis Advance* to retrieve any state or federal case, as well as to validate, not only ensure the case is good law but also to determine if a more recent case exists that also references/interprets/describes your rule of law.
- When researching with *Westlaw* or *Lexis,* make certain you search using specific terms rather than general topics of law, which could yield thousands of unwanted and unnecessary results.
- Become familiar with using the terms and connectors used in a Boolean search, and make certain that certain phrases such as "medical malpractice" are placed in quotes in a Natural Language search.
- Remember that other than *WestlawNext* and *Lexis Advance*, many other legal online subscription services exist as well that offer monthly, weekly, or even daily rates.
- Be certain to utilize all the free quality legal online services that post many state and federal cases as well.
- You learned the many different ways to access an opinion from the US Supreme Court, which establishes legal precedent of each opinion handed down upon release to every state and federal court in the nation. Be certain to become familiar with the methods in obtaining a slip opinion from the Court if needed.

KEY TERMS

CRITICAL THINKING AND APPLICATION

1. You should be able to recognize the origin of an opinion by its citation. Match the following citations with their identifying/descriptive name.

   _____ Parallel citation   **A)** 123 U.S. 456 (2006)

   _____ US Supreme Court   **B)** 734 S.E. 2d 548 (Ga. Ct. App 2012)

   _____ *Lexis Advance*   **C)** 222 P.2d 34, 38 (Az. 1999)

   _____ Unofficial reporter   **D)** *Jones v. Lee*, No. 3442 (3rd Cir. May 8, 2012)

   _____ *WestlawNext*   **E)** 2009 PA Super 42; 123 A.2d 334

   _____ Pinpoint citation   **F)** 2007 PA Super 89

   _____ Official reporter   **G)** 2013 Va. App. LEXIS 51

   _____ Slip opinion   **H)** 2013 WL 59977

2. Look up the following case online: *Brown v. Entertainment Merchant's Association*, 131 S.Ct. 2729 (2011). This is a US Supreme Court case concerning free speech and the sale of video games to minors. This is a good example for reading, comprehending, and summarizing the information in a case. This is also a good case to read, review, and discuss in class.

   a) Read the **majority** opinion only. Take notes and highlight as you read. (Remember to have your legal dictionary with you). Do not brief the case. If someone asked you what the case is about, the issues presented, and the court's reasoning, how would you answer?

3. You work for a criminal defense attorney who is representing a defendant charged with numerous drug offenses, as well as criminal conspiracy. The defendant claims that he was present with his co-defendants when they planned to engage in a drug deal, but he also claims he did not agree to participate. Your attorney needs the elements of criminal conspiracy.

   a) Using the digests of your state, conduct a general word search for criminal conspiracy. Explain your research trail?

   b) When you find a case summary of interest, use the citation and look up that case in the official/unofficial print reporters.

   c) Read and brief the case.

4. You work for a workers' compensation attorney who is representing a claimant who was refused workers' compensation benefits after he was injured in the course and scope of his duties. The claimant was involved in an accident while driving his tractor-trailer on a local interstate. However, the truck company is refusing to pay benefits because it claims the claimant was intoxicated and caused the accident. Blood tests conducted at the hospital confirm the claimant was legally intoxicated. However, an accident recreation expert asserts that the opposing vehicle involved in the accident drifted into the claimant's lane forcing him to swerve out of the way, thus crashing the tractor-trailer. Your attorney needs to know what the *employer* needs to prove to deny workers' compensation benefits in this type of situation.

   a) Using the digests of your state, conduct a search for intoxication as a defense in denying benefits to an injured claimant. Remember that you would not begin a print search with such a specific and narrow topic. What term would you begin with? Explain your research trail?

   b) When you find a case summary of interest, use that citation and look up that case in the official/unofficial reporters.

   c) Thereafter, insert the citation into *WestlawNext* or *Lexis Advance* and validate the case by utilizing the *KeyCite* or *Shepard's* feature. Is the case good law?

   d) Can you find a more recent case while validating that addresses/answers your issue? If so, state its full citation.

   e) When you find a case of interest concerning this issue, brief it.

5. Researching **either** the *conspiracy* or the *workers' compensation* issue above, conduct both a **Boolean** and **Natural Language** search for either issue on *WestlawNext* or *Lexis Advance*. Explain your research trail.

6. You work for a solo practitioner who recently opened a new practice specializing in estate and family law. Your supervising attorney is representing a mother (the client) who currently shares legal and physical custody with her child's father. Both parties currently live in close proximity. The client wishes to relocate from one state to another, approximately 50 miles away. The client argues that the child has special education needs, and a school in the new state is far more superior than where child currently attends school. However, the father argues that if the court grants relocation, the move would not be in his best interest, as he will have to take significant time off work to pick up and drop off the child during his custodial time. Your supervising attorney needs to successfully argue that the client should be permitted to relocate with the child. Before arguing the case in court, the attorney needs the following information:

a) Using the print sources of *your state*, find a family law case that is similar in facts/issues to this situation. Find a case that enumerates and explains what factors, if any, a court must consider prior to granting a "relocation" petition. How are those case decisions similar to this hypothetical?

b) Using *WestlawNext* or *Lexis Advance*, conduct the same search and validate the case(s). Was your search similar or different from the print search?

c) Brief the case(s).

d) How would you explain to your supervising attorney the client's chances of successfully winning the relocation petition from reading the cases you found?

LEARNING OBJECTIVES

After completion of this chapter, you should be able to

1. Explain what a federal regulation is and the functions and powers of the agencies that create them.

2. Describe the purpose of the Federal Register and how to search it in print and online.

3. Explain how to search for federal regulations using the Code of Federal Regulations in print and online.

4. Explain how to cite and validate a regulation.

5. Describe how to locate state regulations in print and online.

REGULATION

AGENCY

ENABLING ACT

FEDERAL REGISTER

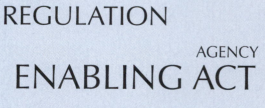

Administrative Law | CHAPTER 8

The majority of your daily research will include locating statutes and case opinions. However, you also need to know that administrative law is another important primary source of authority. They are similar to statutes in appearance, creation, and publication, but different in content, as these laws regulate specialized and unique areas of society.

■ AN INTRODUCTION TO ADMINISTRATIVE LAW

As the United States continues to grow and expand in the areas of consumer protection, food and drug consumption, as well protection of the environment, just to name a few, Congress alone lacks the ability to create the laws to regulate these areas of society. Therefore, Congress has created specific agencies to regulate these important areas that directly affect all of us on a daily basis. For example, in 1970, Congress, in an effort to protect our air and water, passed the Clean Air Act (42 U.S.C. §7401). However, with the millions of cars, trucks, motorcycles, and buses on the road, as well as the thousands of factories located across the country, Congress knew that it would be nearly impossible to regulate and monitor the provisions of the Act nationwide. So Congress created the Environmental Protection Agency (EPA) to do the monitoring and regulating, thereby giving the federal government authority to clean up air pollution *through* the EPA.

The EPA is what is known as an **administrative agency**. Congress has essentially delegated its lawmaking power to the EPA to pass its own laws, called **regulations** (also called rules) in order to monitor and regulate the provisions of the Clean Air Act, such as the regulation of fuel additives and control of air pollution from aircraft or locomotives. A regulation is a rule enacted by an agency, similar to how a statute is enacted by a legislative body. The members of Congress lack the experience, time, manpower, and knowledge to enforce such technical regulations. So, the EPA itself is comprised of numerous employees who possess a high level of scientific expertise in order to investigate and inspect thousands of vehicles and factories to ensure they all comply with the regulations created by the EPA.

Administrative law, also referred to as regulatory law, includes the body of rules, regulations, and decisions, issued by these administrative agencies. Perhaps some of the cases you will work on may involve a federal, state, or local rule or regulation.

Federal regulations are mandatory requirements that apply to individuals, businesses, and corporations, and carry the same weight and authority as any other source of primary authority. Regulations are passed not only on a federal level, but

LEARNING OBJECTIVE 1
Explain what a federal regulation is and the functions and powers of the agencies that create them.

administrative agency
A governmental entity, created by Congress, state legislatures, and local governing bodies, to oversee complex matters of governmental regulation that fall beyond the expertise of legislators.

regulations
Rules and administrative codes, having the force of law, that are created, monitored, and enforced by governmental agencies at the federal, state, and local level.

245

enabling acts
A piece of legislation by which a legislative body empowers a government agency to carry out specific actions, such as to create, monitor, and enforce rules and regulations.

also on state and even local levels. On the state level, your state's turnpike commission or public utilities commission are examples of state agencies. As you will see below, Congress, as well as state legislatures, has created numerous agencies just like the EPA in order to monitor and regulate many areas of our society.

Legislative bodies have the power to create agencies through what are called **enabling acts**. An enabling act is legislation by which a legislative body (Congress) authorizes an entity to have specific powers and to take specific actions. Because of this, agencies lack the power to act beyond the scope of its enabling legislation. For example, the EPA cannot attempt to regulate what we watch on television, which is monitored by another federal administrative agency—the Federal Communications Commission (FCC).

Federal administrative agencies include executive agencies and independent agencies. Both perform the same functions. However, executive agencies fall under the command of the executive branch (the President) and help to carry out executive functions. Conversely, independent agencies (also called Boards or Commissions) exist outside the control of the executive branch and are established through separate statutes passed by Congress.

Executive Agencies

executive agencies
An agency of the executive branch of government subject to the authority of the President that regulates and affects many matters on a national level, such as national security, food and drugs, and counterterrorism.

The **executive agencies** are subject to the authority of the President, who can appoint and remove the head officers of these agencies.

Many of these executive agencies are familiar to us, as we hear about them in the news on a daily basis. For example, Congress, in an effort to make sure all the food we consume as a nation is properly grown, tested, and packaged prior to consumption, created the Department of Health and Human Resources to regulate that area. Specifically, the Food and Drug Administration (FDA), a subdivision of that agency, regulates and monitors our nation's food supply on a daily basis. In addition, many of the executive agencies in Figure 8-1, in

Figure 8-1 The 15 Executive Agencies

Executive Agency	One Subdivision of that Agency
Department of Agriculture	Food and Nutrition Services
Department of Commerce	US Census Bureau
Department of Defense	National Security Agency (NSA)
Department of Education	Office of Federal Student Aid
Department of Energy	Federal Energy Regulatory Commission
Department of Health and Human Services	Food and Drug Administration (FDA)
Department of Homeland Security	Immigration and Customs Enforcement (ICE)
Department of Housing and Urban Development	Federal Housing Administration
Department of Justice	Federal Bureau of Investigation (FBI)
Department of Labor	Occupational Safety and Health Organization (OSHA)
State Department	Bureau of Counterterrorism
Department of the Interior	National Park Service
Treasury Department	Internal Revenue Service (IRS)
Department of Transportation	Federal Aviation Administration (FAA)
Veterans Affairs	Veterans Health Administration (VHA)

addition to having multiple subagencies, can also have *bureaus* or *offices* under them. For example, under the Department of Housing and Urban Development (HUD), in addition to its subagencies, the Office of Equal Opportunity (to enforcement the elimination of all forms of discrimination in the departments' employment practices), and the Office of General Counsel (which helps to ensure that safe and affordable housing is available for all Americans) also report to HUD.

Independent Agencies

Unlike the executive agencies, the head officers of the independent agencies serve a fixed term and cannot be removed by the president. Citizens have more contact with the **independent agencies** than the executive agencies. For example, the Social Security Administration alone serves millions of individuals each day concerning retirement and death benefits.

independent agencies
An agency independent of the executive branch of government that regulates and affects many everyday matters, such as social security, transportation, banking, and postal service.

Some of these independent agencies include: the US Department of Agriculture (USDA); The Central Intelligence Agency (CIA); Equal Employment Opportunity Commission (EEOC); Federal Deposit Insurance Corporation (FDIC); Federal Election Commission (FEC); Consumer Product Safety Commission (CPSC); Environmental Protection Agency (EPA); Federal Trade Commission (FTC); National Aeronautics and Space Administration (NASA); National Transportation Safety Board (NTSB); Federal Emergency Management Agency (FEMA); Federal Communications Commission (FCC); National Labor Relations Board (NLRB); Nuclear Regulatory Commission (NRC); Securities and Exchange Commission (SEC); Social Security Administration (SSA), and the US Postal Service (USPS).

In addition, not only do the independent agencies regularly monitor certain industries to make sure they comply with their regulations, but these agencies have also been granted the power to conduct their own investigations following an incident or accident. For example, when a natural tragedy such as a hurricane or tornado destroys a city, the FEMA agency will be one of the first agencies on the scene to access the situation and to help the citizens who may have been displaced by the disaster. Likewise, the NTSB is the first on the scene to investigate any and all aircraft tragedies.

Figure 8-2 The Creation of Agencies and Regulations

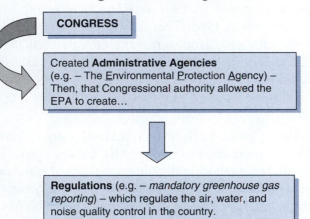

CONGRESS

Enabling acts grant Congress the authority to create the agency.

Created **Administrative Agencies** (e.g. – The Environmental Protection Agency) – Then, that Congressional authority allowed the EPA to create…

Regulations (e.g. – *mandatory greenhouse gas reporting*) – which regulate the air, water, and noise quality control in the country.

Agency Powers

After an agency has been created and designated with a specific regulatory agenda, all agencies themselves have been granted the power of:

- Rulemaking;
- Enforcement; and
- Adjudication

Rulemaking

rulemaking
A power instilled in a governmental agency to create rules and regulations.

Simply put, agencies have the power create the rules and regulations necessary to effectively regulate a particular industry. These regulations have the power of law, equal to that of a congressional statute. The process of creating regulatory law, known as **rulemaking**, includes multiple steps to ensure the rule is necessary to regulate a particular activity. The overall process has been simplified below.

First, a determination is made on whether a particular regulation is needed and what activity the rule would regulate. Thereafter, the agency proposes a rule that would create, add, supplement, or amend an existing regulation. The proposed rule is included in the *Federal Register* so that any member of the public can view the proposal and make any comments and/or objections to it (usually within 60 days). This information is also included on the specific agency website. Next, the agency considers all the commentary, possibly holds a hearing if needed, and issues a final rule (The Office of Management and Budget (OMB) reviews the proposed rule to determine if the rule is necessary. However, the OMB only reviews the proposed rules of the executive agencies, not the independent agencies). The final rule is published in the Federal Register as a "final rule," as well as online. A final rule issued by an agency has full binding legal effect, which is why you are learning them. Lastly, the regulation is codified and added to the Code of Federal Regulations.

Enforcement

enforcement power
A power instilled in a governmental agency to enforce the rules and regulations they create.

What makes these agencies so unique is that they also have the power to enforce the regulations they enact, which is known as **enforcement power**. They achieve this through investigative and prosecutorial powers. For example, in exercising their investigative powers, employees from the EPA routinely inspect businesses and corporations to make certain they follow the strict regulations. It monitors waste being dumped into lakes and rivers and the amount of smog billowing out from factory smokestacks. Further, if any violations are discovered, the agency can exercise its prosecutorial powers. For example, the EPA's criminal enforcement program was created in 1982 and was later granted "full enforcement authority" by Congress in 1988. That means that if anyone violates any of the provisions of the EPA's regulations, it is the EPA that has the power to adjudicate criminal behavior by establishing a criminal case file and submitting it to federal, state, or local prosecutors.

Adjudication

adjudication power
A power instilled in a governmental agency to enforce the rules and regulations they create through negotiation, settlement, or by formal complaint.

Under other agencies, given the highly technical and scientific knowledge of many of these regulations, disputes are not decided by the judicial courts. These agencies are created with their own methods of dispute resolution and **adjudication power**. If an agency fails to resolve a matter through negotiation or settlement, the agency can file a formal complaint against a violator. If the matter is not resolved at this level, judges referred to as **administrative law judges (ALJ)** will hear the claim in a proceeding similar to a trial. However, case decisions and sanctions can be appealed to the judicial courts (Federal Appeals Court) only after all levels of administrative law are exhausted, which includes appeal to the agency Board or Commission. For example, if someone informed the government that you forgot to include your Grandmother's $25 birthday gift last year as income, it is the IRS that contacts you and allows you a specific time period to rectify the situation before taking you to tax court!

administrative law judges
judges who both preside over trials and adjudicate the claims or disputes involving administrative law.

> ## SIDE NOTE
>
> Federal regulations, like statutes, are enacted and amended to adapt to changes and advances in society. For example, in 2015, the Federal Aviation Administration (FAA) permitted the use of drones for many business people, including real estate agents, aerial photographers, farmers, as well as insurance agents and claim adjusters, who can now use the drones to survey unsafe conditions, such as the site of a fire or natural disaster.

■ SEARCHING FEDERAL REGULATIONS

Now that you know and understand what a regulation is and how regulations are created and the powers granted to them, you will now see how to search for a federal regulation in print and online.

LEARNING OBJECTIVE 2
Describe the purpose of the Federal Register and how to search it in print and online.

The Federal Register

The Federal Register is referred to as a journal-type publication for all administrative agencies and is published by the Office of the Federal Reporter. This publication is printed and updated daily. The register includes information concerning proposed and newly enacted federal rules and regulations and notices of federal agencies and organizations, containing summary and commentary material concerning proposed regulations. All documents are published in chronological order and not yet codified into an official publication. Therefore, the register *does not* include the actual text of the regulations that you find in the official Code of Federal Regulations (CFR).

the federal register
An official government publication printed and updated daily that includes all newly enacted rules and regulations, as well as summary, explanation, and commentary of proposed regulations.

The register begins a new volume each year. The page numbering sequence of the register is "continuous;" therefore, they are not cumulative. The first issue of the year will begin at page one, but the final issue could reach page 80,000! In fact, in its first publication back in 1936, one volume of the register was published consisting of an entire 2,620 pages. In 2014, 79 volumes were published consisting of 79,066 pages. Therefore, as you will see below, a researcher must have a *volume* and *page number* (which you can obtain from the index), because the index will nearly prove impossible to use without that information.

The Federal Register in Print

There are many different research tools you can use in order to find information you need. The register includes an *Index* that is published monthly and is cumulated for 12 months. In other words, an index published in April would include the information from January through April, and so on until the last issued index would include all the entries for the year from January through December. The front cover includes the current month, the volume number, and the range of pages within that issue of the register. As you can see in Figure 8-3, the entries within the index are

Figure 8-3 The Federal Register Index

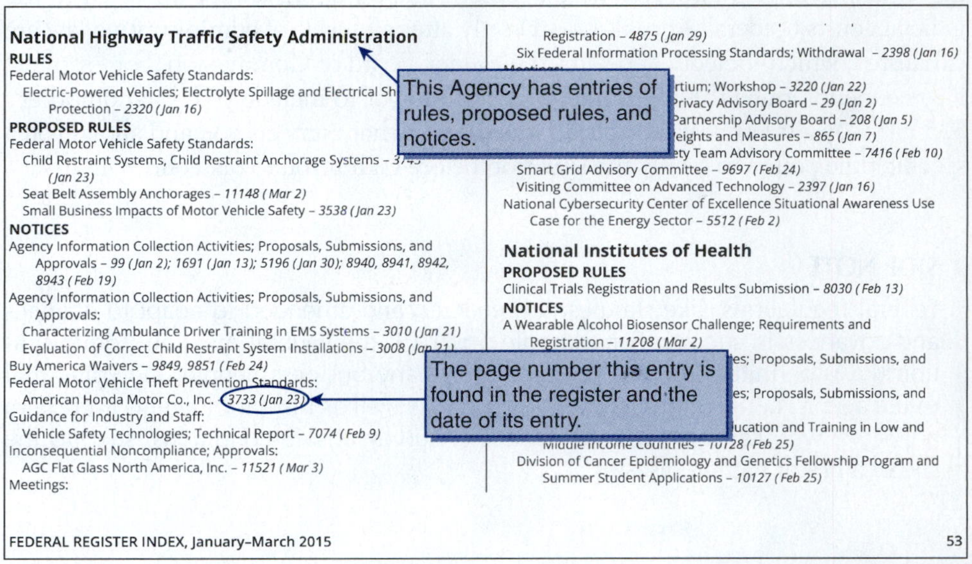

National Highway Traffic Safety Administration
RULES
Federal Motor Vehicle Safety Standards:
Electric-Powered Vehicles; Electrolyte Spillage and Electrical Sh
Protection – *2320 (Jan 16)*
PROPOSED RULES
Federal Motor Vehicle Safety Standards:
Child Restraint Systems, Child Restraint Anchorage Systems – *374*
(Jan 23)
Seat Belt Assembly Anchorages – *11148 (Mar 2)*
Small Business Impacts of Motor Vehicle Safety – *3538 (Jan 23)*
NOTICES
Agency Information Collection Activities; Proposals, Submissions, and
Approvals – *99 (Jan 2); 1691 (Jan 13); 5196 (Jan 30); 8940, 8941, 8942, 8943 (Feb 19)*
Agency Information Collection Activities; Proposals, Submissions, and
Approvals:
Characterizing Ambulance Driver Training in EMS Systems – *3010 (Jan 21)*
Evaluation of Correct Child Restraint System Installations – *3008 (Jan 21)*
Buy America Waivers – *9849, 9851 (Feb 24)*
Federal Motor Vehicle Theft Prevention Standards:
American Honda Motor Co., Inc. *3733 (Jan 23)*
Guidance for Industry and Staff:
Vehicle Safety Technologies; Technical Report – *7074 (Feb 9)*
Inconsequential Noncompliance; Approvals:
AGC Flat Glass North America, Inc. – *11521 (Mar 3)*
Meetings:

Registration – *4875 (Jan 29)*
Six Federal Information Processing Standards; Withdrawal – *2398 (Jan 16)*
rtium; Workshop – *3220 (Jan 22)*
Privacy Advisory Board – *29 (Jan 2)*
Partnership Advisory Board – *208 (Jan 5)*
eights and Measures – *865 (Jan 7)*
ety Team Advisory Committee – *7416 (Feb 10)*
Smart Grid Advisory Committee – *9697 (Feb 24)*
Visiting Committee on Advanced Technology – *2397 (Jan 16)*
National Cybersecurity Center of Excellence Situational Awareness Use
Case for the Energy Sector – *5512 (Feb 2)*

National Institutes of Health
PROPOSED RULES
Clinical Trials Registration and Results Submission – *8030 (Feb 13)*
NOTICES
A Wearable Alcohol Biosensor Challenge; Requirements and
Registration – *11208 (Mar 2)*
es; Proposals, Submissions, and
es; Proposals, Submissions, and
ucation and Training in Low and
Middle Income Countries – *10128 (Feb 25)*
Division of Cancer Epidemiology and Genetics Fellowship Program and
Summer Student Applications – *10127 (Feb 25)*

FEDERAL REGISTER INDEX, January–March 2015 53

Source: https://www.federalregister.gov

arranged first under the name of the agency that issued the document. Under each agency, the entries are then listed alphabetically within the categories of *Rules*, *Proposed Rules*, and *Notices*. Some agencies may have none, one, or all of those categories. All Executive Orders, Proclamations, and other documents from the president are listed under *Presidential Documents*. Each entry contains the page number in the register where the document begins, followed by the date it was published.

Other helpful and informative research tools and finding aids within each issue of the register include a Table of Contents, CFR Parts Affected in This Issue, and Reader Aids.

1. The **Table of Contents** (TOC) section found at the beginning of each issue and contains a comprehensive alphabetical and descriptive listing of all the documents in that issue listed by agency name. Under each agency name, the documents are arranged by *Rules*, *Proposed Rules*, or *Notices*, and each entry includes the page number of where the document begins in that issue of the register.
2. The **CFR Parts Affected in This Issue** section, found at the front of each issue following the TOC, lists any part of a regulation that was affected, in numerical order by CFR title and part, and the page number where the relevant document begins. This section also indicates whether the documents affecting the CFR parts are rules or proposed rules.
3. The **Reader Aides** section, located at the back of each daily issue, includes *Customer Service and Information*, which provides helpful phone numbers, relevant web addresses, and e-mail addresses if you have any questions searching the register or need to access the register online. *Federal Register Pages and Date* is a table of the inclusive page numbers (left side) and corresponding dates (right side) for the current month's register. Also, the *CFR Parts Affected During (the Current Month)* provides a cumulative list of the CFR parts affected and corresponding page number affected during the current month that are organized numerically by title. It is important to note that because any changes to a federal rule or regulation are listed in the federal register first, if you are researching in print, you must search *both* the monthly and daily LSA for any parts

affected within the agency you are researching. This section also includes *Reminders* concerning rules that will be going into effect and the time remaining to submit comments.

So how do you navigate the Federal Register in print? Just follow the easy steps below.

STEP 1: Search the index to determine and narrow down which AGENCY has published information concerning the proposed or newly enacted rule. *Hint*—you can also check the enabling statute as a cross-reference.

STEP 2: Find that particular agency in the index. For example, if you needed to review the latest proposal to ban a certain dangerous drug found in a common over-the-counter pain reliever, you would look under the FDA. Or suppose you needed to review the latest final regulations enacted concerning eligibility for unemployment benefits, you would look under the Department of Labor. Once you find the agency, determine what entry you need under the rules, proposed rules, or notices headings.

STEP 3: After you locate the appropriate entry you need, you will see the page number where the entry appears in the register and the date it was included in the register. From there, you can locate the appropriate page number in the register itself.

As you can see in Figure 8-4, when you do find the entry you are seeking, the description provided by the register includes five specific headings, which include: The main **Heading/Caption**, which includes *agency* that enacted/proposed the regulation; the CFR citation for the rule; the name of the rule, and the current *action* of the regulation (proposed or final rule); The other headings include the **Summary** of the regulation (a very brief but helpful understanding of the rule); the **Effective Date** (the date the regulation becomes effective as law); and the **Contact Information** (which includes contact addresses and phone numbers of the individuals within that particular agency). The last heading includes **Supplementary Information** which includes where the actual rule, or proposed rule, can be located, as well as a more detailed description of the rule and the reasoning behind the need for the regulation.

The Federal Register Online

The Federal Register can also be accessed online for free at two official government websites. However, there is a difference between the two.

GPO Website (www.gpo.gov/fdsys)

STEP 1: On the homepage, click on "Federal Register" from the right-hand column under the "Browse" tab.

STEP 2: Choose the year of the desired regulation (from 1994 to the present).

STEP 3: Choose the month that the desired issue of the Register was published.

STEP 4: Choose the specific day and date of the Register you need.

STEP 5: Choose the specific agency, which will give you a mini index for the regulatory activity for only that agency, or click on the *Table of Contents*.

Once you find the regulatory material, it will look exactly as it appears in the print version of the Register.

Figure 8-4 A Newly Enacted Regulation in the Register

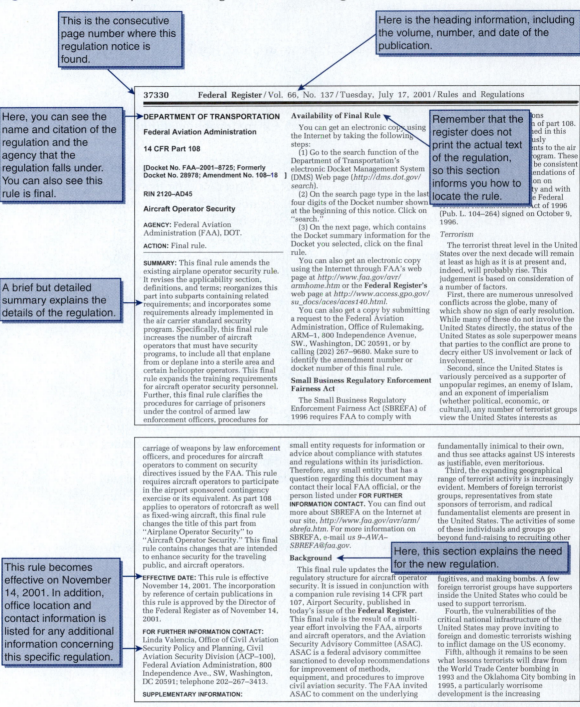

This is the consecutive page number where this regulation notice is found.

Here is the heading information, including the volume, number, and date of the publication.

Here, you can see the name and citation of the regulation and the agency that the regulation falls under. You can also see this rule is final.

A brief but detailed summary explains the details of the regulation.

This rule becomes effective on November 14, 2001. In addition, office location and contact information is listed for any additional information concerning this specific regulation.

Remember that the register does not print the actual text of the regulation, so this section informs you how to locate the rule.

Here, this section explains the need for the new regulation.

Source: http://www.gpo.gov/fdsys

Federal Register Website (www.federalregister.gov)   Although it is an official government site, it offers many features from the home page as you can see in Figure 8-5. On the **Browse** tab at the top of the home page, you can search by *agencies*, *topics*, and *dates*. If you choose *agencies* or *topics*, you can:

■ Enter any term into a search bar to search any regulation relating to that agency;
■ Be directed directly to that agency's website;

Figure 8-5 The Federal Register Online

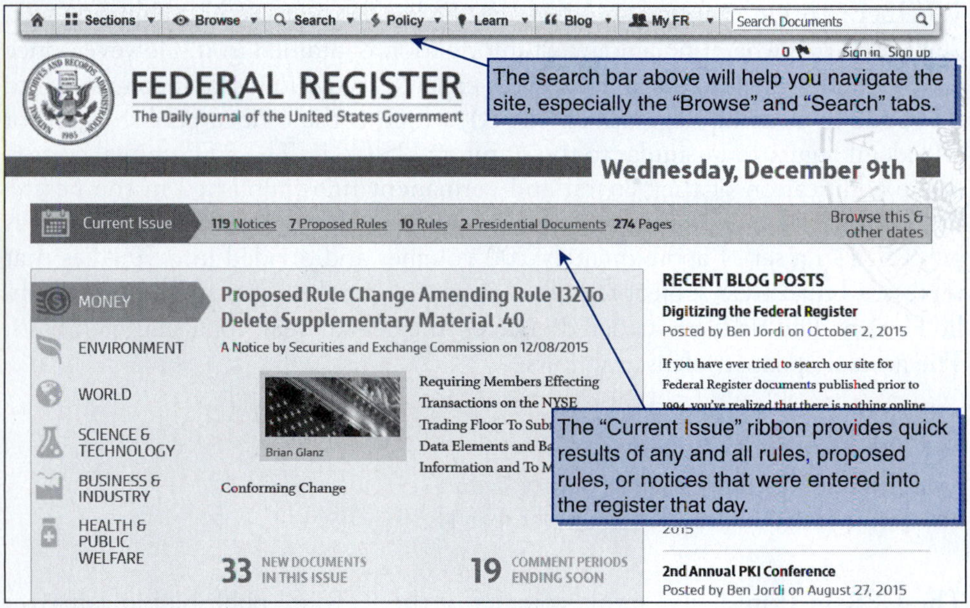

Source: https://www.federalregister.gov

- View every document pending publication;
- View the most recent and significant documents, and
- View all documents where the comment period is near closing, as well as all documents opening for comments.

Under the **Search** tab, you can conduct a *document search*, *advanced document search*, or view the entire index, which is updated daily.

Be mindful that the *Federal Register*, in print or online, does NOT include the actual full text of any regulation. It does, however, act somewhat like a secondary source by explaining the reason for the regulation and by providing a brief yet detailed summary of the regulation.

If you have a subscription, you can also access the *Federal Register* on *WestlawNext* and *Lexis Advance*. The documents are in PDF format and are available from 1936 through 1980 and in Boolean search format from 1980 to the present. *Bloomberg Law* also has the register online from 1936. However, as stated previously, the *Federal Register* can be accessed for free at the above offical government websites—use them. You should always consider a free official government website (federal or state) for your research needs, rather than unnecesarily conducting a search on a paid subscription website. That is why a good researcher knows all the print and online sources of law available.

Although information is updated fairly quickly on the *Federal Register* online, you may be able to find a newly approved regulation even faster on the website of the particular agency itself. Remember, every agency maintains its own public website.

Lastly, if you want or need to keep an eye on a particular regulation for an upcoming case or your attorney needs to advise a client, you can bookmark that agency's website or you can subscribe online to the *Public Laws Electronic Notification Service (PENS)* and receive free daily e-mails concerning the newly enacted and proposed laws by sending an e-mail request to **www.listserv@www .gsa.gov**.

The Code of Federal Regulations (CFR)

code of federal regulations
An official print and online government publication that compiles every newly enacted regulation into a code, consisting of multiple volumes organized into 50 titles.

Whether in print or online, searching the *Federal Register* can be a daunting task, due to the overwhelming amount of information contained in it. However, once enacted and made into a final rule, every enacted regulation is later compiled into the **Code of Federal Regulations (CFR)**, which is the official published set for all federal regulations, similar to the statutory US Code. The CFR annual edition is the codification of the general and permanent rules published in the *Federal Register* by the departments and agencies of the federal government. The set is published in a set of approximately 200 volumes and divided into 50 titles that represent broad areas subject to federal regulation, such as Transportation or Public Health. The titles are updated once each calendar year, on a staggered basis. The annual update cycle is as follows:

- Titles 1–16 are revised as of January 1;
- Titles 17–27 are revised as of April 1;
- Titles 28–41 are revised as of July 1; and
- Titles 42–50 are revised as of October 1.

LEARNING OBJECTIVE 3
Explain how to search for federal regulations using the Code of Federal Regulations in print and online.

The CFR in Print. The print volumes of the CFR are published in softcover books and updated by a different color every year; that is, 2013 (red), 2014 (purple), and 2015 (green). One title can include multiple volumes within the set. Each final enacted regulation is divided into multiple subsections. The actual breakdown is as follows:

The Federal Regulation Numbering System:

Title – The broad subject/topic area of regulation (Title 21: Food and Drugs);
Chapter – The individual rules of the agency (Chapter 12: Meat Inspection);
Part/Subchapter – The specific rules (Subchapter 1: Inspection Requirements);
Section – One particular provision or function of the rule (Section 607: Labeling);
Paragraph – The detailed specific requirement of the rule ((a) Labeling receptacles or coverings of meat or meat food products inspected and passed . . .).

In addition to the volumes, the print set also includes an annual *CFR Index and Finding Aids*. The **Index** portion is organized by subject with references to CFR parts. The **Finding Aids** portion is divided into four sections, including: *List of Agency Prepared Indexes Appearing in Individual CFR Volumes; Parallel Table of Authorities and Rules; List of CFR Titles, Chapters, Subchapters, and Parts,* and *Alphabetical List of Agencies Appearing in the CFR.*

On an important note, because regulations "regulate" many statutory laws, the US Code and the CFR usually run parallel to each other. This means that **Title 7 of the US Code** includes **statutes relating to agriculture**, whereas **Title 7 of the CFR** relates to **agriculture regulations**. So, the *Parallel Table of Authorities and Rules* is quite helpful in locating the CFR title if you know the corresponding statutory citation, as you can see in Figure 8-6.

So, how do you navigate the CFR in print? Searching the CFR for enacted rules and regulations is not difficult. Suppose your attorney needed to know the federal passport and visa document requirements for immigrants and

Figure 8-6 The Parallel Table of Authorities and Rules

CFR Index

5 U.S.C.—Continued	CFR	5 U.S.C.—Continued	CFR
5553	5 Part 550	7204	5 Part 300
5561—5568	32 Part 718	7301	3 Part 100
5569	22 Part 192		5 Parts 251, 715, 731, 735, 771, 772,
5570	22 Part 192		930, 1001, 1300, 1633, 1900, 2635, 3101,
5570	5 Part 550		3901,
The citation for the federal statute 5 Part 178		*The corresponding CFR citation* 4701,
5595	5 Part 550		5001, 5101, 5201, 5202, 5301, 5501, 5502,
5596	5 Part 550		5601, 5701, 5801, 6001, 6201, 6301, 6401,
5701—5709	12 Part 412		6501, 6601, 6701, 6801, 6901, 7001, 7101,
	41 Part 101–7		7301, 7401, 7501, 7601, 7701, 7801, 8001,
5701 *note*	41 Parts 301–51, 301–52, 301–54, 301–		8101, 8301, 8401, 8601, 8701, 9001, 9201,
	70, 301–71, 301–76		9303, 9401, 9601
5703	49 Part 5		10 Part 1010
5706b	5 Part 572		12 Parts 264, 336, 400, 601, 1401, 1600
5707	41 Parts 300–1, 300–2, 300–3, 300–70, 300–		13 Part 105
	80, 300–90, 301–1, 301–2, 301–10, 301–		14 Part 1207
	11, 301–12, 301–13, 301–30, 301–31, 301–		15 Part 0
	50, 301–51, 301–52, 301–53, 301–54, 301–		16 Parts 5, 1030
	70, 301–71, 301–72, 301–73, 301–74, 301–		22 Parts 705, 1001, 1100, 1504
	75, 301–76, 304–1, 304–2, 304–3, 304–		24 Part 0
	4, 304–5, 304–6		28 Part 45
5711	41 Part 300–90		29 Parts 100, 1600, 2703
5721—5738	41 Part 303–70		34 Part 73
5723	5 Part 572		36 Parts 400, 811
5724b	41 Part 302–17		43 Part 20
5738	41 Parts 300–1, 300–2, 300–3, 300–70, 300–		45 Parts 73, 680
	80, 302–1, 302–2, 302–3, 302–4, 302–5,		46 Part 508
	302–6, 302–7, 302–8, 302–9, 302–10, 302–	7302	5 Parts 534, 7302
	11, 302–12, 302–14, 302–15, 302–16, 302–	7312	5 Part 732

Source: http://www.gpo.gov/

non-immigrants for an upcoming case. Before your supervising attorney can proceed, she needs to know how these documents are required and regulated by the federal government.

STEP 1: Go to the *CFR Index and Finding Aids.* The most obvious general search terms would be "PASSPORT" or "VISA," and "IMMIGRANT."

STEP 2: In Figure 8-7, under the term "passports and visas," you see the subtopic "documentary requirements," which includes the requirements for immigrants and non-immigrants. That subtopic also lists the relevant citation of **8 CFR 211** and **212.** The **8** refers to the particular volume in the set, and the **211/212** refers to the specific Part. Now you are ready to go the volume set.

STEP 3: After you pull Volume 8 from the set, you would see that the cover lists the topic of **Aliens and Nationality.**

STEP 4: After you locate "**Part 211 – Documentary Requirements: Immigrants; Waivers**," you would see that the Part is further broken down into five Sections, including **211.1 Visas, 211.2 Passports, 211.3 Expiration of immigrant visa or other travel document, 211.4 Waiver of documents for returning residents, and 211.5 Alien commuters.** As you can see in Figure 8-8, under Section 211.1, it explicitly states the visa requirements for arriving aliens into the country. Thereafter, section 211.2 follows directly after section 211.1, When informing your supervising attorney of this information, similar to reading statutes, always read the *definitions* section which will interpret any terms for their intended meaning within *that* particular regulation, and be mindful of any language including, "and/but/shall/must/may/or" within the regulation as well.

Figure 8-7 The CFR Index

Passports and visas	CFR·Index

Intact stability and seaworthiness, 46 CFR 178

Lifesaving equipment and arrangements, 46 CFR 180

Machinery installation, 46 CFR 182

Operations, 46 CFR 185

Subdivision, damage stability and watertight integrity requirements, 46 CFR 179

Vessel control and miscellaneous systems and equipment, 46 CFR 184

Small passenger vessels carrying more than 150 passengers or with overnight accommodations for more than 49 passengers

Construction and arrangement, 46 CFR 116

Electrical installation, 46 CFR 120

Fire protection equipment, 46 CFR 118

General provisions, 46 CFR 114

Inspection and certification, 46 CFR 115

Lifesaving equipment and arrangements, 46 CFR 117

Machinery installation, 46 CFR 119

Operations, 46 CFR 122

Vessel control and miscellaneous systems and equipment, 46 CFR 121

Subdivision and stability, special rules pertaining to vessels carrying passengers, 46 CFR 171

Subdivision load lines, 46 CFR 46

Vessel control and miscellaneous systems and equipment, 46 CFR 77

Passports and visas

Aliens, medical examination, 42 CFR 34

Documentary requirements

Immigrants and waivers of requirements, 8 CFR 211, 1211

Nonimmigrants, waivers, admission of certain inadmissible aliens, parole of aliens into U.S., 8 CFR 212, 1212

Irish peace process cultural and training program, 22 CFR 139

Operational contract support, 32 CFR 158

Immigrant documentation, 22 CFR 42

Nonimmigrants, 22 CFR 41

Regulations pertaining to both nonimmigrants and immigrants, 22 CFR 40

Labor condition applications and requirements for employers using nonimmigrants on H-1B specialty visas in specialty occupations and as fashion models, 29 CFR 507

Waiver program, 8 CFR 217

Patent and Trademark Office, U.S.

Assignment, recording and rights of assignee, 37 CFR 3

Foreign mask works protection, requests for Presidential proclamation, 37 CFR 150

Goods and services classification under Trademark Act, 37 CFR 6

Government information disclosure, 37 CFR 102

Invention promoters, complaints regarding, 37 CFR 4

Legal processes, 37 CFR 104

Madrid Agreement, international registration of marks, rules of practice in filings pursuant to protocol relating to, 37 CFR 7

Patent cases practice rules, 37 CFR 1

Patent Trial and Appeal Board

Judicial review, 37 CFR 90

Practice before, 37 CFR 41

Trial practice before, 37 CFR 42

Representation of others before Patent and Trademark Office, 37 CFR 10, 37 CFR 11

Secrecy of certain inventions and licenses to export and file applications in foreign countries, 37 CFR 5

Trademark cases practice rules, 37 CFR 2

Patents

See Inventions and patents

Paving and roofing materials

Source: Code of Federal Regulations (CFR), CFR Index and Finding Aids (revised as of 1/1/13), Page 586.

Similar to other primary sources in print, the legal authority contained in the CFR needs to be updated on a regular basis, as the rules and regulations are frequently updated and amended. The CFR maintains its currency by publication of the **List of CFR Sections Affected (LSA).** Years ago, updates were placed in the cumulative pocket parts. Thereafter, in the 1960s, monthly and annual issues of the LSA were published as their own volumes. The LSA updates follow the same staggered format as the titles of the CFR in January, April, July, and October. Check with your local library, as many retain the annual LSA volumes as well. As you can see in Figure 8-9, an LSA search was conducted as to the regulation search on passport and visa document requirements, specifically, **8 CFR 211.** According to the LSA as of that date, there were no changes made to that regulation.

Figure 8-8 Volume 8, Section 211 of the CFR

Department of Homeland Security   **§211.1**

be filed with the regional processing facility within thirty (30) days after the service of the notice of termination. If no appeal is filed within that period, the Forms I–94, I–688 or other official Service document shall be deemed void, and must be surrendered without delay to an immigration officer or to the issuing office of the Service.

(ii) Termination proceedings must be commenced before the alien becomes eligible for adjustment of status under §210.5 of this part. The timely commencement of termination proceedings will preclude the alien from becoming a lawful permanent resident until a final determination is made in the proceedings, including any appeal.

[53 FR 10064, Mar. 29, 1988, as amended at 55 FR 12629, Apr. 5, 1990; 60 FR 21975, May 4, 1995; 61 FR 46536, Sept. 4, 1996; 65 FR 82255, Dec. 28, 2000]

§210.5. Adjustment to permanent resident status.

(a) *Eligibility and date of adjustment to permanent resident status.* The status of an alien lawfully admitted to the United States for temporary residence under section 210(a)(1) of the Act, if the alien has otherwise maintained such status as required by the Act, shall be adjusted to that of an alien lawfully admitted to the United States for permanent residence as of the following dates:

(1) *Group 1:* Aliens determined to be eligible for Group 1 classification, whose adjustment to temporary residence occurred prior to November 30, 1988, s[...] perma-nent [...]1, 1989. Those [...]o tem-porar[...] Novem-ber 30 [...] lawful permane[...] [...]om the date of the adjustment to temporary residence.

(2) *Group 2.* Aliens determined to be eligible for Group 2 classification whose adjustment to temporary resi-

the date of the adjustment to temporary residence.

(b) *ADIT processing*—(1) *General.* To obtain proof of permanent resident status an alien described in paragraph (a) of this section must appear at a legalization or Service office designated for this purpose for preparation of Form I–551, Permanent Resident Card. Such appearance may be prior to the date of adjustment, but only upon invitation by the Service. Form I–551 shall be issued subsequent to the date of adjustment.

(2) Upon appearance at a Service office for preparation of Form I–551, an alien must present proof of identity, suitable ADIT photographs, and a fingerprint and signature must be obtained from the alien on Form I–89.

[53 FR 10064, Mar. 29, 1988, as amended at 54 FR 50339, Dec. 6, 1989; 63 FR 70315, Dec. 21, 1998]

PART 211—DOCUMENTARY REQUIREMENTS: IMMIGRANTS; WAIVERS

Sec.
211.1 Visas.
211.2 Passports.
211.3 Expiration of immigrant visa or other travel document.
211.4 Waiver of documents for returning residents.
211.5 Alien commuters.

AUTHORITY: 8 U.S.C. 1101, 1103, 1181, 1182, 1203, 1225, 1257; 8 CFR part 2.

SOURCE: 62 FR 10346, Mar. 6, 1997, unless otherwise noted.

§211.1 Visas.

(a) *General.* Except as provided in paragraph (b)(1) of this section, each arriving alien applying for admission (or boarding the vessel or aircraft on which he or she arrives) into the United States for lawful permanent residence, or as a lawful permanent resident returning to an unrelinquished lawful permanent residence in the United States, shall present one of the

Callout boxes:

The relevant "Part" follows the Title, Chapter, and Sub-chapters.

All of the "Sections" included within a particular "Part" will be listed.

Here, the relevant "Section" that includes the text of the actual primary law.

Here, the statutory authority of the particular regulation and its original citation found in the Federal Register.

Source: Code of Federal Regulations (CFR), CFR – Volume 8; Section 211, Page 187.

Please note that just because there was no amendment found in the LSA, keep checking the LSA each month, and check the *Federal Register* online to make certain no new rules are being proposed for that particular regulation. This would be information your attorney needs to know.

The LSA is also available online at **The Office of the Federal Register** at **www.ofr.gov**. You can access *List of CFR Sections Affected* directly from the home page, which will take you directly to monthly lists from 1997 to the present on the GPO website. Also, remember that you can also access the **Electronic Code of Federal Regulations (e-CFR),** which updates all federal regulations online *daily*.

Conduct the same search yourself (the document requirements for passports and visas for immigrants and non-immigrants) in the library to become accustomed on how to search for a regulation in print using the index. You will also have practice at the end of the chapter to test your research skills navigating the CFR.

Figure 8-9 LSA Search for 8 CFR 211

	DECEMBER 2014			29

CHANGES JANUARY 2, 2014 THROUGH DECEMBER 31, 2014

Part	Changes	Part	Changes
948	60117	1942	6740, 18482, 56020
959	14440, 64335	1944	6740, 18482, 56020
980	60117	1948	6740, 18482, 56020
983	15050	1951	6740, 18482, 31884
984	14440	1955	6740, 18482
985	14441, 710	1962	6740, 18482
987	19028	1970	6740, 18482
1005	12963, 12985, 25032, 26638	1980	6740, 18482, 56020
1006	12963	3201	63841
1007	12963, 12985, 25032, 26638	3202	63846
1150	75006	3550	6740, 18482, 28851
1160	75006	3560	6740, 18482, 47383
1205	36241, 75006	3565	6740, 18482
1206	35296, 75006	3570	6740, 18482
1207	75006	3575	6740, 18482
1208	67103, 75006	4274	6740, 18482, 31884
1209	75006	4279	6740, 18482, 55316
1210	75006	4280	6740, 18482
1211	2805	4284	6740, 18482
1212	68636, 75006	4287	55316
1214	75006	4290	6740, 18482
1215	75006		
1216	3139, 75006		
1217	27212, 75006		
1218	75006		
1219	75006		
1220	75006		
1221	75006		
1222	75006		
1230	75006		
1250	75006		
1260	16236, 75006		
1280	75006		
1436	52239		
1703	6740, 18482		
1709	6740, 18482		
1710	6740, 18482		
1717	6740, 18482		

TITLE 8—ALIENS AND NATIONALITY

Chapter I—Department of Homeland Security (Immigration and Naturalization) (Parts 1—599)

100.4 (a) amended 42451
103 Authority citation revised 27174
103.2 (b)(19) revised; eff. 1-27-15
.... 64306
103.7 (b)(1)(ii)(N) added; interim
.... 27174
214 Policy statement 58241
217.2 (a) amended 17854

> Any changes to regulation 8 CFR 211 would have fallen here between parts 103 and 214.

Source: http://www.gpo.gov/fdsys/

The CFR Online

The quickest and easiest way to look up the CFR online is through the Government Printing Office at **www.gpo.gov/fdsys**. *The Code of Federal Regulations* (Annual Edition) can be accessed directly from a link from the home page. You can research any year of the CFR from 1996 to the present. The code is divided into the 50 titles and the range of parts is included. A square box preceding each title is also color coded by year the same as the covers of the print set. As you can see in Figure 8-10, once you find the title you need, you can continue to break the title down into chapters, subchapters, parts and sections. Every entry can be viewed in PDF format.

The GPO website not only includes the actual CFR code, but also the *Parallel Table of Authorities and Rules for the Code of Federal Regulations*, and the *List of CFR Sections Affected (LSA)*, which can be accessed from the same page as the CFR under **Related Sources**. Remember that the LSA is an important validating device to ensure your regulation is current, especially the monthly LSA update found in the *Federal Register* in print and online.

The GPO also maintains a daily up-to-date service called the **Electronic Code of Federal Regulations (e-CFR)** at **www.ecfr.gov**, which is, as of the date of this publication, still in "public beta mode," meaning it has yet to be categorized

Figure 8-10 The CFR at GPO Online

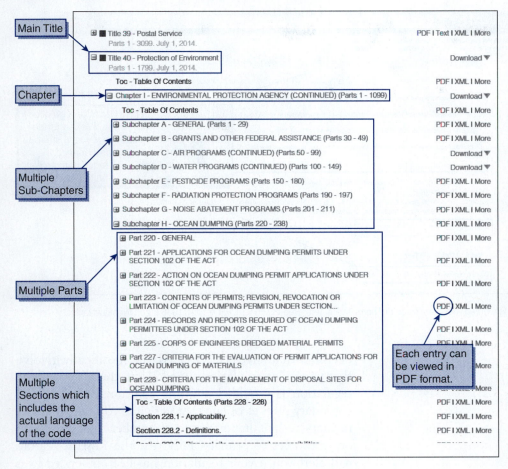

Source: http://www.gpo.gov/fdsys/

as an official government website. Individuals can use the site and try it out, but they also can expect some bugs to be worked out. However, as the e-CFR continues to improve, there is no reason why you cannot use it to search and navigate the site for what you need. Just be certain *to double check your results against the official CFR (you will already have the title and part number) and the LSA for any changes or updates to the regulation.*

Although you can retrieve the official CFR code online for *free*, you can also obtain the same information from other online subscription services.

WESTLAWNEXT: the CFR can be accessed either by citation in the main search box, or by clicking on *Regulations* under the **All Content** tab under the **Browse** section on the home page. You then have the option of choosing the *Code of Federal Regulations*. If you know what title your search falls under, you can click on the title then essentially keep breaking the main title down into *chapters, parts,* and *sections,* until you find what you need. If you do not know the title that you need, you can search the *CFR Index* also located on that page, which provides hundreds of key terms and words to choose from to conduct your search. As you can see in Figure 8-11, every regulation provides the "currency" of the rule, as well as any case

Figure 8-11 The CFR on *WestlawNext*

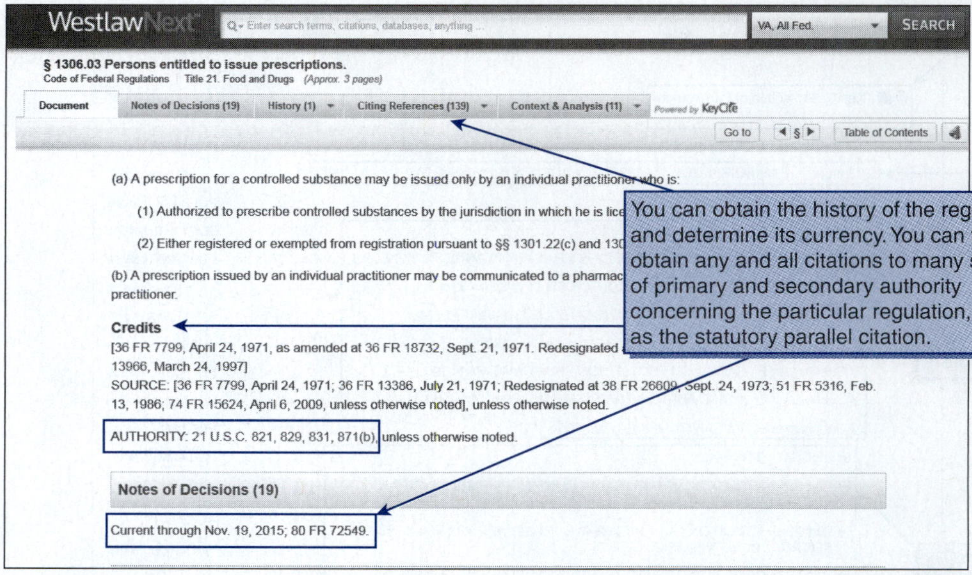

Source: Reprinted with permission of Thomson Reuters, Regulation 21 CFR section 1306.03 on WestlawNext.

decisions that have been decided that specifically involve that particular regulation. In addition, the history of the regulation is provided and any additional primary and secondary sources of law that are cited to that particular regulation. It is important to remember, that similar to other sources of primary authority, the *KeyCite* feature will alert you if your regulation has been amended by a recent rule or repealed or superseded (red flag), or that a proposed rule affecting the regulation is available, or that the regulation has been reinstated, corrected or confirmed (yellow flag).

LEXIS ADVANCE: You can easily access the CFR by typing: CODE OF FEDERAL REGULATIONS into the main search box on the home screen. A drop-down option will not only suggest the CFR, but it also will ask if want to use it as a filter. Go back to the main search box and enter any words/terms/phrase to search the CFR. On the search results page, you can narrow and specify your search with the use of the multiple filters available to you. As you can see in Figure 8-12 when you find the regulation you need, the "currency" of the document will be provided as well as the history of the regulation and any and all references to numerous sources of primary and secondary authority, especially case decisions that explain and interpret the regulation. In addition, you can *Shepardize* the document at the top of the page to make certain it is still valid law.

The Legal Information Institute (Cornell) also maintains the CFR online including all 50 titles and includes a *Table of Popular Names*, a *Parallel Table of Authorities*, and a direct link to the e-CFR website. Cornell does state, as with all its sources of law, that the information provided is not guaranteed to be accurate or up-to-date,

Figure 8-12 The CFR on *Lexis Advance*

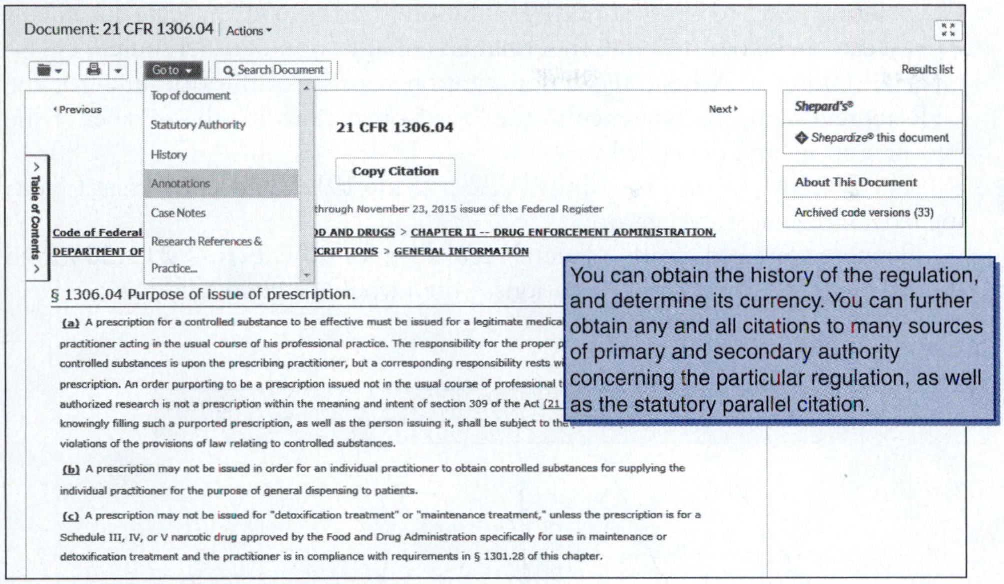

Source: Reprinted with the permission of LexisNexis.

even though the database is refreshed weekly. There are other online preferences as stated above, but just know that the LII is also a source. If you do use the LII, always be certain to back it up by checking the information against the official code.

Lastly, other similar online sites also maintain the CFR, such as **www.LoisLaw .com**, **www.VersusLaw.net**, and **www.TheLawNet.net**. If you do search the CFR from any online commercial source, the view format will not be as it appears in the official CFR in print or online, as any commercial online source is not considered an official government website.

Researching Older Regulations

Suppose your supervising attorney is working on a case involving a client who was severely burned by an electric space heater in his home. An expert involved in the case states that the manufacturer violated multiple consumer product liability regulations during the manufacturing of the heater. Your supervising attorney needs to see the regulations that were in place when the unit was made back in 2003 to determine if ABC Company did in fact commit any violations. Therefore, you would need to research the particular product liability regulation not in effect *today*, but the regulation as it appeared in 2003. As you now know, you can access prior versions of the code back to 1996 on the GPO website. Just keep in mind that any litigation involving a regulation requires the regulation that was in place **at the time of the cause of action**; not the present regulation, as they frequently change or are repealed over time.

PRACTICE TIP

In addition to the official government websites mentioned, the federal government also maintains a website at **www.regulations.gov**. The purpose of the website is to encourage citizens to make their voice heard by submitting comments on proposed regulations and related documents, which are important to help improve the regulations passed daily that affect everyday citizens. The site informs you about the closing period and when to submit comments, as well as a "What's Trending" section based on the high number of comments regarding a particular regulation. Let your voice be heard!

How to Cite a Federal Regulatory Law

A regulation needs to be identified by a citation when used in any legal document. As you can see below, the citation format is similar to that of other sources of law, especially statutes. A basic regulation citation consists of the title number, the CFR abbreviation, the reference to the "part" or section "§", the number of the part or section, and the coded year.

LEARNING OBJECTIVE 4
Explain how to cite and validate a regulation.

The *Bluebook* (Rule 14) and the *ALWD* (Rule 19) dictate the format for citing federal regulatory material.

Suppose you need to cite a federal regulation for **40 C.F.R. § 211.204** from the official Code of Federal Regulations, which would be cited as follows:

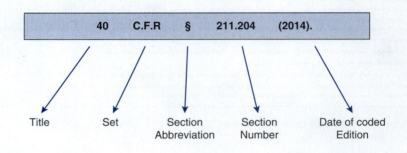

The basic federal regulation citation is composed of three main parts—the title number, the set from which the citation was obtained, and the specific section/part. The first number 40 identifies **Title 40** taken from the 50 titles of the code. The citation was taken from the official code as denoted by the **C.F.R.** The number **211.204** defines the actual location of the section that is found under Subpart B (Hearing Protective Devices) within the code. Keep in mind that if you are citing a range of section numbers, use the double (§§) symbol. The **date** closes the citation. Always cite to the most recent version of the CFR. Please note that you will not leave gaps between the elements in any citation. This is done merely for demonstrative purposes.

Suppose you wanted to cite a specific *part* under the title (Part 211- Product Noise Labeling), rather than the specific *section* under that title, you would use the following:

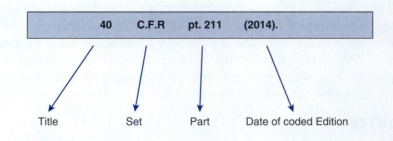

You would not typically cite to a **Chapter** or **Subchapter** under a title of the CFR, as the information is too general and abundant and can include numerous Parts and Sections. When citing a regulation you usually cite the particular **Part** or **Section**.

If a **final** regulation has not yet been published in the CFR, cite to the Federal Register, which would be as follows in *Bluebook* format:

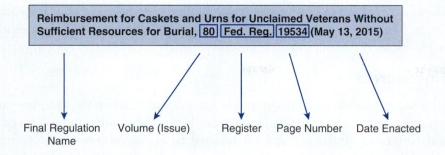

Reimbursement for Caskets and Urns for Unclaimed Veterans Without Sufficient Resources for Burial, 80 Fed. Reg. 19534 (May 13, 2015)

Final Regulation Name | Volume (Issue) | Register | Page Number | Date Enacted

In addition, the *Federal Register* will likely provide the rule's future location in the official CFR as well. In that instance, include the following:

> **Reimbursement for Caskets and Urns for Unclaimed Veterans Without Sufficient Resources for Burial, 80 Fed. Reg. 19534 (May 13, 2015) (to be codified at 38 C.F.R. pt. 38)**

If you need to cite a **proposed** rule, use the same citation as above with the addition of the following:

> **Reimbursement for Caskets and Urns for Unclaimed Veterans Without Sufficient Resources for Burial, 80 Fed. Reg. 19534 (proposed July 2, 2014) (to be codified at 38 C.F.R. pt. 38)**

However, the *ALWD* format for the same citation (**80 Fed. Reg. 19534**) would be as follows:

> **80 Fed. Reg. 19534 (May 13, 2015)**

Use the citation examples as a guide for citing federal regulatory material. If you have any questions, please consult the citation guide assigned to you (*Bluebook* or *ALWD*), or ask your instructor for guidance.

■ SEARCHING STATE REGULATIONS

Now that you know and understand why regulations exist under federal law, state regulations are similar in nature to their federal counterparts. Although the federal regulatory agencies are abundant, it is much more likely that you will have to research state and local regulations in practice. For instance, although federal agencies enforce public welfare regulations concerning eligibility for federal assistance programs though social security, each state has also enacted similar regulations to assist those in need through state public welfare agencies. Even though they are different in form, state regulations monitor and enforce areas of society similar to many federal agencies. For example, state agencies regulate the health, safety, and welfare of its citizens and regulate certain professions within the state, such as massage therapists, real estate agents, and chiropractors.

On the state level, these regulations are created by the state legislature, and similar to federal regulatory law, many states have both executive and

LEARNING OBJECTIVE 5
Describe how to locate state regulations in print and online.

independent agencies and possess rulemaking, investigatory, and enforcement powers. Also, where the federal code may also include executive orders issued by the president, state codes include executive orders issued by the state governor.

Print Sources

Many states publish their enacted regulations with their state statutory codes. However, some of the larger and more heavily populated states publish an official regulatory code similar to the CFR referred to as *Administrative Codes*. Similar to the CFR, these codes are typically arranged alphabetically by topic found in an index at the end of a multivolume set. In addition, some states publish a state Register, similar in form and purpose as the *Federal Register*. State registers provide information on newly enacted rules, as well as important comment information on proposed laws and notices for public meetings concerning proposed regulations.

Suppose you had to research the requirements or procedure a child day care manager must follow in releasing a child to the care of an adult who arrives to pick up the child at the end of the day. Conduct a search similar as you would a federal regulation.

STEP 1: Begin with the terms: DAY CARE, RELEASE OF CHILD. As you can see in Figure 8-13, using the index, under the main topic of *Child Care at Day Care Centers*, you found the requirements that a day care center must enforce when releasing any child to an adult under the subtopic of *Release of Children*.

Figure 8-13 The Pennsylvania Code Index

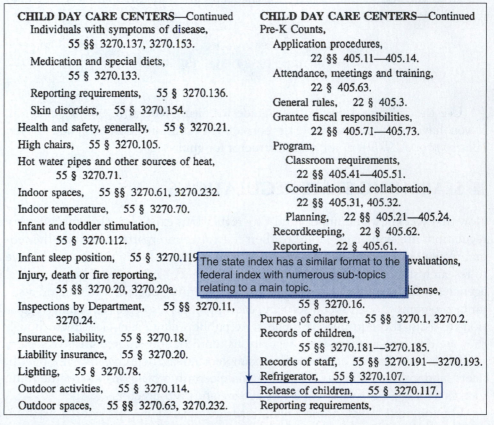

CHILD DAY CARE CENTERS—Continued
Individuals with symptoms of disease,
    55 §§ 3270.137, 3270.153.
Medication and special diets,
    55 § 3270.133.
Reporting requirements, 55 § 3270.136.
Skin disorders, 55 § 3270.154.
Health and safety, generally, 55 § 3270.21.
High chairs, 55 § 3270.105.
Hot water pipes and other sources of heat,
    55 § 3270.71.
Indoor spaces, 55 §§ 3270.61, 3270.232.
Indoor temperature, 55 § 3270.70.
Infant and toddler stimulation,
    55 § 3270.112.
Infant sleep position, 55 § 3270.119.
Injury, death or fire reporting,
    55 §§ 3270.20, 3270.20a.
Inspections by Department, 55 §§ 3270.11,
    3270.24.
Insurance, liability, 55 § 3270.18.
Liability insurance, 55 § 3270.20.
Lighting, 55 § 3270.78.
Outdoor activities, 55 § 3270.114.
Outdoor spaces, 55 §§ 3270.63, 3270.232.

CHILD DAY CARE CENTERS—Continued
Pre-K Counts,
    Application procedures,
        22 §§ 405.11—405.14.
    Attendance, meetings and training,
        22 § 405.63.
    General rules, 22 § 405.3.
    Grantee fiscal responsibilities,
        22 §§ 405.71—405.73.
    Program,
        Classroom requirements,
            22 §§ 405.41—405.51.
        Coordination and collaboration,
            22 §§ 405.31, 405.32.
        Planning, 22 §§ 405.21—405.24.
    Recordkeeping, 22 § 405.62.
    Reporting, 22 § 405.61.
    evaluations,
    license,
    55 § 3270.16.
Purpose of chapter, 55 §§ 3270.1, 3270.2.
Records of children,
    55 §§ 3270.181—3270.185.
Records of staff, 55 §§ 3270.191—3270.193.
Refrigerator, 55 § 3270.107.
Release of children, 55 § 3270.117.
Reporting requirements,

> The state index has a similar format to the federal index with numerous sub-topics relating to a main topic.

Source: The Pennsylvania Code Reporter, Master Index (MI) – "Child Day Care Centers", MI-49. Used with permission.

Figure 8-14 Section 3270.117 of the PA Code

---

55 § 3270.117   CHILDREN, YOUTH AND FAMILIES   Pt. V

§ 3270.117. Release of children.

(a)   A child shall be released only to the child's parent or to an individual designated in writing by the enrolling parent. A child shall be released to either parent unless a court order on file at the facility states otherwise.

(b)   In an emergency, a child may be released to an individual upon the oral designation of the parent, if the identity of the individual can be verified by a staff person.

(c)   If a child is released upon the oral designation of the parent, the following information shall be logged in the child's record:

    (1)   The name of the parent making the request.

    (2)   The date and time of the request.

    (3)   The name of the individual to whom the child is to be released.

    (4)   The name of the staff person taking the call.

    (5)   The name of the staff person releasing the child.

Authority

The provisions of this § 3270.117 amended under Articles IX and X of t [the protocol for the release] (62 P. S. §§ 901—922 and 1001—1087).

> In this example, the particular section explains the protocol for the release of a child to an adult.

Source: The Pennsylvania Code Reporter, Title 55 – Section 3270.117 – Part V, Page 3270–44. Used with permission.

STEP 2:   Now that you have the title and section number you need, go to Title 55 within the set and find the heading of *Children, Youth, and Families*. In particular, as you can see in Figure 8-14, you find the section concerning the specific subtopic of *Release of children*. There, the regulation states explicitly the protocol a day care manger must follow concerning the release of children to an adult who arrives to pick the child up at the facility.

State regulations are broken down and arranged similarly to federal regulations. If you remember in the beginning of this chapter, a federal regulation is broken down into *titles, chapters, subchapters, parts, sections, and paragraphs.* Many of the state regulations typically follow similar format, with some variation, including *division* and *articles,* as you can see in the box below.

Possible State Regulation Organization:

Title » Chapter » Sub-chapter » Part » Section

Or,

Title » Chapter » Sub-chapter » Article » Section

Or,

Title » Division » Chapter » Article » Section

Figure 8-15 The Pennsylvania Code of Regulations Online

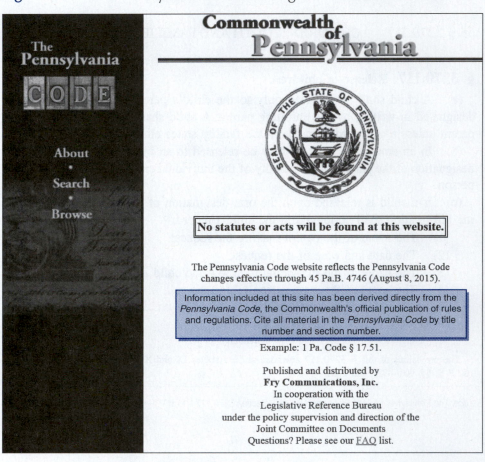

Source: http://www.pacode.com/-. Used with permission.

Online Sources

In print, state regulatory codes are difficult to navigate because they are not usually updated as frequently as they should be in the law library. If your state does publish a set, then there is a good chance that the code is available online, where it can be updated with more frequency. As you learned in previous chapters, just conduct a Google search for: YOUR STATE NAME, CODE OF REGULATIONS.

Some states publish an online regulatory **code** and state **register** as well. However, if your state does publish your code online, make certain it is an official version—it will state that information on the home page of the code, as you can see in Figure 8-15. In addition, similar to federal agencies, many state agencies maintain their own website for individual departments and agencies. For example, the Department of Human Services enforces, among other things, the protection of children residing within the state.

As a follow up, your instructor will inform you as to how the regulations are published in your state and where they can be found in print or online.

Subscription services such as *Lexis Advance* and *WestlawNext* publish and update state regulatory codes as well. You can always search the state materials for free to obtain the citation you need. Just enter the citation into the *Lexis Advance* and *WestlawNext* systems to validate the regulation and use its annotated material, which would save you a great deal of research time. For example, suppose you conducted the same search online as you did in print for what protocol a day care manager must follow when releasing a child to an adult at the day care facility. Refer back to the initial search in Figure 8-13. If you found what you needed in the print material, then you could take the citation (55 § 3270.117) and insert it into either *WestlawNext* or *Lexis Advance* and retrieve the regulation quickly. Suppose that you did not access the print material and you needed to conduct an actual search on either system. Please follow the steps below.

WESTLAWNEXT: You can search state regulations by either citation in the main search box, or you can search by clicking on *State Materials* under the **Browse** section on the home page. Thereafter, you can choose your state, which will take you to the home page for all the legal resources available for that state. Choose your state's code and any title of the regulatory code. In addition, you can view any proposed or adopted regulations, as well as track the status of a current regulation under **Tools & Resources**. You also have the option of using the main search box to enter terms and search a particular title. In this example, once you are on the Pennsylvania page, by entering the terms: PUBLIC WELFARE, RELEASE OF CHILDREN, DAYCARE, you found the regulation as you can see in Figure 8-16. The text of the regulation is the same as that within the print version, with the added benefit of ensuring the regulation is current, as well as the option of viewing multiple sources of annotated material, similar to the federal regulations.

Figure 8-16 State Regulation Law on *WestlawNext*

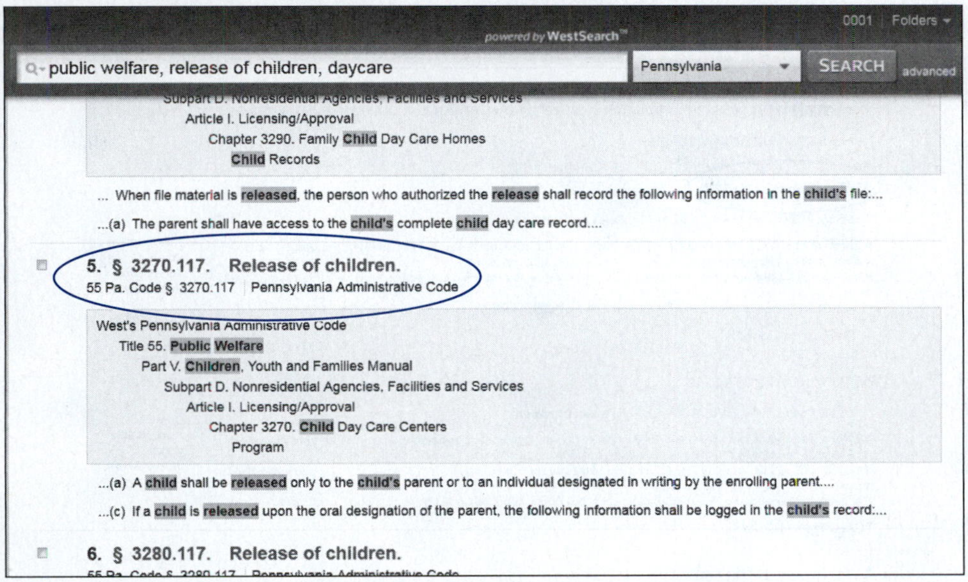

Source: Reprinted with permission of Thomson Reuters, Search results of the CFR on WestlawNext.

LEXIS ADVANCE: You can access any state regulations by choosing **Category** from the **Browse** tab at the top of the page, or use a citation in the main search box. By choosing **Category,** options will appear to access *administrative codes*, *administrative material*, *regulation text*, *regulation tracking*, or *legislative histories*. If you choose *administrative codes*, you can choose your state from the alphabet bar at the top of the page. Once you have established your state as a filter, enter the specific terms in the main search box to retrieve what you need, or choose the main index and conduct your search. Again, in this example, once you are on the Pennsylvania page, by entering the terms: PUBLIC WELFARE, RELEASE OF CHILDREN, DAYCARE, you found the regulation as you can see in Figure 8-17. The text of the regulation is the same as it is in the print version, with the added benefit of ensuring the regulation is current, as well as the option of viewing multiple sources of annotated material, similar to the federal regulations.

As you can see, in using either *WestlawNext* or *Lexis Advance*, your search terms will always be highlighted, which helps you to see how "on point" your searches are on the search results page. If you are conducting a word search without a citation, always be sure to utilize the filters available on both systems so that you can effectively and quickly find what you need.

Agencies/departments are also created on local/municipal levels, which include counties, districts, boroughs, and townships. An example of such a regulation is

Figure 8-17 State Regulation Law on *Lexis Advance*

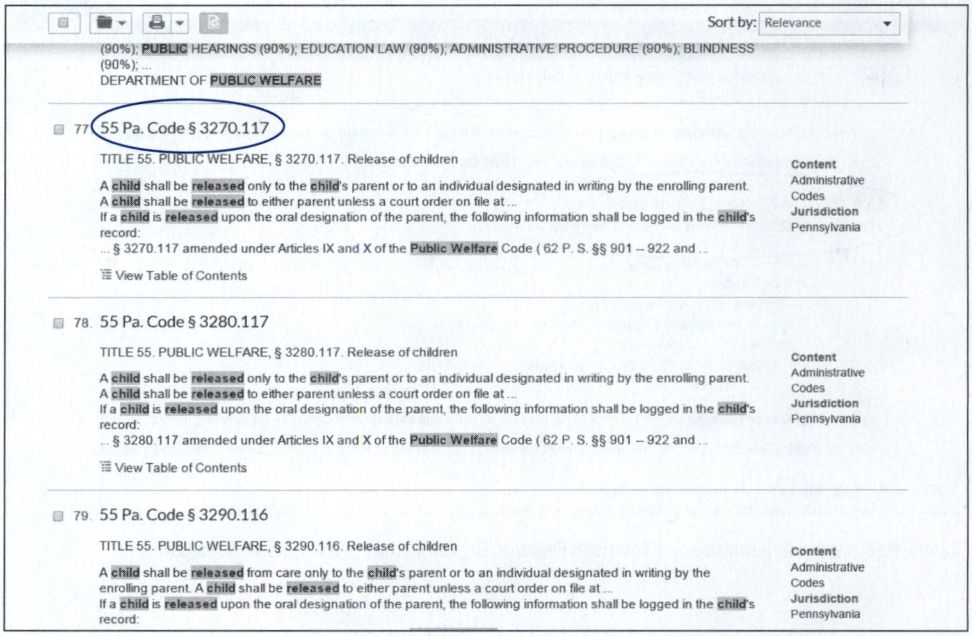

Sort by: Relevance

(90%); PUBLIC HEARINGS (90%); EDUCATION LAW (90%); ADMINISTRATIVE PROCEDURE (90%); BLINDNESS (90%); ...
DEPARTMENT OF PUBLIC WELFARE

77. 55 Pa. Code § 3270.117

TITLE 55. PUBLIC WELFARE, § 3270.117. Release of children

A child shall be released only to the child's parent or to an individual designated in writing by the enrolling parent. A child shall be released to either parent unless a court order on file at ...
If a child is released upon the oral designation of the parent, the following information shall be logged in the child's record:
... § 3270.117 amended under Articles IX and X of the Public Welfare Code (62 P. S. §§ 901 -- 922 and ...

View Table of Contents

Content: Administrative Codes
Jurisdiction: Pennsylvania

78. 55 Pa. Code § 3280.117

TITLE 55. PUBLIC WELFARE, § 3280.117. Release of children

A child shall be released only to the child's parent or to an individual designated in writing by the enrolling parent. A child shall be released to either parent unless a court order on file at ...
If a child is released upon the oral designation of the parent, the following information shall be logged in the child's record:
... § 3280.117 amended under Articles IX and X of the Public Welfare Code (62 P. S. §§ 901 -- 922 and ...

View Table of Contents

Content: Administrative Codes
Jurisdiction: Pennsylvania

79. 55 Pa. Code § 3290.116

TITLE 55. PUBLIC WELFARE, § 3290.116. Release of children

A child shall be released from care only to the child's parent or to an individual designated in writing by the enrolling parent. A child shall be released to either parent unless a court order on file at ...
If a child is released upon the oral designation of the parent, the following information shall be logged in the child's record:

Content: Administrative Codes
Jurisdiction: Pennsylvania

Source: Reprinted with the permission of LexisNexis.

zoning, which regulates how a residential, commercial, or industrial property can be built or used in a certain neighborhood. Other areas of regulation may include requirements for building permits and flood management. You may not have thought about it, but strict regulations are even in place for the builders and operators of carnivals and state fairs who pass through towns all across the country every summer.

Regulatory law, whether it is enacted on a federal, state, or local level, affects citizens across the country every day. This is why it is an important area of primary law that you should understand and know how to research in print and online so that you are prepared if you need to research this area of law for your supervising attorney.

Chapter Checklist ✔

- Regulations affect citizens every day as they are created, monitored, and enforced to protect our health, safety, and welfare, whether they are enacted on a federal, state, or even local level.

- On the federal level, Congress created executive agencies (subject to the authority of the president or the governor), and independent agencies (which affect citizens more directly), to regulate areas such as education, public welfare, transportation, and the environment.

- Federal and state agencies create their own rules and regulations and have been granted enforcement powers and adjudication powers.

- The *Federal Register* is a journal-type publication for all agency activity concerning any and all newly enacted rules, proposed rules, and notes, as well as summary and commentary content concerning regulatory activity. Therefore, the *Register* does not include the actual content of the regulation itself.

- The *Federal Register* is available in print and online for free by accessing the official GPO government website. You can conduct searches in either print or online though the use of an index.

- Remember that you can sign up though the PENS service for updates on newly enacted regulations and keep up-to-date on proposed regulations.

- All newly enacted regulations are codified into the CFR, which is available in print and online for free at the same official GPO website. The CFR is divided into 50 titles and includes more than 200 color-coded and by-year volumes printed in soft back pamphlets.

- The CFR also includes important finding aids, as well as the Parallel Table of Authorities and Rules, which is helpful if you have the citation for the statute that corresponds with the regulation you need.

- Keep in mind that the e-CFR website provides great search options for the code and is updated daily, but it remains in beta mode and is not yet considered an official government website. However, because it is so easy to use—use it—just make certain to double check the research against the official code in print or the GPO website.

- The CFR is also available on other subscription websites such as *Lexis Advance* and *WestlawNext,* among others. When retrieving any primary authority from a non-official government website, ensure that it is correct and current.

- In order to update and validate any information you obtain from either the *Federal Register* or the *CFR*, be sure to check the daily and monthly LSA for any parts recently affected.

- Although states also publish their own regulations with their statutory code or alone as an "Administrative Code," remember that districts, towns, cities, and boroughs also enact their own regulations, particularly in the area of zoning.

KEY TERMS

Administrative agency   245

Regulations   245

Enabling acts   246

Executive agencies   246

Independent agencies   247

Rulemaking   248

Enforcement power   248

Adjudication power   248

Administrative law judge
 (ALJ)   248

Federal Register   249

Code of Federal Regulations
 (CFR)   254

CRITICAL THINKING AND APPLICATION

1. Search the online version of the *Federal Register*. Choose one of the new rules recently enacted in that particular issue. View the information in PDF format, and answer the questions below:

   a. On what page of the *Federal Register* does the newly enacted rule appear?

   b. What is the agency that the new regulation was enacted under?

   c. Where in the *CFR* will the new law be included? (volume and section/part)

   d. What is the full name of the new regulation?

   e. When was the new regulation effective?

   f. Explain to your class, in your own words, what the new rule regulates and why it was enacted.

2. Your supervising attorney is representing a plaintiff in a product safety case where a minor was injured using sporting equipment. It must be determined if the child, who is 12 years old, was using sporting equipment designed for adult use at the time of injury. Search the *CFR* concerning "consumer product safety." In particular, you are looking for how a "child's product" is defined in the federal code.

   a. At what age does the *CFR* determine whether a consumer product is a "child's product," or a "general use product?"

   b. What are the four (4) factors to determine whether a product is primarily intended for children?

   c. How does the *CFR* specifically determine whether "sporting goods and recreational equipment" are designed for children's use or for adult use? Explain.

3. Your supervising attorney is representing a client whose home sustained serious fire damage after the client installed and operated a new wood stove in the home. The stove was positioned on a brick floor protector; however, the client placed the stove flush against a wood-paneled wall. After extensive damage, the client discovered a WARNING label, which was beginning to peel, glued to the back of the stove toward the bottom of the unit. The label warned that the stove must be placed at least 6-8 inches (local building and fire code regulations) from any wall as a fire safety precaution.

   a. Search the topic of "consumer product safety" in the *CFR* in print or online. Remember that each regulation is broken down into titles, chapters, subchapters, parts, and sections. Find the section of the code that regulates the issue of coal and wood burning stoves and appliances. Explain your search trail, detailing how you arrived at the particular section that addresses this issue.

   b. According to the applicable *CFR* section, what are the specific requirements of a manufacturer of such coal and wood burning stoves to inform prospective buyers of the dangers of not properly operating a stove that would apply in this case?

   c. Was the manufacturer at fault in this case? Why or why not?

4. Every state has laws and regulations enforcing pharmacy standards and requirements. Locate the regulations enacted in your state and search for the pharmacist licensing requirements in your state. What are they?

5. Locate the regulations enacted in your state and search for the rules that regulate how day care facilities are operated. Specifically:

   a. What are the required qualifications for the individuals who are employed in those day care facilities?

   b. Do the regulations state anything concerning the nutrition requirements for the children who attend a day care facility?

   c. Do the regulations state anything concerning liability insurance that the owner must have and maintain in order to operate a day care facility?

   d. Do the regulations state anything concerning reporting requirements as to a child who sustains an injury or sickness while at the day care facility?

LEARNING OBJECTIVES

After completion of this chapter, you should be able to

1. Describe where to find the state and federal rules of court and evidence in your jurisdiction.

2. Understand how to properly cite and validate the rules of court and evidence.

3. Explain how to locate, validate, and cite the professional rules of conduct.

4. Explain what a docket is and how to conduct a search for one in your jurisdiction.

5. Explain the importance of non-legal sources of information and where to find these sources in print and online.

CHAPTER 9

Court Rules, Docket Searches, and Non-Legal Sources

> As a paralegal, there will be numerous times when you will be called upon to research "non-legal" sources of information vital to your attorney's case. In addition, a paralegal must be well educated in where to find the rules of court and evidence. These rules drive the litigation process. Also, although you may learn what the rules of professional responsibility are in another course, here you will see where to find those rules.

■ RESEARCHING RULES OF COURT AND EVIDENCE

In sports, players must know the rules. If not, they will commit enough penalties to lose the game. Rules also govern the legal profession. Without the rules of court, your supervising attorney could lose the case. Without knowing the rules, you would not know how many days a defendant can file an answer to the plaintiff's complaint, or the acceptable length of an appellate brief. Similarly, the rules of evidence dictate what type of questions your supervising attorney can ask an expert witness, or if a diagnosis in a medical report is considered hearsay. You should not worry about knowing every civil and criminal rule of law—the attorney will handle that. However, there may be some instances where you may need to look up a rule for the attorney prior to, during, or after trial. Either way, you have to know *where* you can find the rules.

At the trial and appellate level, the state and federal courts are governed by the "rules of court and evidence" in order to keep the courts running smoothly and efficiently. These rules are considered *primary* sources of law because they can be cited in legal arguments.

LEARNING OBJECTIVE 1
Describe where to find the state and federal rules of court and evidence in your jurisdiction.

The State Rules

Each state has compiled a book that includes all the **state rules of practice**. These include the rules of court and evidence pertaining to the trial and appellate courts of that state.

In print, the office you work in will undoubtedly have a copy of these rules. These softbound books contain all the rules in a very easy and straightforward format, usually with an index on the back cover. These books can also be found at your local court house as well as your local law library. The books are published annually and are printed each year in a different color to differentiate a new edition.

state rules of practice
The rules of court and of evidence that all state trial and appellate courts must follow in practice.

273

Online, as you now know, you can find any state information by conducting a simple Internet search. Just insert: STATE NAME, RULES OF COURT AND EVIDENCE into the search bar of any search engine. The results will yield the information you need. Just follow the online directions and hyperlinks to navigate the website. The rules of practice for each state can also be accessed online at **www.ncsc.org**.

Every state has posted their rules of court and evidence online, and the example in Figure 9-1 is one example. Conduct a search of your own state's online rules of court and evidence and be sure to bookmark it on your computer/laptop/tablet for easy access. Lastly, you can also access the state rules for every state through direct links on Cornell's Legal Information Institute (LII) website.

It is also good to inquire as to the "local rules" implemented by the courts within your jurisdiction (city or county) as to the procedures for filing court documents and such. Many judges may implement their own rules concerning their own court procedures. For instance, some judges may only conduct oral arguments instead of accepting written briefs, or they may require the brief to only be a certain number of pages in length. Once you access your state and local rules of court in print or online, you can easily find any court information.

The Federal Rules

The **Federal Rules of Civil Procedure** govern the conduct of all *civil* litigation at the trial level in the US District Courts. The federal rules are found in both annotated versions of the federal code. Similarly, all matters of *criminal* law are governed solely by the **Federal Rules of Criminal Procedure**.

At the appellate level, the federal appellate courts are governed by the **Federal Rules of Appellate Procedure**. All the rules of civil appellate procedure are included, as well as all appellate rules applicable to *each* circuit court.

---

federal rules of civil procedure
The rules that govern civil procedure for federal civil lawsuits in the United States district courts.

federal rules of criminal procedure
The federal procedural rules that govern how prosecutions are conducted in the United States district courts and the general courts of the federal government.

federal rules of appellate procedure
The rules that govern all appellate procedures in cases in the United States Court of Appeals.

federal rules of evidence
The rules, shared between the federal civil and criminal courts, that govern the admission of evidence at trial.

Figure 9-1 Florida Rules of Court Online

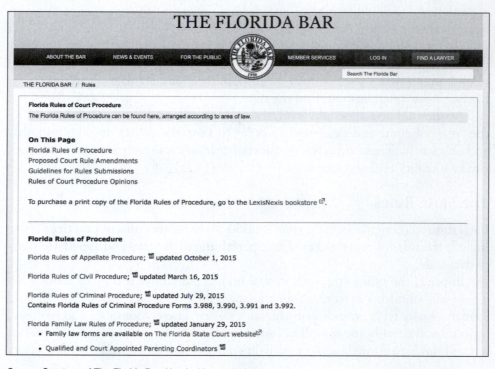

Source: Courtesy of The Florida Bar. Used with permission.

Figure 9-2 The Federal Rules

Federal Rules of Civil Procedure	These "general" rules govern how all civil cases are conducted concerning issues before trial through the end of trial.
Federal Rules of Criminal Procedure	These rules govern how a defendant is arrested, charged, tried, and sentenced.
Federal Rules of Appellate Procedure	These rules govern the proper form and procedure for filing a federal appeal.
Federal Rules of Evidence	These rules govern the evidence that is admissible during civil and criminal trials.
Federal Local Rules of Court	The individual courts can also adopt "local" rules to govern the procedures in their jurisdiction, including the length of a brief.

Also at the trial and appellate level, matters of evidence are covered by the **Federal Rules of Evidence**. Please review Figure 9-2 for a complete list of all the federal rules of court.

You can find the federal rules of civil, criminal, and appellate procedure, as well as the rules of evidence, in the official and the annotated versions of the federal statutory code. Similar to the statutes, the annotated versions provide legal authority that explain and interpret the rule.

You can also access the federal rules online at **www.uscourts.gov**. Just click on the link for "overview" in the left-hand column of the page. You will find "quick links" at the bottom right-hand corner, including links to the federal *appellate rules*, *civil rules*, *criminal rules*, and *evidence rules*. Of course, you can also find the rules of court on *WestlawNext* and *Lexis Advance*.

Keep in mind that the federal trial courts can also create rules of court. These rules are minor in comparison to the actual federal rules and can include matters such as the particular form of citation used, according to each particular judge's preference. These rules can also be found on the Legal Information Institute (LII) website at Cornell University, as you can see in Figure 9-3. Finally, the rules applicable only to the US Supreme Court can be found at **www.supremecourtus.gov**.

PRACTICE TIP

West's Federal Practice and Procedure, and *Moore's Federal Practice* (*Lexis*), are both highly regarded in the legal field explaining and interpreting the federal rules of procedure and evidence. Although the books themselves are considered *secondary sources,* both print sets are quite useful in understanding the federal rules. Be sure to ask the law librarian for assistance in locating these books.

Figure 9-3 The Federal Rules of Evidence on the LII

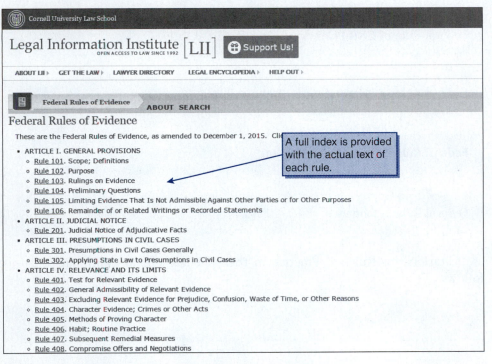

Source: Courtesy of Cornell University Law School. Used with permission.

Citing the Rules

Similar to citing statutes and cases, you must also cite any state and federal rules of law when used in your research. You can cite rules of procedure or evidence in a mix of capital and lower case letters, and no date is necessary.

Proper citation for state rules of evidence and procedure can be found in the state rule book itself for each individual state. In fact, in the beginning of each section, the book shows you how the particular rules are to be cited in your state.

For example, in Pennsylvania, the rules of procedure and evidence would be cited in the following format (all in accordance with *Bluebook* Rule 12.8.3):

PA Rules of Civil Procedure – Pa. R. C. P. 205.5

PA Rules of Criminal Procedure – Pa. R. Crim. P. 134

PA Rules of Appellate Procedure – Pa. R. A. P. 1116

PA Rules of Evidence – Pa. R. E. 104

Each state has a different format. Your local law library as well as the reference desk at your local court house should also have copies of the rules of court and procedure. Remember that once you fill out the appropriate chart in Appendix B with your instructor, you will possess an easy access personal citation guide specific to your jurisdiction.

On the other hand, the federal rules, which are universal and should be applied in any federal court, are listed and organized as follows:

Federal Rule of Civil Procedure - Fed. R. Civ. P. 12(b)

Federal Rule of Criminal Procedure - Fed. R. Crim. P. 36

Federal Rule of Appellate Procedure - Fed. R. App. 10

Federal Rule of Evidence - Fed. R. Evid. 404

Citations for Rules of Practice in the appellate circuit courts are listed as follows:

3rd Cir. R. 3

The *ALWD* citation requires the abbreviation of the rule, the corresponding number, *as well as the publisher and date* (Rule 27.3). For example:

Federal Rule of Civil Procedure - Fed. R. Civ. P. 12(b) (West 2010)

Validating the Rules

As you know, the law continually changes, as do the state and federal rules of practice. The rules found in any print source will be updated with the use of pocket parts, which will be found *within* the statutory code, usually at the beginning of each volume or index. Online, the LII will alert you to changes in the rules and to follow up with a visit to your state's legislative website. *WestlawNext* and *Lexis Advance* also update their databases daily and will always post the most current rules.

LEARNING OBJECTIVE 3
Explain how to locate, validate, and cite the professional rules of conduct.

■ RESEARCHING THE PROFESSIONAL RULES OF CONDUCT

Just like the rules of court and evidence are important to an attorney practicing the law, the professional rules of conduct, or "ethical rules" are equally important. In addition to the ethical canons that paralegals should follow, your supervising attorney is also governed by a strict code of ethics. An instance may arise where you may be asked to research these rules concerning any attorney who may have committed an ethical violation.

Suppose your attorney has just taken on a new client concerning an automobile accident case against a defendant. Your supervising attorney just found out that he previously represented that defendant two years ago in a slip and fall case at a local supermarket, and your supervising attorney is concerned about whether this is a conflict of interests? Or, suppose your attorney (a solo practitioner) received a $10,000 check from an insurance company paid out to a client, but the client is away on vacation for two months. The attorney has a firm bank account, but wants to know if he is permitted to deposit the check in his personal bank account for safekeeping until the client returns. Is the attorney ethically permitted to do so?

When researching legal ethics, there are no "national" or "universal" set of rules. Rather, each state has compiled its *own* ethical code to regulate the conduct of lawyers. These rules of professional responsibility are usually created and regulated by the state's highest appellate court. Although each state compiles its own ethical rules, these rules are all modeled after the American Bar Association's (ABA) **Model Rules of Professional Conduct**. The ABA rules can be located for review at your local library in print—just ask the reference librarian. The print books also are printed in an annotated version, which offer excellent citations to many case opinions that explain and interpret the rules.

Online, the rules can be accessed and viewed at **www.americanbar.org**. The ABA rules are good to view since they provide a good foundation of the general ethical rules of law. In addition, the ABA website has a specific link to each state's attorney and judicial codes, as well as each state's disciplinary board. On the home page, click on *Resources for Lawyers* at the top of the page, then choose the heading *Ethics and Professionalism*. Also found on that ABA website is the option to order an "annotated" version of the Model Rules of Professional

model rules of professional conduct
The set of rules of professional conduct that serves as a model for the ethical rules for most states.

PRACTICE TIP

It is good practice to know that judges have their own set of ethical rules that they must follow, and like the ethical rules for attorneys, each set of judicial canons are unique to each state, although they are similar in content. If you need to review the rules in your state concerning possible judicial misconduct, using your Internet search engine, type in the terms YOUR STATE NAME, JUDICIAL CANONS, which will reveal the search results for the sources of these state judicial canons.

Conduct, which is a good resource that not only includes the rules, but explanations and citations of sources that have applied those rules.

In addition, by conducting a basic Internet search, you can find any state's website listing the rules of professional legal conduct in that state. You can also access the state rules on *WestlawNext* and *Lexis Advance* by adding the term LEGAL ETHICS to your search terms in the main search box on *WestlawNext* or *Lexis Advance*. Researching the ethical rules on *Westlaw* or *Lexis* is good because you have access, within your search, to numerous case opinions that explain and interpret the rules of professional responsibility. The LII at Cornell also posts the ABA rules as well as the ethical rules for each state. As with any free online site, make certain the content is updated. If not, please refer back to the rules in print published in your state, or from an official governmental website.

Ethics Reminder

As a paralegal, always remember to conduct your research with competency, diligence, honesty, and objectivity. However, also remember that if you do become certified and become a member of an official national paralegal organization, you will be expected to abide by the ethical canons of that organization. If you ever see or hear any instance of impropriety in the law firm or office in which you work, always discuss the matter with your supervising attorney.

Validating the Rules

The professional rules of conduct can be supplemented or amended, although it is a rare occurrence. If the rules have been recently subjected to amendment, both *WestlawNext* and *Lexis Advance* regularly update each state's ethical rules. If you do not subscribe to either legal database, you can conduct an Internet search to determine if any recent changes have been made to the code in your state. Remember to only use valid governmental online sources.

Citing the Rules

Like any other primary source of law, each ethical rule (canon) is clearly identified by a unique citation. The rules for the citation of ABA ethical rules in the *Bluebook* can be found in Rule 12.8.5, and in Rule 27.3 found in the *ALWD* citation manual. Some examples of the individual state citation rules include the following:

Maryland Rules of Professional Conduct 1.3.

Texas Disciplinary Rules of Professional Conduct 1.15.

You should not have to conduct any research for the rules of professional responsibility for attorneys with any regularity, but now you know where to look for those rules, and how to cite them, should an issue arise concerning them.

■ DOCKET SEARCHES

In practice, there will be many times when you will have to conduct a docket search. A **docket** is simply a formal record of the proceedings and filings of a particular court case. When a case is filed with the court, it is assigned a "docket number" which is the numeric identifier for that trial level case. If a case decision is appealed, then the case will also be given an appellate docket number as well (refer to Figure 6-7 in Chapter 6 for an example of a case opinion assigned with various docket numbers). Once the trial case is assigned a docket number, the clerk of court will update the docket daily concerning the "procedural history" of a case, which is sometimes referred to as a "docket sheet." A docket will include the particular judge on a case, the parties and attorneys involved, and the details of the case. If you need to track the activity of a case, most docket entries provide information by an *event date* that corresponds to a specific *event description*. For example:

docket
An official yet brief summary of all the proceedings and filings of a court case.

LEARNING OBJECTIVE 4
Explain what a docket is and how to conduct a search for one in your jurisdiction.

CASE NAME:	Williams v. Peterson Trucking Company
DATE:	FILING/HEARING:
Mar-8-2013	Complaint filed by Plaintiff.
Apr-3-2013	Defendant granted extension to file Answer.
Apr-23-2013	Answer filed by Defendant.
Jun-15-2013	Interrogatories to be completed by Plaintiff by Aug-1-2013.

By referring to the docket sheet, you can track every event of the case in question of any past, present, and future filings, hearings, or motions. Court dockets will also include the contact information of all of the attorneys in the case if you should need an address or phone number.

State Dockets

On the state level, almost every county within each state maintains an electronic docket via a state website. Most court dockets are public record and can also be accessed for free or for a small fee at the county clerk's office. State dockets vary by jurisdiction, the actual information recorded, and availability of that information to the public. Most state docket entries available include:

- Civil or criminal trial information;
- Liens and judgments;
- Criminal extracts (background checks);
- Matters involving domestic relations (foreclosures, liens, or injunctions);
- Child custody

However, the following docket information may not be permissible to view concerning the following issues due to privacy reasons:

- Juvenile court decisions;
- Mental health proceedings;
- Adoption and paternity matters;
- Domestic violence matters;
- Psychological evaluations;
- Drug treatment.

To conduct a docket search online, similar to other Internet searches, simply enter the correct search terms in your search engine to locate these websites. For example, to search the civil docket in Arizona, enter the terms ARIZONA

DOCKET SEARCH. If you ever have difficulty locating what you need from a state docket, contact the court clerk's office or a reference librarian at your local state law library. Be sure to check with someone to learn exactly which information is viewable in your jurisdiction.

Federal Dockets

PACER
An electronic public access service that permits users to obtain case and docket information from the federal courts.

On the federal level, case dockets can be obtained through the **Public Access to Court Electronic Records (PACER)** database at **www.pacer.gov**. For a fee, the PACER system allows users to access case and docket information from federal appellate, district, and bankruptcy courts for any information including judgments, liens, foreclosures, and so on. Any user can access PACER by signing up for an online registration account. Similar to the state systems, not all information on the federal dockets are available to the public, such as social security numbers, financial account numbers, certain addresses, and children's names, ages, and addresses.. If you are unable to access any particular information, you can call or e-mail the PACER Service Center at **www.pacer@psc.uscourts.gov**.

Docket Access through Online Subscriptions

You can also conduct a docket search through the subscription legal databases. On *WestlawNext,* you can access any federal docket information (same data as PACER) as well as state court coverage, which varies from state to state. To begin your search, click on *Dockets* in the **All Content** tab on the *WestlawNext* homepage. There, you can click on any state name or federal court. Once selected, be sure to utilize the available filters to narrow your search.

On *Lexis Advance,* dockets can be accessed through a separate product system called **CourtLink**. On the home page, you can enter any keywords with terms and connectors that will reveal any and all state and federal (same data as PACER) docket entries for the keyword/person/company name entered in a single search. Multiple filters will narrow your search. However, *Lexis* is in the process of integrating its docket information into the *Lexis Advance* system as well. On the home page, select *Dockets* from the **All Content** menu. There, you can click on any state name or federal court. Once selected, be sure to utilize the available filters to narrow your search.

You can also access docket entries on *Bloomberg,* which, similar to *WestlawNext/Lexis Advance,* provides access to any federal docket information (same data as PACER) as well as state court coverage, which, as mentioned, varies from state to state. On the home page, just click on *Dockets* from the top menu. If a link appears in blue, then the user can access that information. However, any link in green is unavailable to search/view.

In practice, you will also learn that the term "court docket" is also used to describe a *court calendar*. Simply stated, every court lists, in advance, (sometimes for the entire month) the cases to be heard in that particular trial or appellate court. The clerk of courts then compiles and uploads all those lists on a weekly basis on the court webpage. The calendar usually lists which judges will be in which courtrooms on a particular day, and which cases will be heard in that courtroom by case name or docket number. Attorneys like to know which judges are available within the courthouse, and which judge will be hearing their case.

You will learn the specifics of docket searching and court calendars within your particular jurisdiction in practice. For now, just be familiar with what a docket is and how to begin a basic search for one.

■ RESEARCHING NON-LEGAL SOURCES OF INFORMATION

Non-legal sources have no authoritative weight but may still assist you in your research task. You can *never* use a non-legal source as authority, no matter which jurisdiction. However, along with researching actual sources of law, a paralegal is often called upon to conduct "non-legal" research during preparation of a case. Suppose your supervising attorney asks you to find an expert witness in your state who deals exclusively in traumatic brain injury. In another situation, suppose your supervising attorney is representing a plaintiff who is suing a car manufacturer for a defect, and you are asked to research if that same make and model vehicle had ever been recalled in the past. Sometimes searching for non-legal sources of information is just as important as researching cases and statutes in helping the attorney prepare her case.

Although you will be able to utilize the top Internet search engines for obtaining most general information, there are numerous directories and websites to assist paralegals to secure particular information they need online quickly and efficiently.

non-legal sources
Information that paralegals are called upon to research that concern information about clients, trial opponents, experts, or medical information.

Local Resource Information

Every state/city/county has a local paralegal association from which you can obtain numerous local resource information including, the names, addresses, and phone numbers of the local departments of health and safety, municipal offices, as well as the mayor's office. You should know the name of the organization's director and the brick-and-mortar location of your local chapter as well. These organizations usually hold many informative meetings and seminars about the paralegal profession throughout the year. Also, in the county where you work, the county court will also post important information you may need on its local government website, which will include many local and municipal numbers and addresses. In addition, the firm or office you work in should have a large directory of frequently called numbers and addresses. You can always ask any paralegal or legal secretary in the office for any information you may need.

LEARNING OBJECTIVE 5
Explain the importance of non-legal sources of information and where to find these sources in print and online.

> ### PRACTICE TIP
>
> Rather than keeping numerous names, phone numbers, or addresses on sticky notes forming a multicolor frame around your computer monitor, there is a better way to organize any information you obtain from the Internet—bookmarks! A bookmark allows you to quickly access a previously viewed webpage with a click of the mouse. Any page of interest that you visit allows you to save it as a bookmark with a single right-click. It would be wise to organize your bookmarks into categories such as by client, legal issue, or state or county court offices. There are even bookmark manager programs available to assist you such as the *Yahoo Bookmark Manager, LinkaGoGo, BookMax,* and *iKeepBookmarks*—check them out!

People

If you need to locate a particular person while helping your supervising attorney prepare his case, such as a private investigator, you can search a basic search engine for local investigative agencies. Perhaps your supervising attorney needs to hire a videographer to film a "day in the life" video of a severely injured client to show to a jury. You will have to "shop around" online for someone with great credentials. However, always make sure you find and read any online reviews before securing the services of an outsider. Also, be sure to ask your supervising attorneys first if they have a preference as to who they want to hire or if they have utilized a particular individual in the past.

On the other hand, you may need to locate someone involved in your supervising attorney's case who, for example, was a bystander walking his dog by the scene of your client's accident with first-hand knowledge of how it occurred, but who now cannot be located, or a third party in your client's case who needs to be issued a subpoena for a deposition. Either way, rather than perform a basic Internet "people search," which could cost a lot of time and money, narrow the particular identifiers that make people distinct and unique—someone's full name, age, birth date, drivers' license, or social security number. Check with neighbors or past employers for a last known address, or, if you can, obtain any personal information from a public record document, such as a property or real estate deeds or even a prior criminal or civil case docket record.

If you do utilize a basic "people search," there are many websites to choose from to help locate someone such as, **www.peoplefinders.com**, **www.411.com**, **www.switchboard.com**, and **www.anywho.com**, among numerous others. Some of these sites are free, but most charge a fee for their information and it could take a few days or even weeks to generate a report.

Experts/Consultants

Seeking an expert or consultant to use at trial is an important and expensive decision. Experts are used in cases involving medical malpractice, workers' compensation, personal injury, and cases involving professions, such as engineers, architects, lawyers, or accountants. An expert's opinion can make or break a case. There are numerous websites that can assist you in locating experts or consultants in your state or city. One good way is to search local university websites and read the faculty profiles to see who is qualified as an "expert" in a certain area. This may also be less expensive than someone who makes a living by testifying in court or at depositions. However, if money is not a factor, you can find hundreds of areas of expertise listed from A-Z at **www.experts.com**. That site provides lists of highly qualified experts in those areas from across the country. Also online, **www.findlaw.com** always advertises expert witnesses when researching any authority within your particular jurisdiction. Other helpful websites include **www.expertpages.com** and **www.jurispro.com**. Lastly, it is good practice to establish a working relationship with other paralegals at other firms (especially large firms) to get names and numbers of experts they used at trial so you and your supervising attorney can receive positive or negative feedback before securing an expert. Lastly, as you will see below, *WestlawNext* and *Lexis Advance* also provide numerous experts from which to choose within your jurisdiction.

Attorneys

If your supervising attorney needs to discuss or refer a case to another attorney who is an expert in a particular area of law, or if you need any information about any attorney, such as malpractice complaints or award recognition, the best resource is online at **www.martindale.com**. This site allows you to search the experience, credentials, and overall profile of thousands of attorneys across the country.

Medical Information

Obtaining medical or pharmaceutical information for litigation can prove cumbersome for an entry-level paralegal. If your supervising attorney is representing a victim of medical malpractice for an eye injury, he or she has to become an *expert* of the medical surgical procedure that the defendant's physician performed. The attorney must also know every muscle of the eye in order to represent the plaintiff with success. No worries—you do not need a medical degree to research such information, but you may be called upon to locate medical definitions and descriptions of body parts and surgical procedures in preparation for trial. You may also be called upon to contact local hospitals to quickly secure hospital and medical records, if needed (you will learn how to draft letters and communicate with such third-parties in Chapter 13). If your supervising attorney specializes in personal injury and medical malpractice, he/she may have the hardcover version of the American Medical Association's *Complete Medical Encyclopedia* complete with thousands of medical terms, procedures and up-to-date medical information, which can be purchased online. In addition, the National Institutes of Health Medicine is also available with the same information and can be found at **www.nlm.nih.gov**. Concerning online databases, *WestlawNext* created *Medical Litigator*, which allows you access to numerous amounts of medical information, charts, photos, jury verdicts, and medical expert witness lists. *Lexis Advance* recently developed *MedMal Navigator*, which provides medical litigators with interactive Q and A technology, new tool guides to guide the legal team through the issues and values of a medical malpractice case, and help to formulate a cost-effective trial strategy. Both are accessible with a subscription to either legal database.

WestlawNext and *Lexis Advance* Software

If you have a subscription, *WestlawNext* and *Lexis Advance* both recently developed software to track and monitor all of the above information, including the names, addresses, and resumes of attorneys, judges, and experts in your jurisdiction. The software provides important facts, reviews, biases, behaviors, and case outcomes to assist your supervising attorney to prepare for litigation and improve the outcome of a case.

On *WestlawNext*, under the **Directory** tab are numerous lists and reports of information, including arbitrators, attorneys and judges, and experts, all for review. On *Lexis Advance*, the **Litigation Profile Suite** has similarly compiled volumes of data, including expert witness profiles, attorney profiles, and judge profiles, as well as a large collection of verdict and settlement documents at your disposal. If your subscription does not permit you access to any expert's address and/or phone information, you can always take the name and conduct a general Internet search for office information.

Lastly, there is one more "non-legal" source available for finding changes or updates in the law: *Blogs*. Almost every law office/firm across the country provides up-to-date information on their website or an extended website (a blog) concerning their specific area of practice. If your supervising attorney practices a specific area of law, it would be wise to bookmark that blog for any changes or updates in the law that you may have missed, or to have update e-mails sent directly to you concerning any changes in the law. For example, a law firm that specializes in DUI law might state on its blog, among other things, that the state recently enacted a new "ignition lock law" where certain first-time offenders and all second and subsequent offenders will be required to use an ignition lock device installed by the state. With that information, you could then research the criminal state statutes for the text of the actual law to update your attorney.

It is very important to note that although the attorneys in these firms specialize in the law they summarize on their websites and blogs, there is always, or there should be, a legal disclaimer that the law stated on the website is not to be considered legal advice. As a paralegal, you should also know that THE LAW

PRACTICE TIP

In addition, there are other legal medical resources available at your local law library. For instance, if your local law library carries it, the *Attorney's Textbook of Medicine* (3rd ed.) by Mathew Bender is a good resource for all information relating to medical litigation. Also, for help with actual litigation concerning a medical issue, there are two other trial resources: the *Lane Medical Litigation Guide* (6 volumes) published by *West* and the *Lane Medical Trial Technique Quarterly*. Both of these are great resources for you and your supervising attorney if needed.

SUMMARIZED FROM A BLOG CAN NEVER BE CITED OR USED AS LEGAL AUTHORITY WITHOUT CONDUCTING RESEARCH FROM AN ACTUAL PRIMARY SOURCE OF LAW. The information on those websites is purely informational for the average person, but it can prove helpful to you in keeping up with any changes in the law, which is why this section is included under "non-legal" sources of law.

Although all these rules of practice and non-legal sources of information may seem overwhelming, do not feel that you need to *know* all the rules of law, or how many muscles are in the leg—that is the job of your supervising attorney. Your attorneys will handle the legal arguments, as it is *their* job. However, you should be ready to locate, find, and research anything and everything needed to prepare for a case, as that is *your* job. You do not need to know it all, but you do need to know how and where to find it if needed. You are equipping your supervising attorneys with everything they need to battle in court or in the office at settlement. The better you are at researching legal and non-legal sources of law, the better the attorney will be at performing in the case. Once you become familiar with researching multiple sources, it will become second nature to you, and you will prove to be an invaluable asset to your attorney and to the firm.

Chapter Checklist ✓

- Remember that knowing where to find the rules of court and evidence are just as important as locating the primary sources of law, because the rules *are* primary sources of law.

- The state rules of court and evidence can easily be found in print and online sources complete with easy-to-read and easy-to-follow indexes.

- Keep in mind the "local" rules of court and specific rules of court implemented by certain judges concerning miscellaneous rules such as the procedures during oral motions or the appropriate length of a brief filed with the court.

- The federal rules of court and evidence are also available and easily accessible in print and online.

- During your research, do not forget the Cornell LII online website for any and all state and federal rules.

- Your instructor will review the format for the rules of court and evidence with you in class. The federal citation formats are demonstrated in this chapter.

- Either the print material or the online material will also provide you with any updates on the rules. In addition, most every state website that posts the rules will include or alert you to any amendments.

- It is also important to know where you can locate the rules of professional conduct if your supervising attorney should ever need them. Conduct a basic Internet search to locate the professional ethical code for that particular state. There are also websites included in this chapter at your disposal.

- Remember your own ethical duties as a paralegal. Keep in mind the two golden rules—do ***not*** engage in the practice of law and always be professional, honest, diligent, and competent in your work.

- There is no paralegal code for ethics but if you do become certified in the field or become a member of a paralegal organization, know the organization's ethical code, as you will be expected to abide by it.

- Locating non-legal sources are just as important as researching legal sources of law.

- Create and maintain a good online rolodex of the names and addresses of judges, local attorneys, and other paralegals in other firms for easy and quick access.

- Utilize the information provided in this chapter to look for expert witnesses, consultants, as well as any medical information you may need to assist your supervising attorney in a case.

- Remember that a snapshot search is only to provide you with a quick summary of a specific area of law found on a law firm's website. It can NEVER be used or cited as legal authority, but it can provide you with a quick and easy answer concerning a basic point of law.

KEY TERMS

CRITICAL THINKING AND APPLICATION

1. Knowing the rules of evidence is crucial for your supervising attorney to advocate for a client during trial. Many times, you may be asked to review the rules of evidence prior to, or during trial. Your supervising attorney wants to use a tire expert in an automobile accident case. Look to the "rules of evidence" in *your state* in **print** or **online** and explain what the court must consider in admitting the testimony of an expert witness at trial.

2. Look up the "federal rules of criminal procedure" in **print** or **online** and explain to your supervising attorney the court's procedure of determining whether a criminal confession is voluntary—in other words, what are the five "elements" that the court must take into consideration to determine the voluntariness of a confession?

3. Your supervising attorney is filing her first appellate brief and needs some guidance. Go to the rules of court in *your state* in **print** or **online**. Explain to your attorney the required "form of the brief," and what needs to be included in the brief to be filed with the state appellate court.

4. Concerning the "federal rules of evidence," what *character evidence* can be used during trial? Are there any restrictions? If so, what?

5. Look up the professional rules of conduct of your state **online**. Navigate the site and look through the rules to become comfortable with them. Discuss in class the main topics of ethical concerns.

6. Conduct research on *WestlawNext* or *Lexis Advance* concerning the ethical rules for attorneys. Locate and read a case found in that search concerning the topic of "attorney–client privilege." What is this privilege? How would you explain it someone?

7. Your supervising attorney is upset because she recently found out she may be called as a potential witness in a case she recently obtained concerning the drafting and signing of a will. Your attorney does not know whether she can now represent the client. She has asked you to review the ethical rules in your state. Can the attorney represent the client or is it considered a conflict of interests if she is called as a witness in a case where she represented one of the parties? Are there any exceptions?

8. Conduct an online search and find the local government website that allows you to perform a case docket search for civil trials within your jurisdiction. What are the search options for looking up a case? Navigate the site and become comfortable with it.

9. Conduct an online search for the city clerk in the county in which you live. What is the name of the city clerk and his or her office phone number?

10. On *WestlawNext* or *Lexis Advance*, look up an expert witness who specializes in traumatic brain injury. What did you find out about this expert? Ratings? Cases in which she or he testified? Thereafter, locate the address and phone number for that expert.

11. Using the website *experts.com*, locate an expert in "knee and shoulder surgery." Experts are listed from cities around the country. Choose an expert who is close to your city. What is that expert's name and contact information? Is there a website link for that expert? Can you access a CV (resume) for that expert? Explain.

12. Your supervising attorney is preparing for a medical malpractice case and needs you to perform some "non-legal" research for a case. He is unfamiliar with the drug "Baclofen." Go to the appropriate website to begin your search. What is Baclofen? What is it used in the treatment of?

COMPREHENSIVE CASE STUDY
Part II   Finding the Law

OVERVIEW

In the first installment of the case study, you were introduced to the facts of the case. You and your instructor also developed the issues to be resolved. Now, after learning the primary and secondary legal resources, you can now outline a plan and begin your research.

The Research Plan

Before you begin to research Lena's issues, or issues for any assignment, you need three things:

- The **facts** of the case;
- The **issues** to be resolved;
- The **jurisdiction** of the case

Once you know and understand the facts and issues of the case, you also need to determine the jurisdiction of the case. The jurisdiction will direct you to either the federal, state, or local areas of law, which immediately narrows your research sources. In this case, because Lena is a federal employee, you would most likely begin researching federal law.

Thereafter, take the legal words/terms/phrases from your legal issues to generate the "buzz" words or "key" words/terms/phrases you would use to begin your research. Remember what you learned about the "word search method" in the case law chapters and apply it here. For example, in this case study, what key words, based on your issues, would be appropriate and useful in conducting your search?

You will generate these search words with your instructor in class.

Keep in mind that in practice, as you become more familiar with the law, you can base your word search on actual legal claims or "causes of action," which you can always ask your supervising attorney to provide for you. For example, if you are researching whether a contract was breached when one party made a counteroffer for a used car sale, you would begin your search with the main general area of *contract law* and look for the subtopics of *offer, acceptance, breach, counteroffer*.

Keep in mind that whether your supervising attorney provides you with the pertinent legal terms/words/phrases to guide you in your research, or you generate them your own, it is best to know the definition of each term or phrase prior to beginning the research. For instance, if needed, consult a **legal dictionary** for any term you are unsure of, or to possibly learn a term or phrase before you engage in your research. Remember, legal dictionaries are great secondary sources at your disposal.

Furthermore, a **thesaurus** is also a great help in formulating your search terms. For example, if you were researching employment issues concerning a *teacher*, you can also include the terms *instructor*, *lecturer*, or *professor* to help to narrow your search.

Once you have your key words/terms/phrases, you can determine your research "plan of attack." If you are familiar with the area of law you are researching, or your attorney has provided that information, you may be able to dive right into the primary sources of law. If not, it is always best to educate yourself with the secondary sources of law to become better acquainted with the area of law you are researching.

You can determine, with your instructor, your research plan for the case study.

Now, you can complete the remaining sections of your research worksheet, including your *key terms* and *research plan*. Please complete the sections. You now have a complete one-page worksheet to begin your research.

Research Assignment

Lena Mitchell—client

Facts—client needs time off (3 days a week) from her federal position to care for her sick father—time off could be around 6 months—told by manager she has to use all her sick/vacation time—needs medical documentation—***removed from her position that pays much less and lost her title**. Is there any legal remedy?

Issues

1. _____

2. _____

3. _____

4. _____

5. _____

Key Terms _____

_____

Research Plan _____

_____

Timetable—*In the e-mail you received in the first part of the case study, your attorney told you they would get back to the client "next week." However, make sure in practice that you know the **exact** timeframe for the assignment so you can plan your research accordingly!

The following steps will assist you, not only with this case study, but also in general with any type of research assignment you receive from your supervising attorney. Refer to this flowchart each time you begin your research until you have it memorized.

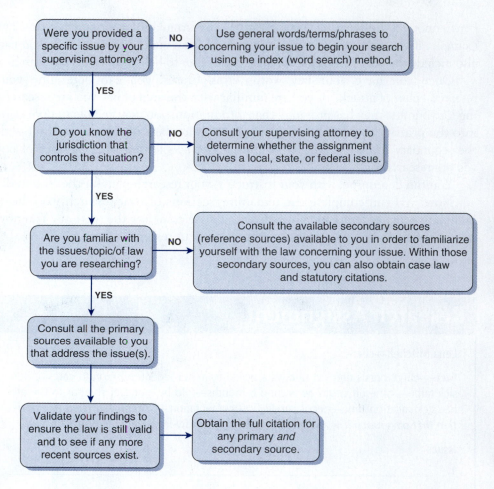

Secondary Sources

Remember that one of the ways these sources are useful is to educate you in a particular area of law. Secondary sources help when you are unsure of where to begin your research of primary law. One of those sources you could consult is the **legal encyclopedia**. Whether state or federal, a legal encyclopedia will "instruct you" on the area or topic of law you seek. Most importantly, if you are unfamiliar with, or have never heard of a particular legal topic, the legal encyclopedia will not only provide a definition, **but also will reference cases and/or statutes with citations for easy access to the law you need**.

1. What are the words/terms/phrases you created to begin your search? In reading the facts of the case, you know that *federal* law should govern these issues. As you know, Lena is a federal employee and is employed as an HR manager in a federal office. Utilize the federal legal encyclopedia using the terms you generated to begin your search. What did you find? Explain your search.

Primary Sources

After consulting the legal encyclopedia to learn about the law, you can then plan which primary sources to reference within your search. Hopefully at this point, you have a good idea of the particular federal statute that will address and answer the issues in this case study. Therefore, you should also be in possession of a statutory citation in order to find that law.

TIP

When you are reading any secondary source, or a particular statute, always note and write down the any case citations for later reference.

Below, begin your actual research in the case study by answering the following questions. Think carefully, and utilize all the knowledge you learned about the primary sources of law.

2. Whether you have secured the citation for the federal statute in question or not, to keep your research skills sharp, search the **index** of the federal statutory code to find what you need. What words/terms/phrases did you use? What did you find?

3. In locating the federal statute, what does it state? Read it *completely* and *carefully*. Does it begin to address your issues? Explain fully. As you have previously learned, go the **Definitions** section to learn the meanings of the terms included within the statute. There are a few definitions that should be of particular interest to you concerning Lena's issues. Read each definition. Does it appear from this information that Lena may be at least eligible to take the leave of absence she requires? Why? Explain your answers fully.

4. What about the other issues you formulated. Does the federal statute address those as well? Explain your answers fully.

5. Suppose you could not get to the law library and had to access the statute online. Locate the statute using **government** or **academic websites**. Which did you use? Did you find the federal statute? Where? Explain.

6. Locate the statute using (*Westlaw*) (*WestlawNext*) or (*LexisNexis*) (*Lexis Advance*) using a *Boolean* or *Natural Language* search. Did you find the federal act? Explain your search process.

If you found the federal statute and answered all the questions, congratulations! Although locating the statute alone should address and answer each of Lena's issues, you are not finished. Remember that statutes and cases complement each other and work together. When you find the statutory law that addresses a particular issue, it is best to find case law to back up and support the statutory law. Case opinions are very important because the courts *explain* and *interpret* the language in the statute.

Remember when you were told to write down any relevant case citations you found? Look up those cases in print or online, which will be easy if you have the citation. Read and brief the case opinions. Gather any cases that support the statutory law found in addressing Lena's issues, along with a brief holding in the case. In particular, look for cases that specifically reinforce the language in the statute.

7. In print, consult the **federal digests** for any additional helpful cases that support the statute. List and briefly describe any case you find.

8. Online, retrieve any of the cases you found in print and **validate** them. As you validate, see if any more recent cases exist addressing your issues. In addition, conduct a *Boolean* or *Natural Language* search for any cases that relate to Lena's issues under the statute. List and briefly describe each case.

Ending the Search

Hopefully, you found a good amount of law to address and answer Lena Mitchell's issues. So how much law is enough? One of the more difficult tasks for paralegals to perform in legal research is to know when to *stop* researching. Initially, paralegals will want to exhaust each and every source of law in order to avoid missing anything that may be of use. It is not the *quantity* of the research, but the *quality*

TIP

Always remember that whether you are searching in print (*pocket parts*) or online (*KeyCite /Shepard's*) be sure to always make certain your law is still valid and determine if more recent law exists to use within your search.

of the research. Your supervising attorney only wants the research that *answers* the legal issue. If your attorney needs a specific answer to a question, such as the elements to the crime of conspiracy, or how many days a plaintiff has to file a civil complaint, you know your answer will include only the elements for conspiracy, or you will find out that the plaintiff has 20 days to file a complaint. You will likely find those answers in a single rule of law. However, if your issue is more general, or you are answering multiple issues, such as in this case study, your search results may include multiple statutes and/or numerous cases, which will require more research.

Some tips to determine when you have exhausted all of your legal resources:

- When you search and the same sources of law reoccur; and/or
- When validation of your sources yield no new results.

In addition, make sure you inquire as to how much time is allotted for research. The client may tell the attorney that she or he will spend no more than X dollars in legal research. Know you parameters before beginning the task. It is best to be proficient in both the print and online methods of research so that you know the most effective and efficient research process to complete an assignment.

In a basic legal research assignment concerning a local, state, or federal issue, it is best, after utilizing the secondary sources, to provide some statutory and case law for your attorney. However, if you find only one statute or one case in a 5- to 7-page legal memorandum, it will not produce a very strong argument. Conversely, a legal memorandum that includes multiple cases and statutes will better support your argument.

You have now successfully researched and retrieved all the necessary law to address Lena's issues. You undoubtedly have multiple pages of the statute, as well as many case decisions, in no particular order. That's ok. At this point, you should have all the information you need. It will be organized and drafted into the legal memorandum later in the next installment of the case study.

LEARNING OBJECTIVES

After completion of this chapter, you should be able to

1. Understand and explain the concept of legal analysis and its purpose in legal research.

2. Understand the two methods utilized in legal analysis.

3. Explain how to utilize the primary sources of law together in your legal analysis.

INTERPRET

ANALYZE

ELEMENTS

EVALUATE

Legal Analytical Skills | CHAPTER 10

Now that you have learned how to research and find the law, it is important to learn how to organize and synthesize all your sources prior to drafting the legal memorandum. You will learn not only the process of legal analysis, but also the methods used. In particular, you will see how to extract and synthesize the rule of law from cases and statutes and how those two main sources are used together when conducting legal analysis.

■ WHAT IS LEGAL ANALYSIS?

One of the more important skills that a paralegal can possess is the ability to analyze legal information. Throughout the litigation process, the lawyer will handle most of the heavy lifting by analyzing overall trial strategy, as well as decide which legal arguments to pursue in the case. However, attorneys have found that the litigation process moves more quickly and efficiently when their paralegal can retrieve the legal sources of law as well as read, understand, and analyze their legal findings. This saves the attorney more time to concentrate on trial strategy and legal argument based on the paralegal's analysis of the legal research.

How do we analyze information? Analytical ability is the process of sorting through facts and deciding what is and what is not important and relevant. In general terms, the process of analysis includes breaking down a whole into its individual parts. We never analyze anything based on assumptions, only facts. We analyze information all the time. For example, suppose you cannot print a document from your laptop. What do you do? Instinctively, you check to make sure the printer is turned on and that there is paper in the tray. If you still cannot print, then you check the network connection from the laptop. If the printer is connected, then you perform a diagnostics test, and so on. When all else fails, it may be time to invest in a new printer! Without realizing it, you are engaged in the process of analysis by breaking the situation down into its individual parts in order to find a solution.

So what is **legal analysis**? Before paralegals begin their research, they have in their possession the facts of the case given to them by their supervising attorney. As you can see illustrated in Figure 10-1, once the legal research is complete, it must be determined if the law can be applied to the facts of the case in order

LEARNING OBJECTIVE 1
Understand and explain the concept of legal analysis and its purpose in legal research.

legal analysis
The application of the law to the facts of the case in order to identify and resolve legal issues.

Figure 10-1 The Formula for Legal Analysis

to address and answer the legal issues presented. That process is known as legal analysis. In this chapter, you will learn two specific ways to extract and analyze a legal issue during your legal research.

If you recall, in Chapter 4, you first learned the various components of a statute, and later in that same chapter you learned how to properly read and understand the language in a statute. Likewise, in Chapter 6, you first learned the multiple components of a case opinion, and later in that same chapter you learned how to properly read and brief a case opinion. You can revisit those chapters if you need to in order to refresh your memory on how to *read* statutes and cases in order to understand the process of legal analysis.

When paralegals can engage in effective legal analysis, they become an invaluable asset to their supervising attorney, as they can help move any client's case more quickly and efficiently. Below you will see the main methods used to analyze your legal research in order to resolve your legal issues.

■ THE METHODS OF LEGAL ANALYSIS

LEARNING OBJECTIVE 2
Understand and utilize the two main methods utilized in legal analysis.

As a paralegal, in a typical law firm or office, your daily research will primarily include case opinions and statutes. You may also be asked to look up some local rules, and codes, which as you know, are both similar to statutory law. There are two methods of legal research/analysis concerning case opinions and statutes: analysis by fact and analysis by law.

Similar Facts Analysis

similar facts analysis
The process of comparing the facts of your case to facts found in previously decided cases to determine if they are sufficiently similar to be used as legal authority.

The **similar facts analysis** method is used only with case law because the courts, can create law to supplement enacted statutory law. For example, suppose you needed to determine if the crime of conspiracy can be committed if one of the parties engaged in the conspiracy is an undercover police officer. You could look up the crime of conspiracy in your state criminal code, which would only state the elements of the crime—that is, a conspiracy is complete when two or more parties enter into an agreement to commit a crime, and one of those parties commits an overt act (an act in furtherance of the conspiracy). The crimes code would *not* tell you if the crime is compete if one party is an undercover officer, which is a unique fact that would have to be addressed by the courts. Therefore, you would need to research case opinions to see if the appellate courts ruled on such an issue in order to determine if a defendant can be convicted of the crime under these facts.

In the common law system, nearly every written opinion becomes part of the large body of case law that can be used for future decisions—this is known as creating **legal precedent**.

legal precedent
A decided case that provides the basis for determining the rule of law in subsequent cases involving similar facts or issues.

What is precedent and how is it created? As each appellate court issues a decision, it is added to the collection of thousands of available cases that can be researched within the realm of case law. Once a court issues an opinion announcing a rule of law, that case can be followed by all the courts of equal and lower jurisdiction in all future cases that are similar in nature. This concept is known as mandatory/binding authority. Precedent ensures that all parties in all cases be treated with consistency and fairness in the court system, in that a court cannot arbitrarily create its own law. In other words, if you find a case that includes facts A, B, and C, precedent requires that all subsequent cases that also include facts A, B, and C be decided the same way.

To see precedent in action, consider the following example: Philip and Davidson are neighbors. Davidson empties his aboveground pool and releases 5,000 gallons of water onto his property. Davidson could not control the flow of water, which washed onto Philip's property destroying his wood fence and flooding his property. Philip (the plaintiff) sues Davidson (the defendant) in court for the damage to his property. Your supervising attorney is deciding whether to represent the plaintiff. The issue is whether Davidson is liable for the damage to Philip's property after releasing the water destroying Philip's property. The attorney asks you to conduct some research on this issue. You find the case of *Jones v. Brown*, decided by an appellate court in the same jurisdiction.

1998: In the case of *Jones v. Brown*, the plaintiff (Jones) sued the defendant (Brown) after Brown blasted rocks onto Jones' property while clearing a rock bed near his property. The debris caused damage to Jones' roof, and he sued for the cost to repair it. The court ruled that Brown was at fault and ordered Brown to pay damages to Jones' property. The rule of law used in that case stated when one "causes" a "physical invasion" onto another's property, that person has committed a tort and is liable for any damage caused due to his actions.

As you can see, the facts found in the *Jones* case are similar to your case. Even though the facts are not exact (rocks vs. water), both were "things" *intentionally* released by the defendant in both cases, and as a result, both **damaged** the plaintiff's property. Remember this: the facts do not have to match *exactly*, only *similarly*. Once you find a case with facts similar to your case, then you may use the *rule of law* found in that case and apply it to address the legal issues in your case.

The "rule of law" in the *Jones* case states that when one "causes" a "physical invasion" onto another's property, that person has committed a tort and is liable for any damage caused due to his actions. That rule of law fits the facts in your case and provides a good legal argument from which your attorney can argue his case. Therefore, your supervising attorney could use the *Jones* case as **precedent** and argue that Davidson should pay for the damage of Philip's property.

By engaging in this type of analysis, the idea is to:

1. Read the facts of the case you find during your research and compare them with the facts of your case;
2. Look for any key differences and/or similarities in the facts;
3. Determine if the differences in the facts are of such a significant degree that the case cannot be used, or if the facts are similar enough that the case can be used as precedent.

Let us look at another example utilizing this type of analysis. Suppose your supervising attorney is representing a client who has been charged with the crime of first-degree murder (FDM) generally. The client has informed the attorney that he shot the victim once in the leg over a drug dispute, and that he had no intention of killing his drug rival, but to only scare him away from his territory. The attorney wants to know if he can persuade the judge to allow the jury to consider manslaughter in the deliberations. The attorney will argue that the defendant did not possesses the intent to kill and cannot, therefore, be convicted of FDM.

In order to persuade the judge, your supervising attorney must have legal authority to back up his argument—this is where you come into the picture.

In general, the crime of murder in the first degree is committed when a person kills another person with premeditated intent. The courts, in almost every state, have supplemented the criminal statute by amending the crime to include that premeditation can be formed "in an instant," and that the intent to kill is proven when the victim is killed on a "vital part of the body," including the head or chest.

You would need to find a case (precedent) that includes facts where a defendant shot the victim in the leg to see how the court ruled.

Keep in mind that you are searching for exact facts, but it is not a necessity. Remember, facts that are merely similar will suffice. For instance, if you could not find a case where the defendant was charged with FDM after *shooting* the victim in the *leg*, you may also use a case where the defendant was charged with FDM after *stabbing* the victim in the *leg*. You know you are generally getting cooler in your search if you find a case where the victim was *shot* in the *arm*, or even *stabbed* in the *arm*. Review the chart in Figure 10-2 for a clearer understanding.

The cases in Figure 10-2 become less useful as you read down the list. The first four cases include the victim getting shot or stabbed in the main extremities—the leg and arm—this could be used as they are exact or similar facts. Thereafter, your search runs cold when you find cases that include the victim getting shot or stabbed in the leg and back, which are dissimilar facts.

Suppose that after you conduct a complete search of the criminal cases in your jurisdiction using the similar facts analysis, you find the following case:

> **2002:** In the case of *State v. Lowe*, the defendant's first-degree murder conviction was affirmed after defendant Lowe stabbed the victim on the playground during a game of pick-up basketball. Premeditation was established when defendant ran over to his gym bag, pulled a knife, and stabbed the victim 4-5 times in the leg, severing a major artery. The appellate court held that premeditation can be formed in an instant, or in the moment the defendant makes the conscious decision to kill. Further, a strike on a vital part of the victim's body is clear evidence of the intent to kill. However, a strike on the victim's extremities (hands, arms, legs, or feet) is not an indication of intent to kill, except when the defendant strikes the victim multiple times in any of these areas on the victim's body.

Based on the analysis of the statute, the case, and your facts, you can, at this point, inform your supervising attorney that it could be argued that the killing may *not* satisfy the elements of first-degree murder. Although the defendant shot the victim, which could clearly establish premeditation, it could be argued that the intent to kill may not be satisfied because the defendant struck the victim one time in the leg, possibly negating the necessary "intent to kill" element based on the *Lowe* decision.

Figure 10-2 A Sliding Scale for Factual Research

FACTS NEEDED: Case where the victim was shot in the leg – FDM?		
CASE 1 – victim shot in the leg.	→	Hot Search (exact facts – on point)
CASE 2 – victim stabbed in the leg.		
CASE 3 – victim shot in the arm.	→	Warm Search (similar facts – ok)
CASE 4 – victim stabbed in the arm.		
CASE 5 – victim shot in the back.	→	Cold Search (dissimilar facts – not ok)

Similar Law Analysis

The **similar law analysis** is primarily used with statutory law, but it can also be used with case law. This type of analysis is used when the facts of the case are NOT unique and can be easily inserted into the elements of a particular law.

similar law analysis
The process of determining if the law found in the primary sources can be applied to your case.

Suppose your attorney asked you to research whether her client could be convicted for the crime of trespassing after the client was arrested for sleeping in an abandoned warehouse. The facts are simple enough. You could read and review the elements of trespass then apply the facts of the case to each element of the crime. Then, you can inform your supervising attorney, with some good accuracy, whether the client has a good chance of being convicted or acquitted according to the law. The attorney can then evaluate all the options and trial strategy in the case.

This method works best when you have facts that are easily identifiable and fit easily into the elements of the particular law, meaning that there is no uncertainty or ambiguity as to any of the requirements of any of the elements of the law. For example, read the facts and applicable law for the crime of kidnapping.

You work for a criminal defense attorney who is representing a man who is charged with the kidnapping his supervisor at work. One evening after he was fired from his job, the client forced the supervisor into the client's car with a handgun. He drove the victim into another state (400 miles away) and called his employer demanding $25,000 for the supervisor's release. The victim broke free and escaped unharmed. He later called police and the client was arrested.

You find the statute that defines the crime of kidnapping in your state:

> **22 A.B.C. §998 – KIDNAPPING** – person is guilty of kidnapping if he unlawfully removes another a substantial distance, or if he unlawfully confines another for a substantial period in a place of isolation for any of the following reasons: (1) to hold as ransom/reward/hostage; (2) to facilitate the commission of a felony; (3) to inflict or to terrorize the victim.

You must break down the statute into its multiple "elements" using the facts of the case. First, the defendant did *unlawfully remove the victim* (threaten with gun) a substantial distance, as 400 miles into another state would clearly constitute a substantial distance. If the client moved the victim only three miles away, would that be considered a "substantial distance?" What about if the victim was taken just around the block? You would have to look up case law to determine what constitutes a "substantial" distance using the similar facts analysis. As you can also see from the statute, a defendant can also be convicted if he "unlawfully confines" another for a "substantial period" to hold the victim as ransom, which was the case here. Of course, you would have to read the facts of the case to see how long the victim was held hostage, which would again require a similar facts analysis.

In another example, suppose you work for an attorney who practices civil tort law. One day, the attorney tells you that the parents of a 19-year-old son arrived and needed some legal advice. Apparently, the son was driving his car down the street and suddenly swerved onto the sidewalk barely missing a neighbor as he walked his dog. The neighbor is furious and says that he was very frightened by the incident (cannot sleep or eat), and he wants to sue the client's son.

During some preliminary research, you learn that the elements of negligence include (1) a duty of care owed by the defendant to the victim, (2) a breach of that duty, (3) the defendant caused the breach, and (4) the victim suffered personal injury or property damage.

Figure 10-3 The Elements for Negligence

Elements of the Law	Facts of the Case
✓ Duty of Care	The defendant had a duty to keep his eyes on the road at all times and to obey all the traffic rules and regulations.
✓ Breach	The defendant took his eyes off the road and continued to operate the vehicle as he attempted to pick up a cigarette he dropped on the floor mat.
✓ Causation	The action of the defendant looking down caused him to veer off the road and swerve onto the sidewalk.
X Damages	However, the plaintiff did not sustain any physical injury or loss of property. The neighbor was only frightened, and therefore this element cannot be satisfied.

You would have to analyze the facts and insert them into each element to see if the defendant could be held liable for his or her actions. If it is easier for you, you can create a chart to help you keep track of each element, as you can see in Figure 10-3.

As you can see, the defendant will unlikely be held liable under a theory of negligence, but he could possibly be liable for another tort such as negligent infliction of emotional distress. Charts like the one above are quick to create and can help you keep track of the multiple elements in any civil or criminal cause of action.

Lastly, if you happen to find a case opinion that includes sufficiently similar facts *and* if the same rule of law found in that opinion applies to your case, then you have found a decision that is known to be a **case on point**. You will be fortunate to find such a case, as they are rare, but they are out there.

case on point
A decided case that is sufficiently similar to your case as to both the facts and the law.

■ UTILIZING PRIMARY SOURCES TOGETHER

LEARNING OBJECTIVE 3
Explain how to utilize the primary sources of law together in your legal analysis.

Now that you know how to analyze your legal findings with the facts of your case from both statutes and cases, you will see how to use statutes, cases, and other sources together to complete and strengthen your legal argument.

Suppose you locate a statute in your research that addresses your legal issue. Even though the statute enumerates all the elements required to satisfy that particular law, it is still good practice to find a case to explain, interpret, or even support the statute.

For example, suppose your supervising attorney is not certain as to whether a lay person can testify as to their opinion while testifying on direct examination. You are working on a case where the plaintiff is suing the defendant for speeding, running a red light, and crashing into the plaintiff's car. A witness on the scene is willing to testify as to the approximate speed of the defendant's car immediately prior to the crash. The witness arrived immediately after the crash and is willing to testify as to the defendant's rate of speed due to the damage and position of both cars, as he was involved in a similar accident himself last year. You find the rule of evidence addressing this issue.

Rule of Evidence 701 – OPINION TESTIMONY BY LAY WITNESSES – If the witness is not testifying as an expert, the witness' testimony in the form of opinions or inferences is limited to those opinions or inferences which are rationally based on the perception of the witness, helpful to a clear understanding of the witness' testimony or the determination of a fact in issue, and not based on any scientific or technical knowledge . . .

So you think you understand the rule, but some more clarification would help. If the rule itself is not clear, or you do understand the rule but you need some further clarity or support, look up cases that have dealt with this issue. You conduct a search for the rule and find the following case.

> **2000** – In the case of *Peterson v. Ellis*, it was improper for the trial court to permit Officer Wilkes to testify as to the rate of speed of the car driven by the defendant, as he arrived on the scene *after* the crash in which both the defendant and plaintiff's cars sustained the same amount of front-end damage. It would have been impossible to determine which car, if not both, had been speeding, and the testimony should have been stricken.

It appears that the witness in your case *cannot* testify as to the approximate rate of the defendant's car because the witness did not see, firsthand, the actual rate of speed of the defendant's car immediately prior to impact. In other words, the witness did not perceive the event, but is only willing to provide a guess or estimate, which is not permitted under the law. Keep in mind that even if you could not find the above case that is factually on-point, suppose you found the following case instead.

> **1999** – In the case of *Commonwealth v. Simpson*, it was error for the trial court to permit witness O'Donnell to testify as to the number of patrons in the club the evening of the shooting. O'Donnell testified that "there had to have been at least 180-200 people in the club since it was a Friday night . . . " However, O'Donnell was not at the club that night and only made an "educated guess" only because he is a patron at the club every Friday night. That information cannot be deemed reliable as to the night in question, as two other witnesses who were present estimated the crowd to include over 300 people.

Although you are dealing with apples and oranges here, the facts, although different from your case, still establish when a witness can and cannot testify as to details of an event. If you found nothing in the realm of a case including a vehicle accident, the *Simpson* case above will let your supervising attorney know that the only way a witness is permitted to testify is if the witness actually observed the event.

Legal analysis is similar to putting together a jigsaw puzzle. You open the box, dump all the pieces, then look to see which pieces fit together to form the picture. You have to carefully examine each piece to see its unique ridges and cuts to determine where each piece fits into the puzzle. The same holds true with analyzing your legal findings. You must carefully read each case and statute to determine which fits perfectly with the facts of your case in order to resolve the legal issue. Like everything else you learn in this text, the more you do it, the better you will understand it.

Chapter Checklist ✔

- Legal analysis is the process of combining the facts of your case with the rule of law found in cases and/or statutes in order to resolve your legal issue.
- Any source of primary law can be included in a legal analysis, but a paralegal will most likley engage in the research of cases and statutes on a daily basis.
- Before you begin the actual analysis process, you first need to be in possession of the facts and issues in the case.
- There are two main methods for conducting legal analysis: factual analysis and analysis by rule of law.

- In factual analysis, you look for factual similarities between your present case and the researched opinions.
- In utilizing factual analysis, do not quit if you cannot find a case "on-point" because this rarely happens. Utilize your word searching skills and find a case that is *similar* to the facts in your case, then when analyzing the situation you can argue why the opinion is relevant to your present case.
- In using an analysis by law, you are extracting the rule of law directly from the primary source.
- In order to strengthen your argument in resolving your legal issue, always use a combination of statutes and case opinions.
- Remember that it is good to use a combination of statutes and cases because statutes state the law, and opinions explain, interpret, and supplement the law.
- You can combine any sources of primary law; the more sources you use, the stronger the legal argument.

KEY TERMS

Legal analysis   293
Similar fact analysis   294

Legal precedent   294
Similar law analysis   297

Case on point   298

CRITICAL THINKING AND APPLICATION

Please read the hypothetical problems below and answer the questions.

1. You are employed at a local law firm that specializes in workers' compensation law. Please read the fact pattern below and decide which case best addresses the factual situation.

   Officer John Baker (29), a member of your city police force for five (5) years, received a dispatch call around 1:30 a.m. concerning a possible domestic violence dispute. As John and his partner arrived at the address, they heard shouting coming from the home. John approched the porch and saw that the front door was opened. John announced himself and entered the home. As John stepped over the threshold, he witnessed a man shoot another man in the chest. As John drew his weapon, the shooter looked at John and said, "I ain't going to jail," and shot himself. The crime scene was later secured and John was interviewed. John always experienced extreme violence on the job, but he never witnessed a double shooting. Thereafter, John could not eat or sleep, and he also experienced nightmares and became distant with his own family. John filed for workers' compensation benefits for "mental stress" on the job. The issue presented is whether or not a police officer can receive benefits due to the result of a work-related psychological injury. Which case(s) support the facts of this hypothetical? Why?

   a. *Harris Case* - Benefits were properly awarded to a seventeen (17)-year-old lifeguard who witnessed an adult have a seizure and drown in the city pool during his watch. The claimant proved a mental injury after proving he needed to be hospitalized, he lost weight, and became clinically depressed following the incident. Under workers' ccompensation law, benefits can be awarded to a claimant who suffers a psychiatric injury caused by work-related stress.

   b. *Bower Case* - It was held that the claimant, a firefighter, failed to prove that he had been exposed to abnormal working conditions where he responded to a call and found a man who had committed suicide by hanging. Thus, if a claimant's job is the type of work typically associated with a high amount of stress, the claimant must prove that the job was unusually stressful for that type of job.

   c. *Russell Case* - It was held that the claimant failed to prove he had experienced abnormal working conditions, thus sustaining a psychiatric work injury, after providing documentation that as a prison guard, he experienced threats, profanity, and fighting among the inmates on a daily basis at the prison. Although unfortunate, those type of working conditions were to be expected being employed as a prison guard at a maximum state institution.

2. You are employed at a local law firm that practices and specializes in family law. Your supervising attorney needs you to analyze some research. Please read the brief fact pattern and choose which case best supports the facts of your case.

Father filed a custody petition seeking primary physical and legal custody of his child (age 6). Mother and father were both originally residents of Florida. After the child's birth, the mother relocated to Virginia where the child lived with her for five years. Thereafter, the child lived with the father in Florida for one year. The father states that the mother recently became addicted to drugs and painkillers and is unfit to raise the child. Presently, the child has been living in North Carolina with his paternal grandfather for the past three months, who also wants to spend time with the child. Father has come to your office for advice, as he does not know which state to file his custody petition. Which case best addresses this situation for what the client needs answered? Why?

   a. *Case A* - Mother, living in Virginia, filed a custody petition seeking sole physical and legal custody of Child. Father is incarcerated in Pennsylvania. Filing custody petition in Virginia proper.

   b. *Case B* - Mother, living in New York, files for primary physical custody of Child. Father, also a resident of New York, relocated to Michigan for work and took Child with him. Child was enrolled in school in Michigan for one year. Court held that jurisdiction was proper in New York, the child's "home state," which is defined as the state where Child has lived at a residence for at least two consecutive years.

   c. *Case C* - Mother, living in Texas, filed a custody petition for primary physical and legal custody of Child. Mother also temporarily lives, and takes Child with her, to her new paramour's house in California. Father, also living in Texas, files a cross-petition for custody. Court held that jurisdiction was proper in Texas, the child's home state.

3. You are employed at a local defense firm that practices and specializes in criminal law. Your supervising attorney needs you to analyze some research. Please read the brief fact pattern and choose which case best supports the facts of your case.

Defendant was charged with the crime of arson after setting fire to his business. No one was inside the business or injured when the fire erupted. Defendant was arrested after he attempted to file a false claim to collect the insurance money. Defendant asserts that his business partner called Defendant and told him that he had his wife with him and that he would kill his wife if he did not commit the crime. The business partner put Defendant's wife on the phone who pleaded for help. Which case below addresses the issue of whether Defendant has a valid defense? Why?

   a. Defendant's conviction for burglary affirmed after Defendant was arrested attempting to break into Victim's home. Defense of duress was not warranted, as no evidence existed of any duress placed upon Defendant even though he testifed that he received a handwritten note demanding him to complete the job. Although the note was produced in court, there was no evidence of an "immediate and definite threat" on Defendant's life.

   b. Defendant's convictions for forgery and theft reversed after Defendant was deemed to have been under duress when his life was immediately threatened to fill out the bank withdraw slip at the bank to steal $5,000 of Victim's money. Defendant had a loaded gun to his back as he filled out the bank slip.

   c. Defendant's defense of duress was proper as he was threatened with imminent threat of death as he was instructed to hit Victim with his car. Duress can be used as a defense when the defendant faces an "imminent and real threat" of harm or death to himself or to someone else if they refuse to carry out the crime.

4. Assume that you are working as a paralegal at the local prosecutor's office. You are working on a case for your supervising attorney concerning the crime of "possession of an instrument of crime (PIC)." The client is charged after being arrested for repeatedly striking his neighbor with his cane, causing physical injury. Which case could be used to support a conviction for this crime? The question is whether a cane can be considered an "instrument of crime?"

   a. *State v. Williams* – the defendant's conviction for PIC, among other crimes, affirmed after the defendant stabbed the victim repeatedly with a kitchen knife.

   b. *State v. Hane* – the defendant's conviction for PIC affirmed after the defendant struck the victim with a tree-cutting pole equipped with a blade, causing severe physical injury to the victim.

c. *State v. Banner* – the defendant's conviction for PIC affirmed after the defendant used a laptop computer to download multiple files from ABC Bank, resulting in the theft of $110,000.

d. *State v. Jones* – the defendant's conviction for PIC affirmed after the defendant attacked the victim repeatedly with a tennis racket causing physical injury.

e. *State v. Peterson* – the defendant's conviction for PIC affirmed after the defendant shot the victim twice in the leg with a handgun, causing physical injury.

5. You are employed in a criminal defense firm. Suppose the crime of "theft" in your jurisdiction is as follows: "The crime of theft is committed when a person takes or removes, however slight, the personal property of another, with the intent to permanently deprive the victim of that property . . . [t]he intent element must be present to permanently deprive . . . a good faith and reasonable belief by the defendant that the property is their own defeats a conviction for theft." In which of the brief fact patterns would the defendant most likely be convicted of a theft? Why?

a. *Case A* - Making the mistaken assumption that the titanium golf club was his, which looked similar to his own club, the defendant took the victim's golf club from the crowded locker room, placed it in his bag, and exited the club.

b. *Case B* – The defendant saw an expensive watch fall from the victim's handbag as she walked down the street, and after the victim walked out of sight, the defendant picked up the watch and intended to sell it for a profit.

c. *Case C* - Making the mistaken assumption that the titanium golf club was his, which looked similar to his own club, the defendant took the victim's club that he found in a different color golf bag than his, and in the seat of another golf cart, placed it in his bag, and exited the course.

d. *Case D* – The defendant, a college student, hurriedly left class, jumped on his bicycle and sped off across campus. Once at his destination, he realized he took the wrong bicycle and promptly returned it to where he found it before the actual owner even realized it was missing.

LEARNING OBJECTIVES

After completion of this chapter, you should be able to

1. Demonstrate the basic rules of grammar in your writing.

2. Demonstrate the basic rules of punctuation in your writing.

3. Explain the print and online sources available to help improve your use of grammar and punctuation in your writing.

GRAMMAR

PUNCTUATION
RULES

FORMAT

The Basic Rules of Writing

After you have researched and resolved the legal issue, you must be able to effectively communicate your findings to your supervising attorney, judge, client, or any member of the legal community.

Therefore, prior to learning the "specifics" of legal writing, such as drafting a legal memorandum, you must master the "basics" of writing in order to ensure that your legal writing is grammatically correct.

We learn the basics of grammar and punctuation early in our education. Thereafter, many of us become lax in utilizing those basic skills on a daily basis. However, as a paralegal, you must understand and utilize the basic mechanics of grammar and punctuation in order to draft a legal document properly and professionally. Your supervising attorney can edit or question your research, but you do not want them to edit or question your writing skills. Make certain that your writing is at a professional level, as many people within the legal profession will be reading your work at different times.

Although you may already be familiar with and utilize many of the basic writing rules included in this chapter, take the time to review and understand all the points presented below.

◼ GRAMMAR

The basic rules of grammar that you will be utilizing in your everyday writing are reviewed in this section.

LEARNING OBJECTIVE 1
Demonstrate the basic rules of grammar in your writing.

Verbs

The **verb** is the most important word in any sentence, as it is the grammatical centerpiece that denotes action or being.

verb
A word that expresses action or being.

Action Verbs

The attorney *read* opposing counsel's brief.

I *walked* to the courthouse for jury duty.

Being Verbs

We *were* anxiously awaiting the jury's verdict.

I *am* a summer intern in family court.

---

subject/verb agreement
The rule of grammar that states that in a sentence, singular subjects must have singular verbs, and plural subjects must have plural verbs.

Subject/Verb Agreement

It is important when constructing a sentence to use a singular subject with a singular verb and plural verbs and pronouns when the subjects are plural. This is referred to as **subject/verb agreement**.

CORRECT: The law firm of Harrison, Martin, and Wright sent Jeremy Rainer, lead counsel, and Gwynn Harvey, *its* newest associate, to the settlement conference.

INCORRECT: The law firm of Harrison, Martin, and Wright sent Jeremy Rainer, lead counsel, and Gwynn Harvey, *their* newest associate, to the settlement conference. (*The singular subject "law firm" requires a singular verb*).

Consider also . . .

> Billy **has** a criminal record. (*Singular subject - Billy*)
>
> Judges **are** the referees at trial. (*Plural subject - Judges*)
>
> William's name **was** not included on the jury list even though he was mailed a notice to serve. (*Singular subject - William's* **Name**)
>
> The jurors' names **were** included on the court crier's list. (*Plural subject – Juror's* **names**)

It is a simple formula—just make sure that whatever your subject is, singular or plural, the verb follows.

Every verb in a sentence must have at least one subject. But some verbs can have multiple subjects, also known as **compound subjects**. Compound subjects joined by the word *and* will most likely use a *plural* verb. When using the words *anybody, anyone, each, every, each one, everybody, everyone, neither,* or *nobody,* use a *singular* verb. Also, when using the word *all* as a subject, you use a *plural* verb. Consider the following examples.

compound subjects
A compound subject occurs when multiple subjects in a sentence are all involved in a singular action.

> *Each* company that **was** subpoenaed mailed their discovery before January.
>
> After only three years in practice, *Samantha* **and** *Jackson* **have** a new law partner.
>
> "Can I ask if *everyone* **has** filled out a jury questionnaire sheet?"
>
> "I understand that *nobody* on the jury **has** decided on a verdict of guilty or innocent?"
>
> The witness testified that *all* of the drugs **were** sold in New York over a period of three years.

When compound subjects are joined by the "neither/nor" or "either/or" combination, the verb must agree in number with the subject closest to it.

> *Neither* the **secretary** nor the **law clerk was** present when the client began yelling and threatening the attorney. (*The words "secretary" and "law clerk" are singular.*)

A good tip to keep in mind is that when you use the "neither/nor" combination, use a plural noun that is closest to the verb so that the verb is plural and vice versa.

For example, "Neither the **defendants** nor the plaintiff *was* prepared for trial." It sounds better and less awkward. You can also say, "Neither the **plaintiff** nor the **defendants** *were* prepared for trial."

Nouns and Pronouns

A **noun** denotes the object or "thing" discussed in a sentence. There are *common* nouns (book, table, car) and *proper* nouns (Monday, Peter, January).

> The **courthouse** is located three blocks from here.
>
> The trial is set for **Monday**, November 18, 2013.

noun
A word that denotes the object or thing discussed in a sentence.

That was easy enough. However, be careful when dealing with **collective nouns**, which are nouns that define a collective number of people in one group, including a *jury, committee, group, team,* or *board.* These nouns are not plural, but *singular,* as they are considered one collective group. Therefore, they always require a singular verb.

> The ethics *committee* **is** reviewing the judge's case.
>
> The *jury* **was** excused for lunch at noon.

collective noun
A word that denotes a collective number of people in a single group.

Within that same family, a **pronoun** is used as a substitute for nouns. Pronoun errors are the most common grammatical errors found in writing. For instance, consider the following sentence: *"Parker was late for the client interview and Parker forgot his pen and paper."* It sounds awkward. Instead of repeating Parker's name a second time, which is unnecessary and breaks the flow of the sentence, you use a pronoun. When a pronoun is used, it must agree in person, number, and gender. If you have a singular subject, then each pronoun in the sentence that describes the subject should be singular.

Personal pronouns can be *singular* and include *I, me, you, she, he, her, him, it, that, this, that, myself, yourself, himself, herself, itself, my, your, his, her,* and *mine.* They can also be *plural,* including *we, us, you, they, them, these, those, ourselves, yourselves, themselves, our, your, their, ours, yours,* and *theirs.*

Consider the following examples.

pronoun
A word used in place of a noun that must agree in person, number, and gender, that makes a sentence less repetitive and cumbersome.

CORRECT:	The **jury** rendered **its** verdict. (*The jury is one singular unit*)
INCORRECT:	The jury rendered **their** verdict.
CORRECT:	**Jason** and **I** want you to come back to the jury room after lunch.
INCORRECT:	Jason and **me** want you to come back to the jury room after lunch.
CORRECT:	In order to receive consideration to be hired as a paralegal, a **person** must demonstrate that **he** or **she** can perform quality research and writing.
INCORRECT:	In order to receive consideration to be hired as a paralegal, a person must demonstrate that **they** can perform quality research and writing.

However, make sure you only use a pronoun *after* using a specific subject first. Otherwise, your reader will be quite confused. For example, you could not write, "*I hate it, yet I buy it in order to stay healthy.*" What is *it*?! Try instead, "I hate **spinach**, yet I buy it in order to stay healthy."

Another type of pronoun is the **indefinite pronoun**, which does not refer to a specific person or thing. Examples include *any, all, anyone, each, either, everyone, none, nobody, something,* and *nothing.* Most of these pronouns refer to a **singular subject** and therefore take a **singular verb**.

indefinite pronoun
A pronoun that does not refer to any particular person, amount, or thing.

> *Nobody* **was** present. *Each* of the jury rooms **was** empty.

relative pronoun
A word used to connect a clause or phrase to a noun or pronoun.

Likewise, **relative pronouns** are used to link a relative (subordinate) clause to the main clause in the sentence. It is relative because it "relates" to the word it is modifying. Examples include, *who* and *whom* (people), *whose* (possession), and *which* and *that* (things).

> *"The person who arrived at court this morning was my co-worker."* (The phrase "the person" modifies "who arrived at court this morning").

interrogative pronoun
A pronoun used to ask a question.

On the other hand, **interrogative pronouns** are used to ask questions (interrogate). Both of these pronouns include, *that, what, whatever, which, who, whom, whose, whichever, whosever, whoever,* and *whomever.*

In dealing with the "who/whom" dilemma, just remember to use the pronouns *who* and *whoever* if you are referring to the **subject in the sentence**, and use *whom* and *whomever* if you are referring to the **objects of a verb**. Another helpful trick to remember is if the decision to use "who/whom" lies *before* the verb, then use "who" or "whoever." On the other hand, if the dilemma to use "who/whom" lies *after* the verb, then use "whom" or "whomever."

> Thomas was the only one **who** *voted* not guilty.
>
> "**What** are you talking about?"
>
> "**Which** witness did you believe more?"
>
> **Whichever** seat you choose is fine with me.
>
> Please *give* this to **whomever** you choose, thank you.

Adjectives and Adverbs

modifier
A group of words that describes or limits a verb, noun, adjective, or adverb.

adjective
A word related to a noun to describe it.

adverb
A word that describes a verb, an adjective, or another adverb.

A **modifier** is a word(s) used to "explain" a noun or a verb, therefore modifying it. Modifiers include **adjectives**, which describe nouns and answer the questions *which, what,* or *how many.* Some examples include *heavy, windy,* and *healthy.* **Adverbs** describe verbs usually describing "when" or "where" and answer the questions *how, how often, when, and where.* Some examples include *yesterday, everywhere, quickly,* and *forcibly.* Although you will learn that less is more and that brevity is good when writing, some modifiers are necessary in order to explain important information.

> ### Adjectives
>
> The **center city** office monitors the internet activity of every office in the firm. (*Answers the question of which office?*)
>
> The plaintiff, upon inspection of the machine, noticed multiple **decayed** wires inside the back panel. (*Answers the question: "What was the condition of the wiring?*)
>
> ### Adverbs
>
> The jurors lost interest because the witnesses' testimony was **unbearably** long. (*Answers the question of how long?*)
>
> Please place each exhibit **here** after showing it to the members of the jury. (*Answers the question of where the exhibits belong?*)

Be careful of "misplaced modifiers" in your writing also. When describing an object, the meaning may be clear to you, but the reader does not possess the same background knowledge as you. Therefore, improper placement of the modifier can change and alter the meaning of the sentence.

Consider the following example.

> **CORRECT:** The judge scolded the defense attorney, who was unprepared as usual.
>
> **INCORRECT:** Unprepared as usual, the judge scolded the defense attorney.

The phrase "unprepared as usual" should apply to the attorney, not the judge, but because the modifier is "hanging" the meaning is unclear.

In addition, consider the following sentence:

> **CORRECT:** Tim and John were in the process of being arrested when Tim slipped and fell onto the pavement.
>
> **INCORRECT:** Tim and John were in the process of being arrested when he slipped and fell onto the pavement. (*Who slipped – Tim or John?*)

Further, an **infinitive verb** is basically a verb with the word "to" in front of it (*to run*, *to read*). In this case, the word "to" is not a preposition, but is referred to as a sign of the infinitive. An infinitive can be used as a noun, adjective, or adverb. However, be sure not to "split an infinitive." Some writers incorrectly position an adverb between "to" and a verb. For example:

infinitive verb
A verb used with the word "to" directly before it.

> **CORRECT:** The attorney wanted *to forcibly take* the exhibit from the witness as she testified.
>
> **INCORRECT:** The attorney wanted *to take the exhibit forcibly* from the witness as she testified.

Conjunctions

The purpose of a **conjunction** is to "connect" or "divide" words and phrases from each other. Just as conjunctions are important when read within a statute, they are just as important when used in everyday language, especially in legal writing.

conjunction
A word used to connect clauses or sentences or to coordinate words in the same clause.

The conjunction *and* is used to connect words or groups of words of equal emphasis; the conjunctions *but* and *yet* are used for the opposite effect to indicate a contrast between words or groups of words; the conjunctions *or* and *nor* are used to denote that either word or groups of words can be considered separately or individually. Many writers are not familiar with the fact that the words *so* and *because* are also used as conjunctions.

> The attorney instructed the paralegal to **either** come with him to court **or** stay in the office and finish her research memo. *("Either" is always used with "or.")*
>
> The final prosecution witness testified in the morning, **but** the defense attorney called three witnesses in the afternoon.
>
> **Neither** the judge **nor** the jury could hear the soft-spoken witness as she testified. *("Neither" is always used with "nor.")*
>
> The defendant refused to settle the case, **yet** he arrived at the office this morning to talk about the case.

Preposition

preposition
Words used to connect nouns and pronouns that are used to introduce additional information in a sentence.

A **preposition** joins a noun, pronoun, or phrase to another part of a sentence and is often used to demonstrate "place" or "location" or to convey other relationships within the sentence. Prepositions usually begin what is called a *prepositional phrase*. The list of simple prepositions includes: *aboard, about, above, across, after, against, along, amid, among, around, as, at atop, before, behind, below, beneath, beside, between, beyond, by, despite, down, during, for, from, in, inside, into, like, near, of, off, on, onto, out, outside, over, past, regarding, round, since, than, through, throughout, till, to, toward, under, unlike, until, up, upon, with, within,* and *without.*

> Grab the witness list **off the table.**
>
> **Despite being tired**, Mark did his best to stay awake during trial.

It is also not recommended to *end* a sentence with a preposition, and the practice should be avoided even though you may be tempted to do so.

> **CORRECT:** Turn *off* the lights.
>
> **INCORRECT:** Turn the lights *off*.

Articles

article
A word that introduces and provides information about a noun.

An **article** can introduce a noun (*a, an, some,* or *the*). Articles can be used for "general" or "specific" reference. For example, "*Grab a book from the shelf.*" (Meaning, grab *any* book). Whereas, "*Grab the book from the shelf.*" (Meaning, grab a *specific* book).

Rules for i.e and e.g.

There will be times when you will use either (i.e.) or (e.g.) within your everyday writing, but do you know what they mean and when and how to use them?

You use (i.e.) when you want to clarify something in your sentence. It is the abbreviation for the Latin phrase meaning "that is." Many people mistakenly use it for listing an example. You use it to clarify your thought in the sentence.

Developing a good rapport with the jury is crucial, *i.e.,* make eye contact and always be respectful.

On the other hand, you use (e.g.) when you want to say "for example."

The attorney was cited on multiple counts by the ethics committee (*e.g.* fraud, mishandling of client funds, and bribery).

In both instances, you can use the comma after each, or either can be used in parenthesis without the comma.

The use of proper grammar is essential to maintaining good writing skills. By utilizing these rules properly, your writing will rise to a professional level.

■ PUNCTUATION

Imagine reading your favorite novel, the newspaper, or even a legal document without any punctuation. It would be very difficult to read or understand. Punctuation gives your sentences and dialogue structure. Below you will learn (or refresh your memory) on the correct usage of some of the most important areas of punctuation.

LEARNING OBJECTIVE 2
Demonstrate the basic rules of punctuation in your writing.

Apostrophe

Everyone knows what an **apostrophe** is, but most confusion stems from the dilemma of when to use it as a singular or plural possessive.

The possessive form of singular nouns, abbreviations, and acronyms take the (**'s**).

apostrophe
A mark of punctuation used to denote possession.

The jury**'s** verdict sheet was taken from the deliberation room. *(It was the sheet that was in the possession of the jury).*

The prosecution**'s** star witness refused to take the stand and ran from the courthouse.

On the other hand, the plural possessive is used in the following instances, especially in words already ending in (s).

The judges**'** decisions.

The prosecutors**'** exhibits.

The witnesses**'** statements.

The witness was given three months**'** notice to secure the check.

All contractions also require an apostrophe, although the use of contractions is **not** advised in legal writing (i.e. *I'd – I would*). Many writers confuse *its* (a plural possessive) and *it's* (the contraction for "it is/has"). For example, "**It's** *illegal when a county board comingles* **its** *finances with personal bank accounts.*" Also remember that the word "cannot" is always one word, not two.

The Hyphen and Compound Words

hyphen
A sign used to join words to indicate that they have a combined meaning.

compound word
A word created out of two words that can stand independent of each other.

Some words used today require a **hyphen**, but when and when not to use a hyphen can become confusing. Hyphens are used to link words and parts of words, and are used in many compound words. A **compound word** is simply a word made up of two independent words that come together to make one new word. For example: court + room = courtroom. Compound words can fall within one of three categories: *closed*, *open*, and *hyphenated*.

Some "closed" compound words that are NOT hyphenated include, *bookcase*, *anyplace*, *keyboard*, *notebook*, *newspaper*, *caretaker*, and even words you would not think of as compound, including *become*, *cannot*, and *herein*.

Some "open" compound words that are also NOT hyphenated include *post office*, *real estate*, *living room*, and *coffee mug*. An open compound word is the only type of word where the second word can be capitalized, for example, *North America* or *Native American*.

Many everyday "hyphenated" words include, *Editor-in-chief*, *X-ray*, *over-the-counter*, *able-minded*, *ex-wife*, *great-aunt*, *ten-year-old*, *fuel-efficient*, *mayor-elect*, *T-shirt*, and *mid-August*.

You will learn that many legal terms require hyphens, including *cross-examination* (although **not** direct examination), *quasi-contract*, *all-inclusive*, *well-established rule*, *counter-petition*, *post-trial*, *cross-claim*, and *counter-claim*.

Some common words you may be tempted to hyphenate, but **cannot** include, *codefendant*, *interoffice memo*, *proactive*, and *preexistence*.

Knowing which words require hyphenation can prove tricky at times, as there are so many words that fall under this rule. When in doubt, always take a second and consult a print or online dictionary.

Comma, Period, Semi-colon, and Colon

comma
A mark of punctuation indicating a pause within a sentence, or used to separate items in a series in a sentence.

A **comma** is typically used to divide a series of items within the same sentence.

> The forgetful attorney lost his witness deposition, trial transcripts, and subpoenas.

Commas are also used to separate parenthetical phrases. This means that if you remove the phrase *within the commas* the sentence can still stand on its own and make sense to the reader.

> The witness, *Janice Myer*, was reprimanded by the judge for not answering the prosecutor's questions.

The idea is that the sentence still makes sense when you take out the phrase *Janice Moore*, although it allows the reader to understand *who* you are talking about, especially if multiple witnesses testified at that trial.

Here is another example.

> Judge Marshall Fink, *who recently retired*, agreed to speak at the conference.

And of course, all dates include necessary commas as well.

In 2013, 281 cases were disposed of by the entire criminal court division.

The trial is set to begin on Tuesday, November 12, 2013. *(Always use a comma between the day and month of a specific date.)*

In addition, if a description, such as a title, follows a proper name, use a comma.

The parents decided to initiate a class action lawsuit against Paula Harris, the school administrator.

Further, when you are tempted, as many of us are, to write a long sentence feeling that the use of many commas will help us, like this sentence, try using shorter sentences with periods instead.

The horrific accident was reported sometime around midnight, and even though there were no witnesses to be found, the crash was loud enough to wake some of the residents on the quiet street, none of whom are willing to testify as to what they heard or saw that evening.

Instead, construct smaller sentences and eliminate numerous commas.

The accident occurred around midnight. No witnesses were willing to testify concerning the loud crash that occurred on this quiet street that evening.

Speaking of the **period**, it is universally known and understood as the mark of punctuation that ***ends*** a sentence and, therefore, the end of a particular thought or idea. Readers understand that when they see a period, they know to stop briefly before they continue reading.

The **semicolon** is a unique form of punctuation, but rarely used properly. Many people confuse when to use a semicolon and a comma. The purpose of the semicolon is similar to that of the comma—both ask the reader to pause briefly before continuing to read. But unlike a comma, the semicolon separates two independent sentences.

The semicolon is also used to separate phrases in a list of information.

period
A mark of punctuation that ends a thought in a sentence.

semicolon
It is a mark of punctuation, more pronounced than a comma, used to indicate a pause between two main clauses.

The defendant's criminal record was extensive; it included robbery, burglary, and arson.

The ethics board includes James Harris, litigation attorney; Sheila Williams, criminal defense attorney; and Gerry Aponte, unit chief with the Cook County prosecutor's office.

colon
A mark of punctuation that either indicates the writer is introducing a quote or list of items, or separating two clauses.

On the other hand, the **colon** is used between two sentences when the second sentence explains or illustrates something in the first sentence. It is used when introducing a formal quotation, rule, or question. Specifically, use a colon:

- When introducing a quotation;
- To explain or to elaborate the information; or
- When presenting a list of items.

> The attorney stepped in front of the jury: "Ladies and gentlemen . . . "
>
> To ensure success, a defense attorney needs the following qualities: an objective mind, intelligence, patience, and knowledge of the law.
>
> The paralegal had two assignments: a deposition summary and to edit a client interview.

Parentheses, Quotation Marks, Ellipses

There are a few other marks of punctuation with which you should be familiar in your everyday and legal writing.

A set of **parentheses** is primarily used to explain a thought or an idea within a sentence.

parentheses
A mark of punctuation inserted as an explanation or afterthought into a sentence.

> The new Havertown Justice Center (completed in June) already has an 85% occupancy rate of office space on the first 10 floors.

You will learn that in writing your research memos or any legal document, parentheses are used to direct the reader to additional information or, more importantly, the *source* of your legal authority.

> The victim testified that although the defendant did not take any personal property from her person, he threatened her with a handgun (Notes of Testimony, 3/14/13, pg. 4). *The reader knows that information will be found on page 4 of the trial transcript.*
>
> The federal statute in question ensures that veterans' families are entitled to disability benefits upon the medical discharge of the claimant (***15 U.S.C. §112***).

Lastly, parentheses are used when ***first*** introducing an abbreviation or acronym.

> The Occupational Safety and Health Administration ("OSHA") representative inspected the factory to ensure that there was adequate ventilation being circulated through the entire factory. In its mission to help employers and employees reduce on the job injuries, OSHA routinely inspects such factories for possible safety violations.

quotation marks
A set of single or double punctuation marks inserted to denote the beginning and ending of a quote.

Another important form of punctuation used in any legal document is **quotation marks**. Quotes are used to emphasize a speaker's exact words, or to emphasize a particular word, or to quote any information from a particular source of law. *Remember that **any** punctuation used in a sentence is always placed **within** the quotation marks, NOT outside.

> The witness testified that she was afraid of the defendant since she had locked him out of the house. She stated: "He owned many firearms and he would return with one of them."
>
> The witness stated, "He grabbed my arm and yelled, 'You aren't getting full custody of our children'." (*If the person making a statement is quoting someone else, you use singular quotes within double quotes*).
>
> During his closing argument, the prosecutor improperly defined the defendant as an "animal" who needed to be placed behind bars for life. (*The use of italics is also permissible in emphasizing a particular word*).
>
> The criminal statute clearly states that, "[a] conspiracy is complete as soon as two or more people agree to make the conscious decision together to commit a crime . . ."

Lastly, another form of punctuation you need to be made aware of and that is used in legal writing is the **ellipsis**, which consists of the three dots at the beginning or end of a quote. The ellipsis informs the reader that you have only cited a portion of the full content of the material. An important rule to remember is that if you are using ellipsis at the beginning of the quote use a bracket for the first letter of the first word to indicate that the first letter was capitalized as it was a new sentence, but you are using it in the middle of your sentence so it becomes lowercase.

ellipsis
A mark of punctuation used to indicate omitted material from a quote by the use of three evenly spaced dots.

> In its opinion, the appellate court stated that, " . . . [w]e are not persuaded by the appellant's argument that the evidence was insufficient to support his verdict . . ." (*This allows the reader to see that there is additional content before and after the selected quote*).

Good grammar and punctuation are necessary to ensure a successful career as a paralegal. A prospective employer will not only request a research memo from you to see your research skills, but to also evaluate your writing skills, which begins with a solid foundation of the rules of grammar and punctuation.

Proper grammar and punctuation is necessary in order for you to communicate in writing within the legal profession. Keep these tips and rules in mind, and refer back to this chapter if needed.

■ ADDITIONAL RESOURCES

To further supplement the instruction in this chapter, there are other valuable outside resources from which you can sharpen and maintain your knowledge of proper grammar and punctuation.

LEARNING OBJECTIVE 3
Explain the print and online sources available to help improve your use of grammar and punctuation in your writing.

There are two very informative websites devoted to the study of grammar and punctuation. First, *Core Grammar for Lawyers* is an online self-directed learning tool designed to not only assist lawyers, but also paralegals and students. After you register a new account, you will be given a pre-test of general and law-specific grammar skills; online lessons on various topics; interactive practice sessions; a detailed and descriptive index to locate exactly what you need, and multiple post-tests to evaluate your progress. Check out this website which can be located at **www.coregrammarforlawyers.com**.

A second good resource is *The Blue Book of Grammar and Punctuation*, currently in its 11th edition as of 2014. The book parallels its companion website at **www.grammarbook.com**. Both sources provide in-depth coverage of the many rules of grammar and punctuation along with hundreds of quizzes to test your knowledge of the material. The instruction on the uses of grammar and punctuation and quizzes are free. In addition, you can purchase a plan for additional quizzes and test banks, or you can purchase individual quizzes for only .99 cents each.

Lastly, a popular and informative publication, *The Redbook, A Manual on Legal Style*, is currently in its 3rd edition as of 2013. First published in 2002, this manual has helped many in the legal profession understand and apply the various rules of writing. The easy-to-read chapters are broken down into multiple sections, including *Mechanics* (which includes the rules of punctuation), *Grammar, Usage, and Editing* (which includes grammar, wording, editing and proofreading), *Legal Documents* (which includes research memos, case briefs, legal letters, motions, and judicial opinions), and *Scholarly Writing* (which includes instruction on student research papers and law review articles). The book is written in what has been referred to as "Restatement Form," meaning that the black-letter rules are followed by multiple examples demonstrating the rules in action, similar to the format of the Restatements of Law which you learned in Chapter 3.

Now that you have learned the basic mechanics, complete the problems below to test your knowledge in these areas.

Chapter Checklist ✓

- Knowledge of the basic rules of grammar and punctuation are very important in the legal profession, as many people can and will be viewing your writing for different reasons.

- A verb is the "action" word in a sentence and a noun denotes the "subject/object" of the sentence. Every sentence should include at least one verb and one subject.

- It is important to remember that the verb and noun should be "in agreement" with each other—singular subject pairs with a singular verb, and plural subjects are paired with plural verbs.

- Before using a pronoun, make certain you have first identifed the person/object so that the reader understands your meaning.

- Adjectives modify/descibe nouns and typically ask *which, what,* or *how many.* Adverbs modify/describe verbs and typically ask *how, how often, when,* and *where.*

- Beware of the "split infinitive"—keep the infinitive verb (*to run*) undisturbed.

- Conjunctions connect or divide words and phrases. Remember that *so* and *because* are also conjunctions.

- A preposition joins a noun, pronoun, or phrase to another part of a sentence and is used to demonstrate "place" or "location."

- Remember that articles introduce a noun and can be used for specific or general reference.

- Know when to use the apostrophe as a singular or plural possessive.

- Compound words can be categorized as *closed, open,* and *hyphenated.*

- Commas are typically used to divide a series of items, whereas the semi-colon seperates two independent sentences.

- The colon is used between two sentences when the second sentence explains or illustrates something in the first sentence.

- Parentheses (used properly) are used to explain a minor point or thought within the sentence, as well as used at the end of a sentence to state the source of your legal authority, or to *first* introduce an abbreviation or acronym.

- Double quotation marks are placed at either end of a quote, and single quotation marks are place at either end of a quote *within* a quote.

- When quoting a *portion* of another's writing, be sure to use the ellipsis which denotes that the quote was taken out of its full context.

KEY TERMS

CRITICAL THINKING AND APPLICATION

Please read each sentence carefully. Choose the proper grammar and punctuation to complete the sentences below.

Choose the correct form of grammar

1. A good law firm should conduct background checks of (its / their) applicants.

2. None of the elevators (is / are) working today.

3. If Gordon (were / was) angry, he did not have to come to court to support the family.

4. The Petersons' names (was / were) included on the list.

5. The voluminous medical reports (were / was) summarized by Kate.

6. The firm's headquarters (are / is) located in Wilmington, Delaware.

7. The jurors names (were / was) included on the list.

8. The jury rendered (their / its) verdict yesterday morning.

9. Laura and (me / I) need you to return to the office.

10. In order to be considered for a clerkship, an attorney must demonstrate that (s/he / they) can perform quality legal research and writing.

11. Each of the jury rooms (is / was) empty.

12. Please give this paper to (whoever / whomever) you choose.

13. Sam is the one (who / whom) we believe will be acquitted.

14. (Who / Whom) is calling?

15. Everyone (was / were) seated in their assigned section in the courtroom.

Rewrite inserting the proper punctuation

16. The prosecutions witness was the last to testify today.

17. The witnesses statements were recorded.

18. The committees report was submitted for editing.

19. John Browns complaint was filed with the court yesterday.

20. Greg spilled coffee on his nine year old computer keyboard.

21. Henry was sent to the post office to mail information concerning marital property to his ex wifes attorney back in mid September.

22. The attorney was effective at cross examination, but not at direct examination.

23. The attorney forgot his paperwork transcripts laptop and his lunch.

24. The partner Harvey Keller was reprimanded by the executive board for not answering the questions posed by the member of the ethics committee.

25. Attorney Karl Fisher who recently wrote two briefs to the Supreme Court offered his advice to the young attorneys on brief writing.

26. The committee includes Paul Davis criminal expert Barbara Williams chief of the juvenile unit and Kenneth Samuels defense attorney.

27. The attorney had two goals take a deposition in the morning and attend a sentencing in the afternoon.

28. The witness stated I saw the defendant enter the yard I recognized his distinctive yellow sweatshirt he always wore outside.

29. The attorney informed the paralegal that she misspelled the word easement in her legal memorandum.

30. In 2013 355 cases were disposed of in civil court most of which were personal injury cases.

Determine if the following sentences are correct or incorrect in their grammar and punctuation.

31. The following sentence was taken directly from a portion of a trial brief with additional material before and after this sentence: " . . . [t]herefore, as the appellate court held in the *Johnson* case, a breach of contract exists when one party refuses to honor the exact terms of the agreement."

32. The client asked: "Is there any way we can just settle the case and not have to endure a long trial"?

33. In its opinion, the court specifically held that the term "conspiracy" was not the same as the term "accomplice" according to the law.

34. The witness stated: "The defendant grabbed me and threw me into the alley. He looked at me and growled, 'Give me your purse!"

35. On Friday, the paralegal had two assignments. Finish a deposition summary and type up a client interview.

36. The lawyer's academic record was impressive; it included a perfect grade point average, multiple honors, and an honorable mention in moot court.

37. The client; James Harris; had a reputation for filing frivolous lawsuits.

38. The attorney was attempting to be pro-active by circulating the inter-office memo before the partner's meeting on Thursday.

39. The witness was given three months' notice to secure the check.

40. All the witnesses' statements were recorded by the court reporter.

41. The judge's decisions will not be disturbed on appeal.

42. The defendant has an extensive criminal history (*i.e.* fraud, forgery, bribery, and theft of services).

43. He said; "Turn off the lights".

44. Neither the judge or the jury could hear the soft-spoken witness.

45. Cynthia was running late for a meeting with Cynthia's new client.

LEARNING OBJECTIVES

After completion of this chapter, you should be able to

1. Describe the various rules that develop and maintain clarity in your writing.

2. Explain how eliminating unnecessary words make your writing more concise and readable.

3. Utilize the rules to avoid slang, clichés, idioms, and euphemisms in your writing.

4. Demonstrate how to improve your spelling and how to properly use capitalization and numbers and figures in your writing.

5. Apply your knowledge of how to properly construct sentences and paragraphs for clear, understandable, and efficient writing.

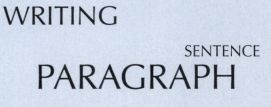

WRITING

SENTENCE

PARAGRAPH

CLARITY

The Rules for Effective Writing

In addition to proper grammar, punctuation, and spelling, there are additional rules that need to be mastered in order to ensure that your legal writing is understandable to the reader, which is crucial in the legal profession.

In this chapter, you will see how to maintain proper sentence and paragraph form by utilizing the important rules of clarity, brevity, and word usage.

■ BEING CLEAR

Although knowing the proper rules of grammar, punctuation, and spelling are important, there are other rules of basic writing that are equally important. Clarity, brevity, word usage, as well as proper sentence and paragraph structure are all necessary components to professional writing.

LEARNING OBJECTIVE 1
Describe the various rules that develop and maintain clarity in your writing.

The Noun/Verb Format

Words are the foundation of the legal profession. It is always best, especially in legal writing, to be clear in your writing. A large part of ensuring that you maintain clarity is through the use of **concrete verbs**. A concrete verb denotes a single, completed action.

concrete verb
A word that describes a single completed action.

I *went* to court.

I *drove* to the prison.

The client and attorney *discussed* the terms of the settlement.

Rather than,

There was a *discussion* between the client and the attorney concerning the terms of the settlement.

When maintaining clarity, you are always safe using the noun/verb format. For example, "The *bell rang*." "*He ran* from the police." "*They* ate together."

Being clear in your writing is important, as you never want your supervising attorney, a partner, the client, or another staff member guessing or speculating as to what you are saying with your words. A key piece of advice to remember is not to attempt to impress anyone by being creative, colorful, or unique in your writing. That is not to say you need to be boring, but clear action words get to the point more quickly and are more easily understood. Some other examples of action verbs include:

Say "Paid"	instead of . . .	" . . . in making a payment."
Say "Decided"	instead of . . .	" . . . made a decision."
Say "Bought"	instead of . . .	" . . . in making a purchase."

Active and Passive Voice

In that same vein, you also need to understand the difference between writing in active and passive voice, which relates in using concrete verbs. Basically speaking, **active voice** is used when the subject of the sentence is "doing the action" of the verb. Conversely, **passive voice** is used when the subject of the sentence is being "acted upon," and is not as strong and direct as active voice.

active voice
This is used when the subject of the sentence is performing the action.

passive voice
This is used when the subject of the sentence is being acted upon by the verb.

> **WEAK:** The settlement options were to be discussed by the parties.
>
> **BETTER:** The parties discussed possible settlement options.

Now, the first sentence above is grammatically acceptable. However, the second sentence is clear and gets directly to the point—the noun/verb format. Using active voice makes the sentence cleaner, and it is easier to comprehend. Some other examples include the following:

The [judge] *ruled* in favor of the defendant.

Instead of,

The case was ruled in favor of the defendant by the judge.

Or,

[Aaron] *testified* for the prosecution.

Rather than,

The testimony was given by Aaron.

However, you can use passive voice in your writing as well, as it is acceptable. For example, you use passive voice to make the action itself the focal point of the sentence and the person/object remains in the background.

For example,

The offer of 5–10 years imprisonment was rejected by the defendant. (*Here, the author is emphasizing the prison sentence itself and not the person who rejected it.*)

Furthermore, if the object/person of the sentence is assumed or known, then it could also be eliminated from the sentence if it is not needed. For example, if you were drafting a legal memorandum concerning a particular defendant, who is the object of the memo, you could write:

The offer of 5–10 years imprisonment was rejected. (*Here, it is assumed that the offer is referring to "the" defendant who rejected the offer, and not "a" defendant. The sentence is complete and yet clear.*)

Parallel Construction

Another important issue concerning clarity is the concept of **parallel construction**. The basic idea is that all parts of a sentence should be "parallel" to each other. This means that all words in a sentence should appear in the same tense, which makes the sentence streamlined and easier to read and comprehend.

parallel construction
This is obtained when all of the words within a sentence appear in the same tense.

> **CORRECT:**   Your duties as a paralegal will include the following: *interview* clients, *research* the law, and *write* legal memoranda.

Notice that each verb (*interview*, *research*, and *write*) is in parallel agreement with one another.

> **INCORRECT:**   Your duties as a paralegal will include the following: *interview* clients, *researching* the law, and *write* legal memoranda.

Notice that the action verbs are NOT in parallel agreement. Whatever tense you use for one verb, use for all the verbs in the sentence. For example, "John walk**ed** to the courthouse, sign**ed** into the visitor's log, and attend**ed** the meeting on the fifth floor.

Verb Tense

Speaking of verb tense, let us discuss that rule as well. Do you recall learning about verb tense in grammar school? Well, get ready for review because those rules still apply, so make sure you maintain consistency in your **verb tense**.

verb tense
The tense of a verb is determined by *when* the action took place in the sentence.

> **SIMPLE TENSE:**   These verbs do not use auxiliary verbs, which include *past tense* (I sit), *present tense* (I sat), and *future tense* (I will sit).

> **PERFECT TENSE:**   These verbs use **have**, **has**, or **had** as an auxiliary verb, which include *past tense* (I had sat), *present tense* (I have sat), and *future tense* (I will have sat).

> **PROGRESSIVE TENSE:**   These verbs use **is**, **are**, **was**, or **were** as an auxiliary verb, which include *past tense* (I was sitting), *present tense* (I am sitting), and *future tense* (I will be sitting).

Now that you know the basic rule, make certain that you maintain verb tense consistency throughout your sentences, as many writers make that mistake.

For example, "*During the jury's verdict, Rodger* **stood** *up and* **yells** *the verdict so loudly that he was* **reprimanded** *by the judge.*" This sentence is incorrect because the tense is inconsistent. The words "stood" and "reprimanded" denotes past tense, yet the word "yells" suggests present tense. Unfortunately, many people speak this way and it is transferred into their writing.

Just remember that when discussing a present event, use the present tense, and when discussing a past event, use a past tense, and so on. You need to know this rule not only for your own writing, but also for any editing you may perform on other's work, as you will need to recognize another's misuse of verb tense.

Consider the following portion of a legal memorandum:

> " . . . the client **had** a strange and unique experience as a teenager many years ago. While he **was** working on a scaffolding painting the side of a warehouse, a gusty wind wrapped around the building and shook the scaffolding so violently that the client **was** thrown to the ground and head his head on the concrete. He **survived** the incident, but **suffered** a moderate to severe brain injury as a result.

Notice that the excerpt was written in the *past* tense, which is proper as the author is recalling a past incident. However, there are times when you must alternate tenses, which is proper and permissible, in order to indicate *different* time periods.

> " . . . the client **had** a strange and unique experience as a teenager many years ago. He **was** sitting in my office and **told** me the strangest story. He **said**: "**I am** standing on a scaffold painting when a gust of wind knocked the scaffold and **I fell** fifteen feet straight down and hit my head on the concrete." **I remember** the look on his face in telling that story. He **survived** the incident, but **suffered** a moderate to severe brain injury as a result.

Notice in that example that someone is recalling the story from the individual who experienced the event. As the individual spoke, he was recalling the incident as it happened, thus the present tense was appropriate in this situation.

Vagueness

vagueness
This occurs when the words within a sentence are not clear enough to understand the intended meaning of the writer.

Another aspect of maintaining clarity includes avoiding **vagueness** in your writing especially legal writing. For example, consider the following sentence written by a paralegal in a memorandum concerning workers' compensation law.

> "On October 8, 2013, the claimant suffered an injury to his lower arm after using the machine on the factory floor, which was later determined to be defective."

If you were the attorney reading that sentence, what red flags go up immediately? What do you need answered specifically? In a case for workers' compensation, a few issues need to be addressed that are necessary for a claim. First, what type of arm injury? Was it an internal injury or a superficial laceration? Second, where was he injured on the lower arm? Was it as high as the elbow? Was it his forearm? Was it bone break or muscle pull? Third, what type of machine was the claimant injured on? How does it operate? Lastly, what is meant by defective? How?

As you can see, clarity and specificity are equally necessary in your writing. Now see how that same sentence can be written below providing the necessary information and maintaining clarity.

"On October 8, 2013, the claimant, employed as a printing press mechanic, sustained a second degree burn to his lower forearm after reaching his arm inside to inspect a complaint that the machine had overheated to 108 degrees that day. The claimant had performed numerous inspections and repairs on that same machine without incident in the past. However, it was later determined that the machine's temperature was running unusually hot due to a malfunction in the wiring system."

Remember that in the legal profession, the writing should be clear, brief yet informative, and understandable.

Nominalizations

Remember the purpose of a noun in a sentence; the noun is object of the sentence and the verb is the action. However, when writers turn a verb or adjective into a noun they have created a **nominalization**. Nominalization makes the sentence less concise, wordy, and difficult to understand. Drop the nominalization and use an action verb instead.

For example, you would not say, *"The commencement of the trial will be at 9am."* You are using the verb "commence" as a noun, but it is not the object/subject of the sentence. The "trial" is the subject of the sentence and action verb is "commence." Rather, you would say, *"The trial will commence at 9am."*

CORRECT:	"We expected the trial to be finished by Friday."
INCORRECT:	"Our expectation was that the trial would be finished by Friday."
CORRECT:	"The witness was calm despite facing her attacker in court."
INCORRECT:	"There was an overall calmness about the witness even though she was facing her attacker in court."

Again, it is not that these sentences are "technically" incorrect, as people do write and even speak this way. However, by using fewer "action" words, you would be surprised how much clearer your writing will be to those who will read it.

nominalizations
This occurs when the writer converts a verb or adjective into a noun which creates confusion and a lack of clarity within a sentence.

■ BEING CONCISE

Brevity and clarity go hand in hand with each other. By striving for clarity, you need to be brief, and vice versa. So, the logical place to begin when discussing brevity would be to learn how to omit all overused, unnecessary, redundant, dead-weight, empty words in your writing.

LEARNING OBJECTIVE 2
Explain how eliminating unnecessary words make your writing more concise and readable.

Word Choice

Since many legal documents can be quite long, **wordiness** occurs when you use two or three words when only one will make your point. Always drop or avoid useless words. One of the many mistakes writers make is beginning a sentence with "*I believe*," or "*I feel . . .*" The reader knows what you have written is what you have thought, pondered, or analyzed because you wrote it! If these are not your thoughts or ideas, then whose are they? The only time this may be acceptable

wordiness
This occurs when the writer inserts multiple words in a sentence to complete a thought when fewer words would establish the same thought.

is beginning a sentence with "*In my opinion . . .* " which denotes a more careful analysis of a situation by the author or an analysis by an expert.

Along those same lines, many people also overuse the phrase "**I just wanted to let you know** *that I really, really appreciated your speech today at the luncheon.*" Instead, try "*Dear Kate, I really appreciated your speech today – thanks!*"

Other needless "wordy" phrases include:

"Large in size . . . " –Just say (big)	"In the event that . . . " – Just say (if)
"Due to the fact that . . . " – Just say (because)	"At this point in time . . . " – Just say (now)

Many writers also use *too many words* to express what they are trying to say. Writing instructors across the country have expressed this concern when editing a student's work. Many writers feel that they need to emphasize their point and thus, they create unnecessary redundancy. For example, look at some examples of when writers use two words when only one is sufficient.

"previously wrote"	"end result"	"plan ahead"
"most unique"	"cooperate together"	"added bonus"
"absolutely certain"	"true and correct"	"completely finished"
"basic fundamentals"	"revert back"	"final completion"

These words do not emphasize your point any better; rather, they are merely redundant and unnecessary to clear writing.

■ WORD USAGE

LEARNING OBJECTIVE 3
Utilize the rules to avoid slang, clichés, idioms, and euphemisms in your writing.

In the middle of writing something, do you ever have to stop and think of just the right word, or ask someone, "What's another name for . . .?" In addition to the other rules included in this chapter, building a strong vocabulary is also an important skill to possess. Having a strong vocabulary will help you communicate effectively, help you to understand what you read, and prevent you from using the same words over and over again. Having a strong vocabulary also will improve your speaking skills so you can eliminate all the "uhs" and "ums" in your conversation.

However, building an impressive vocabulary is not achieved overnight. The best way to improve your vocabulary skills is to read, read again, then read some more. Read your favorite novels and informative magazines such as *Time* or *Newsweek* (not the supermarket tabloids) and complete the daily word puzzles in the local newspaper. You can also build your vocabulary easily by purchasing a thesaurus and utilizing it anytime you need to look up a word in a dictionary. Also, listen to when people speak. You may pick up on a few new words even in casual conversation. Then, use those same words with someone else you later engage in conversation. Those new words will eventually find their way into your writing.

In building your vocabulary, you have to make certain you are using the *correct* words as you write. Many **synonyms** (two or more words that have the same meaning) and **homonyms** (two or more words that are spelled and sound alike but have different meanings) cause confusion for writers. Please review the

synonyms
Two or more words that have the same meaning.

homonyms
Two or more words that are spelled and sound alike but have different meanings.

following chart in Figure 12-1 of frequently "misused" words by writers in their everyday writing.

To help even more, **www.myvocabulary.com** and **www.wordsmith.org** are some great online tools for building your vocabulary to impressive levels, complete with vocabulary builders and daily word puzzles. If you are pressed for time, you can also subscribe to many online sites to enroll in the "word-of-the-day" by e-mail.

Slang, Clichés, Idioms, and Euphemisms

Many of us have unfortunately abandoned the proper and correct word usage of the English language and instead have filled our vocabulary with slang, clichés, idioms, and euphemisms—all of which we are accustomed to but have no place in formal professional writing.

Unfortunately, we have become so immersed in using these slang words and terms so often (especially in e-mails and texts) that when we need to write a formal and professional piece of writing, we are all . . . well, at a loss for words.

Slang consists of arbitrarily changed words and phrases developed over time to produce some extravagant and colorful language.

slang
The inclusion of words and phrases that are regarded as very informal.

> "literally" (although a legitimate word in the English language, people today have abused it to the point that it has **literally** lost its intended meaning). Some other slang terms include,
>
> "freaked-out" "kudos" "grossed-out" "my bad" "newbie" "hater" "the third degree"

Figure 12-1 Commonly Misused Words

Accede – *to agree* (verb) Exceed – *to go beyond* (verb)	Any way – *possibility* (noun) Anyway – *any case* (adverb)	Farther – *distance* (adverb) Further – *quantity* (adverb)
Latter – *final, end* (adj) Later – *in a while* (adverb)	Capitol – *legislature* (noun) Capital – *money* (noun)	Foreword – *book intro* (noun) Forward – *direction* (adverb)
Access – *admission* (noun) Excess – *overflow* (adj)	Cite – *quote* (verb) Sight – *vision* (noun) Site – *specific place* (noun)	Good – *fine, ok* (adj) Well – *healthy* (adj) Well – *fine, ok* (adverb)
Advice – *suggestion* (noun) Advise – *suggestion* (verb)	Conscience – *own internal decision* (noun) Conscious – *awake* (adj)	Device – *object* (noun) Devise – *to bequeath* (verb)
Eminent – *prominent person* (adj) Imminent – *immediate* (adj)	Council – *official group* (noun) Counsel – *to advise* (verb)	It's – *contraction for "it is"* Its – *possessive pronoun*
All ready – *prepared* (adj) Already – *in the past* (adverb)	Imply – *mean* (verb) Infer – *assume* (verb)	Accept – *to receive* (verb) Except – *other than* (prep)
Use – *to consume* (verb) Use – *function* (noun)	Disinterested – *impartial* (adj) Uninterested – *no interest* (adj)	Liable – *accountable* (adj) Libel – *written defamation* (noun)
Among – *three or more* (prep) Between - *at least two* (prep)	Affect – *make happen* (verb) Effect – *end result* (noun)	Passed – *past part. "to pass"* Past – *previous time* (noun)
Precede – *lead* (verb) Proceed – *to continue* (verb)	Principle – *rule* (noun) Principal – *primary* (adj/noun)	Than – *comparison* (conjunction) Then – *next, after* (adverb)
Their – *possessive pronoun* There – *a place* (adverb) They're – *contraction for "they are"*	To – *toward* (preposition) Too – *also* (adverb)	Allude – *indirect hint* (verb) Elude – *to evade* (verb)
Formally – *official* (adverb) Formerly – *past* (adverb)	Appraise – *evaluate* (verb) Apprise – *explain* (verb)	Averse – *reluctant* (adj) Adverse – *unpleasant* (adj)

You may even be using slang without realizing it. Consider using *man* or *gentleman*, rather than *guy* or *dude*. Also, use the word *child* rather than *kid*. It is not difficult to adapt to these rules, and once you become familiar with them and use them often, they will become second nature to you.

A famous author once wrote: "Writing is a war against clichés." Many writers try their best to avoid **clichés** but it is difficult. Because we speak a certain way, that language is transferred into our writing. Hopefully, we are all lucky enough to realize that point when we are writing, which again causes us to pause and think, "What's another name for . . . ?" The following clichés, although used repeatedly in our speech, have no place in professional writing.

clichés
A phrase or metaphor that is characterized by its overuse.

"hit the nail on the head"	"been there, done that"	"sound like a broken record"
"think outside the box"	"short but sweet"	"last but not least"
"back against the wall"	"too close for comfort"	"a stone's throw away"
"right on the money"	"fall on deaf ears"	"it is what it is"

On the other hand, an **idiom** is a word or phrase that is considered informal English and includes many words that have a different meaning from their intended original meaning. Do you know the meanings of the following idioms?

idiom
An exaggerated word or phrase that cannot be taken literally.

"A loose cannon"	"high as a kite"
"Drive me up a wall"	"woke on the wrong side of the bed"
"Play your cards right"	"a chip on his shoulder"
"It's raining cats and dogs"	"works like a charm"
"I'm under the weather"	"hit the nail on the head"
"Hold your tongue"	"a piece of cake"

Lastly, a **euphemism** is a word or words used to replace a word or phrase that may be socially inappropriate to say, or for when the speaker/writer wants to avoid an unpleasant word or phrase.

euphemism
A mild or indirect word or expression substituted for one considered too harsh or unpleasant.

"Misspoke" – Rather than . . . (lie)

"Between jobs" – Rather than . . . (unemployed)

"Put to sleep" – Rather than . . . (euthanize)

"Correctional facility" – Rather than . . . (prison)

"On the street" – Rather than . . . (homeless)

"Passed away" – Rather than . . . (died)

Both idioms and euphemisms should also be avoided in professional legal writing.

Legalese/Legal Jargon

You will see in Chapter 13 and Chapter 14 how and when to use legal terminology properly when drafting a memorandum of law, and legal correspondence. You will be using many legal words/terms/phrases in your writing, but you should stay clear of using **legalese**. You will learn in those later chapters how to use legal terminology properly.

legalese
The use of formal or technical legal language that is too difficult to understand.

■ ADDITIONAL WRITING RULES

Below are some additional rules to utilize in your writing.

Capitalization

You may not think it is important, but in an age of texts and e-mails, we have virtually abandoned the use of capitalization.

LEARNING OBJECTIVE 4
Demonstrate how to improve your spelling and how to properly use capitalization and numbers and figures in your writing.

- First and foremost, the first word of a sentence is ALWAYS capitalized.
- The first word of a quote is also capitalized, even if the quote begins in the middle of the sentence. For example: *Peter stated, "The lunch break is over so I'm heading back to court."*
- Any title (*President, Judge, Doctor*), family name (*Joshua*), proper names (*Dad, Mom, Grandfather*) are capitalized.
- Any state, city, or county name (*New York, Paris, Niagara Falls*) and street names and directions (*Main Street, Northwest*) are always capitalized, as well as the name of any language (*English, Romanian, Irish*).
- The pronoun (*I*) is always capitalized—a rule we have completely abandoned in texting.
- Any days of the week, names of months, and holidays (*Monday, October, Christmas*) are capitalized. However, the four seasons are NOT capitalized unless found in a specific title (*A Lion in Winter*).
- Any membership of a national or political group or organization (*Greenpeace, Grand Old Party*) is capitalized.
- Similar to the first word of a quote, the first word of an independent phrase that follows a colon is capitalized. For example, *"The attorney met his clients for the first time: The two defendants were identified as Joe Brown and Sam Smith."*

Be sure to use proper capitalization when needed in your writing.

Spelling

More often than not, you hear many people claim that they are not good "spellers." We all began to spell at a young age when we began to read, but over the years many of us have become lazy spellers and have relied too much on various "spell-check" software. When we do have to write a handwritten note, letter or card, we panic because we have forgotten to spell many basic words, such as someone who asks you: *"Is there an "e" at the end of the word "proceed?"* In addition, many of us have become careless spellers. For example, suppose you wrote the following note in an email or Word document: *"The attorney will meet you at the courthouse at half past tow to discuss the case."* Even though you meant to write "half past two," the spell-check did not pick up that you incorrectly spelled the word "two." That sentence also passed the grammar check. Always take a moment and re-read and edit anything you write before sending it to anyone.

One way to sharpen your spelling skills is through the use of a dictionary. This helpful source can be used not only to help you learn the meaning of a particular word, but also to ensure the word is spelled correctly.

Figure 12-2 includes a list of the most commonly misspelled words. The list is unique in that although it includes many everyday words, many of these words are also used within the legal profession.

As you write, pick up on the words that are tagged *misspelled* (another commonly and ironically misspelled word) with your spell-check software and learn how to spell them correctly for future use. Further, make sure you read and edit anything you write. Lastly, if you know how to spell the 50 words in Figure 12-2, your spelling ability will improve greatly.

Numbers and Figures

You will undoubtedly use numbers and figures in your legal writing, so here are a few general rules.

- If you can write a number with one/two words, you should (*There were twelve jurors in the jury box*);
- If a number or figure requires more than two words, you can use digits instead (*The settlement check was written in the amount of* **$16,877.98**, *excluding the attorney's fees*);
- However, do not mix numbers and words in the same sentence or paragraph (*Of the* **12** *jurors, only* **three** *have come back from lunch early*);
- All fractions should be written out as words (*Only* **one-third** *of the prosecutor's cases resulted in convictions*);
- Do not begin a sentence with digits, but you can use them within the sentence (**2013** *was the year the judge was transferred to civil court*);
- When using a decimal point with percentages, place a zero before the decimal point to make it easier for the reader to see (*This year, the prosecutor's conviction rate increased by only* **0.8%** *last summer*);
- Always use digits when writing out a date (*The client is scheduled for a deposition on Tuesday, November* **19, 2013**);
- All addresses should also be written as digits (*The subpoena was sent to the witnesses' house at* **123** *Main Street*);
- In legal writing, it is always best to use words **and** digits concerning important numbers so that the meaning is clear (*The defendant received* **six (6)** *notices from the city to cease operation of his business on his property*).

Figure 12-2 Commonly Misspelled Words

Accommodate	Column	Guarantee	Mortgage	Precede
Acceptable	Concise	Harass	Maintenance	Proceed
Accidentally	Consensus	Hierarchy	Noticeable	Questionnaire
Acknowledgement	Conscience	Inadvertent	Occasion	Recommend
Argument	Conscientious	Incidentally	Occurrence	Referred
Bankruptcy	Deductible	Indispensible	Personnel	Relevant
Calendar	Definitely	Judgment	Perseverance	Separate
Category	Embarrass	Liaison	Possession	Suppress
Commitment	Exceed	Libel	Privilege	Supersede
Committee	Foreclosure	License	Prominent	Statute

■ SENTENCE CONSTRUCTION

Now that you have learned all the basic rules for grammar, punctuation, as well as the main rules for effective writing, you will now see how to properly utilize all those rules to construct your sentences.

Rule One: Use clear **declarative sentences**.

Each sentence you write should be lean and mean. At the very least, each and every sentence should include a verb and a noun and should be able to stand on its own as a complete thought. All sentences are either *simple* (noun/verb) or *compound* (noun/verb connected by a conjunction).

> The first prosecution witness was Mary Carroll. She appeared nervous but understood each question and responded in a loud clear voice. After nearly two hours on the stand, Mary was excused. The judge adjourned for the day.

Rule Two: Use a combination of both short and long sentences.

This method works best and keeps the reader engaged in your writing. No one wants to read long sentences, especially in a legal document, that drag on and on. Just remember that each short sentence must stand on its own as a complete thought.

> John's brother Peter contested the will. Although Peter had argued that John had unduly influenced their father to change the will, it could not be proven. No evidence existed.

Rule Three: No fragments or run-on sentences

Speaking of complete thoughts, a **sentence fragment** is a sentence lacking a subject, verb, or both, and is therefore an incomplete thought.

> After she was released of jury duty.
>
> When the trial ends next week.
>
> The deposition, lasting more than an hour.

As you can see, all of these sentences are incomplete thoughts. Do not leave the reader in suspense. Make each sentence complete.

On the other hand, a **run-on sentence** combines two or more complete thoughts, but is lacking a conjunction or mark of punctuation to divide them. For example:

> "My attorney prefers to argue his cases before Judge Kennedy she is very fair, honest, and conducts her trials with integrity."

The reader knows what the writer is saying, but there is no pause between these two separate thoughts. The writer is combining two thoughts into one, thus creating a run-on sentence. So what is the cure?

> *"My attorney prefers to argue his cases before Judge Kennedy; she is very fair, honest, and conducts her trials with integrity."* (semi-colon).
>
> *"My attorney prefers to argue his cases before Judge Kennedy, as she is very fair, honest, and conducts her trials with integrity."* (comma).

LEARNING OBJECTIVE 5
Apply you knowledge of how to properly construct sentences and paragraphs for clear, understandable, and efficient writing.

declarative sentences
A sentence that makes a statement or establishes a complete thought that ends with a period.

sentence fragment
A sentence that fails to create a complete thought due to the lack of a subject, verb, or both.

run-on sentence
A sentence in which two or more independent clauses (complete sentences) are joined without appropriate punctuation or conjunction.

> *"My attorney prefers to argue his cases before Judge Kennedy because she is very fair, honest, and conducts her trials with integrity."* (subordinate conjunction).
>
> *"My attorney prefers to argue his cases before Judge Kennedy. She is very fair, honest, and conducts her trials with integrity."* (separate sentences).
>
> *"My attorney prefers to argue his cases before Judge Kennedy - she is very fair, honest, and conducts her trials with integrity."* (dash).

Any of those examples will correct the problem. Just remember not to combine your sentences into a head-on collision!

Remember to utilize the rules of grammar, punctuation, and all the rules for effective writing in constructing your sentences. This skill is not only beneficial to you in your everyday writing, but also is beneficial in your legal writing.

■ PARAGRAPH CONSTRUCTION

When you combine multiple sentences that discuss a particular thought or idea, you have created a paragraph. Similar to sentence structure, paragraphs also have a certain structure in order to make the reading clear, concise, and understandable. A good paragraph consists of three important parts: the topic sentence, the body, and the closing sentence.

topic sentence
A sentence that introduces a new topic or thought at the beginning of a new paragraph.

Think of the **topic sentence** as the "preview" for what is to come within that particular paragraph. The topic sentence introduces the topic or idea that will be discussed in that paragraph. This sentence must be a clear and understandable thought. Not only does the topic sentence guide the reader, but it also is helpful in guiding you as the writer. A good topic sentence will prevent you from branching off, rambling, or combining too many issues, topics, or points into a single paragraph.

An appeal filed with an appellate court will not be reviewed if the matter is deemed moot by that court.

Suppose that was the topic sentence of a particular paragraph on page 4 of a 10-page brief. Just by reading that sentence alone, the reader knows that the paragraph that follows will explain (1) what type of cases would be deemed as moot (possible examples) and (2) why those cases are not heard by the appellate court.

Remember that the idea is to write an interesting "teaser" in which the reader will be intrigued and will want to read the entire paragraph. You do not want to give away all the information in the first sentence because there may be no need or interest in reading the entire paragraph you have written.

An appeal filed with an appellate court concerning a defendant whose has served his sentence and has been released from prison will not be reviewed, as the matter will have been deemed moot by that court.

As you can see from this example, the writer attempted to cram all the information of the paragraph into the topic sentence. That sentence is overburdened with information. Now the readers (lawyers, judges, or clients) may read that opening sentence and feel that they do not have to read the rest of the paragraph. The reader may miss an important detail or example that you have discussed further. A good topic sentence will show the reader that you are making a statement that expresses a certain topic or view, and that you will expand on that point and provide detail and examples concerning the information in that topic sentence.

The body of the paragraph includes the **supporting sentences** which support, describe, and explain the information in the topic sentence. It is important to note that the second sentence and every subsequent sentence in the paragraph that follows the topic sentence *must* directly support the first sentence. Do not introduce a new topic or idea—stay focused.

supporting sentence
A sentence that supports, describes, and explains, in detail, the main thought or idea of the topic sentence.

> The crime of conspiracy includes multiple elements, which must all be satisfied in order the prosecution to secure a conviction. First, there must be an agreement between two or more persons. It is important to note that if one of the persons is an undercover police officer, the crime cannot be completed. Further, the agreement must be to commit a crime. Second, one of the parties who entered into the agreement must commit an over act in furtherance of the conspiracy. An overt act is defined as . . .

In this example, the topic sentence states a particular topic. In order for a person to be convicted of the crime of conspiracy, certain elements must be satisfied. The reader knows that the paragraphs that follow will include those details. Also in this example, the use of a **transitional sentence** is important to bridge the ideas together smoothly and in an orderly fashion. In particular, when discussing elements to a crime, or elements to any law, the best transitional sentences begin with: *First, ... Second, ..., Third, ..., and so on.* The reader knows that each new sentence is introducing a new idea. Other good transitional sentences begin with: *In addition, . . . Further, . . .* or *Therefore, . . .*

transitional sentence
A sentence that alerts the reader that the writer is changing to a new thought or idea in a smooth and coherent way.

Just remember to stay focused on your particular idea or topic within that paragraph. However, you may asking, "If I am drafting a in-depth legal memorandum where each issue may be several pages long, how do I know when to end the paragraph and begin a new one?" Good question. Just remember the rules above and put them together. One paragraph should be as long as it takes to explain the details of the information in the topic sentence. When you are ready to begin a new thought or idea, then you can begin a new paragraph. However, the typical rule is no more than five to seven sentences in a single paragraph—just be certain you have discussed and developed your idea/point in the topic sentence.

> The crime of conspiracy includes multiple elements, which must all be satisfied in order for the prosecution to secure a conviction. First, there must be an agreement between two or more persons. It is important to note that if one of the persons is an undercover police officer, the crime cannot be completed. Further, the agreement must be to commit a crime. Second, one of the parties who entered into the agreement must commit an over act in furtherance of the conspiracy. An overt act is defined as any act performed by any member of the conspiracy that furthers the conspiracy. For example, if three bank robbers agree to commit a bank robbery, and one of the men steals a car to be used for the get-away, then he has committed an overt act in furtherance of the crime. Therefore, once those elements are satisfied, the crime of conspiracy is complete.
>
> In this case, the defendant has committed the crime of conspiracy. On July 17, 2012, the defendant called his co-defendant on the phone to meet at the local diner. There, the two men discussed stealing a valuable painting on loan at the city museum. After discussing the plan, the defendant called his brother, who works at the museum, and told him to copy the floor plans of the museum. After the brother was apprehended trying to access the blueprints, all three men were properly charged with conspiracy and attempted robbery.

Keep the paragraphs tight if you can. Long paragraphs wear a reader down. The idea is to hold the readers' interest, not bore them.

closing sentence
A sentence that is the last in a paragraph that restates the main idea of that paragraph.

Therefore, be certain that you "signal" when you ending one paragraph by using a proper **closing sentence**, which neatly ends the thought, point, or idea of the original topic sentence. You cannot just end a paragraph because it is too long if you are in the middle of a thought. In that case, you would have an uneven break or disruption in the flow of the material. The closing sentence wraps up the idea or topic of that paragraph. Notice the two closing sentences of the two paragraphs in the example above. Both sentences end the idea or thought included in the paragraph.

Now that you know the basic rules of sentence and paragraph construction, you will see these rules again in Chapter 13 when you learn how to draft a legal memorandum. You will learn the specific key words to include in your topic sentences, as well as when to specifically break your paragraphs. For now, you have a good start in understanding the basics of writing, which can be applied to any type of writing.

As a final thought, whatever type of writing you create—whether in a law office or even in another course at school—get into the habit of outlining your thoughts and ideas *before* putting pen to paper or fingers to the keyboard. ***Always organize your ideas before you write***. You will be surprised how clear, logical, and easy it will be to write your sentences and paragraphs after you first gather and organize the material.

Chapter Checklist ✔️

- It is important to use clear and direct language in your writing. Remember the the noun/verb format and always use concrete verbs, which denote a single direct completed action.

- Along those same lines, get into the habit of using active, rather than passive voice, in your writing. Remember, especially in legal writing, active voice is best because the subject of the sentence is "doing the action" of the verb which is more clear and direct.

- Make sure that all of your verbs within a sentence are "parallel" with one another, and maintain consistency in your verb tense.

- However, remember that you can alternate tenses when you are writing about different time frames, for example, if someone speaking in the present tense is discussing an event that happened in the past, which would require past tense of those verbs.

- Clarity, especially in legal writing, is crucial. Avoid vagueness at all costs. After you have read something you have written, make sure that the reader would have no questions as to what you have written, and that everything is clear and understandable.

- Being concise in your writing goes hand-in-hand with clarity. Avoid using useless and empty phrases such as, *I believe, . . . I feel that, . . . I just wanted to say or let you know . . .* Just say what you mean and get to the point. Stay away also from "wordy" phrases that use two to four words when one will suffice; for example, rather than writing *Due to the fact that . . .* Just say *because*.

- Avoid redundancy in your word usage as it impairs clear and concise writing.

- Know the different homonyms in Figure 12-2—that is important.

- Although you may feel tempted, especially in writing e-mails, stay clear of slang, cliches, idioms, and euphemisms.

- Know the rules of capitalization and the use of numbers/figures.

- Do not rely on your computer's "spell-check" feature—learn how to spell correctly, as a spell checker will not alert you to homonyms (two words that are spelled and sound alike but have different meanings, such as *sight* and *site,* or properly spelled but misplaced words, such as a *beach of contract.)*

- Review the rules of proper sentence construction—avoid fragments and run-ons.

- Know how to construct a quality paragraph, and know the purpose of a topic sentence, the paragraph body, and the closing sentence.

KEY TERMS

CRITICAL THINKING AND APPLICATION

Please read each sentence carefully and follow the directions below.

Wordiness: The following sentences are very cumbersome and wordy. Rewrite each sentence by tightening the language – for example:

Take the sentence: *"Julia was paid by ABC Company every two weeks."*

And rewrite it as: *"ABC Company paid Julia bi-weekly."*

1. In the situation where a paralegal is well trained, that particular paralegal can be asked by an attorney to perform legal research for the purpose of determining a response to the client's question.

2. The judge had made a decision stating that the various settlement options were to be discussed by the parties.

3. In considering whether or not Jason is considered an employee of ABC Hospital, we believe that he will most likely have to submit employment verification to his attorney.

4. Jefferson was presented with a citation by the police for speeding, and at the same time he was also cited for running a red light.

5. I truly and honestly believe that if the witness, who took the stand under oath and provided testimony, was telling the truth, he would not have been continually and nervously wiping his brow.

6. At this point in time, in the event that testimony will be provided by Aaron, court will need to be adjourned now for lunch, as Aaron's testimony will prove to be quite lengthy.

7. The attorney previously wrote the client that they would need to plan ahead and cooperate together and review the basic fundamentals in preparing for trial.

8. There was a very calm and overall peacefulness and tranquility about the witness even though for the fact she was facing her attacker in court.

9. I just wanted to let you know and to make you aware that it was my great expectation that the trial would be completely finished by Friday.

10. On the date in question, January 31, 2012, John Morris, informed the police that he did indeed witness the crash with his own eyes. John told the police that the driver of the red car quickly and hurriedly traversed through the red light at a very high rate of speed, and that the driver of the blue car had the absolute right of way and was sideswiped by the red car, which resulted in the crash.

Choose the correct word usage:

11. The overall consensus (between / among) the twelve jurors was that the defendant was guilty.

12. There are just (to / too) many people in this room.

13. The judge stated: "Your attorney will (apprise / appraise) the situation to you."

14. If the witness is ready she may (proceed / precede) with her testimony.

15. Some may (infer / imply) by her stance that she is quite upset with him.

16. After the operation his (cite / site / sight) had not improved. Therefore, he testified that he had only visited the construction (cite / site / sight) on one occasion. However, he was able to (cite / site / sight) the proper building code regulation at issue in the case.

17. In the (past / passed) the attorney would only conduct a client interview over the phone.

18. This courtroom is much smaller (than / then) our previous room.

19. The new law clerk has really (exceeded / acceded) my expectations.

20. The will was clear in that Laura intended to (device / devise) her entire estate to charity.

21. (Between / Among) he and I, we prosecuted over fifty cases this year.

22. The (principle / principal) rule is that complaints must be filed within two years from the date of injury.

23. The witness stated: "I ran over to him to ask what happened but he was not (conscience / conscious)."

24. One who physically and intentionally invades another's property is (liable / libel) for trespass.

25. I hope the judge is feeling ok because he does not look (good / well) to me.

Spell each word in bold correctly (without spellcheck):

26. After checking his **calander**, the attorney agreed to meet next week.

27. An **arguement** ensued between the families of the victim and defendant.

28. The **comittee** is set to meet next Monday.

29. The defendant was arrested for driving without a **lisence**.

30. The defendant was told not to **harrass** the victim anymore on her way to work.

31. The motion to **supress** was denied by the court.

32. The co-defendants argued for **seperate** trials.

33. The attorney informed his client that there was no **guarante** he would receive a life sentence.

34. The prosecutor asked the defense attorney if the offer was **aceptable** to his client.

35. Write your name in left-hand **collumn**.

36. This room can only **acommodate** fifty people at one time.

37. The man testified that he was part of the **maintanence** crew.

38. The plaintiff told the judge that his attorney was **reffered** to him last week.

39. My attorney has **exceded** my expectations.

40. I hate that judge because he likes to **embarras** the attorneys during trial.

41. The client was told to bring all the **personel** records for the employees.

42. **Judgement** was granted in favor of the plaintiff.

Proper Sentence and Paragraph Construction:

43. The main components of legal research include, forming the issue, determining the search method, citation, and validation. Describe and explain each of those components of legal research. Be certain to use proper paragraph structure, as well as topic, supporting, transitional, and closing sentences.

44. Please research and locate the crimes of theft, robbery, and burglary in your jurisdiction. Explain what each crime is, and the differences between them. Be certain to proper paragraph structure, as well as topic, supporting, transitional, and closing sentences.

LEARNING OBJECTIVES

After completion of this chapter, you should be able to

1. Explain what a research memorandum is as well as its purpose and use in the legal profession.

2. Identify the components of a research memorandum and apply the proper format when drafting a memorandum.

3. Understand the proper use citation within a research memorandum.

4. Explain the importance of using a research memorandum as a writing sample for prospective employers and how to prepare one for submission.

MEMORANDUM

STRUCTURE
COMPONENTS

OBJECTIVE

The Research Memorandum | CHAPTER 13

Now that you have learned all the foundational concepts concerning legal research, as well as how to find the law, read it, and analyze it, you are now ready to prepare and communicate those findings in a written document called the legal memorandum. It is important to learn how to properly draft a memo for employment in the legal field. The legal memorandum is also an excellent writing sample to present to any prospective employer, as it demonstrates your cumulative legal research and writing abilities.

■ WHAT IS A RESEARCH MEMORANDUM?

A **research memorandum** (also referred to as a *legal memorandum, internal memorandum, or interoffice memorandum*) is a written document in which the researcher provides the legal findings that govern a particular situation or answer a specific legal question or issue. The memorandum can also inform your supervising attorney how to initiate or defend a lawsuit. It can further provide the information needed for any motions that will arise prior, during, or after trial.

Objective Writing

The memo is a form of **objective writing**, meaning that the memo is written to answer the issue by providing both the positive *and* negative aspects of the question or issue. The memo is not a form of persuasive writing. By writing the memo objectively, your supervising attorney can be made aware of the strengths *and* weaknesses of the case prior to taking any action. This may save time and money later on during litigation.

During your research, if you find any authority that is *adverse* to the client's interests you must tell your supervising attorney. Again, you need to inform your attorney of all authority found, good or bad, so that he or she is properly equipped to handle the case. Do not hold back any information, as attorneys by nature do not like surprises, and withholding negative findings could be detrimental to the case. In addition, stay focused on answering the issue at hand. No matter how passionate you are about a particular case, avoid inserting your own personal opinions into the memo. Keep the contents to the findings of law. Only by following these rules can the attorney make truly informed decisions and determine the best course of action in representing the client.

LEARNING OBJECTIVE 1
Explain what a research memorandum is as well as its purpose and use in the legal profession.

research memorandum
A written document in which the researcher provides the legal findings that address and resolve a specific legal question or issue.

objective writing
Writing that is unbiased and presents both the strengths and weaknesses of an issue.

Purpose and Use

The research memo has many purposes in the law office. First and foremost, the memo answers the legal question/issue. As you are now aware, locating and reading numerous primary and secondary sources of law can become quite overwhelming. The process of drafting the legal memo "filters out" the unnecessary legal findings and provides a clear and concise rule of law in order to answer the issue or specific question presented. Rather than explaining your findings from memory or from your notes, the memo allows you to organize your research in an understandable and readable format. A well-drafted memo saves your supervising attorney time to pursue other avenues in the case.

The research memo can also be used to decide whether or not to pursue a client's case. Following the initial client interview, your supervising attorney may ask you to look up the elements for a particular cause of action, or review the statutory and case law concerning a particular criminal or civil action. In addition, the memo can also address and resolve an issue during trial before filing or defending a motion, or to assist in determining the correct legal strategy prior to filing a trial or appellate brief. So as you can see, the legal memo serves multiple purposes in assisting your supervising attorney and client.

Audience

Although the research memo is a communicative document between an attorney and his or her researcher, there may be occasions when multiple attorneys, partners, and support staff at the firm or office are working on the same case. Therefore, the memo must be written clearly and concisely so that any member of the legal team can read and understand the findings. In drafting a legal memo, your writing should be professional, clear, and concise with a formal tone. Remember to always use plain English and avoid ambiguous language. Also, making small adjustments like using the word "children" rather than "kids," or "man" rather than "guy" makes a difference in maintaining a professional tone.

It is also possible that the memo will be sent to the client in the form of an opinion letter, which you will learn in the next chapter. The opinion letter is a formal letter written by your attorney to the client explaining the current situation of the case. Instead of attaching your legal memo, which the client may not understand, your attorney may ask you to summarize the results of the research, but omit any legal terminology. Thereafter, the attorney could include your summary of the law into the opinion letter.

For example, you perform research for a client's sale of her property. The contract states, . . . *an implied covenant of a lessor as to delivery of possession means that there shall be, at the time the lessee's right to possession attaches, no legal impediment to the lessee's taking possession . . . "* What?! The clause could be summarized to simply state that the party selling the property must be free of any existing liens or mortgages on the property prior to sale.

Prior to drafting a legal memorandum, remember the key summary points found in Figure 13-1.

■ FORMAT AND COMPONENTS

Similar to case briefing, the legal memo follows a particular format. Before you draft the memorandum, you should have four items in your possession: (1) the facts of the case; (2) your completed research; (3) a citation manual; and, if necessary, (4) a legal writing manual.

Figure 13-1 Important Aspects of the Research Memorandum

Objectives	Uses	Audience
To find authority and provide supportive **and** possible adverse research in your legal findings.	To decide whether or not to pursue a client's case.	The supervising attorney who assigned the research assignment.
To maintain objectivity, and to **not** argue a specific or persuasive point of view.	To answer/solve a particular legal question or issue prior to, during, or after trial (appeal).	Any attorney, partner, or staff member also working on the case or on a different case with a similar legal issue.
To provide only the rule of law that addresses the issue and to **avoid** inserting any personal opinions.	To help the attorney to develop a legal strategy in deciding how to argue/ defend the case.	The client, who wants/needs updates on the progress of the case.

Components of a Memorandum

Unlike a document that is filed with the court, the memo is an "internal" document, so there is no required format. However, it is a good idea to request a copy of a memo from your law office, as it can provide a useful template for your own work.

The following is a standard format used by many legal professionals. Please see the sample memorandum in Appendix A for an additional example with variations on the format.

LEARNING OBJECTIVE 2
Identify the components of a research memorandum and apply the proper format when drafting a memorandum.

Heading

The **heading** of the memo includes many pertinent details. As you can see in Figure 13-2, at first glance, the document needs to identify the *recipient*, the *researcher*, the *date*, and the *subject matter* of the memo.

Note that when filling in the "Re" line, you list both party names and at least the purported cause of action. The subject line is just that—one line, but it should at least be informative so that any member of the law office who reads or glances over the memo will know what the document is addressing. It is also helpful to insert the case file number that the firm uses to identify each case.

heading
The portion of the memorandum that includes the name of the recipient of the memo, the name of the author of the memo, the date when the memo was complete, the subject heading, and the file number, if applicable.

Question/Issue Presented

The **question/issue presented** is very important, as it is the reason you are drafting the memo. The issue will always be presented as a question that needs to be answered, similar to determining the issue while briefing a case. Sometimes you will be given a direct question to research and other times you will have to conduct your research prior to formulating the issue, again, similar to when you learned how to brief a case. Read the following fact pattern to see how a basic legal memo is constructed.

You are a paralegal working in a large litigation firm in Philadelphia, Pennsylvania. The firm represents Dorothy Harrison (*Patient* – age 78) who recently

question/issue presented
The portion of the memorandum that includes the issue or legal question that was addressed and answered.

Figure 13-2 Memorandum—The Heading

Memorandum

To: Jackson Palmer, Supervising Attorney
From: Carrie Jenkins, Paralegal
Date: March 22, 20_ _
Re: Patient vs. Doctor (medical malpractice) Our File # 123-456-7

underwent cataract surgery at a local hospital on December 15, 2011. Dr. Jason Williams (*Doctor* – age 49) and his surgical team successfully performed the procedure. Doctor examined Patient after the operation and told her that the eye looked "very healthy," and gave Patient medication for her eyes to be used twice a day and told her to return to the hospital in five (5) days for an evaluation. Doctor left Philadelphia to attend a medical conference in Atlanta. Five (5) days later, he met Patient for her post-op appointment. Patient complained of soreness in her right eye and blurred vision. Doctor was running behind in his schedule and told Patient the soreness was normal and sent her home. Patient was unable to resume her duties as a volunteer librarian. A few days later, Patient still experienced pain and continued blurred vision in her right eye, and she made another appointment. Patient's daughter, Julie brought her to the hospital where Doctor discovered a major infection in the eye. Due to the intensity of the infection, as well as her age, Patient has permanently lost vision in her right eye. It was determined that Patient took her medication as prescribed, and that it is standard medical procedure that a surgeon must schedule a post-op appointment within forty-eight (48) hours of any surgical procedure. Your firm must determine whether to bring suit against Doctor.

Your supervising attorney has to decide whether to take Patient's case and represent her in a civil suit against Doctor. After a brief discussion of the facts, your supervising attorney wants you to perform research to determine if a case exists.

Issues are sometimes presented in the form of an actual question such as:

GOOD: *Can Doctor be held liable to Patient after failing to properly diagnose and treat her eye?*

BETTER: Other attorneys prefer the method used by judges in their court opinions stating an indirect question, such as: *The issue is **whether** Doctor is liable to Patient after failing to properly diagnose and treat her eye?*

BEST: However, an informative and detailed issue is the best issue, such as: *Whether Doctor is liable to Patient after failing to schedule a required post-op evaluation of her infected eye, in which she eventually lost her vision?*

You would **not** simply state, "*Is Doctor negligent?*" Also, do not include any legal terms, such as *negligence*, or *medical malpractice*, as you do not want to jump to any "legal conclusions." As you can see in Figure 13-3, try to frame the issue in a *neutral* manner as to not "lean" toward a particular answer, such as *Is Doctor liable after failing to properly treat an elderly patient who suffered a very painful eye infection and eventually lost her vision in that same eye?*

Addressing Multiple Issues. Although you are learning the basic format of a memorandum concerning a single issue, there may be instances where **multiple** issues need to be analyzed and discussed. If you recall, you were first introduced to the possibility of resolving multiple issues in the Comprehensive Case Study. There is no need to draft multiple memos addressing each issue—all issues can be addressed in the same memo as long as you number them and maintain consistency in your format.

For example, change the facts **only to demonstrate this point** and consider the following: As the condition of her eye began to worsen, Patient did not take the eye medication that was prescribed to her by Doctor. Now you have two potential issues to address.

Figure 13-3 Memorandum—The Issue/Question Presented

Memorandum

To: Jackson Palmer, Supervising Attorney
From: Carrie Jenkins, Paralegal
Date: March 22, 20 _ _
Re: Patient vs. Doctor (medical malpractice)
        Our File # 123-456-7

Question/Issue Presented:
Whether Doctor is liable to Patient after failing to schedule a required post-op evaluation of her infected eye, in which she eventually lost her vision.

Your "issue" section may now look like this:

1. Whether Doctor is liable to Patient after failing to schedule a required post-op evaluation of her infected eye, in which she eventually lost her vision; and
2. Whether Patient contributed to the loss of vision in her eye after failing to take her prescribed eye medication.

Therefore, you would also number the remaining sections of the memo to correspond to the numbered issues to provide the reader with an understandable and clear format. Your supervising attorneys will tell you how they want the issues broken down for ease of analysis. If not, as you research the law, you will be able to tell which issues need to be addressed.

Brief Answer

The **brief answer** is just that—an answer to the question/issue presented. Because you provide a full analysis on the issue or topic you are researching, the answer must be *brief*; however, it should never be a "yes" or "no" answer. Your attorney may not have time at first to read the memo. Therefore, a well-crafted issue and answer will suffice until the memo can be read fully. The brief answer should actually answer the issue and not just "mimic" the issue. For example, *Doctor is liable under a theory of medical malpractice for failing to schedule Patient's post-op evaluation, resulting in loss of vision in her eye.* By only removing the "whether," you are left with the equivalent of a "yes" or "no" answer. The answer does not give any indication "why" Doctor is liable.

However, a proper "brief answer" could be stated as, *Doctor is likely liable under a theory of **medical malpractice**, as he **breached** his **duty of care** to Patient by not scheduling the required timely post-op evaluation, resulting in failure to diagnose and treat her eye infection.* Since the brief answer will be drafted *after* you have researched and analyzed the issue, you can now include "legal terms" such as *medical malpractice, breach,* and *duty of care.* As you can see in Figure 13-4, it answers the issue but also requires the reader to read further in the analysis.

Statement of Facts

Other than the information required in the *heading*, the **statement of facts** can immediately be completed as soon as you receive the assignment. Again, similar to a case brief, the facts consist of the "storyline" of the case. The facts include

brief answer
The portion of the memorandum that includes the answer to the issue/legal question presented.

statement of facts
The portion of the memorandum that includes the "storyline" in order to place the legal issue in proper context for the reader.

Figure 13-4 Memorandum – The Brief Answer

Memorandum

To: Jackson Palmer, Supervising Attorney
From: Carrie Jenkins, Paralegal
Date: March 22, 20 _ _
Re: Patient vs. Doctor (medical malpractice) Our File # 123-456-7

_____

Question (Issue) Presented:
Whether Doctor is liable to Patient after failing to schedule a required post-op evaluation of her infected eye, in which she eventually lost her vision.

Brief Answer:
Doctor is likely liable under a theory of medical malpractice, as he breached his duty of care to Patient by not scheduling the required timely post-op evaluation, resulting in failure to diagnose and treat her eye infection.

---

the *what, where,* and *when* of the events that give rise to the issue to be resolved. As you can see in Figure 13-5, the facts section is also helpful for anyone who is not familiar with the case to understand the context of the issue.

If you recall from Part One of the Comprehensive Case Study, the facts are either given to the paralegal by the supervising attorney after the client interview, or obtained by the paralegal themselves following an initial meeting and interview. Either way, the notes of the meeting will be in "shorthand" or "bulleted" form so you would have to reorganize and assemble the facts in proper grammar and sentence structure. Again, similar to the brief answer, the facts should be delivered objectively and not biased in any way. The facts section should be brief yet thorough.

It is good to practice your writing skills by reorganizing and rewriting the facts. Follow these three main components to effective paragraph writing when drafting the facts, or any writing.

- First, when beginning any new paragraph, always **indent** and begin with a *topic sentence* that introduces the subject material of the paragraph.
- Second, the **body** of the paragraph expands on the topic sentence and explains the material introduced by the topic sentence.
- Last, the ***conclusion*** sentence summarizes the main idea of the paragraph.

Legally Significant Facts

In reviewing the facts of the case, you only want to utilize the facts that possess any "legal significance" to the case. Not all facts are important to the issues at hand. You should also be familiar with legally significant facts from the Comprehensive Case Study and case briefing.

As you can see in Figure 13-5, some of the facts in the hypothetical were omitted from the original fact pattern given to you. The reason for this is that the memorandum should only contain the **legally significant facts** of the case. This means only the facts that have a direct impact on the case should be used, and all unnecessary facts can be "filtered out."

legally significant facts
The facts of the case that allow the researcher to specifically target and address the legal issue presented.

Figure 13-5 Memorandum—The Statement of Facts

Memorandum

To: Jackson Palmer, Supervising Attorney
From: Carrie Jenkins, Paralegal
Date: March 22, 20 _ _
Re: Patient vs. Doctor (medical malpractice) Our File # 123-456-7

_____

Question (Issue) Presented:
Whether Doctor is liable to Patient after failing to schedule a required post-op evaluation of her infected eye, in which she eventually lost her vision.

Brief Answer:
Doctor is likely liable under a theory of medical malpractice, as he breached his duty of care to Patient by not scheduling the required timely post-op evaluation, resulting in failure to diagnose and treat her eye infection.

Statement of Facts:
Patient (78) underwent cataract surgery on December 15, 20_ _. Doctor and his surgical team successfully performed the procedure and examined Patient after the operation and told her that the eye looked "very healthy," and gave her medication for her eyes to be used twice a day and told her to return to the hospital in five (5) days for an evaluation. Five (5) days later, he met Patient for her post-op appointment. Patient complained of soreness in her right eye and blurred vision. Doctor was running behind in his schedule and told Patient it was normal and sent her home. A few days later, Patient still experienced pain and continued blurred vision in her right eye, and when she made another appointment at the hospital, Doctor discovered a major infection in the eye. Due to the intensity of the infection, as well as her age, Patient has permanently lost vision in her right eye. It was determined that Patient took her medication as prescribed, and that it is standard medical procedure that a surgeon must schedule a post-op appointment within forty-eight (48) hours of any surgical procedure.

For example, this is the original set of facts you received: The firm represents Patient (78) who recently underwent cataract surgery at a local hospital on December 15, 2011. Doctor and his surgical team successfully performed the procedure. Doctor examined Patient after the operation and told her that the eye looked "very healthy," and gave Patient medication for her eyes to be used twice a day and told her to return to the hospital in five (5) days for an evaluation. Doctor left Philadelphia **to attend a medical conference in Atlanta.** Five (5) days later, he met Patient for her post-op appointment. **Patient arrived late for her appointment due to traffic, but Doctor did examine her that day.** Patient complained of soreness in her right eye and blurred vision. Doctor was running behind in his schedule and told Patient it was normal and sent her home. Patient was unable to return to work **as a volunteer librarian.** A few days later, Patient still experienced pain and continued blurred vision in her right eye, and she made another appointment. **Patient's daughter, Julie brought her to the hospital** where Doctor discovered a major infection in the eye. Due to the intensity of the infection, as well as her age, Patient has permanently lost vision in her right eye. It was determined that Patient took her medication as prescribed, and that it is standard medical procedure that a surgeon must schedule a post-op appointment within forty-eight (48) hours of any surgical procedure.

PRACTICE TIP

It is good practice to always notate from where in the file you take certain facts and information, as a litigation case file can be massive with pages of documents, transcripts, depositions, reports, and so on. This is so you can quickly and easily locate those same facts and information later if necessary for yourself or your supervising attorney.

The words or phrases in **bold** are *omitted* from the facts in the memo because they serve no purpose to the issue at hand, which is the doctor's negligence. It is not important or relevant "where" Doctor attended a conference; rather, it is important that he wasn't at the hospital to evaluate Patient. In addition, it is not relevant to know that Patient volunteers at the local library, as it would not have any impact on her case. It does not matter that she was late for her appointment, only that the doctor examined her. Lastly, it is also irrelevant who brought Patient to the hospital, only what happened there.

Let's review a different hypothetical in order to understand this "legal facts" concept. Suppose Mike, a potential client, comes to your office wanting to bring a *negligence* suit against a home improvement store. In a negligence claim, the plaintiff must prove that the defendant (store) had a duty to keep the plaintiff (Mike) safe on the premises; the defendant breached that duty by directly causing the plaintiff to become injured; and the plaintiff did suffer physical injury. Two weeks ago, Mike drove to the store to purchase lumber for a deck he and his brother were building in Mike's backyard. After purchasing the necessary nails, paint, and sealant, Mike walked to the lumber section to hand pick the lumber for the deck. As Mike and his brother were pulling lumber from the metal shelves, which customers were permitted to do, Mike slipped on sawdust on the floor, spraining his ankle. The employees of the store were required to maintain a clean floor for its customers, especially in the lumber area.

Can you distinguish the unnecessary facts from the legally significant facts?

As you can see in Figure 13-6, it is irrelevant as to what Mike was purchasing at the store for a claim of negligence. It was the duty of the employees to keep the floor free of debris, which was breached when they failed to keep the floor clean. Therefore, the fact that Mike slipped on the floor due to fact it was *not* cleared of debris *is* relevant. Remember to only include the facts that have legal significance to your analysis. If you know the cause of action you are researching, it is not difficult to determine the important facts. It is also good to review the facts section in the case law you find to determine the important or legally relevant facts.

Analysis/Discussion

analysis/discussion
The portion of the memorandum that applies the facts of the case to the researched authority in order to resolve the legal issue.

IRAC
The step-by-step outline of how the analysis section is constructed within the memorandum.

The **analysis/discussion** is the most important section of the memorandum. This is where your legal issue/question is analyzed. This section can only be written after you have gathered the relevant facts and the law.

The analysis/discussion section of the memorandum typically follows what is referred to as the **IRAC** format. IRAC is an acronym that stands for the following: *Issue*, *Rule*, *Analysis*, and *Conclusion*. As illustrated in Figure 13-7, you use the IRAC method to form the "framework" for your analysis section of the memo. IRAC helps you write the best possible analysis section, and most importantly, keeps your thoughts and arguments organized.

Figure 13-6 Unnecessary Facts vs. Legally Significant Facts

Unnecessary Facts	Legally Significant Facts
Mike was at the store to purchase lumber to build a deck with his brother.	Mike slipped on sawdust, injuring his ankle, while pulling lumber, a task customers were permitted to do.
At the store, Mike purchased nails, paint, and sealant.	Employees at the store were to maintain a clean floor, especially in the lumber area.

Figure 13-7 The Components of IRAC

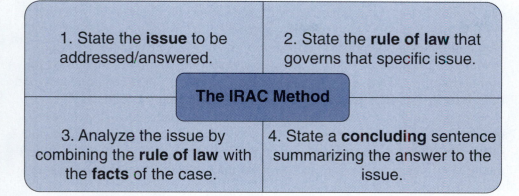

The process of legal analysis occurs when you combine the facts with the law—the two necessary ingredients. The analysis or discussion section "explains" the most current state of the law and how the law relates to the facts of the case in order to answer the legal issue. All authority, including cases, statutes, and rules will be inserted in this section in order to analyze the issue(s).

The legal memorandum is an *internal* legal document (not filed with the court). Therefore, you may utilize *secondary* sources if needed, but just remember to cite those sources appropriately so the attorney knows the difference.

In the analysis/discussion section, it is best to "summarize" the law. **Do not just copy or cut and paste entire statutes or cases directly into the memorandum**. Your attorney could copy a statute or case without you. You are being trained to read, understand, digest, and summarize information, which is a great and invaluable skill. Summarizing the information helps to train you to read and understand your legal findings, and it helps your supervising attorney to not have to read through a 5-page statute or a 20-page case opinion.

Ok, so going back to the medical malpractice example included in this chapter, suppose you found the law you need concerning medical malpractice liability.

Medical Malpractice - Professional malpractice is comprised of the same elements as negligence, including, (1) the defendant owes a particular duty to the plaintiff to act according to the law; (2) the defendant breached that duty of care by doing something not according to the law; (3) the defendant's actions directly or indirectly caused the negligent act;, and (4) the plaintiff suffered actual harm or injury. In professional medical malpractice claims, the breach of duty is established when the physician deviates from the standard medical practices in his or her field (*please note that this may not be the law for medical malpractice in all jurisdictions; however, a uniform provision may be similar in many states*).

Now that you know the law, follow the formula and **apply the law to the facts of the case**. You are striving to satisfy ALL the elements to successfully sustain a cause of action. In this example, we know that Patient did suffer physical injury so the fourth element is satisfied. Also, we know that the duty owed by Doctor is not only to treat the patient, but also to follow all the required medical standards and guidelines following surgery. According to the law, it would appear Doctor may be liable, as he breached his duty of care when he instructed Patient to return to the hospital three days beyond the required standard of a necessary post-op, 48 hours following surgery. This deviation likely contributed to Patient developing an eye infection, which ultimately resulted in loss of vision in that eye. If the doctor would have met with her sooner, he likely would have seen the infection and could have treated it. It could also be argued that Doctor could have instructed another doctor to evaluate Patient while he was out of town.

Use the authority to analyze the issue and support your point of view. If you do find anything adverse to the client's interest, figure out a way to overcome that setback. This may reveal new issues. If so, analyze them as well.

Remember, if you were researching and analyzing multiple issues, you would **number** each issue and analyze each issue separately. For instance, suppose your supervising attorney was informed that Patient never took her prescribed eye medication prescribed by the doctor. This may reduce Patient's damages and would need to be addressed separately.

In Figure 13-8, notice the words/terms in **bold** that begin each paragraph in the analysis section in the memo. If you use those words/phrases to begin each section of IRAC, it will keep you on track with your analysis, and anyone reading the memo will understand it clearly.

Remember to not merely state a conclusion, but *analyze* the problem. This can be a difficult concept, but with practice, you will be able to work through a legal problem slowly in order to arrive at your answer. For instance, you would not state that "the defendant is not liable according to the law." While that statement is technically true, it does not "show the work" necessary to see *how* you arrived at your answer. Remember in elementary school, when your third-grade math teacher would not give you credit for your answer unless you showed your work? Well, she was right. The same concept applies here. Just remember the IRAC method prior to drafting the analysis/discussion section. A quick outline will suffice. For example, here is another IRAC analyzing a criminal issue.

ISSUE - Whether the defendant can be convicted of assault, and to what degree, after punching the victim in the face, causing a black eye.

RULE OF LAW - *Simple Assault* occurs when the defendant causes "bodily injury" to the victim; whereas *Aggravated Assault* occurs when the defendant causes "serious bodily injury," by the use of a deadly weapon, or causing permanent physical injury.

ANALYSIS - The defendant punched the victim in the face, which only resulted in a black eye. This type of injury would most likely not cause permanent physical injury, nor was a deadly weapon used in the attack.

CONCLUSION - The defendant most likely will not be convicted of aggravated assault. He will, at most, be convicted of the lesser charge of simple assault for his actions.

Overall Conclusion

conclusion
The portion of the memorandum that summarizes the overall findings of the memorandum.

At the end of the memorandum, you close out the findings by inserting an overall **conclusion** (optional), which need not be long. Although they are similar, a conclusion is different from a brief answer. As you can see in Figure 13-9, the brief answer directly answers the particular corresponding issue, whereas the conclusion is usually longer and includes concluding language in accordance with the memo as a whole—not one particular issue.

Figure 13-8 The Analysis/Discussion

Memorandum

To: Jackson Palmer, Supervising Attorney
From: Carrie Jenkins, Paralegal
Date: March 22, 20 _ _
Re: Patient vs. Doctor (medical malpractice)
          Our File # 123-456-7

Question (Issue) Presented:
Whether Doctor is liable to Patient after failing to schedule a required post-op evaluation of her infected eye, in which she eventually lost her vision.

Brief Answer:
Doctor is likely liable under a theory of medical malpractice, as he breached his duty of care to Patient by not scheduling the required timely post-op evaluation, resulting in failure to diagnose and treat her eye infection.

Statement of Facts:
Patient (78) underwent cataract surgery on December 15, 20 _ _. Doctor successfully performed the procedure and examined Patient after the operation and told her that the eye looked "very healthy," and gave her medication for her eyes to be used twice a day and told her to return to the hospital in five (5) days for an eva [You do not actually write out the letters I.R.A.C. in the analysis. This is done here to demonstrate the IRAC format used in the memo.] ient for her post-op appointment. Patient complained of soreness ir [...] or was running behind in his schedule and told Patient it was normal [...] Patient still experienced pain and continued blurred vision in her rigl [...] ppointment at the hospital, Doctor discovered a major infection in the eye. Due to the intensity of the infection, as well as her age, Patient has permanently lost vision in her right eye. It was determined that Patient to [...] that it is standard medical procedure that a surgeon must schedule a [TIP: use the highlighted phrases to help guide you to create the proper IRAC structure and format each time you write the analysis section of a memo.] t (48) hours of any surgical procedure.

Analysis/Discussion:
(I)The issue is whether Doctor is liable under a theory of medical malpractice after failing to schedule Patient's required post-op evaluation, resulting in the development of an infection causing loss of vision in her eye.
(R)The rule of law in (*insert your state here*) states that a cause of action for medical malpractice is similar in nature to a claim of negligence, which requires that (1) a duty of care owed to the plaintiff, (2) a breach of that duty, (3) the defendant's actions directly or indirectly caused the injury, and (4) the plaintiff suffered physical harm/injury.
(A)Here, (In this case,) it would appear Doctor may be liable, as he breached his duty of care when he instructed Patient to return to the hospital three days beyond the required standard of a necessary post-op forty-eight hours following surgery. This deviation more than likely contributed to Patient developing an eye infection which ultimately resulted in loss of vision in that eye.
(C)Therefore, it is likely that Doctor could be held liable for malpractice after failing to schedule Patient's required post-op evaluation, resulting in the development of an infection causing loss of vision in her eye.

Figure 13-9 Memorandum—The Conclusion

Memorandum

To: Jackson Palmer, Supervising Attorney
From: Carrie Jenkins, Paralegal
Date: March 22, 20 _ _
Re: Patient vs. Doctor (medical malpractice) Our File # 123-456-7

_____

Question (Issue) Presented:
Whether Doctor is liable to Patient after failing to schedule a required post-op evaluation of her infected eye, in which she eventually lost her vision.

Brief Answer:
Doctor is likely liable under a theory of medical malpractice, as he breached his duty of care to Patient by not scheduling the required timely post-op evaluation, resulting in failure to diagnose and treat her eye infection.

Statement of Facts:
Patient (78) underwent cataract surgery on December 15, 20 _ _. Doctor successfully performed the procedure and examined Patient after the operation and told her that the eye looked "very healthy," and gave her medication for her eyes to be used twice a day and told her to return to the hospital in five (5) days for an evaluation. Five (5) days later, he met Patient for her post-op appointment. Patient complained of soreness in her right eye and blurred vision. Doctor was running behind in his schedule and told Patient it was normal and sent her home. A few days later, Patient still experienced pain and continued blurred vision in her right eye, and when she made another appointment at the hospital, Doctor discovered a major infection in the eye. Due to the intensity of the infection, as well as her age, Patient has permanently lost vision in her right eye. It was determined that Patient took her medication as prescribed, and that it is standard medical procedure that a surgeon must schedule a post-op appointment within forty-eight (48) hours of any surgical procedure.

Analysis/Discussion:
The issue is whether Doctor is liable under a theory of medical malpractice after failing to schedule Patient's required post-op evaluation, resulting in the development of an infection causing loss of vision in her eye.

The rule of law in (**your state**) states that a cause of action for medical malpractice is similar in nature to a claim of negligence, which requires that (1) a duty of care owed to the plaintiff, (2) a breach of that duty, (3) the defendant's actions directly or indirectly caused the injury, and (4) the plaintiff suffered physical harm/injury.

Here, (In this case,) it would appear Doctor may be liable, as he breached his duty of care when he instructed Patient to return to the hospital three days beyond the required standard of a necessary post-op forty-eight hours following surgery. This deviation more than likely contributed to Patient developing an eye infection which ultimately resulted in loss of vision in that eye.

Therefore, it is likely that Doctor could be held liable for malpractice after failing to schedule Patient's required post-op evaluation, resulting in the development of an infection causing loss of vision in her eye.

Conclusion (optional):
Therefore, it is likely that Doctor's deviation from the required standard of care resulted or at least contributed to Patient's injury.

PRACTICE TIP

After drafting a legal memorandum, it is best to ask your supervising attorneys if they want you to copy/print/attach any authority used in the event they want or need to review it themselves.

■ USE OF CITATION

Another important detail of writing a quality legal memorandum is including the proper citation for all authority used in the analysis portion of the memo. Remember that using proper citation not only allows the reader to know that the law you assert is relevant authority from **trustworthy sources**, but also is from the **proper jurisdiction** as well.

Figure 13-10 Inserting Case Citation Into the Memorandum

Analysis/Discussion:

The issue is whether Doctor is liable under a theory of medical malpractice after failing to schedule Patient's required post-op evaluation, resulting in the development of an infection causing loss of vision in her eye.

The rule of law in (*your state*) states that a cause of action for medical malpractice is similar in nature to a claim of negligence, which requires that (1) a duty of care owed to the plaintiff, (2) a breach of that duty, (3) the defendant's actions directly or indirectly caused the injury, and (4) the plaintiff suffered physical harm/injury. **Smith v. Regent Hospital, 123 A.2d 456 (Pa. 2009)**. In professional medical malpractice claims, the breach of duty is established when the physician deviates from the standard medical practices in his or her field. **Grossman v. Parkview Medical Center, 123 A.2d 456 (Pa. 2008)**.

Here, (In this case,) it would appear Doctor may be liable, as he breached his duty of care when he instructed Patient to return to the hospital three days beyond the required standard of a necessary post-op forty-eight hours following surgery. This deviation more than likely contributed to Patient developing an eye infection which ultimately resulted in loss of vision in that eye.

Therefore, it is likely that Doctor could be held liable for malpractice after failing to schedule Patient's required post-op evaluation, resulting in the development of an infection causing loss of vision in her eye.

For the majority of the memorandums you draft, you will likely utilize case law and statutes as your authority. In writing the "rule" portion of IRAC, when you state a rule of law, it requires a citation. However, never begin a new paragraph or sentence with a citation.

For instance, in Figure 13-10, notice the insertion of the necessary citation in **bold**. Anytime you assert a rule of law, you cite that authority, which is referred to as a **citation sentence**.

citation sentence
A sentence that stands on its own citing to a particular source of law, beginning with a capital letter and ending with a period.

Using Citation Within a Memorandum

The following list includes the 10 formats commonly used for inserting the proper citation when drafting a legal memorandum. Let's use a simple concept. Suppose you were drafting a memorandum concerning the law of "first degree murder" in Pennsylvania.

LEARNING OBJECTIVE 3
Understand the proper use citation within a research memorandum.

1. Remember the number one rule: You use a citation sentence anytime you assert a rule of law:

> First degree murder is a killing by premeditation. ***Commonwealth v. Jones,* 123 A.2d 456 (Pa. 2000).**

This lets the reader know you cited the law from actual legal authority.

2. To strengthen your argument, you can use multiple cases as sources of authority:

> First degree murder is a killing by premeditation. ***Commonwealth v. Jones,* 123 A.2d 456 (Pa. 2000), and *Commonwealth v. Matthews,* 987 A.2d 654 (Pa. 2000).**

See Practitioner's Note 4 in *Bluebook*. Only **underscoring** and *italics* is permitted with use in legal memoranda; however, **bold** is also widely used to highlight case law. You want the authority used to "stand out" on the page.

3. To further strengthen your argument, you can use statutory and case law as sources of authority:

> First degree murder is a killing by premeditation. *18 Pa.C.S. §2502; Commonwealth v. Jones, 123 A.2d 456 (Pa. 2000).*

Notice in this example, always place statutes before case law. (Always arrange sources according to the "hierarchy" of authority—constitutions, statutes, regulations, case law).

4. If you refer to the same rule of law *immediately* after you provide the full citation, you do not have to provide the full citation a second time:

> First degree murder is a killing by premeditation. *Id at 457.*

See Rule 4.1 in the *Bluebook*. You must use (*Id.*) with the page number of the case or portion of the statute you are citing *if* different from the first citation.

5. If you refer to the same rule of law *subsequently* in the memo after you provide the full citation, you do not have to provide the full citation multiple times:

> First degree murder is a killing by premeditation. *See Jones, Supra.*

See Practitioner's Note 4 in *Bluebook*, which does not permit the use of "supra" concerning cases and statutes. However, it is widely used by attorneys and judges in the legal field.

6. If you *cite* a case within a case, it must have a proper citation, meaning if you are reading/briefing a case and the appellate court cited a case within its opinion, you must cite both cases:

> First degree murder is a killing by premeditation. *Commonwealth v. Jones, 123 A.2d 456 (Pa. 2000), citing Commonwealth v. Matthews, 987 A.2d 654 (Pa. 2000).*

This citation is used to allow the reader to know that the *Jones* case cited law from the *Matthews* case.

7. If you *quote* a case within a case, it must be properly cited:

> First degree murder is a killing by premeditation. *Commonwealth v. Jones, 123 A.2d 456 (Pa. 2000), quoting Commonwealth v. Matthews, 98 A.2d 54 (Pa. 2000).*

8. You can use "*See*" if the cited authority contains the same idea but uses different wording—it is good to use an *abstract* (brief explanation of the case in parenthesis) to allow the reader to see *how* the case you are citing is relevant:

> First degree murder is a killing by premeditation. ***See, Commonwealth v. Jones,* 123 A.2d 456 (Pa. 2000) (conviction affirmed when defendant, following a fistfight with the victim, walked two blocks to his home, loaded a gun, returned to the scene and fired at the victim, killing him, thus satisfying premeditation).**

9. You use the phrase "*See also*" if the source contains "related" information that supports your claim:

> First degree murder is a killing by premeditation. ***Commonwealth v. Jones,* 123 A.2d 456 (Pa. 2000), *See also Commonwealth v. Matthews,* 987 A.2d 654 (Pa. 2000) (conviction for first degree murder affirmed after defendant formed intent to kill minutes prior killing the victim, thus establishing the necessary premeditation).**

10. Finally, you can use "*but see*" the same way, but only when you introduce authority that **contradicts** the previous cited authority:

> First degree murder is a killing by premeditation. ***Commonwealth v. Jones,* 123 A.2d 456 (Pa. 2000) (Premeditation can be formed in an instant),** *but* see ***Commonwealth v. Matthews,* 987 A.2d 654 (Pa. 2000) (conviction for first degree murder reversed after defendant punched the victim one time during a street fight, killing him instantly).**

Let's use another example, using proper citation of statutory law and case law concerning a criminal issue in Figure 13-11. Notice the use of many of the rules you just learned.

Also, remember what you learned about *pinpoint citations* if you need to insert them into the analysis. If the case you are citing is particularly long, you can insert a pinpoint cite so that the reader can go immediately to that particular point in the case.

Figure 13-11 Using Case and Statute Citation Together

Analysis/Discussion:
The issue is whether the defendant is guilty of first degree murder after approaching the victim as he sat in his car, and fired three shots, then fleeing the scene.

In (state), first degree murder is defined as a premeditated, intentional killing. *bf 12 A.B.C. §1234; see also, Commonwealth v. Henderson,* 123 A.2d 456 (1998).

Here, the defendant approached the victim's car with a loaded gun, raised it and fired three shots, killing him. Premeditation can be formed in an instant. *Commonwealth v. Lewis,* 123 A.2d 456 (2009). Premeditation does not equal prolonged planning. *Id.* Further, the victim was shot in the chest, which also raises the inference of an intentional killing. *See, Commonwealth v. Jones,* 123 A.2d 456 (2006) (conviction for first degree murder affirmed after defendant shot victim twice in the chest, a vital part of the body). Lastly, the defendant fled the scene, which also can be used as evidence in a first degree murder case. *See, Lewis, supra.*

When you are citing authority, it is better to summarize the rule of law in the case, or to summarize the statutes. Use of quotes is permitted, but should be reserved for the most important quotes. Do not fill the analysis section with only quoted cases and statutes with no analysis or thought.

Like anything else, citation will become easier the more you do it. It is always good to get into the practice of using citation **whenever** you assert any point of law. Anyone reading the memo will know your authority is trustworthy, and once you cite any law, you will not have to return to the source at a later date to retrieve it. Always remember that when inserting citation into the memorandum, you have multiple citation sources to reference in print and online. If you ever have any questions or doubt on how to cite any authority, refer to this textbook your *Bluebook* or *ALWD* guide, as well as Cornell University' online citation guide.

You have learned a lot of material throughout this text, and hopefully, it was presented in a very simple and understandable format. Legal research is a complex subject; however, you have been provided all the basic tools you need to succeed in researching any legal topic or issue. You are not expected to know everything about legal research. Many in the legal field, as in any profession, are continually learning. However, you should now know *where* to look to find the legal research you need quickly and efficiently.

Learn to develop your own style and research in whatever way is most comfortable for you. You have learned an invaluable skill that you will exercise and practice each day in the legal field.

■ THE MEMORANDUM AS A WRITING SAMPLE

Submitting a good writing sample alone will not get you the best paralegal position available, but a poorly written, unedited, and unorganized writing sample may prevent you from getting the best paralegal position available. In drafting the legal memorandum for the textbook case study, you will be presenting a professional memorandum to a future employer that will highlight your research and writing ability and will make you stand out from the competition.

Preparing the Memorandum

Draft a complete, clear, and concise memo of three to five pages, ideally. A prospective employer can usually determine the quality of your work after a few pages. You want the writing sample to highlight your writing and research abilities and nothing else. You do not want to submit a sample that discusses a difficult or complex area of the law. Remember, it is a potential employer you are attempting to impress, not the United States Supreme Court.

Be prepared to edit and rewrite multiple times, and ask your legal research and writing professor for help if needed. The key to a good writing sample is a quality document that presents a clear analysis and answer to a legal issue. Do not be discouraged because the writing sample is not a product of the "real world." It is good that the samples provided are fictional and are not written for actual clients, as those samples would tend to include confidential or complex information and analysis. They would also need to be edited extensively or redacted, which would take away from the overall content and quality of the memorandum. Also, the writing sample should have been written recently, as one's legal research and writing skills progress over time.

PRACTICE TIP

Remember that the firm or law office you work in will have numerous examples of legal memorandums on file. Review the memos written for the supervising attorneys you work for to see exactly how they want the memos written, as well as to see examples of the IRAC method and use of citation. It would be wise to make some copies and review them.

LEARNING OBJECTIVE 4

Explain the importance of using a research memorandum as a writing sample for prospective employers and how to prepare one for submission.

When to Submit

When sending a resume and cover letter, almost everyone sends a writing sample, especially for a legal position. If your resume and grades are good then only send those items. Send your writing sample if and when the potential employer asks for it. Another good reason to hold onto the writing sample is that if you are called in for an interview, you can present the sample during the interview and not walk in empty handed. This way, you have the full attention of the interviewer and he or she can scan the memo briefly in front of you. This is also to your benefit because if the interviewer has any questions about the memo or its topic, this can generate good conversation during the interview.

Another suggestion might be to wait a day or two after sending the resume and grades, and if you do not receive a call, then send the writing sample separately, whether it was requested or not. This is good practice because once you send an entire packet (resume, cover letter, grades, writing sample) all at once, that information can be overwhelming, especially if it includes information not requested. Your packet could end up in the discarded pile. By sending the writing sample a day or two later, it allows the potential employer to see your name again and your interest in the position. If you do send the writing sample separately remember to put your name on it, as so many students forget. Lastly, do not send the memo in any type of binding or folder. It will not impress anyone; rather it makes you look unprofessional and makes it cumbersome for the potential employer to read—you are not submitting a high school paper. Most, if not all, employers today ask that you send your resume, cover letter, and writing sample by e-mail. However, if you do send it "snail mail," use a single staple in the upper left-hand corner of the memorandum and send it unfolded in an 8 ½ by 11-inch yellow manila envelope.

Chapter Checklist ✔

- Prior to engaging in writing your legal memorandum, make certain you have all the authority you need to answer the issue(s).
- Make certain you have "summarized" the rule of law from all your authoritative sources.
- Remember that the memo is to be written in an "objective" format, and do not insert any personal opinions or bias.
- Offer both sides of the argument. Show the weaknesses as well the strengths of the arguments.
- Whether you are writing the memo to your supervising attorney or summarizing the law for an opinion letter, keep your audience in mind.
- Prior to actually writing the memorandum, have the facts of the case, your completed and summarized research, and a citation reference.
- You can "fill in" the heading, the issue/question presented, and facts, prior to even analyzing the issue.
- If you are addressing multiple issues, be sure to number them within the memorandum.
- Only utilize the "legally significant facts" in the memorandum.
- Make certain you outline your analysis prior to drafting the memorandum—this will save you time.
- Analyze the issue(s) using the IRAC method to ensure clarity and conciseness in your writing.
- Do not merely "cut and paste" law from your authoritative sources into the memorandum; summarize the law and use quotes, but sparingly.
- Most importantly, make certain you have **answered the issue presented to you**!
- As always, if you encounter any difficulty or problems, talk with your supervising attorney for guidance or assistance.

KEY TERMS

CRITICAL THINKING AND APPLICATION

Please read the hypothetical problems below. Apply the concepts you learned in this chapter. Perform the necessary research and draft a short memorandum for each. Some of the questions only have a single issue, so do not concentrate on the length of the memo, but rather concentrate on getting the format and content correct.

1. Read the following fact pattern of this hypothetical concerning civil law. Using the format you have learned in this chapter, draft a legal memorandum. Use the law of *your state* to analyze and answer the issue that follows. Concerning your heading, address the memo to "supervising attorney" and the case file is #44555-21.

Fact Pattern

Peter Hiller (age 47) has been working for ABC Construction Company as a driver for five (5) years. He originally worked as a construction worker, but a leg injury forced him into driving a truck. Peter drives back and forth in his 2001 flatbed truck to various construction sites operated by ABC workers and picks up and/or drops off lumber, metal, or any large quantities of building supplies and/or material used by the workers during construction.

Last week, Peter picked up a large load of rotted lumber extracted from the deck of an old restaurant that was being rebuilt by the river. Peter and some of the construction workers loaded the truck to capacity, which included many large pieces of lumber, and tied down the exposed lumber with heavy rope. Tom, a driver himself, told Peter to be careful since the load was "piled up high" and included many "loose pieces of wood." Tom suggested that Peter make two trips, but Peter said his truck could handle it. Thereafter, Peter and some of the workers stopped and had lunch. Peter checked the load twice to ensure that no lumber

was movable or could fall from the truck, and drove off to the dumping site, approximately eight (8) miles away.

As Peter was traveling along interstate, he hit a few unusually deep potholes in the road which caused the truck to shift its load a few times. Peter heard the lumber shift and thought to pull over, but the load looked secure in the rearview mirror, and he didn't want to be late to the dumping ground.

Sarah Filmont (age 29) was also driving along the same interstate in her 2012 Chevy Cruze. She was behind Peter when one of the pieces of lumber slid underneath the rope and fell off the truck onto the hood of Sarah's car. Sarah swerved to the right, just missing another car, and drove onto the shoulder hitting the guardrail. Peter heard the crash and stopped the truck a few hundred feet in front of the accident. Emergency crews arrived on the scene and transported Sarah to the hospital, where she sustained several lacerations, a fractured arm, and broken collarbone.

It was determined that highway and transportation regulations state that any vehicle carrying loads on a flatbed must be chained and secured to the truck. It was also determined that Peter was traveling 53 mph at the time of the accident, and the speed limit was 55 mph.

Issue

a. Is Peter liable to Sarah under a theory of **negligence**?

2. Read the following fact pattern of this hypothetical concerning criminal law. Using the format you have learned in this chapter, draft a legal memorandum. Use the law of *your state* to analyze and answer the issues that follow. Concerning your heading, address the memo to "supervising attorney" and the case file is #44555-21.

Facts

Defendant (age 32) was a drug user and was desperate to get money to support his addiction. Defendant entered a bar, and recognized Neighbor sitting on a stool drinking beer. Defendant approached Neighbor and asked him if he had any money he could lend him, to which Neighbor replied, "Get lost! You still owe me money!" Defendant and Neighbor began to argue, and the owner told Defendant to get out.

Defendant got in his car, and drove away. Around 2 a.m., Defendant's car broke down, and he was left stranded, exhausted, and had no money for a bus. It was cold outside and his only intent was to find a location to sleep unnoticed for a few hours until morning. Defendant found a house with no lights on and no car in the driveway. He walked around the back of the house, and found the garage unlocked. He went in and fell asleep in the corner. The next morning, Defendant awoke to Homeowner opening the garage to get to her car.

Upon seeing Defendant, she screamed and tried to run. Defendant grabbed Homeowner by the arm and forced her back into the house and down to the basement. Defendant bound Homeowner's hands, feet, and mouth, pushed her in the closet and locked it. Defendant ran back up the stairs, where he saw a new Rolex watch on the table and put it in his pocket. Defendant ran out the door and hitched a ride back to his neighborhood.

Before entering his apartment, Defendant knocked on Friend's front door and asked if he wanted to buy a new watch. Defendant removed the Rolex from his pocket and while handing it to Friend said, "Here, fifty bucks." Friend handed Defendant fifty dollars and closed the door. Upon close examination, Friend saw that the inside of the watch was engraved "*Best of Luck in Retirement.*" Friend knew that Defendant never worked a day in his life. He closed the door, shrugged his shoulders and put the watch on his wrist.

It took three days, but the police eventually arrested Defendant at his apartment. Homeowner was eventually discovered in the closet by a neighbor six (6) hours after the incident. Homeowner passed out due to not taking her insulin shot, and struck her head on the floor. Once freed, she was immediately given her insulin and received multiple stitches at a local hospital. She was expected to make a full recovery.

Issues

   a. Can Defendant be convicted of **kidnapping** of Homeowner?

   b. Can Friend be convicted of **receiving stolen property** of the watch?

   c. Can Defendant be convicted of **burglary** for initially entering Homeowner's residence?

3. Read the following fact pattern of this hypothetical concerning civil law. Using the format you have learned in this chapter, draft a legal memorandum. Use the law of *your state* to analyze and answer the issues that follow. Concerning your heading, address the memo to "supervising attorney" and the case file is #6671-33-00.

Facts

Nathan Hudson (age 23) was a young and talented baseball pitcher who played ball in the minor leagues and was being scouted by some professional teams. Nathan always dreamed of becoming a star pitcher, but he knew that his less than perfect vision may prevent him from playing at a pro-level, as he was required to wear protective prescription "sports glasses" while on the mound. The glasses would at times steam up and could prove to be uncomfortable to wear during games in high humidity and summer heat. The pro scouts looked beyond the glasses and saw a young man with unequaled skill and talent. However, Nathan wanted to impress the scouts and correct his vision and improve his chances of playing on a professional level.

During the offseason, Nathan met with Dr. Jules Levine regarding corrective eye surgery. Dr. Levine explained the entire procedure to Nathan, including the procedure itself, the possible effects following the procedure, and post-operative steps to be taken by Nathan. However, it is a medical requirement that *anyone* considering corrective eye surgery must undergo a series of pre-screening tests to determine if the patient is a candidate for the procedure, as many patients do not qualify for the surgery. Dr. Levine did conduct a few basic tests, but failed to conduct the required testing to determine if Nathan possessed any pre-existing conditions that could affect the corrective eye procedure. Dr. Levine assumed that due to Nathan's age, his conditioning as a professional athlete, and the selective pre-operative tests performed, he was a perfectly healthy candidate for the surgery.

Dr. Levine performed the procedure with success, and informed Nathan of his post-op instructions.

Nathan followed the doctor's orders, but three days after the procedure, the vision in his right eye appeared worse than prior to surgery. After performing some tests, it was determined that Nathan had recently developed a degenerative corneal condition in his right eye; a condition that would have been discovered by conducting the proper pre-screening testing.

The surgery has now worsened the condition in Nathan's right eye and he will not be able to pitch again anytime in the near future. He will undergo testing and undergo treatment for the degenerative condition of the cornea, and has stopped playing baseball.

Nathan has come to speak with your supervising attorney concerning a possible lawsuit. The surgery performed by Dr. Levine was a success. However, Nathan sustained an injury that threatens, if not ends his chance at a professional baseball career.

Issue

a. Can Dr. Levine be held liable under a theory of **medical malpractice** for Nathan's injury? If so, how?

4. Read the following fact pattern of this hypothetical concerning criminal law. Using the format you have learned in this chapter, draft a legal memorandum. Use the law of *your state* to analyze and answer the issues that follow. Concerning your heading, address the memo to "supervising attorney" and the case file is #CP-332-11-2013.

Facts

John Brown was attending a fundraiser at a hotel in the city, which he helped to organize. He was in the hotel manager's office as the manager placed a large amount of cash into the hotel safe. John pretended to look away, but watched and memorized the combination the manager used to open the safe. Later that evening, John saw Mrs. Gloria Fontaine, a very wealthy socialite, and introduced himself. John noticed the expensive diamond-studded necklace she wore, which was worth $5,000. John was invited to her table, and they talked and had dinner during the event.

After the fundraiser, John went home to get the tools he needed to return to the hotel to break into the safe. John arrived at the back door of the hotel around midnight with a crowbar. Just before John was about to touch the lock on the door, he heard someone inside. He immediately dropped the crowbar and went around front to the entrance of the hotel. At the front desk, he lied to the concierge and said that he lost his wallet at the fundraiser. He displayed his ticket from the event and asked to go to the banquet room to search for the wallet. Seeing that John had the proper credentials, the concierge gave him permission to search the ballroom on his own. As John pretended to look for the wallet, he saw an open side door that provided direct access to the manager's office. John walked through the door and went straight to the safe. He dialed the combination and removed $10,000 in cash.

After he hid the money on his person, he saw the guest list from the fundraiser on top of the manager's desk. He scanned the list and wrote down Mrs. Fontaine's address. John returned to the front desk and said that he did not find his wallet, so he thanked the concierge and left.

Around 1am, John drove out to the home of Mrs. Fontaine. He turned off the lights to the car and parked on the street. After walking up the long driveway, he climbed the trellis to Mrs. Fontaine's bedroom window. He carefully and quietly removed two glass panes from the window and entered the room as Mrs. Fontaine lay sleeping. He saw the diamond necklace she wore that evening on her dresser. He took the necklace and quietly exited the room and back down the trellis to his car.

After a lengthy investigation, John eventually was charged and arrested on two separate counts of felony burglary. John's fingerprints were identified on the discarded crowbar and the necklace.

Your supervising attorney has agreed to defend this case, but he needs you to conduct some research prior to trial. Analyze the following issues.

a. Whether Defendant can be convicted of **burglary** at the hotel and/or the home of Mrs. Fontaine? Be sure to analyze both crimes, and discuss the differences between them. Make certain that your memorandum is well organized and develop the issues fully. Remember to utilize the facts within your analysis.

5. Read the following fact pattern of this hypothetical concerning workers' compensation law. Using the format you have learned in this chapter, draft a legal memorandum. Use the law of *your state* to analyze and answer the issues that

follow. Concerning your heading, address the memo to "supervising attorney" and the case file is #WC3329-2013.

Facts

Jackson Hughes (age 42) was a painter for ABC Construction Company, located in *your state*. ABC hired Jackson last summer, as Jackson's solo paint business was not generating any clients and, therefore, not generating any money. ABC would send Jackson out on multiple jobs per month. After the ABC construction crew would complete a job, Jackson would return to the site and paint the recently constructed area.

A few weeks ago ABC sent Jackson to an ABC site that required a large area to be painted inside and two outside walls that needed to be painted, all in two days. Jackson was upset at the order and asked if he could pull in a few extra painters as well as have an extra day to complete the job. ABC approved the request for extra painters, but the deadline remained. Upset, Jackson hung up the phone and left the site to drive to the paint store for a few supplies. Afterwards, on the way to the new job, Jackson stopped at a local bar and had a few beers on an empty stomach, as he did not stop to eat lunch that day. After he left the bar, he didn't feel well and decided to make a stop home to sleep for an hour or so before driving to the new site to set up.

As Jackson was turning the corner at an intersection, he didn't make the turn completely and ended up hitting a traffic light pole, which crashed onto the roof of the ABC truck. Jackson sustained a broken collarbone, separated right shoulder, and multiple lacerations from broken glass. Jackson was treated and released from the hospital, but has been unable to work. He filed a workers' compensation petition stating that the truck's steering mechanism was faulty, which caused him to steer into the pole. Your supervising attorney, representing ABC, seems to think the five beers Jackson consumed had something to do with the "faulty steering."

Upon inspection, there appeared to be no defects to the steering mechanism or steering column. It was also determined that Jackson's blood alcohol content (BAC) exceeded the legal limit. However, Jackson's attorney is now asserting that Jackson was in the course and scope of his employment at the time of the accident and, therefore, is entitled to benefits. There are a couple of issues to be resolved. Using the workers' compensation laws of *your* state, answer the following:

a. Was Jackson injured during the "course and scope" of his duties at the time he was injured? Explain fully.

b. How does the fact that Jackson was "legally intoxicated" affect his claim for benefits, if at all? Explain fully.

COMPREHENSIVE CASE STUDY
Part III   Drafting the Legal Memorandum

OVERVIEW

In the first installment of the case study, you were introduced to the facts of the case and you formulated the issues to be researched. In the second installment, using the secondary and primary sources, you conducted the research necessary to address and answer Lena's issues. Now, after having the results you need, you can organize your research to formulate a rule of law and communicate the research results in the form of a legal memorandum.

Organizing the Results

After compiling all the necessary research during the last installment of the case study, you undoubtedly have numerous sections of a particular federal statute as well as a few cases to supplement the statutory law. Now, as you previously learned, organizing and synthesizing your research is crucial as you prepare to draft the legal memorandum.

Follow the steps and answer the questions below as you begin the process of transferring your legal findings into the legal memorandum. Keep in mind what you learned about legal analysis and apply it here.

1. You have read all the pertinent sections of the statute and have either printed out the statute online or either scanned or photocopied the statute from the printed books. Either way, match up the sections of statute with each corresponding issue—this will ensure that you have all your issues covered.
2. Gather any relevant case law opinions that support the statutory law. Make sure you brief the case and extract the rule of law that interprets and/or explains the language in the statute. Hopefully, you have even found cases with a similar fact pattern.

Synthesize the rule of law and create short blurbs that include the primary law that addresses each issue. For example, if you found that Lena must provide medical documentation to her employer detailing her father's illness under the federal statute, you could write the following:

Must provide medical documentation in order to take her leave of absence – *Federal Statute XX, Section XX; Smith v. Jones, (federal worker needed to produce treatment schedule and diagnosis of her son's illness to take leave of absence under the federal act); Johnson v. Brown (court defines what is meant by sufficient "medical documentation").*

Remember what you learned about legal analysis—you are only providing quick references for yourself as you begin to **organize** your research. You want to make sure that you have valid primary authority that addresses and answers each issue. It does not have to look great, just make sure all the puzzle pieces fit at this time.

Drafting the Memorandum

The task of drafting a legal memorandum does not have to be a daunting one. Remember all that you learned in drafting the memo in the previous chapter. Whether the memo briefly addresses a single issue or contains multiple pages addressing numerous issues, the *process* is the same. There are sections of the memorandum that can be immediately filled in prior to analyzing the issues. Recall the basic format of the legal memorandum below. Before you begin any analysis, all the sections in **bold** below could be filled in immediately.

Memorandum

To: **Supervising Attorney**
From: **Paralegal**
Date: **XX-XX-XXXX**
Re: **Lena Mitchell (federal employment - leave of absence)**

_____

Question (Issue) Presented:

Brief Answer:

Statement of Facts:

Analysis/Discussion:

Conclusion:

---

3. Draft the **heading** for your memorandum including all the relevant identifying information for the Lena Mitchell case. You may not have a case (file) number at this point, as the attorney is deciding, based on your memo, whether to even take the case.

4. Under the **question (issues) presented** section, write out the three main issues in the Lena Mitchell case. Remember, now the issues are written out more *formally* and inserted into the memo. Up to this point, your notes most likely have been scribbled in your own shorthand, which is fine. Now, you are writing for an audience, that is, your supervising attorney and possibly the client.

5. Under the **facts** section of this case study, feel free to copy them as they are presented, or condense and rewrite them in your own words. In practice, draft the facts in your own words and remember to synthesize the information and omit any facts that have no relevance to the issues (weather, irrelevant backstory, etc.) This will help you practice how to read, synthesize, and condense a large amount of material into a more streamlined set of facts that relate directly to the issues.

You are now ready to address the issues by organizing and drafting the **discussion/analysis** section. It is always best to outline your arguments for each issue *prior* to writing them out in the memorandum.

As you draft your analysis/discussion section of the memorandum, remember to use the basic writing skills you learned in this text. Remember to use proper sentence structure including topic and closing sentences. In addition, indent each new paragraph every time you begin a new thought (discussion). Also, utilize all the skills you learned, including the IRAC method and proper insertion of citation. A combination of both basic and legal writing methods will ensure success in drafting your legal memorandum. For example, follow this simple outline for each issue you are required to address and discuss:

> The issue is whether Lena is permitted by law to take a leave of absence from her position to care for her ailing father.
>
> Under federal law, *(explain the federal law here)*.
>
> In this case, *(include the specific facts relevant to the specific issue that relate to the law. This is your detailed analysis section—you can also use rules of law here as well)*.
>
> In conclusion, *(briefly wrap up the issue and offer a conclusion and whether the law is or is not favorable to the issue)*.

In addition, as you have previously learned, do not forget to provide an *objective* argument, meaning that if you locate any adverse legal authority, you must include that information. Your supervising attorney can only decide whether to take the case of s/he knows the good and the bad as well as the strengths and the weaknesses of the issues. When drafting the analysis/discussion section, provide a well-reasoned, well-developed, and comprehensive analysis/discussion for each issue. Take your time and use the **proper format**, an **appropriate amount of legal authority**, **proper citation**, and, above all, **answer the issues**.

6. Now that you have fully analyzed and answered each issue, return and write out the **brief answer** section. Do not write a yes/no answer. Remember that the brief answer "briefly" answers the issue, providing the reason, but it does not include all the analysis and authority as found in the analysis/discussion section.

7. After completing the first draft of the memorandum, read and edit it yourself and correct any mistakes, or strengthen any weak areas you find in your argument. Show the next draft to your legal research and writing instructor for corrections/edits.

Following multiple drafts, you will have a quality, professional legal research and writing sample to show and impress any prospective employer.

■ Three sample memoranda are included in **Appendix A** so that you can see acceptable variations for drafting the legal memorandum.

LEARNING OBJECTIVES

After completion of this chapter, you should be able to

1. Explain the different types of letters that a paralegal will draft in practice.

2. Explain the basic components of a letter.

3. Explain how to correspond by email and text messaging in a professional manner.

LETTERS

CORRESPONDENCE
FORMAL

RECEPIENT

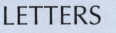

There are many important skills within the realm of legal research that are important to being a highly marketable and successful paralegal. One of those skills is the ability to draft various types of legal letters with many individuals within the legal profession, including attorneys, clients, and judges, among others.

Any correspondence must be written in a professional manner because you are not only representing yourself but also your supervising attorney and the reputation of the firm/office.

■ LEGAL LETTER WRITING

An important and necessary skill, other than conducting legal research, is the ability to clearly and effectively communicate with other individuals within the legal profession in a competent and professional manner.

Drafting a **legal letter** may appear an easy task, as everyone is familiar with writing letters, but in drafting a legal letter, your audience dictates the tone and language included in the letter. Daily you will be responsible for communicating primarily with clients, but also with attorneys and judicial staff. Although many individuals today are more comfortable writing e-mails and text messages to communicate, the legal profession is different; communication is more formal and professional. For example, if you were paying your attorney hundreds of dollars an hour and requested an update concerning settlement negotiations, would you rather receive a formal letter from your attorney or an e-mail? A formal letter demonstrates the professionalism you demand as a paying client.

As a paralegal, there are also different *types* of letters you will be responsible for sending to clients, including:

- Sending out important information for the client to review or sign;
- Confirming client information, such as scheduling a deposition, settlement negotiations, or trial dates;
- Enclosing information/forms to be completed by the client with specific directions;
- Informing the client of the current status of the case and any new developments;
- Requesting information that was not ascertained during the client's initial interview or information needed as the case progresses;
- Requesting a continuance or specific hearing with the trial judge on your case; or

legal letter
The mode of professional correspondence between individuals in the legal field and multiple third parties.

LEARNING OBJECTIVE 1
Explain the different types of letters that a paralegal will draft in practice.

- Informing your medical expert witness to the facts and issues of the case in preparation for trial.

These are just a few examples. Each type of letter has its own purpose, and that information needs to be communicated clearly. Consider the following three individuals whom you could send a formal letter.

- **A *Client***: always assume that the client is unfamiliar with certain aspects of the legal profession. Therefore, the language used must be clear, formal, and professional, but do not use legal terminology, as most clients will not understand what you are saying to them. You can simplify important legal information in easy to understand layman's terms.
- **A *Judge***: On the other hand, when writing to a judge or to other attorneys, you must still maintain clarity and formality, but legal terminology can be used, due to the legal expertise of your audience.
- **A *Third Party***: A third party can be a fact-based witness who is a landscaper, or an expert witness who is a brain surgeon. Regardless of the profession, use *everyday ordinary language* in a letter, but still keep it formal. Do not assume someone's educational level based on their profession or line of work.

In discussing the specific aspects of quality legal letter writing, any letter that leaves your desk must always be **clear**, **professional,** and **formal**. It is not professional to use slang so make certain you always use proper grammar, punctuation, and topic and sentence structure. Also, never insert any personal feelings about the case or opposing counsel, anything prejudicial or negative about anyone, or promises or opinions about the case or outcome.

Ethics Reminder

Another ethical rule that a paralegal must follow is to never offer any legal advice to a client. This includes giving opinions as to case strategy or speculating or promising certain results in the case in any legal correspondence. Also, every letter you draft must be signed by you, and any letter drafted by your supervising attorney must be signed by that attorney. It is important to avoid any confusion for the client about who is providing the information in the letter.

The Components of a Legal Letter

In every legal letter, there are some basic components that should be included, which are enumerated below. As for the *style* of the letter, there are several different formats, but more than likely you can write each letter in what is referred to as **full block format**. This means that **all** the information in the letter (from the date to closing) is flush left, as you can see in Figure 14-1 below. This makes for a more professional and uniform letter adopted and followed by many legal professionals.

However, the firm or law office in which you work will inform you as to the style of the legal letters drafted in that particular office. If no style is dictated to you, full block is universally used in the legal profession.

Please review Figure 14-1 to see all possible basic components that can be included within a legal letter written to a client. The letter is directing the client

full block format
A typical legal letter style where all the information is flush left and single spaced.

Figure 14-1 Example of the Components of a Full Block Style Letter

Smith, Jones, and Harris **(1)**
123 Main Street
New York City, New York 10023
(212) 555-5555

March 18, 20_____ **(2)**

***Via Facsimile and United States Mail* (3)**

Ms. Francesca Brown **(4)**
456 Diamond Avenue
Brooklyn, New York 11220

Re: Interrogatories of *Brown v. Samuels* **(5)**
    Case Number, JT-6632-13

(7)

Dear Ms. Brown: **(6)**

As we discussed on the phone last week, enclosed please find the interrogatories to be completed in full. This is part of the discovery process in your case against Mr. Samuels. Answer each question honestly and to the best of your knowledge. When you are finished, sign at the end where I have inserted the yellow tab. Please return the completed and signed documents by Friday, April 4, 2013. I have included an envelope addressed to the firm with the appropriate pre-paid postage for your convenience.

If you have any questions, please feel free to call me at (212) 555-5555.

Sincerely, **(8)**

Ilana Donahue, CP
Certified Legal Assistant

cc: Martin Smith **(9)**

Enc. **(10)**

ID/id **(11)**

to complete a set of interrogatories enclosed by the paralegal and to return them completed by a certain date.

1. **The Letterhead** — All correspondence sent as part of your paralegal duties should be drafted on official firm letterhead, which the firm will provide for you. It identifies the firm's name, address, and telephone numbers. It symbolizes the authoritative of the letter and lets the client know where to respond. If a letter is more than one page, the subsequent pages should carry the firm's header rather than the letterhead, which generally appears on the first page only.

2. **The Date** — The date of mailing should be the first item directly beneath the letterhead. The date is extremely important in determining the timeline of sending and receiving documents in a proceeding. Include the date you know the letter will be ***mailed***, or sent, even if you type it out a day or two before.

3. **The Mailing Method** — If you are sending the letter by anything *other than* the United States Postal service, such as via facsimile, e-mail, or by certified letter, include the method of transmission in underlined font. It should appear below the date.

4. **The Recipient's Address** — Include the recipient's business title and business name if he or she has one. If you are writing a letter to a third party, make certain you have that person's full position, title, and address/location.

5. **The Reference Line** — Before the body of the letter, include a reference line that functions as the "subject line" of the letter. It will alert the recipient to the matter addressed. If the case has an ongoing case or claim number, you firm may also want you to include it here.

6. **The Greeting (Salutation)** — Respectfully address the client or opposing party with his or her appropriate title and last name ("Mr.," "Ms.," or "Dr.") following "Dear." If you are unsure who to send it to, you may begin the letter with "To Whom it May Concern," although it is not advised. Be professional and always take the time to obtain a specific name and position, which will speed up your response time as well.

7. **The Body of the Letter** — Keep the text of your letter as concise as possible. Make sure to mention (1) your purpose for sending the letter, (2) what you would like the recipient to do, and (3) direct the recipient to call or write if there are any questions. Keep your audience in mind when drafting a letter. The purpose of the letter will vary according to the type, as you will see from the examples that follow.

8. **The Closing** — End the letter cordially. Other options include "Best regards," "Kind Regards," or "Very Truly Yours." Place your name approximately four lines below this to allow room for an original signature. Include your title so that you are not mistaken for an attorney. Remember to avoid representing yourself as an attorney to avoid confusion and violation of ethical codes.

9. **Carbon Copies** — Similar to the "cc" function in an e-mail, this is to alert the recipient that a third party will also receive a copy of the document and to identify that third party. You will usually copy (cc) your supervising attorney.

10. **Enclosures** — Include "Enc." if you are enclosing a document such as a court order, contract, release, or litigation materials. If there is more than one enclosure, use "Encs."

11. **Author and Typist** — The final item should denote the initials of the author of the letter in all capitals. Include your middle initial even if you do not use it in your signature. The second set of letters denotes the initials of the person who typed the letter, which may occasionally differ from the author.

LEARNING OBJECTIVE 2
Explain the basic components of a letter.

modified block format
A typical legal letter style similar to full block format but each new paragraph is indented.

In addition to the full block format above, a **modified block format** is the same as full block except that in part #7 above, each topic sentence beginning each new paragraph would be *indented*. This will not be an issue since your supervising attorney will not likely be concerned with the *style* of the letter. Rather, the attorney **will** be concerned with the *content* of the letter, which is important. When in doubt, use the full block style.

As previously mentioned, although the style may be similar for each letter, paralegals draft different *types* of letters. As you will most likely be drafting letters mostly to clients, make certain you keep the following three points in mind while writing any type of letter to a client. For instance,

1. Keep the language clear and concise, as a legal case can prove overwhelming, intimidating, and confusing to the client who is unfamiliar with the law.

   > **Instead of:** "The attorney in your case will begin to engage in the process of evaluating the value of your current residence and determine forthwith whether or not any prior titles, easements, deeds, liens, or mortgages may or may not be still attached to the residence in question prior to any sale."
   >
   > **Try instead:** "The attorney in your case will make the determination whether any outstanding legal obstacle, such as a past title or deed, remains attached to the property before sale."

   Remember, you are not writing to an attorney or judge. Always assume the client is a lay person with no knowledge of the law. It is not your job to educate on the law, but to provide important information that is understood.

2. Speaking of educating the client, never use any type of legal citation in a client letter. It will mean nothing to clients and will only confuse them.

   > **Instead of:** "According to a recent case decided in the state appellate courts, which has also been upheld in three other states as well, a homeowner in a residential neighborhood is prohibited from building and operating a smoke house, which was deemed a public nuisance for all neighbors in the immediate surrounding area. *See, Howard v. Balwer,* 223 P.2d 330, 335 (2013); *see also,* **12 A.B.C.§233.1(a)**."
   >
   > **Try instead:** "A law was recently passed that is similar to your case, which holds that a homeowner cannot build and operate a smokehouse on their property. In doing so, the homeowner was held liable for public nuisance."

   The client does not care that the case comes from the appellate courts, or the name of the case citation, or the accompanying statutory law—he just wants to know the status and progress of *his* case.

3. Do not use legalese; in other words, do not try and impress the client with Latin terminology.

   > **Instead of:** "The attorney proved a *prima facie* case *ipso facto* and the judge awarded partial temporary custody to you, the grandparent, in *loco parentis* since the mother was deemed *in absentia* at the hearing." What?! What happened?!
   >
   > **Try instead:** "At today's hearing, the judge awarded you, the grandparent, partial temporary custody due to the mother's failure to appear at the hearing."

   Keep all your correspondence clear and understandable.

General Correspondence Letters

Letters of **general correspondence** include either a request for information from someone or provide specific information to someone. These letters include the most typical type of communication in the profession. For example, after the attorney and client meet and both agree to legal representation, the first type

general correspondence
A legal letter that either provides information or requests information.

engagement letter
A legal letter written by an attorney to define the specifics of the contractual relationship with the client.

of general correspondence between the client and attorney is contained in the **engagement letter**, which is illustrated in Figure 14-2. It is a basic letter informing the new client of all the terms, conditions, and fees concerning representation (providing specific information). The letter will usually accompany many additional forms for signature that you must alert the client to fill out and sign before returning to you (requesting specific information). Although this type of letter may be written by a paralegal, it must be reviewed and signed by the paralegal's supervising attorney before it is mailed to avoid the paralegal engaging in the unauthorized practice of law.

Beginning with Figure 14-2, and continuing through Figure 14-8 carefully review each letter of **general correspondence**, to see the reason and purpose of each letter. Please take note of all the helpful hints in the boxes within each figure as well.

Figure 14-2 Example of an Engagement Letter in Full Block Style

---

Gold & Ellis
123 Main Street, Suite 118
Philadelphia, Pennsylvania 19117
(215) 555-5555

November 4, 20___

Via Federal Express
Mr. and Mrs. Theodore and Joanne Ackers
6544 Callowhill Road
Philadelphia, PA 19138

Re: Representation Agreement, Case Number, TJA-6019-110

Dear Mr. and Mrs. Ackers:

It was a pleasure meeting both of you. This letter will confirm the content of our meeting on Friday, November 1, 20___. As we discussed, after researching your issues, it is in my opinion that both of you have a valid property claim against ABC Corporation. Therefore, as we agreed, our office will represent you in the above-mentioned case.

I have included two forms for signature. The form titled "Attorney/Client Agreement" includes the terms of representation that we discussed in this case, and the form titled "Fee Agreement," outlines our legal fees. Both forms need to be reviewed and signed by both of you. If you have any questions before signing anything, please contact our office. We have included a self-addressed stamped envelope for your convenience in order for you to return the forms.

A confidential file will be opened in your case and you may view any of the contents upon request. After the final disposition of your case, the file will be destroyed.

We will keep you up to date concerning any legal action. If you have any questions, at any time, please feel free to contact me or my paralegal, Katrina Smith, at 215-555-5554. Thank you for choosing us, and I look forward to representing you both.

Sincerely,

Kevin Ellis, Esq.

cc: Katrina Smith, CP

Figure 14-3 Example of a Letter Confirming a Deposition in Full Block Style

---

Smith, Jones, and Harris
123 Main Street
New York City, New York 10023
(212) 555-5555

March 26, 20___

Via Federal Express
Ms. Francesca Brown
456 Diamond Avenue
Brooklyn, New York 11220

Re: Plaintiff's Deposition in *Brown v. Samuels*
        Case Number, JT-6632-13

Dear Ms. Brown:

This letter is to confirm our conversation yesterday in which we scheduled your required deposition at the law offices of Smith, Jones, and Harris for Friday, April 18, 20___ at 2:30 pm.

If you recall, the deposition will be conducted by Samuels' attorney, who will ask you questions related to the above-referenced court case. You will provide answers while under oath and in the presence of a court reporter. Your attorney, Mr. Smith, will also be present to represent you during the deposition.

Mr. Smith and I would like to meet with you at least once before the deposition to discuss your case and this important step in the litigation process, so I will call you on Monday of next week to schedule an appointment for you to come to the office.

Please remember to bring any documents relating to the case, such as accident and medical reports, if you have not already provided them to us.

Best regards,

Ilana Donahue, CP
Certified Legal Assistant

cc:

ID/id

It is good practice to fully explain what will happen during the deposition so that the client is not unsure or apprehensive.

The attorney may want to bring the client in to go over the facts of the case and what questions could be asked prior to the actual deposition.

Always make certain to ask the client to bring *any* legal documents in their possession such as accident reports, doctor's evaluations, etc.

Figure 14-4 Example of a Letter Enclosing a Deposition Transcript in Full Block Style

Smith, Jones, and Harris
123 Main Street
New York City, New York 10023
(212) 555-5555

April 21, 20___

Via Federal Express
Ms. Francesca Brown
456 Diamond Avenue
Brooklyn, New York 11220

> If you are asking clients to do anything, make certain you explain in detail what is needed from them.

Re: Transcript of Deposition from April 18, 20___
        Case Number, JT-6632-13

Dear Ms. Brown:

Enclosed is a copy of the transcript of your April 18, 20_____ deposition. Please review it carefully and note anything that was incorrectly transcribed. You may not rewrite your testimony, but you should note any inaccurate transcriptions on a separate sheet of paper. You may correct the spelling and names of places, and/or any substantive information concerning your actual testimony. Please note the page and line of any mistakes; they will be re-typed and discussed before submitted to the court reporter. Any changes must be received by the court reporter within 30 days, or the chance to correct the record will be forfeited.

Therefore, I would appreciate your prompt review of the transcript by Friday, May 2, 20___. If you find any serious discrepancies, please call me immediately. I have included an envelope addressed to the firm with the appropriate pre-paid postage for your convenience.

Kind regards,

Ilana Donahue, CP
Certified Legal Assistant

cc: Stuart Jenkins

ID/jag

Figure 14-5 Example of a Letter of a Status Report in Full Block Style

Smith, Jones, and Harris
123 Main Street
New York City, New York 10023
(212) 555-5555

May 7, 20____

Via Facsimile and United States Mail
Ms. Francesca Brown
456 Diamond Avenue
Brooklyn, New York 11220

> In providing a status report, be certain not to provide any legal advice, or to make any promises as to the outcome of the case.

Re: Status Update of *Brown v. Samuels*
        Case Number, JT-6632-13

Dear Ms. Brown:

This letter is to provide you with a status report concerning the progress of your case against defendant Samuels. To date, we have received a completed interrogatory and deposition review from you. We have requested the same from the opposing side. Samuels' deposition is currently scheduled for May 14, 20____.

After we review his testimony, we will likely proceed with our settlement conference to be scheduled by the court by the end of June.

Please feel free to call with any concerns or questions.

Sincerely,

Ilana Donahue, CP
Certified Legal Assistant

> Always remember that dates and deadlines are very important. Never state that an event is scheduled "sometime in the near future." Always be specific and give a definite date.

cc: Stuart Jenkins

ID/id

Figure 14-6 Example of a Letter Enclosing a Request for Information in Full Block Style

Smith, Jones, and Harris
123 Main Street
Wilmington, Delaware 10023
(212) 555-5555

May 9, 20____
Mr. Ryan Farraghut, Custodian
of Records
First Metropolitan Hospital
Office of Records
789 Industrial Road
Wilmington, DE 11220

> You may also have to engage in written correspondence with third parties in a case. Remember to remain professional in your tone. In this example, you are seeking medical documents from a third party.

Re: Request for Medical Documents

> In seeking specific legal information from a professional third party, you can use legal jargon and citation when necessary.

Mr. Farraghut:

Pursuant to the Health Insurance Portability and Accountability Act (HIPAA) of 1996, codified at 42 U.S.C. §300gg and 29 U.S.C. §1181, et seq, I am requesting that your office provide copies of the following:

All documents, medical and insurance related, specific to the treatment of Ms. Francesca Brown of 456 Diamond Avenue, Brooklyn, New York 11220. In particular, we are seeking the records specifically from February 8, 20_____ through February 11, 20___. These documents are not located at the hospital. They should, however, be at your Albany, NY office records office.

These documents are needed in this office by May 15, 20___. If any portion of this request is denied, please provide a detailed statement of the reasons for denial and an index or similar statement concerning the nature of the documents withheld.

Thanking you in advance,

Ilana Donahue, CP
Certified Legal Assistant

ID/jag

Figure 14-7 Example of a Letter for Settlement Agreement in Full Block Style

Smith, Jones, and Harris
123 Main Street
New York City, New York 10023
(212) 555-5555

July 1, 20____

Via Certified Mail
Ms. Francesca Brown
456 Diamond Avenue
Brooklyn, New York 11220

Re: Settlement Agreement in *Brown v. Samuels*
          Case Number, JT-6632-13

Dear Ms. Brown:

This letter is to provide you with the enclosed settlement agreement which was negotiated between you and the defendant Joshua Samuels.

Please read the entire agreement to make certain no mistakes have been made. Afterwards, as we agreed, please come to the office on July 15, 20_____ so the settlement agreement can be signed and dated by you before opposing counsel. Thereafter, you should receive your settlement check in the mail in the <u>actual amount to you of $18,322.32</u> (minus attorney fees) within one week. As we also discussed, if you would prefer to come back to the office to receive the check rather than have it mailed, please let us know on the 15th. We look forward to seeing you at that time.

Please feel free to call with any concerns or questions.

Sincerely,

Ilana Donahue, CP
Certified Legal Assistant

cc: Stuart Jenkins

ID/id

Figure 14-8 Example of a Letter to a Judge Requesting a Dismissal in Full Block Style

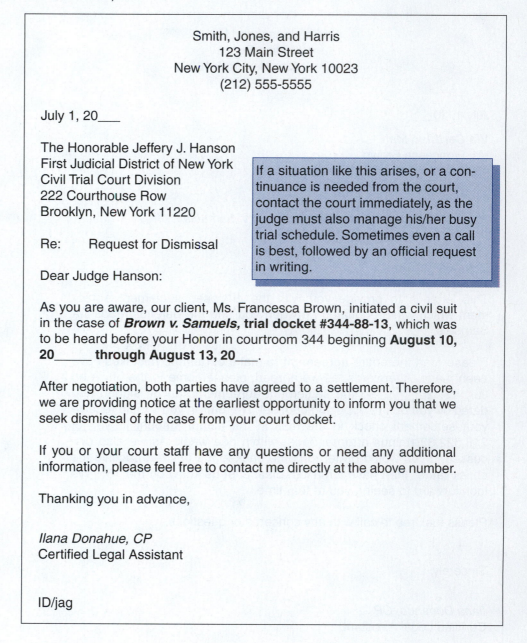

Smith, Jones, and Harris
123 Main Street
New York City, New York 10023
(212) 555-5555

July 1, 20____

The Honorable Jeffery J. Hanson
First Judicial District of New York
Civil Trial Court Division
222 Courthouse Row
Brooklyn, New York 11220

Re: Request for Dismissal

Dear Judge Hanson:

> If a situation like this arises, or a continuance is needed from the court, contact the court immediately, as the judge must also manage his/her busy trial schedule. Sometimes even a call is best, followed by an official request in writing.

As you are aware, our client, Ms. Francesca Brown, initiated a civil suit in the case of **Brown v. Samuels, trial docket #344-88-13**, which was to be heard before your Honor in courtroom 344 beginning **August 10, 20_____ through August 13, 20___**.

After negotiation, both parties have agreed to a settlement. Therefore, we are providing notice at the earliest opportunity to inform you that we seek dismissal of the case from your court docket.

If you or your court staff have any questions or need any additional information, please feel free to contact me directly at the above number.

Thanking you in advance,

Ilana Donahue, CP
Certified Legal Assistant

ID/jag

Be sure to ask your supervising attorney or another paralegal in the office if there are templates for certain types of letters. If not, use the following letters included here as guides in practice.

Please note that any correspondence (letter, fax) you send to a judge's chamber should be *addressed to the judge* even though the document will likely NOT be read by the judge, at least not initially. All judicial correspondence is opened and read by the judge's staff, including the legal secretary and law clerk that act as the "gatekeepers" of the judicial chambers. If you do need any information concerning that particular court, you will be dealing mostly with the judge's staff, so know their names and responsibilities as well.

Other than general correspondence, there are other types of legal letters that address important and specific issues.

Demand Letters

A **demand letter** is exactly what it sounds like—you are "demanding" someone to take action or cease performing an action. A demand letter sets forth the client's demands, and if those demands are not met, the attorney will threaten legal action. For example, demand letters can be written to a landlord, who has wrongly violated a tenant's rights, or to a collection agency who is harassing a client, or to the car mechanic who took hundreds of dollars from your client to fix the client's engine, but didn't complete the job, or finished it incorrectly.

Although the person on the receiving end of your demand letter has done something "improper," you must maintain a professional tone and demeanor throughout the letter. You cannot draft a letter filled with derogatory terms or a multitude of expletives—keep it professional. In addition, because these individuals are not filled with elation to receive such a letter, it is best to send this type of letter by certified or registered mail, preferably at their office or place of business.

In drafting a demand letter, feel free to maintain the same *format* as a general correspondence letter in block format. However, the *content* in the body of the letter will obviously be different. In writing these letters, your attorney will certainly want input and may even tell you what to write, or will want to review it before you send it out. That is not because the attorney does not trust you—rather, these letters are sensitive in nature and you must strike the right balance of firmness and professionalism. A few tips to keep in mind when drafting this type of letter include:

- Be clear on the facts. This is very important. The receiver needs to know exactly what he or she is being accused of and why this is detrimental to your client. Be specific, and include relevant dates, receipts, and so on.
- Be specific in the demand the client is seeking. This is where the attorney will assist you. If you want the landlord to fix the plumbing system, state that the tenant will withhold rent until it is fixed. Or, to the collection agency, you could state that the agency must stop the harassing letters and phone calls, as the client has paid the money owed in full. Be sure to include a copy of the receipt and the amount paid on a specific date.
- We all know that in life there are consequences to our actions. Be clear as to what will happen, or what action the attorney will take if the problem/situation is not rectified. The attorney will also provide input here, as the consequence will most likely be legal in nature.
- Always end with some type of action by a definite date. Do not end the letter stating, "Thank you for your prompt action in this matter." If you do that, the letter will be ignored, until you have to write another letter. End the letter strongly with an ultimatum such as, "Please contact the firm by June 1, 20_____ with your decision." Or, you could say, "Please make all necessary repairs by January 15, 20___, which is four weeks from the date of this letter. If the repairs are not made by that time, we will be forced to initiate legal proceedings at that time."

In addition, when drafting the actual letter, make certain that you have not only the facts, but also the correct and legally significant facts of the case. Sometimes when clients are explaining what happened, their mind may become clouded due to frustration or anger. Therefore, make sure you double check the facts concerning *exactly* what action was taken by the potential defendant. If you want, send a copy of the demand letter to the client for review *before* you send it out to the potential defendant.

demand letter
A letter formally demanding that the person to whom the letter is addressed perform a legal obligation or to act on a contractual commitment by a specific date.

Make certain you also have researched the law before demanding action. If the law does not address the situation, or the law fails to offer the client any remedy, then sending a demand letter is pointless.

Keep in mind that a demand letter is *not* a legal document filed with the court that *initiates* any legal action—it is, however, a letter seeking action *before* taking legal action. Look at Figure 14-9 and Figure 14-10 for examples of demand letters addressed to a collection agency and a commercial business.

Figure 14-9 Example of a Demand Letter in Full Block Style

Smith, Jones, and Harris
123 Main Street
Hamden, Connecticut 10023
(212) 555-5555

March 28, 20___

Via Certified Mail
Mr. Jason Winters, Collection Agent
Allied Collection Agency
The Allied Building
331 South Mason Street
Hamden, Connecticut 12281

Re: Account for Peter Newsome
          Allied Case Number, 33-224332-12

Dear Mr. Winters:

This letter is to provide you with the current status of the case file of our client, **Peter Newsome, case number, 33-224332-12**. As you are aware, Mr. Newsome had an outstanding medical account with First Metropolitan Hospital in the amount of $1,088.12, which was transferred to you to collect payment.

Our client has informed us that as of February 15, 20___, his account was ***paid in full***. Please find the ***enclosed receipt*** and ***canceled check*** in the amount of $1,088.12. However, Mr. Newsome has informed us that your office has repeatedly called his house on a daily basis, three times per day, for the last two weeks stating that he must pay the balance owed. We ask that you please check and update your records to terminate Mr. Newsome's account with your office. We would kindly ask that no one contact Mr. Newsome further, and any and all questions and inquires can and will be answered by our firm.

Please contact me by April 5, 20_____ after you have checked your records and have confirmed that the balance was paid in full. Thank you for your assistance in this matter.

Sincerely,

Ilana Donahue, CP
Certified Legal Assistant

Figure 14-10 Example of a Demand Letter in Full Block Style

Smith, Jones, and Harris
123 Main Street
Atlanta, Georgia 10023
(212) 555-5555

May 1, 20____

Via Certified Mail
Mr. William Banks, Manager
XYZ Commercial Storage Center
882 Churchville Road
Atlanta, Georgia 30309

Re: Account for David Arnold
        Account Number, 77648-321

Dear Mr. Banks:

As you are aware, David Arnold was a tenant at unit 64A at your storage facility from July 23, 20_____ to March 13, 20_____ (see attached agreement). As the legal representatives of Mr. Arnold, this firm is writing this letter pursuant to the Georgia General Laws, Chapter ___; Section ____. Because you demanded and accepted a security deposit from Mr. Arnold in the amount of $4,750.00, you are required to comply with the appropriate security deposit laws of this state (see attached statute Chapter ___; Section _____).

In the state of Georgia, you have thirty (30) days to return a security deposit from the day the tenant vacates the premises, or in the alternative, provide the client with an itemized statement as to why the deposit was not returned. As of the date of this letter, it has been forty-five (45) days since Mr. Arnold has vacated the premises and removed all of his equipment. At this time, you have neither returned Mr. Arnold's deposit, nor provided him for a reason of why it was not returned, despite Mr. Arnold's repeated requests. Please be advised that if the amount is not paid in full within five (5) business days of receipt of this letter, this firm will be seeking the full amount of the deposit plus penalties under Georgia law.

Please contact this office as soon as you receive this letter. We will expect that Mr. Arnold will receive a check for $4,750.00 by May 9, 20___. Thank you in advance for your cooperation.

Sincerely,

Ilana Donahue, CP
Certified Legal Assistant

> You can attach relevant documents to support and strengthen the facts in the letter.

Opinion Letters

opinion letter
A formal letter by an attorney expressing their opinion about a specific case based on their knowledge of the law and the facts of the case.

An **opinion letter** is typically drafted by the attorney or written out by the attorney for the paralegal to type and/or add any legal authority. This is because an opinion letter is just that—your attorney giving the client an "opinion" and advice about the law/rules that apply to a specific fact situation. For example, if a client wants to open a new business, the attorney, through the opinion letter, will explain all the legalities concerning the new business, such as tax requirements, safety regulations, and corporate filings.

In addition, attorney opinion letters may be required for transactions with lenders, contracts between individuals, and as a type of defense against malicious wrongdoing in litigation. The attorney acts as the "mediator" between the client and the new business venture.

The attorney will likely write the letter, but may need legal authority or various citations from you in order to complete it. It is important that because the content of the opinion letter does offer *legal advice*, it must be written, or reviewed by the attorney. Please review Figure 14-11 for an example of an opinion letter drafted by an attorney to his client.

Ethics Reminder

You have an ethical duty to never offer a client any legal advice. The client letter must only state the law researched, and must not provide any legal advice or strategy unless written and/or signed by your supervising attorney. An opinion letter can include legal strategy and/or legal advice, but those types of letters must be reviewed and signed by the attorney.

Collection Letters

collection letter
A letter stating a request to settle an outstanding account.

On occasion, individuals will default on paying their credit card, mortgage, student loans, and so on. On those occasions, the company/bank will put the individual on notice and attempt to collect the debt through legal counsel. This is done through the use of a **collection letter** In essence, the law firm is retained to collect the debt.

As you can see in Figure 14-12, since these are not letters of general correspondence, it may be written by a paralegal, but most likely will be reviewed and signed by your supervising attorney.

Even if you are asked to draft a particular type of letter that is not included in this Chapter, just remember the basic elements that need to be included in a letter and adapt accordingly. In addition, always ask your supervising attorney for clarification if necessary before guessing what is expected of you.

■ ONLINE CORRESPONDENCE

Although legal letters are the general mode of communication between members of your firm and the outside world, it is not advisable to "shoot the client a quick e-mail," as a mode of communication. Your supervising attorney may regularly keep in contact with certain clients by e-mail, but unless you are permitted for a specific reason, or if client has requested correspondence by e-mail, you should maintain all communication in letter form.

Figure 14-11 Example of an Opinion Letter in Full Block Style

The Law Office of Peter K. Hughes
123 Main Street
Wilmington, Delaware 19931
(302) 555-5555

June 3, 20____

Mr. Michael Davidson
443 Homestead Avenue
Apartment 3-D
Wilmington, Delaware 19932

Re: Case File #FAM-51-44543-2013

Dear Mr. Davidson:

Thank you for reaching out to me and requesting my services. After review of your case, I will provide you, in this letter, with my legal opinion concerning your situation. My legal analysis will provide you with the information to make an informed decision in your case. I will first summarize the facts of the case. Second, I will summarize and explain the law that governs your situation. Lastly, I will provide my legal opinion on the possible outcome of your case.

You and your wife are the paternal grandparents of Lucy Davidson (age 4), who has lived with you and your wife since last June after your son, Lucy's father, was incarcerated around that same time. The child's mother, Miranda Johnson, also lost her job around that same time. Therefore, you and your wife have supported and provided a home for the child for the past eight (8) months here in Wilmington. The child's mother has recently secured gainful employment and has relocated to a new residence approximately fifteen (10) miles from her prior address. The mother now has filed a petition for sole physical and legal custody of the child. At this time, the mother is upset and does not wish for her child to be raised or cared for by you and your wife. However, the mother is refusing you and your wife to visit and spend time with the child. You are now requesting if you and your wife can file a counter petition for visitation rights.

The Delaware statutes allow third-party visitation rights, which include grandparents. In order to successfully obtain visitation rights, grandparents must have "a substantial and positive and prior relationship with the child," and visitation must "be in the child's best interest." In addition, specifically where a parent objects to visitation, the grandparent (petitioner) must show by a "preponderance of the evidence" (a "more-than-likely" burden of proof) that the visitation "will not substantially interfere with the parent/child relationship."

It appears that the mother cannot provide any legitimate reason to deny you and your wife visitation rights. She is most likely denying visitation due to her anger and frustration at her husband. Legally, you have standing to file a petition for visitation, which the court should approve. We can demonstrate that you have a substantial and positive prior relationship with the child, as Lucy was in your care for eight months where you cared for all her needs. Furthermore, we can also demonstrate, by a preponderance of the evidence (more likely than not) that any visitation would not "substantially" interfere with the parent/child relationship, as you all still reside in the same state.

Based on this evaluation, please let me know if you want me to pursue filing a petition on your behalf. I will work with you and develop your case. Please do not hesitate to call me with any questions or concerns. If there are any misstated facts in this letter, please inform me immediately by contacting my paralegal Cassie Kaplan. She can be reached at 302-555-5550. Again, it was a pleasure to speak with you, and I look forward to representing you in this matter.

Sincerely,

Peter K. Hughes, Esq.

cc: Cassie Kaplan, CP

Figure 14-12 Example of a Collection Letter in Full Block Style

Smith, Jones, and Harris
123 Main Street
Austin, Texas 10023
(212) 555-5555

June 8, 20____

Via Certified Mail
Mr. Francis Harper
123 North Main Street
Austin, Texas 16654

Re: Home Loan #664-88GTD34-19
Property Address: 123 North Main Street
Payoff: $102,887.54

THIS FIRM IS ACTING ONLY AS A DEBT COLLECTOR AND IS
ATTEMPTING TO COLLECT SUCH DEBT. ANY INFORMATION
OBTAINED BY THIS FIRM WILL BE USED FOR THAT PURPOSE

Dear Mr. Harper:

This law firm represents Big City Bank, the creditor on the above referenced loan. This letter is to advise you that this firm has been retained
to collect the debt secured on the above referenced property, which
may involve foreclosure against said property.

As of the date of this letter, you owe $102,887.54, but due to interest,
late fees, and other charges accrued daily, this amount may be greater
than what is listed. Therefore, if you do pay the amount in this letter, an
adjustment may be necessary to recoup the additional money.

This letter is providing notice of an attempt to collect the debt. If you
fail to notify us within thirty (30) days after receipt of this letter, it will be
assumed that the debt is valid. If you dispute the debt, we will forward
a copy of the loan agreement from the bank. Please be advised that,
without notice to you, we may initiate the foreclosure action within thirty
(30) days if requested by our client. If this debt has been discharged
in bankruptcy proceeding, then please disregard this notice. However,
please call our office to inform us of the discharged debt.

Our client may permit you to reinstate the loan on conditions, payments,
and terms in order to cure the debt. Please call the bank to see if this
option is available to you. Other alternatives, if you qualify, may include
full or partial payoff. The bank will consider any and all individual hard-
ships and circumstances and will be flexible in resolving the debt.

In addition, please feel free to contact our office with any questions or
concerns that we may be able to address and answer for you.

Sincerely,

Peter K. Hughes, Esq.

cc: Cassie Kaplan, CP

Correspondence by E-Mail

If you do communicate with anyone within the legal profession by e-mail, even other attorneys or support staff within your office, keep these rules in mind:

LEARNING OBJECTIVE 3
Explain how to correspond by email and text messaging in a professional manner.

- Remember to use a professional format. Always address the individual by "Mr., Ms., or Mrs." Never draft an e-mail beginning with, "Hey, or Hi." Also, be careful in using ALL CAPITAL LETTERS! Even if your intention is to merely *emphasize* something, this can be construed as yelling or anger!
- Use proper topic sentences, and use different paragraphs for each new thought or idea. Always close with stating your full name, title, and phone number and/or address.
- Keep in mind that unlike a letter, an e-mail can be forwarded to hundreds of people. Make certain you check with your attorney, if you are permitted to send an e-mail, that the e-mail does not include any personal or confidential material concerning the client.
- Include any relevant contact information so that the recipient can easily reach you if needed, including your title, office address, and direct phone extension after your name.
- Make certain that if you do send e-mails on a regular basis, that you attach a disclaimer at the end of every e-mail you send out, such as the following:

> This message is confidential. It may also be privileged or otherwise protected by work product immunity or other legal rules. If you have received it by mistake, please let us know by e-mail reply and delete it from your system; you may not copy this message or disclose its contents to anyone. Please send us by fax any message containing deadlines as incoming e-mails are not screened for response deadlines. The integrity and security of this message cannot be guaranteed on the Internet.

- It is wise to also attach a return receipt to any e-mail that leaves your computer. If not, you have no idea whether the message was received or not. For example, there could be a computer glitch on the recipient's end, or you may have inserted an incorrect or different e-mail address. So rather than wait all day and curse out the recipient for not responding, just save the worry and send a return receipt.
- If you have to send an important e-mail, or you are not sure how to word it, let it sit. Minimize the window and take a break or go to lunch. When you return, open it and read it again with fresh eyes. If it still looks good, then send it. If not, include what information you missed or forgot to include.

Your supervising attorneys will discuss with you the acceptable methods of communication with them, other members of the firm/office, and clients. Also, the firm may have letter templates for certain types of legal letters. If not, please use the formats in this chapter.

Text Messaging

To date, millions of text messages are sent and received every day in this country, and the practice is slowly but steadily being used in the professional world. The use of smartphones has allowed many in the legal field to communicate more quickly and efficiently using text messaging.

However, keep one very important point in mind: If permitted, use text messaging as a quick and convenient method to communicate with your supervising attorney and staff, but do not lose the formalities and professionalism expected in the legal field. Of course, that does not mean you need to begin a text message with, *"Dear Sir, . . . "* However, do not text your supervising attorney like you would your best friend. If the attorney allows the two of you to text to stay in contact, do not forget that he/she is your supervisor and maintain professionalism within the communication. Just keep the following top five tips of business texting etiquette in mind during your legal employment. First, do not text anyone you work with after hours or late at night unless otherwise directed. Second, do not use slang or acronyms such as (TYVM, GR8, L8R). Third, do not text during a client interview, meeting with your supervising attorney, or in court. Fourth, never use a text to communicate urgent or important information to your supervising attorney - always call them. Lastly, text sparingly, and never text when an email or call will suffice.

As with any and all electronic correspondence communicated through a smartphone, tablet, or computer, everything you send over the Internet cannot be taken back, deleted, or permanently erased. Be smart and protect your character and reputation. If you keep that rule in mind, you will never have to be concerned with the content you send online.

Chapter Checklist ✔

- You learned the importance of legal letter writing—a skill that requires three important elements: formality, professionalism, and above all, clarity.

- Always be mindful of your audience, whether it be a client, judge, attorney, or a third party in a case. Although you always maintain a formal and professional consistency, the degree of legal content included will differ for each person.

- Be sure to be clear as to what you or the attorney need from the person, or what you are requesting. Do not include any unneccessary information. Also, do not insert any personal feelings, bias, or promises of a particular outcome in the case.

- You learned the various elements of a legal letter—be sure to know each part.

- Always use the full block format unless otherwise directed.

- Be sure to reference the letters of general correspondence in this chapter when needed in practice, as each includes typical examples used daily.

- In a demand letter, always be clear on what the client is seeking or address the specific problem, the consequences for noncompliance, and a definite time frame for the person to compete your request.

- Remember that opinion letters are to be written by the attorney, as those letters offer legal advice and/or legal strategy. If the attorney does permit you to write such a letter, make certain the attorney reviews, edits, and signs the letter.

- You also learned that e-mail can be another form of legal correspondence. Maintain formality and professionalism, and only e-mail a client if specifically directed by the client or the attorney.

KEY TERMS

CRITICAL THINKING AND APPLICATION

1. Your supervising attorney's clients, Mr. and Mrs. Joseph and Mildred Hampton, were recently in your office outlining the financial details of their new business, a bed and breakfast. Draft a letter to them collectively, stating that the attorney has completed the preparation of all the legal and financial documents, which are enclosed for their review. Ask them to examine the documents and to inform you with any mistakes or changes. Tell them that if no changes or mistakes are found, to call and set up an appointment to finalize and sign the documents at the office. If they do find any mistakes, tell them to call the office immediately so that the changes can be made, and a new set of documents were be sent out immediately. The client's address is 377 Main Street, South Carolina, 23321. Your heading/address is Tamber, Miloe & Stash, 123 Kings Court, South Carolina, 23321. Send the letter via United States mail and certified mail.

2. Your supervising attorney recently conducted a deposition of Mr. James McKeenan, a client who is engaged in an intellectual property dispute concerning the creation and development of a particular video game. You recently sent Mr. McKeenan a copy of his deposition transcript to review, but you just realized that you found the last three pages of the deposition on your desk under some papers, which were not sent out for review. Draft a letter informing Mr. McKeenan of the mistake, and that the remaining pages are included for his review. The client's work address is The Allied Corporation, Development Office, 443 Concord Drive, Wilmington, DE 28811. Your heading/address is the same as in question #1.

3. Your supervising attorney has a case scheduled for trial from June 1st of this year until June 4th of this year. However, all the depositions are not yet complete, the attorney is having a difficult time tracking down two witnesses to testify, and an expert witness has revealed new information that must be investigated further. Because of this, your attorney will not be ready for trial on June 1st of this year. Send a letter to the trial judge apologizing for the recent events, and ask if the trial can be postponed until July 1st of this year providing the judge's docket can accommodate the case. Mention also that the defense is in agreement as to the July 1st date and will not assert any objection. The judge's address in chambers is, The Honorable Martin K. Stevenson, Jr., Trial Court Division, First Judicial District of Philadelphia, Room 772 City Hall, Philadelphia, PA 19107. The trial court's docket number is TC-33299-13. Send a carbon copy also to the Clerk of Courts Office and to the defense attorney, Sheena Davis, Esq., 339 Packard Building, Suite 221, Philadelphia, PA 19102.

4. Your supervising attorney has a new client who recently came to the office with a problem. He is a graduate student at a local university, and he, his wife and five-year-old son rented an apartment near the university. The client, Desmond Jones, signed a two-year lease with the landlord. However, upon moving in, Mr. Jones discovered extensive mold in the bathroom behind the wallpaper; oil, dirt and grease under the lid of the stove which caught fire twice; and if the apartment upstairs uses water, Mr. Jones has no hot water for up to four hours. Mr. Jones' son also suffers from asthma.

The attorney wants you to look up the law concerning warranty of habitability, and draft a demand letter to the landlord. Inform the landlord of each problem specifically, in detail, and state that Mr. Jones's attorney will initiate a lawsuit against him if the problems are not rectified in full in two weeks from the date of your letter. In the meantime, inform the landlord that the attorney is requesting that the Jones family stay at another of the landlord's rentals, rent free, until the problems are fixed. Inform him also that your attorney will call him in one week to check on his progress. Send the landlord's letter certified only, signature requested. The landlord's contact information is: Jackson Walker, 3223 Jenkins Street, Apartment 3-D, City, State 44312. The law concerning a warranty of habitability in that state is as follows: "Every landlord in the state warrants that the premises he is offering for rent are fit for human habitation, and to do necessary repairs during tenancy to maintain them in that condition." **ABC State Compiled Laws, §554.139**. The tenant, by law, can also withhold rent, or initiate a lawsuit as a remedy for the breach of warranty. Send a carbon copy to Mr. Jones at 550 University City Building, Apartment 3-B, City, State 44312.

5. You are employed as a paralegal in a large law office in the city in which you live. A new client, Marcus Walker, recently visited your office to speak with your supervising attorney, Cassandra Fells. Marcus is a computer software developer who recently created software that will make it easier for consumers to make safe and secure purchases online. A rival company is suing Marcus for copyright infringement. At the meeting, your supervising attorney has agreed to represent Marcus and defend against the lawsuit. Draft a typical engagement (representation) letter to Marcus welcoming him as a new client. Marcus signed all the necessary paperwork, but Cassandra has told you that he forgot to read and sign the fee agreement! Tell Marcus to carefully read and sign the agreement and either mail, fax, or scan the form back to the office as soon as possible. Be courteous and remind Marcus to call anytime he has any questions or concerns.

6. You are employed as a paralegal in a law firm that specializes in defense workers' compensation law (The defendant's attorney will always send the claimant to an independent doctor to assess the claimant to make certain the claimant is, in fact, injured and not a malingerer). You must draft a letter to Dr. Harold Levin, M.D. who is scheduled to perform an independent medical examination (IME) on the claimant of the case, Kevin Miller, on January 15, 20___. Dr. Levin's offices are located at Allied Health West, 333 Grove Pike, Suite 221 Philadelphia, PA 19112. You must provide detailed information to the doctor prior to his examination, including Claimant's work injury history and medical history. Inform the doctor that you are sending, along with the letter, all medical reports from the UIP Medical Center, Pennsylvania Department of Corrections, and Valley Orthopedic Associates.

Use headings in the letter—concerning Claimant's **work injury history**, inform the doctor that:

- Claimant allegedly sustained a work-related injury on November 1, 20_____ working as a laborer at Company X.
- Claimant allegedly slipped on stairs and injured his back.
- The alleged incident was not witnessed by anyone.

- Following the alleged injury, Claimant was convicted of a felony and incarcerated for one (1) year, which is the reason for the delay in the IME.

Concerning Claimant's **medical history**, inform the doctor that:

- Claimant was admitted to UPI Medical Center and treated for a back injury, but was released that same day.
- Dr. Jeffery Knowles diagnosed Claimant's injury as "local pain and mild swelling in the lower back."
- X-rays showed no fracture in the back area.
- Claimant was also prescribed Percocet for pain.
- At State Correctional Institute Haswell, Claimant was also treated by prison physician Daniel Straus, M.D., whose diagnosis was "mild lower back pain."
- Medical restrictions by both doctors included only "rest, and no repetitive stooping, bending, or twisting of the lower back."
- Upon his release from prison, Claimant also attended physical therapy for traction therapy twice a week.

Inform the doctor that your supervising attorney needs for him to perform a full and complete IME on Claimant, paying particular attention to the lower back area, and to provide the attorney with an opinion, within a reasonable degree of medical certainty, as to whether he believes Claimant:

- Sustained any type of work-related injury,
- Suffers any disability concerning his lower back,
- Can return to work as a laborer with or without restriction at the time of the IME,
- Requires any ongoing treatment or therapy, or
- Requires any surgical intervention.

As always, inform the doctor that if he has any questions or concerns, to contact you the paralegal on the case. Send a carbon copy to your supervising attorney, Keith Watson, Esq. and John Bower, insurance representative. The case number is 91130-00331.

LEARNING OBJECTIVES

After completion of this chapter, you should be able to

1. Explain what is included in proofreading and editing a legal document.

2. Demonstrate how to cite check a legal document in print and online.

3. How to validate citations within trial records.

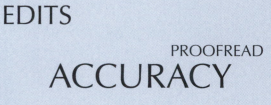

EDITS

PROOFREAD
ACCURACY

CITE-CHECK

Proofreading, Editing, and Cite Checking

Not only must paralegals be proficient in legal research and writing, but they must also be proficient in other correlative skills as well.

In this chapter, you will learn the importance of proofreading and editing your own work, as well as the work of others. In addition, paralegals need to be able to properly cite check their supervising attorney's documents. This is a crucial skill for any document that is officially filed with the court.

■ PROOFREADING AND EDITING SKILLS

Paralegals need to be proficient in proofreading and editing skills not only for their own work, but also so they can proofread and edit the work of their supervising attorneys.

Proofreading and Editing

Proofreading is an important but difficult task. Mostly because there is a difference in what a legal document *should* say and what it *does* say. Whether the attorney is writing a trial brief, an appellate brief, or any legal document filed with the court, the document needs to be clear, concise, error free, and professionally polished before the document is filed with the court.

LEARNING OBJECTIVE 1
Explain what is included in proofreading and editing a legal document.

Proofreading includes:

- Checking for any grammatical errors, spelling, and missing punctuation;
- Checking that any homonyms are used correctly (such as the correct use of the words "to" "too" and "two");

Editing includes:

- Ensuring that the names of both parties and any addresses, locations, and property measurements included in the document are written and spelled correctly, especially in real estate documents and contracts;
- Ensuring that any and all dates are correct to the exact date and year;
- Ensuring that all monetary amounts are correct (to the exact penny) in a business, personal injury, real estate, or contract document;
- Checking that all injuries are written and spelled correctly in a workers' compensation or personal injury case;
- Checking that all references to notes of testimony or deposition transcripts are correct, including the correct page and line numbers.

proofreading
The act of reading a written document for the purpose of finding errors in grammar, punctuation, spelling, or syntax.

editing
The act of preparing written material to make it acceptable for presentation to a particular audience by correcting and revising its content and organization.

As you can see, proofreading does not only include making certain every sentence ends with a period. More than likely, the attorney will be concentrating on developing the legal argument and getting it down on paper, which is the attorney's job. Attorneys will not have the file in front of them, which will include case details such as money totals, dates, names, or the names of injuries. However, those details *are* very important and must be analyzed with strict scrutiny—this is the job of the paralegal.

Ethics Reminder

> Proofreading and editing skills are not only important, but are also included under the ethical duties of a paralegal, which fall under competence and professionalism requirements. When proofreading or cite checking any legal document, always take the time to carefully read the information. Never quickly scan any document, as you run the risk of missing something important.

If any mistakes are made due to inattentiveness to detail, it will affect the reputation of the law office and possibly adversely affect the case itself. Opposing counsel and their staff are trained to look through the documents filed by their adversaries to see if any mistakes exist to use against them.

To ensure you are drafting an error-free document, it helps to clearly see what you are writing. Try magnifying the zoom level of the Word document from 100% to 150%. Once finished, the best way to proofread and edit a legal document is to have the document in your hands. It is difficult to concentrate and read any document on a computer screen. Double-space the entire document, print it out, and read it. This way you can grab your red pen or highlighter and make as many notes or edits in the margins and in between the lines. This format will also be easier for your attorney to read. However, if you and your supervising attorney prefer reading documents on a computer monitor then maintain that format.

There are other helpful tips to proofread and edit your documents. For example, print the document and read it backwards. It may seem odd but it works. You will catch all the misused words that the "spell checker" will miss, even if spelled correctly. Another good tip is to read the document out loud (when you are alone of course). You will also pick up on misused words or missing information as you read aloud rather than merely scanning the pages, in which case you may miss something.

Another important tip to remember when drafting/proofreading any document is to make certain that the proper "case content" is included in the document. For example, many paralegals send out numerous standard letters, complaints, and so on and may have Word document folders housing those specific templates. However, a mistake is often made when the last client's name was never deleted in the letter or document, or a date within the body of the letter was never changed from the last letter, and so on. Please do not make this mistake. It not only demonstrates poor proofreading skills, but clear incompetence as well. In addition, make certain that you understand the meaning and difference between certain terms used in many documents such as,

- offeror/offeree,
- grantor/grantee,
- mortgagor/mortgagee.

Do you know what each word means? Each is distinctive, so the correct term must represent the correct party and each must be used properly within any legal document.

Lastly, proofreading and editing is time consuming and tedious work. Take a break if you need to—legal proofreading and editing is a marathon, not a sprint. Did you ever get to a good point in a novel when you want to read what happens in a particular scene, but your eyes get tired and you end up reading the same page two or three times? And that is when you are reading for pleasure, so the chance of it happening when you are proofreading a legal document is even greater. After reading so many pages of legal content, it can become monotonous, so get up, take a walk, and recharge the battery. Come back with fresh eyes and continue the editing process.

Always discuss with the attorney all the recommended edits/changes prior to making the change in the document. It is important here to point out again that you would be amazed how efficient you can be just by having open communication with your attorney. Rather than guessing at anything, you can always send an e-mail, tap on their door, send a text, grab them before going to lunch, or whenever, and ask your question. Do not wait for that "perfect time" to talk with your supervising attorney, and do not guess or assume anything concerning your immediate task or general duties—you are a team, and attorneys immensely rely on you to assist them.

Online Assistance

Authors like Charles Dickens and Mark Twain had something in common other than great literary talent. They wrote without the use of "Spell Check!"

We all know and rely on these online tools while writing in a Word document, but they can only assist to some degree. As you may know, even if you spell an injury, city, person's name, or legal term *correctly*, the spell and grammar check will not recognize it and will underline it as incorrect. This is because a pre-set database of "common words" is included within the Microsoft software. However, based on your legal practice, and common legal words you use, you can add terms/ words and "customize" your online dictionary in Word, so that you do not run into this problem. You can simply enter the phrase into your search engine, "add words to your spell check dictionary—Word." The directions will show you how to customize your dictionary in *Word, Access, Excel, OneNote,* and *Publisher*.

Spell Check is helpful in catching misspelled words, errors in grammar, as well as finding things you may not catch, such as an extra space between words, two periods at the end of a sentence, and double words (the the). However, you should not become dependent on it. It is best to learn the rules of grammar, punctuation, and word usage so that you do not become reliant on online assistance. Another reason not to solely rely on Spell and Grammar Check is because certain conjunctions, such as *or, and, if,* and *but* may be spelled correctly, but if they are misplaced within a contract, they can make the difference between winning and losing a case.

As you can see in Figure 15-1, the *Chicago Manual of Style Online* can be used for a handy reference list of all the commonly recognized proofreader's marks, which you should know. Those marks may be utilized by your attorney in proofing your documents so you should know what they symbolize, as they are universal in the publishing world.

In addition to proofreading and editing legal documents for content, grammar, and punctuation, make certain the document you are editing follows the correct format set by the courts within your jurisdiction. For example, the length of the

Figure 15-1 Proofreaders' Marks – 16th Edition of the Chicago Manual of Style

Proofreaders' Marks

OPERATIONAL SIGNS

Mark	Meaning
⸍	Delete
⌣	Close up; delete space
⸍	Delete and close up (use only when deleting letters *within* a word)
(stet)	Let it stand
#	Insert space
(eq #)	Make space between words equal; make space between lines equal
(hr #)	Insert hair space
(ls)	Letterspace
¶	Begin new paragraph
□	Indent type one em from left or right
]	Move right
[	Move left
][	Center
⌐	Move up
⌣	Move down
(fl)	Flush left
(fr)	Flush right
═	Straighten type; align horizontally
‖	Align vertically
(tr)	Transpose
(sp)	Spell out

TYPOGRAPHICAL SIGNS

Mark	Meaning
(ital)	Set in italic type
(rom)	Set in roman type
(bf)	Set in boldface type
(lc)	Set in lowercase
(caps)	Set in capital letters
(sc)	Set in small capitals
(wf)	Wrong font; set in correct type
X	Check type image; remove blemish
V	Insert here *or* make superscript
Λ	Insert here *or* make subscript

PUNCTUATION MARKS

Mark	Meaning
⌃	Insert comma
⌄ ⌄	Insert apostrophe *or* single quotation mark
⌄ ⌄	Insert quotation marks
⊙	Insert period
(set) ?	Insert question mark
;	Insert semicolon
⌃ or :|	Insert colon
═	Insert hyphen
M	Insert em dash
N	Insert en dash
{|} or (|)	Insert parentheses

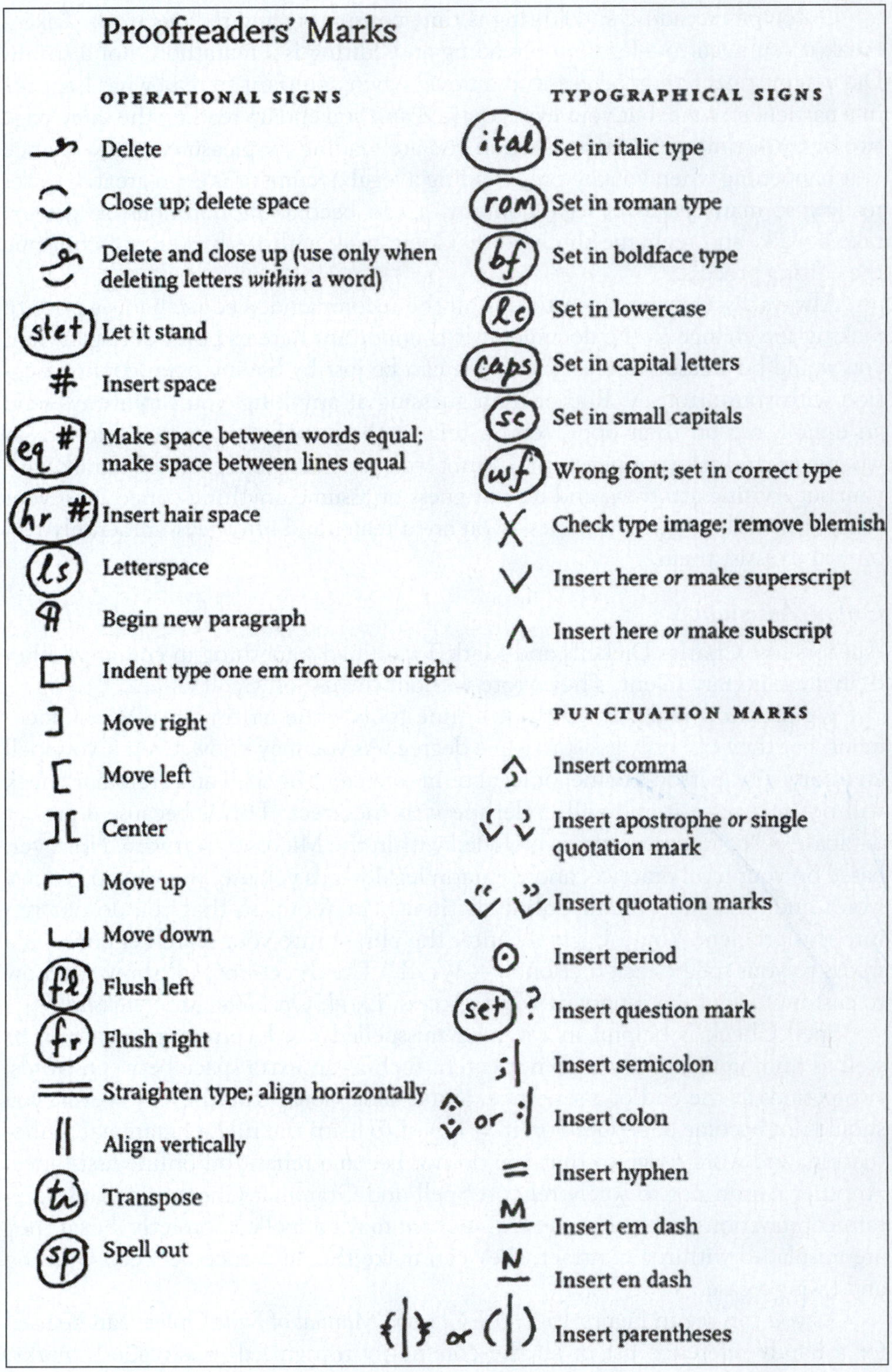

Source: http://www.chicagomanualofstyle.org. Used with permission of the University of Chicago Press.

document, acceptable font and style, possible cover page, and so on. These rules can be found in print or online in the local rules of court within your state or federal jurisdiction.

Proofreading and editing not only your own documents, but those of your attorney, is a very important task. In the legal profession, the smallest incorrect detail can lose a case. Therefore, excellent reading and comprehension skills are also a must. The attorney provides the arguments, but the paralegal provides the details—together, you create a highly professional legal document.

■ CITE-CHECKING SKILLS

LEARNING OBJECTIVE 2
Demonstrate how to cite check a legal document in print and online.

Other than internal research memoranda, which you learned in Chapter 13, there are many external legal documents that are filed with the courts by your supervising attorney. These documents include briefs (trial and appellate), documents referred to as findings of fact/conclusions of law (FOF/COL), and trial memoranda attached to motions. Unlike research memoranda which are considered objective writing, briefs, FOF/COL, and trial memos are considered *persuasive* writings, meaning that your attorney is arguing a specific point of law. In all these documents, the facts of the case are presented followed by legal argument. Within the legal argument section, numerous points of legal authority are included, which need to be verified.

Writing these types of documents is not a task typically given to an entry-level paralegal due to the complexity of the assignment. However, after gaining the necessary experience, your supervising attorney may permit you to draft such documents on your own. In the meantime, that does not mean that you cannot provide important assistance to expedite the filing of these documents.

Ethics Reminder

Another ethical rule that a paralegal must keep in mind is that a paralegal cannot engage in the practice of law. Therefore, if your supervising attorney permits you to draft any type of persuasive legal document, it MUST be read, edited, and SIGNED by the attorney prior to filing it with the court.

In this section, you will learn many important skills that will enable you to assist your attorney in preparing these various documents.

Cite checking includes both validating existing authority within a document, as well as inserting legal authority into a document. Aside from checking the grammar and punctuation of a legal document, it is equally crucial to proofread or insert all the authority contained in that document. You must make certain that all the authority included in the document is valid and accurate.

cite checking
The process of carefully reading the legal citation included within a legal document to determine if the sources of law are proper and valid authority.

Inserting and Validating Citations

You and your supervising attorney can work together in drafting these documents to be filed with the court. As you are creating the "facts" section, the attorney will draft the "legal argument" section. Because the attorney's job is very busy handling multiple cases and juggling different tasks on the case, he or she may just type or even write out the legal argument, and leave space with notes to you to fill in the appropriate authority. This saves the attorney a great deal of time. The reason for this is because the attorney will not be able to recall the citations of specific statutes or the names of specific cases to insert into the document to support his or her argument.

For instance, you may receive a portion of a case brief like the following:

> . . . However, the defendant in this case has failed to abide by the rules of court specifically stating that all defenses to the assertions made in a complaint must be filed within thirty (30) days of receiving the complaint. See, State Rules of Court, (add the rule here). Moreover, the defendant fails to satisfy any of the elements in proving a breach of contract in his counterclaim. See, (add case law here holding that a defendant must prove certain elements for a breach of contract in a counterclaim) . . .

As you can see, the lawyer will create the actual legal argument, which is her job. As the attorney is writing the document, she is not going to spend time researching all the authority as well; this is your job. You may receive an entire document that is peppered with highlighted notes within the document directing you to what authority is needed.

The practice of inserting legal authority into a document requires that you understand what the attorney is arguing/asserting. Make certain attorneys do not just leave blank spaces—they need to at least make a brief note of "what" to insert. You will be surprised by engaging in this practice how much you will learn about a particular area of law.

In another instance, as the attorney is drafting the argument, he may insert a prior document he wrote which includes legal authority, into the new document. In those instances, simply highlight each point of authority yourself (mostly case law) and look each case up to validate it, making sure the authority "matches up" with how the attorney is using the source.

Figure 15-2 Cite Checking Authority in a Brief

presumption is "one of necessity" to be applied only in cases of the party's "inability to present direct testimony regarding the exchange of *verba in praesenti*." *Id.* at 1021. There is no basis to resort to the presumption if the claimant is available to directly testify to the words allegedly exchanged with the decedent. *Giant Eagle v. Workmen's Comp. Appeal Bd. (Bahorich),* 602 A.2d 387, 389 (Pa. Cmwlth. 1992). The validity of a common-law marriage is a mixed question of law and fact. *PPL v. Workers' Comp. Appeal Bd. (Rebo),* 5 A.3d 839, 843 (Pa. Cmwlth. 2010).

Employer first argues that the WCJ in establish a common-law marriage "by substantial e and convincing evidence," equating the appella applicable burden of proof.

> Upon receiving the document, you would highlight or circle the appropriate authority (usually case law) and verify it for accuracy and content.

Citing *Gibson v. Workers' Compensation Appeal Board (Armco Stainless & Alloy Products),* 861 A.2d 938 (Pa. 2004), which involved a fatal claim petition filed by the decedent's surviving wife, the WCJ stated that Claimant was

Source: http://www.pacourts.us

By engaging in the process of cite checking sources or inserting the authority into the document, you are also strengthening your comprehension of legal terminology. However, if you encounter any word/term/phrase with which you are unfamiliar, be sure to look it up—do not guess or assume anything.

Not only will you be responsible for cite checking the work of your own attorney, but you will also cite check the documents filed by *opposing* counsel. Anything that is filed in court by the opposing party will also be mailed to your supervising attorney. The idea behind this is that many times opposing counsel may inadvertently include a case that is directly on point to help them win their issue, but it may have been recently overturned and therefore be considered invalid law. If you find such an error, notify your supervising attorney immediately. Sometimes winning your case is not only about a good offense but a good defense as well.

Figure 15-3 Cite Checking Opposing Counsel's Brief

481 U.S. 739 (1987) 25

Wash. State Grange v. Wash. State Republican Party,
552 U.S. 442 (2008) 25

Weinschenk v. State,
203 S.W.3d 201 (Mo. 2006) 27

Winston v. Moore,
244 Pa. 447, 91 A. 520 (1914) ....

CONSTITUTIONAL PROVISIONS AND STATUTES

Pa. Const. art. I, §§ 1 and 26 ....

Pa. Const. art. I, § 5 ....

Pa. Const. art. III, § 1 (1838) ....

Pa. Const. art. VII, § 1 ....

25 P.S. § 2626(b) ....

25 P.S. § 3050(a.2)(1) 15

25 P.S. § 3050(a.4)(5)(ii)(D), (E) 16

Act of March 14, 2012, P.L. 195, No. 18 1

75 Pa. Cons. Stat. § 1510(b) 2, 11, 12, 13

Ind. Code § 3-11-10-24 .... 17, 26

OTHER AUTHORITIES

Black's Law Dictionary 1584 (8th ed. 2004) 8

Jacob Gershman, *Judge Posner Walks Back Comments to HuffPost*,
Wall St. J. LawBlog, Oct. 28, 2013, *at* http://blogs.wsj.com/law/2013/10/28/judge-posner-walks-back-comments-to-huffpost/ 28

Pa.R.C.P. 227.1 .... 1, 3, 6, 39

Richard A. Posner, *I Did Not 'Recant' on Voter ID Laws*, New Republic, Oct. 27, 2013 28

> When your attorney receives a brief from opposing counsel, it is good to go immediately to the "Table of Authorities" at the beginning of the brief. As you can see here, counsel uses cases, constitutions, statutes, as well as secondary authority. You would cite-check each source to validate that it is good law, and that the source was used properly. The page numbers provided direct you to the page in the brief where the authority is used.

Source: http://www.pacourts.us

Therefore, any legal document your attorney receives from opposing counsel, will be given to you to make certain:

- The authority used is still good law and has not been overturned (this happens more than you think);
- The citations are correct, including all quotations used;
- The authority stands for the point of law being argued.

Cite checking is a very important task and a paralegal can spend much time ensuring that all legal documents filed with the court are correct. While you are employed, be certain to inform your supervising attorneys that you are familiar with cite insertion/checking—they will be not only impressed, but grateful as well.

You may be called upon to check any and all authority located in an opposing attorney's document in order to tell the attorney how to rebut his argument, or to show your attorney where his argument is weak.

Online Assistance

With a subscription, both *Lexis Advance* and *WestlawNext* have created cite-checking software that can be installed directly into your Microsoft Word document. Both *Lexis* and *Westlaw* offer online step-by-step tutorials on how to use the software.

Lexis for Microsoft Office offers many helpful cite checking and validating features that allow you to cite check any document within minutes. As you can see in Figure 15-4, the software works in a "split-screen" format so you never have to leave your Word document. The software can *Shepardize* your entire document to ensure every citation is not only valid law, but that it is in its proper format with the jurisdictional format you set. The system can also read and validate any quoted authority to make certain it matches its official legal source of law. In addition, if your attorney requires help with gathering all the citations for an appellate brief, you can create a Table of Authorities for every source of authority included in the brief right within your Word document.

Figure 15-4 Lexis for Microsoft Office

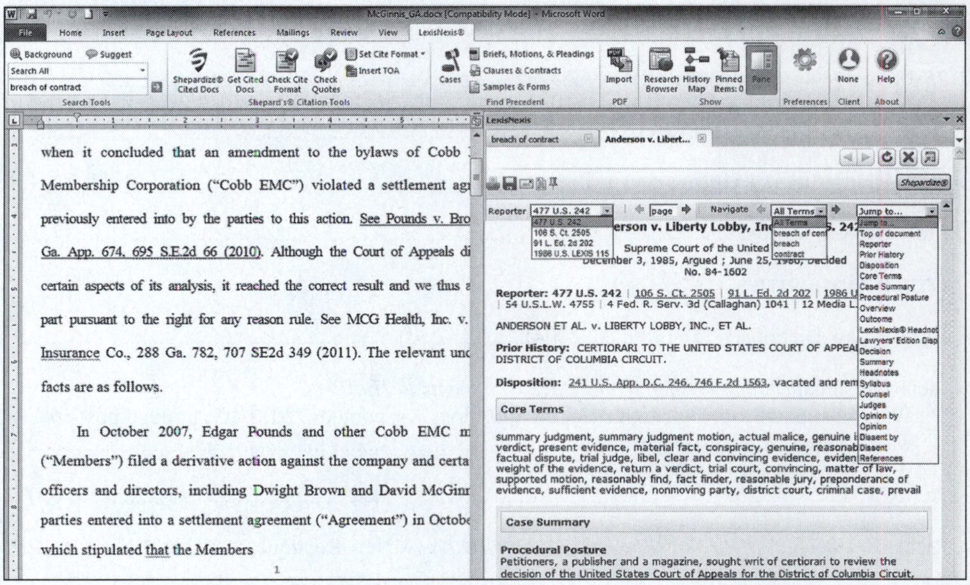

Source: Reprinted with the permission of LexisNexis.

Figure 15-5 Westlaw Drafting Assistant

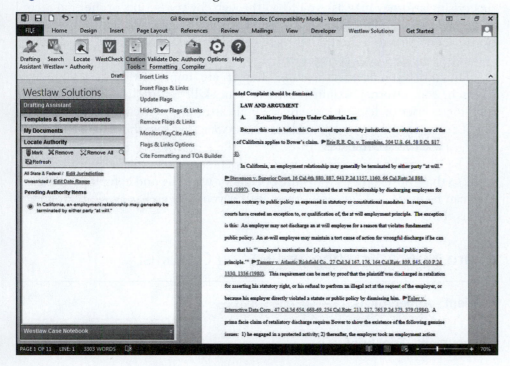

Source: Reprinted with permission of Thomson Reuters, from Westlaw Legal Solutions.

In addition, *WestlawNext* created **Westlaw Drafting Assistant**, which performs essentially the same tasks as the *Lexis* software. As you can see in Figure 15-5, you can perform a "split-screen" search of all authority and quickly and efficiently validate it within minutes using *WestCheck*. You can also verify the accuracy of all quoted material within the document using *QuoteRight*, as well as build a Table of Authorities if needed from all the authority within that particular document. In addition, you can format the document, including all citations, according to the jurisdictional guidelines you set.

You can utilize all these features from both systems in a Word document that you *create*, as well as in a document you *receive* from opposing counsel to cite their work for possible errors. Both *Lexis* and *Westlaw* offer a quick and efficient way to cite check, format, validate authority, and create a Table of Authority within your Word document.

Validating Citations to a Record

Other than cite checking authority within a document, paralegals also validate citations to the trial record. If you are drafting the facts of the case into any legal document, you have to cite to a specific note, deposition, interrogatory, medical report, and so on, just as you would for legal authority.

LEARNING OBJECTIVE 3
How to validate citations within trial records.

When you are drafting the facts section for any legal document, there is constant cross-referencing between documents throughout the file. For example:

> "On August 15, 2013, Dr. Levin stated at his deposition that he instructed the plaintiff to see a specialist to evaluate her arm." (N.T. 8/15/13, pg. 34).

The "N.T." stands for "notes of testimony," or "T.N." is also used indicating "transcript notes." So, for instance, if the opposing counsel and the judge in your case read the above sentence, they should be able to quickly go to the deposition of August 15th to read that portion of the doctor's testimony. At other times, your supervising attorney may ask you to go through the transcripts of the trial record to find references that the attorney wants to use in his or her brief. In those situations, when you cite to trial notes, deposition notes, exhibits, or medical records, you must provide a correct document and page number to that source.

The skills you learned in this chapter are important. Other than legal research, your attorney requires many of your skills during litigation. If you are proofing a brief or legal document for your attorney, you can create your own template to ensure you have addressed *everything* within the document before filing, as you can see in Figure 15-6.

The list can be made specific for each document and attached with the document so that the attorney knows the document was fully and completely proofed, or it can be made as a "general" checklist for you to keep handy. Check off each task as completed.

Figure 15-6 A Proofing and Editing Checklist

Client - Anderson, C.

Document - Trial brief

Date -

_____ Proofread (spelling, grammar, punctuation)

_____ Edit (correct names, titles, dates, injuries, monetary amounts, medications, etc.)

_____ Correct case references (notes of testimony, transcript references)

Cite Checking:

_____ Accurate quotes

_____ Accurate citation format

_____ Accurate and valid authority

_____ Cite check any additional authority (statutes, rules of court)

_____ Any and all legal authority inserted where needed

Chapter Checklist ☑

- Proofing and editing skills are also very important in the legal profession, whether editing your work or the work of your attorney. You have to be a sharp and careful reader, and make certain that every name, date, injury, medication, and especially every monetary amount or figure is correct.

- There are many online programs that exist to assist you in proofing and editing legal douments—use them.

- Remember that athough the paralegal is responsible for any in-house writing and legal correspondence, any legal document filed with the court, such as a brief or complaint, is written by the attorney. As you become more seasoned, your supervising attorney will expand your responsibilities, but if you do assist in writing a legal document to be filed, it is **always** to be reviewed, edited, and signed by the attorney.

- Cite checking is a skill that requires careful reading. Always cite check all citations for accuracy, validity, and recency.

- *Lexis* and *Westlaw* both have software that can be inserted directly into your Word document to assist with cite checking, as well as a host of other helpful features. If your supervising attorney has a subscription to either company, sign up for this feature.

- Inserting case citation when needed is equally important. Make sure that the authority you locate directly relates to the legal argument the attorney is asserting.

KEY TERMS

Proofreading   389   Editing   389   Cite checking   393

CRITICAL THINKING AND APPLICATION

Please read each question and follow the directions.

1. Your instructor will obtain a document (trial or appellate brief, findings of fact, or trial memoranda) that was filed with the court in your state, and redact all the authority from that document. Read the document carefully, and **insert** all of the redacted authority within the document.

2. Your instructor will obtain another brief or portion of a brief from a case within your jurisdiction where all of the authority will be included in the document. Locate all the authority and cite check it to be certain it is accurate, valid, and in the proper *Bluebook* citation format. As you are validating the law, see if you can find more recent cases that stand for the same point of law.

3. If you have a subscription to either *Lexis* or *Westlaw* in your paralegal academic program, install the system's cite-checking software. Navigate through the program and utilize the software using a Word document that you create —maybe your legal memorandum or your comprehensive case study from this text. Become familiar with the program.

4. You are employed as a paralegal in a small general practice firm that handles real estate transactions. The client is coming to your offices this week to sign an agreement to purchase real estate. The attorney has drafted the agreement, but she needs you to carefully proofread this very important document.

Read the following facts of the agreement below. Thereafter, sharpen your proofreading skills and see if any mistakes have been made in the agreement. If so, what are the corrections, if any? Highlight or circle and explain the errors.

- Address: 123 County Line Road.
- Location: Beginning at an iron pipe marked A and thence running South 7 degrees 13 minutes East 85 feet to a pipe marked B, thence North 74 degrees 21 minutes East 33 2/10 feet to a pipe marked C, thence North 10 degrees 21 minutes West 75 7/10 feet to a pipe marked D, thence South 88 degrees 27 minutes West 27 1/10 feet to the place of beginning containing 2310.4 square feet.

- Purchase price: $295,500.00 to be paid in cash at time of sale. If not, purchaser's ability to obtain a mortgage loan within 30 days after acceptance of the offer by the seller in the amount of $200,000.00, payable in not less than 60 monthly installments at an interest rate not to exceed 3.4%.

- Purchaser down payment: $95,000.00 with a balance of $200,000.00 to be paid at the rate of 3.4%.

- No existing mortgages exist.

- Ernest money: negotiable, but not to exceed $35,000.00.

- Possession: Purchaser takes physical possession on August 1, 2013; and if seller is not prepared to transfer ownership, a breach of contract fee of $250.00 per day will be incurred.

- Additional "improvements and fixtures:" split-rail fence only along creek side; work-shed (8 feet by 6 feet).

- The agreement is void if not accepted by the seller no later than noon on August 1, 2013.

- Closing of the sale to take place 10 days after Purchaser's receipt of an abstract.

AGREEMENT TO PURCHASE

The undersigned ("Purchaser") hereby offers to purchase form the owner (herein "Seller") the real estate located at 123 County Line Road, in City, County, and State. The legal description includes: Beginning at an iron pipe marked A and thence running South 7 degrees 13 minutes East 85 feet to a pipe marked B, thence North 74 degrees 21 minutes East 33 2/10 feet to a pipe marked C, thence North 10 degrees 21 minutes West 75 7/10 feet to a pipe marked D, thence South 88 degrees 27 minutes West 27 1/10 feet to the place of beginning containing 2310.4 square feet.

A. The purchase price shall be two hundred and ninety-five thousand dollars ($295,500.00). The entire purchase price to be paid in full at the time of sale. If not, Purchaser may obtain a mortgage within thirty (30) days after acceptance of this offer in the amount of two hundred thousand dollars ($200,00.00), payable in not less than sixty (60) monthly installments, including an interest rate not to exceed 3.2%.

B. No existing mortgages exist on record.

C. The down payment to be made at the time of sale shall be ninety-four thousand dollars ($95,000.00) and the balance of two hundred thousand dollars ($200,00.00) shall be paid.

D. As earnest money, Purchaser deposits thirty-five thousand ($35,000.00) with the broker which shall be applied to the purchase price at the time of closing the sale. In the event this agreement is not accepted by Seller, this earnest money is to be promptly returned to the Purchaser by the broker. In the event the offer is accepted by Seller, and Purchaser shall fail to perform the terms of this agreement, the earnest money shall be forfeited as liquidated damages suffered by Seller.

E. Purchaser to take possession of the property on August 1, 2013. In any event that the Seller does not perform according to the closing of this agreement, Seller is ordered to pay two-hundred dollars ($250.00) per day as damages for breach of contract.

F. This offer to purchase includes all improvements, buildings and fixtures presently on the real estate including, electrical, gas, heating, air conditioning, plumbing, equipment, appliances, screens, storm windows, interior and exterior doors, awnings, attached carpeting, trees, shrubs, flowers, split-rail fence, and a work-shed (6' × 8').

G. This offer is void if not accepted by Seller in writing on or before August 1, 2013 by 5pm.

Signatures:

Seller _____,

Purchaser _____

5. You are a paralegal working in a real estate firm and your supervising attorney needs you to review a client's real estate lease for any error. Read the attorney's notes below concerning the important portions of the agreement then proofread the lease itself to ensure that the attorney's notes correctly match the information in the lease. Is there anything that you would bring to the attorney's attention?

Thomas Devlin (Landlord) and Michael Williams (Tenant) entered into a lease agreement for the dates of June 14, 20__ through March 10, 20 __. The landlord leased to the tenant three garages (A, B, and D) located at 1567 Ridge Avenue. The landlord recently painted the garage doors and the floor of each garage. The tenant is to not make any marks on the floors or walls and is not permitted to nail, screw, or drill into any of the walls. The tenant may use the shelving units within each garage. The tenant is not permitted to store any explosive or flammable liquids or containers within the garage at any time. The tenant shall pay the landlord $675.00 per garage for a total of $2,025.00 per month. If any payments are late (after the first of the month) then the parties agree to a penalty of $120.00 per day after the first of the month until paid in full. The tenant will pay a security deposit of $250 per garage for a total of $750 which will be held and disbursed to the tenant at the end of the lease. After the lease has expired, the landlord and tenant agreement will automatically renew on a month-to-month basis. The landlord agrees to maintain the garage areas structurally, including the garage doors, walls, ceiling, and floors of each garage, working outside lights surrounding the garage, ice and snow removal by a third party independent contractor of the landlord's choosing, and a working and updated alarm system. The tenant agrees to be responsible for the garage door lock. The Landlord agrees not to enter the premises in possession of the Tenant (Garage A, B, or D) during the lease period without the presence of the Tenant during the lease period. However, the Tenant agrees that the Landlord may enter the premises without the Tenant in the case of an immediate emergency and/or and Act of God or disaster. The tenant agrees not to assign or sublet any of the leased property without the prior written consent of the landlord. The landlord may terminate this lease upon thirty (30) days notice to the tenant that the entire property has been sold. The lease shall be construed and governed by the laws of the state of X.

LEASE AGREEMENT

This lease agreement (Lease) is made effective on June 14, 20__ by and between Thomas Devlin (Landlord) and Michael Williams (Tenant). The parties agree as follows:

TERM: The lease is to begin on June 14, 20__ and will terminate on March 10, 20__.

PREMISES: Landlord leases to the Tenant, Garage A, B, and D, located at 1567 Ridge Avenue.

RENT: On the first of every month, the Tenant will pay $675.00 per garage for a total of $2,205.00 per month. If the payment is late a daily penalty will be imposed of $120.00 per day until rent and penalties are paid in full.

FURNISHINGS: Prior to Tenant's possession of the property, the landlord painted each garage door and floor of each garage. The Tenant is prohibited to paint either the garage doors or floors a different color or mark up the garage doors or floors in any way. In addition, the Tenant is prohibited from nailing, screwing, of drilling into any of the walls of any garage, but may have use of the shelving units in each garage.

DUTIES: The Landlord agrees to maintain the garage areas structurally, including the garage doors, walls, ceiling, and the floors of each garage, the working outside lights surrounding the garage, ice and snow removal by a third party independent contractor whom the Landlord and Tenant agree upon, and a working and updated alarm system. The Tenant agrees to the responsibility for the garage door lock, but is not permitted to add any additional alarm or security measures.

RENEWAL: Upon termination of the lease on March 10, 20__, the Landlord and Tenant agree that the lease will automatically renew on a month-to-month basis.

SECURITY DEPOSIT: The Tenant will pay a security deposit of $250.00 per garage for a total of $750.00 which will be held then disbursed to Tenant at the end of the lease.

ACCESS BY LANDLORD: The Landlord agrees not to enter the premises in possession of the Tenant (Garage A, B, or D) during the lease period without the presence of the Tenant.

However, the Tenant agrees that the Landlord may enter the premises without the Tenant in the case of an immediate emergency and/or and Act of God or disaster.

DANGEROUS MATERIALS: The Tenant agrees not to store any material that is considered dangerous, flammable, or of an explosive nature, or anything that would increase the likelihood of fire that would cause damage to any unit on the Landlord's property unless the Tenant provides prior written consent of Landlord is obtained and proof of adequate insurance protection is provided by the Tenant.

ASSIGNABILITY: The Tenant agrees not to assign or sublet any of the leased property without the prior written consent of the Landlord.

TERMINATION UPON SALE: The Landlord may terminate this lease upon thirty (30) days notice to the Tenant that the entire property has been sold, with notice including written correspondence mailed to or served to the Tenant.

GOVERNING LAW: This lease shall be construed and governed by the laws of the state of X.

COMPREHENSIVE CASE STUDY
Part IV   Drafting Legal Correspondence

OVERVIEW

Welcome to the final installment of the Comprehensive Case Study. In the initial installment, you formulated the issues based on the facts of the case. In the second installment, you researched the law in order to address and resolve those same issues. In the third installment, you gathered and organized your research findings and drafted a legal memorandum. Now, in the final installment, you will draft legal correspondence to Lena's supervisor and to Lena, utilizing your letter writing skills.

■ THE FIRST LETTER

As you learned in Chapter 14, a demand letter consists of the plaintiff's attorney "demanding" that the potential defendant correct the wrong committed upon the plaintiff. This type of letter allows the defendant to make the situation right before any legal action is initiated. If you recall, "demanding" does not mean being rude, callus, or demeaning to the potential defendant. Rather, the letter should remain professional, yet firm in your request.

In a case such as this where a managing supervisor oversees a federal office, and there is a grievance by an employee, the employee may file a complaint with the US Department of Labor or bring a private lawsuit against the employer. However, in many situations such as this, a demand letter may prevent any legal action and the employee can return to work.

So in the first letter, you are to draft a demand letter to Lena's supervisor including the following points:

- Explain the facts fully and clearly. Briefly inform the supervisor of the reason for Lena's requested time off, as well as any legally significant facts in the case in order to help refresh the supervisor's mind of the case;
- Be specific in what you are demanding for the client. This is where your supervising attorney (your instructor) will assist you. In researching Lena's issues, what should you "demand" from the supervisor? Be sure to include:
  - Reinstating her managerial position;
  - Payment of any lost wages;
  - Remove any and all possible discipline reports in Lena's employment records due to this situation.
- Explain the detrimental effects for not complying with the law, and suggest to the supervisor that he comply with the law you found or be faced with having to defend his actions in a court of law.

- State a definite date for his response (one week from the date of the letter), and explain that if your supervising attorney does not hear from him, legal action will be initiated by the attorney.
- Send the letter certified mail. Lena's file number is 44-5546. Your firm's address is Wallace, Kennedy, & Pittman. 123 Main Street, Your City, Your State, Your Zip. (111-555-1234). Send a copy to the client as well.

The supervisor's information is as follows:

Mr. Craig P. Sullivan
The Haswell Building
442 One Way Road
Your City, Your State, Your Zip

As with all demand letters, it would have to be read, edited, and approved by your supervising attorney.

■ THE SECOND LETTER

As you also learned in Chapter 14, another type of letter commonly drafted by a paralegal is the status letter. If you recall, the status report letter is different from an opinion letter in that the opinion letter is drafted by the attorney, contains information specific to trial strategy, and includes legal advice by the attorney, which is something a paralegal is prohibited from doing according to the ethical rules. On the other hand, the purpose of the status update letter is to merely keep the client up-to-date on the status of the case, nothing more.

Draft a status update letter to the client, Lena Mitchell, and be sure to include the following:

- Inform the client that all research has been performed on her case, and that the results proved favorable for her to take the requested leave of absence;
- Inform her of the research results of the supervisor's actions;
- Inform her that a demand letter has been drafted and sent to the supervisor, and that she will be receiving a copy;
- Explain that you will again contact her (by phone) after one week to see if the supervisor will comply with the law;
- If not, explain that the attorney will contact her as to her legal options at that time;
- End the letter stating that if you can be of any assistance to her, to please contact you.

The client's information is as follows:

Ms. Lena A. Mitchell
321 Main Drive
Your City, Your State, Your Zip

Utilize your best grammar and punctuation in drafting these letters.

Congratulations on completing the textbook case study!

"That which we persist in doing becomes easier, not that the task itself has become easier, but that our ability to perform it has improved."

–Ralph Waldo Emerson

SAMPLE LEGAL MEMORANDA

In Chapter 13, you learned how to create a memorandum of law. In this appendix, you will see three additional memos, each ranging from easy to advanced levels. Each memo will also highlight helpful tips. Read them carefully and pay particular attention to the *analysis* section in each, as it is the most important.

You will also notice that the format may differ slightly from the memorandum example you read in Chapter 13. These variations are acceptable in the legal profession, but it is good to view a memorandum from your office to see what the attorneys prefer to use. If your supervising attorney has no preference, consider some of the following options found in this appendix.

■ SAMPLE ONE – CIVIL LAW (LEVEL: EASY)

This memorandum example demonstrates an easy and brief analysis. When you receive an assignment from your supervising attorney, not every memo written will be a complex, five-page memo including multiple issues. Some can be simple; therefore, the memo should also be succinct yet clearly address and answer the issue.

Memorandum

TO: Supervising Attorney

FROM: Paralegal

DATE: June 24, 20xx

RE: Peter v. David - #58856-001

Question Presented

> If you are only analyzing a single issue, you do not have to number it, but you may if you feel more comfortable.

1. Whether David can be held liable for assault and battery against Peter?

Brief Answer

David cannot be held liable for assault or battery against Peter, as Peter was not aware of an imminent apprehension to satisfy the claim of assault, and David did not engage in any actual intentional contact to satisfy the claim of battery.

Statement of Facts

Peter and David are neighbors who have lived next door to each other for five (5) years. The men would routinely engage in arguments and disputes concerning their respective properties. One day, Peter informed David that he wanted to plant trees along the centerline of the two properties, and Peter asked David to "go in half" since they would be planted on both the properties. David became enraged and said that he would not put out the money for trees and have to contend with raking the leaves, as well as having the leaves clogging up his drains and gutters every year. David insisted that he and his neighbor Peter build a tall fence between the properties instead, to which Peter disagreed. At that point *Peter's wife, Linda, exited their home to help Peter with some landscaping in the front garden.* David went into his garage, grabbed a small garden shovel, and went over to Peter, who had his back turned away from David and was kneeling in the flower garden. David said that he wish Peter were dead and swung the shovel at Peter's head, missing him by about six (6) inches. Afterward, Peter turned around, pulled the earbuds out from his MP3 player and said, "What do you want?!" David threw the shovel on his lawn and walked away yelling, "I'm going out to shop for the tallest fence I can find!" *Linda informed Peter of David's actions.*

> This is another good example of using only the *legally significant facts*. Even though all the facts here are true, are they really significant and directly related to whether or not an assault and/or battery had been committed? The issue is brief, so make the facts brief as well. Consider all the facts in italics—are they necessary? Now, read the facts not in italics.

Analysis/Discussion

The issue presented is whether David can be held liable for assault and/or battery against Peter after David picked up a shovel and swung it at Peter's head, although David did not cause any physical contact with Peter, and Peter did not see or hear the threat.

In Pennsylvania, an assault occurs when (1) the defendant acts intending to cause a harmful or offensive contact with another, or an imminent apprehension of such contact; and (2) the other person is placed in such apprehension of a harmful or offensive contact; and (3) the other person is aware of such contact. *Ford v. Jacobs*, 999 A.2d 432 (Pa. 2003). On the other hand, a battery is committed when the defendant creates intentional contact that is harmful or offensive without the other person's consent. *Jones v. Peterson*, 222 A.2d 778 (Pa. Super. 1998).

> **Notice here that you could have discussed the assault claim first, then discussed the claim of battery, or combined the discussion of the two torts as you see here**

In this situation, David, following a heated argument, picked up a shovel and swung it at Peter's head. That act could have very well constituted an assault. However, one crucial element of assault is that the plaintiff is "aware" of the imminent fear of an immediate harmful or offensive contact. *See, Vonn v. Miller*, 556 A.2d 443 (Pa. Super. 2002) (no assault occurred after defendant grabbed a brick, approached plaintiff from behind, and held it over plaintiff's head in a threatening manner; plaintiff was unaware of the threat and did not sustain any imminent fear of an immediate harmful or offensive contact). Because Peter was unaware of David's actions, as his back was turned away from David, the "awareness" element cannot be sustained, and therefore the claim must fail. Even David's offensive words and tone (wishing he was dead) cannot sustain a claim for assault. It is well settled that words alone do not constitute an assault. *Smith v. Walker*, 334 A.2d 339 (Pa. 1999). According to the law, and after a review of the relevant facts, no assault was committed.

Furthermore, David cannot be held liable for the tort of battery, as David caused no actual physical contact with Peter in order to satisfy the elements of the tort. The facts clearly state that David swung the shovel directly at Peter's head, but no actual contact was made. The main and crucial element of a battery is that a "contact" must be made against the plaintiff.

Therefore, it is more than likely that David cannot be held liable for the torts of assault or battery against Peter.

■ SAMPLE TWO – CRIMINAL LAW (LEVEL: MODERATE)

This memorandum example demonstrates a slightly more difficult analysis. Just remember to follow the "basics" of memo writing, which can be applied to any type of memorandum analyzing any type of issue.

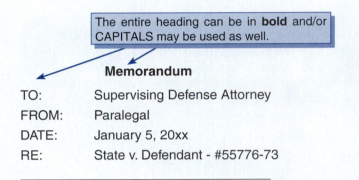

The entire heading can be in **bold** and/or CAPITALS may be used as well.

Memorandum

TO: Supervising Defense Attorney
FROM: Paralegal
DATE: January 5, 20xx
RE: State v. Defendant - #55776-73

You can use either "question" or "issue" presented.

Questions (Issues) Presented

1. Whether Defendant can be convicted of first-degree murder after stopping, aiming, and shooting Victim on a vital part of the body?
2. Whether Defendant can be convicted of robbery as he did not take Victim's money but committed the crime by force with a deadly weapon?

Brief Answers

1. Defendant can be convicted of first-degree murder because he committed the killing with premeditation on a vital part of the victim's body, thus satisfying the necessary elements of the crime.
2. Defendant can be convicted of robbery in the first-degree because even though he did not take the victim's money, he committed the crime by force, thus satisfying the necessary elements of the crime.

The various headings can be in **bold** or **underlined**. But whatever you choose, be consistent!

Statement of Facts

Defendant was fired as a parking attendant after failing a drug test for the third time. He was angry at being unemployed and wanted to "get even." Defendant asked Friend, to drive him to pick up his last paycheck. Friend was suspicious since it was 10:30 p.m. Saturday evening, and he did not believe anyone could retrieve the paycheck at such a late hour, but he agreed to drive Defendant anyway.

Defendant instructed Friend to park just outside the parking lot. Defendant told Friend that he was going to rob the parking attendant. He knew at least $400 would be in the cash drawer since he previously worked in the booth. Friend said, "What?! You got to be kidding, I'm not going to jail for you." Defendant told Friend to "keep an eye open" for anyone approaching. Friend saw Defendant load a full magazine clip into an automatic handgun, and pull a plastic bag from his pants pocket. Defendant said, "Don't worry. I'm not killing nobody. Just stay put." Defendant took Friend's cell phone and car keys, and exited the car. Friend remained in the vehicle.

As Defendant walked up to the booth, he said to the attendant, "Hey, nobody is working the front desk inside, can you validate my parking ticket?" As the attendant turned away for a moment, Defendant pulled out his gun, pointed it at the attendant and said, "Hey, I know you have the key to the cash box, so open it up." The attendant lied and said he didn't have a key and stood up to run from the booth. Defendant yelled, "Open the box!" The attendant threw the whole cash box at Defendant, which broke open at Defendant's feet, and the attendant ran from the booth yelling to get the attention of the security guards. Defendant left all the money, and as he ran toward the car, he stopped, turned, aimed, and fired a single shot at the attendant who momentarily turned around, striking him in the center of his chest. The attendant collapsed and Defendant jumped into the car.

Defendant threw the car keys at Friend and told him to drive. The two men stayed at the apartment of Defendant's girlfriend, but both were captured and arrested two days later.

Attendant died from the gunshot wound, but no firearm was recovered. No witnesses were present at the crime scene except for a man walking his dog across the street and saw Defendant run into Friend's car after hearing a gunshot. After his arrest, Friend provided a statement to police implicating Defendant. Friend told police that he did not plan or participate in any of the crimes.

Analysis/Discussion

1./ Issue One

> Whichever format you use, make certain you **always** number multiple issues so that the reader can differentiate each issue.

The issue is whether Defendant can be convicted of first-degree murder after stopping, aiming, and shooting the parking attendant on a vital part of the body.

In Pennsylvania, to sustain a conviction for first-degree murder, the Commonwealth must prove that the defendant acted with a specific intent to kill, a human being was unlawfully killed, and that the accused committed the killing. **18 Pa.C.S.A. §2502.** An intentional killing is defined as a killing by means of poison, lying in wait, or any type of willful, deliberate, premediated killing. *See, Commonwealth v. Simpson,* 754 A.2d 1264 (Pa. 2000).

Here, Defendant approached the parking attendant and demanded the cash box. After the parking attendant said he did not have the key and attempted to flee the scene, Defendant pulled out his gun, pointed it at the attendant and said, "Hey, I know you have the key to the cash box, so open it up." The attendant attempted to flee and threw at Defendant the whole cash box, which broke open at Defendant's feet, and the attendant ran from the booth. Defendant left all the money, and as he ran toward the car, he stopped, turned, and fired a single shot at the attendant, striking him in the chest. The attendant collapsed and Defendant jumped into the car.

In deciding whether the defendant had the specific intent to kill, the fact finder may consider all relevant evidence, including the defendant's words and conduct and the attending circumstances that may show his state of mind. *Commonwealth v. Gibson*, 951 A.2d 1110 (Pa. 2008). The prosecution will most likely argue that Defendant could have easily run into Friend's car to make his escape, and the facts state that he was not himself in any immediate danger when he shot the parking attendant so self-defense is not an option. The prosecution does have a strong case for first-degree, as Defendant stopped, turned and aimed at the parking attendant, which constitutes premeditation. Further, the prosecution will argue that if our client wanted to silence the parking attendant from calling for assistance, he could have shot him in the leg, arm, or even in the air to scare him. Rather, Defendant shot the victim in the chest. *See, Commonwealth v. Jones*, 886 A.2d 689 (Pa. Super. 2005) (specific intent may be inferred from the defendant's use of a deadly weapon upon a vital part of the victim's body). In addition, Defendant fled the scene after the shooting and did not call for help or offer assistance to the victim. *See, Commonwealth v. Markman*, 916 A.2d 586 (Pa. 2007) (flight and concealment can be circumstantial proof of consciousness of guilt). The defense can attempt to argue the lesser charge of second-degree murder (murder committed during the course of committing a felony) but may not prove successful, as the prosecution can easily make out the elements of first-degree murder.

Therefore, it is very likely that Defendant can be convicted of first-degree murder after he committed the killing with premeditation on a vital part of the victim's body, thus satisfying the necessary elements of the crime.

Issue Two

The next issue is whether Defendant can be convicted of robbery, as he did not take the victim's money but committed the crime by force with a deadly weapon.

In Pennsylvania, a person commits the crime of robbery when, in the course of committing a theft, he (1) inflicts serious bodily injury (SBI) upon another, or (2) threatens another with or intentionally places the fear upon another of SBI, or (3) commits or threatens to commit any felony in the first or second degree, or (4) physically takes or removes property from another by force however slight. **18 Pa.C.S.A. §3701**.

Here, Defendant demanded the cash box from the parking attendant with the threat of force—a firearm, thus satisfying the crime. However, in the course of committing the theft, Defendant shot and killed the victim during the robbery, thus elevating the grading of the crime to a first-degree felony. It is irrelevant whether or not the defendant actually takes the property of the victim during a robbery; the crime is satisfied by the defendant using force or acting with a threat of force. *See, Commonwealth v. Lloyd*, 545 A.2d 890 (Pa. Super. 1987) (defendant found guilty of robbery even though a "completed theft" is not necessary; force or threat of force is sufficient).

Therefore, it is likely that Defendant can be convicted of first-degree robbery after he used deadly force in taking the property of another, thus satisfying the necessary elements of the crime.

> Remember that each case/statute must stand out. It is best to **bold** or *italicize* cases and <u>underline</u> statutes, but remember, whichever you do choose – be consistent throughout the memo.

■ SAMPLE THREE – CIVIL LAW (LEVEL: ADVANCED)

This memorandum example demonstrates a slightly more difficult analysis. It involves a medical malpractice case that involves the actions committed by the doctor, the patient, and a third party—all of which must be analyzed.

Memorandum

TO: Supervising Defense Attorney
FROM: Paralegal
DATE: March 19, 20xx
RE: Patient v. Doctor - #776-22-399

Questions (Issues) Presented

1. Whether Doctor can be held liable for plaintiff's injuries after he performed a surgical procedure on the plaintiff.
2. Whether Patient contributed to her injury caused by Doctor by not following Doctor's proscribed postsurgical instructions?
3. Whether Doctor can be held liable for the actions of Nurse who engaged in routine postoperative care following after surgery, which caused injury to Patient?

Brief Answers

1. Doctor can be held liable under a theory of medical malpractice after he committed numerous negligent actions during and following Patient's surgical procedure.
2. Patient did not contribute to her injury as her failure to follow Doctor's post-operative instructions were independent of Doctor's negligent actions, and had no adverse affect on her injury.
3. Doctor cannot be held liable for the actions of Nurse as she was not under the immediate and direct supervision of Doctor's instructions.

Statement of Facts

Doctor, a licensed surgeon, has been practicing at Temple University Hospital in the city and state of Philadelphia, Pennsylvania for eighteen (18) years. Patient (age 82) was referred to Doctor by her family physician after sustaining a broken ankle. After examining her ankle, Doctor determined that Patient sustained a complex break and that he would need to re-set the ankle bone. Due to her age, Doctor informed Patient that her bones would not heal properly on their own, so he would have to insert three (3) screws and a metal plate to fuse the bones together during an operation.

The operation was scheduled for 4 p.m. on Friday. Doctor was notified Tuesday of that same week that he was needed as a last-minute replacement at a national medical conference in Miami on Saturday and Sunday of that same week.

Doctor was thrilled by the opportunity to speak at such a prestigious event, so he was determined to complete all his surgical procedures before flying out for the conference on Friday night. Doctor was tired after performing all his surgical procedures that week, but he knew that his last surgical procedure, Patient's ankle re-set, could be performed quickly, as he considered it a routine procedure.

After two (2) hours, the surgery was performed without any difficulty or complication. Three (3) hours following the procedure, Nurse, who specialized in post-op care and treatment, removed Patient's IV bandage, which due to Patient's age, tore open her skin, causing Patient to cry out in pain. Before Patient was discharged, Doctor informed her that the operation was a success and instructed her to keep her foot elevated at home for three (3) days until the stitches began to heal. Patient was also prescribed different anti-inflammatory and pain medications. At home, Patient did take her prescribed medication, but did not keep her foot elevated, as she complained to her daughter that the ankle "hurt constantly" and the whole area inside the foot "felt tight." Doctor never called Patient from the conference to follow up after the operation, nor did he call the hospital to have any physician look at Patient post-op. Doctor remained in Florida after the conference to take a vacation for three additional days.

Upon his return to the hospital six (6) days after Patient's operation, Doctor examined Patient. After hearing her complaints of tightness and pain, he took x-rays of the ankle and determined that the plate had been secured too tightly to the bone, thus impinging on various nerves and muscles around the ankle. As a result, Patient suffered irreversible injury and will need to undergo a second operation to repair the plate. Thereafter, she will be required to undergo intensive physical therapy and will have to use a cane for at least one year thereafter. In addition, Patient developed a serious infection where the bandage was ripped from her skin, which may require a minor skin graft to heal.

It was determined that by keeping her foot elevated, Patient would still have sustained and suffered from the injury caused by Doctor, and the lack of constant elevation did not worsen Patient's condition. It was also determined that it is standard medical procedure to evaluate a patient 48-72 hours post-op, and that the screws used during Patient's procedure were produced from a new manufacturer. Doctor did not examine the screws prior to surgery, but he stated that the screws and plate were "standard" and did not deviate from the screws he was familiar with using during surgical procedures.

Analysis/Discussion

> If you are analyzing a civil or criminal cause of action that includes multiple elements, make sure you discuss *each* element.

Issue One

The first issue is whether Doctor can be held liable for medical malpractice for his actions during and after surgery as Patient sustained irreparable damage following a surgical procedure. It is well settled that a case of medical malpractice requires evidence of "'a negligent or unskillful performance by a physician . . . in the performance of a professional act'." *Keech v. Mead Johnson*, 580 A.2d 1374 (Pa. Super. 1990) quoting *Collins v. Hand*, 246 A.2d 398 (Pa. 1968). Specifically, in order to prove a claim of medical malpractice, it must be shown that (1) a duty of care was owed by the physician to the patient, (2) the physician committed a breach of that duty, (3) the breach of that duty was the cause of the harm to the patient, and (4) the patient suffered direct physical damage as a result. *Cruz v. Northeastern Hospital*, 801 A.2d 602 (Pa. Super. 2002).

In this situation, Doctor had a duty of care to Patient to operate in a well rested state. Patient's age alone should have warranted more care, even though Doctor determined the operation to be "standard." However, Doctor breached that duty of care and was negligent in rushing to perform and complete Patient's operation, although he had performed many surgeries that week, and was tired. Doctor further caused injury as the screws were secured too tightly to the ankle bone. That action directly caused physical harm and damage to the ankle, which will have to be subsequently operated on in the future. Clearly, the elements of malpractice can be made out in this case.

In addition, owing a duty of care also includes knowing and examining the proper tools used during surgery. Doctor failed to examine or even inquire as to the screws and plate used during the operation, which were recently purchased by the hospital from a new manufacturer. It will have to be determined if the screws were different from what Doctor was used to using, as their tightening strength may have been different from the older models. Further, it was determined that standard medical procedure includes evaluating a patient 48-72 hours following surgery. Doctor again breached his duty of care by failing to evaluate Patient within the required time period post-op, nor did he contact the hospital or have another surgeon examine Patient during that time, especially since he decided to take a vacation after the medical conference.

Typically in medical malpractice cases, expert testimony is required but not for claims of negligence that are so obvious. *See, Maurer v. Trustees of University of Pennsylvania*, 614 A.2d 754 (Pa. Super. 1992) ("expert evidence is not required in a medical malpractice action where the matter in dispute is so simple and the lack of skill or want of care is so obvious as to be comprehensible by a layperson"). However, although it may not be necessary, it might prove beneficial to secure expert testimony in this case to strengthen Patient's claim. A claim of medical malpractice can be made out against Doctor for his multiple negligent actions against Patient.

Issue Two

The second issue is whether Patient contributed to her injury caused by Doctor for not following Doctor's proscribed postsurgical instructions.

Pennsylvania has adopted a modified rule of comparative negligence. A plaintiff's recovery is barred only if his contributory negligence is *greater* than the causal negligence of the defendant. **42 Pa. C.S.§7102(a)**. Even if the plaintiff *did* contribute in some way to the injury, such negligence will not bar any recovery by the plaintiff. It will diminish the recovery of compensation by that percentage of fault. *Id.; see also Ruparcich v. Borgman*, 547 A.2d 1279 (Pa. Cmwlth. 1988).

However, the plaintiff must first be deemed to have contributed to his or her own injury. In doing so, it is the defendant's burden to prove the plaintiff's conduct as a contributing factor, who must show both the negligence of the conduct alleged and the causal relationship of that conduct to the injures for which damages are sought. *Angelo v. Diamontoni*, 871 A.2d 1276 (Pa. Super. 2005). Contributory fault may stem either from a plaintiff's careless exposure of himself to danger or from his failure to exercise reasonable diligence for his own protection. *Gorski v. Smith*, 812 A.2d 683 (Pa. Super. 2002).

Here, Patient took all her prescribed medications. However, the actions of Patient not keeping her foot elevated cannot be deemed to have contributed to her injury, as that post-op instruction was separate and distinct from Doctor's negligent actions. Keeping the foot elevated would not have healed or corrected the internal injury caused by Doctor. It is clear from the case law that comparative negligence can *only* be determined if the plaintiff did in fact perform an action, or omit from doing a prescribed action, which in turn would create or worsen the plaintiff's injury. Even if Doctor intends to use this as an affirmative defense, it will fail, as failure to keep the foot elevated cannot be deemed to have "contributed" to Patient's injury and will not absolve Doctor of his independent negligence.

Issue Three

The third issue is whether Doctor can be held liable for the actions of Nurse who engaged in routine postoperative care hours following surgery, which caused injury to Patient.

In an earlier, but still relevant case, it was held that a surgeon's liability "does not apply, after an operation is concluded, to treatment administered by floor nurses and interns in the regular course of the services ordinary furnished by a hospital, as all such care and attention would clearly be acting exclusively on behalf of the hospital, and not as assistants to the surgeon . . . " *Shull v. Schwartz*, 73 A.2d 402 (Pa. 1950). In addition, " . . . hospital employees are not generally servants of private physicians when administering treatment to patients . . . " *Gillis v. Metro Hospital*, 441 A.2d 445 (Pa. Super. 1981).

Here, hours after surgery was complete, Nurse checked on Patient as a routine procedure and, thereafter, removed the bandage holding her IV in place. Although Nurse removed the bandage improperly and without due care, submitting Patient to infection and skin graft treatment, it was solely the actions of Nurse acting as an agent of the hospital. Nurse was not acting on behalf of Doctor, nor did she remove the bandage per Doctor's order. Interns, residents, and nurses "who are full time employees of the hospital, assigned their duties by the hospital, paid by the hospital, and subject to discharge by the hospital, are deemed subjects of the hospital." *Tonsic v. Wagner*, 329 A.2d 497 (Pa. 1974). It will have to be determined if a second lawsuit could possibly be filed against Nurse/Hospital for the negligent removal of the bandage and the injury to Patient, but at this time and for this analysis, Doctor cannot be held liable for such action.

> Notice that the cases cited in the third issue are quite old. However, if you ever find a case that is directly *on point* and is still *good* case law that has not been overturned, use it! If your supervising attorney notices and says anything, explain that the case is on point and good law. You can always validate the case to obtain a newer case as well.

APPENDIX B

"MY LAW"—A STATE-SPECIFIC CITATION AND JURISDICTION GUIDE

In many of the chapters in this book, you learned how to cite federal material. This appendix is designed to include all the specific citations of **your** state that you may need for reference in class and in practice. In Part I, the first chart below includes the following:

- At the top of the chart, please fill in your state name/jurisdiction;
- The first column includes the particular source of law;
- The second column includes a space for you and your instructor to fill in the appropriate citation for your particular state; and
- The last column includes the standard *Bluebook* citation reference to help guide you, where appropriate.

Always refer to the *Bluebook* for any further assistance or guidance when needed.

Next, in the second chart found in Part II, fill in the appropriate state and federal courts from which you can retrieve case law research from **your** jurisdiction.

Your instructor will assist you in completing the charts below.

Part I—Citation Guide

SOURCE OF LAW	CITATION EXAMPLE	BLUEBOOK REFERENCE
STATE NAME		
State Slip Opinion		Rule 10; T.1; T.6, T.7
Intermediate State Appellate Court Opinion		Rule 10; T.1; T.6, T.7
State Supreme or Highest State Court Opinion		Rule 10; T.1; T.6, T.7

STATE NAME		
SOURCE OF LAW	**CITATION EXAMPLE**	**BLUEBOOK REFERENCE**
Newly Released Opinion on *WestlawNext*		Rule 10 and 18
Newly Released Opinion on *Lexis Advance*		Rule 10 and 18
Example of a Parallel Citation		Rule 10 and P.3
Example of a Pinpoint Citation		Rule 3
State Statute		Rule 12; Rule B5; T.1
Ordinance		Rule 12
State Constitution		Rule 11; T.1
State Regulation		Rule 14; B5; T.1
Local/Municipal Regulation		Rule 14; B5; T.1
State Ethics Rule		Rule 12

STATE NAME		
SOURCE OF LAW	**CITATION EXAMPLE**	**BLUEBOOK REFERENCE**
State Legal Encyclopedia		Rule 15
Restatement		Rule 12
State Civil Jury Instruction		(see instructor)
State Criminal Jury Instruction		(see instructor)
State Rule of Evidence		Rule 12
State Rule of Civil Procedure		Rule 12
State Rule of Criminal Procedure		Rule 12
State Rule of Appellate Procedure		Rule 12

Part II —Jurisdictional Guide

STATE APPELLATE COURTS	FEDERAL APPELLATE COURTS
Supreme (Highest) State Court	Federal Circuit Court (include all the states included in your circuit, as you can retrieve research from *any* of those states)
State Intermediate Appellate Court(s) or N/A	

All state and federal jurisdictions must follow any decision handed down by the US Supreme Court.

APPENDIX C

MORE PRACTICE: AN ADDITIONAL CASE STUDY

The Comprehensive Case Study (CCS) included in this textbook was designed for you to apply the skills needed to research any assignment. You learned each step of the research process from the initial issue formulation to the drafting of the legal memorandum addressing and resolving those issues. You now have another opportunity to apply those skills with: An Additional Case Study.

◼ OVERVIEW

The CCS involved a research assignment concerning *federal* law. In this section, the issues pertain to an assignment involving *state* law. After reading the facts, please follow the guidelines to complete the assignment.

◼ INTRODUCTION

You are employed as a paralegal with a medium-sized firm in your state. One day, a potential client, Keith Saunders (33) discusses possible representation with your supervising attorney. After meeting with Keith, your supervising attorney calls you into his office (*remember to always have a pen and legal pad with you to take notes*). The attorney relates the basic points of the meeting, and he also requires some research from you. Please begin by reading the facts outlined below.

The Facts

Keith has been working at ABC Company for five (5) years. Every summer, the company holds an annual company picnic for all of the employees of ABC, which includes approximately 150 people. The company has held this event for the past three (3) years on the first Friday in August during normal working hours. The picnic is an opportunity for the employees to mingle with each other in a more relaxed atmosphere and to discuss new ideas with the management team, which has resulted in increased productivity at the company. In fact, every idea created and discussed at the annual picnic has been implemented the following year with great success. During the afternoon, the company also presents merit awards to employees for their work over the past year. The company advertises the picnic at work, and any employee who wishes to attend must sign up. The employees are encouraged to attend, but are not required. Any employee who does not attend must use one of their vacation days. The event is held on the scenic company grounds, which is situated on three (3) acres of land. The company sets up numerous tents for the event and provides all the food and drinks. The company does not provide alcohol for the picnic, and no employee is permitted to bring any type of alcoholic beverages to the event.

Keith arrived at the picnic and had a great time with his coworkers. Keith also discussed a number of new ideas he had with his immediate supervisor, Ralph Kline.

During the awards presentation Keith was presented with two merit awards for submitting all his projects on time and for keeping them under budget.

Later that afternoon, the annual "touch-football" (no tackling) game began. Keith and some of his fellow employees played against their company supervisors. Keith was in good physical condition and enjoyed playing a variety of sports.

Everyone had a great time playing the football game. After about an hour of play, the score was tied. Keith made an impressive one-handed catch for a score and won the game for his team. Thereafter, without Keith knowing, all of his teammates ran up behind him and tackled him to the ground in a celebratory "pile-up" while chanting, "Keith . . . Keith . . . Keith..!" After everyone got up, Keith remained on the ground. His right leg was twisted under his body and he was in agonizing pain. His coworkers carried Keith to one of their cars and laid him across the back seat and drove him to the hospital.

After an extensive evaluation, it was determined that Keith sustained a broken tibia bone (lower leg), a dislocated knee joint, and a fractured femur bone (upper leg). He would require at least one (1) surgery to insert numerous pins and plates, and at least 1-2 additional surgeries at a later date. Keith also sustained extensive nerve damage in his leg.

Keith's injury has prevented him from performing his duties at ABC Company. After discussing the facts of the case with your supervising attorney, Keith wants to file a claim for workers' compensation with your supervising attorney for his lost wages due to his injury.

The Issues

You now need to develop the issues to be researched in this case. What questions need to be answered in order to address/answer/resolve the legal issues? What questions do you have and need answered after reading the facts?

Before you begin any research, the basic premise of workers' compensation is that an employer must pay any lost wages and medical expenses of an employee who is injured on the job. An injury is only compensable if the injury occurred during the course and scope of the employee's duties for his employer. Remember that you are researching how Keith *can* receive workers' compensation benefits. In this situation, there are two major issues to be researched. Now that you know the basic premise of workers' compensation law, consider the following:

1. What thoughts come to mind concerning Keith's injury occuring during a company picnic?
2. What thoughts come to mind concerning Keith's injury itself, which was the result of "horseplay?"

Do not forget to create a quick research guide. What are the *legally relevant facts*? What is the issue(s) you have developed?

The Research Plan

Remember that you need to know the *facts*, the *issues*, and the *jurisdiction* before you begin your research assignment. Thereafter, take the legal words/terms/phrases from your legal issues to generate the "key" words/terms/phrases you would use to begin your research. Remember what you learned about the "word search method" in the case law chapters and apply it here. For example, in this case study, what key words, based on your issues, would be appropriate and useful in conducting your search?

Update your research guide chart and review the research flowchart provided to you in the original CCS prior to beginning your research.

Remember that this issue is a state issue. Workers' compensation law is governed by statutes in every state. Although the specifics in the law will vary from state to state, the basic legal principles are the same. If you are not familiar with your state's workers' compensation statutes, and you want to "learn" about workers compensation, begin to search the secondary sources of law in your state legal encyclopedia and state digests. You will also obtain some good citations for statutes and cases.

Thereafter, go and find those statutes and cases in print and online. Be certain to read the statutes carefully, as each is composed of *elements*. Recall what you learned about how to "read" a statute. Read the "*and*," "*if*," "*or*," and "*but*" carefully. Make sure you read each case opinion to extract the rule of law. Do not take the rules from the headnotes. Read the entire opinion.

Keep researching until you feel you have firmly answered the issues. Remember what you learned about knowing when to stop. Locating what you need in the statutes is not too difficult, but if you are finding the same cases over and over again, then you should end the search. Find the sources of law that help to analyze and answer the issue. Remember, it is the *quality*, not the *quantity* of the research.

Organizing the Results

Once you have finished your search of the secondary and primary sources of law, you need to organize your results. Remember how to synthesize the law in the statutes with the rule of law found in case opinions. The law found in the statute is the rule of law, and the rules in the case opinions interpret, explain, support, and supplement those laws.

Drafting the Memorandum

If you recall, the legal memorandum is an *objective* piece of writing. This is to ensure that your supervising attorney can decide how to address the legal issues, and whether to even take the case. The attorney must know the pros and cons of the issues in order to create an effective legal strategy.

Review the chart below for the overall format of the legal memorandum.

Memorandum

To: **Supervising Attorney**
From: **Paralegal**
Date: **XX-XX-XXXX**
Re: **Keith Saunders—Workers' Compensation Research**

Question (Issue) Presented:

Brief Answer:

Statement of Facts:

Analysis/Discussion:

Conclusion:

After completing the basic sections of the memo, pay careful attention to the most important section—the analysis/discussion. Write out your thoughts/ arguments on a legal pad, and draft the content into the memo. Use the example below and the IRAC method when writing each issue.

EXAMPLE

The issue is whether . . . (*create defined and detailed issue(s)*).

Under state law, (*explain the state law here*).

In this case, (*include the specific facts relevant to the specific issue that relate to the law. This is your detailed analysis section—you can also use rules of law here as well*).

In conclusion, (*briefly wrap up the issue and offer a conclusion and whether the law is or is not favorable to the issue*).

When drafting the analysis/discussion section, provide a well-reasoned, well-developed, and comprehensive analysis/discussion for each issue. Take your time and use the **proper format**, an **appropriate amount of legal authority**, **proper citation**, and above all, **answer the issue**.

Once finished, you will re-read the memo and make some edits. Remember what you learned in your basic writing skills chapter—keep the sentences short yet informative. Create sentences that get directly to the point, and make sure you write in an active, not passive voice. After some fine tuning, you will again possess a high-quality and professional piece of writing.

INDEX

Note: Page numbers with *f* indicate figures.